STARKE'S
GUIDE THROUGH
ITALY,

ETC., ETC.

Printed by J. Smith, rue Montmorency, N° 16.

INFORMATION AND DIRECTIONS

FOR

TRAVELLERS ON THE CONTINENT.

BY MARIANA STARKE.

NEW EDITION,
THOROUGHLY REVISED, AND WITH CONSIDERABLE ADDITIONS.

PARIS:
PUBLISHED BY A. AND W. GALIGNANI,
AT THE ENGLISH, FRENCH, ITALIAN, GERMAN, AND SPANISH LIBRARY,
18, RUE VIVIENNE.

1828.

ADVERTISEMENT.

The chief object of the following Work is to comprise, within the compass of One Portable Volume, all the information necessary for Travellers on the Continent of Europe, and the Island of Sicily.

To accomplish this purpose it was requisite to examine with exactness, and give a detail, calculated to be read upon the spot, of the ancient edifices, principal museums, and galleries, public and private, in the above-mentioned countries. It was also requisite to copy all the most frequented routes from the post-books lately published by Royal authority; and this has been the Author's employment during the last three years.

The favourable reception given to the fifth Edition of her "Information and Directions for Travellers on the Continent," leads her to hope that the ensuing pages may, in some degree, answer the purpose for which they were written; and exonerate Travellers from the necessity of encumbering themselves, in every metropolis of the Continent, with books published to serve as Guides. At Paris, Strangers are in the habit of purchasing the Post-book, the List of Pictures in the *Musée Royal*, and the List of Sculptures in the same Museum, added to Galignani's excellent Paris Guide, and equally excellent Guide through France. At Florence Molini's accurate description of the Royal Gallery, and Gargiolli's account of the City, are usually purchased. At Rome Vasi's Itinerary (two volumes), and the description of the Museum of the Capitol, besides Nibby's highly and justly estimated publications, are deemed almost indispensable; as are from ten to twelve Guides at Naples, for the City and its Environs.

No complete printed description of the sculpture, frescos, and oil-paintings in the Vatican, and private galleries at Rome, being at the present moment attainable, the Author of the ensuing Work has endeavoured to supply this deficiency: and a Guide for Sicily being much wanted, she has given a concise historical account of that Island, and its antiquities, added to Information and Directions for Travellers who may intend going thither.*

Exmouth, September, 1827.

* Vide Addenda, following the Index.

INFORMATION AND DIRECTIONS

FOR

TRAVELLERS ON THE CONTINENT.

CHAPTER I.

FRANCE.

Calais—Best Road to Paris—Abbey of S. Denis—Paris—Most prominent improvements—Musée Royal des Arts—Musée du Luxembourg—Ecole Royale des Beaux Arts—Public Libraries—Musée d'Histoire Naturelle et Jardin du Roi—Académie Royale de Musique, and other Theatres—Manufacture Royale des Glaces—Manufacture Royale des Tapisseries aux Gobelins—Colonne de la Place Vendôme—Arc de triomphe de l'Etoile—Port S. Denis—Port S. Martin—Tribunal du Corps-Législatif—Basilique de Nôtre-Dame—Basilique de la Nouvelle S. Geneviève—Garde-meuble—Hotel Royal des Invalides—Institution Royale des Sourds-Muets—Hospice de la Salpêtrière—Hôpital des Enfans trouvés—Observatoire—Palais du Temple—Palais de la Bourse—Greniers de Réserve—Abattoirs—Halle au Blé—Halle aux Vins—Marché à la Volaille et au Gibier—Bridges—Fountains—Burial-places—S. Cloud—Sèvres—Versailles—Present state of Society at Paris—Passports.

ON revisiting Calais, in May, 1817, after an absence of twenty years, I discovered no apparent change, either in the town or its inhabitants; except that the latter, at least the lower order of persons, have acquired a habit of smoking incessantly, like the Germans; while the former boasts a larger number of good inns than it possessed under the government of Louis XVI.; and has been ridded of all its conventual institutions, and likewise of the host of mendicants by whom travellers were formerly annoyed.

Understanding that the route through Beauvais to Paris was smoother, less hilly, and shorter by three posts, than that through Amiens, I turned off at Abbeville, (where the roads divide,[1]) and pursued my way to Granvilliers; passing near a mound which commands the adjacent country, and is denominated Cæsar's Camp. The entrenchments are well preserved; and medals and other antiquities have been found on this spot. Granvilliers contains 3,000 inhabitants; the road from Calais thither is excellent; and, owing to its great breadth, perfect straightness, and thickly-planted borders of trees, possesses an appearance of grandeur for the same reason common to most of the high-roads in France. The country had hitherto presented nothing remarkable; but, after quitting

---

[1] Travellers who go by way of Beauvais to Paris, lose seeing one of the handsomest churches in France, the Cathedral at Amiens; and frequently experience bad treatment at Granvilliers; where the proprietor of the only tolerable inn the town can boast (*l'Hôtel d'Angleterre*), is neglectful and imposing.

Granvilliers, I passed through fine sheets of corn, interspersed with convents transformed into manufactories of various descriptions; objects frequently seen now in the French territories, and, generally speaking, disadvantageous to a landscape; but this disadvantage is counterbalanced by the improved state of agriculture, the increase of towns and villages, and the air of comfort which pervades even the humblest peasant's cottage.

Beauvais, seated on the banks of the Therain, is celebrated on account of the siege it sustained in 1472; when Jeanne Hachette headed the women of the town, and defended it against an army of 80,000 men, commanded by the Duke of Burgundy, whom she compelled to abandon his enterprise; and, in memory of this heroine, there is every year at Beauvais, a procession in which the ladies take precedence. The Cathedral, though unfinished, merits notice: it contains the tomb of Cardinal Forbin, by Coustou; fine painted glass; and good specimens of the tapestry for which Beauvais has long been famous. The Church of S. Etienne is likewise ornamented with fine painted glass.

From Beauvais I proceeded through avenues of fruit-trees, and a country rich in corn and vineyards, to Beaumont, pleasantly situated on the left bank of the Oise; and from Beaumont through avenues of fruit-trees, and well cultivated plains, to S. Denis, whose venerable Abbey has long been celebrated for containing the burial place of the monarchs of France. During the Revolution, however, this Abbey was stript of its treasures, its church was unroofed, its altars were levelled with the dust, and its royal Dead torn from the depositories of departed greatness. But the Emperor Napoleon having determined to restore the church to its pristine use and splendour, repaired and improved the royal vaults, securing them with gates of bronze, and at the same time re-establishing the subterranean chapels, in which he erected three expiatory altars; one dedicated to the Race of Clovis, another to that of Charlemagne, and a third to the princes of the Capetian dynasty: he likewise ordered prayers to be offered daily at the expiatory altars: and no change has been made in his plans by the present government, except that the bronze gates, with which he secured the royal vault destined to receive himself and his family, have been removed for a door of black marble. The Church is repaired with elegant simplicity, and contains two old monuments near the great door, and two of less ancient date; one being that of Louis XII., near which is a kneeling statue of the late Queen Marie Antoinette.—Good pictures adorn the Sacristy, and the conventual buildings of the Abbey are converted into an establishment for the gratuitous education of the daughters of the members of the Legion of Honour. Strangers who inquire for one of the Swiss Guards, (always in attendance at S. Denis,) are conducted by him into the royal Burial-place; where Napoleon's classic taste has supplied the tombs destroyed by republican frenzy; thus making the three dynasties complete, twelve princes excepted. The remains of Louis XVI. his Queen, two Aunts of Louis XVI. who died at Trieste, the Duke of

Berry, two of his Children, and Louis XVIII. have been deposited in this royal mausoleum.

Between S. Denis and Paris, (almost one continued street,) the splendid dome of the *Hôtel des Invalides*, Mont Martre, Belleville, and S. Chaumont, are the most striking objects; the second still exhibits marks of having made a desperate stand against the allied armies of Europe, when they united to dethrone Napoleon: and the two last were bravely defended on the 29th of March, 1814, by the pupils of the *Ecole Polytechnique*.

Paris, anciently called *Lutetia*, is watered by the Seine, anciently *Sequana*; and previous to the dethronement of Louis XVI., was supposed to contain from seven to eight hundred thousand inhabitants; but since that period, the number has considerably increased. The improvements this city owes to Napoleon are innumerable: and on entering the *Place Vendôme* (adorned with a fine imitation of Antoninus's column), on advancing to the *Garde-meuble*, and the palace of the Tuileries, viewing that superb edifice, its princely gardens, and the magnificent façades of the Louvre (deemed one of the most perfect specimens of modern architecture), then contemplating, from the Pont Louis XVI., the *Palais Bourbon*, the front of the *Tribunal du Corps Législatif*, the *Champs Elysées*, the stately dome of the *Hôtel des Invalides*, the noble quays of the Seine, and the beautiful bridges thrown over that river (which traverses Paris from east to west), it is impossible not to think this metropolis the rival of ancient Rome; especially when we recollect that the vast and splendid apartments of the Louvre, though recently despoiled of many treasures, still boast one of the largest and finest collections in the world of paintings and sculpture.

At Paris, however, grandeur is more common than consistency; for ere the eye be sated with gazing on the above-described magnificent panorama, it discovers streets narrow, insignificant, and filthy; disgraceful, in short, to any capital.

Among the most prominent improvements made during the imperial reign, are the noble Gallery intended to unite the immense palaces of the Louvre and the Tuileries; the triumphal Arc de l'Etoile, (not finished); the Exchange; the Establishment for the Orphans of the Legion of Honour; the Fountain of the Elephant, on the site of the Bastile, unfinished, but worthy of the colossal Mind by which it was projected; the Storehouses for Grain, called *Greniers de réserve*; the Slaughterhouses, called *Abattoirs*, magnificent in size, and particularly beneficial, as, previous to the reign of Napoleon, there was nothing of this description at Paris; the Cupola of the Corn-market; the general Magazine for wines; the Poultry and Game Market; the great Market; the Market of S. Germain, of S. Martin, etc. etc.; the *Rue de la Paix*; the *Pont du Jardin du Roi*; the *Pont de la Cité*; the *Pont des Arts*; the *Pont des Invalides*; the new Quays; the Fountain of the *Esplanade du Boulevard de Bondy*; and the already mentioned Column in the *Place Vendôme*.

The triumphal Arch in the *Place de Carrousel*, also, ranks

among the embellishments of Paris; though devoid of that magnitude and simplicity which distinguish the Roman edifice it was meant to imitate.

But what especially charms the eyes of strangers in the French capital, is a beautiful Belt, called the *Boulevards*, which encircles the town, and consists of drives and walks, bordered with forest-trees and gardens, and which, from the number of shops, and the profusion of flowers, whereby it is adorned, has a peculiar air of gaiety during winter; and possesses, during summer, a salubrious coolness, rarely met with in a vast metropolis. The circumstance of all others, however, most conducive to the healthfulness of Paris, is the purification of the water of the Seine; which, though perfectly wholesome now, was seldom drank with impunity in its natural state.

Judging by appearances, I should think Paris as much improved in wealth as in magnificence; the shops being far more numerous, and far better stocked, than in time past; the manufactories greatly improved; the hotels (which amount to upwards of three hundred) furnished with an elegance heretofore unknown; the coffee-houses displaying the most expensive embellishments; the tables of Restaurateurs abounding with luxuries; and the opera-house exhibiting a splendour, with respect to stage-decorations, which no other theatre in Europe can boast.

Having enumerated the most striking changes in this metropolis, I will now enter into a few particulars respecting the objects best worth notice.

Musée Royal du Louvre.[1] This immense collection of sculpture and paintings is placed in the magnificent palace of the Louvre: several rooms on the ground floor, princely in size, and rich in marbles and mosaics, being appropriated to the efforts of the chisel; and a suite of splendid apartments up stairs to those of the pencil. Among the sculpture are the choicest treasures of the Villa Borghese, and many other highly va-

---

[1] For the benefit of travellers restricted in point of time, I shall mark (as I have already mentioned) with one or more exclamation-points, according to the merit of the work in question, those productions of the chisel and the pencil which are generally deemed most worthy of notice in the public and private galleries of the Continent: and, for the use of travellers who may visit those galleries, I will here subjoin a short account of the origin of the Art of Sculpture.

Asia seems to have given birth to this art; but its progress appears to have been slow in all countries. During its infancy, in its native soil, the heathen divinities were represented by nothing more than square stones. Grecian sculpture began in a similar manner; after which, Bacchus, and other pagan gods, were worshipped under the form of a column. The next improvement consisted in placing the representation of human heads upon these columns: Hermes was worshipped under this form; whence comes the word *Herma*. The most ancient representations of the human figure, at full length, were of potters' clay. Dedalus, however, and, after him, Domophon, worked in wood; following artists worked in ivory; and their successors made statues of bronze; but, during the infancy of bronze sculpture, the component parts of statues were fastened together with nails; this is exemplified by six female figures, found in Herculaneum. After bronze, stone was used; and last of all, marble; but, for a considerable period, the heads, hands, and feet only of statues were marble, the trunks being wood. This custom prevailed so late as the days of Phidias; and even when sculpture had reached its zenith of perfection, several of the finest statues of marble, instead of being cut, each of them, out of one block, were made in separate pieces, and subsequently joined together. This is exemplified in the celebrated Niobe and two of her daughters; in the Albani Pallas; and in the Faustina, found near Ostia, among ruins supposed to be the remains of Pliny's Villa, called Laurentum. Very ancient statues were frequently painted, and sometimes draped with real stuffs, like the Madonnas of modern Italy.

lued works of art, which once embellished Rome.

Vestibule. No. 1, colossal bust of a vanquished Province.[1]—5, ditto of Domitian.[2]—6, ditto of Alexander Severus.[3]—7, statue of a Barbarian Prisoner.[4]—9, colossal bust of Lucius Verus.—11, statue of a Barbarian Prisoner.[5] 13, colossal bust of Jupiter Serapis.—18, Vase adorned with bacchanalian emblems![6]

Arcade leading to the Hall of the Emperors. No. 19, statue of Apollo, called *Sauroctonon*, or Lizard-killer; supposed to be one of the finest imitations extant of a bronze statue of Apollo, by Praxiteles![7]—22, statue of the Genius of eternal sleep.[8]

Hall of the Roman Emperors. No. 26, statue of Marcus Aurelius.[9]—26, a Barbarian Prisoner.[10] —28, bust of Vespasian.—31, statue of Nero.—33, ditto of Trajan.[11] The *basso-rilievo* on the Pedestal of this statue represents a husband and wife dining, and reposing on their couch; and is curious, because it exhibits ancient Roman costume.—34, bust of Claudius.—41, *basso-rilievo* found at Rome, and representing a religious ceremony performed before the temple of Jupiter Capitolinus; of which the three doors indicate the three naves consecrated to the three associated divinities, Jupiter, Minerva, and Juno.[12]—42, statue of Trajan.[13]

Hall of the Seasons. No. 46, statue of Venus Genitrix!—47, bust of Commodus.—50, statue of a wounded Combatant.[14]—55, an Egyptian divinity, in oriental alabaster![15]—59, bust of Venus![16]— 65, statue of Euripides![17]—73, ditto of a Nymph.—74, statue of Bacchus.[18]—75, a Sarcophagus, representing the Voyage of the Good to Elysium.—76, *basso-rilievo* of Mithras (a Persian divinity), the Genius of the sun, accomplishing the mystic sacrifice of the bull! Mithras was worshipped by the Romans, who erected altars to him; and this *basso-rilievo* was found near the Forum Romanum.—82, *basso-rilievo* taken from the Temple of Minerva at Athens; it represents the Panathenæa, and was composed by Phidias, and executed under his orders![19]

Hall of Peace. No. 85, a Candelabrum, taken from the Vatican Museum.—89, statue of Posidonius![20]—92, ditto of Demosthenes![21]—95, ditto of Trajan![22]

Hall of the Romans. No. 97, bust of Geta, very rare.[23]—98, Inopus, a fragment found at Delos.[24]—100, statue of Augustus.[25] 101, bust of a Roman Warrior.[26] 102, statue of Rome.—111, ditto of Tiberius, found at Capri: drapery fine, head restored.—113, statue of Augustus![27]—115, bust of Faustina the Elder.[28]—116, colossal bust of Rome![29]—118, statue of Julia, the consort of Septimius Severus.—120, group representing Thetis, etc. and worth notice, on account of the ancient

---

1 From the Villa Borghese.
2 From the Villa Albani.
3 From the Braschi Palace, at Rome.
4 Vil. Borg.   6 Ibid.
5 Ibid.   7 Ibid.
8 This statue does not express the idea it is intended to convey.
9 From Gabii. 13 Gabii.
10 Vil. Alb.   14 Vil. Borg.
11 Gabii.   15 Vil. Alb.
12 Vil. Borg. 16 Vil. Borg.
17 Vil. Alb.   18 Vil. Borg.
19 The Panathenæa were festivals in honour of Minerva, the patroness of Athens.
20 Vil. Borg.
21 From the Museo Pio Clementino.
22 Vatican.   23 Gabii.
24 Inopus, a river of Delos, supposed, by the inhabitants, to be a branch of the Nile.
25 Vatican.   26 Vil. Borg.
27 Mu. Pio Clementino.
28 Braschi Palace.   29 Vil. Borg.

galley on which the goddess is placed.[1]—123, bust of Lucilla.[2]—124, statue of Chastity.—126, bust of Antinous, found near Frascati!—128, Metope, taken from the Parthenon, at Athens!

Hall of the Centaur. No. 130, statue of a Roman, name unknown.—132, herma of Alexander the Great, found at Tivoli.—134, group of the Centaur!!! This master-piece is supposed, by the Chevalier Visconti, to have been executed in the time of Adrian by Aristeas and Papias, natives of Aphrodisias, in Caria.[3]—135, colossal head of Apollo.—138, ditto of Marcus Aurelius.[4]—140, ditto of Lucius Verus.[5]—141, statue of Germanicus.[6]—142, ditto of Claudius.[7]—144, ditto of Achilles.[8]—146, statues of Fauns.[9]—149, bust of Lucius Verus.[10]—150, statue of Sextus Pompeius, found near Tusculum, and executed by Ophelion, a Greek artist!—151, one of the largest and most beautiful Candelabra of antiquity, found in Magna Græcia.

Hall of Diana. No. 154, statue of Bacchus.—162, ditto of Minerva.—164, bust of a Roman, name unknown.—165, group of three Nymphs suspending their wet garments on a column!!![11]—167, statue of Thalia.[12]—168, *Basso-rilievo* of Hercules stealing the tripod of Delphos.—170,[13] bust of Rome.—171,[14] statue of Venus.—175, a Greek *basso-rilievo*.—176, *Basso-rilievo*, representing the Suovetaurilia, a sacrifice among the ancient Romans, which consisted of the immolation of a sow (*sus*), a lamb (*ovis*), and a bull (*taurus*), whence the name. It was usually observed every fifth year.—178, Diana *à la Biche*!! so called because the goddess is represented at the moment when she has rescued the celebrated Hind with golden horns from Hercules, and reprimanded him for molesting an animal sacred to her. This beautiful work, found between Genzano and Aricia, amidst the ruins of a temple consecrated to Diana, is of Parian marble, and stands upon a pedestal ornamented with fine *bassi-rilievi*: that part which represents three cities, personified by three female figures wearing crenated diadems, is particularly admired!!!—180, group called Venus victorious![15] The *basso-rilievo*, which serves as a pedestal to this group, is in the Etruscan style.—182, *basso-rilievo* denominated the Conclamation; a ceremony which took place at the funerals of the ancient Romans, and consisted in calling the Departed loudly and repeatedly by name; and likewise endeavouring to rouse them by the noise of music, in order to ascertain whether they were really dead.—185, group of Venus and Cupid, supposed to be an imitation of the draped Venus of Praxiteles!—192, statue of Minerva! This fine piece of sculpture is supposed, by Visconti, to be a copy of the bronze Minerva of Phidias, surnamed The Beautiful.[16]—196, bust of Marcus Agrippa.[17]—197, statue of the Lycian Apollo!—199, statue of Diana.—201, bust of Demosthenes, supposed to be one of the best likenesses extant of that philosopher.[18]—207, Fountain in the form

---

1 Vil. Alb.
2 Gabii.
3 Vil. Borg.
4 Ibid.
5 Ibid.
6 Gabii.
7 Ibid.
8 Vil. Borg.
9 Ibid.
10 Ibid.
11 Vil. Borg.
12 Ibid.
13 Ibid.
14 Ibid.
15 Vil. Borg.
16 Ibid.
17 Gabii.
18 Vil. Alb.

of a tripod, found among the ruins of Adrian's Villa.

Hall of the Candelabrum. No. 208, a Candelabrum, which, if found in its present state, would have ranked among the largest and most beautiful ancient works of its kind; but, though the materials of which it is composed are antique, they were put into their present form by Piranesi.—210, bust of Venus![1]—212, *basso-rilievo* of Antiope reconciling her sons Zethus and Amphion.[2]—213, statue of Diana.[3]—214, an Altar consecrated to Diana-Lucifera, or the moon.[4]—215, bust of Isis.—216, statue of a Dog, found at Gabii![5]—218, statue of Pollux.[5]—220, Tripod of the Delphic Apollo, found at Ostia!—224, statue of a Wild Boar, being an antique copy of the celebrated boar at Florence.[6]—229, Tripod found at Gabii.—230, statue of Marsyas!!! This is deemed one of the finest pieces of sculpture extant; and, like every other antique representation of Marsyas, is supposed to be imitated from a picture by Zeuxis, which Pliny mentions as having graced the temple of Concord at Rome.[7]—232, *basso-rilievo* of Jupiter.[8]

Hall of the Tiber. No. 233, statue of Æsculapius![9]—234, statue of Antinous in the character of Hercules, found near Tivoli.—238, statue of Flora.[10]—241, Chair consecrated to Bacchus![11]—242, statue of Ceres.[12]—244, statue of a Bacchante.[13]—245, Chair consecrated to Ceres.[14]—246, statue called the Diana of Gabii.—249, the Tiber, a colossal group found at Rome, on the site of the temple of Isis and Serapis, near the Via-Lata!!![15] This fine group, together with that of the Nile (in the Vatican Museum), adorned two fountains which embellished the avenue of the temple. The Tiber is represented in a recumbent posture, resting his right arm on an urn, near which reposes the wolf of Mars, with her nurslings, the founders of Rome: the oar in his left hand indicates that the river is navigable.—251, four statues, called Caryatides, which once adorned the Villa Albani.

Arcade which leads to the Hall of the fighting Warrior. No. 258, statue of Antinous.—259, *basso-rilievo*, representing the Birth of Bacchus.[16]—260, statue of Mars.

Hall of the fighting Warrior. No. 262, statue of a Warrior, called the Gladiator of the Villa Borghese!!!! He is represented as combating with an enemy on horseback; his left arm bears a shield, with which he is supposed to parry the strokes of his opponent, whom, with the right hand, he is about to wound with all his force. The attitude of the statue is admirably calculated for this double action; and every limb, every muscle, is said to wear more precisely the appearance of life, than does any other masterpiece of the Grecian chisel. The author of this transcendent and inimitable work was Agasias of Ephesus, whose name is engraved on the trunk which supports the figure; and whose design, according to Visconti, was not to repre-

---

1 Vil. Borg.
2 Ibid.
3 Ibid.
4 Ibid.
5 Ibid.
6 Vil. Borg.
7 Ibid.
8 Ibid.
9 Vil. Alb.
10 Vil. Borg.
11 Mu. Pio Clementino.
12 Vil. Borg. 13 Ibid.
14 Mu. Pio Clementino.
15 Ibid. 16 Vil. Alb.

sent a gladiator, but a warrior. Winckelmann is of the same opinion; and says, that the statue in question appears to have been executed before the period when gladiatorial shows were first exhibited in Greece. During the commencement of the seventeenth century, this *chef-d'œuvre* was discovered at Antium, where the Roman Emperors had a Villa; and where the Apollo of Belvedere was found about a century before.[1] — 263, statue of Mercury.[2] — 267, bust of Clodius Albinus.[3] — 269, bust of Marcus Aurelius.[4] — 270, a Sarcophagus representing the death of Meleager![5] — 272, group of two Romans in the costume of Mars and Venus.[6] — 276, statue of Adrian![7] — 279, ditto of Cupid, in the character of Hercules.[8] — 281, statue of a wounded Amazon! The upper part of this figure is said to be an antique imitation of the wounded Amazon of Ctesilas; but the sculptor, by whom it was restored in the sixteenth century, has deviated from the costume appropriate to female warriors. — 282, statue of the Venus of Arles, so called, because found at Arles, in Provence; and, supposed to be Venus victorious, the device of Cæsar. — 284, statue of an Infant Mercury.[9] — 287, statue of Lucius Cæsar![10] — 290, group of a Faun and a Satyr: the pedestal is supposed to have been an ornament with which the tops of ancient wells were sometimes embellished.[11] — 297, statue of Mercury: the subject of the *basso-rilievo* on the Pedestal is taken from the Odyssey, and represents Ulysses in the Shades below.

Hall of Pallas. No. 299, statue of a Female petitioning the gods.[12] — The sculptor who restored the hands of this statue has converted it into an Euterpe. — 301, statue of Ceres.[13] — 302, ditto of the Genius of Bacchus![14] — 304, bust of Trajan.[15] — 306, statue of Polymnia, upper part modern, drapery antique, and very fine.[16] — The Muse of Memory, and the Inventress of Harmony, seems stationed to watch over a Sarcophagus, numbered 307, and called that of Homer; because the father of heroic poetry is here represented as conversing with Calliope, and indicating, by the two fingers he holds up, that he composed only two epic poems. Figures of all the other Muses adorn this Sarcophagus; which was discovered, at the commencement of the last century, near Rome, on the road to Ostia. — 310, a colossal statue, called The Pallas of Velletri, because it was found near that town, in 1797!!! The goddess is represented as possessing the dignified beauty which accords with wisdom; and, though armed with her helmet, ægis, and lance, she seems, from the mildness of her countenance, to indicate that the arts of peace are not less dear to her than the glory of war. This statue is of the finest Greek workmanship; and the pedestal on which it rests merits observation. — 314, statue of a female Musician, supposed, by the costume, to have been executed in the time

---

1 Vil. Borg.
2 Ibid.
3 Vil. Alb.
4 Vil. Borg.
5 Ibid.
6 Vil. Borg.
7 Gabii.
8 Ibid.
9 Vil. Borg.
10 Gabii.
11 The receptacles for the ashes of victims in heathen temples seem to have been usually thus adorned.
12 Vil. Borg.
13 Ibid.
14 Ibid.
15 Vil. Alb.
16 Vil. Borg.

of Trajan or Adrian![1]—315, Sarcophagus, called that of Acteon.[2] —317, bust of Adrian.[3]— 318, statue of Nemesis.[4]—319, ditto of an Infant Hercules.[5]—321, statue supposed to represent Hope. The *basso-rilievo*, which adorns the pedestal, displays the formation of man by Prometheus, and Minerva giving him life, under the emblem of a butterfly.—328, the cinerary urn of Clodius; Egyptian workmanship, as appears from the hieroglyphics.[6]—331, a triangular Altar, representing three of the signs in the zodiac, namely, Virgo, the Scorpion, and Sagittarius, with the three divinities, Ceres, Mars, and Jupiter.[7]—332, a Grecian Vase, executed by an Athenian artist, called Sosibius.[8] —339, a sepulchral urn, which contained the ashes of Fundanius Velinus.[9]—340, group representing a Peasant cutting up a Deer.[10] —341, statue of Euterpe.[11]—343, Basin or Bath of Porphyry. Baths were sometimes used as sepulchres, when properly shaped for the purpose.[12]

Hall of Melpomene. The floor of this apartment is ornamented with Mosaics, chiefly executed at Paris by Belloni, and representing Minerva in her car, followed by Peace and Abundance; with river Gods, etc., forming a border to the picture. No. 344, bust of Isis.—345, statue of a Female petitioning the gods, and supposed to be the portrait of a Roman Empress.[13]—347, bust of the Nile.— 348, colossal statue of Melpomene, supposed originally to have adorned Pompey's theatre, and found on its site!!![14]—351, bust of Jupiter-Serapis!—353, altar consecrated to Diana.—354, statue of a Negro Slave.[15]

Hall of Isis. Four columns of Spanish marble are placed in the four corners of this apartment, and serve as pedestals to four Egyptian Statues; the most remarkable of which is an Isis, with a lion's head, in black basalt.— No. 359, statue of Isis, found in Adrian's Villa.—361, statue of an Egyptian Priest.— 363, ditto, in green basalt.[16]—367, statue of an Egyptian Priestess kneeling, with the throne of the gods in her hand; found near the *Via Flaminia*, about ten leagues from Rome.— 378, large Altar of twelve gods, supposed to be a production of the Ægina school!—380, statue of Venus, supposed to be an antique imitation of the Venus of the Capitol.[17]

Hall of Psyche. No. 381, Altar of twelve gods, found at Gabii!! This valuable piece of sculpture is adorned with busts of the twelve principal divinities of the Greeks and Romans, namely Jupiter, Minerva, Apollo, Juno, Neptune, Vulcan, Mercury, Vesta, Ceres, Diana, Mars, and Venus; the two last of whom Love is uniting: it is likewise adorned with the twelve signs of the zodiac, and with symbols of the divinity supposed to preside over the month which each sign indicates.—383, statue of a dancing Faun.[18]—387, statue of Psyche![19]—398, statue of Minerva, supposed to be a production of the Ægina school.— 399, statue of Cupid trying his

---

1 Vil. Borg.
2 Ibid.
3 Gabii.
4 Ibid.
5 Vil. Borg.
6 Ibid.
7 Gabii.
8 Vil. Borg.
9 Vatican.
10 Vil. Alb.
11 Vil. Borg.
12 Ibid.
13 Vil. Borg.
14 Mu. Pio Clementino.
15 Vil. Borg.
16 Ibid.
17 Ibid.
18 Vil. Borg.
19 Ibid.

bow; probably an antique copy of the bronze Cupid of Lysippus.[1] —403, statue of a dancing Faun.

Hall of the Augur. No. 417, statue of Cupid.[2]—418, *basso-rilievo*, representing the funeral of Hector.[3]—439, *basso-rilievo*, representing one of the Roman Augurs consulting the entrails of an ox, and unique with respect to its subject.[4]—442, statue of Commodus, found at Gabii.

Hall of Hercules and Telephus. No. 450, a colossal group of Hercules and Telephus.[5]—458, statue of Minerva.[6]—461, recumbent statue of an Hermaphrodite: this seems to be an antique imitation of the celebrated Hermaphrodite in the Hall of the Caryatides. The mattress is antique.[7]—462, statue of Diana, formerly called the Zingarella.[8]—465, statue of Julius Cæsar, found at Gabii.—466, statue of Pertinax.

Hall of Medea. No. 470, group of the Graces; the heads are modern.[9]—478, *basso-rilievo* representing the vengeance of Medea.[10] —488, group of Mercury and Vulcan.[11]—491, a sleeping Nymph.[12] 496, group of Cupid and Psyche.[13] —498, statue of a Muse.[14]

Corridor of Pan. No. 501, statue of a priestess of Isis, found at Athens.—504, statue of a young Faun.[15]— 506, statue of Pan.[16]— 514, bust of an Egyptian Priest. —517, herma of the Indian Bacchus, found at Rome.—522, statue of Urania.

Hall of the Caryatides, so called, because one end of this immense apartment exhibits four Caryatides, the work of Jean Goujon. No. 523, a triangular Altar, adorned with *bassi-rilievi*, representing three Lacedæmonian Virgins.[17]—526, herma of Socrates. —527, the celebrated Hermaphrodite of the Villa Borghese, supposed to be the finest imitation extant of the bronze Hermaphrodite of Polycletus!!! This statue was discovered, at the commencement of the seventeenth century, near Dioclesian's Baths. The mattress on which the figure rests was done by Bernini, who, likewise, restored the left foot.—528, herma of Homer, from the Museum of the Capitol.—530, herma of Diogenes.—533, statue of a Lion, in green basalt![18]— 559, statue of Hercules; upper part fine.[19]— 560, herma called Hercules; but supposed, by Winckelmann, to represent Xenophon.—592, herma of Thucydides.—593, statue of Sabina, the consort of Adrian![20] —595, statue of an African Fisherman, heretofore denominated the death of Seneca![21]— 596, a column of red porphyry, surmounted by a fragment of a statue of Minerva, apparently of the Ægina school.—597, Choiseul Marble, discovered at Athens, in the year 1788. — 622, statue of Livia.—623, herma of Zeno.[22] —655, herma of Pittacus.—657, ditto of Epicurus.[23]—681, statue of Venus rising from the bath.[24] — 682, bust of Tiberius, found at Gabii.—684, statue of Alexander the Great![25]—The *Basso-rilievo* fixed in the wall, above this statue, represents Achilles arming

---

1 Vil. Borg.	8 Vil. Borg.	15 Vil. Borg.	21 Vil. Borg.
2 Ibid.	9 Ibid.	16 Ibid.	22 Ibid.
3 Ibid.	10 Ibid.	17 Ibid.	23 Ibid.
4 Ibid.	11 Ibid.	18 Albani collection.	24 Vatican.
5 Ibid.	12 Ibid.	19 Vil. Borg.	25 Vil. Alb.
6 Ibid.	13 Ibid.	20 Gabii.	
7 Ibid.	14 Ibid.		

himself for battle; and was taken from the Villa Borghese.—694, group of a Child strangling a goose, supposed to be an antique copy of a work in bronze, which Pliny mentions as having been executed by Boëthus, a Carthaginian sculptor! This group was found near Rome, on the spot now called Roma Vecchia, the ancient *Pagus Lemonius*.— 698, statue of Venus rising from the bath; supposed to be an antique copy of a celebrated Venus, by Polycharmus, which adorned Rome in the days of Pliny!— 699, bust of Marcus Aurelius.[1]— 703, torso of Jupiter, supposed to be an antique imitation, in marble, of the famous Jupiter-Olympius of Phidias!—704, statue of a Discobolus, found in the *Via Appia*.—705, 706, and 708, Vases found at Marathon. —709, group of Silenus with the infant Bacchus!!!! This master-piece of art was discovered, during the sixteenth century, in the gardens of Sallust.—710, statue of Jason, improperly called Cincinnatus!! This *chef-d'œuvre* was found at the Villa Negroni, and is thought to be in the style of Agasias the Ephesian.—711, Vase of the Villa Borghese!! The *bassi-rilievi* on this beautiful Vase, which was found in the gardens of Sallust, represent a Bacchanalian ceremony.—712, statue of a Roman, in the character of Mercury, and improperly called Germanicus!! This *chef d'œuvre*, which appears to be the work of the younger Cleomenes, does not, in point of features, resemble any of the statues, nor any of the medals, of Germanicus: it was found in the Villa Negroni.

The staircase, leading to the apartments which contain the paintings, was built according to the design of Fontaine; and consists of four distinct flights of steps; two leading to the Gallery of Apollo, and two to the Exhibition-rooms of living Artists, which are interesting, because they contain a greater number of historical pictures than do our Exhibitions at Somerset-House. Beyond these rooms is the Gallery, called Italian; in size one of the most magnificent apartments existing; and adorned with columns, mirrors, candelabra, altars, busts, ancient and modern vases, all of the most costly description; besides upwards of eleven hundred and fifty pictures, which clothe its walls. This Gallery is divided into nine parts; the three first containing the works of the French School; the three next being appropriated to the works of the German, Flemish, and Dutch Schools; and the three last to the Italian Schools.[2]

French School. No. 13, the Descent from the Cross, by Bourdon.—22, the Nativity, by Le Brun.—25, the blessed Virgin preparing a meal for the Infant Jesus.—26, Jesus served in the Desert by Angels.—27, the Magdalene renouncing the vanities of life, supposed to represent Madame de la Vallière!—31, the Dream of Anne of Austria.—33, Pentecost.—34, the Lapidation of S. Stephen!—and, 37, the tent of Darius! all by Le Brun.—49, a Painter's *Studio*, by Cochereau.— 57, the Last Judgment by Cousin! —63, Joas acknowledged king of Israel, by Antoine Coypel.—69, a Kitchen, by Drolling, a self-taught

---

[1] Gabii.
[2] Engravings of a considerable number of the pictures in this Museum have been taken; and proof impressions are sold, for the benefit of the establishment, at the *Calcographie du Musée Royal*.

Painter.—80, David anointed king over Israel, by Claude Lorrain!—81, the Disembarkation of Cleopatra, to present herself before Antony!—82, 83, 84, and 85, all by Claude.—107, the Descent from the Cross, by Jouvenet.—123, *La Vièrge à la Grappe*, by Mignard!—126, S. Cecilia, by ditto.—139, portrait of Nicholas Poussin, by himself.—140, the Deluge, a particularly fine and poetical picture.—142, the Preservation of the Infant Moses.—149, the Judgment of Solomon!—151, Our Saviour, the blessed Virgin, S. John, Elizabeth, and Joseph!—154, the Blind Men of Jericho!—157, the Death of Saphira!—159, the Assumption of the Virgin.—161, S. François Xavier, recalled to life!—166, the Death of Eurydice.—167, Shepherds of Arcadia.—168, Time rescuing Truth from Envy and Calumny, and bearing her to the regions of eternity!—171, Diogenes throwing away his tankard! all by Nicolas Poussin.—199, S. Paul preaching at Ephesus, by Le Sueur.—202, Simon, the Cyrenian, coming to the aid of Our Saviour, who is represented as sinking under the weight of his cross, while S. Veronica offers him a handkerchief, which receives the impression of his countenance!—and 203, the Descent from the Cross; both by Le Sueur.—257, Antibes, by Vernet.—258, 259, 260, Toulon.—261, Bandol.—262 and 263, Marseille.—264, Cette.—265 and 266, Bayonne.—267 and 268, Bordeaux.—269, La Rochelle.—270, Rochefort.—271, Dieppe.—275, a Sea-port at sunrise!—273, a Sea-port at Sunset!—281, a Moonlight-scene—282, a Sea-view by moonlight!—283, a Tempest; and, 285, a Tempest; all by Vernet.

Flemish, German, and Dutch Schools. No. 341, View at sunset, in Italy, by Both!—353, the Garden of Eden, by Breughel.—359, a Landscape, the figures in which are by Annibale Caracci, the other part by Paul Brill.—372, *Les Religieuses*, by Philippe de Champaigne.—373, the Repast at the house of Simon the Pharisee.—374, the Last Supper—and, 379, a large Landscape, likewise by Philippe de Champaigne.—389, a Landscape, with Cattle, by Cuyp!—390, a Gentleman mounting his horse; and, 391, the same Gentleman returning from his ride; likewise by Cuyp.—404, the Dropsical Woman, by Gerard Dow!! (this picture is deemed his chef-d'œuvre.)—409, a Philosopher, by the same Artist!—410, the Interior of a Guard-house, by Jean le Duc.—413, Charles I. of England, by Anthony Vandyck.—415, Isabella, daughter to Philip II. of Spain.—425, Sketch of Our Saviour dead in the arms of the blessed Virgin, and Angels weeping!—326, the Infant Jesus receiving homage from a Saint and a King! and 328, (*Ex Voto*), the Infant Jesus receiving homage; all by Anthony Vandyck.—432, Hagar banished to the Desert, by Philip Vandyck.—444, an Angel announcing the Birth of the Messiah to the Shepherds, by Flinck.—451, a Landscape, by Glauber!—470, a Portrait of Sir Thomas More, by John Holbein.—471, a Portrait of Erasmus.—472, ditto of an Archbishop of Canterbury.—473, ditto of Nicholas Kratzer, Astronomer to Henry VIII. of England; and, 478, the Descent from the Cross, with two other paintings in the same frame, all by John Holbein.—484, the Interior of a Dutch dwelling, by Peter de Hooch!—487, and all the intermediate numbers to 496, by Van Huysum.—498, the Crucifixion, by Jardin!—522, the Descent from the Cross, by Lucas de Leyden.—526, a Jeweller weighing gold, and his Wife examining a book illuminated with miniatures, by Quintin Matsys.—577, Interior of the Cathedral at Anvers, by Peter Neff!—578, 579, 580, and 581, by the same Master.—582, a Landscape, by Aart Vanderneer: the cows in this landscape are attributed to Cuyp.—588, S. Carlo Borromeo administering the sacrament to persons infected with the plague at Milan, by Van Oost the Elder.—590, the Family of Adrian Van Ostade, by himself.—597, Travellers stopping at an Inn, by Isaac Van Ostade.—604, an Angel announcing the Birth of the Messiah to the Shepherds, by Poelenburg.—609, Portrait of Guillaume du Vair, by Probus the Younger.—615, two Horses fastened to a Trough at an Inn-door, and a man bringing them water, by Paul Potter!—616, Cattle, by ditto!—617, a Landscape, with Cattle, by Pynaker.—620, 621, 622, and 623, Portraits of Rembrandt, by himself.—626, Head of a man with a fur cap.—627, Head of an old person with a long beard.—628, Tobit and his Family prostrate before the Angel of God!—629, the good Samaritan.—630, Our Saviour at Emmaus.—632, S. Matthew writing, and an Angel dictating to him.—633, Venus and Cupid!—634, a Philosopher in meditation; and, 635, the Interior of a Tradesman's dwelling; all by Rembrandt.—637, a Wolf devouring a Sheep, by Rosa di Tivoli; the landscape in this picture was painted by Tempesta.—640, Lot and his Daughters leaving Sodom, by Rubens.—641, Elias succoured by an Angel in the Desert.—642, the Adoration of the Magi.—643, the Flight into Egypt;—and, 644, the blessed Virgin and our Saviour surrounded with groups of Children; all by Rubens; as are twenty-four pictures, taken from the Luxembourg Palace, and representing the life of Mary of Medicis. The first number is 650, and the most striking of these fine pictures are numbered 661, 664, 670, and 671—the Portrait of Richardot, numbered 674—and the representation of a Village Fête, numbered 678! are likewise by Rubens.—683, a Landscape, by Ruysdael, with Figures and Cattle, by Berghem!—684, another Landscape, by Ruysdael, with Figures by Wouvermans!—685, a Tempest, by Ruysdael!—687, Our Saviour at Emmaus, by Santwoort!—688, the Holy Family, by Schalken!—701, Animals entering the Ark, by Sneyders.—705, a Kitchen, by ditto.—711, the Inside of a Church, by Steenwick!—724, the Temptation of S. Anthony, by David Teniers.—734, Head of an old Man, by ditto.—762, a Hare and other Game, by Weenix the Younger.—763, a Peacock, Game, and a Dog, by ditto!—765, Pharaoh's Daughter finding Moses, by Adrian Vanderwerf!—767, an Angel announcing to the Shepherds the Birth of the Messiah!—768, the Magdalene in the Desert!—and, 770, Nymphs dancing! all by Vanderwerf.—778, an Attack of Polish Cavalry, by Philip Wouvermans.

Schools of Italy. No. 815, the Infant Jesus embracing S. John, by Albano.—818, Venus impatient to try the effect of her beauty on the heart of Adonis.—819, Vulcan reposing at the feet of Venus, while the Loves forge arms for the latter.—820, the Loves, while sleeping after their labours, disarmed by Diana's Nymphs.—821, the Loves, after having recovered their losses, and become triumphant, conducting Adonis to the feet of Venus; all by Albano.—838, the blessed Virgin and our Saviour listening to S. John, who is presented to them by Elizabeth— and 839, Charity; both by Andrea del Sarto—857, the blessed Virgin, by the Cav. Batoni.—868, the resurrection of Lazarus, by Bonifazio.—880, 881, and 882, views of Venice, by Canaletto.— 868, the blessed Virgin dead, and the Apostles weeping, by M. A. Caravaggio.—888, a young Woman telling a Youth his fortune, by ditto.—895, the Nativity, by Annibale Caracci.—898, the blessed Virgin recommending silence to S. John, that he may not disturb the repose of our Saviour! —902, our Saviour ascending to Heaven, after his resurrection.— 906, the Martyrdom of S. Stephen;—and 907, the same subject, all by Annibale Caracci.— 919, the Infant Jesus and his Mother, by Lodovico Caracci.—926, S. Cecilia, by Cavedone.—932, Jesus presenting the ring for his mystic marriage, to S. Catherine of Alexandria, by Antonio Allegri, da Correggio!—934, Antiope asleep, Love sleeping by her side on a lion's skin, and Jupiter standing near, transformed into a Satyr, by ditto!!—940. David vanquishing Goliath; a double picture on the same subject, by Daniello da Volterra.[1]—941, Jesus consecrating the bread, by Agnese Dolci.—945, a Landscape representing the flight into Egypt, and attributed by some persons to Domenichino, and by others to Ann. Caracci.—948, S. Cecilia, by Domenichino!—956, a Concert; attributed to Leonello Spada.—975, the Adoration of the Shepherds, by Spagnoletto.—981, Melancholy, by Domenico Feti! —986, and 987, portraits of Benvenuto Garofolo, by himself.— 990, a mystic subject, likewise by Garofolo.—991, a Landscape, by Gasparo Dughet, called Gasparo Poussin.—997, the Messiah accepting the instruments of the Passion, by Luca Giordano!— 1004, a portrait of Guercino, by himself.—1008, the blessed Virgin and S. Peter, deploring the death of the Messiah;—and 1016, Circe, both by Guercino.—1021, the Salutation, by Guido.—1022, the Infant Jesus sleeping on his Mother's knees.—1025, Jesus and the Samaritan.—1026, Jesus giving the keys of Heaven to S. Peter.—1027, Jesus crowned with thorns.—1030, Jesus in the Garden of Olives.—1031, the Magdalene.—1032, the same subject; —and 1036, an Allegory representing the union of Design and Colour — all by Guido.—1044, portrait of Giulio Romano, by himself.—1045, the Adoration of the Shepherds, by Giulio Romano.—1057, portrait of Monna Lisa, a celebrated Florentine Beauty, by Leonardo da Vinci.[2] —1058, S. John Baptist!—1059,

---

1 It is said that Monsignor Giovanni della Casa, a Florentine prelate, employed Daniello da Volterra to model a group in plaster of David vanquishing Goliath; and then desired him to represent in painting the two sides of the model; which seems to have been done in this double picture.

2 Francis I. of France gave for this picture 4,000 gold crowns; a sum exceeding 45,000 francs.

S. Anne, the blessed Virgin, and Infant Jesus!—1060, the Infant Jesus blessing S. John—all by Leonardo da Vinci.—1062, Jesus receiving a cross of rushes from S. John, School of Leonardo da Vinci.[1]—1065, the Holy Family, by Bernardino Lovini, more commonly called Luini.—1066, the Messiah sleeping, by ditto.—1076, the blessed Virgin showing the Messiah to the Angels and Shepherds, by Carlo Maratta.—1079, the marriage of S. Catherine, by ditto.—1090, the Infant Jesus on his Mother's lap, playing with a chaplet, by Murillo!!—1091, God the Father, and the Holy Ghost, contemplating the Messiah while he receives a cross of rushes from S. John!—1092, the Messiah on the Mount of Olives, presented by an Angel with the Chalice and the Cross.—1093, S. Peter imploring pardon of the Messiah;—and 1095, a young Beggar seated!!—all by Murillo.—1102, the blessed Virgin and Joseph presenting the Infant Messiah to be adored by a Shepherd, Palma Vecchio.—1119, the Messiah sinking under the weight of his Cross, by Paolo Veronese.—1136, the blessed Virgin, with the Infant Jesus and S. Martina, by Pietro da Cortona.—1138, Faustulus, the Shepherd of Amulius, presenting Romulus and Remus to his wife Laurentia, by ditto.—1149, portraits of Raffaello Sanzio d'Urbino, the founder of the Roman School, and his Master Pietro Peruzino, by Raphaël.[2]—1151, portrait of Count Balthasar Castiglione.—1154, the Archangel Michael vanquishing Satan.—1157, the Holy Family, called *La belle Jardinière!*—and 1158, the same subject, painted for Francis I. of France!!—all by Raphaël, who finished the last mentioned work only two years before his death.—1159, the Infant Jesus reposing;—and 1160, the Infant Jesus caressing S. John; both by Raphaël.—1175, a Sportsman shooting a bird, and Soldiers reposing on a rock, by Salvator Rosa.—1178, the Infant Jesus sleeping on his Mother's knees, with Cherubim in the angles of the picture, by Sasso Ferrato!—1179, the Apotheosis of the blessed Virgin, by ditto.—1181, head of S. John Baptist, by Schiavone.—1182, the Holy Family, by Schidone.—1186, the blessed Virgin visiting Elizabeth, by Sebastiano del Piombo.—1192, the Prodigal Son imploring his Father's pardon, by Leonello Spada.—1198, portrait of Tintoretto, painted by himself.—1205, portraits supposed to be those of Titian and his Mistress, painted by himself.[3]—1207, portrait of Cardinal Hippolito of Medicis.—1209, portrait of Alphonso d'Avalos.—1210, portrait of a man dressed in black.—1214, another Portrait.—1215, the Soldiery insulting the Messiah at the door of his prison!!—1217, the Messiah carried to the tomb!—1218, the Pilgrims of Emmaus.[4]—1219, the blessed Virgin, the Infant Jesus, S. Stephen (the first Dalmatian martyr), S. Ambroise, and S.

---

[1] Leonardo da Vinci founded the Milan School.

[2] According to some opinions this picture represents Raphaël and Pontormo, and was painted by the latter.

[3] Titian (Vecellio Tiziano) was one of the founders of the Lombard School.

[4] According to tradition, the pilgrim on the right of our Saviour represents the emperor Charles V.; the pilgrim on the left, Cardinal Ximenes; and the page, Philip II. of Spain.

Maurice!—1220, two Angels worshipping the Messiah.—1221, the blessed Virgin holding a rabbit, for which the Infant Jesus seems to ask;—and 1222, S. Agnes presenting her palm of martyrdom!—all by Titian.—1233, the martyrdom of S. Irene, by Francesco Vanni!—1235, portrait of the Infanta Marguerita Theresa, daughter of Philip IV. of Spain, and of his consort, Maria-Anne of Austria, by Velasquez.

Several pictures belonging to this magnificent collection have suffered considerably, from being ill-restored and over-varnished; and several statues, belonging to the Museum of Sculpture, are, in appearance, still more hurt, by having been partially cleaned.

Admission may usually be obtained gratis, to the *Musée Royal*, every morning, Mondays excepted, from ten o'clock till four, by Foreigners; provided they show their passports. Admission is given to the public in general every Saturday and Sunday, from two o'clock till four.

Musée du Luxembourg. These Galleries, formerly adorned with the works of Rubens and Le Sueur (now removed to the Louvre), are at present destined to receive the works of living Artists: and, in addition to the most admired pictures of the three last Exhibitions, here are other celebrated works of the modern French School.

Ecole Royale des Beaux Arts, Rue des Petits Augustins, ci-devant Musée des Monumens Français. Monsieur Lenoir, to whom Paris was indebted for the last-named Museum, arranged, in chronological order, all the sepulchral monuments he was able to rescue from the sacrilegious grasp of the infatuated leaders of the French revolution: thus exhibiting a series of memorials of the most distinguished characters to whom France has given birth, from the days of Clovis, to the present era: and, at the same time, forming a history of the commencement and progress of sculpture, and the art of painting upon glass, among his countrymen. But since the re-establishment of the monarchy, the tombs contained in this repository have been replaced in the churches whence they were taken; and the remaining part of this interesting Museum enriches the *Musée Royal*.

Bibliothèque du Roi, Rue de Richelieu. This Library (perhaps the finest existing), contains nearly eight hundred thousand printed volumes, eighty thousand volumes of manuscripts, five thousand five hundred volumes of prints, and a Cabinet of Antiquities, enriched with Isiac Tables, Pagan Deities, and the most rare and valuable collection of Medals in the world. The Gallery appropriated to the Manuscripts is adorned with paintings, by Romanelli; and the Apartment next to the *Cabinet des Estampes* contains a portrait of King John, considered as the most precious relic of French painting in the fourteenth century.[1] This Library is open to the public every day, from ten till two, festivals and vacation-times excepted.

Bibliothèque Mazarine, Palais des Beaux-Arts, Quai Conti.—This Library, which originally contained about sixty thousand volumes, has lately been enriched

---

[1] The portfolio of Gaignieres, containing a collection of the *costume* of the French nation, from the days of Clovis to the present period, may be found among the prints.

with the Library of the Institute; and possesses a fine terrestrial Globe of copper, executed by the brothers Bergwin, under the direction of Louis XVI. for the Dauphin.

Bibliothèque de S. Geneviève, Place S. Geneviève, Bâtimens du Collège Henry IV. This Library contains an hundred and twelve thousand volumes; and is adorned with Busts of distinguished characters; among whom are Jules Hardouin, Mansard, the Chancellor Letellier, by Coysevox, and Doctor Arnauld, by Girardon. Here likewise may be found a plan of Rome in rilievo, executed by Grimini, in 1776. This Library is open to the public every day from ten in the morning till two, festivals and vacation-times excepted.

Bibliothèque de l'Arsenal, Rue de Sully, à l'extrémité du Quai des Célestins. This Library, supposed to contain an hundred and fifty thousand printed volumes, and five thousand manuscripts, is particularly rich in history and Italian poetry; and open to the public every day, Sundays and vacation-times excepted, from ten in the morning till two in the afternoon.

Bibliothèque de la Ville, Place du Sanhédrin, derrière l'Hôtel de Ville. This Library is open to the public from twelve in the morning till four in the afternoon.

Bibliothèque du Musée d'Aistoire Naturelle, Rue du Jardin du Roi. This Library is particularly well stored with books relative to natural history, and likewise with herbals, and drawings representing plants. Strangers are admitted on Mondays Wednesdays, and Saturdays, upon producing their passports.

Bibliothèque de la Faculté de Médecine, Rue de l'Ecole de Médecine. This Library, rich in works on the art of healing, is open to the public daily, from ten in the morning till two.[1]

Musée d'Histoire Naturelle, et Jardin du Roi, Quai S. Bernard, et Rue du Jardin du Roi. The Botanic Garden, belonging to this Museum, contains a large collection of plants from various countries; together with buildings which serve as dens for wild beasts; and a menagerie, so constructed that tame animals, not natives of France, and birds of all kinds and countries are provided with habitations analogous to their modes of life: and in the midst of this appropriate spot, the French naturalists have erected a modest monument to Linnæus. The Amphitheatre of Anatomy stands in this garden; as does the Museum of Natural History; on the first floor of which is the finest collection of fishes in Europe; together with lizards, serpents, shells, minerals, fossils, etc.: and on the second floor the most magnificent assemblage imaginable of Birds and Quadrupeds, preserved to admiration.

The Botanic Garden is always open to the public, gratis; the Museum of Natural History on Tuesdays and Fridays only, from three o'clock in the afternoon till six in summer, and till dusk in winter; and the Menagerie every day, from eleven o'clock till six during the summer; and from eleven till three in winter. Artists, and students belonging to the Museum, and foreigners are

---

[1] The Library of *l'Ecole Polytechnique*, that of *l'Ecole des Mines*, and that of *la Cour de Cassation*, are accessible to foreigners who apply for leave to visit them.

admitted on other days upon obtaining permission. The fine bridge of Austerlitz, now called *Pont du Jardin du Roi*, is a great ornament to the Botanic Garden.

Académie Royale de Musique, ou l'Opéra, Rue Lepelletier. This Theatre, which is spacious and sonorous, presents the most brilliant *spectacle* in Europe, with respect to scenes, machinery, dresses, accuracy relative to costume, and excellence relative to the composition and execution of the ballets represented. It is open on Sundays, Wednesdays, and Fridays.

Italian Opera, Place Favart. Open on Mondays, Tuesdays, Thursdays, and Saturdays.

Théâtre Français, Rue de Richelieu. This Theatre is dedicated to the representation of French dramas.

Théâtre de l'Opéra Comique, Rue Feydeau. This Theatre contains seventeen hundred spectators; and is well calculated for music.

Théâtre de l'Odéon, près le Luxembourg. French dramas are represented in this Theatre.

Théâtre du Vaudeville, Rue de Chartres S. Honoré. This Theatre generally exhibits a variety of little dramas, songs, etc.

Théâtre des Variétés, Boulevard Montmartre.

Manufacture Royale des Glaces, Rue de Reuilly. This Manufacture is well worth notice; as it employs eight hundred workmen; who have attained such perfection in their art as to make Mirrors of 120 inches in length, by 80 wide.

Manufacture Royale des Tapisseries de la Couronne, aux Gobelins, Rue Mouffetard. This Manufacture also is well worth notice; as it exhibits the most beautiful Tapestry existing; and may be seen on Saturdays, after two o'clock.

Colonne de la Place Vendôme. This stately column, 135 Paris feet in height, and 12 in diameter,[1] is made of the cannon taken from the enemies of France, in the battles fought by Napoleon and his Generals: it represents those battles in bronze *bassi-rilievi*; and on its summit originally stood a colossal statue of the Emperor: which, after his dethronement, was taken down; and has, according to report, been carried to Moscow. A winding staircase of 176 steps, leads to the top of this column; from which the view of Paris is beautiful.

Arc de Triomphe de l'Etoile. On the 15th of August, 1806, Paris began to erect this fine Arch, in order to perpetuate the fame obtained in Germany, by the French Armies, during the former year: it was intended to be 135 Paris feet in height; but unfortunately is not finished.

Porte S. Denis. The conquests of Louis XIV., in 1672, induced the city of Paris to erect this magnificent triumphal Arch to perpetuate his fame. The *bassi-rilievi* represent military trophies, (remarkably well-executed,) personifications of Holland and the Rhine, the passage of the Rhine, and the taking of Maestricht.

Porte S. Martin. The continued success of Louis XIV. induced the city of Paris to erect, in 1674, another monument to his fame: this Arch, though less

---

[1] A Paris foot is nearly thirteen English inches.

adorned than that of S. Denis, is, in point of architecture, equally harmonious and dignified. The *bassi-rilievi* represent the taking of Besançon, the triple alliance, the taking of Limbourg, and the defeat of the Germans; figured by the god of war repulsing an eagle. Great artists were employed in executing both these Gates.

Tribunal du Corps Législatif. Opposite to the bridge of Louis XVI., rises a magnificent Peristyle, formed by twelve Corinthian columns surmounted by a triangular pediment: a superb flight of steps, adorned with colossal statues of Minerva and France, leads to the entrance of the building; and opposite the bridge are statues of Sully, Colbert, l'Hôpital, and d'Aguesseau. This peristyle forms the approach to the Hall of the Deputies.

Basilique de Nôtre-Dame. This ancient edifice, surmounted by twin-towers of a majestic height, contains some good paintings of the French school, and a descent from the Cross (in sculpture) by the elder Coustou.

Basilique de la Nouvelle S. Geneviève, ou le Panthéon. This elegant building, erected by command of Louis XV., after the design of Soufflot, in the form of a Greek cross, is 340 Paris feet in length, peristyle inclusive, and 250 feet wide: in the centre rises a dome, nearly 63 feet in diameter, supported within, and adorned without, by pillars, which produce a pleasing effect. The exterior height of the dome is 282 feet; and the interior height of the nave 170 feet. The peristyle consists of 22 Corinthian columns 58 feet high, and five and a half in diameter, supporting a triangular pediment.[1]

Garde Meuble de la Couronne, rue des Champs Elysées. This deposit for the furniture belonging to the crown, is worth notice.

Hôtel royal des Invalides. This edifice was erected by command of Louis XIV., as a retreat for old and deserving soldiers of the French army; and exhibits a magnificence most honourable to its Founder. The dome, deemed a master-piece of architecture, was designed by Jules Hardouin Mansard; and (measuring from the pavement to the cross on the top of the lantern) is 300 Paris feet high: the lead which covers it was originally gilt, by order of Louis XIV.; and re-gilt by command of Napoleon. Round the interior of this dome are six chapels. In the great cupola Charles de Lafosse has painted the apotheosis of S. Louis, and likewise the four Evangelists, placed between the principal arches. J. Jouvenet has represented, on the ceiling, the twelve apostles; Boullongne painted the chapels of S. Jérôme, S. Ambroise, and S. Augustin, in which the history of these Fathers of the Church is given; and the Chapel of S. Grégoire, painted originally by Le Brun, has been retouched by Doyen. The ceiling of the sanctuary, painted by Nicolas Coypel, represents the mysteries of the Trinity, and the assumption of the Virgin. The groups of Angels, forming concerts, in the embrasures of the windows, are by Louis and Bon Boullongne. The inlaid pavement of the dome and chapels particularly merits notice. This building

---

[1] The Church of S. Eustace is bold and light in point of architecture; and the churches of S. Roch and S. Sulpice, built about the middle of the eighteenth century, are handsome.

likewise contains the monument of the great Turenne; who is represented dying in the arms of Victory; while Wisdom and Valour stand on each side, deploring the loss of the Hero. In front is a bronze *basso-rilievo* of the battle of Turckeim; and the only inscription on the monument is the word, "TURENNE." The remains of Marshal Vauban have been honoured with a place opposite those of Turenne.

The Hôtel des Invalides, which gives shelter and comfort to seven thousand Veterans, is open to the public every day, from ten in the morning till four in the afternoon.

Institution Royale des Sourds-Muets, Rue S. Jacques. The benevolent idea of teaching the deaf and dumb to speak, was formed by the Abbé de l'Epée, who, with a fortune of only twelve hundred livres per annum, maintained at his private expense, forty scholars of the above description; and thus founded one of the noblest charities in France: but all the sacrifices he was compelled to make, in order to accomplish his purpose, would, at length, have proved fruitless, had not his talents and virtues been renewed in the late Abbé Sicard, who brought the plans of his predecessor to such perfection that he enabled the Deaf and Dumb, not only to read, write, and cast accounts, but likewise to understand turning, working in mosaic, drawing, and painting, so as to get their own livelihood: he also taught them French and English grammatically; geography, history, geometry, and metaphysics; and, at the conclusion of every month, his Pupils had a public exhibition, to which Strangers were always admitted, on applying to the Director of the Establishment for tickets.

Hospice de la Salpêtrière, Boulevard de l'Hopital, près le Jardin du Roi. This vast and well-regulated Hospital, nobly endowed by Louis XIV., and enriched by private contributions, is capable of containing nearly eight thousand persons; and receives females of all descriptions, incapable of earning their bread.

Hopital des Enfans-Trouvés, Rue d'Enfer. The exemplary Vincent de Paul erected, in 1640, a Hospital for Foundlings; which was afterwards greatly assisted both by private and public bounty; but, nevertheless, in 1792, out of eight thousand children, placed in this asylum, four thousand died ere they had attained their second year: and to check the course of this afflictive mortality, Monsieur Hombron conceived the idea of uniting the Mothers with their Children; and thus preserving both: ceasing, therefore, to make a lying-in Hospital of the *Hôtel-Dieu*, the French Government formed the Foundling-Hospital into a double establishment; the one part for pregnant Women, and the other for deserted Infants. These two establishments are, however, now divided, the Lying-in Hospital being in the Rue de la Bourbe.

Observatoire, Rue du Faubourg S. Jacques. This building was erected by the order of Louis XIV.; and has, of late years, been much improved in point of convenience, and amply furnished with astronomical instruments.

Palais du Temple. Except the Palace of the Grand Prieur, nothing remains of the edifice which, about the middle of the twelfth century, belonged to the Knights

Templars; and was given, after their abolition, to the Knights of Malta. The Palace of the Grand Prieur, however, has been repaired at a large expense, and is now a convent.

Palais de la Bourse, Rue des Filles S. Thomas. Paris long wanted an Exchange worthy of her riches and extensive commerce, and this fine building does honour to its architect, Bronguiard.

Greniers de Réserve, Boulevard Bourdon. This immense storehouse for grain, whose appellation alone bespeaks its importance, was begun in 1807; and such is its size, that, although not carried to half the elevation intended, the expense of materials and labour only has amounted to twelve millions of livres.

Abattoirs, ou Tueries. Those buildings, constructed by the Romans to give health to the ancient capital of the civilized world, were not more magnificent than the *Abattoir* or Slaughter-house of Mont Martre, situated at the top of the Rue de Rochechouart: the length of the ground on which it stands being 1078 Paris feet, and the breadth 385 feet. It contains a number of courts, watered by the Ourcq, four sheep pens, four ranges of stalls for oxen, commodious slaughter-houses, and ample storehouses for fodder, etc. The *Abattoir de Popincourt*, situated in the Rue des Amandiers S. Antoine, already boasts seven sheep-pens, and seven ranges of stalls for oxen. The *Abattoir d'Ivry*, less vast, rises on the outside of the barrier des Deux Moulins: the *Abattoir de Vaugirard*, on the Place de Breteuil, equals the others in convenience if not extent. The *Abattoir du Roule*, erected in the Plaine de Mouceaux, at the extremity of the Rue de Miroménil, is one of the most spacious.

Halle au Blé, Rue de Viarmes. The cupola of this market, built in 1782, by Molinos and Legrand, was 377 Paris feet in circumference; and from the pavement to its summit, 100 feet: it consisted of wood, placed in a hemispheric form, and apparently so slight, that it was impossible to contemplate this extraordinary piece of architecture without wondering how it held together. After standing twenty years, it fell a prey to fire; and has been restored on a plan wholly new, and particularly well worth observation, from rendering it invulnerable to the attacks of the element by which it was, in 1802, destroyed. Great additions have likewise been made to the size of the market; which was, previously, too small for the consumption of the metropolis.

Halle aux Vins, Quai S. Bernard. The ancient emporium for wines having fallen to decay, Napoleon ordered the first stone of the present building to be laid on the 15th of August, 1813; and this immense edifice, constructed to hold four hundred thousand wine casks, is divided into numerous magazines and cellars.

Marché à la Volaille et au Gibier. Nothing can be more elegant of its kind than this market; which generally receives fresh supplies of game, etc., on Mondays, Wednesdays, Fridays, and Saturdays.

Of the sixteen Bridges which are seen at Paris, the *Pont-Neuf*, erected by Henry IV., is the longest;[1] the *Pont Louis XVI*, and that of the *Ecole Militaire*, the boldest with respect to design; and the *Pont des Arts*, and that of the *Jardin du Roi*, the most remarkable on account of their lightness, elegance, and arches of iron. A fine suspension bridge, called that of *Les Invalides*, is now building.

Fontaine de l'Esplanade du Boulevard de Bondi. The composition of this fountain is simple; the execution good; and the effect produced by the water, falling in sheets from basin to basin, particularly pleasing.

Fontaine des Innocens. This fountain was erected in 1551, according to the designs of Lescot and Goujon; and afterwards removed from its original situation, added to, and placed in the centre of the *Marché des Innocens*, where it now stands.

Fontaine de Grenelle, Rue de Grenelle. This work, executed by Bouchardon, and erected in 1739, is admired with respect to the sculpture and architecture; but so sparingly provided with water, as to destroy the effect of the fountain, which is embellished with statues representing the city of Paris, the Seine, and the Marne.

Fontaine de la Bastille. This magnificent fountain, designed by the emperor Napoleon, and, like too many of his works, unfinished, rises on the site of the Bastille, in a commanding situation; and was to have been surmounted by an enormously colossal elephant, whose proboscis was to have dispensed the water. The model of this elephant may be seen in a building near the fountain.

Cimetières et Catacombes.— Paris formerly exhibited no burial-grounds adorned with funereal monuments; the cause of which seems to have been, that the possessors of riches and honours were entombed within the walls of consecrated buildings; while the mortal remains of the poor were thrown into the vast and common grave of the respective cemeteries; and even grudged a little earth to cover them. These receptacles of corruption, by constantly evaporating putrid air, produced epidemic maladies; and thus punished the living for their want of piety toward the dead: in 1773, therefore, the Parliament of Paris ordered the *Cimetière des Innocens* (the largest and most noxious of these receptacles), to be closed: and soon after all the cemeteries within the city were closed likewise; though pride and interest still produced burials in the churches: the remains of the poor, however, were transported, without scruple, from the ancient cemeteries, into vast and profound stone-quarries, on the outside of the city: and, during the revolution, even the asylum of a church did not preserve the bones of the deceased from the touch of sacrilege; the remains of the prince, and those of the peasant, finding, in the before-named quarries, a common grave. In 1800 a decree was issued for cemeteries to be formed without the city walls, and in 1804, Government empowered the friends of the deceased to erect monuments to their memory in the cemeteries; a circumstance which soon changed the aspect of these chambers of death. The hand-

---

[1] The statue of Henry IV. has been recently re-erected on one side of the Pont-Neuf.

somest cemetery in the environs of Paris is that of Père Lachaise; and here lie united all sorts and conditions of men; Jews, Infidels, Papists, and Protestants, forming one common dust.

To the south of Paris, under a spot called *La Tombe Issoire*, is a funereal receptacle of another description. Nothing above ground announces this abode of melancholy; which lies amidst vast stone-quarries; and is denominated The Catacombs, from the resemblance it bears to burial-places so called at Rome and Naples. Since the year 1806, this spot has been the receptacle for all the human bones which, during several ages, were accumulating in the cemeteries and suppressed churches within the walls of Paris. A dark staircase, just wide enough for one person, and penetrating ninety feet under ground, leads to the principal gallery, which admits two persons abreast. To the right and left are vaults of great extent: and that strangers may not lose themselves in this dangerous labyrinth, a black line has been traced on the roof of the principal gallery, to serve as a guide. Rocks jutting out, here and there, relieve the too great uniformity of this gallery; which leads to another, called that of Port-Mahon, from containing a model of the last named place, made by an old soldier who worked in the quarries, and was at length crushed to death, by an enormous stone which fell upon him. Picturesque and terrific rocks next meet the eye, and lead to a vestibule, at the end of which is a black door, the entrance to an apartment where millions of human bones, forming a kind of mosaic work, are placed in straight lines between the pillars which support the ponderous roof of the cavern; whose walls exhibit, at intervals, religious sentences, descriptive of the immortality of the soul, and the blessings of the life to come. Here is likewise a small Chapel with an expiatory altar, on which are these words: "*Second Septembre*, 1792."

The environs of Paris contain a variety of objects that merit notice; the most prominent of which are the following:

S. Cloud. The furniture of this royal Château (about two leagues from Paris, on the road to Versailles), is peculiarly splendid and elegant; and its park merits attention, particularly when the water-works are exhibited.

Sèvres. This town, which is very near S. Cloud, contains the celebrated manufactory of China; long deemed the most beautiful in Europe.

Versailles. This is a fine town, four leagues distant from Paris; and contains 28,000 inhabitants: its royal Château was despoiled and deserted during the revolutionary government; but is now undergoing repair. The Ceilings and Theatre of this Palace merit notice; the Orangery is particularly beautiful; the Water-Works are celebrated; the *Châteaux* of *Grand Trianon* and *Petit Trianon* (both in the grounds), are objects of curiosity; and the public Library of the town deserves attention.

I will now close my account of Paris by saying, that it has gained much during the last twenty years, in point of wealth, convenience, and external grandeur, and also with respect to society. The Parisians have paid England the compliment of adopting her taste, with respect to laying out gardens, shrubberies, etc.: they have likewise profited by her agricultural knowledge; and also adopted many of her modes of life.

Paris, like Calais, has been ridded, within the last twenty years, of that multitude of Mendicants who formerly filled its streets: and, if we may judge by appearances, there are fewer individuals of the French nation who have any need, at present, to depend on alms for their support.

It is necessary that British Subjects, previous to leaving Paris, should go to the *Préfecture de Police*, near the Pont-Neuf, to reclaim their Passports; which are taken from them at the frontier, and sent hither: this Office is open from nine in the morning till four. Hence, every Passport must be sent to the British Ambassador (whose signature can only be obtained from eleven in the morning till one); then it must be taken once more to the Police Office. Persons going into Italy should likewise have their Passports countersigned by the Austrian Ambassador at Paris.[1]

---

[1] The trouble and detention, with respect to Passports, which frequently occur at Paris, may be avoided, if a traveller provide himself, previous to his departure from London, not only with the necessary passport from the French Ambassador, but likewise with another, from the Sardinian Ambassador, if he purpose crossing either Cenis, or the Estrelles; or, if he intend to cross the Simplon, from the Austrian Ambassador. A traveller thus provided, is authorized to direct the Police-Office, either at Calais or Boulogne, or any other French port where he may land, to forward his passport to the last Custom-house in his road through France: he is also authorized to demand a provisional passport; on showing which, at the Pont de Beauvoisin, or any other frontier Custom-house, whither he may have ordered his original passport to be sent, he receives that passport again, and is thereby enabled to enter Italy.

CHAPTER II.

SWITZERLAND, THE SIMPLON, MILAN, ETC.

Journey to Fontainebleau—State of the road from Paris thither—Royal Château at Fontainebleau—Sens—Joigny—Auxerre—State of the road between the last-named town and Fontainebleau—S. Bris—Grottoes of Arcy—State of the road between Vermanton and Lucy-le-Bois—Rouvray—Pont-de-Pany—Dijon—Description of that city—Genlis—Auxonne—Dôle—Poligny—Military road over the Jura-Alps—French frontier Custom-house—Magnificent view on descending to Gex—Geneva—Description of that city—Lake of Geneva—Voltaire's Villa at Ferney—Excursion to Chamouni, and the Mont-Blanc—Description of the military road from Geneva, and over the Simplon, to Domo-d'Ossola—Lago-Maggiore—Borromean Islands—Colossal Statue of S. Carlo Borromeo—Description of the road from Sesto-Calende to Milan—Triumphal Arch intended as a termination to the Simplon-road—Milan—Description of that city—Monza—Lodi—Custom-house near the Po—Piacenza—Description of that city—Parma—Description of that city—Reggio—Modena—Description of that city—Castel Franco—Custom-house there—Bologna—Description of that city and its environs—State of the road between Milan and Bologna—State of the road between Bologna and Florence—Volcano near Pietramala—Country round Florence—Approach to that city.

BEING anxious to see the new military route, made over the Jura-Alps and the Simplon to Milan, and finding that the road from Dijon to the base of the Jura, though not good, was passable, my friends and I determined to go that way into Italy.[2]

After quitting Paris, we crossed the Orge on a fine bridge, drove through the village of Essonne, seated on the Juine (observing the Seine at a little distance), crossed the Ecolle at Ponthiery; and then drove through the village of Chailly to the immense forest of Fontainebleau; than which nothing can be more picturesque, nor, in some parts, more gloomily magnificent. On each side of the road are lofty ranges of grey rocks; and at their very summits beeches, and other trees, of an astonishing magnitude; the richness of whose foliage, contrasted with the rude and barren appearance of the huge and shapeless masses of stone in which they vegetate, exhibits one of the most extraordinary scenes imaginable.

After driving several miles, through this singular forest, we discovered in its centre, the town of Fontainebleau; and soon found ourselves housed at a comfortable inn, *l'Hôtel de la Ville de Lyon*; where the charges are moderate; a circumstance worth recollecting, at a place famed for the rapacity of its innkeepers.

The road, from Paris to Fontainebleau, is paved, and in excellent condition: the royal château in the last mentioned town merits notice; as it contains

---

1 From Auxonne to Poligny the road is, generally speaking, bad after a continuance of heavy rain; though it has been so well repaired, subsequent to June, 1817, that when I repassed it, during May, 1819, I found it one of the best roads in France.

2 The most profitable money travellers can take from Paris into northern Italy is Napoleons; as they pass current for their full value throughout that country; neither does any loss accrue from taking them into southern Italy.

magnificent apartments beautifully painted in arabesque; splendid furniture; peculiarly fine specimens of Sèvres china; and some few good easel pictures; among which is the blessed Virgin and Infant Saviour, S. John, and Elizabeth, by Raphael. The Gallery contains a bust of Henry IV., said to be the best likeness extant of that great prince; and, in the same apartment, are busts of Francis I., Sully, Washington, and the celebrated Duke of Marlborough. In this château, likewise, is a small mahogany table, on which Napoleon signed his abdication; and which still bears marks of a penknife it was his custom, while thinking deeply, to strike into the table or desk he wrote upon.

Fontainebleau is supposed to contain 9,000 inhabitants.

On quitting this town, we reentered the forest; and drove several miles, amidst scenery not unlike parts of the Pyrenees, to Fossard; thence proceeding, by the side of the Yonne, to Villeneuve-la-Guiard,[1] Pont-sur-Yonne, and Sens; between the two last of which places the country is rich in vineyards.

Sens, anciently the capital of the Sennones, contains 11,000 inhabitants, is seated at the confluence of the Yonne and the Vanne, and encircled by handsome promenades, and Roman works, which deserve the notice of antiquaries. Its cathedral is adorned with fine painted glass, namely, two roses, the one representing Heaven, the other Purgatory (these are placed above the two side-doors of the church); and the windows in the Chapels of S. Eutrope and N. D. de Loretto, which were executed by J. Cousin. The Chapel of S. Savinien contains an excellent representation, in stucco, of a curtain; and in the centre of the choir is a monument, by Coustou, erected to the memory of the unfortunate parents of Louis XVIII., and embellished with statues of Religion, Immortality, Conjugal Love, and Time, whose mantle covers the Dauphin's urn, and seems ready to envelope that of the Dauphiness; she being alive when this monument was begun. The cypress wreaths are remarkably well executed, and the statues of Time and Religion much admired; especially the latter, but the shape of the monument wants elegance.[2]

On quitting Sens, we crossed the Vanne, driving through a fine valley watered by the Yonne; the graceful sinuosities of which river, combined with the vineyards on its banks, greatly embellish this part of France. After passing through a magnificent avenue of poplars to Villeneuve-sur-Yonne, a pretty town containing a large, and, judging from the outside, a handsome church, we reached Villevallier; thence traversing a bold and picturesque country to Joigny,[3] anciently *Joviniacum*, built on each side of the Yonne, and joined together by a handsome bridge; the circumstance, perhaps, from which it may derive its modern name. The Château here, erected by the Cardinal di Gondi, commands an extensive view; and the adjoining church of S. Jean contains a curious Sar-

---

[1] A good inn here, the *Hôtel de la Souche*.
[2] The best inn here is the *Hôtel de L'Ecu*, kept by Goisset, fils.
[3] A good inn here, the *Hôtel des Cinq Mineurs*.

cophagus; on the cover of which is a recumbent figure, apparently designed to represent our Saviour; while surrounding three parts of the Sarcophagus, are several statues, which, owing to their situation, appear gigantic.

From Joigny we proceeded, through Bassou, to Auxerre;[1] which is seated on the left bank of the Yonne, and contains 12,000 inhabitants. It stands amidst wide-stretching vineyards; as do all the large towns in this part of France; and but for the extreme ugliness of Gallic architecture, when uncorrected by Italian taste, might be called a handsome city: its public edifices seem to have been considerably injured by the late revolutions: its Cathedral, however, merits notice; and contains fine painted glass. The three Gothic churches of S. Pierre likewise deserve attention; as do the Quai-Condé, the Quai-Bourbon, and the Promenades.

We found the road between Fontainebleau and Auxerre paved in some places, well-kept throughout, and peculiarly exempt from steep hills; but, between the last-named town and S. Bris, it becomes hilly, and continues so for several leagues. After quitting S. Bris, we proceeded to Vermanton;[2] two leagues south of which, are the celebrated grottoes of Arcy; and either from Vermanton, or Lucy-le-Bois,[3] the Post-master will allow his horses to go round by these grottoes, which contain fine stalactites; but cannot be seen to advantage without the aid of torches; and are, during winter, full of water, and at all times damp. Vermanton is seated on the right bank of the Cure; and from this town to about one league beyond the next post (Lucy-le-Bois) the road, unless frequently repaired, becomes bad after heavy rain: a new branch, commencing near Lucy-le-Bois, has, however, been lately made to this road: and, though longer, it should always be preferred to the old road, because harder and smoother.

Having passed Avallony,[4] which is pleasantly situated on the banks of the Cousin, and contains 5,500 inhabitants, we proceeded through an uninteresting country, to Rouvray;[5] thence driving by the side of the Cousin, and then crossing the Serein, on our way to Maisonneuve,[6] and Vitteaux[7] on the Brenne, which contains 2,000 inhabitants. After this, we traversed a hilly country, embellished with vineyards, to La Chaleur (called *Mal-nommée*; it being a very cold place); hence proceeding to Pont-de-Pany; and observing no objects that particularly deserved attention, till, on coming to a château, once magnificent, but now reduced to ruins, we were agreeably surprised to discover, at an abrupt turn of the road, beautiful Alpine scenery, continuing the whole way to the Post-house[8] at Pont-de-Pany, a bridge thrown over the Ouche, near the head of the Canal of Burgundy. Hence we drove for a short time between rocks and mountains;

---

[1] Here are good inns, namely, *Le Léopard* and *L'Hôtel de Beaune*.
[2] *L'Hôtel de S. Nicolas* is a good inn; and there are others.
[3] Lucy-le-Bois contains two inns, the *Post-house* and *L'Hôtel des Diligences*.
[4] Two inns, *Le Lion d'Or*, and *La Ville de Dijon*.
[5] Two inns, *L'Hôtel de la Poste*, which is remarkably good, and *L'Hôtel du Raisin*.
[6] Inn, *La Poste*, and tolerably good.
[7] Inn, *La Poste*, and good.
[8] The *Post-house* at Pont-de-Pany is a tolerably good inn.

and then traversed a fine country to Dijon; passing, as we approached that town, some curious rocks on the left.

Dijon (anciently *Dibio*), the capital of Burgundy, and supposed to contain 21,600 inhabitants, is seated in a fertile plain, between the rivers Ouche and Suzon, and must formerly have been handsome, but has suffered so severely from the late revolutions, that few of its public edifices now merit notice, except the spires of S. Benigne and S. Jean; the former of which, 375 Paris feet in height, is called the finest piece of architecture of its kind in Europe; the latter does not measure quite 300 Paris feet. The Promenade du Cours merits notice; and on the City Gate, leading to Pont-de-Pany, is the Car of Victory, not long since placed there in honour of the duke d'Angoulême. Commerce appears to flourish at Dijon; and wines, together with eatables of every kind, are particularly good; but the climate, to persons who suffer from a cold and cutting wind, is ungenial.[1]

Soon after quitting this city we discovered the Jura Mountains: and, on entering the next town, Genlis, observed to the right, a château, said to belong to the Comtesse of that name, so much distinguished in the literary world by her writings for the use of young people. Genlis is a pretty village, adorned with neat houses, and a handsome bridge over the Norge.[2] Hence we proceeded to Auxonne, seated on the Saône, and containing 5,000 inhabitants.[3] A battle was fought in this neighbourhood, between the French and the Allies; and bones of men and horses were, not long since, sufficiently discoverable to mark the field of action.

The road is hilly to the next post, Dôle: that town, built on the Doubs, was once strong, but Louis XIV. demolished its fortifications. The College, one of the finest in France, the Promenade, called Le Cours, and the Canal of the Rhine, merit observation: and near Dole are remains of the ancient Roman road which extended from Lyon to the banks of the Rhine.[4] On quitting Dole we crossed a wooden bridge, according to appearance recently erected; and observed, both to the right and left, stone bridges broken down. After passing the rivers Doubs, Clause, Louve, and Cuisance, and driving through a particularly long and beautiful avenue of poplars terminated each way by a bridge, we arrived at Mont-sous-Vaudrey; thence descending, not rapidly, but almost constantly, to Poligny, amidst corn-fields and vineyards.

Poligny is situated at the extremity of an extensive plain, near the source of the Glantine, and at the base of the Jura; it contains 5,300 inhabitants.[5]

On quitting Poligny we began to ascend the Jura Mountains, through a fine road, constructed by order of Napoleon, to form part of the *Grande Route militaire*, leading to the Simplon: and so judiciously are the ascents and descents of this pass managed, that a drag-chain is seldom requisite even for heavy carriages, though be-

---

[1] Here are several inns; the *Hôtel du Parc* and the *Hôtel de la Cloche* are very good ones.
[2] Best inn, *L'Hôtel de la Côte d'Or*.
[3] Inns, *L'Hôtel du Grand Cerf*, very good; and *L'Hôtel du Mont-Jura*.
[4] Best inn at Dole, *L'Hôtel de la Ville de Paris*.
[5] Here are two inns, *L'Hôtel de Genève*, and *L'Hôtel du Grand Cerf*. The former is the best.

tween Morez and Les Rousses the road, in some few places, would be rendered much pleasanter, and indeed much safer, by the addition of parapet walls.

The base of the Jura presents, near Poligny, thorns, briers, gooseberry-bushes, beech-trees, and enormous rocks of granite. The commencement of the ascent exhibits bold and beautiful Alpine scenery, together with a magnificent view of the vast and fertile plains of France: while, not far distant from Poligny, are picturesque ruins of a spacious convent, seated amidst rich vineyards, and encircled by luxuriant woods. Having reached the summit of the first ascent, and passed Boreau, where the rocks are strikingly fine, we traversed a comparatively tame country to Champagnole, a town of considerable size, situated on the right bank of the Ain.[1] Much of this town appears recently built, as indeed do the greater part of all the towns, villages, and pretty detached cottages on the Jura Mountains. At Champagnole we crossed the Ain; thence proceeding through a country adorned with pasturages, cottages, villages, and woods, to a magnificent gallery, cut through the side of lofty rocks, clothed with firs to their summits; while opposite to this gallery rise woods and mountains still more elevated; and in a deep dell, at the base of the road, runs a torrent, whose waters further on, at the bridge of Dombief, form a beautiful cascade. Continuing our course through wild and sublime scenery, we reached a romantic village, called Maison-neuve;[2] beyond which, to the left, among woods of peculiarly beautiful firs, are rocks worth notice, on account of their whimsical shape. Having passed another village, and driven through a fine grazing country, bounded by woods, we crossed the Pont-de-Leme, and arrived at S. Laurent.[3] The road from Champagnole hither is excellent, and, generally speaking, a gradual ascent; and no sooner does the winter-snow begin to disappear in this country, than the hedges and pasturages are adorned with such a variety and profusion of beautiful flowers as no other part of the Alps can boast.

Quitting S. Laurent, we recrossed the Leme, driving amidst cottages and pasturages to another magnificent gallery, cut through woods of beech and fir, and terminated by a plain. Hence we descended for five miles, between rocks and mountains, clothed with beeches, to Morez, a considerable town, seated on the river Bienne, and close to a brawling torrent, called Le Bief de la Chaille, in a valley so narrow as merely to admit two rows of houses and the street which divides them. The mountains that form this valley rise almost perpendicularly, like walls of a stupendous height, and give Morez the appearance of being entombed in the lowest dell of the Alps; it contains, however, some good houses, together with 1,200 inhabitants.[4] Here we were obliged to continue nearly two days, because our passports had neither been signed by the

---

[1] Here are two small inns, namely, *The Hôtel de Genève*, and *The Hôtel de Lyon*, at either of which travellers might breakfast or dine, but they would be comfortless sleeping-places.

[2] Maison-neuve contains an inn where travellers might breakfast or dine, but it is not a sleeping-place.

[3] Inn, *La Poste*, and very comfortable.

[4] Inn, *La Poste*, and very comfortable.

Austrian Minister at Paris, nor the French Minister of the Interior; nor yet at the gates of the different cities through which we had passed. In vain I urged that they had been granted by the French Ambassador in London, expressly for the purpose of enabling us to travel through France to Italy, and that we never were asked to show them at the gates of the cities through which we had passed; in short, after consulting every person in the town who seemed capable of giving advice with respect to this vexatious detention, we were compelled to send one of our servants fifteen miles, through a dangerous road, to the Sub-Prefect of the district, entreating him to let us proceed: and though our petition was immediately and most handsomely granted, we, nevertheless, found, in all the remaining part of our journey, great inconvenience from the want of Austrian passports; and this, indeed, is not surprising, as the Emperor of Austria may now be called the Ruler of Italy.

Having obtained leave to quit Morez, we proceeded to Les Rousses by a steep ascent, parallel with a noisy torrent, and between immense rocks, above which tower the mountains of Rezoux and Dôle,[1] resplendent with snow, while the near prospect presents Alpine trees, shrubs, and flowers. This road, for some miles beyond Morez, is too narrow to be perfectly safe, either in the dark, or after heavy rain.

Having passed Les Rousses, which contains the frontier custom-house of France, where, however, on quitting that kingdom, travellers meet with no detention, we traversed several valleys to La Vattay; thence proceeding to Gex,[2] through a magnificent road, or (more properly speaking) gallery, which passes under a deep archway hewn out of a granite rock; and exhibits, for nearly a mile, an upper gallery made to catch the earth and stones, which are continually falling from the more elevated parts of the Alp. On the descent stands the *Fontaine Napoléon*, bearing an inscription nearly obliterated.

This side of the Jura is embellished with luxuriant pasturages, neat cottages, and noble woods of beech and fir, which clothe its summits: but what particularly arrests the attention of travellers on descending towards Gex, is a prospect, abruptly presented to their view, of the Pays de Vaud, the Lake of Geneva, and the stupendous Glaciers which surround it; a prospect so perfectly unique, rich, beautiful, and sublime, as neither to be described nor imagined; and all I shall say of it is, that I am persuaded there are few persons who would not think themselves recompensed for almost any degree of fatigue by seeing this prospect to advantage.

Having passed Gex, and the villa once belonging to Voltaire at Ferney, we entered Geneva; crossing, on the way to our hotel in that city, two bridges, whose arches are bathed with the waters of the lake, which, under the appellation of the Rhone, continue their course through France to the Gulf of Lyons.

---

[1] The Dôle rises 3948 Paris feet above the level of the Lake of Geneva, and is one of the loftiest summits of the Jura Alps.
[2] Best Inn, *Les Balances*.

Geneva, said to contain near 30,000 inhabitants, and anciently a strong town, belonging to the Allobroges, is delightfully situated on the immense lake which bears its name, and divided into unequal parts by the Rhone. It possesses fewer public buildings worth notice than almost any other large city of Europe: but this deficiency is counterbalanced by the fine views from its ramparts, and the peculiar richness and beauty of its environs; which boast a considerable number of handsome villas, and a great variety of delightful walks, rides, and drives.

The public Library, open every Tuesday morning from one till three, merits notice; as it contains rare and curious books; and an ancient Roman silver shield, adorned with *bassi-rilievi*, and found in the bed of the Arve, during the year 1721.[1] The Hydraulic Machine, which supplies the fountains of the city with water, likewise merits notice.[2]

The Leman, or Lake of Geneva, anciently called *Lemanus*, is computed to be about nineteen leagues in length, and between three and four in breadth at the widest part, near Rolle: it abounds with fine fish, and its banks are said to be visited by forty-nine kinds of birds.

The object generally thought best worth notice, in the immediate vicinity of Geneva, is Voltaire's villa at Ferney; which house, since the death of its first owner, has had many masters; but they have all deemed it sacrilege to change any thing: and consequently the rooms are furnished just the same as when he died. On entering the hall my attention was caught by a large picture, *composed* by Voltaire himself, and executed by a wretched artist whom he met with at Ferney. That Voltaire was the vainest of men I have always heard; but that any man could have the overweening vanity to compose such a picture of himself is scarcely credible. In the fore-ground stands this celebrated philosopher, holding the Henriade, which he is presenting to Apollo, who has just descended from Olympus, in order to receive it: in the back-ground is the temple of Memory, toward which flies Fame, at the same time pointing to the Henriade.—The Muses and Graces are surrounding Voltaire; and seem in the act of carrying his bust to the temple of Memory—the heroes and heroines of the Henriade are standing astonished at his wonderful talents—the authors who wrote against him are falling into the infernal regions, which gape to receive them and their works; while Envy and her Imps are expiring at his feet: the family of Calas likewise is exhibited in this picture. From the hall we entered a handsome saloon, ornamented with a bust of Voltaire; and a design in china for the tomb of a lady supposed to have died in child-birth, but who was, in fact, buried alive: it represents the lady and her child bursting through the tomb; which is broken by the artist in so natu-

---

[1] The Library belonging to Barbezat and Delarue, Rue de derrière le Rhône, No. 177, facing the Post Office, where most of the European newspapers may be found, contains a large collection of books. Those of M. Ledouble and M. Cherbulier are also well furnished.

[2] The best hotels in the city of Geneva are, *Les Balances* and *L'Ecu de Genève*; at the latter of which the charges are moderate, the dinners well served, and the beds good; but the smells in this house render it unpleasant. We paid three francs a-head for dinner at the *Ecu de Genève*.

ral a manner, that one feels ready to exclaim, "What a pity it is that this beautiful monument has met with an accident." In Voltaire's bed-room are portraits of his friends; and the vase wherein his heart was placed before its removal to Paris: this monument is of black marble, plain, but neat; and immediately under that place which contained the heart is written: "*Mon esprit est partout, et mon cœur est ici.*" Over the vase is written: "*Mes mânes sont consolés, puisque mon cœur est au milieu de vous:*" alluding, I presume, to the surrounding portraits; namely, Frederic the Great of Prussia; Le Kain, the celebrated French actor; Catherine II. of Russia; and Madame du Chastelet. Voltaire himself is in the centre; and in various parts of the room are Newton, Milton, and several other great men, both English and French.

After resting ourselves, for a day, at the *Hôtel d'Angleterre*, at Sécheron, one of the best inns on the Continent, and about a quarter of a league from Geneva, we hired a landau and four horses for three days, in order to visit the celebrated Valley of Chamouni, and see as much of Mont-Blanc as is practicable during so early a part of summer as the commencement of June.[1] At five o'clock, therefore, on a cloudless and delightful morning, we set out from Sécheron; drove through Geneva the moment the gates of that city were opened,[2] and almost immediately entered Savoy; finding the road good, the ascents gentle, the country abounding with corn, vineyards, and fruit-trees; rosemary and barberry-bushes growing in and near the hedges, and beeches, mingled with firs, crowning the heights. At the distance of half a league from Geneva we passed through Chêne; and, one league further on, discovered, in profile, the Salève; passing, soon after, the château of Mournex, and the hill and château of Esery. We then crossed the Menoge, a river which rises at the base of the Voirons; traversed the villages of Nangi and Contamine; and saw, towering above us, the ruins of the castle of Fossigny.

Our first stop was at Bonneville; rather a large town, containing two inns; either of which can furnish a good breakfast and delicious honey. After baiting our horses for an hour and a half, we resumed our journey; crossing the Arve on a stone bridge, 500 feet in length, passing through the small town of Cluse, and then traversing the delightful valley of Maglan, rich in corn, vineyards, and fruit-trees, enamelled with flowers, and encircled by enormous and fantastically-shaped Alps, crowned with woods of beech and fir, and exhibiting the most wild and picturesque scenery imaginable. These Alps seemed gradually to increase in magnitude as we advanced; while the glens, through which our road lay, gradually grew narrower. Three quarters of a league beyond Maglan we perceived, on our left, a magnificent cascade, called Nant d'Arpenas, falling from a height of 800 feet; and, shortly after, we were presented with a view of Mont-Blanc, which

---

[1] A Swiss cabriolet, called *un char-à-banc*, is an excellent carriage for this excursion; because it can go the whole way to Chamouni; which a coach or post-chaise cannot.

[2] The gates of Geneva are usually opened about five in the morning, during summer, and shut at ten in the evening.

continues to exhibit its awful and stupendous beauties the whole way to Chamouni. We now saw the town of Salenche, seated near a noisy torrent, at the base of cultivated mountains, above whose lofty summits rise pyramids of eternal snow. Leaving this town on our right, we drove to S. Martin, and found there a good inn, the *Hôtel de Mont-Blanc*, containing a considerable number of beds, and commanding a particularly fine view of that part of the mountain denominated the *Dôme du Goûté*. This inn likewise contains a small cabinet of natural history for sale.

From S. Martin, or Salenche, to Chamouni, is a journey of six or seven hours; which can only be accomplished on foot, on horse, or mule-back, or in a *char-à-banc*: we therefore left our Geneva carriage at S. Martin, where we slept; hiring, instead, a *char-à-banc*, at eighteen French livres per day; three mules, at seven livres each per day; and three Guides, at six livres each per day; beside the driver of the *char*. Our guides were Jean Riant, Vinence Riant, and Colas Dufour; and we found them all civil, careful, and intelligent.

At a very early hour in the morning we left S. Martin; and not long after crossed the Nant Sauvage, a dangerous torrent when swollen with rain: generally speaking, however, the road, though rough, is safe; but the aspect of the country between S. Martin and Servoz, particular spots excepted, is wild and gloomy; though here, and indeed throughout our whole excursion, we saw an infinite number of flowers, intermingled with barberry and rosemary-bushes. On approaching the village of Chède, we crossed another delicious plain; and passed through several hamlets, which, in times of civil discord, afforded shelter to the ancient Romans. The magnificent cascade of Chède is about a quarter of a league from that village; and the lake of Chède, situated near the road, though small, is pretty, and serves to reflect on its bosom the majestic summits of Mont-Blanc, which is easily distinguished from its neighbours by being the only triple-headed monster among them.

Proceeding to the beautiful and fertile valley of Servoz, we could not behold, without shuddering, the ruins of an Alp, which, in its fall, menaced this luxuriant spot with destruction; insomuch that the inhabitants fled precipitately; though not quick enough to prevent some of their children from being crushed to death: and the dust produced by rocks thrown violently against each other, led people at first to imagine that this terrific crash of nature proceeded from the eruption of a volcano.

We breakfasted at Servoz, a small village containing one solitary inn, somewhat like a hedge-alehouse in England, but where good honey and eggs may be procured, and likewise good coffee. Continuing our route, we passed a stream called the Servoz; and then, crossing the Arve on a picturesque bridge, discovered, to our right, the ruins of the Château de S. Michel; and, to our left, an abyss, where, impaled in jagged rocks of the most sombre hue, interspersed with fir-trees, flows the Arve, exhibiting a scene sublime even to horror. After ascending some way, by the side of this ravine, we at length entered the far-famed valley of Chamouni; first observing the glacier of Taconai; then, that of Bossons; and, at a distance, that of Bois; then traversing the torrent of Nagin, the hamlet of Ouche, the torrents of Gria, Taconia, and Bossons, and the Arve, previous to our arrival at the town of Chamouni. This town owes its existence to a convent of Benedictines, founded, in 1099, by a Count of Geneva; but the valley in which it stands might probably have been unknown at the present period, if two English gentlemen, Messrs. Windham and Pocock, had not, in the year 1741, discovered it; and given to modern Europe details respecting a place which even the natives of Geneva, though only eighteen leagues distant, had never heard of. It is situated 3,174 feet above the level of the Mediterranean sea, and contains two inns, both tolerably good.

The verdant clothing of the singular valley of Chamouni is beautifully contrasted with cloud-capped mountains, silvered by eternal snow; gloomy forests, chiefly composed of firs; cottages and hamlets scattered here and there; brawling torrents and rocks of red porphyry and granite, interspersed with glaciers of a dazzling whiteness, whence rise sea-green pyramids of ice, which, when illuminated either by the sun or moon, exhibit a prospect unique and wonderful; but, nevertheless, so much has been said in praise of this valley, that I own I felt disappointed on seeing it.

The botanist and mineralogist may find ample amusement at Chamouni: and here, as at S. Martin, there is, for sale, a cabinet of natural history, containing minerals of Mont-Blanc and S. Gothard; seals, necklaces, etc. made of the crystal of Mont-Blanc; together with insects and plants indigenous to the higher Alps. The honey of Chamouni is excellent.

Every part of the valley presents a view of Mont-Blanc; this gigantic Alp, primeval with a world whose several changes it has quietly witnessed, is said, by M. de Luc, to be fifteen thousand three hundred and three English feet, and, by M. de Saussure, seventeen thousand seven hundred Paris feet above the level of the Mediterranean sea: while the crust of snow, on its sides and summits, is supposed to exceed four hundred feet in depth. The first persons who ever reached the top of this stupendous mountain, seem to have been Jacques Balmat, of Chamouni, and Dr. Paccard: they went in the year 1786, and in 1787 were followed by M. de Saussure and an English gentleman. Without aspiring so high as to think of following their steps, we felt a great inclination to ascend to the *Mer de Glace*: but, on inquiry, it appeared that the Montanvert, which leads to the *Mer de Glace*, was so much clogged with snow, and threatened by avalanches, as to be impassable: our guides, however, assured us, that, by mounting the *Chapeau*, a giddying eminence opposite to Montanvert, we might obtain the gratification of our wishes, so far as to see the *Mer de Glace*; though we could not, by that path, reach it. Taking a hasty dinner, therefore, at Chamouni, we ordered our mules and *châr-à-banc*, bidding the guides provide the customary walking-sticks at Chamouni, which are six feet in length, with a sharp iron spike at the end of each. We then mounted our *char*, attended by the guides; who, when seated on their mules, and armed with our spear-like walking-sticks, very much resembled knights-errant of old, though not arrayed quite *comme il faut* for a tournament. We drove during half an hour through a good road, but were then obliged, owing to the rapidity of the ascent, to leave our carriage, and mount the mules: these animals conveyed us safely through a dirty hamlet, and up part of the Chapeau, till the road became so rugged, and the ascent so very steep, that we deemed it more prudent to trust to our own feet than those of the mules; and, each of us taking the arm of a guide, we pursued our way by walking at the extreme edge of terrific precipices, through a path so rugged, that nothing but the spiked sticks, with which we penetrated the ground at every step, could have prevented us from falling. By perseverance, however, we attained the wished-for height, and discovered, immediately above us, the *Mer de Glace*, though not that part which exhibits an unequal surface, but the smooth margin, whence descends an immense glacier; opposite to which we stood a full half hour, listening to the noise of distant and near avalanches, which the stillness of the scene rendered doubly audible, and contemplating the extraordinary appearance of the glacier, which I can compare to nothing but a narrow and tempestuous ocean, whose towering waves have been suddenly rendered motionless by an All-powerful hand.

Our journey to and from the Chapeau occupied three hours and a half: we therefore returned late to Chamouni: and, after having entered our names, and made our remarks in the travellers' book, which is a curious composition, we rested a few hours; and then set out early next morning for Geneva, under a sky perfectly serene and cloudless.

From Chamouni to Servoz we were three hours in returning—from Servoz to S. Martin three and a half—from S. Martin to Bonneville four—and from Bonneville to Geneva three and a half.

The price charged for dinner, at S. Martin and Chamouni, is five francs a-head—for beds, two francs a-head—and for breakfast, two francs and a half per head.

There is a mule-road, nine leagues in distance, from Chamouni to Martigny, which leads to S. Bernard and the Simplon.[1]

Having determined to pursue

---

[1] Persons who visit Chamouni at the proper season for ascending the *Montanvert*, should engage careful and judicious guides; and likewise hire a porter to carry cold provisions and wine. Ladies sometimes go part of the way in *chaises-à-porteur*; for each of which it is requisite to have six chairmen; but good walkers had much better trust to their feet.

It being a work of full three hours to ascend the *Montanvert*, and then descend to the *Mer de Glace*, it is advisable to set out from Chamouni by seven in the morning. For about one league and a quarter, there is a safe mule-road, passing through forests of firs, which exhibit traces of ancient avalanches, enormous blocks of granite, and large trees laid prostrate; but on entering a narrow and rugged path, called *Le Chemin des Crystalliers*, it is no longer practicable to go on mules: here, therefore, these animals are usually sent back to the *Source of the Arvéron*. The view near a little Fountain, called *Le Caillet*, merits notice: as the Arve, in the plain beneath, appears, from this elevated spot, like a thread; the Bourg like card-houses; and the fields and meadows like the squares of a chess-board, or beds in a flower-garden embellished with various shades of green. Beyond this fountain the road is excessively steep and rugged, though not dangerous; and after passing the *Hôpital de Blair*, built by an English genthe shortest route from Geneva to the Simplon, by passing through Savoy, instead of going round by Lausanne and the Pays de Vaud, we set out for Coligny; traversing a fine road, bordered with fruit-trees, corn-fields, and vineyards, and bounded by the Jura mountains on the right, and the Lake of Geneva, with its stupendous glaciers, on the left. We then crossed a bridge, which marks the limits between the territories of Geneva and Savoy; observed a finely situated old castle, and discovered Cenis, with great part of the lofty chain to which that Alp belongs. On arriving at Dovaine in Savoy, where the custom-house officers expect to be feed by travellers, we had our trunks plumbed, in order to secure them from examination, and then proceeded to Thonon; the road to which place exhibits a particularly fine view of the Lake, encircled by the Pays de Vaud, the Jura, the plains of Savoy, and the great Alps; and winds through a country abounding with corn and vines, trained in the Italian manner, from tree to tree.

Thonon, the ancient capital of the Duchy of Chablais, is pleasantly situated on the Lake. The site of the castle merits notice; and at a small distance from the town is the Convent of Ripaille. Hence we drove to Evian (celebrated for its mineral waters); crossing the Dranse, on a long narrow bridge, apparently built by the ancient Romans: but what especially charmed us in this part of the road, was the bold and varied outline presented by the Alps; together with the picturesque ruins of an ancient castle, beautifully surrounded with woods

tleman of that name, the Traveller is presented with a sight of the *Mer de Glace*; to reach which, occupies a full quarter of an hour; and persons who venture to walk upon its surface should be especially careful to avoid the cracks and chasms with which it abounds: the colour these chasms assume is a beautiful sea-green; and the waves of this frozen ocean, which from the top of *Montanvert* appear like furrows in a corn-field, are now discovered to be hillocks from twenty to forty feet high. The *Mer de Glace* is eight leagues in length, and one in breadth; and on its margin rise pyramidical rocks, called Needles, whose summits are lost in the clouds; they likewise are denominated the Court of their august Sovereign, Mont-Blanc; who glitters, on the opposite side, in stately repose; and being far more exalted than her attendants, veils in the heavens, which she seems to prop, a part of her sublime and majestic beauties. From the *Mer de Glace* travellers usually reascend the *Montanvert*, and dine either at *l'Hôpital de Blair*, or *La Pierre des Anglais*; an immense block of granite, so called because Messrs. Windham and Pocock, in 1741, made it their dinner-table, after they had penetrated, without a guide, into these unknown regions. Hence is the descent to the *Source of the Arvéron*, through the *Chemin des Chèvres*; a short but extremely rugged path; on pursuing which it is not uncommon to see avalanches fall from the surrounding mountains, and pyramids of ice tumble with a tremendous crash and roll to the bottom of *Montanvert*, at whose base is the *Source of the Arvéron*; after examining which, travellers usually re-mount their mules, and return to Chamouni.

The inhabitants of this country are well-looking, sensible, honest, and remarkably fearless. The woods are peopled with rabbits, white hares, martens, and ermines; the rocks with marmots and the sagacious chamois. These last-named animals live together in flocks, and generally feed in valleys where no sportsman can penetrate; while a few are constantly detached from the main body, as scouts; and others perform the duty of sentinels. The courage and agility with which the chamois leaps from precipice to precipice, and scales rocks almost perpendicular, should teach the boldest Alpine travellers not to feel vain of their achievements.

Persons who wish to vary their route back to Geneva, may return by the *Col de Balme*; from whose summit the Valais, the Rhone, the great and the small S. Bernard, the passages of Cenis and the Simplon, S. Gothard, and the Alps of Berne and Unterwalde, are all discoverable; while the sublimity of this extensive view is greatly heightened by a near prospect of Mont-Blanc and her surrounding Needles. I would, however, rather advise travellers to return by Six, Samoëns, and Thonon; whence it is easy to embark upon the Lake, and proceed to Geneva. Going all the way by land, the distance is fifteen leagues.

1 Inn, *Les Balances*, and not very comfortable as a sleeping-place.

of intermingled walnut and chesnut trees. Soon after passing this ruin, our road conducted us to the very brink of the Lake, shaded by trees of the before-named description; the town of Morge being exactly opposite; and, still further to the left, that of Lausanne. A fishing-boat, rowed by women and children, and a vessel laden with wood for Geneva, gave additional interest to this delightful scene.

Continuing our course by the side of the Lake, we reached the rocks of Meillerie[1] (immortalized by Rousseau); which exhibit striking proofs of the obstacles presented by nature, to the formation of the new military road made by Napoleon, and cut through masses of stone 200 feet high; which tower on one side, above the traveller; whilst on the other, rise two walls, the first serving as a parapet, the second strengthening the foundations of the road, and preventing them from being washed away by the Lake, on whose bed they rest. Near S. Gingoux a gorge in the mountains (which are here broken into forms indescribably wild and magnificent) discovers the source of the Amphion, celebrated for the before-named mineral waters, which enrich Evian. Vevey is seen on the opposite shore. S. Gingoux belongs to the Valais; and the post-house, a good inn which contains twenty beds, is situated beautifully, near the termination of the Lake, where it loses itself in the Rhone. Immediately after leaving S. Gingoux we noticed some pretty streamlets; which, as they trickle down the rocks, form themselves into chrystallizations. Pursuing our way to Vionnaz, we found the prospects gradually increase in sublimity as we approached the Alps, at whose feet the road winds in the most picturesque manner possible, amongst well-planted orchards enamelled with flowers. From Vionnaz we proceeded to S. Maurice; crossing a wooden bridge, curiously constructed, with a roof somewhat resembling such as are used in England to cover farm houses; and thrown over one of the most noisy and rapid torrents I ever beheld. We then passed a hermitage, which had long presented itself to view, and particularly attracted our notice, from its romantic situation on a lofty eminence crowned by woods, with a majestic mountain forming a vast screen behind them. The Rhone shortly after discovered itself; adding much to the interest of the scenery; as its opposite shore presented bold overhanging rocks, richly adorned with foliage: while before us rose a magnificent stone bridge, two hundred feet in length, and a Roman work; one end being bounded by a tower, now converted into a chapel, and the other by a castle, through part of which the road to S. Maurice has evidently been cut, and now passes over a draw-bridge. This town is placed in a peculiarly wild and beautiful situation, at the base of a long chain of rocks; some of which are excavated to form houses. The only antiquity I heard of at S. Maurice, is a curious mosaic pavement.[2] The Theban Legion was massacred near this spot by order of the

---

[1] A fish, called the *Lotte* of Meillerie, is much admired by epicures.

[2] S. Maurice contains a remarkably good inn, *L'Hôtel de l'Union.*

Emperor Maximian. On our way hence, to Martigny, the country at first presented no striking objects, except the Dent du Midi, and the Dent de Morcles (two Alps which rise seven thousand feet above the level of the Rhone), and at a distance, Mont-Velan and Mont-Valsoray, which make part of the group of the *Grand S. Bernard*, and rise more than ten thousand feet above the level of the sea. We had not, however, driven long amidst this Alpine solitude, ere our road conducted us to the bottom of a magnificent Cascade, called The Pissevache; and formed by a river, named the Salanche, falling from an immense height, though not above an hundred feet perpendicularly. This cascade is illuminated, in the forenoon, by the sun; and displays all the colours of the rainbow: but after twelve o'clock, these terrestrial rainbows cease; while the river, broken by its fall, seems transformed into a brilliant sheet of gauze, with which it veils the rocks from whose summits it rushes.

Report says, that, at the top of this cascade, are frequently found trout; which could in no way get thither, but by leaping, or rather flying upward.

Not far distant from the Pissevache we passed the Pont du Trient, exhibiting a rivulet that issues from a remarkable opening in the rocks; the two sides of which, thus divided by the stream, are quite perpendicular, and nearly twelve hundred feet high.

Martigny, seated near the entrance of the great Valley of the Rhone, where the roads from France, Italy, and Chamouni meet, was a well-built and flourishing town, till nearly destroyed by a sudden and dreadful inundation of the Dranse; which occurred not long ago. Liberal subscriptions, however, from the benevolent inhabitants of the neighbouring countries, have enabled the people of Martigny to rebuild several of their houses, which were thrown down and swept away; and likewise to repair other ravages caused by the inundation. There is an old fortress here, separated from the town by the Dranse, which issues from the adjacent mountain of S. Bernard, and unites its waters with those of the Rhone near this spot. The valley of the Rhone is the most extensive in Switzerland; as from the Alps of *La Fourche*, where it commences, to the Lake of Geneva, where it terminates, is thirty-six leagues. Two excellent wines are made near Martigny, the one called *Coquempin*, and the other *La Marque*; and a great variety of rare plants may also be found in this neighbourhood.[1]

On quitting Martigny, to proceed through Riddes to Sion, we drove, for a short time, between steril rocks and mountains: but the face of the country soon changed, exhibiting luxuriant pasturages, vineyards, villages, churches, oratories, and remains of ancient castles: indeed, this approach to Sion, through the Valley of the Rhone, displays the height of cheerful beauty, united with almost every object that may be called sublime: the flat ground is intersected with rivers, and

---

[1] *La Grande Maison* at Martigny is a good inn; and *Le Cigne*, though small, is clean and comfortable.

enriched by cultivation; the near mountains are studded with villas, and other buildings, of a dazzling whiteness; and the horizon is bounded by Alps of an enormous magnitude, blanched with eternal snow.

Sion, anciently *Sedunum*, and in German *Sitten*, the capital of the Haut-Valais, and built partly on the right bank of the Rhone, and partly on the river Sitten, is a very old Swiss Bishoprick; and contains several convents, six churches, a hospital, and an hôtel de ville. The town stands on the declivity of three hills; each being crowned by a Castle: in the lowermost, called Mayoria, or Meyerbourg, the Bishop usually resides: the second bears the name of Valeria; and the third, called Tourbillon, contains portraits of all the Bishops of Sion since the year 300. Several Roman antiquities are discoverable in this town; among which, and near the great door of the cathedral, is a half-effaced inscription in honour of Augustus.[1] Above Sion, to the right, and seated on rocks difficult of access, are the castles of Séon and Montorges; objects particularly calculated to attract the attention of a landscape-painter: and, on the opposite side, in the Commune of Brémes, is a curious Hermitage, comprehending a church and cloister, with several cells, all hewn out of the solid rock. Near Sion flows the river Morges, which marks the limits between the Haut and Bas-Valais.

From Sion we proceeded to Sierre, through a beautiful country, rich in vineyards and pasturages, and watered by the Rhone. Sierre, seated on the banks of the stream whose name it bears, is one of the prettiest Bourgs of the Haut-Valais: but its inhabitants are particularly liable to goitrous swellings; owing, it is said, to the unwholesomeness of the water they are compelled to drink.[2] German is the language spoken at Sierre, and throughout the Haut-Valais. After quitting Sierre, we crossed the Rhone, traversed the forest of Finges, and passed the town of Leuck, behind which opens the gorge of the Dala, and part of the lofty and steril Mont-Gemmi. We then drove to Tourtemagne;[3] on approaching which we were presented with a view of the whole chain of Alps that connects the Simplon and S. Gothard: but the country, as the valley narrows, becomes marshy and barren. Within half a mile of the hotels at Tourtemagne, but not in the high-road, is a Water-fall, less magnificent than the Pissevache, though more beautiful in point of situation, and well worth notice.

Hence we drove to Viege, in German *Visp*, or *Vispack*, standing on the banks of the Visp, a river equal in size with the Rhone, and, beyond the bridge which crosses the Visp, towers the summit of Mont-Rose. From Viege

---

[1] *Le Lion d'Or* is a good inn; and *La Croix Blanche*, though less good, is tolerable.

[2] I have observed that women who carry heavy burdens on their heads are generally afflicted with this malady; not only in the neighbourhood of the Alps, but in other situations where the height of the mountains is, comparatively speaking, moderate: and I am therefore inclined to think, that goitrous swellings may sometimes originate from a strain given to the throat by an over-burden carried on the head.

[3] In German, *Turtmann*. Here are two inns, *Le Soleil* and *Le Lion d'Or*, the former of which, though small, is clean and comfortable.

we proceeded to Brigg: for though Glise is the regular post, Brigg (a post-town likewise) is the better stopping place, and not more than half a mile out of the great road. Soon after quitting Viege, we passed Gambsen, and the entrance to the valley of Nantz; crossing a torrent, called the Saltine, near which the country is marshy; and then traversing the bed of the Rhone, till our arrival at Brigg,[1] one of the handsomest towns of the Haut-Valais, and situated opposite to the base of the Simplon; the lower part of which exhibits luxuriant meadows, interspersed with fruit and forest-trees, oratories, and cottages; while the heights are adorned with hermitages, cascades, and noble woods of fir.

To the left of Brigg is the pretty village of Naters, washed by the Rhone, which descends from the summits of the Fourche and the sombre valleys of the Axe. This river receives, in the vicinity of Brigg, the waters of the Saltine, which come from the Simplon, together with those of Kelchback, which descend from the Belp-Alp and the Blatten. The adjacent mountains abound with deep dells; and, to the north, rise the rocks of Nesthorn, and part of the Upper-Glacier of Aletsch.

In order to appropriate an entire day to the passage of the Simplon, anciently called *Mons Cæpionis*, or *Sempronii*, and one of the loftiest of the Italian Alps, we slept at Brigg; and set out with the dawn next morning, equally favoured in point of weather as during our expedition to Mont-Blanc. The journey, either from Glise or Brigg, over the Simplon to Domo-D'Ossola, a distance of fourteen leagues, generally occupies about twelve hours. The new military road, planned by Napoleon, in 1801, was finished in 1805, at the joint expense of the kingdoms of France and Italy;[2] its breadth throughout is twenty-five Paris feet; the number of bridges, thrown across the rocks, is fifty; and the number of grottoes (chiefly hewn out of solid masses of granite), five: and so gradual, on both sides of the mountain, is the inclination of this wonderful road, that to drag the wheels, even of heavy carriages, is needless. The work was conducted, on the side of the Haut-Valais, by French Engineers; and, on the Italian side, by the Cavaliere Giovanni Fabbroni; who, though long distinguished for devoting his eminent abilities to the service of his country,[3] has, in this instance, exceeded himself; as, beside every other impediment, he had Herculean difficulties to surmount even in the soil; for he was compelled to pierce through, and blow up the hardest and most refractory rocks existing; while the French artificers, generally speaking, met with no obstacle, except

---

[1] The *Post-House* at Brigg is a comfortable inn; as is *L'Hôtel d'Angleterre*.

[2] As this is the shortest practicable route from German Switzerland and the Haut-Valais into the Milanese, it has always been the track pursued by the Milan courier, though frequently at the peril of his life; for the earthquake of 1755, which destroyed Lisbon, nearly blocked up this passage of the Alps; so that Napoleon found it needful to employ three thousand men between three and four years in constructing the new road.

[3] To this gentleman Florence owes the celebrated anatomical wax-work which enriches the Museum of Natural History in that city: though the invention was ascribed to the Cav. Fontana.

masses of slate, in many places already decomposed.[1]

This road is the only passage of the Alps which human labour has made practicable for heavy waggons and artillery: and, when we contemplate the stupendous height of the Simplon, the numerous and appalling precipices with which it abounds, the impetuous torrents which deluge its sides, and the tremendous avalanches by which its woods are frequently rooted up, and its rocks overthrown, we cannot but acknowledge that men, who, in defiance of obstructions such as these, could form a road exempt even from the appearance of danger, capable of braving the most furious storms, resisting the giant hand of Time, and conducting human beings, cattle, and every kind of carriage, quickly and safely, during all seasons of the year, through regions of eternal snow, deserve, in point of genius, to be ranked not only with, but even above, the ancient Romans; whose works of this description, surprising as they are, can, in no instance, vie with the descent into Italy, from the cloud-capped village of Simplon to the rich vale of Domo D'Ossola—and yet, to the shame of the nineteenth century, nations inimical to France attempted, at the close of the last dreadful war, to destroy the parapet-walls, and burn the bridges—in short, to annihilate the road—happily, however, these acts of barbarism have hitherto done no material mischief; but, unless the Glacier gallery and grotto be cleared of snow towards the commencement of every summer, as was the practice during the reign of Napoleon, this eighth wonder of the world, this universal benefit to Europe, will ultimately be rendered useless.

But to return to the description of our journey: after taking a cross-road from Brigg, to get into the great military route, we passed, on the right, one of the first works of the ascent to Simplon; a bridge thrown over the Saltine; and consisting of a lofty and beautiful single arch, covered, at the top, to preserve from rain the timber of which it is composed. We then passed on the left a chapel, with several small oratories leading to it; and began to ascend, by bold and beautiful windings, to a dark forest of firs; the openings of which presented us with views of the Valley of the Rhone, encircled by snow-crowned Alps; their gigantic Empress, Mont Blanc, proudly towering above them all; and, in consequence of her enormous height, appearing close to us, though really far distant. Engrossed by the sublimity of the scene, we continued to ascend, almost imperceptibly to ourselves; till, on traversing precipices whose bases are washed by a roaring torrent, we discovered, with surprise, that we had attained an eminence which hindered us from distinguishing the sound of its brawl.

This part of the road is cut through crumbling rocks; and in order to prevent the loose fragments above from falling upon travellers, broad paths are made in the upper part of these rocks, to catch whatever may be thrown down, either by tempests, or cas-

---

[1] The quantity of gun-powder used in blowing up the rocks, to form the road on the Italian side of the Simplon, is said to have been 17,500 pounds.

cades, or avalanches; while the road itself is supported by a strong wall of granite, varying in height according to the inequalities of the ground upon which it rests; and in some places measuring two hundred feet.

After reaching what is called the first Gallery (though in fact, the whole road might properly be denominated a continued series of serpentine galleries and grottoes, rising one above the other, and united by stupendous arches of the most chaste and elegant construction;) we crossed the Kanter on a bridge eighty feet in height; and so built, as to be incapable of receiving any injury from the annual melting of the winter-snow; there being, at certain distances, cavities, through which the water discharges itself, without hurting the work: and this judicious plan is likewise pursued with respect to all the parapets and foundation-walls.

Fine cascades and beautiful glens alternately presented themselves to view, till we reached, in four hours from the time of our departure from Brigg, the third Refuge; where we breakfasted. These Refuges, placed at short distances from each other, in the most exposed situations on the Simplon, are small buildings, meant to shelter men, cattle, and carriages, in case of sudden storms; and numbered "1st Refuge," "2d Refuge," etc.; an appellation particularly well chosen, as its meaning is the same in almost every modern language.

After passing the third Refuge, we observed an infinite variety of Alpine flowers growing amidst lawns of turf, short and soft as velvet; we then crossed the bridges of Oesback and the Saltine (near the former of which is a magnificent cascade); and, soon after, entered a Grotto thirty paces in length; leaving to our left the Glacier of Kaltwasser, from which descend four cascades, whose waters traverse the route, in aqueducts of a masterly construction, and then precipitate themselves into chasms below. Continuing to ascend through easy, bold, and beautiful sinuosities, we reached an eminence exposed to violent gusts of wind, where trees cease to flourish, and flowers no longer enamel the earth; and where a recent avalanche has rooted up and blighted firs and larches, and suspended them on each other, over the yawning abyss underneath, in a manner we shuddered even to contemplate.

Not far distant from this picture of desolation is the Glacier Grotto, fifty paces in length; on coming out of which, we ascended to the most elevated point of the whole passage; and found ourselves on every side surrounded by eternal snow. Here, and here only, that is immediately previous to entering, and immediately after quitting the Glacier Grotto, the road was bad; not, however, in consequence of any radical defect; but merely because the *Cantonniers* had neglected to clear the snow away.[1] On the right of this spot we discovered, beneath us, the ancient Hospice, now peopled by Monks belonging to the

---

[1] The *Cantonniers*, instituted by Napoleon to keep this route in repair, have been cruelly reduced in number by the King of Sardinia; although the tax imposed for their maintenance is still paid at the barrier. Voituriers pay ten francs per horse.

Grand S. Bernard; and, on the left, above us, the magnificent foundations of the new Convent and Barracks. We then passed the bridge of Senkelbach; and descended to the village of Simplon; noticing, on our way, a vast reservoir of water; one part of which flows down, into Italy, while the other irrigates France, by forming a ramification of the Rhone.

From the third Refuge to the sixth, which stands at the most elevated point of the passage, near the Barrier, we were two hours in going; and thence, to the inn at Simplon, half an hour. This inn is situated three thousand two hundred and sixteen Paris feet above the level of the Mediterranean sea: but neither here, nor even while passing the Glacier Grotto, and the heights beyond it (which are four thousand six hundred and ninety Paris feet above the level of the Mediterranean), did I experience the slightest sensation of cold: the day, however (as has been already noticed), was especially favourable; affording us continual sunshine, without one gust of wind;—*agremens* seldom met with by the Alpine traveller.

After dining on delicious trout at the village of Simplon,[1] a little hamlet encircled by the summits of the enormous Alp whose name it bears, we set out to descend into Italy, through a pass which exhibits scenes it would be vain to attempt particularizing, as they beggar description.

The commencement of the descent exhibits, on each side, lofty and barren rocks, with a considerable space between them; and, on the left, a thundering torrent: but, soon after quitting the village of Simplon, we found these rocks gradually approach each other, becoming perpendicular, and scarcely leaving sufficient space for the road.

Having crossed the bridges of Lowibach and Kronbach, we arrived at Steig, where the union of the Kronbach and the Quirna, which descend the glacier of Lavin through a gorge in the rocks to the right, form the river Vedro, or Diverio, whose wild and impetuous course the road follows, till within a short distance of Domo-D'Ossola. About a league and a half from Steig is an isolated inn; soon after passing which we entered a narrow ravine, and crossed the river several times, by means of stupendous bridges, till we came to the third Grotto, eighty paces in length; after quitting which, we approached the magnificent cascade of Frissinone; whose waters precipitate themselves from a rock so high that they seem lost in æther ere they reach the foaming bed of the Diverio which receives them. After passing this cascade, we entered the fourth Grotto, deemed the most wonderful work of the Simplon; it being two hundred and two paces in length, lofty in proportion, and cut, with exquisite taste and skill, through solid rocks of granite. Scarcely had we passed this grotto, before a sudden turn of the road presented us with another cascade, formed by the torrent which issues from

---

[1] The inn here, *Le Soleil*, is particularly good; and travellers are, I believe, likewise received at *L'Hospice*.

the gorge of Zwischbergen, and falls perpendicularly, and with such clamorous violence close to the traveller, that, startled and alarmed by the scene, we felt for a moment as if it would be impossible to proceed with safety. Below the gloomy village of Gondo is a chapel which marks the Italian confine; and further still are the Italian hamlets of S. Marco and Isella; at the latter of which travellers are visited by Milanese custom-house officers, for the purpose of obtaining money. After quitting these sombre hamlets, we entered the still more sombre gorge of Yeselles, empaled by perpendicular rocks, from whose summits fall cascades sufficient to supply whole rivers; and echoing with the tremendous roar of the Diverio, whose waters rush furiously through enormous fragments of dissevered rocks, sometimes exhibiting all the colours of the rainbow, and at others boiling and foaming into gulfs, which can only be compared to the Chaos of Milton and the *Inferno* of Dante. This narrow, awful, and appalling gorge extends to Divedro, a place said to stand at the height of one thousand seven hundred and eighty-two Paris feet above the level of the Mediterranean sea; but situated on a fertile, and indeed a pleasant spot, notwithstanding the gloomy aspect of the mountains by which it is encompassed.[1] From Divedro we descended into another equally wild and narrow glen, called Val-Divedro; crossing two bridges, and driving through the fifth and last Grotto, eighty paces in length. We then proceeded to Crevola, once more crossing the Diverio on a magnificent bridge, sixty paces in length, and deemed a masterpiece of architecture. Hence, as we approached Domo-D'Ossola, the rocks and mountains gradually receded, till the base of the Simplon presented a landscape thickly studded with villages and vineyards; and the rich and extensive plains of Italy opened to our view; forming a delicious and most striking contrast to the sublime and terrific solitude from which we had so recently emerged.

The descent, from the village of Simplon to Domo-D'Ossola, is usually accomplished in five hours and a half; and the latter town contains two good inns.[2]

Wishing to visit the Borromean Islands, on our way to Milan, we embarked at Baveno,[3] on the Lago Maggiore, previously pursuing the great military road (which extends to Milan), and passing two fine bridges, opposite to the latter of which is the Val-

---

[1] Divedro contains a tolerable inn.

[2] The *Hôtel de la Ville*, and The *Hôtel d'Espagne*.

I have passed the Simplon twice; namely, in May, 1817; and in June, 1819: the first time travelling *en voiturier*, the second time going post: and the number of hours employed in crossing this Alp, was both times precisely the same. From Brigg to the village of Simplon (as I have already mentioned), we were six hours and a half in ascending; and thence to Domo-D'Ossola five hours and a half in descending: from Domo-D'Ossola to the village of Simplon we were seven hours in ascending; and thence to Brigg five hours in descending. The most favourable season for passing the Simplon is between the middle of June and the end of October. During winter, carriages are usually dismounted, and put into Traîneaux, if the snow be deep.

[3] It is possible to embark at Fariolo, the post previous to Baveno; but the latter is the more convenient place; because boats are always in waiting there to convey Travellers to the Borromean Islands and the Lake of Como: the price of a boat, for the former expedition, being four livres per rower; and the time requisite for seeing the islands five or six hours. The inn at Baveno is tolerably good.

ley of Mont-Rose, an Alp very little inferior in height to Mont-Blanc.[1]

The Lago Maggiore, sometimes called Lago Locarno, and anciently *Verbanus*, is reputed to be about fifty-six Italian miles in length, about six in breadth, and, toward the centre, about eighty fathoms deep. The picture presented by this Lake, is enchanting; its banks being adorned by forest-trees, olives, and vineyards, interspersed with hamlets, white as snow, and enriched with villas and other edifices, remarkable for the variety and elegance of their construction, while, on its bosom, rise three little Islands, two of which contain palaces and gardens belonging to the family of S. Carlo Borromeo. Isola Bella generally strikes travellers as the most beautiful of these islands.[2] Half a mile distant from Isola Bella, toward the west, is Isola Pescatori; and about a mile distant, toward the north, Isola Madre. The passage from Isola Bella to Isola Madre seldom occupies more time than half an hour. The latter, at which we landed first, is about half a league from the shore, and consists of four gardens, or rather terraces, one above the other, embellished with luxuriant flowers, shrubs, and forest-trees; and crowned by a Palace, where the objects best worth notice are—a Madonna and Child, with other pictures, all painted on marble, and attributed to Perugino—S. Thomas Aquinas, ascribed to Guercino—S. Geronimo, ascribed to Correggio—Erasmus and Belisarius, ascribed to Schidone—a painting on marble, supposed to have been done by Albano—the Prodigal Son, ascribed to Guercino—a portrait, ascribed to Titian — a Smith's Shop, by Bassano—the Madonna, Our Saviour, etc. ascribed to Giordano. —Landscapes, by Tempesta[3]— four cattle pieces, together with some paintings attributed to Giovanni Belino, Andrea del Sarto, and Annibale Caracci.

We proceeded next to Isola Bella, which consists of eight terraces, one above the other, carpeted with odoriferous flowers, enriched with exotics, refreshed by fountains, shaded with forest-trees, and crowned by a noble palace, which contains Paintings by Tempesta, a fine Bust of S. Carlo Borromeo, by Franchi;[4] and a large subterranean apartment, fitted up to imitate a series of grottoes, in a manner equally singular and tasteful; and which, during hot weather, must be delicious. After viewing this abode of Calypso, we embarked for Sesto-Calende; landing, however, by the way, at Arona; and then walking about three-quarters of a mile, through a beautiful country, to see the celebrated colossal Statue of S. Carlo Borromeo, which was executed, in bronze, by Zonelli, and measures one hundred and twelve feet in height, reckoning

---

[1] The valley of Mont-Rose possesses gold-mines; and the grapes here are trained round trees whose branches are so managed as to resemble baskets.

[2] This island contains an inn furnished with clean beds, and where good dinners may be procured at four francs a head.

[3] This artist, after having murdered his wife, in order to espouse a prettier woman, took refuge here.

[4] S. Carlo Borromeo is universally acknowledged to have been a peculiarly benevolent character; one of his family was as notoriously wicked; and the rest, though worthy, in the common acceptation of the word, were not in any respect distinguished: a circumstance which occasioned the following remark, —"That one Borromeo belonged to Heaven, another to Hell, and the remainder to Earth."

the pedestal. This statue is erected on a hill that overlooks Arona, the birth-place of S. Carlo, who is represented as giving his benediction, with one hand, to the mariners of the lake, and holding a book with the other. This is one of the largest statues now existing in Italy; and so enormous are its dimensions, that the head alone will contain four persons seated round a table, and one person may stand in the nose.

At Sesto, we rejoined our carriages; which went by land to Belgirata[1] and Arona, and then crossed the Ticino, in a *pont-volant*, at the entrance of the first-named town. The road between Baveno and Sesto exhibits another fine work of the Simplon, walls of an immense height, which prevent the waters of the Lake from overflowing the country.—Sesto-Calende is beautifully situated on the Ticino, at the commencement of the plains of Lombardy; and persons, who like water-carriage, may go from this town, or even from Baveno, or Fariolo, to Milan, in the boats of the Lago Maggiore:[2] we, however, proceeded by land, through a delightful country, to Somma; where, close to the great road, grows a cypress of extraordinary magnitude, and, according to tradition, planted previous to the birth of Our Saviour. Scipio's first battle with Hannibal took place near Somma. Hence, to Gallarate, we passed over heaths adorned by fine woods interspersed with beautiful broom; and between Gallarate and Castellanza, part of the country is of the same description, except that it exhibits pretty paths cut through underwood of chesnut and oak. On approaching Ro, we drove between corn-fields, meadows, hamlets, and villas, to *the Church of Nostra Signora de' Miracoli*; built after the designs of Tibaldi, and adorned with good paintings, by Procaccino, etc. The inside of this church does honour to its architect; and the façade, erected by Pollach, is adorned with two *bassi-rilievi*; one of which represents the Salutation, and the other the Presentation in the Temple. The country between Ro and Milan is flat, well cultivated, and beautifully adorned by acacia and tulip-trees, which flourish here with peculiar luxuriance. But the greatest ornament of the approach to Milan, the Triumphal Arch, intended as a termination to the avenue of the Simplon, on one side, and as a decoration to the Forum, on the other, is, alas, unfinished! The commencement of this magnificent work, however, particularly merits attention. Four gigantic columns, each hewn out of a single block of marble, were designed to support its two façades, the bases of which alone are completed; one side being adorned with beautiful figures in *basso-rilievo*, representing France, Clio, Calliope, and Italy; and the other side, embellished with *bassi-rilievi*, almost equally beautiful, and representing Hercules, Mars, Minerva, and Apollo; while, in surrounding outhouses, are deposited still finer *bassi-rilievi*, relative to the achievements of Na-

---

[1] A good inn here, *L'Albergo Borromeo*.
[2] Public boats go from Sesto to Milan every morning, between the hours of five and seven, and take Passengers at one Paul a-head. Private boats, large enough to contain a carriage, may be hired at Baveno for twenty-eight, or, at most, thirty francs, to go down the Lago Maggiore to Sesto.

poléon; together with capitals of pillars, and other architectural decorations, highly creditable to the talents of Cagnola, under whose orders this work was begun.

Milan, in Italian Milano, and anciently denominated *Mediolanum* (supposed to have been founded by the Gauls 590 years before the Christian era), is seated on a peculiarly fertile spot, between the rivers Adda and Ticino, and intersected by three navigable canals, one of which extends to Pavia. Milan contains about 130,000 inhabitants; and may be called a handsome town, though its buildings, in point of architecture, are, generally speaking, faulty: its climate, during winter, is very cold; during summer, extremely hot; and frequently damp and unwholesome during autumn and spring.[1] Its *Duomo*, or Cathedral, the largest church in Italy, S. Peter's excepted, is a Gothic edifice of white marble, begun in the year 1386: but the exterior part was left unfinished till the reign of Napoleon, who ordered it to be completed, after the designs of Amati; and though much had been accomplished, much still remained undone, when the Emperor of Austria resumed the government of the Milanese: it is said, however, that Napoleon's plan will still be followed. This cathedral, in length 449 Paris feet, in breadth 275, and in height 238, to the top of the cupola, is divided into five parts, by an hundred and sixty immense columns of marble, and paved with the same material. The interior ornament of the principal door is supported by two columns of granite, called Migliaruolo, and found in the beds of the neighbouring lakes and torrents. The interior and exterior distribution of the choir were executed under the orders of Pellegrini; the Sarcophagus of Gian-Giacomo de' Medici was designed by Buonaroti; and the bronze ornaments were made by Leoni. The Statue of S. Bartholomew is by Agrati; the Cupola, situated in the centre of the choir, is by Brunellesco; and, immediately underneath, in a subterranean chapel, most sumptuously decorated, rest the mortal remains of S. Carlo Borromeo, enclosed by a crystal sarcophagus adorned with silver gilt: his countenance, part of the nose excepted, is well preserved; his robes, crosier, and mitre, are superb; and silver *bassi-rilievi*, executed by Rubini, after the designs of Cerano, and representing the great features of the exemplary life of S. Carlo Borromeo, embellish the walls of this chapel. A staircase, consisting of 468 steps, leads to the top of the cathedral; and it is impossible to form a just idea of the exterior decorations of this immense and venerable marble pile, without ascending to its roofs; where alone the fretwork, carving, and sculpture, can be viewed to advantage. The three finished sides of the exterior walls are covered with *bassi-rilievi*, statues, and groups of figures; several of them well executed: while every spire, or needle, is crowned with a statue, rather larger than life; and among these, there appears to be more

---

[1] The irrigation of the rice-fields, with which the Milanese abounds, contributes to render the air, at times, insalubrious.

than one likeness of Napoleon.[1]

The Church of S. Alessandro possesses considerable merit with respect to architecture, together with good frescos in its cupola; and its high altar and Ciborio[2] are remarkably handsome.

The Church of S. Lorenzo, an octagon edifice (adjoining to which is a building that resembles an ancient bath), is embellished by handsome columns, whose bases appear to have been originally the capitals of pillars, belonging, as tradition reports, to a Temple of Hercules, which once stood near this spot; and, before the church of S. Lorenzo, is the only specimen of ancient Roman architecture now remaining at Milan; namely, a Portico, supported by sixteen beautiful fluted columns of the Corinthian order, with an entablature, which bears an inscription in honour of the Emperor Verus.

The Refectory of the suppressed Convent of S. Maria delle Grazie is embellished with Leonardo da Vinci's celebrated fresco of the Last Supper; and although this masterpiece has suffered cruelly from time and ill treatment, it is still in sufficiently good preservation to be highly interesting.[3]

The College of Brera, now the Gymnasium, or Palace of Arts and Sciences, contains a fine collection of pictures, among which are the following: *First room.* (Frescos) three boys playing on musical instruments, by Gaudenzio Ferrario. *Second room.* The Magdalene and Our Saviour, by Lodovico Caracci—two pictures of Saints, by Procaccino—Our Saviour bearing his Cross, by Daniello Crespi—S. Sebastiano, by M. A. Caravaggio—Our Saviour and the Woman of Samaria, by Annibale Caracci—Abraham dismissing Hagar, by Guercino!!!—The Madonna, Our Saviour, God the Father, etc. by Albano—Head of Our Saviour, by Guercino!—The Madonna, Our Saviour, S. John, and S. Petronio (the patron of Bologna), by ditto—a Dance of Winged Loves, by Albano!!—the Last Supper, by Rubens—the Woman detected in Adultery, by Agostino Caracci—the Ascension of the Madonna, by Paris Bordone—the Ascension of Our Saviour, by Giulio Romano—the Nativity, by ditto—the Baptism of Our Saviour, by Paris Bordone—Our Saviour dead, by Salmeggia—S. Peter and S. Paul, by Guido!—*First division of the second room.* Saints adoring the Cross, by Tintoretto—the Madonna, Our Saviour, and Saints, by Savoldi—the Woman detected in Adultery, by Palma Vecchio—Our Saviour supping with the Pharisee, by Paolo Veronese—S. Francesco, by Palma il Giovane—the Marriage in Cana of Galilee, by Paolo Veronese—Our Saviour dead, by Tintoretto—The Madonna, Our Saviour, and Saints, by Giulo Romano!—Our Saviour dead, by Benvenuto Garofalo!—*Second division.* Se-

---

[1] Cathedrals, in Italy, are always open from sun-rise till sun-set; other churches are usually opened at six or seven in the morning, shut at twelve; opened again at three in the afternoon, and shut at five or six. From the middle of Lent till Easter, the finest altar-pieces are covered. The common fee, to the Sacristan of a church, is from one to two pauls. Palaces are usually shown from nine or ten in the morning till twelve, and from three till five in the afternoon. The common fee, at a palace, is from three to five pauls, according to the size of the party.

[2] The tabernacle wherein the Host is kept.

[3] The late Viceroy of Italy had a fine copy taken of this fresco, and did every thing in his power to preserve the original.

veral curious old pictures.—*Third division.* Portrait of Solomon—ditto of Ann. Caracci—ditto of Procaccino—the Madonna and Saints, by Pompeo Battoni—S. Girolamo, by Subleyras—Souls delivered from Purgatory, by Salvator Rosa!—a large Landscape, by N. Poussin—ditto, by Salvator Rosa—the Madonna, our Saviour, and Saints, by Luca Giordano.—*Third room.* The Madonna, Our Saviour, and S. Francesco, by Vandyck—the Head of a Monk, by Velasquez! *Fourth room.* The Madonna, Our Saviour, etc. in the first manner of Correggio—the Marriage of the Madonna, in the first manner of Raphael—Our Saviour dead, by Giovanni Bellino; and a Sketch, by Andrea del Sarto.

The Gymnasium contains casts of all the finest statues of antiquity, a particularly well furnished Observatory, a good Library, and a Botanic Garden.

The Ambrosial Library, founded by Cardinal Federigo Borromeo, contains above thirty-five thousand printed volumes, together with between fourteen and fifteen thousand precious manuscripts, among which are those of Leonardo da Vinci, accompanied by his drawings—a Virgil, with annotations by Petrarca, in his own hand-writing—a Pliny—a Plato and a Cicero of the second century—and a Josephus written on papyrus, and written on both sides of each leaf. This library likewise contains the following paintings:—A Holy Family, by Titian—Sketches, by Pietro da Cortona—the original Sketch of the School of Athens, by Raphael, well preserved, and most valuable!!—a fine copy of Leonardo da Vinci's painting of the Last Supper—a Sketch, by Raphael, of part of the Battle of Constantine!—a Holy Family, by Bernardino Luino, the contemporary and rival of Leonardo da Vinci!—the Head of Our Saviour, by Luino—Our Saviour dead, by Titian—Sketches of the Last Judgment, by Buonaroti—Sketches, by Polidoro da Caravaggio, and other great masters—a Miniature of the Celestial Regions, by Albano!!—and a fresco, by Luino, representing our Saviour crowned with thorns.

The Great Hospital and *the Lazaretto* merit notice; the latter is just beyond the eastern gate of the city.

The Marengo Gate, a simple and elegant specimen of Ionic architecture, bears the following inscription: "*Paci Populorum Sospitæ.*"

The Amphitheatre, situated near the Forum, is a magnificent building, erected, after the designs of Canonica, and large enough to contain 36,000 spectators. The *pulvinare,* and the principal entrance of this edifice, especially deserve attention.

The Theatre of La Scala, built after the designs of Piermarini, is deemed, with respect to architecture, the most beautiful opera-house in Europe; and, except the great theatre at Parma, and that of S. Carlo at Naples, it is the most spacious. The stage decorations also are particularly splendid and classical, and the orchestra is, generally speaking, the best in Italy: but the circumstance most creditable to this, and indeed to every other theatre on the Continent, is that perfect decorum which enables ladies (though unattended), to go, return, and even walk, from box to box, without the slightest chance of receiving an insult.

Milan contains other theatres; namely, the *Canobiana*, shaped like La Scala, but not so large; *the Teatro Re;* and *the Carcano*, built by Canonica.

The principal promenades are the Ramparts, the Corso, and the Esplanade, between the town and the Forum.[1]

The environs of Milan boast a considerable number of handsome villas, among which is that which was presented by the citizens to Napoleon.

Monza, about three leagues north of Milan, likewise contains a superb royal residence, built after the designs of Piermarini; and another, called *Pelucca*, celebrated for its stud of horses. At Monza Charlemagne was crowned king of Lombardy; and in the Cathedral there is the ancient crown of the Lombard kings, commonly called "The Iron Crown," because its inside is lined with some of that metal, said to be composed of the nails with which Our Saviour was fastened to the cross. The outside of this diadem is gold, studded with precious stones.[2]

On quitting Milan we took the Bologna road, traversing a luxuriant country, which abounds with fields of rice, and every other kind of grain, vineyards, and streamlets, for the purposes of irrigation, and exhibits not a single inch of fallow land; this last, however, is a thing rarely seen in Italy, where the husbandman no sooner reaps one crop than another succeeds, to the number of four or five in a twelvemonth. The road is, generally speaking, flat, and bordered with towns and villages, so far as Lodi, which stands on an eminence, near the Adda, is well built, and contains about 12,000 inhabitants. The most remarkable of its churches, *L'Incoronata*, was erected according to the design of Bramante, and adorned with frescos and paintings in oil by Callisto, the pupil of Titian: but what chiefly renders this town interesting is that, at the bridge of Lodi, Napoleon gained one of his most memorable victories.[3] The little province, of which Lodi is the capital, usually gives food to 30,000 cows; and its cheese, improperly called Parmesan, is most excellent. Hence we proceeded to a troublesome Austrian custom-house, near the Po; and then crossed that fine river, on a *pont-volant*, to Piacenza. This town, seated in a rich and pleasant country, contains several objects of interest; namely, the *Cathedral* and the *Church of La Madonna della Campagna*, both adorned with good paintings, the cupola of the former being by Guercino, the angles by Francesconi, and the ceiling above the great altar, and frescos behind it, by Lodovico Caracci and Procaccino. This church is likewise adorned with a picture of S. Corrado, by Lanfranco, and another of S. François Xavier, by Fiamingo; the Angels, in fresco, which surround the latter, being likewise by Fiamingo; and the As-

---

1 Among the principal hotels are, *The Albergo Reale, The Albergo della Gran-Bretagna, The Croce di Malta, I Tre Re*, and *Il Pozzo*.

2 From Milan it is easy to make an excursion to Pavia, either by land or water; the latter town being only seven leagues distant from the former.

3 From Lodi there is a road, by Cremona and Mantua, to Bologna: and to the east of Lodi is the road through Brescia and Verona to Venice.

cension, on the ceiling of one of the chapels, by the same master. *The Church of the Canonici regolari di S. Agostino*, designed by Vignola; *the Town-hall*, by the same architect; and *two equestrian Statues*, the one representing Ranucolo, and the other Alessandro Farnese, by Francesco Moca, also merit notice. Piacenza, though large, is built entirely of brick, not even its palaces excepted; it contains a pretty theatre and good hotels.[1] Here commences the ancient *Via-Flaminia*, constructed during the consulate of Lepidus and Flaminius, and leading to the *Via-Emilia* in Romagna; and not far hence flows that memorable torrent, the Trebbia, whose immense bed travellers drive through on their way to S. Giovanni, in the road to Tortona.

At the distance of half a mile from Piacenza, we crossed a bridge thrown over the Po, having, to our right, the lofty mountains of the Apennine, with villages and farms at their base; and to our left a plain, watered by the above-named river. Midway to Fiorenzuola we traversed, on a stone-bridge, a torrent called the Nura, and thence drove through the bed of the Larda, always dry in summer, and provided with a narrow bridge, over which carriages pass when the stream is swoln by winter rain. We then proceeded through Fiorenzuola, a small town where, however, there are good inns, to Borgo-San-Donino, seated on the Stirone, and not far distant from what are supposed to be the ruins of the ancient *Julia Chrysopolis*. The cathedral at S. Donino merits notice, as does the edifice converted, by order of Napoleon, into an Asylum for the Poor.[2] A few miles from this town stands Castel-Guelfo, celebrated for having given its name to the Guelfs, whose strife with the Ghibelines bathed Italy in blood. Beyond Castel-Guelfo we passed, on a *pont-volant*, the Taro, after heavy rains a dangerous torrent, but over which a magnificent bridge, begun by Napoleon, is now on the point of being finished by Maria-Louisa.

After traversing a rich and beautiful valley, adorned with villages and vineyards, we arrived at Parma, a handsome town, which derives its appellation from the river that runs through it. The walls of Parma are between three and four miles round, and the inhabitants are said to amount to thirty-five thousand; but, nevertheless, this city looks deserted and melancholy.

The Cathedral, built, like all the other public edifices, of brick, is a spacious Gothic structure, containing a high altar, richly decorated with precious marbles, and a cupola finely painted by Correggio, but cruelly injured. Over the organ are the families of Correggio and Parmigianino, painted by themselves, and tolerably well preserved; and on the sides of the principal door are portraits of those great artists, likewise painted by themselves. This church also contains a monument to the memory of Petrarca.

The Church of S. Giovanni Evangelista, built with majestic simplicity, is embellished with frescos by Correggio and Parmigianino; the former of whom has

---

[1] The *Albergo delle Tre Ganasce*, and *S. Marco*.

[2] S. Donino contains two inns,—*La Croce Bianca*, and *The Albergo del Angelo*.

represented, in the cupola, Our Saviour ascending to Heaven, and the Apostles witnessing his ascension!

The Stoccata, built after the design of Bramante, does honour to the taste of that distinguished architect, and is adorned with fine paintings, namely, Moses breaking the Tables of the Law, by Parmigianino; three Sibyls, by ditto; another Sibyl, by Mazzuolo, and frescos in the cupola by Correggio.

The Convento delle Monache di S. Paolo contains a room adorned with frescos by Correggio, and deemed the most beautiful work of its kind he ever executed: the subject seems to be Diana triumphant, accompanied by Genii.

The Royal Academy contains a fine collection of pictures, among which are the Adoration of the Magi, by Agostino Caracci—the Ascension, by Raphael—the Marriage of the Madonna, by Procaccino—the Deposition from the Cross, by Schidone—the Martyrdom of two Saints, by Correggio—the Repose in Egypt, by ditto—the Descent from the Cross, by ditto—the Holy Family, by Parmigianino—a fresco, representing the Madonna and Our Saviour, by Correggio!!!—a fresco, representing the Madonna crowned, by Annibale Caracci!!—and S. Girolamo, by Correggio.

The Library belonging to the Academy is adorned with a fresco by Correggio, representing the Madonna crowned; and another room contains the death of the Madonna, by Lodovico Caracci.

The great Theatre, designed by Vignola, and built of wood, is the most spacious, and, in point of architecture, the most perfect edifice of its kind in Italy: it contains, with ease, five thousand spectators (some authors say, nine thousand), all of whom can see every thing which passes on the stage, and hear every syllable spoken by the actors, even though uttered in a whisper. This fine specimen of architecture, however, is now so entirely out of repair, that a few years may probably reduce it to a heap of ruins.

Adjoining to the great Theatre, is another, built after the design of Bernini, and, comparatively speaking, small, as it does not hold more than two thousand spectators.

Parma contains good hotels.[1]

Just beyond one of the city gates is the *Palazzo-Giardino,* embellished with fine frescos by Agostino Caracci: nine miles distant, on the way to Casal-Maggiore, is *Colorno,* a large palace, adorned with two statues; one representing Hercules, the other Bacchus; and both found in the Orto Farnese, at Rome: and thirteen leagues distant, at the base of the Appennine, are the ruins of *Velleia,* a Roman municipal city, which was buried by the sudden fall of a mountain supposed to have been undermined by a subterraneous watercourse. This melancholy event took place in the fourth century; and from the number of human bones found at Velleia, when it was excavated in 1760, there seems reason to fear the inhabitants had no time to escape.[2]

From Parma we traversed a rich and beautiful country to S. Ilario; passing, on quitting the Duchy of Parma, the Lenza on

---

[1] *La Posta* is the best.
[2] Velleia is much nearer to Fiorenzuola than to Parma.

a magnificent bridge; and then crossing the Crostolo, on another bridge, previous to our arrival at Reggio. This town, anciently *Regium Lepidi,* and seated on the Crostolo, is said to contain nearly 16,000 inhabitants. *The Cathedral* here merits notice; as one of its chapels contains good pictures: but what particularly renders this spot interesting, is its having given birth to that greatest of Italian poets, Ariosto: indeed, the soil seems to have been prolific of genius, for between Reggio and Modena we passed within a league of Correggio, the birthplace of the great painter who bears its name. Reggio contains three hotels.[1]

Driving through Rubiera,[2] where travellers who arrive after dark find the gates shut, and are compelled to wait till permission be obtained to have them opened, we traversed a fine bridge thrown over the Secchia, and then passing near a splendid column erected (as we are told) in honour of Napoleon, found ourselves at Modena, anciently *Mutina;* a small but handsome city, situated amidst luxuriant pasturages; and, of late years, much improved. The gates are handsome; the ramparts form a beautiful promenade round the town; the streets, in general, are straight, wide, and clean; and the Strada-maestra (part of the ancient *Via-Emilia*) is magnificent. *The Cathedral* contains a picture of the Presentation by Guido; and the *Campanile,* built of marble, is one of the loftiest towers in Italy. *The Churches of S. Vincenzo* and *S. Agostino* merit notice; as does the *public Library,* which is well stored with valuable manuscripts and rare editions of printed works. The university has long been celebrated; and *the Palazzo Ducale* contains a sumptuous hall, painted by Francesconi; together with a small but choice collection of pictures; among which are, the adoration of the Magi, by Procaccino—the crucifixion, by Andrea Mantegna—the Madonna, the Saviour, and several other figures, by Garofalo—the Holy Family, by Andrea del Sarto—four landscapes, by Salvator Rosa—five paintings, by Annibale Caracci—the Saviour on the cross, by Guido—the martyrdom of S. Peter, by Guercino—S. Rocco, by Guido—Roman charity, by Sacchi—a small painting of the Saviour on the cross, and the Madonna standing near, by Guido—and the head of the Madonna, by Carlo Dolci. Modena contains public Baths, a Theatre, a public Walk, and several private Collections of pictures, most of which are said to be upon sale. It likewise still contains the *Secchia,* or Bucket, immortalized by Tassoni; but this object so interesting to lovers of poetry, is now removed from the cathedral, where it used to be exhibited, and withheld from public view, because placed under the care of the Municipality.

Modena afforded an asylum to Brutus after the assassination of Cæsar; and is also famous for having given birth to Muratori, Vignola, and Tassoni, the author of the *Secchia Rapita.*[3]

After bidding adieu to this city, we crossed the Panora, on a fine bridge newly constructed, which

---

[1] *La Posta—Il Giglio*—and *l'Albergo di San-Giovanni.*

[2] Rubiera, or Mursalla, for it seems to have both names, boasts but one tolerable inn; and that stands beyond the bridge, on the road to Modena.

[3] *The Grande Albergo Reale,* at Modena, is an excellent hotel.

marks the limits of the Duchy; thence proceeding to Castel-Franco; where we observed the lotus growing luxuriantly in the ditch that encompasses the Fort: and this being the first town of the Papal dominions, we were obliged to fee the Custom-house Officers, that our baggage might escape examination. We then crossed the Reno, on another fine bridge, and entered Bologna, by the ancient Roman road, through a rich and beautiful Alpine country.

Bologna, seated on the Reno, at the base of the Apennine, is supposed to have derived its name from the Galli-Boïonienses, who called it *Boïona*, which time changed first into *Bononia-Felsinia*, and at length into Bologna: but, be this as it may, the city is of high antiquity, well peopled, commercial, wealthy, and situated in a salubrious, though not a warm climate: its walls are from five to six miles round; and its population is supposed to amount to 60,000 inhabitants; indeed, some authors rate it much higher. Bologna has twelve gates; the handsomest of which are those of Modena, Ferrara, and Bonaparte.

The Cathedral, erected in 1600, contains the last work of Lodovico Caracci, namely, a fresco representing the Annunciation! it adorns the sanctuary. In the Chapter-room is a picture of S. Peter and the Madonna bewailing the death of our Saviour, by the same master; who has likewise adorned the bottom of the choir with a fresco of our Saviour giving the keys of Paradise to S. Peter. Below the choir is a curious Crypt.

The Church of S. Petronio, built in 432, and repaired in 1390, is large; and, on account of its antiquity, curious. Charles V. was crowned here, by Clement VII.; and this edifice contains the celebrated meridian of Cassini, the gnomon of which is eighty-three feet in height.

The Dominican Church contains good paintings; among which is the Paradise of Guido, one of his finest compositions in fresco!

Lo Studio, the Palace of the University, was designed by Vignola, and contains a Statue of Hercules in bronze; a Museum of Natural History; an Anatomical Theatre; a Cabinet of Antiquities; and a Library rich in manuscripts and books of Science. This celebrated University, supposed to have been founded by the Countess Matilda, once contained six thousand Students, and seventy-two Professors.

The Academia delle belle Arti is adorned with a fine, though not a numerous, collection of pictures; among which are the conversion of S. Paul, by Lodovico Caracci—S. Girolamo, by Agostino Caracci—S. Bruno, by Guercino—the Madonna della Pietà, by Guido—S. Cecilia, by Raphael—the massacre of the Innocents, by Guido—a fine picture, by Parmigianino—the head of Guido, by Simone da Pesaro—the portrait of S. Andrea Corcini, by Guido; and two large pictures, by Domenichino.

The Palazzo-Marescalchi, and the *Palazzo-Ercolano*, likewise contain good pictures.

The Tower of Asinelli, built in 1119, is three hundred and twenty seven feet high, and said to be the loftiest edifice of its kind in Italy. *The neighbouring Tower,* built in 1110, is an hundred and forty feet in height, and from eight to nine feet out of the perpendicular.

A handsome Fountain, adorned by a *colossal statue of Neptune*, called the *chef-d'œuvre* of Giovanni di Bologna, embellishes the Piazza del Gigante; and through this city runs a Canal, by the aid of which travellers may go by water to Ferrara, and thence embark on the Po for Venice.

The Theatre here is one of the largest in Italy; and the façades of the palaces, and other buildings, are magnificent; but the streets appear narrow, from being lined almost universally with porticos; and this circumstance, combining with the want of spacious squares, diminishes the beauty of the town, by giving it a sombre appearance.[1] Travellers, on arriving here, are greeted by an excellent band of musicians; who, after having played a few tunes, are well satisfied with a fee of two or three pauls.

Bologna gave birth to Guido, Domenichino, Albano, Annibale, Lodovico, and Agostino Caracci,[2] and Benedict XIV.: and among its natural curiosities is the phosphorescent stone, found near the city, on Monte Paderno.

About one mile distant from the walls is *the Campo-Santo*, once the Certosa-Convent: and here lies the celebrated singer, Banti, whose vocal powers not long since captivated Europe. This repository of the dead is well worth notice; and its Church contains paintings by Cesi, Guercino, Guido, etc.

The Church of the Madonna della Guardia also merits notice; as it is approached by a Portico, consisting of six hundred and forty arches, built at the expense of various individuals, corporations, and ecclesiastical establishments; the whole being three miles in length, and extending from the city to the church, which is magnificently placed, and somewhat resembles the Superga near Turin.

Persons who enjoy fine scenery and good paintings should likewise visit *S. Michele in Bosco*, once a Convent belonging to the Olivetans. The Portico of the Church is adorned by the pencil of Cignani; and one of the chapels contains a picture, by Guercino, representing Bernardo Tolomei, the Founder of the Order, receiving his statutes from the hands of the Madonna. In the Convent are several fine works by Lodovico Caracci; and one picture by Spada. The situation of this building is delicious.

I will now close my account of Bologna, by observing, that persons who visit Italy for the purpose of educating their children, would do well to reside in this last-named city, where masters of every description may be obtained on moderate terms.

Between Milan and Bologna the road is excellent, and does not pass over one high hill: and from Bologna we crossed the Appennine to Florence by a road which, though hilly, is excellent, and in great measure newly constructed, under the direction of the Cav. Fabbroni.

The time usually employed in accomplishing this journey, either with post-horses, or *en voiturier*,

---

[1] The best hotels here are, *The Grande Albergo Imperiale*, and *S. Marco*.

[2] Annibale Caracci was designed for a goldsmith; but his uncle, Lodovico, observing that both Annibale and his brother, Agostino, were blessed with great abilities, took upon himself the office of instructing them in painting; and so much did they profit by his lessons, that their memory must be for ever honoured by true lovers of the Arts.

is from fourteen to fifteen hours. The ascents and descents are more rapid than those of the Simplon; though not sufficiently so to render a drag-chain often requisite, even for heavy carriages; and the paved gutters intersected by small wells, made to receive the streams which descend from the heights above the road, keep the latter dry, and in good repair.

From Bologna to Pianoro, the first post, we found the country rich and flat; but at Pianora oxen were added to our horses, and we began to ascend the Apennine, whose summit presented us with a magnificent view of the plains we had recently traversed, the Alps, and the Mediterranean and Adriatic sea. The wind on this spot is, generally speaking, strong, and particularly cold. Hence we proceeded to the next post, Lojano, where travellers should not sleep, as the inn affords no comfortable accommodation. From Lojano to Pietramala, the frontier Custom-house of Tuscany, the ascent continues; and the road winds amidst bold scenery, less sublime than the Alps, but more beautiful. The inn at Pietramala (about midway between Bologna and Florence), is provided with several clean beds; and persons wishing to visit the little Volcano, in this neighbourhood, would do well to sleep here. The Volcano is situated on a hill, called Monte di Fo, covered with rocks, and about one mile distant from the inn; but there being neither a carriage nor a mule road to the spot, it is necessary to walk; and less than an hour and a half cannot be allowed for going and returning. The mouth of this little volcano disgorges, unceasingly, clear flames, sometimes spreading fifteen feet in circumference, and always burning brightest in wet and stormy weather.

From Pietramala we descended the Apennine to Le Maschere, another inn, provided with good beds; thence proceeding through a country gradually increasing in richness, till, at length, Val-d'-Arno opened to our view, and exhibited, in its centre, the beautiful city of Florence, seated amidst fields teeming with almost every production of the vegetable world, and surrounded by hills clothed with olives and vineyards, and studded with an innumerable host of splendid villas.

Ariosto says of Florence, that, on seeing the hills so full of palaces, it appears as if the soil produced them. "And if thy palaces (continues he), which are thus dispersed, were concentrated within one wall, two Romes could not vie with thee."

The approach to Florence for several miles displays a richness of cultivation unrivalled, perhaps, in any country, (the environs of Lucca excepted): and the entrance to the city, this way, through the Porta-San-Gallo, is strikingly magnificent.[1]

---

[1] All the Gates of Florence are shut when it becomes dark, except the Porta-San-Gallo.

CHAPTER III.

FLORENCE.

Origin and present appearance of Florence—Palazzo-Vecchio—Loggia—Piazza del Granduca—Fabbrica degli Ufizi—Magliabechiana Library—Royal Gallery—Palazzo-Pitti—Giardino di Boboli—Museo d'Istoria Naturale—Duomo—Campanile—Baptistery—Chiesa di San Marco—S. S. Annunziata—S. Maria Maddalena dei Pazzi—Santa Croce—S. Lorenzo—New Sacristy—Old Sacristy—Capella de' Medici—Mediceo-Laurenziana Library—Chiesa di Santa Maria Novella—D'Or-San-Michele—Di San-Spirito—Del Carmine—Di S. Trinità—Di S. Ambrogio—Di S. Gaetano; etc.—Reale Accademia delle Belle Arti—Oratorio dello Scalzo—Palazzi Gerini—Riccardi—Corsini—Mozzi—Buonaroti—Strozzi—Uguccioni—Casa dei Poveri—Spedale di Bonifazio—Spedale di Santa Maria Nuova—Spedale degl' Innocenti—Column in Via Romana—Column near the Ponte S. Trinità—Column in the Piazza del Duomo—Bronze Wild Boar in the Mercato Nuovo—Pedestal near the Church of S. Lorenzo—Group of Hercules and Nessus—Statue of Ferdinando I.—Porta S. Gallo—Triumphal Arch—Fresco by Giovanni di San Giovanni—Ponte S. Trinità—Theatres—Florentine Mosaic Work, and Sculpture in Alabaster—Accademia della Crusca—Hotels—Provisions—Water—Climate—List of objects best worth notice, as they lie near each other.

FLORENCE, in Italian, Firenze, which signifies, in the Etruscan language, a red lily (actually the arms of the city), has deservedly acquired the appellation of *La Bella:* it stands (as I have already mentioned) in a luxuriant, beautiful, and extensive plain, encircled by the Apennine; and is said, by some authors, to have been an ancient town of Etruria, afterward inhabited by the Phœnicians; while others suppose it to have been founded either by Sylla's soldiers, or the people of Fiesole: and one thing seems certain, namely, that the choicest part of Cæsar's army was sent to colonize at Florence (then called *Florentia*), about sixty years before the birth of our Saviour; and under the dominion of the Roman Emperors it became one of the most considerable cities of Etruria, and was embellished with a Hippodrome, a Campus Martius, a Capitol, and a road, called *Via-Cassia*. Its walls are six miles in circumference, and contain above 70,000 persons; and the river Arno (anciently *Arnus*), which runs through it, is adorned with four handsome bridges: its squares are spacious and numerous: its streets, like those of every large Tuscan city, clean, and excellently paved with flat stones; and, were the façades of all its churches finished, nothing could exceed the elegance of this Athens of Italy.

So many changes have lately taken place at Florence, relative to works of art, etc., that I trust it will not appear like arrogance in me to give a minute detail of the objects best worth a Traveller's attention; especially as there exists, at this moment, no accurate Florence Guide.

The Palazzo-Vecchio, adorned with a Tower so lofty that it is deemed a *chef-d'œuvre* of architecture, was built by Arnolfo, the Disciple of Cimabue: and, before the entrance to this palace, is a Statue, in marble, of David, supposed to be in the act of slaying Goliath, by Buonaroti;[1] and a group, likewise, in marble, of Hercules slaying Cacus, by Bandinelli. On the ceiling and walls of the great hall are frescos of the most celebrated actions of the Florentine Republic and the House of Medicis, all by Vasari; except four pictures in oil, one representing the coronation of Cosimo I., by Ligozzi; another, the twelve Florentines, at the same time Ambassadors from different States to Boniface VIII., by Ligozzi; a third, the election of Cosimo I., by Cigoli; and, a fourth, the institution of the order of S. Stefano, by Passignano. In this hall, likewise, is a group of Victory with a prisoner at her feet, by Buonaroti! and another group of Virtue triumphing over Vice, by Giovanni di Bologna! The exploits of Furius Camillus are painted *in tempera*, by Salviati, in the Sala dell' Udienza Vecchia.

The Loggia of the Palazzo-Vecchio was built after the design of Andrea Arcagna; and is adorned with a group, in bronze, called Judith and Holofernes, by Donatello—Perseus with Medusa's head, in bronze, by Cellini! (the *basso-rilievo* on the pedestal which supports this group is much admired), a group in marble, of a young Roman warrior carrying off a Sabine Virgin, and her father prostrate at his feet, with the rape of the Sabines in *basso-rilievo* on the pedestal, by Giovanni di Bologna!!—two lions, in marble, brought from the Villa-Medici, at Rome—and six antique statues of Sabine priestesses.

The Piazza del Granduca contains a noble fountain, erected by Cosimo I., after the design of Ammannati—and an equestrian statue of Cosimo I., in bronze, by Giovanni di Bologna! to whom the sea-nymphs and tritons, which surround the fountain, are likewise attributed.

The Fabbrica degli Ufizi, which comprehends the Royal Gallery, was built by Vasari: the exterior part of the edifice is ornamented with Doric columns, forming two magnificent porticos, united at one end by an arch, which supports the apartments occupied by courts of justice; and, over this arch, is a statue of Cosimo I., by Giovanni di Bologna; together with recumbent figures of Equity and Rigour, by Vincenzo Danti.

The Magliabechiana-Library, rich in manuscripts and printed books of the fifteenth century, (and where the Florentine academy meet), is under the same roof with the Royal Gallery; the latter is usually open to the public from nine in the morning till three in the afternoon, festivals excepted.

Staircase leading to the Royal Gallery. Between the windows is the statue of Bacchus, in marble; and, opposite to it, the statue of a Child.

First Vestibule. A statue of Mars, and another of Silenus, with an infant Bacchus, both in bronze—ten busts of the Princes of the House of Medicis, among which is that of the great Lorenzo —four *bassi-rilievi*.

Second Vestibule. A horse in marble; supposed to have originally belonged to the group of Niobe and her Children! Two quadrangular Columns, which

---

[1] Michelangelo Buonaroti was not only the most eminent Sculptor of modern days, but likewise the Founder of the French School of Painting.

appear to represent the victories by land and sea of the person to whom they were dedicated: on one of these columns rests a head of Cybele; and, on the other, a fine bust of Jupiter—a Wild Boar!! said to be Grecian sculpture—colossal statues of Trajan, Augustus, and a Barbarian King—two Wolf-dogs—a bust of Leopoldo.

First Corridor. The ceiling of this immense Gallery is adorned with arabesques: round the walls, near the ceiling, are portraits of the most renowned characters of antiquity; comprehending generals, statesmen, princes, and literati; and, on the wall to the left, below the portraits, are paintings of the Florentine school. Here, likewise, is a most valuable collection of busts of the Roman emperors, and many of their relatives, which go round the three corridors. The first corridor contains several curious sarcophagi; one of which, in the centre of this apartment, near the entrance-door, is particularly admired. On the left side are statues of a Wrestler, Mercury, and Apollo, all especially worth notice; as are the statues of Apollo, Urania, and Pan, with the young Olyntus, on the right side; and the two seated figures of Roman Matrons,¹ and the group of Hercules killing the Centaur Nessus, at the end.

Second Corridor. On each side near the ceiling, is a continuation of the portraits of the most renowned characters of antiquity; here, likewise, are paintings containing the history of S. Maria Maddalena, together with several pieces of sculpture, namely, Cupid; Bacchus and Ampelos; a Bacchante; Mercury; Leda; Venus rising from the bath; Minerva; or, Pallas-*Athenas*; a round altar! supposed to be the work of Cleomenes; a tripod, dedicated to Mars; a Faun; Ganymede with the eagle; a torso of a Faun! etc.

Third Corridor. The ceiling of this immense Gallery is adorned with paintings, representing the revival of the Arts and Sciences, with other historical subjects; in which are introduced portraits of all the most eminent characters among the Florentines. On each side, near the ceiling, is a continuation of the portraits of the most renowned characters of antiquity; and, on the left side, below the portraits, are paintings of the Neapolitan, and other schools. Here, likewise, is a large number of statues; among which are Marsyas—Bacchus, by Buonaroti—S. John, by Donatello—and a copy of the Laocoon, by Bandinelli—an antique recumbent Statue, in black marble, supposed to represent Morpheus!—David, by Donatello—Bacchus, by Sansovino—Apollo seated—a wounded Soldier—a Discobolus, attributed to Myron! and a Thetis on a sea-horse. This apartment also contains a fine picture of S. Peter healing the lame man at the gate of the temple, by Cosimo Gamberucci; another of the transfiguration, by Luca Giordano; and another of the Madonna, our Saviour, and S. John, copied, by Empoli, from a celebrated fresco, which was painted by Andrea del Sarto, and is now destroyed. Among the most striking busts in the corridors are those of Nero, Otho, Titus Vespasian, and Antoninus Pius.

---

1 One of these is supposed to represent Agrippina, the mother of Nero.

Cabinet of modern bronzes. Mercury standing on the wind, by Giovanni di Bologna!!—Bust of Cosimo de' Medici, by Cellini! *Bassi-rilievi* representing S. Francis Xavier, S. Joseph, and S. Teresa, by Soldani—a recumbent Statue, by Vecchietta of Siena—an anatomical statue, by Cigoli—a Child with wings, attributed to Donatello—David, attributed likewise to Donatello—a copy of the Farnese bull—the sacrifice of Abraham, by Ghiberti!—a small copy of the Laocoon!

Cabinet of antique bronzes; enclosed in fourteen glass cases—the first of which contains, Apis, Jupiter, Neptune, Pluto, and a remarkable head of Saturn; Juno, with Etruscan characters on her hip! a Grecian bust of Minerva, etc. *Second case.* Venus with her attributes—a celestial Venus—a triumphant Venus—an Hermaphrodite!—an Amazon!—Mars armed, etc. *Third case.* Hercules, Bacchus, and Bacchantes—a Faun playing the Doric flute—the labours of Hercules represented by a multitude of small statues—a Genius giving ambrosia to Bacchus! *Fourth case.* Victory, Fortune, Genii, Egyptian divinities; among which is a beautiful Serapis, and Isis, crowned with a disk, holding Horus on her lap. *Fifth case.* Etruscan divinities; a very fine collection. *Sixth case.* Portraits of men and women; fragments of statues, beautifully executed; and a small skeleton. *Seventh case.* Animals of various kinds, which served for votive offerings; symbols, and military ensigns; a hippogriff, a chimæra; a bull with a man's head; a Roman eagle, which belonged to the twenty-fourth Legion—and an open hand, called by the Romans *Manipulus*. *Eighth case.* Sacrificial instruments, altars, and tripods; a curious sistrum; a mural crown, etc. *Ninth case.* Candelabra and lamps. *Tenth case.* Helmets, spurs, bits, etc., for horses; rings, bracelets, ear-rings, all made of gold; mirrors of white metal; and needles made of hair. *Eleventh case.* Ancient inscriptions graven on bronze—a manuscript, on wax, nearly effaced—Roman scales and weights; etc. *Twelfth and thirteenth cases.* Kitchen utensils—a silver disk! on which is represented Flavius Ardaburius, who was Consul of Rome in 342. *Fourteenth case.* Locks, keys, and some monuments of the primitive Christians; among which is a lamp in the shape of a boat, with a figure of S. Peter at the stern. *Middle of the cabinet.* The Head of a Horse! An Orator, with Estruscan characters engraved on his robe!!—this fine statue was found near the Lake of Perugia—a Chimæra, with Etruscan characters engraved on one of the legs!! it was found near Arezzo—An Etruscan statue of a Genius, or, perhaps, a Bacchus, found at Pesaro!!![1] A Minerva; injured by fire, but very beautiful; on the helmet is a dragon, the symbol of vigilance and prudence!! This statue was found near Arezzo, and one arm has been restored. Behind the Chimæra is a Torso! and, before it, a Tripod! supposed to have belonged to a temple of Apollo. This cabinet likewise contains four busts, found in the sea, near Leghorn; they appear to be Grecian sculp-

---

[1] Winckelmann seems to have thought this fine statue the work of a Grecian artist; especially as Pesaro was a Grecian colony.

ture, and one of them resembles Homer.[1]

Hall of Niobe. At the upper end of this magnificent apartment is the celebrated group of Niobe and her youngest child; supposed to have been done by Scopas; and generally considered as the most interesting effort of the Grecian chisel Italy can boast: it is not, however, perfect; as one of the mother's hands, and one of the child's feet, have been restored. Round the apartment are statues of the other children of Niobe; which seem the work of various artists. The daughter, next to Niobe, on the left, is admirably executed; the opposite statue, on the right, has great merit; the dead son is wonderfully fine; but, considering the fable, it appears extraordinary that the sculptor should have placed him on a cushion. The two daughters on each side of Pædagogus, and the third statue, on the left of the entrance door, have great merit. It is extremely to be regretted that these *chefs-d'œuvre* of art are not disposed in such a manner as to accord with the subject.

The second statue on the left of the entrance door is a Psyche, and has nothing to do with the tragedy of Niobe; but was introduced merely to adorn the apartment; as likewise was the statue of a youth kneeling, and apparently wounded.

The walls of this room are adorned with the following pictures. A portrait of a Princess, resembling Mary, Queen of Scotland, by Vandyck. A gipsy telling a young woman her fortune; and the adoration of the Infant Jesus; both by Gherardo delle notti—a Bacchanalian party, by Rubens—a story from Ariosto, by Guido—a man with a monkey, by Annibale Caracci—the Madonna, our Saviour, S. John, etc.; by Fra Bartolommeo della Porta!—a portrait of Lorenzo de' Medici duke of Nemours, by Alessandro Allori—the Dispute in the Temple, by M. A. Caravaggio—Mars armed, by Guercino,—S. Maria Maddelana, by Carlo Dolci—The Madonna entreating our Saviour to bless the Charitable, called the *Madonna del Popolo*, by Baroccio!—a portrait of the Sculptor Francavilla, by Porbus—a Madonna, by Sassoferato—a head of S. Peter in tears, by Lanfranco.—The martyrdom of S. Stephen, by Cigoli!—S. Clovis, of the Cordeliers, by Carlo Dolci—Elizabeth, Duchess of Mantua, by Andrea Mantegna—the Infant Jesus with Angels, by Albano—and the Madonna, our Saviour, etc.; supposed to have been designed by Leonardo da Vinci, and coloured by Bernardino Luino.

Cabinet of Greek and Latin Inscriptions, Egyptian Monuments, etc. Here are two Egyptian divinities in basalt—sepulchral Monuments—Brutus, by Buonaroti, only just commenced; and above it the first work of that

---

[1] The Etruscan Bronzes of the Florentine Gallery are supposed to have been executed at a period when Sculpture of this sort had reached its zenith of perfection in Etruria; where, according to Pausanias, bronze statues existed much earlier than in Greece. We are told that Romulus had his statue made of bronze, probably by an Etruscan artist; we are likewise told that this event occurred about the eighth Olympiad; and it does not appear that the Greeks worked in bronze till about the sixtieth Olympiad. During the infancy of bronze sculpture, the component parts of statues were fastened together with nails: this is exemplified by six female figures of bronze, found in Herculaneum.

artist (the head of a Satyr), executed when he was only fifteen, and the cause of his introduction to the Platonic Academy. Busts of Euripides — Demosthenes — Aratus—Pythagoras—Sappho—Alcibiades—Sophocles — Aristophanes—Plato—Homer—Seneca—Ovid—Solon—Socrates—Anacreon—Hippocrates, etc.

Cabinet containing portraits of Painters, chiefly done by themselves. In the centre of this apartment is the celebrated Vase of the Villa Medicis, adorned with *bassi-rilievi* representing the sacrifice of Iphigenia!! The ceiling is painted by Pietro Dandini: round the walls are portraits of Raphael, Leonardo da Vinci, Buonaroti, Titian, the Caracci family, Domenichino, Albano, Guercino, Guido, Vandyck, Velasques, Rembrandt, Charles Le Brun, Vander-Werf, etc. etc. The apartment which communicates with this, likewise contains portraits of Painters.—The ceiling is painted by Bimbacci; and in the centre of the room is a magnificent table of Florentine Mosaic work.[1] Round the walls are portraits of Mengs, Batoni, Reynolds, Angelica Kaufman, and Madame Lebrun: and here, also, is a marble bust of Mrs. Damer, done by herself.

Cabinet containing pictures of the Venetian School. Portrait of a man with his hand on a skull, by Titian—portrait of Sansovino, by ditto—portrait of an old man, by Monroe—our Saviour dead, by Giovanni Bellino—a figure in a Spanish dress, by Monroe—the Madonna, our Saviour, S. John, etc., by Titian—Venus with her attendants, and Adonis dead, by Bonvicino—portraits of Francesco Duke of Urbino, and his Duchess, by Titian!—four heads, by Paolo Veronese, Paris Borbone, Tiberio Tinelli, and Campagnola — two dogs, by Bassano—portrait of Giovanni de' Medici, the father of Cosimo 1. by Titian!—the marriage at Cana in Galilee, by Tintoretto—portrait of a man in black with red hair, by Bordone—the Madonna, our Saviour, and S. Catherine, who is offering him a pomegranate, by Titian!! and the portrait of a woman with flowers, commonly called The Flora! by the same master—the Crucifixion, by Paolo Veronese—portrait of Sansovino in old age, by Tintoretto — portrait of a Knight of Malta, by Giorgione—portrait of a Geometrician, by Palma Vecchio.

Cabinet of Gems, etc. This apartment is ornamented with fine columns of oriental alabaster, and verde antique; and contains a most valuable collection of medals, gems, etc., together with a table of Florentine mosaic work, executed when the manufacture was in its infancy, and representing the ancient port of Leghorn.

Cabinet containing pictures of the French School. The ceilings of this apartment, and those that communicate with it, were painted by the Poccetti school. Pictures on the walls—Theseus raising the enormous stone, under which his father hid the sword he was to take to Athens! by N. Poussin—Venus and Adonis, by the same master.

Cabinet containing pictures of the Flemish School. Bust of

---

[1] Florentine Mosaic Work, called *Opera di Commesso*, consists of sparks of gems, and minute pieces of the finest marble, so placed as to imitate flowers, insects, and paintings of every description.

a man wrapped in fur, with a cap on his head, by Denner!—a landscape, by Paul Brill—ditto, by Claude Lorrain. The inside of a church, by Peter Neff—and the inside of a prison, where the death of Seneca is represented, likewise by Peter Neff.

Cabinet containing Pictures of the Dutch School. A Schoolmaster teaching a Child to read, by Gerard Dow — nine pictures by Francis Mieris, namely, a Charlatan exhibiting his tricks — an old Lover and his Mistress — a Man seated at Table, with a Bottle of Beer; and, near him, a Woman and a Man asleep—the portrait of the Son of Mieris—his own Portrait—ditto, in another attitude—a Woman sleeping, and two other figures—the Painter's Family—and a Peasant cutting Bread, while his Wife drinks Beer.—The Judgment of Solomon, by Vander-Werf, and the Saviour in the Manger! by the same artist.

Cabinet containing Pictures of the Italian School. The Head of Medusa, by M. A. Caravaggio!—the bust of the Madonna pressing Our Saviour to her Bosom! by Carlo Cignani—the Rape of Europa, by Albano—the Massacre of the Innocents, by Dosso Dossi—the Madonna, the Saviour, and S. John, with Joseph in the background, by Schidone!—the Madonna, the Saviour, and S. John, by Massari—the same subject, by Guido—the Breaking of Bread, by Palma Vecchio—a Landscape, by Salvator Rosa! and an Annunciation, by Garofalo.

Cabinet called the Tribune. This elegant apartment, built after the design of Buontalenti, and paved with precious Marbles, contains admirable specimens of Sculpture and Painting. Here is the Venus de' Medici, found in Adrian's Villa, and supposed to have been done by Praxiteles!!!!—the Apollo (called *Apollino!!*) attributed to the same great artist—the Dancing Faun!!! evidently a production of the best age of ancient sculpture, and excellently restored by Buonaroti—the *Arrotino!!* found at Rome, and supposed to represent the Scythian Slave, when commanded to flay Marsyas—and the group of the *Lottatori*, or Wrestlers!![1] found with the Niobe. The Venus de' Medici is about five English feet in height; the hands are modern; indeed the statue, when first discovered, was broken in thirteen places. Pliny mentions six famous Venuses; one, by Phidias, which stood under the Portico of Octavia, at Rome; another, finished by Phidias, but begun by his pupil; and this stood just without the town of Athens; another, at Rome, in the Temple of Brutus Callaicus; and a fourth, by an unknown artist, which was placed in the Temple of Peace: another, made by Praxiteles, and veiled, was purchased by the people of Cos; and the sixth, an undraped figure, was sent to Gnidus: but this latter, the more excellent work of the two, is supposed to have been destroyed at Constantinople; as was the Olympian Jupiter of Phidias, the Juno of Samos, etc. It seems, therefore, impossible to discover, from the author just quoted, whether the modest and beautiful Venus de' Medici be, or be not, the child of

---

[1] Winckelmann thought this work not unworthy either of Cephissodorus, who made the *Symplegma* at Ephesus; or of Heliodorus, who executed a similar group. These artists were the sons of Praxiteles.

Praxiteles. Among the pictures of the Tribune are, the Epiphany, by Albert Durer—Endymion sleeping, by Guercino—a Sibyl, by the same magic pencil—a Holy Family, by Buonaroti—Venus, with a Loxe behind her, by Titian—another Venus, with Flowers in her right Hand, and at her Feet a Dog! also by Titian—a portrait of the Prelate, Beccadelli, by the same master—a Holy Family, with the Magdalene, and the Prophet Isaiah, by Parmigiano—three pictures, namely, the Circumcision, the Adoration of the Magi, and the Resurrection, by Mantegna—the Madonna, Our Saviour, S. Francesco, and S. John the Evangelist! by Andrea del Sarto—the Madonna in Contemplation by Guido!—the Massacre of the Innocents!! by Daniello da Volterra—the portrait of Cardinal Aguechia by Domenichino!—the Holy Family and S. Catherine, by Paolo Veronese—a Bacchante and a Satyr!! by Annibale Caracci—S. Jerome, by Spagnoletto—the Madonna, Our Saviour, S. John, and S. Sebastiano, the two former seated, the two latter standing, by Pietro Perugino!—six pictures by Raphael, namely, a portrait of Maddalena Doni, a Florentine Lady, in his first style—two Holy Families, in an improved style, though still partaking of the Perugino school—S. John in the Wilderness!!!—a portrait of Pope Giulio II.!—and another of *La Fornarina!!* who was celebrated for her attachment to Raphael, all three painted in his last and best style—a portrait, by Vandyck, supposed to represent Jean de Montford—and another, representing Charles V. on Horseback—a Holy Family, by Schidone—Job and Isaiah! by Fra Bartolomeo della Porta—the Flight into Egypt, by Correggio!—the Virgin adoring the Infant Jesus by ditto!—the Decapitation of S. John, by ditto—Herodias receiving the Head of S. John, by Leonardo da Vinci!—a Madonna and Child, by Giulio Romano—Hercules between Vice and Virtue, by Rubens.

Cabinet containing Pictures of the Tuscan School. Jesus sleeping on his Cross, by Cristofano Allori—the Head of Medusa, with the Hair changed into Serpents, by Leonardo da Vinci!—Our Saviour dead in the Arms of the Madonna, by Angelo Allori—Our Saviour, the Apostles, the Marys, etc. by Carlo Dolci—an Angel playing on a Guitar, by Rosso—a small portrait of Dante—ditto of Petrarca—portrait of Andrea del Sarto, by himself—S. Simon, by Carlo Dolci—S. Peter, by do.—a Child, holding a Bird, by A. Allori—a Sketch, by Leonardo da Vinci!

Second Cabinet of the Tuscan School. The Visitation of Elizabeth, by Mariotto Albertinelli—a Miracle performed by S. Zenobio, Bishop of Florence, by Ridolpho Ghirlandajo!—the Body of the Saint carried to the Cathedral, by ditto!—the Madonna, Our Saviour, S. Zenobio, and other Saints, by Domenico Ghirlandajo.

Cabinet of the Hermaphrodite. A colossal bust of Juno!—a colossal Head of Neptune—an Hermaphrodite of Greek sculpture! and a Satyr of modern sculpture—a group of two Children playing—a bust of Cicero!—a bust of Marcus Antonius, very rare—Ganymede, restored by Cellini—a statue called *Genio delle Morte*—a group of Cupid and

Psyche, found on the Mons Celius, at Rome! — a bust of Antinous — an Infant Hercules — a colossal bust of Jupiter — a bust of Berenice, the wife of Titus, and queen of part of Judea! — a bust of Alexander the Great!! — a sleeping Love! — a recumbent statue of an Hermaphrodite!

The Palazzo Pitti, where the Grand Duke of Tuscany usually resides, was begun after the design of Filippo di Ser Brunellesco, the most celebrated architect of the fifteenth century, and finished by Ammannati. In the quadrangle is the *basso-rilievo* of a Mule, who constantly drew a sledge which contained the materials employed in the building; and over this *basso-rilievo* is a statue of Hercules, attributed to Lysippus.[1] On the ground-floor is a chapel, which contains a beautiful altar of Florentine work, with the Last Supper, executed in *pietri duri*, in its centre — the ceiling and walls are adorned with frescos, of which that representing the Crucifixion seems the best. The ground-floor likewise contains fine frescos by Sebastiano Ricci, Giovanni da San Giovanni, etc. The first room up stairs contains ten statues taken from the Villa Medicis; and the best of these is a Minerva. The second room contains busts of Roman Emperors, and other sculpture, likewise taken from the Villa Medicis. In the third room are the following paintings: — A portrait, by Rembrandt — another, of Titian's Mistress, by himself — three Landscapes, by Salvator Rosa — a Battle-piece, by ditto!! — two Landscapes, by Rubens — Astrologers, by Zingona — Hunters with Game, by Giovanni da San Giovanni. *Fourth room* — our Saviour at Supper, by Palma Vecchio — a portrait of the Secretary S. Juliano, by Cris. Allori — a Child, by Santo di Tito — Our Saviour dead, S. John, the Madonna, and Mary Magdalene, by Fra Bartolommeo!! — portrait of Giulio II. by Pordenone — the Deposition from the Cross, by Andrea del Sarto — a Holy Family, by Pordenone. — *Fifth room* — the *Madonna della seggiola*!!!! by Raphael — S. Mark, by Fra Bartolommeo!!! — two pictures of Joseph and his Brethren, by Andrea del Sarto — a copy of Raphael's fresco of S. Peter delivered from prison, by Federico Zuccari — the Madonna and Angels, by Luca Giordano — S. Peter, by Carlo Dolci — Our Saviour and other figures, by Cigoli — S. Sebastiano by Titian. *Sixth room* — S. John, as a Child, sleeping on the Cross, by Carlo Dolci! — two pictures of the Assumption, by Andrea del Sarto — the Hours, by Giulio Romano! — a Holy Family, by Titian — S. Sebastiano, by Annibale Caracci — Cleopatra, by Guido — Andrea del Sarto and his Wife, by himself — Giulio II. by Raphael!! — S. John, by Carlo Dolci — Our Saviour and Saints, by Fra Bartolommeo! — a dead Christ, by Pietro Perrugino — a Madonna and other figures! by Raphael — four Saints, by Andrea del Sarto. *Seventh room* — The Madonna, Our Saviour, etc. by Fra Bartolommeo!! — Calvin, Luther, and Catherine a Boria! by Giorgione da Castel-Franco, one of the Founders of the Lombard School — the Madonna, etc. by

---

[1] According to Winckelmann, this statue, though ancient, is of a time posterior to that of Lysippus.

Andrea del Sarto — a Head, by Carlo Dolci! — Leo x., by Raphael!! *Eighth room*—the Fates, by Buonaroti!!—Our Saviour and the Madonna crowned, by Carlo Dolci — a Holy Family, by Raphael!—a Magdalene, by Titian—a Child, by Correggio—S. John, by Andrea del Sarto. *Ninth room* — Our Saviour in the Garden, by Carlo Dolci!!—a Holy Family, by Schidone! The ceilings of these apartments, up stairs, painted by Pietro de Cortona and his scholars, represent the patriotic actions of the Medici family under emblems taken from heathen mythology.

Ceiling of the Camera di Venere. Minerva forcing a Youth (by whom is meant Cosimo I.), from the arms of Venus, to place him under the guidance of Hercules, while the Genius of War shows him the Laurel Wreath he ought to aspire after—the Continence of Scipio—Antiochus quitting his Mistress to go where duty calls him—Crispus, son of the Emperor Constantine, resisting the solicitations of Fausta, his stepmother — Cyrus dismissing his prisoner, Panthea, that he might not be seduced by her charms—Augustus showing Cleopatra that her beauty had not power to captivate him — Alexander receiving the Mother and Wife of Darius with humanity, but without being betrayed into faulty admiration of the latter—Massinissa sending poison to the Queen of Numidia, that she might avoid, by death, the disgrace of swelling Scipio's triumph.

While Pietro da Cortona was employed in painting the Camera di Venere, Ferdinando II., who came to view the work, expressed great admiration of a child drowned in tears. " See," replied the painter, " with what facility children are made either to laugh or weep!" and, so saying, he gave one stroke with his brush, and the child appeared to be laughing; till, with another stroke, he restored the countenance to its original form.

Ceiling of the Camera d'Apollo. A Youth, who again represents Cosimo I., inspired with poetic fire, and Apollo showing him the celestial globe, that he may sing of its wonders—Cæsar attending to instructive books as he walks, that he may not waste time—Augustus, after having shut the Temple of Janus, cherishing the Muses, and listening to the Æneid—Alexander preparing to march, and taking with him part of the Iliad— the Emperor Justinian forming a code of laws.

Ceiling of the Camera di Marte. Cosimo I., under the form of a young warrior, leaping out of a boat, and combating with his lance; while Mars assists him, by darting lightning at his enemies—Castor and Pollux carrying the spoils of the vanquished to Hercules, who makes them into a trophy — Captives loaded with chains, supplicating the Goddess of Victory; Peace, with the olive-branch in her hand, giving them comfort; while Abundance revives, and scatters blessings among the conquered people.

Ceiling of the Camera di Giove. Jupiter receiving a young Hero, who still represents Cosimo I., and is conducted to Olympus, by Hercules and Fortune, in order to receive a crown of immortality. A Genius holds his hands before the Hero's eyes, to prevent their being dazzled by the splendour of the Thunderer; while another

Genius presents the young man's armour, perforated with javelins, to the Goddess of Victory, who engraves his name upon a shield: she is supposed to have just begun, and only written the initial letter of the word *Medicis*. The frescos, in form of a fan, represent the emblems of peace; namely, Minerva planting an olive-tree—Mars mounted on Pegasus—Castor and Pollux with their horses coupled together—Vulcan reposing in his forge—Diana sleeping after the chase.—Apollo, god of arts, and Mercury, god of commerce and wealth, appear among the emblems of peace; while the General of the Vanquished is represented as making ineffectual efforts to snap his chains; in which attempt he is aided by Discord, who carries in her hand a torch to relume the flames of war.

Ceiling of the Stanza di Ercole. Hercules on the funeral-pile; above which is the apotheosis of that Hero, whom Mars and Prudence conduct to Olympus, where he receives a crown of immortality.

The Palazzo Pitti may usually be seen from eleven till twelve in the morning, and from three till five in the afternoon. The Custode up stairs expects from four to six pauls, according to the size of the party he attends; and the servant below stairs expects two or three pauls.

The Giardino di Boboli, open to the public on Sundays and Thursdays, is very large, and contains several pieces of sculpture; the most remarkable of which are two Dacian prisoners, in oriental porphyry, at the entrance; a colossal Ceres; the Fountain at the end of the principal walk, decorated with a colossal Neptune standing on a granite basin above twenty feet in diameter, with the Ganges, Nile, and Euphrates' beneath, all by Giovanni di Bologna; Neptune, in bronze, surrounded with sea-monsters, by Lorenzi; and four unfinished statues by Buonaroti.

The Museo d'Istoria Naturale, collected by the Grand Duke Leopoldo, is said to be the finest museum existing, with respect to the anatomical preparations in wax and wood, the petrifactions and minerals, and the thick-leafed, milky, and spongy plants; which cannot be preserved in the common way, and are therefore beautifully represented in wax, to complete the botanical part of this princely collection. All the anatomical preparations, in wax and wood, were executed under the orders of Cav. F. Fontana, except the famous representation of the Plague, which was done by the Abate Lumbo in the days of the Medici, and is so painfully fine that few persons can bear to examine it. This masterly performance owes its present place to Cav. Giovanni Fabbroni, a gentleman already mentioned, who has not only contributed essentially to the improvement of the museum, but likewise to that of arts and sciences in general. *Below stairs* is a Laboratory. *On the first floor* are two rooms filled with large quadrupeds, fishes, etc.—a Library—rooms destined to Mechanics, Hydraulics, Electricity, and Mathematics; together with a Botanic Garden: and *on the second floor* are twenty rooms, containing the representation of the Plague and anatomical preparations; all of which may be avoided by persons not inclined to see them. *In another suite of apartments, on the same floor*, are Birds, Fishes,

Reptiles, Insects, Shells, Fossils, Minerals, Wax-plants, etc. The observatory makes a part of this Museum, which is usually open to the public every day, festivals excepted, from eight in the morning till twelve; and again from three till five in the afternoon.

Santa Maria del Fiore, or the *Duomo*, was begun about the year 1294, by Arnolfo, and finished about the year 1445, by Brunellesco; it measures 426 feet in length, and in width 363. Its cupola was completed by the last-named architect; who has gained immortal honour by the performance. Its lantern, designed by Brunellesco, is of solid marble, finely carved. The outward walls of this vast church are incrusted with black and white polished marble; the pavement is marble, and the balustrades and pillars which surround the tribuna were designed by Buonaroti, and ornamented with *bassi-rilievi*, by Bandinelli and Giovanni del Opera. Toward the Via de' Servi, over a door of curious workmanship, is an Annunciation in mosaic, called by the ancients, *lithostratum*, and executed by Ghirlandajo: another specimen of the same kind is placed within the church, above the great door. Over the southern door is a group of the Madonna and our Saviour between two Angels, by Giovanni Pisano. At the upper end of the choir is a crucifix, by Benedetto da Majano; behind the high altar, a marble *Pietà*, said to have been the last work of Buonaroti, which death prevented him from completing! and on the altar are three statues, by Bandinelli, of God the Father, our Saviour, and an Angel. This edifice contains statues, portraits, and monuments of celebrated characters of the Florentine Republic. On the right, near the great door, is a bust of Brunellesco; next to this, a bust of Giotto; further on, are Pietro Farnese, General of the Florentines, and Marsilio Fecini, the Reviver of the Platonic philosophy; a man, as remarkable for his learning, as for the lowness of his stature. Near the door leading to the Via de' Servi, is an antique portrait of Dante, the father of Italian poetry; whose tomb, however, is at Ravenna, where he died in exile. This portrait was done by Andrea Orgagna; and so highly do the Florentines venerate the memory of Dante, that the place where he often sat, in the Piazza del Duomo, is carefully distinguished by a white stone.[1] Near to this great Poet, is a picture of Giovanni Acuto, the Pisan General; and another of Niccolo da Tolentino; and under the first-named picture is an inscription, which says, Acuto was a British Knight.[2] In the Chapel of S. Zenobio is a bronze ciborio, by Ghiberti; and the door of the Sacristy was executed by Luca della Robbia.[3]

The Campanile, a quadrangular tower of black, white, and red marble, designed by Giotto, and begun in 1334, is 280 feet in height, and the most beautiful edifice of its kind in Italy. The four statues, on the side nearest to the Baptistery, are by Donatello; and

---

[1] Dante was born at Florence, A.D. 1261. He fought in two battles; was fourteen times appointed Ambassador, and once Prior of the Republic: but, nevertheless, without having committed any crime against his country, he was stripped of his fortune, banished, and even condemned to be burnt alive.
[2] Supposed to have been Sir John Hawkwood, who died in the reign of Richard II.
[3] The Meridian in this church is said to be the largest astronomical instrument in Europe.

one of these (called, by its author, his *Zuccone*, or Bald-pate) he preferred to all his other works, partly from the beauty of the sculpture, and partly because it resembled one of his friends. The other statues are by Niccolo A●●tino, Andrea Pisano, Giottino, and Luca della Robbia.

S. Giovanni, or *the Baptistery*, supposed to have been originally a temple of Mars, is of an octangular form, with a roof somewhat like that of the Pantheon. The exterior walls are incrusted with polished marble; and the two bronze doors, done by Ghiberti, after the designs of Arnolfo, and formerly gilt, are so peculiarly beautiful, that Buonaroti used to say, they deserved to have been the gates of Paradise. The other door was executed by Andrea Pisano, after the designs of Giotto. The foliage and festoons, round the first-named doors, are by Ghiberti's son, Bonacorsa; the *bassirilievi* represent scriptural histories. On the outside of the Baptistery is a celebrated group, in bronze, by F. Rustici, representing S. John Baptist with a Scribe and a Pharisee. The two porphyry columns, on the sides of the principal entrance, were presented by the Pisans to the Florentines, in consequence of the latter having guarded Pisa while its inhabitants were engaged in subduing Majorca and Minorca: and the pendent chains, seen here, and in other parts of the city, are trophies won by the Florentines when they conquered the ancient Porto-Pisano. The interior part of the Baptistery is adorned with sixteen immense granite columns, which support a gallery; and between these columns are statues representing the twelve Apostles, the law of nature, and the written Law, all by Ammannati; except S. Simon, which, in consequence of the original statue being broken, was replaced by Spinnazzi. The high altar is adorned with a statue of S. John Baptist in the act of being transported to Heaven by Angels; and this group, and the ornaments of the pulpit, are by Ticciati. On the ceiling are mosaics by Apollonius (a Grecian artist), Andrea Teffi, Gaddo Gaddi, etc. The pavement is chiefly ancient mosaic, and in one part represents the sun, with the twelve signs of the zodiac. In ancient mosaic, likewise, is the following inscription, which may be read either backward or forward: " *En giro torte Sol ciclos et rotor igne.* "[1]

The Chiesa di S. Marco, belonging to the Padri Domenicani, is a handsome edifice, adorned with good sculpture and valuable paintings. On the right of the great door are—a Crucifixion, by Santi di Tito—the Madonna, our Saviour, and Saints, by Fra Bartolommeo!—and an old mosaic, representing the Madonna, etc. The cupola of the tribuna was painted by Alessandro Gherardini; and behind the high altar is the last Supper, by Sacconi. To the right of the tribuna is the Serragli chapel, the ceiling of which was painted by Poccetti! Here, likewise, are, the last Supper, by Santi di Tito, and the Supper of Emmaus, by Cav. Curradi. Further on, is the Salviati chapel, completely incrusted with marble, and containing a picture, by Alessandro Allori, of the return of our Saviour from Purgatory; a statue of S. John Baptist, executed after the design of Giovanni di Bologna, by

---

[1] " Phœbus drives on, oblique, his fiery car."

Francavilla; bronze *bassi-rilievi*, executed after the designs of Giovanni di Bologna, by Portigiani; a cupola, painted by Aless. Allori; two paintings, representing the exposition and translation of S. Antonino, by Passignano; and, under the arch of the chapel, S. Antonino in marble, by Giovanni di Bologna. Leading down the church, toward the great door, is a picture, by Cigoli, representing the Emperor Heraclius, in the habit of a Penitent, bearing the cross; a fine copy, by Gabbiani, of Fra Bartolommeo's celebrated picture of the Madonna, our Saviour, and S. Catherine; S. Vincenzio Ferreri preaching to the people; and the Transfiguration, by Paggi. The ceiling of the nave is painted by Pucci! and the curtain of the organ, by Gherardini. In this church are buried two celebrated men, Angelo Poliziano, and Giovanni Pico della Mirandola, both highly famed for their learning; and the latter was not only styled, "The phœnix of the sciences," but called, by Scaliger, " A prodigy—a man without a fault!"—They both died in 1494. The Sacristy of S. Marco contains a statue of our Saviour, by Antonio Novelli; two *bassi-rilievi*, by Conti; and, over the first door, within-side, a picture, by Beato Giovanni Angelico! The Library is rich in manuscripts—the Cloisters are adorned with frescos, by B. G. Angelico, Poccetti, Fra Bartolommeo, Carlo Dolci, etc.; and near the garden is a chapel, painted by Poccetti, and now the *Spezieria*, where the best essences in Florence are fabricated.

The Church of the S. S. Annunziata contains a fresco of the Annunciation, done by a certain Bartolommeo; who being, it is said, at a loss how to make the countenance of the Madonna properly seraphic, fell asleep, while pondering over his work; and, on waking, found it executed in a style he was unable to equal: upon which, he instantly exclaimed, "A miracle, a miracle!"—and his countrymen were too fond of miracles not to believe him; although the Madonna's face is by no means so exquisitely painted as to be attributed to a heavenly artist. *The open Vestibule*, leading to the church, is ornamented with several frescos; namely, a nativity, by Baldovinetti; S. Filippo Benizzi induced to embrace the monastic life in consequence of a vision, by Rosseli; S. Filippo covering a naked Leper with his own shirt, by Andrea del Sarto; S. Filippo, while travelling toward Modena, reviled by young men sitting under a tree, which, being struck with lightning, two of the revilers are killed;—this is by Andrea del Sarto; as are, S. Filippo delivering a young person from an evil spirit;—a dead child restored to life, by touching the garment which covered the corpse of the Saint— women and children kneeling round a friar, who is adorned with the relics of S. Filippo's clothes;— and seven lunettes, on the other side of the vestibule. The marriage of the Madonna, is by Francabigio; the visit of Mary to Elisabeth, by Pontormo; and the Assumption, by Rossi. This Corridor contains a bust of Andrea del Sarto. The church of the Annunziata is loaded with ornaments: it contains, in the centre of the ceiling, an Assumption, by Volterrano; who likewise painted the cupola of the Tribuna! In the chapel which encloses the miraculous picture, is an altar, adorned with silver *bassi-rilievi;* two silver candelabra, about six feet high; two large silver statues of angels; a ciborio, beautifully worked, and embellished with a head of our Saviour, by Andrea del Sarto; a silver cornice, from which hangs a curtain of the same metal; and an immense number of silver lilies, and lamps, which encircle the altar. The pavement of this chapel is porphyry and Egyptian granite; and, in the adjoining Oratory, whose walls are incrusted with agate, jasper, and other precious stones, is a crucifix, by Antonio di San Gallo. To the left of the great door is a picture of the last Judgment, by Aless. Allori; and another, of the Crucifixion, by Stradano: the ceiling and lunettes of the chapel on this side, at the end of the cross, are painted in fresco, by Volterrano; and contain a curious old picture, over the altar, of S. Zenobio, and other figures. In front of the high-altar (which is adorned with a splendid silver ciborio), are recumbent statues, the one by Francesco da S. Gallo, the other by Giovanbatista Foggini: and behind the altar is a Chapel decorated after the designs, and at the expense, of Giovanni di Bologna, who was buried in it; and whose tomb is adorned with a crucifix and *bassi-rilievi*, in bronze, executed by himself, for the Grand Duke by whom they were thus handsomely and judiciously appropriated. The chapel contains a picture of the Resurrection, by Ligozzi; a *Pietà*, by Passignano; a Nativity, by Paggi; and a Cupoletta, by Poccetti! Leading from the high-altar, toward the great door in the opposite side of the cross to that already described, is a Chapel, painted by Vincenzio Meucci: and near this, is the Chapel of Bandinelli, containing a dead Christ, in marble, supported by Nicodemus; the latter being a portrait of Bandinelli, by whom this group was executed. The curtain of the organ, representing the canonization of S. Giuliana, is by Romei. In a Corridor on the left side of the church, is the celebrated fresco, called *La Madonna del Sacco!!!* deemed the masterpiece of Andrea del Sarto; and at which Buonaroti and Titian are said to have gazed unceasingly. It is recorded, that the author of this beautiful work did it for a sack of corn, in a time of famine. Here are other paintings, by eminent artists; and those in the Corridor, which contains the *Madonna del Sacco*, were done by Poccetti, who has represented the most remarkable actions of the Six Founders of the Monastery. Another Corridor contains, Manetto preaching before S. Louis, King of France; and Innocent IV. making his nephew Protector of the order of Servites, both by Rosselli; and the Madonna in a car, by Salimbeni. Another Corridor exhibits Alexander IV. giving Religion power to erect monasteries throughout the world, by Rosselli; Buonfigliulo resigning the government of the Church, by Poccetti; three other paintings, by Salimbeni; and, on the ceiling, small portraits of illustrious Servites. The Refectory is adorned with a fresco, by Santi di Tito; and, on the top of the stairs, leading to the Noviziato, is a *Pietà*, by Andrea del Sarto, deemed one of his best works: this great Painter was buried in the open Vestibule before the church.

The Chiesa di S. Maria Maddelena dei Pazzi particularly deserves notice, on account of the Neri-Chapel, situated on the right side of the Court leading to the church. The altar-piece of this chapel is by Passignano; and its cupoletta contains the *chef-d'œuvre* of Poccetti, representing the mansions of the Blessed!! In the church is a magnificent *Cappella-maggiore*, incrusted with rare and beautiful marbles, and adorned with twelve columns of Sicilian jasper, whose capitals and bases are of bronze gilt. Here rest the remains of S. Maria Maddalena dei Pazzi, surrounded with *bassirilievi* of bronze gilt (expressing the most memorable actions of her life), and four marble statues, representing her most conspicuous virtues; namely, piety, sweetness, penitence, and religion. Sweetness, with the lamb and dove, and Religion with a veil, are particularly worth notice; especially the latter; the features through the veil being finely expressed. The cupola is by Pietro Dandini; and the other paintings, by Ciro Ferri and Luca Giordano. On the right of the high-altar is a Chapel adorned with frescos, by Sorbolini, a living artist; and on the left another Chapel, likewise painted in fresco, by Catani, a living artist. This church also contains a fine crucifix in wood, by Buontalenti; and the curtain of the organ, done by G. B. Cipriani, who has left no other work in Florence, represents S. Maria Maddalena receiving the communion from the hand of our Saviour! The first chapel, on the right, near the great door, contains the martyrdom of S. Romolo, by Carlo Portelli; said to be the only picture he ever painted; and on the opposite side of the church are, the Visitation, by Ghirlandajo; Christ in the garden, by Santi di Tito—and the coronation of the Madonna, by Angelico! The Chapter-room and Refectory of the Monastery, to which this church belongs, are embellished with the works of Perugino, Raffaellino del Garbo, and other celebrated artists.

The Chiesa di Santa Croce, built about the year 1294, by Arnolfo, and afterward repaired by Vasari, is a vast edifice, better calculated to promote religious contemplation than any other church at Florence. Over the middle-door of the façade, is a statue, in bronze, by Donatello—and at the entrance of the church, on the right, is the tomb of Buonaroti; who was born, at Chiusi, near Arezzo, in 1474, and died at Rome, in 1563; but the Grand-Duke of Tuscany, jealous that Rome should have the honour of providing a grave for this great and good man, ordered his body to be removed thence, and buried in the church of Santa Croce. The family of Buonaroti was noble: and Michael Angelo's parents were averse to his becoming an artist; which they deemed derogatory to nobility: he, however, by unceasing importunities, at length prevailed upon them to let him follow his natural genius. Sculpture, Painting, and Architecture, are represented, in mournful attitudes, sitting beneath the tomb of their Favourite; whose bust rests upon a sarcophagus: and a small painting, done by Buonaroti, is introduced among the ornaments at the top of the monument. The statue of Sculpture, by Cioli, is ill done; Architecture, by Giovanni dell' Opera, is more happily executed; and Painting, by G. Batista del Cavaliere, better still: the bust of Buonaroti is by the last-named artist.[1] The second tomb, on this side, is that of Filippo Buonaroti, the antiquary—the third, that of Pietro Michelli, called by Linnæus, "The lynx of botany" —the fourth, that of Vittorio Alfieri, by Canova: who has represented Italy mourning over the sarcophagus of the poet; which is adorned with masks, lyres, laurel-wreaths, and a head of Alfieri, in *basso-rilievo*. The Florentines are not pleased with the shape of this monument; neither do they like the manner in which the figure of Italy is draped: and this last circumstance, united with the late public revolutions, gave birth to the following *jeu d'esprit*:

"Canova questa volta l'ha sbagliata
Fe l'Italia *vestita* ed è spogliata."

The fifth monument, on this side, is that of Machiavelli; erected 266 years after his death, at the expense of the Literati. The sixth monument is that of Lanzi; near which is an Annunciation, in marble, by Donatello. The eighth monument is that of Leonardo Bruni, Aretino, the historian; which bears a Latin inscription to this purport: "Since Leonardo died, History mourns, Eloquence is mute; and it is said that neither the Greek nor Latin Muses can refrain from tears." The ninth monument is that of Nardini, a famous musician; and the tenth that of an equally famous architect, Pio Fantoni of Fiesole. The Castellani-Chapel contains a picture of the Last Supper by Vasari; a monument to the memory of Cav. Vanni; and another to that of M. B. Skotnicki; representing Grief as a recumbent female figure, veiled, and lying on a sarcophagus, which exhibits a pallet, brushes, and an unstrung lyre. This monument is by Ricci, now a distinguished artist; but, not long since, a peasant on the Marchese Corsi's estate, near Florence. The Baroncelli-Chapel contains paintings, on the walls, by Taddeo-Gaddi; and, over the altar, a picture of the Coronation of the Madonna, etc. by Giotto. The Riccardi-Chapel contains good paintings, by Passignano, Rosselli, and Giovanni di San Giovanni. Behind the high-altar are paintings, by Agnolo Gaddi, representing the Invention of the Cross.[2] The Niccolini-Chapel, built after the design of Antonio Dosio, and beautifully incrusted with rare marbles, contains fine pictures by Aless. Allori; statues of Moses and Aaron, by Francavilla! and a cupola, painted in fresco by Volterrano, the four sibyls, in the angles of which are *chefs-d'œuvre*. This quarter of the church likewise contains a celebrated crucifix, by Donatello; together with pictures of the Martyrdom of S. Lorenzo, by Ligozzi;

---

[1] Buonaroti, when an infant, was put out to nurse at the village of Settignano, about three miles distant from Florence, and where the inhabitants were chiefly stone-cutters and sculptors: his nurse's husband followed the latter occupation; so that the child's passion for this art seems to have been sucked in with his milk.

[2] The history of the Invention of the Cross is as follows:—In 356, Saint Helena, the mother of Constantine, being at Jerusalem, ordered the Temple of Venus, which profaned that sacred spot, to be destroyed; in doing which, remains of the Holy Sepulchre were discovered, and likewise three crosses: it seemed, however, impossible to ascertain which of the three was that whereon Our Saviour suffered; till a learned prelate took them all to the habitation of a dying lady, placing her first on one, then on another, and then on the third, which she no sooner touched than the illness eft her.

the Trinity, by Cigoli! and the Descent of the Holy Ghost, by Vasari. Leading toward the great door, and opposite to the monuments already described, are the following:—First, the tomb of Cocchio—second, that of Carlo Mazzopini—third, that of Carlo Marzuppini, Aretino, finely executed by Desiderio da Settignano—fourth, that of Lami, by Foggini—fifth, that of Pompeio-Josephi Signorinio, by Ricci; who has adorned this sarcophagus with a beautiful recumbent figure of Philosophy, whose countenance expresses deep sorrow. Near this tomb is a picture of the Resurrection, by Santi di Tito; together with the monument of the great and much injured Galileo, erected by order of Viviani, his pupil. The bust of Galileo is by Foggini. History tells us that Galileo was at first interred in the Piazza Santa Croce (which is unconsecrated ground), because he lay under suspicion of heresy on account of his philosophical discoveries: nay, it is even asserted that the family of Nelli (Viviani's executors) found some difficulty in obtaining leave to remove his bones into the church, almost a century after his decease. Beyond this tomb is that of Filicajo. At the bottom of the church is a painting of the Resurrection, by Aless. Allori! and the pulpit merits notice, as it was executed by Benedetto da Majano. The Sacristy contains curious pictures, in fresco, by Taddeo Gaddi; and, in the Monastery of Santa Croce are paintings by Cimabue and Giotto.

The Chiesa di S. Lorenzo, built at the expense of a lady, named Juliana, who lived during the reign of the Emperor Theodosius, consecrated in 392, and rebuilt in 1425, by Brunellesco, contains a high-altar of beautiful Florentine work, done by command of the Grand Duke Leopoldo, and designed for the Chapel of Medicis: and, above this altar, are a crucifix, by Giovanni di Bologna; a Madonna, by Buonaroti; and S. John, by one of his scholars. The church likewise contains the tomb of Cosimo *Pater Patriæ*; two pulpits adorned with bronze *bassi-rilievi*, by Donatello; and a ciborio of marble, together with an Infant Jesus, by Desiderio da Settignano.

The new Sacristy, or *Capella de' Principi*, designed by Buonaroti, contains the tomb of Giuliano de' Medici, Duke of Nemours, and brother to Leo x., ornamented with a statue of the Duke; a recumbent figure of Day!! and another of Night!! all by Buonaroti—the tomb of Lorenzo de' Medici, Duke of Urbino; ornamented with a statue of that prince; together with a recumbent figure of Twilight, and another of Day-break! all by Buonaroti! and here, likewise, by the same great master, is a group of a Madonna and Child, which, if finished, might, according to appearance, have proved the finest of his works!!

The old Sacristy, built by Brunellesco, contains a porphyry tomb, with bronze ornaments, made to enclose the remains of Pietro and Giovanni, sons of Cosimo, *Pater Patriæ*, by Verrocchio.

The Capella de' Medici, adjoining to the church of S. Lorenzo, was begun in 1604, by Ferdinando I., after his own design. Three hundred workmen were, for a considerable time, employed upon this building: but, latterly, the number has been lessened: and we have already seen the ducal family of Medicis extinct; nay, perhaps, may see the Dukedom itself annihilated, ere the finishing stroke be given to this magnificent mausoleum of its Princes. The building is octangular; and the walls are beautifully incrusted with almost every kind of precious marble. Six sides of the octagon are embellished with sarcophagi of Egyptian and oriental granite; made after the designs of Buonaroti; and two of them enriched with cushions of red jasper, which bear regal crowns of great value. Here, likewise, are two statues, in bronze, one of which is by Giovanni di Bologna, and the other by Pietro Tacca. The sarcophagi are mere ornaments; the bodies of the Princes being placed perpendicularly under them, in a subterranean repository.

The Capella de' Medici may be seen daily, from ten in the morning till four in the afternoon.

The Libreria Mediceo-Laurenziana, one of the most elegant apartments of its kind in Europe, was built, under the direction of Buonaroti; by whom the designs for the pavement also were executed. The windows are beautifully painted in arabesque by Raphael's scholars; and the manuscripts, which compose this library, are well arranged, highly valuable, and several of them finely illuminated. Here are, a Virgil of the third century, written in capitals—an old Testament of the twelfth century—the celebrated Pisan Pandects of the sixth century—the Psalms of David of the eleventh century—a prayer book beautifully illuminated—a missal, painted by the school of Pietro Perugino—a copy of Dante, written only twenty-two years after his death—a Livy of the fifteenth century, beautifully illuminated—the geography of Ptolomy (of the fifteenth century)—the *Decamerone* of Boccaccio, written two years before his death—a Homer of the fifteenth century—a Horace with Petrarca's own hand-writing in it—a celebrated Syriac manuscript—the Life of Lorenzo de' Medici, etc. etc.

This Library is usually open to the public, except during the vacation and on festivals. A trifling fee is expected, by the Sub-Librarian, for attending travellers.

The Chiesa di Santa Maria Novella, commenced in 1279, by two Domenican Monks, was so much admired by Buonaroti, that he used to call it his *Sposa*. Over the middle door, on the inside, is a crucifix, by Giotto—and, to the right, are the following pictures: an Annunciation, by Santi di Tito—a Nativity, by Naldini!— and the Resurrection of Lazarus, by Santi di Tito. Here, likewise, are the tomb of Villana dei Botti, by Settignano; and a painting of the Madonna, by Cimabue, supposed to have been the first work he ever did in Florence;[1] and near the latter is the Martyrdom of S. Catherine, by Giuliano Bugiardini; several of the figures in which picture were designed by Buonaroti. This part of the church also contains a Madonna, in marble, by Benedetto da Majano. In the choir, behind the high-altar, are paintings representing the lives

---

1 This is in a chapel, to which you enter by steps.

of the Madonna and S. John Baptist, all by Ghirlandajo; they comprise portraits of the painter himself, and of several of his most illustrious contemporaries; among whom are Pietro, Giovanni, and Lorenzo de' Medici. The high-altar was erected in 1804; and the altar-piece is by Sabatelli. The adjacent chapel contains a crucifix done by Brunellesco, for the famous countess who lived with Donatello. In the next chapel is a picture of Christ raising the dead, by Agnolo Bronzino, and a ceiling by the same artist: the tombs and the *bassirilievi* in this chapel are by Giovanni dell' Opera. A chapel on the top of some steps, and immediately opposite to that wherein the Madonna of Cimabue is placed, contains paintings by Andrea and Bernardo Orcagna; who have represented hell in one part, and heaven in another! This church likewise contains, on one of its pillars, the martyrdom of S. Peter, by Cigoli; and a fine painting of the good Samaritan, by Aless. Allori. The paintings over the door of the Campanile are by Buffalmacco; and the adjoining monastery contains several valuable frescos by old masters; among which there is said to be a portrait of Laura.¹

The Chiesa d'Or Sanmichele is esteemed for its architecture; and was built by Giotto and Taddeo Gaddi, as the market for grain. On the outside are several pieces of sculpture, namely: Saints Matthew, Stephen, and John Baptist, by Ghiberti; S. John the Evangelist, by Baccio da Montelupo; Saints Peter, Mark, and George, by Donatello (the last is deemed particularly fine); S. Philip the Apostle, S. Eligio, and four other Saints in one group, by Nanni d'Antonio; S. Thomas, by Andrea Verocchio; S. Luke, in bronze, by Giovanni di Bologna! and another statue of that Apostle, by Mino da Fiesole. The inside of this church contains sculpture, by the revivers of the art.

The Chiesa di San Spirito, built by Brunellesco, is, in point of architecture, the finest church at Florence. On the right of the entrance-door is a copy, by Nanni di Baccio, of Buonaroti's *Pietà*, in S. Peter's at Rome. The picture of our Saviour driving the Profane from the Temple, is by Stradano—the stoning of S. Stephen, by Passignano—and the group, in marble, of the Arch-Angel Raphael and Tobias, by Giovanni Baratta. The second picture, to the right of this group, is by Filippo Lippi—the picture of the Madonna, our Saviour, and S. Catherine, by the same author—and the Virgin appearing to S. Bernardo, is a fine copy of a work of Perugino's. The picture, representing several Martyrs, is by Aless. Allori—that representing the Woman taken in adultery, is by the same author—and the beatified Chiara da Montefalcone receiving the communion from our Saviour, is by Vignali. The Altar of the holy sacrament contains fine sculpture, by Andrea Contucci, da Monte San Savino! near this, is a picture, by Ghirlandajo, of our Saviour bearing his cross! and the Transfiguration, by Pietro di Cosimo. Returning to the nave, in the first Chapel, is a picture

---

1 The *Spezieria* of Santa Maria Novella is celebrated for perfumes, medicines, etc.

by Agnolo Bronzino, of Christ appearing to the Magdalene; and, next to this, is the Madonna, S. Sebastiano, etc. by Petrucci; copied from a work of Rosso's. Beyond the organ is S. Anne, the Madonna, and other Saints, by Ghirlandajo; and, near this, is a statue of our Saviour holding his cross, by Taddeo Landini, from the original of Buonaroti, at Rome. The Cappella-maggiore, by Michelozzi, is beautiful in point of architecture, richly incrusted with precious marbles, and adorned with statues of S. Peter and S. John. The roof of the Vestibule to the Sacristy is one single block of stone. The Sacristy contains an altar-piece, by Filippo Lippi, of the Madonna, our Saviour, Angels, and Saints! and a painting over the door, by Poccetti, of S. Agostino, and an Angel, in the form of a child! The architecture of the Sacristy is particularly fine; and that of the Campanile much admired.

The Chiesa del Carmine, begun in 1268, was nearly destroyed by fire; and, in consequence of that accident, repaired, not many years since. The ceiling and cupola were painted by Stagi and Romei: subjects—the most renowned characters of the old and new Testament—the Prophet Elias conveyed to Heaven in a chariot of fire—the Madonna putting the veil upon S. Maria Maddalena de' Pazzi—the beatified Angelo Mazzinghi in glory —and the ascension of our Saviour into Heaven. On the right side of the entrance-door is a picture of our Saviour on the cross, with the Madonna and Magdalene standing near, by Vassari— a *Pietà* by Antonio Guidotti; and a picture of S. Jacopo, by Lorenzo Lippi! The Cappella della S. S. Vergine del Carmine was painted by Masolino da Panicale, and Masaccio his disciple, the first person who attained perfection in the revived art; but, as he died young, his work was finished by Filippo Lippi, the son of Fra Filippo. Leonardo da Vinci, Fra Bartolommeo, Andrea del Sarto, Buonaroti, and Raphael, are supposed to have derived the greater part of their knowledge from the study of these excellent paintings; which represent the life of S. Peter. In the choir is a tomb, by Benedetto di Rovezzano. The curtain of the organ (which is one of the best instruments at Florence), represents the Madonna giving the sacred habit to Simon Stock; and was painted by Romei. But the most striking thing here, is the Corsini-Chapel, magnificently incrusted with rare marbles, and containing the sarcophagus of S. Andrea Corsini, adorned with silver *bassi-rilievi!* Over the altar is an *alto-rilievo*, representing S. Andrea Corsini, (who, from a Monk, became Bishop of Fiesole), ascending into Heaven; this is by G. B. Foggini; and above it, is God the Father in glory, by Marcellini. On the sides of the chapel are two marble *alti-rilievi*, by Foggini; the one representing the Saint reading his first mass, and the Madonna appearing, and saying, "Thou art my servant; I have chosen thee; and in thee will I be glorified:" the other representing his descent from Heaven to assist the Florentines in the battle of Anghiari! The Cupoletta was painted by Luca Giordano. To the right of this chapel is the Deposition from the Cross, by G. D. Ferretti, un-

G 2

der a Cupoletta painted by Romei: and, on that side of the nave not already described, is a picture of S. Maria Maddalena dei Pazzi receiving the veil from the Madonna, by Fabbrini—a Nativity, by Gambacciani—an Annunciation, by Poccetti—and the Adoration of the Magi, copied, by Viligiardi, from the celebrated picture of Gregorio Pagani. The monastery, to which this church belongs, contains frescos by Vasari, Poccetti, etc.

The Chiesa di S. Trinità contains a nativity, by Ghirlandajo—a *Pietà* by Angelico—a Chapel belonging to the Sassetti-family, representing, in fresco, the life of S. Francesco, of Assisi, by Ghirlandajo!—two pictures in the Cappella degli Usimbardi; one representing S. Peter sinking, by Christofano Allori!—the other S. Peter receiving the keys of Heaven, by Empoli!—with frescos, above, by Giovanni di San Giovanni—a modern painting of S. Giovanni Gualberto, in the act of pardoning an enemy, by Francesco Corsi—the Sermon on the Mount, by Rosselli—and an Annunciation, by Empoli, placed under a cupoletta, finely painted by Poccetti. The Statue of S. Maria Maddalena, between the entrance-doors, was begun by Settignano, and finished by Benedetto da Majano! The refectory was painted by Giovanni di San Giovanni, and Ferrucci.

The Chiesa di S. Ambrogio contains a Chapel adorned with sculpture, by Mino da Fiesole; and paintings representing the miracle of the Cross, by Cosimo Rosselli. The picture in the Cappella del Rosario is by Passignano; and the small fresco, representing the Madonna, our Saviour, and S. Anne, is by Masaccio!

The Church of S. Gaetano contains the best organ at Florence, and some good pictures; *the Church of Ognissanti,* likewise contains good pictures; and the *Conservatorio di Ripoli,* in Via della Scala, merits the attention of travellers who have time to spare.

The reale Accademia delle belle Arti, founded by the Grand-Duke Leopoldo, is open to public inspection at the same hours with the Gallery, and merits notice, not only on account of the liberality of the institution, which gives all possible encouragement to rising genius, but likewise as it contains excellent casts of the Baptistery-doors, and most of the fine statues hitherto discovered in Italy. Here is a noble apartment, fitted up with drawings, etc., for the use of young painters; other noble apartments, containing every necessary accommodation for those who are further advanced; a gallery, containing paintings and sketches, by celebrated masters, among which is a valuable picture by Angelico, another by Giovanni di San Giovanni, of the Repose in Egypt; and a beautiful head of Our Saviour, by Carlo Dolci. This academy likewise contains Schools for Architecture, practical Mechanics, etc.; and here also the Florentine work in *pietri duri,* called *Opera di commesso,* is made.

Not far hence are cloisters which formerly belonged to the suppressed company of S. Giovanni Batista, but are now in custody of the Academy, where the key is always kept; these cloisters, commonly called *l'Oratorio dello Scalzo,* contain fresco paintings of the life of S. John Baptist, all by Andrea del Sarto, except two, which were done by Francabigio. At the entrance of the court are figures representing Faith and Hope; and, on the sides of the opposite door, Charity and Justice, all by Andrea. The history of S. John commences with Zacharias becoming dumb, on account of his incredulity. Second painting, Mary visiting Elisabeth —third, Elisabeth brought to bed —fourth, Zacharias blessing S. John, who departs for the desert (this is by Francabigio) — fifth, S. John meeting Our Saviour, as the latter returns from Egypt (likewise by Francabigio)—sixth, the Baptism of Our Saviour by S. John—seventh, S. John preaching in the Desert — eighth, the converted Jews receiving baptism—ninth, S. John carried before Herod—tenth, Herod's Supper and Dance—eleventh, the Decapitation of S. John — twelfth, Herodias's Daughter with the Head of S. John. It is recorded that Andrea del Sarto received for each of these frescos only twenty livres,[1] though many of them are exquisitely fine; they will, however, shortly be obliterated by the humidity of their situation, unless restored in the manner now practised at Rome.[2]

The Palazzo-Gherini is adorned with valuable pictures, though the finest part of this collection has been recently sold. Among those which remain are, *First room*—Charity, by Cignani; and Hagar in the Desert, by Rosselli. *Second room*—Head of a young Female, by Correggio! *Third room* — four heads, by Nogari; and two pictures, by Bassano. *Fourth room* — a landscape, by Both; ditto, by Swanevelt; and ditto, by Paul Brill. *Fifth room*—Prometheus, by Salvator Rosa! —Head of Our Saviour! by Stradano; Head of a Female, by Carlo Dolci! *Seventh room* — two landscapes, by Both; S. Sebastiano, by Guercino! and the Assumption, by Carlo Maratti. *Eighth room* — Our Saviour in the Sepulchre, by Tiarini! a dead Nun, by Vanni; a little picture, by Rubens! the Madonna, Our Saviour, and S. John, by one of the Caracci Family; two little pictures, by Peter Neff; and two small landscapes, by Vernet; the Madonna, Our Saviour, and other figures, by Fra Bartolommeo; a portrait of Salvator Rosa, by himself; a Peasant playing on a Wind-instrument, by Murillo; a Holy Family, by Raphael; a portrait of a Woman with a Veil, by Santi di Tito; and an old Man with a Child in his Arms, by Guido!!

The Palazzo-Riccardi, which once belonged to the Medici family, is a fine building. The Gallery contains a ceiling beautifully painted by Luca Giordano; the ceiling of the Library is by the same master; and the collection of manuscripts and printed books is valuable.

The Palazzo-Corsini is adorned with some good paintings.

The Palazzo-Mozzi, near the *Ponte a la Gracie*, contains fine paintings, by Salvator Rosa.

The Palazzo - Buonaroti, in Via Ghibellina, is interesting, from having been the residence of so great a man, and likewise

---

[1] Fifteen shillings.
[2] The person who unlocks the door of the Oratorio dello Scalzo expects two pauls for his trouble; and the person who attends travellers round the Royal Academy likewise expects from two to three pauls, according to the size of the party.

from containing some remains of his works.

The Palazzo-Strozzi is a fine piece of Tuscan architecture.

The Palazzo-Uguccioni, built after the design of Buonaroti, contains a painting, by Perino del Vaga, of the passage of the Israelites through the Red Sea!

The Casa dei Poveri, in Via dei Malcontenti, which owes its establishment to the Emperor Napoleon, is an immense edifice, capable of lodging three thousand persons, who, in great measure, maintain themselves, by making caps, or rather Phrygian bonnets, for the Mediterranean mariners, ribbons, cloth, carpets, etc. etc. There are work-shops of almost every description in the house; and the present Grand Duke of Tuscany, much to his honour, supports and benefits this benevolent and useful institution, which has completely cleared Florence of the innumerable troops of mendicants by whom it was formerly infested.

The Spedale di Bonifazio, or great Hospital, near the Porta San-Gallo, receives lunatics, and persons afflicted with chronic disorders, and is spacious, clean, and airy. The sick appear to be comfortably lodged and well attended, but the funds belonging to this charity are not sufficiently ample to supply convalescent patients with a proper quantity of nourishment. Detached from the rest of the building are excellent apartments for lunatics: somewhat less care, however, seems to be taken of these unhappy creatures than of others.

The Spedale di Santa Maria Nuova contains upward of a thousand beds, and the patients are extremely well attended.

The Spedale degl' Innocenti usually contains three thousand children, who have not, however, a sufficient number of nurses; and the custom of binding up every new-born infant in swaddling clothes frequently distorts the limbs, nay, sometimes, produces mortification and death.

The Column of Saravezza-marble, in Via Romana, was erected by Cosimo I. in memory of the battle of Marciano—*the Granite Column, near Ponte Santa Trinità*, was taken from Antoninus's Bath at Rome, and erected at Florence by Cosimo I. in memory of the conquest of Siena. There is, on its summit, a figure of Justice, which gave rise to the following proverb:— " Justice, at Florence, is too high to be reached"—*the Column near the Baptistery, in the Piazzo del Duomo*, was erected to record a miracle relative to the corpse of S. Zenobio.

The bronze Wild Boar, in the Mercato-nuovo, is a copy, by Pietro Tacca, of the famous antique in the Gallery de' Medici. *The Pedestal adorned with bassi-rilievi in marble, which stands near the entrance of the Church of S. Lorenzo*, was done by Bandinelli, and represents Giovanni de' Medici, father of Cosimo I., with prisoners and spoils. *The Group of Hercules killing the Centaur Nessus, which stands near the Ponte-Vecchio*, is by Giovanni di Bologna!!—*the Piazza del Annunziata* contains an equestrian statue of Ferdinando I. *Over the Porta San-Gallo* is a fresco-painting, by Ghirlandajo; and, just beyond the gate, a magnificent *triumphal Arch*, erected in honour of the Emperor Francis I. when Grand Duke of Tuscany. *On the outside of a house, near the Porta Romana*, is a fresco, by Giovanni di San Giovanni, representing the city of Florence, under the form of a woman clothed in royal robes, and the other cities of Tuscany, as females paying homage to their queen.

The Ponte Santa Trinità, built by Ammannati, is remarkably elegant.

Florence contains three theatres, the *Pergola*, or opera-house, a beautiful edifice, well secured from fire, and originally built after the design of Pietro Tacca—the *Cocomero*, smaller than the Pergola —and the *Teatro Nuovo*.

The Florentine Mosaic work, and the Sculpture in alabaster, of the Brothers Pisani, in the Prato, and of Bartolini, in Via della Scala, are much admired. This country is likewise celebrated for a sort of marble which splits almost like slate, and, when polished, the variations of its yellow and brown veins represent trees, landscapes, and ruins of old walls und castles; several petrifactions are also found in this neighbourhood.

A long residence at Florence is deemed injurious to the sight, owing, perhaps, to that glare which proceeds from the reflection of the sun upon white houses, and likewise to the fogs which prevail here in winter.

This city boasts the honour of having given education to Dante, Petrarca, Boccaccio, Corilla, the celebrated *Improvvisatrice*, who was crowned at Rome, Americo Vespucci, (whose voyages to, and discoveries in, the new world obtained him the honour of calling America by his own name), Machiavelli, Galileo, Buonaroti, and a larger number of distinguished artists than any other place in Europe.

The Accademia della Crusca, which has, for a length of years, been established at Florence, is too well known to need description; and this academy is now united with two others, namely, the *Fiorentina*, and the *Apatisti*, under the name of *Reale Accademia Fiorentina*.

There are several good hotels at Florence, [1] and the markets are constantly well stored with excellent eatables, fish excepted, which is never fresh but on Fridays and Saturdays. The Florence wine is good and wholesome, the water much otherwise, except that which comes from Fiesole, and supplies the fountains of the Piazza-Santa Croce, and the Palazzo-Pitti. It is remarkable, however, that all the Florence water, when analysed, appears wholesome; and consequently it seems probable that the noxious quality may proceed from copper vases in which it is drawn, and usually suffered to stand, though large glass bottles, secured by a case of reeds, for the purpose of holding water, might be easily met with.

The climate of Florence is cold during winter, very hot during summer, but delightful in autumn and spring.[2] Doctor Downes, an

---

[1] *Il Pellicano*, also called *l'Hôtel des Armes d'Angleterre*, and kept by Gasperini, is an excellent inn, where dinners are better cooked and more comfortably served than at any of the other hotels. Gasperini repairs English travelling-carriages particularly well. *Schneiderff's* is a very large and good hotel: *The Quattri Nazioni*, and *The Nuova York*, are likewise good inns; and at 4380, Piazza S. Maria Novella, travellers may be comfortably accommodated with board and lodging, for a moderate price, by *Madame Merveilleux du Plantis*, an English lady of high respectability, married to a Captain in the Royal Navy of France.

[2] Persons who wish to preserve health in Tuscany should be careful never to eat sweet things made with *orange-flower water*, falsely so called; it being, in this country, a distillation from the Italian laurel-leaf (the bay), which is poisonous.

English physician, resides in this city.

I will now close this chapter with a list of the preceding churches, palaces, etc., as they lie near each other.

Duomo — Campanile — Battisterio di S. Giovanni — Palazzo Riccardi — Chiesa di S. Marco — Reale Accademia — L'Oratorio dello Scalzo — Spedale di Bonifazio — Porta S. Gallo — Arco trionfale — Statua di Ferdinando I., alla Piazza del Annunziata — Chiesa di S. Maria Maddelena de' Pazzi — Casa dei Poveri — Chiesa di Santa Croce — Chiesa di S. Ambrogio — Palazzo Buonaroti — Chiesa di Santa Maria Nuovo — sua Spedale — Chiesa di S. Lorenzo — Libreria Mediceo-Laurenziana — Capella Reale — Basso di S. Lorenzo — Chiesa di Santa Maria Novella — Palazzo-Corsini — Palazzo-Strozzi — Colonna di granito alla Piazza della Trinità — Chiesa della Trinità — Ponte della Trinità — Palazzo-Gerini — Galleria Ducale — Palazzo-Vecchio — Loggia — Fontana — Statua di Cosimo I. — Palazzo-Uguccioni — Chiesa d'Or San-Michele — L'Ercole and Nessus di Giovanni di Bologna — Palazzo-Mozzi — Palazzo-Pitti — Giardino di Boboli — Chiesa di S. Spirito — Chiesa del Carmine — Porta Romana.

CHAPTER IV.

FLORENCE.

Festa di San Giovanni—Corso dei Barberi—Game, called Pallone—Environs of Florence—Royal Cascini—Careggi de' Medici—Anecdote respecting the Physician of Lorenzo il Magnifico—Poggi Imperiale—Pratolino—Fiesole—Vallombrosa—Abbey of Camaldoli—Convent of Lavernia—Character of the Florentines—Tuscan Peasantry—their behaviour at a Ball—Anecdote relative to a Poor Foundling—Laws of Leopoldo—Population of Tuscany.

I CANNOT close my account of this city, without mentioning the ceremonies of the *Festa di San Giovanni*, the patron saint of Florence, on the vigil of which is the *Corsa dei Cocchi*, or chariot-race, probably an epitome of the ancient Etruscan games. This exhibition takes place in the Piazza of S. Maria Novella. At the upper and lower end of the piazza are obelisks, to each of which is fastened a cord, whose centre is held up by six poles, supported by men clothed in ancient costume. Round the piazza, in an amphitheatrical form, are scaffoldings, ornamented with rough fresco paintings of urns, etc. which produce, however, a good effect; at the upper end is the sovereign's box, handsomely decorated: under the scaffoldings are posted horse and foot-guards, and round the piazza, above the scaffoldings, are balconies, windows, and even house-tops, crowded with spectators. Were the chariots made in the ancient form, this exhibition would be far more interesting; but the carriages are modern in point of shape, and particularly clumsy, exhibiting nothing like antique costume, except the habit of the charioteers.

On the morning of the Festa di S. Giovanni homage used to be paid by all the Tuscan cities to their prince, but this custom is, for the present, abandoned, owing to the pageants which represented the several cities having been nearly destroyed by the French.

In the afternoon of this day is the *Corso dei Barberi,* a race performed by horses without riders, and which, from the multitude of spectators, the splendour of the equipages, and the gallant appearance of the troops who attend their sovereign, is an extremely gay sight. The horses have, fastened to their bodies, little spurs, so contrived that the quicker the animal gallops, the more they run into him. The race-ground is the longest street at Florence, where many of the spectators stand, without any defence whatsoever, frequently meeting with accidents by urging the horses on. When these animals reach the goal, they are stopped by a large piece of canvass, which several men hold up; the sovereign then announces the winning horse, and thus ends this amusement, which is followed by a pretty exhibition of fireworks at the Palazzo-Vecchio.[1]

The game called *Pallone,* a favourite exercise at Florence, also merits notice, because it was played by the ancient Romans; who are described as striking the *follis* with the arm guarded, for that purpose, by a wooden shield: the mode of playing continues precisely the same to the present moment; and this game, like most of the ancient exercises, is well calculated to give courage and strength.

The environs of Florence are extremely interesting. The usual airing of the upper ranks of persons is to the *Royal Farms,* or *Cascini;* which are open to the public at all hours; though it is deemed unwholesome to walk, ride, or drive in these beautiful farms very early in the morning, and equally prejudicial to remain there after sun-set.

Careggi de' Medici, about three miles from the Porta San Gallo, was the favourite retreat of Lorenzo *il Magnifico;* and in the hall of this villa the Platonic Society used to assemble, and form plans for those stately edifices and patriotic institutions by which Lorenzo benefited and embellished his country. The house stands upon an eminence, whence the ground falls gradually almost every way; opening, on one side, to a noble view of Florence; on another, to a boundless prospect of Val d'Arno; while, on another, rise mountains, covered with neat farm-houses and magnificent villas; and, on another, vaults Fiesole, dignified with ruins of ancient Greek and Roman splendour; and, to complete the deliciousness of the situation, cool and refreshing breezes almost constantly blow, about noon, from the Gulf of Spezia, and make the fortunate inhabitants of Careggi unconscious of oppressive heat, even in the dog-days:—no wonder, therefore, that the elegant

---

[1] So universal is the rage for splendour at this festival, that a milliner, at whose house one of my friends lodged, absolutely hired for the day, at a great expense, a coach with two footmen in laced liveries, that she might parade about the streets in style: nay, further, this woman and her apprentices, though generally dressed in the plainest manner possible, were now adorned with diamonds.

and wise Lorenzo should have called this his favourite abode! Careggi, like the generality of Tuscan villas, is built upon arches; and consists of an immense ground-floor, with a spacious hall in its centre, and several surrounding rooms; every ceiling being arched, and every apartment cool. Above stairs is another large hall, with a handsome suite of rooms, terminated by a terrace: and round the third story runs a gallery which commands a prospect so extensive that it seems to overlook all Tuscany. On the outside of the house are noble porticos. The water at this villa is peculiarly fine; owing, in some measure, to the following circumstance. When the great Lorenzo laboured under his last illness, a famous physician of Padua was summoned to attend him, he did so, and exerted his utmost skill; but to no purpose—Lorenzo died! —when some of his household, frantic with grief, met the unsuccessful physician, and threw him down the well in the quadrangle. The dead body was, of course, drawn up; and the well so nicely cleaned, that its water has, ever since, been super-excellent. It is remarkable that the above-named physician, when resident at Padua, had his nativity cast, and was told he would be drowned: he therefore quitted Padua, whence he was frequently compelled to go by water to Venice, and came to settle at Florence, as a place where water-carriage was unnecessary; thus furnishing an example

———— That human foresight
In vain essays to 'scape th' unerring stroke
Of Heaven-directed Destiny!

Poggi Imperiale, about one mile from the Porta Romana, is a royal villa containing an admired statue of Adonis, by Buonaroti; and portraits of Petrarca, and Laura, by Albert Durer. The prospects from this spot are beautiful; and not far hence stands the Monastery of S. Matteo in Arcetri, near which are vineyards that produce the celebrated wine called *Verdea*.

Pratolino, a royal Villa about six miles from the Porta S. Gallo, is famous for its garden; which contains water works, and a statue of the Appennine sixty feet in height, by Giovanni di Bologna.

On the way to Pratolino is the modern Campo-Santo of Florence.

Fiesole, anciently *Fœsulæ*, one of the twelve great cities of Etruria, is proudly seated, on a summit of the Apennine, in a most enchanting situation, about three miles and a half from the Porta Pinti, by the Majano-road. Light carriages may go with perfect ease and safety, so far as Majano, which is two-thirds of the way: but thence, to the Francescan Convent, at Fiesole, the best conveyance is a *traineau;* which the peasants at Majano can always furnish. Between the latter place and Fiesole is the Docia; a monastery built by Buonaroti, and deliciously situated. *The ancient Etruscan town of Fiesole* is supposed to have been destroyed by en earthquake, long before the period when Sylla founded a colony there: the walls of this town, however, are in several places discoverable: and it seems evident, from the manner in which they present themselves, that they were thrown down by some convulsion of nature: they appear to have originally consisted of large stones without cement, like the walls of

Pompeii and Pæstum. Here, likewise, are remains of an Amphitheatre, built on the side of a hill, as was the Grecian custom; the shape and size of the edifice, some of the staircases, seats, and caves for the wild beasts, together with the reservoir of water which belonged to this theatre, may be traced:[1] and here, also, is an ancient Temple, now roofed, and made into a church. Fourteen fine columns with Ionic capitals, the pavement, and the altar of the ancient building still remain; though the altar has been moved from its original situation. This temple is supposed to have been dedicated to Bacchus. The walls of the Roman town may, in some places, be traced; as may the pavement of the streets, which resembles that of Pompeii. The modern town, if it may be so called, contains a Cathedral, built in 1028, apparently on the site of an ancient temple; and adorned with Sculpture, by Mino da Fiesole, and Andrea Ferrucci, Fiesolano; and likewise with a picture of the martyrdom of S. Thomas, by Volterrano; here, also, are an episcopal Palace, a Seminary, and a Francescan Convent, which last stands on the spot called *Rocca dei Fiesolani*.

Vallombrosa, about fourteen miles distant from Fiesole, is well worth notice; not only because it has been immortalized by Milton, but likewise on account of the beauty of the country, and the noble Certosa of Vallombrosa, which still contains fine paintings; though the finest were, I believe, removed when the Convent was suppressed. Vallombrosa itself has suffered very little from being under the dominion of France: but the Certosa is not yet re-established. Mules are the necessary conveyance for persons who cannot walk, there being no carriage road to the Convent.

Lovers of wild scenery would be gratified by proceeding from Vallombrosa to *the Abbey of Camaldoli*, about thirty-six miles from Florence, and thence to the *Convent of Lavernia (mons Alvernus)*, about fourteen miles further. The former of these Convents was suppressed by the French; who cut down much of the fine wood belonging to it: now, however, this Convent is re-established; though its inhabitants, about thirty in number, are too poor to entertain visitors gratis; and therefore Travellers, after eating or sleeping under its roof, usually make a present to the community. The convent of Lavernia never was disturbed by the French, and contains, at present, about sixty Capuchins.

The modern Florentines, like their Etrurian ancestors, are fond of learning, arts, and sciences; and, what is more estimable and endearing to Foreigners, they are, generally speaking, good-humoured, warm-hearted, and friendly; such, at least, have I found them, for many successive years. The Tuscan peasantry, considered collectively, are pure in their morals and pastoral in their manner of living; and the peculiar comeliness of both sexes is very striking, especially in that tract of country which extends from Flo-

---

[1] The Etrurians are famed for having invented Amphitheatres, together with the games called *Curuli*, and *Certami dei Cavalli*: and about the year of Rome 400, comedians were invited, by the Romans, to come from Etruria, and perform plays, for the first time, at Rome; the Romans thinking these new games might appease the gods, and stop a then raging sickness.

rence to Peschia: but it is only among the peasantry that one can form a just idea of Italian beauty; and perhaps I might add, it is only among the peasantry one can form a just idea of the Italian character; inhabitants of populous cities being nearly alike, whether in London, Paris, Vienna, Florence, or Rome. The men are tall, robust, finely proportioned, and endowed with that entire self-possession which inspires respect, and perhaps a more favourable opinion of them than they really deserve. The women are of a middle stature; and were it not for bad stays, would be well made. They have large, languishing black eyes, accompanied by that expressive brow which constitutes the most remarkable and captivating part of an Italian countenance. Their manners are uncommonly graceful; and, instead of curtsying, they gently bow their bodies, and kiss the hand of a superior; a practice common, indeed, throughout Italy. When two young persons agree to marry, the banns are published three times in a parish church; after which they receive the nuptial benediction. The bride's portion is paid three days before marriage, one half in wearing apparel, and the other half in money; which the bridegroom usually expends in purchasing jewels for his lady; which consist of a pearl necklace, cross and ear-rings, frequently intermixed with rubies; and worth from twenty to thirty pounds sterling: these jewels being considered by the man as the woman's exclusive property; indeed, money so invested may be looked upon as placed in a bank; while the interest received is that high gratification which the woman derives from exhibiting her ornaments on gala-days; and these ornaments continue in the family for ages, unless the pressing call of necessity compel them to be pawned, or sold. When the *Sposa* is taken in labour, the husband, after procuring medical help, deems it his next duty to get some of what is called the life-giving plant (*aleatrice* the peasants call it), which he places on her bed; and without which he believes his child cannot be born. This custom is derived from the Greeks.[1] About a fortnight after the birth of the infant, its parents give what they denominate a *seaponata*, or christening dinner,[2] to their relations; on which occasion every guest brings a present, as was the practice at Athens; and the dinner is served dish by dish, likewise an ancient custom. On the husband's demise the eldest son becomes heir-at-law; but is obliged to portion his sisters, and either maintain his mother, or return her dower:[3] all his relations frequently live with him: but the largeness of the family creates no confusion; there being a superior over the men, and another over the women, who allot, to every person, their business; which is thus kept distinct. A Tuscan far-

---

[1] Some of the Grecian ladies used to hold palm-branches in their hands, in order to procure an easy delivery.

[2] Children in Roman-Catholic countries, however, are christened immediately after their birth.

[3] An elder son among the Greeks was obliged either to maintain his mother, or return her dower. Hence Telemachus, though he sustained great losses by means of Penelope's suitors, thinks it imprudent to send her home to her father; because that could not be done without returning her dower:—

"I could not now repay so great a sum
To the old Man, should I dismiss her home
Against her will."

HOMER's *Odyssey*.

mer shares equally with his lord in the produce of an estate; and the owner even provides seeds, plants, manure, implements of husbandry, in short, whatever may be requisite for the cultivation of the land. The upper class of farmers usually possess a horse and a market-cart, a waggon, and a pair of large dove-coloured oxen, who draw the waggon and the plough, whose colour seldom, if ever, varies throughout Italy, and whose beauty is as remarkable as that of their masters. The female peasants, besides working in the vineyards, almost equally hard with the men, often earn money by keeping poultry, and sometimes one or two lambs; whose fleecy coats the children decorate, on the Festa di San Giovanni, with scarlet ribbons tied in fantastic knots: and by the aid of money thus acquired, wearing-apparel, and other necessaries, are purchased. Shoes and stockings are deemed superfluous, and merely ornamental, even by the women; who carry them in baskets on their heads, till they reach a town; when these seemingly embarrassing decorations are put on: for the *Contadina* is as vain of her appearance as the *Dama nobile*; and, no wonder — since the Arcadian dresses and lovely countenances of these peasants arrest every eye, and show them, perhaps too plainly, how strong are their powers of attraction.[1] The phraseology of the Florentine peasants is wonderfully elegant: but the most remarkable quality of these persons is their industry; for, during the hottest weather, they toil all day without sleep; and seldom retire early to rest: yet, notwithstanding this fatigue, they live almost entirely upon bread, fruit, pulse, and the common wine of the country: however, though their diet is light, and their bodily exertions are almost perpetual, they commonly attain old age, especially in the neighbourhood of Fiesole.

My family and I about twenty years ago spent one summer at Careggi de' Medici, and another at Careggi di Riccardi; and during our residence in the latter villa, we invited all the surrounding peasants to a dance. Our ball-room was a lofty apartment sixty feet by thirty; and in the centre of the ceiling hung a lustre, composed of such light materials that every puff of wind gave it motion: indeed it had the appearance of being continually turned round by an invisible hand: this lustre we filled with candles; and the walls, which were adorned with full-length portraits of the Medici Princes, we likewise decorated with festoons of vines, olive-branches, flowers, and lamps, so that the whole apartment resembled an illuminated arbour. At sun-set, on the appointed day, our guests appeared altogether upon a lawn leading to the villa, preceded by their own band of music: and no sooner did this procession reach our hall door, than the musicians struck up a lively tune; while the dancers, as they entered, formed a quadrille, which would have been applauded on any opera-stage. When this dance was finished, the female peasants advanced, in couples, to the top of the hall, where we were seated, paying their compliments to us with as much ease and elegance as if they had been educated in a

---

[1] I am sorry to say that the ancient costume of the Tuscan peasants is less frequently worn than it used to be twenty years since.

court: and then commencing another quadrille, different from, but quite as pretty, as the first. With a succession of these dances we were amused till supper; after which our visitors, who had been regaled with punch, a liquor they particularly relish, came once more to us; when the women returned thanks for their entertainment, kissed our hands, and, presenting their own to their partners, bowed and retired.

I cannot dismiss the subject of Tuscan peasantry, without mentioning another circumstance, which may perhaps serve to show the grateful and delicate turn of mind possessed by these people.

One day, as we were walking near Careggi, we observed a girl, apparently about fourteen years of age, watching a flock of goats, and at the same time spinning with great diligence; her tattered garments bespoke extreme poverty; but her air was peculiarly dignified, and her countenance so interesting, that we were irresistibly impelled to present her with a few crazie. Joy and gratitude instantly animated her fine eyes while she exclaimed: "Never, till this moment, was I worth so much money!"—Struck by her words and manner, we inquired her name; likewise asking where her parents lived? "My name is Teresa," replied she; "but, alas! I have no parents." "No parents!—who, then, takes care of you?"—"The Madonna."—"But who brought you up?"—"A peasant in Vallombrosa: I was her nurse-child; and I have heard her say my parents delivered me into her care; but that she did not know their name. As I grew up she almost starved me; and, what was worse, beat me so cruelly, that, at length, I ran away from her." "And where do you live now?" "Yonder, in the plain (pointing to Val d'Arno); I have fortunately met with a mistress who feeds me, and lets me sleep in her barn: this is her flock." "And are you happy now?" "O yes! very happy. At first, to be sure, it was lonesome sleeping in the barn by myself; 'tis so far from the house; but I am used to it now: and indeed I have not much time for sleep; being obliged to work at night when I come home; and I always go out with the goats at day-break: however, I do very well; for I get plenty of bread and grapes; and my mistress never beats me." After learning thus much, we presented our new acquaintance with a paul—but to describe the ecstasy this gift produced is impossible.—" Now," cried she (when a flood of tears had enabled her to speak), "now I can purchase a *corona*[1]—now I can go to mass, and petition the Madonna to preserve my kind benefactresses!"

On taking leave of this interesting creature, we desired she would sometimes pay us a visit; our invitation, however, was only answered by a bow: and, to our regret, we neither saw nor heard of her again, till the day before our departure from Careggi; when it appeared that, immediately after her interview with us, she had been attacked by the small-pox, and was only just recovered.

During the next summer, although we again resided in the same neighbourhood, we, for a

---

[1] Without a *corona* she informed us that she could not be permitted to go to mass.

considerable time, saw nothing of Teresa. One day, however, we observed a beautiful white goat browsing near our house; and, on going out, perceived our *Protegée* with her whole flock. We now inquired, almost angrily, why she had not visited us before?—"I was fearful of obtruding," replied the scrupulous girl; "but I have watched you at a distance, ladies, ever since your return; and I could not forbear coming rather nearer than usual to-day, in the hope that you might notice me." We gave her a scudo, and again desired she would sometimes call upon us. "No, ladies," replied she, "I am not properly dressed to enter your doors; but, with the scudo you have kindly given me, I shall immediately purchase a stock of flax; and then, should the Madonna bless me with health to work hard, I may soon be able, by selling my thread, to buy decent apparel, and wait upon you, clothed with the fruits of your bounty."—And, indeed, it was not long ere we had the pleasure of seeing her come to visit us, neatly dressed, and exhibiting a picture of content.

According to the excellent laws of the Emperor Leopoldo, father to the present Grand Duke of Tuscany, no man can be imprisoned for debt, though creditors have power to seize the property of their debtors; and no offence is punishable with death, though murderers are condemned to perpetual labour as galley-slaves: and to these, and many other equally wise regulations, made by Leopoldo, are attributable the almost total exemption from robbery and murder which this country has long enjoyed; and the increase to its population of two hundred thousand; an astonishing difference, as the original number was only one million.

CHAPTER V.

PISA.

Situation, supposed origin, and present appearance of Pisa—Duomo—Baptistery—Campanile—Campo-Santo—Sonnet to Grief—Chiesa de' Cavalieri—Palazzo de' Cavalieri—Chiese di San Frediano—di S. Anna—di S. Caterina—di S. Paolo all' Orto—di S. Francesco—Church belonging to the Conservatorio di S. Silvestro—Chiese di S. Matteo—di S. Pierino—di S. Michele in Borgo—di S. Vito—della Spina—di S. Andrea in Chinseca—di S. Martino—Palazzi-Lanfranchi—Tonini—Lanfreducci—Casa-Mecherini—Palazzo-Seta—Royal Palace—Hospitals, etc.—University—Torre della Specola—Botanic Garden—Ancient Vapour-Bath—Suppressed Church of S. Felice—Subterranean part of S. Michele in Borgo—Aqueduct of Caldacolli—Modern Baths—Mountain of S. Giuliano—Modern Aqueduct—Canal—Royal Farm—Character of the Pisans—Hotels—Fountain-Water—Theatre—Bridges—Battle of the Bridge—Illumination in honour of S. Ranieri—Carnival—Climate.

As the road I took, from Florence through La Scala to Pisa, exhibits no particular objects of interest, I shall begin this chapter with an account of the last-named town.

Pisa, one of the twelve great cities of Etruria, stands on the banks of the Arno, forty-eight miles distant from Florence, fourteen from Leghorn, and six from the Mediterranean sea. Strabo says, it was built by the Arcadians, soon after the Trojan war: while other authors suppose it yet more ancient: and, in modern times, it has been the capital of a great republic, whose conquering fleet was a terror to the Saracens, a scourge to the African corsairs, and a check upon the ambition of Genoa; and with innumerable spoils, taken from the first-mentioned people, most of the present buildings at Pisa were erected. This city is, next to Florence, the largest in Tuscany; but though its walls are nearly five miles in circumference, they do not, at the present moment, contain above eighteen thousand persons. The streets are wide, straight, and excellently paved; the bridges elegant; the quay is one of the finest in Europe; and the situation of the Cathedral, Baptistery, Leaning Tower, and Campo-Santo, render these majestic edifices particularly striking and beautiful. The Arno traverses the city in the form of a crescent; and divides it nearly into two equal parts.

The Duomo, a Gothic structure, in the shape of a Latin cross, built (as I have already mentioned), in the eleventh century, under the guidance of Buschetto, a Grecian, is remarkable for the richness and variety of its marbles, and, next to the cathedrals of Milan and Siena, perhaps the finest church of its kind in Italy. The eastern front is ornamented with an immense number of columns; some of which are Grecian marble, others oriental granite, and one is porphyry: among these the most striking are six magnificent columns which adorn the three celebrated modern bronze-doors; and are said to be either Grecian or Egyptian workmanship. The modern doors were designed by Giovanni di Bologna, and cast by P. D. Portigiani: that in the centre, deemed the least beautiful of the three, represents the life of the Madonna; and is surrounded by figures of Saints and Prophets, and embellished with an elegant border of foliage, fruits, and flowers. Those on the right and left represent the life of the Saviour, beginning with his birth, and ending with his crucifixion; they are likewise embellished with a border, nearly similar to the one already described. The mosaics, in the arches above the doors, were done by Filippo di Lorenzo Palidini. The architrave of the eastern door was taken from an ancient edifice: and the bronze-door which fronts the Campanile, is esteemed for its antiquity, though not remarkable for merit of any other kind. The inside of the church is adorned with seventy-four lofty columns; sixty-two of which are oriental granite, and the rest rare marble: and although most of these columns were originally unequal in height, and consequently ill-adapted to match, yet so well has the architect disposed of and added to them, that even the most observing eye perceives no want of symmetry. Twelve altars, designed by Buonaroti and executed by Stagio Stagi, adorn the walls of this edifice. The high-altar is magnificently decorated with lapis lazuli,[1] verde antique, brocatello di Spagna, bronze gilt, giallo di Siena, etc.: the tribuna contains two porphyry columns, whose capitals and bases are peculiarly elegant; that near the episcopal throne is embellished with the best works of Stagi, and bears a bronze angel greatly admired. The decorations of the opposite column were executed by Foggini: and the group of angels on a golden field, which adorn the great arch, by Ghirlandajo, the master of Buonaroti. The seats for the canons (a sort of wooden mosaic introduced into Tuscany in the time of Brunellesco), merit notice. The four pictures of S. Peter, S. John, S. Margherita, and S. Caterina, are by Andrea del Sarto; and the mosaic on the ceiling, representing the Saviour, the Madonna, and S. John, was executed by Gaddo Gaddi and other artists in 1321. On the right side of the great cross is the Chapel of S. Ranieri; whose sarcophagus rests on a pedestal of red Egyptian granite, adorned with other valuable marbles: the sarcophagus is of verde di Polcevera, the altar of giallo di Siena, and the balustrades are of inlaid marble: the whole was executed by B. G. Foggini, at the command of Cosimo III., in honour of S. Ranieri, who died in 1161, and was proclaimed, by the Pisans, their Patron Saint. This chapel contains a mosaic, by Gaddo Gaddi, representing the Madonna enthroned and attended by angels; and an antique Grecian, or Roman statue, said to represent Mars, though now called S. Efeso.

On the left side of the great cross is the Chapel of the Holy Sacrament; which contains a ciborio of massy silver, and an altar adorned with silver *bassi-rilievi;* both well executed, after the designs of Foggini: the balustrades are of inlaid marble; and here, likewise, is a mosaic, by Gaddo Gaddi, representing the Annunciation. At the bottom of the church, over the great entrance-doors, is a beautiful Bar, or gallery, ornamented with *bassi-rilievi,* by Giovanni, the son of Niccolo Pisano; and it is much to be lamented that this fine work, which originally adorned a pulpit, is now placed so high, that its merits are scarcely discernible; it represents scriptural histories. The centre aisle contains a pulpit of inlaid marble, supported by two small columns; the one porphyry, the other oriental brocatello; and the first is deemed particularly curious, from consisting of various pieces so well joined that it may be properly denominated *Breccia porfirea:* the second is deemed the finest specimen of its sort in Italy. The pillar, on the right, which supports the cupola, is adorned with a picture by F. B. Gozzoli, who lived in the fifteenth century; it represents S. Tommas Aquinas disputing with an assembly of doctors; and the pillar, on the left, is adorned with a picture of S. Agnes, by Andrea del Sarto! Among the pictures which I have not already mentioned, those best worth notice are—the Madonna and our Saviour surrounded with saints, attributed to Pierino del Vaga and G. A. Sogliani—S. Ranieri putting on the religious habit, by

---

[1] Lapis lazuli is said to be the *Cyanœum* of the ancients; and Great Tartary is supposed to produce the best.

Cav. B. Luti—the death of S. Ranieri, by Cav. G. Melani, who flourished in the seventeenth century—the three Maries at the foot of the cross, by G. Bilivert—the adoration of the serpent in the wilderness, by O. Riminaldi—Habakkuk borne by an angel, by Bilivert—Judith giving the head of Holofernes to her servant, and the Madonna, our Saviour and saints, originally painted by Passignano, and added to by Tempesti—God the Father, Raphael, and other angels, by Salembini—and the institution of the Lord's Supper, by Tempesti. The bronze Griffin on the top of the Duomo is a curious antique *intaglio*, supposed to be Egyptian workmanship.

The Baptistery, a German-Gothic structure, erected (as has been already mentioned) by Diotisalvi, in the twelfth century, is an octagon of white marble, whose principal entrance is embellished with two large and two small columns, similar to those which adorn the great doors of the Duomo.

The inside of this edifice resembles an ancient temple. Twelve arches, supported by eight vast columns of Sardinian granite, and four pilasters of white marble, serve as the base to a second row of pilasters, on which rests the cupola. The capitals, both of pillars and pilasters, are antique. The Font, elevated on three steps of beautiful marble, is adorned with *intagli* and mosaics, so well executed, that they appear to have been done long before the building. On the margin are four places for the immersion of infants; and in the centre is a large basin for the immersion of adults: this practice of immersion, however, has been abandoned since the thirteenth century. The Pulpit, one of Niccolo Pisano's best works, is supported by nine columns of precious marble, and ornamented with *bassi-rilievi*, formed out of oriental alabaster and Parian marble. The first piece represents the birth of our Saviour—the second, the adoration of the Magi—the third, the Presentation in the Temple—the fourth, the Crucifixion (much inferior to the rest)—the fifth, the last Judgment. This Baptistery was finished in 1153; at which period Pisa is said to have been so populous, that a voluntary contribution of one florin, from every family, sufficed to pay for this noble edifice.[1]

The Campanile, or *Leaning Tower*, begun by Guglielmo, a German, and Bonnano, Pisano, about the year 1174, is of a circular form, nearly 190 feet in height, and declining above 13 feet from its perpendicular. This beautiful edifice consists of eight stories, adorned with two hundred and seven columns of granite and other marbles, many of which have evidently been taken from ancient buildings. According to the opinion of the most respectable writers, it appears that this tower originally was straight; though some accidental cause, such as an earthquake, the great fire of Pisa, or the natural looseness of the soil, has produced its present extraordinary inclination: and in that part of the Campo-Santo where the life of S. Ranieri

---

[1] Pisa, at the period above mentioned, was supposed to contain 13,400 families; and, reckoning five persons to each family, the number of inhabitants will amount to 67,000: but the population of this city, during its most flourishing state, is said to have amounted to 150,000.

is painted, we see this now leaning tower perfectly upright, and consisting of seven stories only: may not, therefore, the eighth story, which rather inclines on the contrary side to the others, have been added, in latter times, as a balance, to prevent the whole edifice from falling? The stairs leading up to the summit of this tower are easy of ascent; and the view from the eighth gallery is very extensive.

The Campo-Santo, or ancient burial-ground, the most beautiful edifice at Pisa, and unique in its kind, is a vast rectangle, surrounded by sixty-two light and elegant Gothic arcades of white marble, and paved with the same. Archbishop Ubaldo Lanfranci, who was contemporary with Richard *Cœur-de-lion*, and his brother warrior in the Holy Land, brought to Pisa a large quantity of earth from Mount-Calvary, and deposited it on the spot round which the walls of the Campo-Santo are now erected. He is, therefore, supposed to have given the first idea of this edifice in 1200; and the present structure, eighteen years afterward, was commenced under the direction of Giovanni, Pisano, who finished it in 1283. The statues over the principal door are by Giovanni, Pisano; they stand in a kind of temple, and, among them, is the sculptor himself, kneeling to the Madonna. The sarcophagi under the arcades are chiefly of Parian marble. Here is the tomb of the Countess Beatrice, who died in 1113, and was mother to the celebrated Countess Matilda, the last descendant from the Counts of Tuscany. On this Sarcophagus is represented, in *basso-rilievo*, the chase of Meleager, according to some opinions, and the story of Phædra and Hippolitus, according to others: however, be this as it may, the merit of the work proves it an ancient production, applied, in latter ages, to its present use; and it is supposed that this sarcophagus was the model from which Niccolo, Pisano, and his son, used to study. Here, likewise, is an ancient Vase, embellished with *bassi-rilievi*, representing Bacchanalian mysteries, and which seems to have been one of the vessels employed by the Greeks and Romans in their religious ceremonies. Round the walls are fresco-paintings of the fourteenth and fifteenth century; which, however deficient in many respects, cannot but yield pleasure to those persons who wish, on their entrance into Italy, to view the works of the Revivers of an art afterward brought to exquisite perfection. In the first division of the arcade, on the western wall, are six large pictures, representing the life of S. Ranieri; the three upper ones being by Simone Memmi; the three under ones, by Antonio, called Veneziano: and they particularly merit notice, on account of the costume accurately preserved throughout them all, and likewise because they show how ships were armed and rigged in the days of S. Ranieri. In one of these pictures is the Campanile: they all are supposed to have been begun in 1300. The second division contains six paintings, representing the life and death of Saints Efeso and Potito, done by Spinello Spinelli, Aretino, about the year 1400. The third division contains six paintings, representing the history of Job, by Giotto; so injured, however, by the hand of time, that it is difficult to distinguish them, although, in 1623, they were retouched, by Maruscelli. The other paintings of this arcade are said to have been done by Nelli di Vanni, Pisano. The two first pictures in the second arcade represent the history of Esther, by Ghirlandajo; retouched, however, by Aurelio, or Baccio Lomi. The second division of this arcade contains the history of Judith; which is modern, ill-done, and damaged. The first division of the northern arcade contains four pictures, representing the Creation, by Buffalmacco, who flourished in the beginning of the fourteenth century. The other paintings which adorn this arcade (those over the doors of the chapels excepted) represent the principal events of the book of Genesis; and were begun by B. Gozzoli, in 1484, and finished in the short space of two years. The first of these numerous pictures contains the famous *Vergognosa* di Campo-Santo; and over the chapel-door is the adoration of the Magi, by which work Gozzoli established his reputation among the Pisans, and prevailed with them to employ him in painting their Campo-Santo; not merely on account of the general merit of the picture, but because it exhibited an excellent likeness of his mistress, a Pisan girl, whom he drew, to display his imitative powers. Over the same door is the Annunciation, attributed to Stefano, Fiorentino; and the fifth lower picture from this, is particularly interesting, as it contains several portraits of illustrious men, and among them that of Lorenzo de' Medici. Over the door of the second chapel is the coronation of the Madonna, by Taddeo Bartoli; and in the fifth lower picture, beyond this chapel, are portraits of other illustrious men, among whom the painter has placed himself, though his figure is almost totally obliterated. These works, by Gozzoli, are, generally speaking, the best preserved of any in the Campo-Santo. The paintings of the eastern arcades so far as the chapel-door, are by Zaccaria Rondinosi, Pisano, and were executed in 1666; they represent the history of King Ozia, and Balteshazzar's feast. Beyond the chapel are three paintings, said to be by Buffalmacco, and representing the crucifixion, resurrection, and ascension of the Saviour. The next picture which is in that part of the southern arcade not already described, represents the triumphs of Death, and was done by Andrea Orcagna, who flourished in the middle of the fourteenth century: it contains several portraits. The second large picture, by the same master, is the universal Judgment, in which Solomon is represented as dubious whether he may go to Heaven or Hell. The next picture, or rather a compartment of the last, represents Dante's *Inferno;* and was painted by Bernardo Orcagna, brother to Andrea, and restored by Sollazino, who flourished about the year 1530. The fourth picture represents the history of the Anchorites, by Laurati, the pupil of Giotto: and over the great door is an assumption, by Simone Memmi, one of the best preserved pictures of the fourteenth century.

It is remarkable that, among the immense number of countenances contained in these paintings, we scarcely find two alike. The faces, generally speaking, are well done; the figures and drapery stiff; the perspective is bad; but the borders, which form the several compartments, are particularly elegant. Among the monuments is that of Count Algarotti, erected by Frederic the Great, of Prussia; but remarkable only for the beauty of the marble: near this is the sarcophagus of G. F. Vegio, by Taddo; and, in the eastern arcade, is the monument of Filippo Decio; who had it erected in his life-time; giving, as a reason, "That he feared posterity would not have done it for him." This monument is by Stagio Stagi. Under Orcagna's picture of the triumphs of Death stands an ancient Roman Mile-stone; which was discovered on the Via-Emilia, near Rimazzano, and thence transported to Pisa; and on each side of this column is an inscription, the one to the memory of Lucius, and the other to that of Caius Cæsar, the adopted sons of Augustus. Six hundred ancient families of Pisa, beside many illustrious characters of different nations, are said to be interred in the Campo-Santo.

The solemn grandeur of this burial-ground, prompted me to compose the following sonnet to Grief; which I am tempted to insert, because it is descriptive of the Campo-Santo:

STRUCTURE unmatch'd, which braves the lapse of Time!
  Fit cradle the reviving arts to rear!
  Light, as the paper Nautilus, appear
Thy arches, of Pisano's works the prime.
Famed Campo-Santo! where the mighty Dead,
Of elder days, in Parian marble sleep,
  Say, who is she, that ever seems to keep
Watch o'er thy precincts, save when mortal tread
Invades the awful stillness of the scene?
  Then, struggling to suppress the heavy sigh,
  And brushing the big teardrop from her eye,
She veils her face—and glides yon tombs between.
'Tis GRIEF!—by that thick veil the Maid I know,
Moisten'd with tears which never cease to flow.

The Chiesa de' Cavalieri, or Church of S. Stefano, from whom the square in which it stands is named, was built by Vasari: the high-altar, by Foggini, is of porphyry; so likewise is the sarcophagus above it, reputed to contain the bones of S. Stephen; and the bronze-chair, suspended over the sarcophagus, was presented by Innocent XII. to Cosimo III. On the ceiling are six paintings relative to the Knights of S. Stefano; the two first by Ligozzi, the two next by Empoli, the fifth, by Cigoli, and the last, which represents Cosimo I., receiving the habit of the order, is by Cristofano Allori. On the walls and ceiling are trophies taken from the Infidels, by the Knights of S. Stefano. This church contains a very curious organ; reputed to be the finest in Europe; a nativity, by Bronzino; and a silver crucifix, by Algardi.

The Palazzo de' Cavalieri, situated in the same square, was built by Vasari; and, over the principal entrance are busts of six Grand Masters of the order, beginning with Cosimo I., who instituted these Knights to defend the Mediterranean against Turks and Corsairs, by means of galleys, on board of which every Knight was compelled to serve three years ere he could be finally received into the order: but, when peace was established between Barbary and the Tuscans, the Knights and their galleys became useless; insomuch that the latter were, in 1755, all broken up and destroyed.

Near to the Palazzo de' Cavalieri, there formerly stood a building, now totally demolished, which was called the Tower of Famine, from having been the prison of Ugolino.[1]

The Chiesa di S. Frediano, which is supported by columns of oriental granite with ancient capitals, contains a painting of our Saviour on the cross, done, in the thirteenth century, by Giunto, Pisano.

The Chiesa di S. Anna contains a curious representation of our Saviour on the cross, wrought in wood, on the tabernacle of the high-altar: and this wooden sculpture, of which there are several specimens in Pisa, is attributed to G. Giaccobi, Pisano.

The Chiesa di S. Caterina, contains a curious picture, by F. Traini, one of the most skilful disciples of Andrea Orcagna: this picture represents S. Thomas Aquinas surrounded by the fathers of the church, among whom is a portrait of Urban VI.; at the feet of these are several philosophers and heretics, with their works torn in pieces; and what seems very incongruous, S. Thomas himself is placed between Plato and Aristotle, who are presenting him with their literary productions.

The Chiesa di S. Paolo all' Orto contains a head of our Saviour, which appears to have been done in the twelfth century.

The Chiesa di S. Francesco, supposed to have been built after the designs of Niccolo, Pisano, contains a Chapel dedicated to S. Antonio da Padova, and painted by Salembini and Maruscelli—a Chapel painted by Passignano; together with a Madonna and Child, said to have been done in the fourteenth century—another Chapel (near the Sacristy), the paintings in which are attributed to Spinello, Aretino, who likewise did the large picture over the Sacristy-door—a picture, in the Sacristy, by Giotto, of S. Francesco receiving the elect: and, in the Sacristy-chapel, the Madonna and saints, painted in 1395, by T. Bartoli. In the Cloister to the right of the little steps which lead into the church, the bones of Ugolino, his sons, and nephews, are, according to tradition, deposited.

The Church belonging to the Conservatorio di S. Silvestro contains two antique paintings, by Guidotti; and a small *basso-rilievo*, in *terra cotta*, attributed to Luca della Robbia, the inventor of painting upon glass.

The Chiesa di S. Matteo, built by the brothers Melani, is remarkable for the fresco-paintings of those artists, which are so skilfully managed as to make the roof appear wonderfully higher than it really is.

The Chiesa di S. Pierino, supposed to have been an ancient heathen temple, contains a Madonna, painted on the wall, and a crucifix, by Giunto, Pisano. The ornaments on the outside of the great door are ancient and beautiful; the pavement is of *pietri duri;* and the edifice stands on an ancient Bone-house, which contains two sarcophagi of Parian marble, together with paintings in the style of those which adorn the Campo-Santo.

---

[1] Count Ugolino, a Pisan nobleman, entered into a conspiracy with Archbishop Rugiero, to depose the Governor of Pisa; in which enterprise having succeeded, Ugolino assumed the government of the city: but the Archbishop, jealous of his power, incited the people against him; attacked his palace, seized his person, and cast him and his family into prison; till, at length, refusing them food, and throwing the key of their dungeon into the Arno, he left them, in this dreadful situation, to be starved to death!

See DANTE's *Inferno*, Canto XXXIII.

The Chiesa di S. Michele in Borgo, said to have been built before the eleventh century, by Guglielmo Pisano, is incrusted with cerulean marble, supported by ancient colums of Granitello, and adorned with a marble crucifix, wrought by Niccolo, Pisano, and originally placed in the Campo-Santo. The Madonna, under this crucifix, is supposed to be one of the most ancient paintings in Pisa. The cupola, the upper-nave, the vision of S. Romualdo, the expedition to Majorca and Minorca, and the institution of the Foundling Hospital, are all painted by Guidotti.

The Chiesa di S. Vito, or, more properly speaking, the Cappella di S. Ranieri, contains a fresco representing the death of the Saint, and executed, not many years since, by Tempesti, in his best manner. The surrounding architectural ornaments are by Cioffo.

The Chiesa della Spina exhibits monuments of the ancient Pisan school of sculpture, namely, the Madonna, our Saviour, S. John and S. Peter, by Nino, Pisano, one of the Revivers of the art; two figures attributed to Moschino; and a half-length Madonna, by Nino.

The Chiesa di S. Andrea in Chinseca contains a valuable monument of the Greco-Pisano school, namely, our Saviour on the cross, which appears to have been done in the thirteenth century.

The Chiesa di S. Martino contains a crucifix, by Giunta, Pisano.[1]

The Palazzo-Lanfranchi, on that side of the Arno called *Parte di Mezzo-giorno,* was built after the design of Buonaroti.

The Palazzo-Tonini contains two paintings, in fresco, from Tasso's *Gerusalemme,* begun by Melani, and finished by Tommasi, his scholar.

The Palazzo - Lanfreducci, which is incrusted with statuary marble, has a chain, and these words over the door: "*Alla giornata*"—many tales are told in consequence; but none of them seem sufficiently authenticated to be worth relating. This palace contains a celebrated picture, by Guido, the subject of which is, sacred and profane love, represented by two boys; perhaps the subject of this picture may have been taken from Plato, who says, there are two Cupids, as different as day and night; the one possessing every virtue, the other every vice.

Casa-Mecherini, on the opposite side of the Arno, and called *Parte di Tramontana,* contains a celebrated Sibyl, by Guercino; with frescos by Tempesti and Cioffo.

The Palazzo-Seta, in Via S. Cecilia, contains frescos by the brothers Melani; as do the *Palazzo del Publico* and the *Palazzo de' Priori.*

In *the regal Palace* the ceilings are painted with elegance; and the furniture, though plain, is handsome.

The Hospitals are spacious; and the *Loggia de' Banchi* and *Casino Nobili,* are fine buildings.

The University of Pisa was founded by the Emperor Henry

---

[1] The Churches at Pisa contain many Paintings, by old Tuscan masters, which I have not mentioned; and a minute description of them may be found in Morrona's History of Pisa.

VII.; though in consequence of civil wars, it became almost annihilated, till the reign of Cosimo I.; by whom it was re-established on the present plan, in 1543: it has produced as many, if not more, learned men than any other public seminary in Italy.

The Torre della Specula, or Observatory, was erected about the year 1735; and is furnished with good instruments.

The Botanic Garden was founded by Ferdinando, second son of Cosimo I.; and has been greatly improved by Sig. Santi, one of the Professors of the University; a Gentleman whose literary productions do honour both to his head and heart; and whose kindness toward the British Nation has ever been such as to command their sincerest gratitude and highest esteem.

There seems little doubt that Pisa was a Roman colony, often visited by the Cæsars: and Nero, about the year 57, is said to have made an excursion to this city, with which he was so much pleased, that he embellished it with a magnificent palace and a temple dedicated to Diana, which stood at the entrance of the Lucca-gate. This temple was built in the form of a rotunda; all of marble without; the ceiling being an imitation of the starry firmament. The internal decorations consisted of oriental marble columns, with various pieces of sculpture and painting; the pavement was Egyptian marble, and the statue of the goddess stood in its centre. Whether the palace did or did not enclose this temple, is unknown; but the former is described as being highly ornamented, and of a vast extent, containing baths, gardens, and fish-ponds: and it is added that Nero, in order to have it amply supplied with water, built the aqueduct of Monti-Pisani, which extended from Caldacolli to the Lucca-gate. Such is the account given of Nero's temple and palace: and it is certain that the buildings of the *Hypocaustum*, extended from the Duomo to the vicinity of the Monastery of S. Zenone. It is equally certain that foundations of immense buildings have been discovered in the gardens which now occupy the space between the church of S. Zenone and the Duomo; that numberless pieces of marble are seen in the walls and buildings, which at present stand upon the above-named space; and two ruins, near the Lucca-gate, one of which has been recently demolished, were evidently parts of the Hypocaustum: these circumstances concur with several others to establish the truth of what I have advanced. The most respectable remains of these antiquities is the *Vapour-Bath*, situated in a garden close to the Lucca-gate: this bath is an octagon, with four semi-circular niches; in the upper part of which are *terra-cotta* tubes of a triangular shape. Opposite to the entrance there appears to have been a place reserved for some marble ornament. The roof forms a semicircle, and contains eight places to admit light, beside an octagon aperture in the centre. The pavement, leading to the great furnace, was made of *calcistruzzo*, with a surface of marble one finger thick, to walk or lie down upon. It is probable that, under this marble pavement, there were vaulted rooms, where the attendants kept up perpetual fires: and some persons imagine that under every niche were vases filled with water, which, on being heated by the fires, impregnated the apartments with vapour. Ancient baths always consisted of four apartments, distinguished by the appellations of cold, tepid, hot, and sudatory; and the apartment called tepid, in the men's bath, always communicated with the same apartment in the women's bath: and there is no doubt that the bath above described consisted of four apartments, as traces of them may yet be discovered. From the appearance of the bath now remaining, it seems to have been lined throughout with marble; and the six Grecian columns on the sides of the bronze doors of the Duomo, together with the other two, which ornament the principal door of the Baptistery, are supposed to have been taken from this building. In the garden adjoining to the bath, stood the Monastery of S. Zenone, vulgarly called S. Zeno; of which, however, the Church only remains; and in it are sarcophagi, which, though mutilated and almost defaced, still possess sufficient beauty to make us execrate the hand of avarice or barbarism which has thus destroyed these valuable remains of Grecian sculpture.

A house, belonging to the noble family Da Paulle, seems to have been formed out of the ruins of an ancient theatre; judging from the granite columns of different orders discoverable in the walls.

In the suppressed Church of S. Felice are two columns of oriental granite, with capitals adorned by mythological figures, supposed to represent Jupiter, Harpocrates, Diana, Minerva, Isis, Ceres, and Genii. They probably belonged to a Roman temple, on the site of which the church of S. Felice is said to have been erected. The sculpture seems to be of Septimius Severus's time.

The subterranean part of S. Michele in Borgo deserves notice; the pillars and walls are of *pietre verrucane*, the roof is tufo, and curiously ornamented with arabesques, resembling those which adorn Livia's baths at Rome, and not unlike, in style, to many of the paintings found in Herculaneum. This building could not have been a Christian church, because the primitive Christians adorned their churches with nothing but quotations from Holy Writ; therefore it must, in all probability, have been erected previous to the time of Constantine.

The Aqueduct of Caldacolli, so called from the hot springs which supply it, is supposed to be that erected by Nero: eight arches may still be seen at the distance of about two hundred yards from the modern baths of Pisa; and ruins of the whole are discoverable between this spot and the Lucca-gate.

No vestiges remain of the ancient Port of Pisa, mentioned by Strabo: but it is supposed to have been near the mouth of the Arno, and not far from Leghorn. We are told that this port was protected neither by mole nor pier; and though open to every wind, yet vessels rode securely on its bosom, owing to the size and tenacity of the weeds, which were so closely interwoven as to exclude the agitation of the sea.

The modern Baths, situated about three miles and a half to the north of Pisa, are elegant, commodious, and surrounded by several good lodging-houses. These baths, the most celebrated in Italy, have the reputation of being particularly beneficial in gouty cases, and diseases of the liver.

Two large fragments of columns with two capitals, which bear marks of remote antiquity, together with several other concurring circumstances, lead us to imagine these modern baths occupy the same ground with those mentioned by Strabo and Pliny.

The Mountain of S. Giuliano, which rises immediately above the baths, exhibits some curious caverns.

The modern Aqueduct, begun by Ferdinando I., and finished by his son, Cosimo II., is a magnificent work, worthy the Princes of the House of Medicis: it commences at a village, called Asciano, and extends to Pisa, a distance of four miles, conveying to that city the most pure and delicious water in Europe.

The canal, which extends from Pisa to Leghorn, was made by Ferdinando I.

The royal Farm, or *Cascina*, near Pisa, situated in an extensive and beautiful forest of cork-trees, ever-green oaks, etc., and washed by the sea, is worth notice; as it contains camels, who, though foreigners, breed here, and are employed as beasts of burden: they are, however, much less numerous at present than they were twenty years ago. The Grand Duke, Leopoldo, was the first person who attempted to breed camels in Italy.

The nobility of Pisa, and all the gentlemen belonging to the University, are remarkably civil and kind to foreigners, the lower classes of people respectful and humane, but exacting.

The two principal Hotels in this city are, *Le tre Donzelle*, and *L'Ussero*, the former of which has the advantage in point of situation, and is, moreover, a tolerably good inn, though by no means so comfortable as private lodgings on that side of the quay called, *Parte di Mezzo-giorno*, for, on the opposite side, and in many of the streets and squares, the houses are damp, and consequently unwholesome.

Travellers should be especially careful to send for the Fountain-Water of Pisa that flows through the Aqueduct; because the well-water, with which the houses are supplied, is seldom fit either for drinking or even for kitchen use.

The Theatre here is capacious, but not elegant.

The three Bridges, as I have already mentioned, are handsome, especially the middle one, which is composed of marble and *pietra verrucana;* and the mock fight, occasionally exhibited on this bridge, is perhaps almost the only remaining vestige of those martial games heretofore so famous among the Greeks and Romans. The amusement consists in a battle fought by 960 combatants, who, clothed in coats of mail, and armed with wooden clubs, dispute, for forty-five minutes, the passage of the bridge. The strongest combatants possess themselves of the field of battle, and when it is possible to employ stratagem they never let slip the opportunity, but to fight in earnest is forbidden; nevertheless this mock encounter frequently costs lives, and is, therefore, but seldom permitted, though one of the most beautiful exhibitions in Italy.— Some authors tell us it was instituted by Pelops, son of Tantalus, King of Phrygia; others think it was established by Nero; while others believe it to have been originally celebrated in memory of the defeat of Musetto, King of Sardinia, which happened in the year 1005, upon a bridge at Pisa: but whoever the institutor might be, the amusement is entered into by the Pisans with a degree of spirit that exceeds all description.¹

There is likewise, every third year, on the 17th of June, a singular and most beautiful illumination here, in honour of S. Ranieri. On this night the whole Lung'-Arno appears like an immense crescent of magnificent and regularly built palaces, studded with innumerable quantities of diamonds; some in the Tuscan, others in the Gothic, and others in the grotesque or Chinese style of architecture (which participates so much of the Egyptian, that many persons believe the Chinese were originally an Egyptian colony).² Add to this, the three bridges ornamented by temples blazing with jewels; and such is the scene which Pisa presents to view at this general illumination—no wonder, therefore, that Ariosto is said to have borrowed images from so splendid and singular an exhibition, which can only be likened to an enchanted city.

The immense length and beautiful curve of the Pisa-quay contribute greatly to the splendour of these two exhibitions, the ground being so shaped that all the spectators are seen at once, whether in balconies, carriages, on foot, or in boats upon the river : and the same cause renders the Carnival at Pisa particularly beautiful; for, during the last week of this whimsical diversion, the whole quay is filled with masks, from three in the afternoon till the commencement of the pastimes at the theatre.

The *Carneia*, or Carnival, appears to have been a festivity observed in most of the Grecian cities, but especially at Sparta, where it took birth about 675 years before the Christian era, in honour of Apollo, surnamed *Carneus*. It lasted nine days.

The climate of Pisa, during winter, is one of the best in Europe, though at other seasons not equally salubrious.

---

1 When a man stands candidate for the honour of being a combatant, he is cased in armour, and then beat for half an hour with wooden clubs ; during which ceremony, should he happen to flinch, or cry out, he is rejected ; but if he do neither, he is chosen.

2 The belief that the Chinese were originally an Egyptian colony, has lately been strengthened by a discovery, in the Cabinet of Medals at Milan, of a Chinese work, containing drawings of nearly a thousand antique Vases, resembling those called Etruscan, and of Egyptian origin.

CHAPTER VI.

GENOA, NICE, TURIN, LEGHORN, LUCCA, ETC.

Excursion from Pisa to Genoa—New Road—Harbour, Fanale, Fortifications, Streets, and Bridge of the latter City—Cathedral, and other Churches—Residenza dei Dogi—Palazzo Durazzo—University—Palazzo-Doria, and other Palaces—Hospitals—Albergo dei Poveri—Theatre—Hotels—Population—Provisions—Climate—Character of the Genoese—Description of Nice, and its Climate—Journey over the Maritime Alps to Turin—Population of that City—Bridge erected by the French—Regal Palace—Cathedral, and other Churches—Theatre—University—Public Garden and Ramparts—Hotels—Climate—Water—Environs—Alessandria—Plain of Marengo—New Road over the Bocchetta—Old Road—Leghorn—Harbour, Light-house, Fortifications, and other objects best worth notice in the Town and its Environs—Inns—Lucca—Population—Cathedral—Other Churches—Palazzo-Publico—Ancient Amphitheatre—Modern Theatre—Character of the Lucchesi—Seminary founded by the Princess Elise—Inn—Marlia—Bagni di Lucca—Environs of the Bagni—Peasantry—Mode of cultivating this part of the Apennine—Villas between the Baths of Lucca and the City—Road through Pistoja to Florence.

The road from Pisa to Lerici is tolerably good, during summer, but at other seasons travellers frequently embark at Via-Reggio (a small sea-port belonging to the Lucchesi, and famous for the excellence of its fish), going thence either in a deck-vessel or a felucca[1] to Genoa, between which city and Lerici there was only a mule-path when we made this excursion; the carriage-road, begun long since, is now, however, passable; though not finished: it lies at the edge of precipices without any fence to guard travellers from accidents; and through torrents difficult to ford; but it commands sublime scenery: and when parapet walls are erected on the height, and bridges thrown over the torrents, (which may probably be accomplished in the course of two years,) this road will vie in excellence with those of Cenis and the Simplon. At present the only good inns on the new road are *La Posta*, at Pietra Santa; *L'Europa*, at La Spezia; and *Il Ponte*, at Sestri.

Between Pisa and Via-Reggio we crossed the Serchio, anciently the *Ansa*, in a ferry; finding, at the latter town, a tolerable inn, though unhealthily situated.

We then proceeded to Pietra Santa, placed in the neighbourhood of a marsh, the exhalations from which are extremely noxious, particularly toward sun-set. The inn here being comfortable, is sometimes preferred, as a sleeping-place, to that at Massa, which cannot be commended; though in point of air and situation, the latter town is infinitely preferable to the former. Not far hence are quarries of Seravezza-marble. Massa, seated in a pleasant valley, near the sea, is small, but well-built; and contains a handsome Royal residence, together with some good pictures in its Churches: and five miles distant from this town is Carrara, whose quarries produce marble,

---

[1] A felucca is an open boat, which makes use both of sails and oars, always keeping near shore, and, in case of bad weather, running immediately into harbour.

perhaps, for the purposes of sculpture, the most beautiful in the world; though, for want of proper care in transporting the blocks, they are frequently split and broken. Carrara contains nearly 3500 inhabitants; and is built of marble, taken from the adjacent quarries, which are well worth seeing, and where fine crystals are often found: it owes much to its late Sovereign, the Princess Elise, who converted her Palace here into an Academy of Sculpture, richly stored with models, both ancient and modern, and well worth observation.

Having passed Lavenza, formerly *Aventia*, the Port whence the Carrara-marble is conveyed to every part of Europe, we proceeded to Sarzana, a large town near the site of the ancient *Luna;* and on arriving at Lerici, formerly *Ericis-Portus*, embarked in a felucca for Genoa;[1] coasting the Riviera, and passing Porto-Venere, defended by two castles, near which ships go through a narrow strait into the Gulf of Spezia, supposed to have been the *Portus-Lunæ* of the Romans; and a peculiarly large and safe harbour, surrounded with towns, villages, and plantations, abounding in olive-trees, vines, and fruit.

Genoa, in Italian Genova, called *La Superba,* anciently a city of Liguria, and the first which fell under the Roman yoke, appears to great advantage when viewed from the sea, about one mile distant from the shore; for, then its numberless and stately edifices represent the seats of a vast amphitheatre, placed on a declivity of the enormous Apennine. The Harbour of Genoa is capacious and beautiful, but not safe, being too much exposed to the Libecio, or south-west wind. *The Fanale*, or Light-house, is a lofty tower, built on an isolated rock at the west side of the harbour. The fortifications, toward the sea, appear strong; being cut out of the rocks: but the naval power of this country, once so formidable, seems now reduced to a few galleys, chiefly employed in fetching corn from Sicily. Genoa is defended by two walls; one of which immediately encompasses the town, while the other takes in the rising grounds that command it. The streets, three excepted, are not wide enough to admit the use of carriages. The roofs of the houses are flat, and frequently adorned with orange-trees. Here is a fine stone bridge over the Bonzevera, and another over the Bisagno; the former stream washing the western, the latter the eastern, side of the city.

The Cathedral, dedicated to S. Lorenzo, is a Gothic structure, incrusted and paved with marble, and adorned with a Crucifixion, by Barocchio. The bones of S. John Baptist are said to be deposited in one of the chapels.

The Annunziata, though built at the sole expense of the Lomellino family, is one of the most costly churches in Genoa, and contains a fine picture of the Last Supper, by G. C. Procaccino.

S. Maria in Carignano, built in obedience to the will of Bendinelli Sauli, a noble Genoese, is an elegant piece of architecture; and

---

[1] The distance, by sea, from Lerici to Genoa, is about twenty leagues; the price commonly given for a felucca, from five to six sequins; and the time usually employed in going, from twelve to fifteen hours: though, if there be no wind, or if the wind be contrary, Travellers are compelled to land, for the night, at Portofino; a pretty, but comfortless, little fishing-town.

the magnificent bridge, leading to it, was erected by a son of the above-named nobleman. The Church contains a statue of S. Sebastiano, by Puget; another of the beatified Alessandro Sauli, by the same artist; and an interesting picture of S. Peter and S. John curing the Paralytic, by D. Piola.

S. Ambroggio is adorned with three celebrated pictures, namely, the Assumption, by Guido—S. Ignatius exorcising a demoniac, and raising the dead, by Rubens—and the Circumcision, by the same master.

S. Domenico contains a picture of the Circumcision, by Procaccino; and the ceiling of the Sanctuary is by Cappuccino.

S. Filippo Neri is a handsome church; the ceiling of which was painted by Franceschini; and in the Oratory is a statue of the Madonna, by Puget.

S. Matteo, built by the Doria family, contains sepulchral monuments, by Mont-Orsoli; a high-altar of Florentine work; and, behind it, a much admired *Pietà*.

S. Giovanni in Vecchio is adorned with a picture, by Vandyck.

S. Francesco di Castelleto contains a celebrated picture, by Tintoretto; together with bronze statues and *bassi-rilievi*, by Giovanni di Bologna.

S. Stefano alle Porte contains a picture representing the Martyrdom of S. Stephen, the upper part painted by Giulio Romano, the lower part by Raphael.

The Rezidencia dei Dogi is a large unornamented modern building, erected in consequence of a fire, which consumed the ancient edifice. The great hall is magnificent in point of size; and once contained statues, in marble, of persons eminent for their liberality to the public: but revolutionary frenzy destroyed these statues. The Arsenal, in this palace, contains the prow of an ancient Roman galley; its length being about three spans, and its greatest thickness two thirds of a foot: it was discovered in 1597, in consequence of the harbour being cleaned. Here, likewise, is the armour of several Genoese ladies, who joined a crusade to the Holy Land, in 1301.

The Palazzo-Durazzo (Strada Balbi) contains noble rooms splendidly furnished, and a large collection of pictures, among which are celebrated works of Vandyck and Rubens, and the Magdalene at Our Saviour's feet, by Paolo Veronese!!

The University is a fine building; and contains, in its Vestibule, two Lions of marble, which are much admired.

The Palazzo-Doria (Strada-Nuova) is a magnificent edifice in point of architecture.

The Palazzo-Rosso contains fine pictures; among which are three Portraits, by Vandyck—Judith putting the Head of Holofernes in a bag, by Paolo Veronese—an old Man reading, by Spagnoletto—the Madonna, by Capuccino—the Adoration of the Shepherds, by Bassano—Our Saviour in the Garden of Olives, by the same—Clorinda delivering the Christians, by Caravaggio—the Resurrection of Lazarus, by the same—Cleopatra, by Guercino—and several works, both in painting and sculpture, by Parodi.

The Palazzo-Brignole, opposite to the Palazzo-Rosso, contains fine pictures.

The Palazzo-Serra boasts a

saloon, deemed one of the most sumptuous apartments in Europe.

The Palazzo-Carega was built after the design of Buonaroti; as was the Palazzo-Pallavicino, at Zerbino.

The great Hospital is a noble establishment for the Sick of all nations; and likewise for Foundlings; the boys remaining till they are able to work; the girls still longer. The number of sick received into this hospital has frequently exceeded one thousand; and the number of foundlings three thousand.

The Hospital of Incurables likewise is a noble establishment.

The Albergo dei Poveri, perhaps the most magnificent hospital in Europe, stands upon a lofty eminence; and was founded by a nobleman of the Brignoli-family, to serve as an asylum for upwards of a thousand persons, from age and other causes, reduced to want. The Chapel is handsome, and contains a *basso-relievo*, by Buonaroti, of the Madonna contemplating the dead body of Our Saviour! and here, likewise, is an Assumption, in marble, by Puget.

The Theatre of S. Agostino is much admired, with respect to its architecture; as, indeed, are a considerable number of buildings, which I have not enumerated; but, though no city of Italy boasts so many splendid edifices as Genoa, though all these edifices are built of marble, and though the Strada-Nuova, the Strada-Novissima, and the Strada-Balbi, are strikingly magnificent, the narrowness of the other streets, and the want of spacious squares, gives an air of melancholy to the town in general: its environs, however, are exempt from this defect; and display a delightful union of grandeur and cheerfulness; the whole road to Sestri, a distance of six miles, exhibiting one continued line of villas, nearly equal, in size and elegance, to the palaces within the city.

Genoa contains good Hotels;[1] and its population, including the inhabitants of San Pietro d'Arena, is supposed to amount to eighty thousand.

An Italian proverb says of this city, " that it has sea without fish, land without trees, and men without faith:" the provisions, however, not excepting fish, are excellent; but the wine is bad, and the climate by no means a good one. The country, though (like Italy in general) thinly wooded, is, in some parts, romantic and beautiful: but as to the people, they certainly vie in faith with their Ligurian ancestors.

The nobles are ill educated, and seldom fond of literature: they rarely inhabit the best apartments of their superb palaces; but are said to like a splendid table: though their chief gratification has always consisted in amassing wealth for the laudable purpose of expending it on public works and public charities.

The common people are active and industrious; and the velvets, damasks, and artificial flowers of Genoa have long been celebrated.

Hence, to Nice, there is a bridle-road, which traverses a delightful country; and from Genoa to Finale, and again from Ventimiglia to Nice there is a carriage-road; but, as the inns are bad, we preferred hiring a felucca with

---

[1] *L'Hôtel d'Europe*, which is excellent; *L'Albergo di Londra; La Croce di Malta;* and *Le Quattri Nazioni.*

ten oars, and pursuing our excursion by sea.[1]

The first night we reached Oneglia, a small town occupied chiefly by fishermen; and the second night we arrived at Nice.

This city is seated in a small plain, bounded on the west by the Var, anciently called the *Varus*, which divides it from Provence; on the south by the Mediterranean, which washes its walls and on the north by that chain of Alps called *Maritimæ*, which seems designed by nature to protect Italy from the invasions of her Gallic Neighbours. The citadel of Mont-Albano overhangs the town; and the Paglion, a torrent which descends from the adjacent mountains, separates it from what is called the English quarter, and runs into the sea on the west.

The situation of Nice is cheerful; the walks and rides are pretty; the lodging-houses numerous and tolerably convenient; the eatables good and plentiful; and the wine and oil excellent: but the near neighbourhood of the Alps, and the prevalence of that searching wind, called *vent de bise*, render the air frequently cold, and even frosty, during winter and spring; while, in summer, the heat is excessive.[2]

From Nice we set out to cross the Maritime Alps to Turin, by a most excellent and wonderful road, constructed during the reign of Victor-Amadeus-Maria, King of Sardinia (who was seventeen years in completing it); and lately altered and improved by the French; especially between Nice and Scarena.[3]

After driving about five miles on the banks of the Paglion, we began to ascend the mountain of Scarena; reaching the village of that name in less than three hours. We then proceeded, for nearly two hours and a half, up a mountain composed of red, grey, and white marble, and, on arriving at its summit, were presented with a view of Sospello, lying at our feet, and apparently not half a mile distant; yet so lofty was the mountain we were upon, that we had nine miles to go ere we could reach Sospello. This village, built on the banks of the Paglion, and surrounded with Alps, contains two tolerable inns. Hence we proceeded up the mountain of Sospello, which, being loftier than Scarena, exhibited a road more wonderful than that we had already passed, winding through immense rocks of marble, some of which were blown up with gunpowder, in order to make room for carriages. Near Sospello stands an ancient Roman castle; but, what seems extraordinary, the old Roman road over these Maritime Alps is no where discoverable. After ascending for three hours, we reached the summit of the mountain; and then descended, in less than one hour, to La Chiandola; a romantic village, situated at the brink of a brawling torrent, and adorned by cascades gushing from jagged rocks of a stupendous height. We slept at La Chiandola; where the inn is tolerably good; and next

---

[1] The usual price for a ten-oared felucca, from Genoa to Nice, is about ten sequins.

[2] The principal inns at Nice are, *L'Hôtel de York, Le Dauphin,* and *La Poste.*

[3] This road, as constructed by Victor-Amadeus, was always passable for carriages at certain seasons of the year, and not only passable, but excellent: if I recollect right, the above-named Prince was the first person who ever attempted making a carriage-road over the great Alps.

morning set out early for Tenda. To describe the road between this town and La Chiandola is impossible: neither do I think it in the power of imagination to picture such scenery as we beheld. Our ascent was gradual, by the side of the already-named torrent; which, from rushing impetuously over enormous masses of stone, forms itself into an endless variety of cascades: while the stupendous rocks, through which this road is pierced, from their immense height, grotesque shapes, and verdant clothing, added to the beautiful water-falls with which they are embellished, present one of the most awfully magnificent grottoes that the masterly hand of nature ever made. Through this grotto we travelled for a considerable number of miles, surrounded by mountains, whose summits the eye cannot reach; though sometimes a brilliant mass of snow, which we guessed to be the peak of an Alp, appeared hanging, as it were, in the sky; but clouds always rested upon, and eclipsed the middle-part. Suddenly, however, we beheld, suspended in the air (for such really was its appearance) a large fortified Castle; and, soon afterward, on turning a point, we discovered the town of Saorgio, built in the shape of an amphitheatre, and apparently poised between earth and heaven; while the lower part of the rocks exhibited such woods of chesnut as, to English Travellers, appear equally uncommon and beautiful. After this, we were continually presented with convents, hermitages, remains of castles, and old Roman causeys, till our arrival at Tenda; which is situated under an immense Alp (of the same name), computed to be eight thousand feet in height; and over the summit of which lies the road. Tanda is a sombre-looking town, resembling what Poetry would picture as the world's end: for the cloud-capped mountain behind it seems to say, "Thou shalt proceed no further." It is prudent to pass the Col-di-Tenda before mid-day; because, at that time, there generally rises a wind very inconvenient to Travellers. This passage, since the improvements made in the road by the French, seldom occupies above five hours; though, formerly, it took up nearly double that time; we, therefore, left Tenda at eight o'clock, that we might reach the summit of the ascent by eleven; and this was easily accomplished. On first setting out we were presented with picturesque prospects embellished by bold cascades. When we had proceeded about three parts up the mountain, the air became chilly; and we perceived, by the fog which enveloped us, that we were passing through clouds; these, on attaining the summit, we found ourselves considerably above; and here the cold was intense. The top of this vast Alp exhibits a barren rock, whence we descried Mont-Viso, with other Alps still more lofty; and at our feet Limone, seated in a valley through which rushes a torrent formed by snow from the Col-di-Tenda. Limone contains a tolerable inn. Hence the road runs parallel with one of those streams which fertilize this wild part of Piedmont, till it enters the luxuriant plain in which stands Coni; a finely situated town, whose fortifications were once deemed impregnable. Here we slept at the post-house; proceeding, next day, to Savigliano, and struck by the change of scenery; rich and tame cultivation succeeding to the sublime and beautiful wildness of the Alps. Savigliano is a large town, with a tolerable inn. Hence we drove to Carignano, through one of the most fruitful valleys imaginable; and after having stopped to dine at the latter place, proceeded to Turin.

This city, seated in a spacious plain loaded with mulberries, vines and corn, and watered by the rivers Po and Dora (the former of which was anciently called *Bodinco*, or bottomless), is approached by four fine roads shaded with forest-trees; while the surrounding hills are covered with handsome edifices, pre-eminent among which towers the magnificent church of La Superga.

Turin was named *Augusta Taurinorum*, by Augustus, when he made it into a Roman colony; before which period it was the capital of the Taurini, a Gallic tribe: the modern walls, or ramparts, are about four miles round, and contain a population of 88,000 persons: the citadel, a particularly fine fortress, which the French nearly destroyed, is now rebuilding. The streets, which are wide, straight, and clean, intersect each other at right angles; so that on one particular spot, in the middle of the town, they may all be seen at once, issuing, like rays, from a common centre. The Strada del Po, the Strada-Nuova, and the Strada del Dora-Grande, are very handsome; so are the Piazza del Castello, and the Piazza di S. Carlo; each being adorned with porticos: and the Bridge thrown by the French over the Po, is one of the most beautiful pieces of architecture of its kind in Europe.

The regal Palace contains an equestrian statue of Amadeus I.; magnificent suites of apartments; and a valuable collection of pictures; among which is a portrait of Charles I. of England — the Children of Charles I., with a Dog — and a Prince of the House of Carignano on horseback — all by Vandyck — Homer, represented as a blind *Improvvisatore*, by Murillo — the prodigal Son, by Guercino — and Cattle, by Paul Potter.

The Cathedral merits notice, on account of one of its Chapels, called La Cappella di S. Sudario, built after the designs of Guarini.

The Chiesa di S. Filippo Neri is a fine edifice in point of architecture, built after the designs of Giuvara, Torinese; and contains a superb high-altar and baldacchino.

The Chiesa di S. Christina contains a statue of S. Teresa, deemed the *chef-d'œuvre* of Le Gros.

The Teatro di Carignano is handsome; and the *gran Teatro* is one of the largest and most beautiful buildings of its kind existing.

The University contains a fine statue of Cupid, supposed to be Grecian sculpture — a very valuable ancient mosaic pavement — the celebrated Isiac Table, found at Mantua, and one of the most precious monuments extant of Egyptian antiquity! — together with sacrificial Vases — Lamps — Medals, etc.

The public Garden, and the Ramparts, are delightful promenades; and were it not for a want of correctness and simplicity in the structure and decorations of the principal edifices, Turin would be one of the most beautiful towns in Europe.

Here are good Hotels;[1] good shops (where the manufactures of the country, namely, velvets, silks, silk stockings, tapestry, porcelain, chamois-leather-gloves, etc. are sold); a good market for eatables, and good wine: but the fogs which invariably prevail, during autumn and winter, make the climate, at those seasons, unwholesome: and the foul and noxious water, too frequently found in the wells and reservoirs of this city, often proves even a greater evil than the fogs: there is, however, before the Po-Gate, near the Capuchin-convent, a well of excellent water.[2]

The objects best worth notice in the environs of Turin are: *Valentino*, where there is a public Garden—*La Villa della Regina*, which commands a fine view—*Camaldoli*, the road to which is very romantic—*La Superga* (five miles distant from the city), a magnificent church, where rest the ashes of the Sardinian Kings; and *La Veneria*, a royal Villa, containing good paintings, and a fine orangery.

The ruins of the ancient town of *Industria* are not far distant from Turin.

Wishing to pass the Bocchetta,[3] one of the loftiest mountains of the Apennine, we quitted Turin by the magnificent new Bridge already mentioned; and travelled on a good and pleasant road, embellished with fine views of the Po and the Alps, to Asti; a large town, seated amidst vineyards which produce the best wine in Piedmont.

Asti, supposed to contain above ten thousand inhabitants, is encircled with extensive walls in a ruinous condition: and of the hundred towers, for which it once was famous, scarce thirty remain; and even these seem nodding to their fall. The people here are poor, because inclined to idleness; and the town, generally speaking, has a sombre aspect, that quarter excepted where the nobility reside, and where the buildings are handsome. Asti boasts the honour of containing the paternal mansion of the Conte Vittorio Alfieri, the greatest, and almost the only distinguished tragic Poet modern Italy ever produced. *The Duomo*, here, has been lately erected, and merits notice; as do *the Churches of S. Secondo*, and *the Madonna della Consolata*, and likewise that of *S. Bartolommeo dei Benedettini*, on the outside of the walls.[4]

On quitting Asti we crossed the Stironne, traversed a beautiful vale richly clothed with grain; and after having passed the village of Annone, were presented with a particularly fine view of the Po. We then passed Felizzano and Solera, and approached the Fortress of Alessandria through a road in some places sandy, but otherwise good.

---

1 *L'Albergo dell' Universo*—*L'Europa*—*La Buona Donna*, etc.

2 Travellers, before they quit Turin, are obliged to have their Passports examined and signed at the Police Office; and likewise by the Austrian Ambassador, if they design going beyond the Sardinian territories. For the latter signature four francs and a half, per Passport, are demanded.

3 Since I took this journey, the new Route of *Val di Scrivia* has been opened; a happy circumstance for Travellers; as the new Road is excellent, and in consequence of its low situation exempt from those dangerous storms which frequently visit the Bocchetta: beside which, the old road is so rough that no carriage, not particularly strong, can pass over it without injury.

4 Asti contains two very tolerable inns; namely, *La Rosa Rossa*, and *Il Leone d'Oro*.

Alessandria, seated in the midst of an extensive plain, and watered by the Tanaro, is a handsome town, particularly celebrated for the sieges it has sustained, for the strength of its citadel, perhaps the finest in Europe, and for a magnificent Bridge covered from end to end, and equally remarkable for its length, height, and solidity. The Sluices of the Tanaro merit notice; the Piazza d'Armi is spacious: and the regal Palace, the Governor's House, the Churches of S. Alessandro, and S. Lorenzo, the new Theatre, and the Ramparts, are usually visited by travellers. This town, (which contains about eighteen thousand inhabitants and two Hotels),[1] was anciently called *Alexandria Statelliorum;* but has, in modern days, acquired the ludicrous appellation of *Alessandria della Paglia;* partly owing to a fable, importing that the Emperors of Germany were in former times crowned here, with a straw diadem; and partly because the inhabitants, being destitute of wood, are supposed to bake their white bread with straw.

On quitting Alessandria, we crossed the Tanaro, and immediately re-entered the above-named plain; called, on this side, that of Marengo; and famous for the decisive victory gained here, by Napoleon, over the Austrians. No ground can be better calculated for the strife of armies than this plain; which is not only extensive but flat, and equally devoid of trees and fences; though either in consequence of judicious cultivation, or the quantity of human blood with which the soil has been fertilized, it bears abundance of fine corn. A quarter of a league distant from Alessandria we crossed the Bormida, a large and rapid torrent; and, half a league further on, passed the hamlet of Marengo. One public-house on this plain is still called The *Torre di Marengo*, and another, The *Albergo di lunga fama;* but the column, surmounted by an eagle, and placed on the spot where Dessaix fell, is now to be seen no more.

At Marengo we quitted the route which leads to Parma; and proceeded through a good, though, in some parts, a narrow road, to Novi; seeing, by the way, the Domenican Abbadia del Bosco, adorned with a few good paintings, and some sculpture; the latter by Buonaroti.

Novi, placed among vineyards at the base of the Apennine, contains six thousand inhabitants, several magnificent houses, which belong to rich Genovesi, who spend the autumn here; and two comfortable inns;[2] it is, therefore, the best sleeping-place between Turin and Genoa, both on account of the last-named circumstance, and likewise from being situated about midway. One tower of the old Castle of Novi alone remains, standing on an eminence, and remarkable for its height.

After driving through the vineyards, orchards, and chesnutgroves, near Novi, we penetrated into the heart of the Apennine, by a road somewhat resembling a saw; traversing ancient watercourses and narrow defiles to Gavi, a town which contains one

---

[1] *L'Albergo Reale Vecchio d'Italia*, and *L'Albergo Nuovo d'Italia;* the former excellent.

[2] *L'Albergo Reale* in Via-Ghirardenghi, and *La Posta*, beyond the town, on the way to Genoa,

thousand six hundred inhabitants and a good hotel. The castle here is proudly seated on a rock, for the defence of the pass: and, according to report, was never taken. Voltaggio, the next town, and where the present passage of the Bocchetta commences, is nearly equal in population to Gavi; and contains two good inns. Hence the road passes through a defile, sometimes surrounded with chesnut-woods, at others exhibiting bad pasturages bordered by the Lemmo, and hovels the very picture of wretchedness; though erected on blocks of beautiful and costly marble, with which this part of the Apennine abounds. The women who inhabit these hovels, are of low stature, with thick legs, broad feet, large throats, and frequently goitrous swellings: the children look unhealthy, and seem to be wholly occupied by watching pigs and goats, and following mules and carriages, to collect dung for manure: the food of these poor mountaineers is chesnut-bread, hog's-lard, and snow-water: and when the chesnuts fail, famine ensues. As we advanced toward the Col, we found the hovels lessen in number; and at length saw no vestige of any habitation except a guard-house on an isolated rock, where, during the period when this passage was infested by banditti, soldiers were stationed to protect travellers. On gaining the summit of the Bocchetta we were presented with a view of the beautiful valley of Polcevera, terminated by the city of Genoa and the Mediterranean Sea: and the rich cultivation exhibited in this valley, by the persevering industry of the Genovesi, produces a most delightful contrast to the savage and barren aspect of the northern side of the Apennine. The descent for two leagues to Campo-Marone is, in some places, very rapid; but thence to Genoa the road constructed by a Doge of the Cambiaso family is excellent: it lies on the left bank of the Polcevera, amidst villas, villages, orange and olive gardens, cypresses, and that most beautiful of all Italian trees, the round-topped maritime stone pine, at length entering the city by the magnificent Faubourg of San Pietro d'Arena. [1]

Having procured a bill of health at Genoa, which is always necessary on quitting this town by sea, we again embarked in a felucca; and were fortunate enough, on the second evening of our voyage, to reach the harbour of Leghorn.[2] The island of Gorgona, and the rock, called Meloria, are both situated on the right side of the entrance into this fine harbour, which is divided into two parts, that furthest from the shore being defended against the violence of the sea by a pier; though large vessels anchor in the roads, about two miles from the pier-head. The Light-house is built upon an isolated rock in the open sea.

Leghorn, in Italian Livorno, the nurse-child of the House of Medicis, called by the ancients, *Liburnus Portus*, and formerly subject to Genoa, was the first free port established in the Mediterranean: and this political establishment,

---

[1] Between Turin and Genoa, a carriage with two places and four wheels goes, generally speaking, with two horses only, according to the tariff; but the postmasters often put on three horses; though travellers do not pay any thing extra in consequence.

[2] We paid for our felucca twelve sequins.

the work of Cosimo I., who exchanged the episcopal city of Sarzano for the then unimportant village of Leghorn, soon rendered the latter a place of great consequence: and by cutting several canals, and encouraging cultivation, he, in some measure, destroyed the noxious vapours which naturally proceeded from a loose and marshy soil. Leghorn, to persons unskilled in the art of war, seems strongly fortified: but various circumstances, I am told, would prevent it from being tenable long, whether attacked by land or sea. This city is two miles in circumference, and contains 60,000 inhabitants, 20,000 of whom are said to be Jews; its ramparts are handsome; and the high-street, from its breadth and straightness, from the richness of its shops, and, still more, from the motley crowd of all nations with which it is constantly filled, presents a picture equally singular and pleasing. The great square is spacious; and *the Duomo* is a noble edifice, designed by Vasary: this Church—*the Jews' Synagogue,* (one of the finest in Europe)—*the Church of the united Greeks—the Monte, or Bank—Micali's Shop —the Coral Manufacture — the great Printing-House — the Opera-House — the four Slaves in bronze*, by Pietro Tacca, chained to the pedestal of the statue of Ferdinando I., which stands in the Dock-yard, and was done by Giovanni del Opera—*the Lazzaretti —the Campo-Santo—the English Burial-ground—the new Aqueduct*, not yet completed, which is to bring wholesome water to the city from the mountains of Colognole (twelve miles distant)—and *the Church of the Madonna di Montenero*, are the objects best worth notice in Leghorn and its environs. Here are several inns:[1] and the English Factory have a Protestant Chapel. From Leghorn we proceeded, by land, through part of the forest of Arno, to Pisa, a distance of fourteen Tuscan miles; though persons who prefer water-carriage may go by the Canal, from the one city to the other. At Pisa we directed our course to Lucca, traversing an excellent road.[2]

Lucca, called *L'Industriosa*, is beautifully situated, about twelve Tuscan miles from Pisa, in a luxuriant valley, encircled by the Apennine, and watered by the Serchio: it is defended by eleven bastions of brick, and ramparts, which, from being planted with forest-trees, give this little city the appearance of a fortified wood with a watch-tower in its centre: the edifice which resembles the latter being the cathedral. The ramparts are three miles in circumference; and form a delightful promenade, either on foot or in a carriage. Previous to the French revolution the word "*Libertas*" was inscribed on the Pisa-gate: this inscription, however, no longer exists: but, nevertheless, it is impossible to enter Lucca without feeling high respect for a town which, even during the plenitude of Roman despotism, maintained its own laws, and some degree of liberty; and which, since that period, till very recently, always continued free. The territory contains about four hundred square miles, and about 120,000

---

[1] *The Albergo di S. Marco*, kept by Thomson, and a good inn—*The Croce d'Ora* and *The Croce di Malta*.

[2] Here there is an Austrian Custom-house, at which I was called upon to pay four pauls for a four-wheeled carriage with two horses.

people. Cæsar wintered at Lucca after his third campaign in Gaul: and, according to Appian of Alexandria, all the magistrates of Rome came to visit him; insomuch that two hundred Roman Senators were seen before his door at the same moment: which circumstance proves Lucca to have been, at that period, a large city.

The streets are broad, well-paved, and clean; but irregular.

The Cathedral, erected in 1070, though unpromising without, is a fine Gothic building within; and contains, on the right of the great door, the tomb of Adalbert, surnamed "The Rich," who lived in the beginning of the tenth century; and was, according to Muratori, the Progenitor of the Princes of Este, and the House of Brunswick Hanover, now Sovereigns of Great Britain. The famous Countess Matilda was a descendant from the above-named Adalbert; and this Princess, the daughter of a Duke of Lucca, who died in 1052, reigned over Tuscany, Lombardy, and Liguria, maintaining desperate wars, for thirty successive years, against the Schismatics and Anti-Popes; till, at length, she drove the Emperor, Henry IV., out of Italy, and restored to the Church its ancient possessions. But to return to the Cathedral: this edifice is adorned with paintings, by Coli and Sancasciani, Lucchesi; a picture, by Zuccari; another, by Tintoretto; statues of the four Evangelists, by Foncelli; a celebrated crucifix, called the *Voto Santo;* fine painted glass windows, and a beautiful inlaid marble pavement.

S. Maria, called *La Chiesa dell' Umiltà*, contains a good picture, by Titian.

The Chiesa di S. Ponziano contains two good paintings, by Pietro Lombardo.

The Palazzo Publico, built by Ammannato and Filippo Giuvara, is embellished with the works of Luca Giordano, Albert Durer, Guercino, etc.—and in the Armoury are several ancient helmets, the smallest of which our courier, an athletic man, attempted to put on his head; but found himself scarcely able to lift it—so much is human strength degenerated!

Remains of the ancient *Amphitheatre* are discoverable on the spot called *Prigioni vecchie*.

The modern Theatre is small, but pretty.

The police of Lucca has long been famed for its excellence. The upper ranks of people are opulent, learned, and well-inclined; the mechanics (instructed by their late Sovereign, the Princess Elise), display great taste and expertness in making household furniture; the lower ranks of people possess more integrity of character, with a stronger sense of religion, than is common now, either in Roman Catholic or Protestant countries; and the peasants are the most industrious and skilful husbandmen of southern Italy.

Lucca contains a *Seminary*, founded by the Princess Elise, for the education of an hundred young ladies, beside children of humble birth: and this Princess had likewise taken measures to establish an Institute, for the encouragement of arts and sciences, when she was called upon to relinquish her throne.

The Pantera is the best inn at Lucca.

Travellers who enter this city

with post-horses are compelled to quit it in the same manner.

The surrounding country is rich in villas; and that called *Marlia*, on the way to the Baths of Lucca, particularly merits notice; as it was built by the Princess Elise, is furnished with peculiar elegance, and stands in a beautiful garden.[1] The road from Lucca to this villa, a distance of between four and five miles, is excellent; and hence to the Bagni-caldi (about eight miles), equally good: it winds almost constantly by the side of the Serchio; and is cut through rocks clothed with olives and chesnuts, and adorned with convents, villas, and cottages. Nothing can be more romantic than this drive; and, on the way, are three extraordinary bridges; the first consisting of two immense arches, not in a straight line with each other, but forming, in the centre, a considerable angle; neither do these arches support a level road: on the contrary, you ascend one arch, and descend it again; you then come to an angle of flat ground; after which you ascend the other arch, and descend that, till you reach a smaller arch, which brings you to the opposite shore of the Serchio. The height of this bridge we could not precisely ascertain; but, judging from the eye, it is nearly equal to that of Augustus at Narni. The second bridge is similar to the first; but the third, which consists of only one large arch, is by far the loftiest; and, according to oral tradition, was the work of the Devil; who seems to have been, in the opinion of the Italians, a great architect; for every extraordinary building is attributed to him. Other accounts, however, say, these bridges were erected by the Countess Matilda: and one of the postilions, who drove us to the Bagni, told me, they were built soon after the year 1000—an extraordinary circumstance that he should have been so accurate a chronologist!—but the common people of Italy are well-informed respecting the history of their country; and, moreover, so fond of its poets, as frequently to know their works by heart.

The Bagni-caldi di Lucca are situated on the side of a romantic and picturesque mountain, thickly clothed with chesnut-woods; where, during summer, the walks are delightful. The *Bagni della Villa* are in the plain, near the banks of the Lima; and the late Sovereign, by making a fine road to these Baths, and inducing her own family to frequent them, has converted a secluded village into a gay public place. At the Bagni-caldi there is one lodging-house, which accommodates from twelve to fourteen families;[2] another, which accommodates three families;[3] several small lodgings; a coffee-house, and a cassino; where, during the season, there is a ball every Sunday night. These baths, therefore, to persons

---

[1] The Empress Maria Louisa visited this Villa, not many years since; slept here, and ordered every thing to be in readiness for her departure at four o'clock the next morning: she, however, lingered in the Marlia-gallery (apparently lost in thought), till ten o'clock; and then, with great reluctance, went away. Her Son's Bust is at Marlin; and, if like him, he must have a countenance replete with sense and animation, and bearing a strong resemblance to his Father.

[2] In this house, which belongs to the Abate Lena, families may either have kitchens to themselves, or employ the *Traiteur* who resides under the same roof.

[3] This house belongs to an excellent *Traiteur*, called Johachino; who furnishes the tables of his Lodgers: his third floor, which is the best, was let in 1817 for thirty sequins a month; and his other floors for eighteen or twenty sequins each.

very fond of society, must be an eligible summer situation. At the Bagni della Villa there are several good lodging houses; some of which accommodate two or three families, others only one; and here the mother of the Princess Elise used to reside.[1] At the Ponte-Seraglio, near the Bagni-caldi, there are lodging-houses; but these, generally speaking, are inhabited by persons of the second rank.

The usual Promenade here is between the Bagni della Villa and the Ponte-Seraglio, on a dusty road; while a delightful drive, made by the Government, under the wood on the opposite side of the river, is totally neglected.

The season commences with July and ends with August; though June and September are months better calculated for the examination of this beautiful spot, which is one of the coolest summer abodes of southern Italy.

Provisions here are not exorbitant in price, even during the season; but good table-wine and good butchers' meat, except veal, are difficult to procure; and fruit, except Alpine strawberries, cherries, and wild raspberries, is neither very fine nor very plentiful.

Lovers of botany should visit, during the month of June, the *Prato Fiorito*, near these Baths; which is, at the above-named time, enamelled with a larger number and a greater variety of flowers than fall to the share, perhaps, of any other spot existing.[2] The best way of seeing this garden of Flora is to set out at an early hour, going by Coltrone, and returning by Monte-Villa, near which several of the chesnut-trees are of so extraordinary a size that they would be fit subjects for landscape-painters to study. The modes of conveyance to the Prato Fiorito are various; ponies and donkies may be easily procured, but people, in general, prefer being carried by *Fortentini*; of whom there is a considerable number at the Baths: three men are requisite for each chair; and their usual pay is five pauls a man, with bread, common wine, and cheese of the country for dinner, wherever the party like to stop; which is generally at the foot of the Prato Fiorito; there being, in this place, a spring of good water.

Another pleasant excursion may be made in the same manner, from the Bagni della Villa to Ponte Nero: the best way of going is to cross the Lima on the Ponte Nuovo, keeping on the far side of the river the whole way; and then returning by Palleggio; as that village, together with the hamlets of Cocciglia and Cosoli di Val di Lima, form a beautiful and most romantic prospect. The party should dine near this spot; and then go back to the Baths by the Palleggio side of the river, as far as the wooden bridge of La Fabbrica; where they should cross to the other side. A guide well acquainted with the country is requisite for this ex-

---

[1] The best apartment in the house of the Signora Lena, at the Bagni della Villa, was let in 1817 for thirty sequins a month: the first floor in the house of Sig. G. B. del Chiappa for twenty-eight sequins a month; and the second floor for eighteen or twenty sequins. Casa-Ambrogio, Casa-Nobile, Casa-Bonvisi, and Casa-Rossi, are good lodging-houses; the last is that in which the Mother of the late Sovereign formerly lived.

[2] Tradition reports that, on this eminence, there once stood a temple dedicated to Æsculapius; whose Priests are supposed to have cultivated round the edifice a large number of flowers; which chance has perpetuated to the present day.

cursion, and may be procured at the Baths.

Loiano, likewise, from its singular situation, is worth visiting.

The peasantry of these mountains are an honest and industrious people: the little land they possess is cultivated with the utmost care, and in the neatest manner; but does not yield sufficient food for the numerous inhabitants of this part of the Duchy of Lucca; who are, therefore compelled, like many other natives of the Apennine, to live chiefly on bread made of chesnuts; and when these fail, the consequence is dreadful; as was exemplified lately, when hundreds perished from want; while those who survived had no sustenance but beans boiled with grass, and herbs collected on the mountains: and yet there was no rioting, no murmuring, no complaint—the famishing peasants prayed to Heaven for relief, and awaited with resignation the approach of better days. The vices and crimes which disgrace more opulent countries are little known amongst these innocent peasants, whose probity and piety are equally exemplary.[1]

The mode of cultivating this part of the Apennine is beautiful: at the commencement of each ascent vines are dressed on terraces cut in the side of the hill; wheat being sown between every two rows of vines: above these there frequently is an olive garden; and on the more elevated parts of the hill are chesnuts.

Mountains are sold here not by measurement, but from a calculation respecting the number of sacks of chesnuts they usually produce. The landlord receives two-thirds of the chesnuts which are collected; and half of the other crops. The richer grounds in the plain produce hemp, from which much coarse cloth, and some of a finer sort, is manufactured; and every peasant has a stock of silk-worms.[2] Wheat is usually cut about Midsummer; and immediately carried off the fields; which are, on the same day, sown with Indian corn; and this comes up in a week, and is fit to be cut in October. In many places rows of Indian corn and French beans, called scarlet runners, are planted alternately; the former serving as a support to the latter.[3]

On our return from the Baths of Lucca, we noticed, between that romantic spot and the city, several villas, with gardens, possessing shady walks; a comfort seldom found in southern Italy: and, on inquiry, I learnt, that the owners of these habitations were usually glad to let them to respectable tenants, from May till the end of September.

Having traversed the beautiful and highly-cultivated plain of Lucca, adorned with forest trees,

---

1 The Rector of the parish in which the Bagni di Lucca are situated, told a friend of mine, that, after a residence of twenty years among his parishioners, who amount to above eight hundred people, he had never heard of the commission of one theft, neither had he heard of more than three children born out of wedlock.

2 The female peasants often manufacture a silk, for their own wear, from the bags of those silk-worms which are allowed to work their way out, in order to produce eggs for the ensuing year. The costume of the inferior peasants is neat; and the wives and daughters of the farmers are, on festival days, handsomely dressed when they go to church, or elsewhere; but this finery is laid by, the moment they return home.

3 It was not in my power to collect much information relative to the Baths of Lucca; because my residence there was short: but from a friend, who spent several months in that vicinity, and is, moreover, a judicious and accurate observer, I received many of the particulars I have, in consequence, been enabled to detail.

from which hang festoons of vines in every direction, we approached Pescia, a small episcopal city at the base of the Apennine, and peculiarly situated amidst mountains cultivated to their summits, and covered with villages, churches, and castles: the episcopal palace here looks handsome; and near this town are the baths of Monte-Catini.

The road, to the end of the Lucchese territories, is excellent; but thence to Pistoja paved, and not well kept. The country between Pescia and Pistoja is bold and romantic; and the latter city finely placed on the side of the Apennine, near the river Ombrone, contains particularly wide, straight, and well-paved streets; palaces, which announce magnificence; and a venerable Gothic Cathedral: but the city looks too large for its inhabitants (said to be only 10,000), and therefore has a gloomy appearance. It was famous among the ancients for the defeat of Catiline; and, in modern times, the factions of the Guelphs and Ghibellines have rendered it no less remarkable. The situation of Pistoja is cool; the air healthy; the country fruitful; and the provisions are cheap and good.

The Cathedral contains a monument erected to the memory of Cardinal Fertoguerra, begun by Andrea Verrochio, and finished by Lorengetti—over the high altar is an ascension, by Bronzino; and on the walls several historical passages of scripture are represented in *basso-rilievo*. The famous Civilian Cino is interred in this church, and his memory perpetuated by two inscriptions, over which are *bassi-rilievi* by Andrea, Pisano.

The Baptistery, which stands in the area before the church, is spacious, and was used, in the first ages of Christianity, for baptizing proselytes.

The Chiesa di S. Francesco di Sala contains seven paintings, by Andrea del Sarto.

The Chiesa di S. Prospero contains a fine Library in the anteroom, to which are *bassi-rilievi*, by Cornaquioi.

The Chiesa dell' Umiltà is admired for its architecture and cupola, by Vasari.

The Chiesa dello Spirito Santo possesses an excellent organ.

The Episcopal Palace contains a statue of Leo XI.

The modern College and Seminary merit notice.

Good organs, cannon, and muskets, are made at Pistoja. The best inn (a very bad one) is the post-house.

From Pistoja we proceeded to Prato and Florence; leaving, to the right, the royal Villa of Poggio-a-Cajano, whose foundations were laid by Leo X.; and this villa merits notice, from its fine situation, and because it is embellished with the works of Andrea del Sarto.

The country between Pistoja and Florence may, with truth, be called the richest and best cultivated garden in Tuscany: and the lofty hedges of vines climbing up forest trees, and forming themselves into magnificent festoons on each side of the road, present the appearance of an immensely extensive gallery, decorated for a ball.

The road from Pistoja to Florence is good.

CHAPTER VII.

SIENA AND ROME.

Journey from Florence to Rome through Siena—Description of the last-named city and its Environs—Radicofani—Viterbo—Tomb of C. V. Marianus—Ponte-Molle—Nasonian Sepulchre—Muro Torto—Porta del Popolo—Rome—Mal' aria—Climate—Water conveyed daily to the ancient city—Size and population of ditto—Size of the modern city—Society—Excavations—Foro-Romano—Colosseo—Arco di Costantino—Chiesa di S. Teodoro—Arco di Settimio Severo in Velabro—Chiesa di S. Georgio in Velabro—Arco di Giano Quadrifronte—Lake of Juturna—Cloaca Maxima—House called that of Pilate—Chiesa di S. Maria in Cosmedin—Tempio di Vesta—Tempio di Fortuna Virilis—Palazzo de' Cesari—Circus Maximus—Chiesa di S. Gregorio sul Monte-Celio—Terme di Tito—Sette Sale—Chiese di S. Martino in Monte—di S. Pietro in Vincoli—di S. Maria della Navicella—di S. Stefano Rotondo—Obelisk of the Piazza del Popolo—Obelisk of the Trinità de' Monti—Villa Medici—Statues and Obelisk of Monte-Cavallo—Chiese di S. Bernardo—di S. Maria degli Angeli—The Pope's Oil-Cellar—Obelisk of S. Maria Maggiore—Column—Basilica—Obelisk of S. Giovanni in Laterano—Battisterio di Costantino—Basilica di S. Giovanni in Laterano—Scala Santa—Triclinium—Amphitheatre Castrense—Basilica di S. Croce in Gerusalemme—Temple called that of Venus and Cupid—Claudian Aqueduct—Chiesa di S. Bibiana—Tempio di Minerva-Medica—Arco di Gallieno—Remains of Aqueducts—Chiesa di S. Prassede—Campidoglio—Tarpeian Rock—Chiese di S. Maria d'Aracoeli—di S. Pietro in Carcere—Palazzo del Senatore—Palazzo de' Conservatori—Museo-Capitolino—Tempio di Pallade—Tempio e Foro di Nerva—Foro e Colonna Trajana—Dogana Pontifica—Obelisk of Monte-Citorio—Colonna Antonina—Mausoleo d'Augusto—Campo-Marzo—Mausoleo-Adriano—Tempio del Sole—Baths of Constantine—Obelisk of S. Maria sopra Minerva—Chiesa di S. Maria sopra Minerva—Casanatense Library—Pantheon—Bagni d'Agrippa—Piazza-Navona—Chiesa di S. Agnese—Teatro di Marcello—Prison of the Decemviri—Portico d'Octavia—Tempio d'Esculapio—Chiesa di S. Cecilia in Trastevere—Basilica di S. Maria in Trastevere—Fountain—Chiese di S. Prisca—di S. Sabina—di S. Alessio—Monte-Testaccio—Sepolcro di Cajo Cestio—Terme di Caracalla—Sepolcro de' Scipioni—Porta di S. Sebastiano alle Catacombe—Cerchio di Caracalla—Sepolcro di Cecilia Metella—Public Ustrina—Scene of combat between the Horatii and Curiatii—Basilica di S. Paolo—Chiesa di S. Paolo alle tre Fontane—Excavations—Chiesa di S. Urbano alla Caffarella—Fontana della Dea Egeria—Tempio di Redicolo—Porta-Pia; Chiesa di S. Agnese—Chiesa di S. Costanza—Hippodrome—Villa Faonte—Ponte Lamentano—Tomb of Menenius Agrippa—Mons Sacer—Porta di S. Lorenzo; Basilica di S. Lorenzo—Porta Maggiore; ancient Temples at the Tor de' Schiavi—Porta S. Giovanni—Aqueducts—Temple of Fortuna Mulcebris—Farm called Roma Vecchia—Gates not already mentioned—Bridges not already mentioned.

BEFORE I enter upon a description of Rome, I will give a brief account of Siena, and other places, through which we passed on our way from Florence to the first-named city.

Siena, formerly called *Sena Julia*, in honour of Cæsar, is by some authors supposed to have been an ancient town of Etruria; while others attribute its foundation to the Gauls who marched to Rome under the command of Brennus. It stands on the acclivity of a Tufo-mountain; or, perhaps, more properly speaking, the crater of an extinct volcano; and once contained 100,000 inhabitants; though its present population does not amount to a fifth part of that number. The buildings are handsome, and the streets airy; but many of them so much up and down hill as to be scarcely practicable for carriages. The wine, water, bread, meat, and fruits, are excellent; the upper classes of people well educated, pleasing, and remarkably kind to Foreigners; and the Tuscan language is said to be spoken here in its utmost perfection.

Some remains of the old walls of Siena are discoverable near the church of S. Antonio; and several ancient grottoes, cellars, subterranean aqueducts, and, as it were, whole streets, excavated under the mountain, merit notice.

The Roman Gate is much admired.

The Cathedral, which occupies the site of a temple dedicated to Minerva, is a master-piece of Gothic architecture, incrusted without and within with black and white marble: it was erected about the year 1250; but, in 1284, the original front was taken down, and that which now stands, commenced by Giovanni, Pisano, and finished by Agostino and Agnolo, celebrated sculptors of Siena. Near the great door are two vases for holy water; the one executed by Giacomo della Quercia, the other an antique, found at the same time with the Graces; and both these vessels contain marble fishes, so well done that they appear to be swimming. The pavement is reckoned one of the most curious works of art in Italy; and consists of scriptural histories, wrought in mosaic. The story of Moses was designed by Beccafumi, surnamed Meccarino, and executed, by various artists, about the middle of the sixteenth century. The story of Joshua is by Duccio di Buoninsegna, Sanese. In this pavement are likewise represented the emblems of cities once in alliance with Siena, namely, the elephant of Rome with a castle on its back—the lions of Florence and Massa—the dragon of Pistoja—the hare of Pisa—the unicorn of Viterbo—the goose of Ovieto—the vulture of Voltera—the stork of Perugia—the lynx of Lucca—the horse of Arezzo—and the kid of Grossetto. Here also is the she-wolf of Siena, borne in memory of Romulus and Remus. This work appears to have been executed about the year 1400. The pavement of the area, under the cupola, and that before the high altar, representing Abraham's intended sacrifice of his son, are particularly celebrated; and the latter is attributed to Meccarino. The art of paving in this beautiful way, or, more properly speaking, of representing figures in black and white marble thus exquisitely, is now lost. Near the entrance of the choir are four large frescos by Salimbeni. The Chigi-Chapel contains a copy, in Roman mosaic, of a painting by Carlo Maratti; a statue of the Magdalene, by Bernini; and three other statues, by his scholars. The chapel of S. Giovanni contains a statue of that saint by Donatello! This cathedral is adorned with painted glass windows, executed in 1549; and busts of all the Popes, down to Alexander III.; among these formerly was the bust of Pope Joan; with the following inscription under it: "*Johannes* VIII., *Fœmina de Angliæ.*"

The Library, or Sacristy, is

now stripped of all its books, except some volumes of church music, well worth notice, on account of the illuminations with which they are decorated; here, likewise, is a celebrated antique group, in marble, of the three Graces, which was found under the church; and on the walls are frescos representing the principal transactions of the life of Pius II., by Pinturicchio, after the designs of Raphael; the first painting on the right is said to have been wholly done by that artist.

The Tower of the Palazzo della Signoria, vulgarly called *del Mangia*, and built by Agnolo and Agostino in 1325, is a fine piece of Architecture.

The Churches of the Spedale di S. Maria della Scala—the Agostiniani—S. Martino di Provenzano—S. Quirino, and *del Carmine*; and *the Church of the Camaldolensi*, on the outside of the town, contain good pictures.

The Church of *S. Lorenzo* is famous for an ancient Roman Inscription, and a well, at the bottom of which is a sort of fountain, supported by columns that appear to be of high antiquity: and the *Domenican Church* contains a painting of the Madonna with our Saviour in her arms, executed by Guido di Siena in 1221, nineteen years before the birth of Cimabue.

The Palazzo degli Eccelsi contains the Sala della Pace, adorned with paintings which represent, on one side, the recreations of Peace; and, on the other, Tyranny, Cruelty, Deceit, and War; all done by Ambrogio, Sanese, in 1338—the Sala di Consiglio, where are paintings relative to the history of Siena, by the same master, and other subjects, by Bartoli—the Sala di Balia, ornamented with paintings which represent the life of Alexander III.; and are highly valuable because they exhibit the costume of the age in which they were done; (they are of Giotto's school)—the Sala del Consistorio, embellished with some of Beccafumi's finest frescos, and the judgment of Solomon, by Luca Giordano; with several other apartments, in which are works of Salimbeni, Casolani, etc. The Theatre makes a part of this palace, and is large and commodious.

The Fountain constructed in 1193, is so famous for the quantity and quality of its water, as to be mentioned in the *Inferno* of Dante: indeed, there are few cities placed in so elevated a situation as Siena, that can boast such abundance of excellent water: and moreover, the climate, for persons not afflicted with weak lungs, is wholesome at all seasons of the year—a recommendation which does not belong to many cities of Italy.[1]

This town contains a celebrated University; several Academies, valuable Libraries, Museums, etc.; and gave birth to Gregory VII., and Alexander III., two of the greatest Sovereigns who ever filled the Papal throne.[2]

The environs of Siena appear to contain several villas, delightfully calculated for summer habitations; but Travellers should be especially careful not to fix themselves near the Maremma: a con-

---

[1] Siena boasts another recommendation,—it is exempt from gnats; as, generally speaking, are all the elevated parts of this country.

[2] The best inns at Siena are, *The Hôtel des Armes d'Angleterre*, and the *Aquila Nera*; the latter is very comfortable.

siderable tract of country, situated near the sea, and deemed particularly unwholesome now; though heretofore remarkably populous.

Beyond Siena, some leagues to the left of the high-road, lies Chiusi, the ancient *Clusium*, near the Lake of Chiana, formerly *Clanius*: but this city, once Porsenna's capital, is at present thinly peopled, on account of its noxious air.

Buonconvento, pleasantly situated on the Ombrone, about fifteen miles from Siena, is likewise infected with *Mal' aria*: and here the Emperor Henry VII. was poisoned by receiving the sacrament from a Domenican monk.

San-Quirico, placed in a healthy air, amidst olive-trees and vineyards, contains a small Gothic Church, the nave and choir of which merit notice; a Palace belonging to the Chigi family; a curious Well, opposite to the palace, and an ancient square tower, supposed to be of Roman origin.[1]

Near the mountain of Radicofani the soil is volcanic, and the country wild and desolate: the road, however, is excellent; the ascent five miles in length, and the descent the same. Radicofani, which rises two thousand four hundred and seventy feet above the level of the Mediterranean sea, exhibits, on its summit, large heaps of stones, supposed to be the mouth of an extinct volcano. The post-house, not far distant from this spot, is a good inn; and the little fortress near it was once called impregnable, though now falling to decay. This is the frontier of Tuscany; and at the foot of the mountain, on the way to Torrecelli, the road traverses a torrent, sometimes dangerous after rain. Beyond Torrecelli is Ponte-Centino, the first village of the Ecclesiastical State: this country is embellished with woods, and a fine bridge, thrown across the Paglia.

To the next town, Aquapendente, the approach is particularly beautiful: this was the *Aquula* of the ancients; and derives its appellation from the water-falls in its vicinity.[2]

Hence, the road traverses a volcanic plain to San Lorenzo-nuovo; a remarkably well-constructed, clean, and pretty village; which possesses the advantages of wholesome air and good water; and was built by Pius VI., that the inhabitants of what is now called San Lorenzo-rovinato might remove hither, in order to avoid the pestilential atmosphere of the latter place.[3]

Not far distant from S. Lorenzo-nuovo is Bolsena, supposed to stand upon the site of the ancient *Volsinium*: one of the principal cities of Etruria; and whence the Romans, 265 years before Christ, are said to have removed two thousand statues to Rome. Here are remains of a Temple, supposed to have been dedicated to the Goddess Narsia; Etruscan ornaments, which adorn the front of the parochial Church; and, opposite to this edifice, a Sarcophagus of Roman workmanship. In the environs are remains of an Amphitheatre; together with an immense quantity of broken cornices, capitals of pillars, ancient

---

[1] The best inn here, *Il Sole*, contains tolerable beds.

[2] At Acquapendente every Passport must be examined and sealed by the Police Officers; who demand, in consequence, one paul per Passport.

[3] Inn, *The Post-house*, and tolerably good.

mosaics, etc. Bolsena, now an unimportant village, is seated on a magnificent Lake, of the same name, anciently called *Lacus Vulsinus*, and thirty-five Roman miles in circumference: this Lake contains two small Islands, both of them inhabited; and said, by Pliny, to have floated in his time; though now they are fixed: it is supposed to be the crater of a volcano. Nothing can exceed the beauty of the views in this neighbourhood; but the air is unwholesome.

Near Bolsena is Orvieto, celebrated for the excellence of its wines; and containing a handsome Gothic Cathedral; adorned, on the outside, with sculpture, by Niccolo, Pisano; and embellished within, by a painting of Signorelli's, which Buonaroti particularly admired.

Between Bolsena and Montefiascone, the road passes close to a remarkable hill, covered with regular prismatic basaltine columns, most of them standing obliquely, and a considerable length out of the ground: indeed, the whole country, so far as Montefiascone, exhibits rocks of basalt, interspersed with forest scenery: and, near the above-named hill, is an ancient Tomb, erected, according to the inscription it bears, by L. Canuleius, for himself and his family.

Montefiascone, a finely situated, though not a handsome town, produces such excellent wine, that a German Traveller, a Prelate, died from drinking it to excess.

Between Montefiascone and Viterbo the country is dreary; and near the latter town, on the right, is a Lake of hot water; the exhalations from which are sulphureous.

Viterbo, supposed to have been the ancient metropolis of Etruria, called *Volturna*, is situated at the base of Monte-Cimino, anciently *Mons-Ciminus*: and encompassed by walls flanked with towers, which give it, at a distance, a splendid appearance: it contains about thirteen thousand inhabitants, is well built, well paved, and adorned with handsome fountains and a fine gate, erected by Clement XIII.[1]

The road from Viterbo to Ronciglione traverses part of the Monte-Cimino, amid flowers, odoriferous herbs, oaks, chesnuts, and other forest-trees; and at the base of this mountain, near Ronciglione, is the Lake of Vico, anciently *Lacus-Ciminus*, encircled with richly wooded hills, and forming a beautiful basin of nearly three miles in circumference, said to have been the funnel of a volcano; and where, as tradition reports, a city once stood.

Nine leagues from Viterbo, but not in the high-road, is Corneto; remarkable for the number of Etruscan antiquities which have been, and still are to be found in its vicinity: and one league north of Corneto is a hill, called Civita-Turchino, upon which the ancient *Tarquinium* is supposed to have stood. Several little eminences lie between this hill and the town of Corneto; and those which have been opened exhibit subterraneous rooms cut in the tufo, lined with stucco, and filled with Etruscan vases and sarcophagi.

Ronciglione is situated near a picturesque valley, in a barren soil; where agriculture seems al-

---

[1] At Viterbo, *The Aquila Nera* is a good inn.

most wholly neglected; and where the Campagna di Roma begins to feel the influence, during hot weather, of that wide-spreading and incomprehensible pest, *Mal'aria*.[1]

Near Monterosi (*Mons Erosus*) is a sheet of lava; not far hence, the Loretto and Siena roads join; falling into the *Via-Cassia*; and immediately beyond the junction of these roads is the Lake of Monterosi, which emits an offensive smell.

Baccano, *placed in a peculiarly noxious air*, is only two posts from Rome; and on the hill above Baccano St. Peter's may be discovered; while in a valley, on the left, near Storta, may be seen a half ruined Castle, erected on the site of the ancient Citadel of Veii.

No country can be more dreary, nor more neglected, than that which lies between Baccano and the Ponte-Molle: but, from the heights near this bridge, Rome presents herself to view; gradually expanding as the road descends to the banks of the Tiber.

Between Storta and the Ponte-Molle is *the tomb of P. Vibius Marianus*.

The Ponte-Molle, anciently *Pons-Milvius*, was built by M. Emilius Scaurus; and is celebrated for the vision seen here by Constantine; and the victory gained by that prince over the Tyrant Maxentius who was drowned in the river near this spot: there are, however, scarce any remains of the ancient bridge, except its foundation.

The approach to Rome is by the *Via-Flaminia*, between the Pincian and the Marian hills;[2] and, about two miles and a quarter from the Ponte-Molle, cut out of rocks which overlook the *Via-Flaminia*, is *the Nasonian Sepulchre*; and near the Porta del Popolo, toward the Porta-Pinciana, is the *Muro-torto*, a part of the city-wall, which declines from its perpendicular, and supposed, by some persons, to have been the Sepulchre of the Domitian Family, where the ashes of Nero were deposited.

Nothing, of its kind, can be more magnificent than the entry into Rome through the *Porta del Popolo*; a gate erected originally by Aurelian (when he inclosed the Campus Martius), and called *Porta-Flaminia*. The outside of the present gate was built by Vignola; and the inside ornamented by Bernini.

Rome has suffered so materially from volcanic eruptions, earthquakes, and the frequent ravages of invading armies, that even the surface of the ground on which it originally stood is completely altered; insomuch, that on digging deep, it is common to discover columns, statues, fragments of edifices, and sometimes even the pavement of the ancient city, from twenty to thirty feet under ground. The stupendous common sewers, through which the offal of Rome was conveyed into the *Cloaca-maxima*, are many of them choked up; and the *Cloaca-maxima* itself is in bad order; this causes pestilential air; and the workmen who, by digging

---

[1] Ronciglione contains two inns, *The Posthouse*, and *The Albergo di S. Agnello*; wretched hovels both; though wholesomely situated; and, therefore, preferable as sleeping-places to the inns nearer Rome, all of which are infected by *mal' aria*.

[2] Three roads led from Rome to Lombardy: the *Flaminian* along the Adriatic; the *Aurelian* along the Mediterranean; and the *Cassian* between these two, through the interior of the country.

deep, have opened apertures to the common sewers, not unfrequently have lost their lives from the putrid effluvia. In the neighbourhood of Rome all the land is ill-cultivated and worse drained; so that fogs and noxious vapours prevail there during night: it likewise abounds with sulphur, arsenic, and vitriol: hence, therefore, in some measure, perhaps, may arise that *Mal' aria* which never affected ancient Rome; because these minerals were either unknown to its inhabitants, or suffered to remain buried in the bowels of the earth. The temperature of the seasons also seems to be changed; for Horace gives us to understand that, in his time, the streets of Rome, during winter, were filled with ice and snow: and it appears, from Juvenal, that to see the Tiber frozen over was not uncommon: whereas, at present, it is deemed extraordinary for snow to lie three days in any part of the city; and, respecting the Tiber, no person recollects to have seen it frozen. These circumstances, added to the want of trees to agitate and improve the air, concur to account for the present unhealthiness of some parts of Rome, and nearly all its Campagna, during summer: beside which, the mouth of the Tiber is choked with mud and sand; while its bed has been considerably narrowed by filth and rubbish, thrown from the houses situated on its banks; so that a strong south wind often makes it overflow, and inundate the city and its environs.—Could this river be turned into another channel, and the present bed cleansed and deepened, what an advantage might Rome derive in point of healthfulness; and what a harvest to Antiquaries might the river's bed afford![1]—So unwholesome now is the Campagna di Roma in July and August, that, during these months, it is dangerous to sleep within twenty miles of the city: Rome itself, however, even at this season, is not usually visited by *Mal' aria*, either on the Corso, the Quirinal Hill, or the streets comprised within the Rioni Monti, Trevi, Colonna, Campo-Marzo, Ponte, Parione, Regola, S. Eustacio, Pigna, and S. Angelo: but at this season the climate is oppressively hot; though, during winter and spring, temperate and delightful.

The ancient Romans had aqueducts sufficient to convey daily to the city eight hundred thousand tuns of water: the three principal aqueducts now remaining are, that of the *Acqua-Vergine;* that of the *Acqua-Felice;* and that of the *Acqua-Paulina;* the first was repaired by Paul IV., and discharges itself into the Fontana di Trevi: the second comes from the neighbourhood of Palestrina, twenty-two miles distant from Rome, and is one of the many works which do honour to the reign of Sextus V., who expended a million of scudi in repairing it: this aqueduct discharges itself into the Fontana di Termine. The third, which derives its name from its restorer, Paul V., is separated into two channels; one of which supplies Monte-Gianicolo, and the other the Vatican: it comes

---

[1] Beside sixty colossal statues which adorned ancient Rome, her streets and forums were lined with porticos, supported by columns of marble, and embellished with busts and statues innumerable; and a large portion of these precious remains of antiquity is supposed to have been thrown into the Tiber. So numerous were the marble columns in Rome, that a tax was put upon them.

thirty miles; and principally discharges itself into the fountain near the church of S. Pietro-Montorio.

Rome, during the reign of Valerian, was surrounded by a wall, said to have been fifty miles in circumference:[1] and the number of inhabitants, during its most flourishing state, was, by some authors, computed at four millions.[2] Modern Rome is not above thirteen miles in circumference; and contains scarce 135,000 inhabitants: but reduced as this ancient Mistress of the world now is, in size and population, reduced too as her Papal throne has been in wealth and power, still, the matchless frescos of Raphael, Buonaroti, Danielo da Volterra, Giulio, Romano, Annibale Caracci, Guido, Domenichino, Guercino, etc., are unalienably hers; still the master-pieces of Grecian sculpture adorn her museums; still her stately palaces, noble churches, beautiful fountains, gigantic columns, stupendous obelisks, and peerless Coliseum, entitle her to be called the most magnificent city of Europe, and the unrivalled Mistress of the Arts!— Her streets, nevertheless, are ill paved and dirty; while ruins of immense edifices, which continually present themselves to view, give an impression of melancholy to every thinking spectator.

The society at Rome is excellent; and the circumstance of every man, whether foreigner or native, being permitted to live as he pleases, without exciting wonder, contributes essentially to general comfort. At Rome, too, every person may find amusement: for whether it be our wish to dive deep into classical knowledge, whether arts and sciences be our pursuit, or whether we merely seek for new ideas and new objects, the end cannot fail to be obtained in this most interesting of cities, where every stone is an historian: and though Rome has, in some respects, suffered from her late Rulers, the French, she is, generally speaking, obliged to them; as they removed the earth with which time had buried part of the Coliseum; disencumbered the temple of Vesta from the plaster-walls which destroyed its beauty; excavated the Forum of Trajan, the Baths of Titus, and the lower parts of the Temples of Concord and Jupiter Tonans; removed from the foundations of the arches of Septimius Severus and Constantine, the earth and rubbish, by which they were in some measure concealed, and ridded the Temple of Peace of an immense collection of earth, which entombed nearly one third of its remains.

I will now endeavour to point out the most convenient way of visiting the Antiquities, Churches, Palaces, etc.; mentioning the objects best worth notice only; in order to prevent Travellers from wasting their time, and burdening their memory, by a minute survey of what is not particularly interesting; and thereby, perhaps, depriving themselves of leisure to examine what really merits the closest attention. I shall begin with the Antiquities; previously

---

[1] The upper ranks of ancient Romans do not appear to have resided so much in the city as in villas not far distant: and this wall of fifty miles in circumference might probably enclose the suburbs of Rome, which must, judging from the remains now left, have been very extensive.

[2] Tacitus says, the Emperor Claudius made a lustrum, by which the number of inhabitants was found to be sixty-eight classes, consisting of one hundred and sixty-four thousand each.

observing, that whoever wishes to see these wrecks of ancient splendour to advantage, should visit them, for the first time, by the mild and solemn light of the moon; which not only assimilates with fallen greatness, but throws every defect into shadow; leaving Imagination to supply every beauty, and array every object in its pristine garb of magnificence.

Foro-Romano. There were two kinds of Forums in Rome, *Fora Civilia,* and *Fora Venalia*; the former serving as ornaments to the City, and likewise as Courts of Justice; the latter as Marketplaces. The forum Romanum was of the first kind; and here stood the Comitium and the Rostrum. The Comitium was a large apartment, for a considerable period, open at the top; it contained the tribunal, and ivory chair, whence the Chief-Magistrate administered justice. The Rostrum was so called because this building contained an Orator's pulpit, garnished with beaks of vessels, taken by the Romans, from the People of Antium.[1] The Forum Romanum is supposed to have extended in length, from the Chiesa della Consalazione to that of S. Adriano; and, in breadth, from the three Columns, called the Temple of Jove Stator, to the triumphal Arch of Septimius Severus.[2] It was built by Romulus, and surrounded with porticos by Tarquinius Priscus: little, however, now remains to be seen, except heaps of ruins, and piles of vegetable earth; the immense accumulation of which cannot be accounted for.

The *Via-Sacra,* so called in consequence of the peace concluded between Romulus and Tatius, and the sacrifices offered to the gods on that occasion, traversed the Forum Romanum, from the side near the Coliseum to the Arch of Septimius Severus; and in the middle of this Forum was the *Lacus-Curtius*; whence the fine *alto-rilievo* in the Villa-Borghese is said to have been taken.[3]

Tempio di Giove Tonante. This beautiful edifice was built by Augustus in consequence of his escape from lightning. Only three columns, with part of the frieze, now remain; and on the side of the latter are sacrificial instruments in *basso-rilievo,* namely, the *præficulum,* the *patera,* the *aspergillum,* the *securis* and *culter,* together with the *albogalerus,* a cap resembling a bishop's mitre, supposed to have been worn by the priests of Jove.

Tempio della Concordia. Furius Camillus erected this temple, in consequence of the reconciliation he effected between the Senate and people of Rome: it was consumed by fire, and rebuilt; but the portico only is remaining now; and consists, in front, of six Ionic granite columns, whose bases and capitals are white marble, with one column on each side. In this temple Cicero is supposed to have convoked the Senate which condemned Lentulus and Cethegus, the accomplices of Catiline.[4]

Arco di Settimio Severo, erected A. D. 205, in honour of the Emperor and his Sons, by the Senate and people of Rome. This arch

---

[1] The Latin word for ship-beaks is *rostra.*

[2] A distance of about 750 feet one way, and 500 the other.

[3] Rome is supposed to have been built in the mouth of an extinct volcano: and this opinion seems justified by the story of Curtius, and the account of the manner in which the Temple of Peace was destroyed.

[4] Some antiquaries imagine this to have been the Temple of Fortune; because the Temple of Concord is said to have fronted the Comitium.

was originally adorned with a triumphal car and six horses; in the car were two figures;[1] on each side was a foot soldier; and on each extremity of the attic, a soldier on horseback. The *bassirilievi* on the arch record the victories of Severus over the Parthians, and other uncivilized nations.

Tempio di Saturno, now *Chiesa di S. Adriano*. This temple, during the time of the Republic, was the treasury: but scarce any part of the original building now remains, except its brazen gate, which adorns the church of S. Giovanni in Laterano. The situation of the Chiesa di S. Adriano merits notice; as, before it, stood, according to Tacitus, the famous golden column, erected by Augustus, and called *Milliarium aureum*: whence the distance to every province was measured, and which is said to have been placed in the centre of ancient Rome. From this column the Roman roads branched off, in straight lines, to all parts of Italy.

Colonna di Phocas. This column, supposed originally to have adorned an ancient edifice, was erected, in the seventh century, on its present site, in honour of the Emperor Phocas, whose statue of bronze gilt is said to have stood on the top of the pillar.

Tempio di Antonino e Faustina, built A.D. 168, by the Roman Senate, in memory of their Emperor, Antoninus Pius, and his Consort, Faustina. The portico of this temple, now the Chiesa di S. Lorenzo in Miranda, is adorned with ten Corinthian columns of marble, called, by the Romans, Cipollino: the sides of the portico seem originally to have been incrusted with marble, now taken away; but a frieze of white marble, adorned with griffins, etc., still remains, and proves the ancient magnificence of the building.

Tempio di Giove Statore.[2] On the north side of the Via-Sacra, toward the Palatine hill, stand three beautiful columns of white marble, supposed to have been part of the portico of a temple consecrated to the above-named deity, by Romulus, on the spot where he rallied his soldiers who fled from the Sabines. Some persons suppose the *Comitium* to have made part of this edifice; but, be that as it may, the now remaining part must have been rebuilt when architecture was in much higher perfection than during the days of Romulus.

Chiesa di S. Maria Liberatrice. This Church is supposed by modern antiquaries to stand on the site of the original Temple of Vesta, erected by Numa, and bordering on the *Lacus-Curtius*. Near this Church are ruins of a square brick edifice, erected by Tullus Hostilius, and called *Curia Hostilia*: and on this side of the Forum, the Rostra,[3] the temples of Augustus,

---

[1] Probably the Sons of the Emperor, because he was prevented by the gout from assisting in the triumphal procession.

[2] Stator (στατωρ), he who makes to stop, or stand. When Cicero, in consequence of Catiline's conspiracy, convened the Senate in the Temple of Jupiter, he concluded his oration there by saying, "Whilst thou, Jupiter, whose worship was established with the foundation of this city; thou, whom we truly call *Stator*, the prop and stay of our empire:—Query, therefore, supposing the Senate to have assembled in the Capitol, whether the Temple of Jupiter Stator was not there?

[3] Pliny informs us, that the first sun-dial, set up for public use at Rome, was likewise placed on this spot, about the year U.C. 491.

and Castor and Pollux, together with the Basilica of Portius, are all supposed to have stood.

Tempio di Remo, now *Chiesa de' S. S. Cosimo e Damiano.* The bronze door, marble door-case, and porphyry columns, which adorn the outside of this building, appear to be antique; as does the rotunda which serves as a vestibule; but the body of the church seems to have been erected about the time of Constantine. In this temple was a pavement containing the plan of Rome, cut on white marble, probably in the reign of Septimius Severus and Caracalla; which plan, mutilated and unmethodized, is now fixed in the stair-case of the Museum of the Capitol.

The subterranean part of this temple merits notice.

Tempio della Pace. Vespasian, after terminating the war with Judea, raised this vast edifice upon the foundation of the portico of Nero's golden house, about the year 75: it was deemed the most magnificent temple of ancient Rome; being of a quadrangular form, three hundred feet long, and two hundred feet broad. It consisted of three naves, with three tribunes on each side; it was incrusted with bronze gilt, adorned with stupendous columns, and enriched with the finest statues and pictures of the Grecian school; particularly the celebrated work done by Protogenes, for the Rhodians, and representing Ialysus. Pliny likewise places here the statue of the Nile with sixteen children; probably that which now enriches the Vatican. The citizens deposited their wealth in this temple; and here, likewise, Titus Vespasian placed the spoils of Jerusalem; in short, it served as a public treasury, till about an hundred years after its foundation, when the whole building, with all the precious contents, are said to have been destroyed by fire, which issued suddenly from the bowels of the earth: and this record of the entire destruction of the temple, added to an idea that the style of architecture is not good enough for the days of Vespasian, has lately induced several persons to conjecture that these ruins, called the Temple of Peace, are, in fact, the remains of the Basilica of Constantine, which stood near the Colisæum. Little now can be traced of the building in question, except three immense arches, or tribunes, with part of the walls and roof, niches for statues, and doors of communication: but what serves to convey some idea of the grandeur of this edifice is one of the eight columns with which its interior was decorated, namely, a fluted Corinthian shaft of white marble, sixteen feet and a half in circumference, and, without base or capital, forty-eight feet high: it now stands before the church of S. Maria Maggiore.[1]

Tempio di Venere e Roma, near *the Chiesa di S. Francesca Romana.* This double temple had two fronts; and each front had a portico adorned with columns of rare marble. There are considerable remains of this temple; namely, two tribunes, great part of one of the side-walls, and the foundation and broken pillars of one of the porticos; all of which indicate that the edifice must have

---

[1] I presume not to judge whether these ruins did, or did not, make part of the Temple of Peace; but the edifice certainly appears to have been built in a style superior to that usually adopted in the days of Constantine, and very similar to the Temple of Venus and Rome.

been extremely magnificent: it was built after the designs of the Emperor Adrian; and the manner in which the roofs of the tribunes were stuccoed and ornamented resembles the style in which the remaining roofs of his villa near Tivoli were adorned.[1]

Arco di Tito, built by the Senate and people of Rome, and dedicated to Titus in honour of his conquest of Jerusalem. It consists of one large arch, over which is an attic story. Each front was originally adorned with four fluted composite columns. On the frieze is represented Titus's triumphal procession, together with the image of a river-god, probably the Jordan. Under the arch, on one side, is the Emperor seated in a triumphal car, conducted by the Genius of Rome, and attended by Victory, who is crowning him with laurels. On the other side of the arch are the spoils of the temple of Jerusalem, namely, the table of shew-bread; the tables of the law; the seven-branched golden candlestick; the jubilee trumpets, etc., copied, no doubt, from the originals, and therefore the only faithful representations extant of these sacred Jewish antiquities. The deification of Titus is represented on the roof of the inside of the arch. This edifice was nearly destroyed, that its ornaments might be placed elsewhere; but, nevertheless, enough remains to prove that it was the most beautiful building of its kind ever erected.[2]

Colosseo. This vast and majestic edifice is supposed to have derived its name of *Colisæum* from a colossal statue, one hundred and twenty feet high, of Nero, in the character of Apollo; which was placed here by Titus Vespasian, who, on the day when it first opened, is said to have had five thousand wild beasts killed in its arena.[3] The building was erected by Flavius Vespasian; and is supposed to stand where once were the fish-ponds of Nero; it consists of four stories, namely, three rows of porticoes, raised one above the other, and terminated by a lofty circular wall. The first story is adorned with Doric columns, the second with Ionic, the third with Corinthian columns, and the fourth with pilasters, between which are windows. The shape is an oval, computed to be one thousand six hundred and forty-one feet in circumference, and one hundred and fifty-seven feet in height. The arena, likewise, is an oval, of two hundred and seventy-eight feet long, by one hundred and seventy-seven wide. The materials of which the edifice is chiefly composed are immense blocks of Travertino,[4] originally fixed together with iron or bronze cramps, now taken away.[5] The entrances were eighty in number, seventy-six being for the people, two for the Gladiators,[6] and two for the Em-

---

[1] The name of the Temple seems allusive to the boasted descent of the Romans from Æneas, the son of Venus.

[2] Judea is always represented, on the medals struck by Titus, as a woman sitting on the ground in a posture denoting sorrow.

[3] So called, because strewed with *sand*, that the blood of the slain might not make the place slippery.

[4] A stone much used in large buildings at Rome.

[5] The cramps were fastened with melted lead.

[6] Gladiatorial shows were exhibited in this Amphitheatre till the year 404; when an Eastern Monk, named Almachius, or Telemachus, rushed into the arena, and endeavoured to separate the combatants: the Prætor, Alypius, who enjoyed these horrid sights, ordered the Gladiators to slay the Monk: they obeyed; but he was canonized; and Honorius abolished the shows.

peror and his suite: and within the walls were twenty staircases, leading to seats appropriated to the different classes of spectators. Round the arena was a high wall; immediately above which stood the *podium,* or balcony, for the Emperor, and the seats for the Vestal Virgins, Senators, and Magistrates, entitled to curule chairs; and behind these seats rose others, in four divisions, the last of which were appropriated to the populace. The seats are supposed to have contained eighty-seven thousand spectators; and the gallery above them twenty thousand. There was an awning which stretched over the whole edifice, in case of rain, or intense heat: and in the wall of the uppermost story are square holes, supposed to have contained the rings for fastening the cords of this awning. The arches of the first row of porticos are numbered on the outside; probably to enable the various classes of spectators to find, without difficulty, their destined place. Two gates led into the arena; the one being opposite to the Temple of Venus and Rome, the other on the side of the *Mons-Cœlius;* and, near the latter entry, Pius VII. has recently raised a noble buttress, to prevent this part of the Colisæum from falling. Soldiers, likewise, are constantly stationed here, to guard the edifice from mischief; and also to protect Travellers, who may wish to examine this stupendous pile by moonlight.

Near the Colisæum, toward the Via-Sacra, are remains of a Fountain called the *Meta Sudans;* which supplied the persons who assisted at the shows with water; and might, perhaps, be used in filling the arena for the *Naumachiæ* frequently exhibited there.

Arco di Costantino, dedicated to that Emperor by the senate and people of Rome, in memory of his victory over Maxentius at the Ponte-Molle. This arch stands at the junction of the Celian and Palatine hills, in the *Via-Appia:* and is the most splendid, because the best preserved edifice, of its kind, remaining in Rome. It has, on each side, four fluted Corinthian columns, seven being giallo antico, and one white marble; and on the pilasters, above these columns, are statues of Dacian warriors. The *bassi-rilievi* on the frieze, representing the conquest of Verona, and the victory at the Ponte-Molle, together with the four figures of Fame, and the two medallions on the side of the arch, are proofs of the decline of sculpture under Constantine: the other *bassi-rilievi,* two excepted below the great arcade (which were also done in the time of Constantine), are finely executed, and supposed to have been taken either from the Arch or Forum of Trajan. One of these, fronting the Colisæum, represents the triumphal entry of Trajan into Rome; and another, on the opposite side, represents him in the act of offering the sacrifice called *Suovetaurilia.* The Statues of Dacian warriors, the Columns of giallo antico, and all the Cornices, were taken from the Arch of Trajan.

Chiesa di S. Teodoro. Immediately behind the *Forum Romanum,* on the way to the *Forum Boarium,* stands this small Rotunda, anciently the Temple of Romulus; and erected on the spot where he was discovered. The bronze wolf, now preserved in the Capitol, originally enriched this temple.¹ On the outside of the door of entrance is a pagan altar. The ancient walls of the Temple are perfect, and exhibit withinside three large niches for statues. The roof is modern. The old Roman custom of carrying sick infants to this Temple still continues; although the building is now consecrated to Christian worship. The interior of the edifice may be seen every Sunday morning, from eight o'clock till ten; and every Thursday morning, from seven o'clock till eight. Near this spot was the Lupercal.

Arco di Settimio Severo in Velabro. This Arch was erected by the *Argentarii*, bankers, and merchants of the *Forum Boarium*, to Septimius Severus, his Empress, Julia, and their Son, Caracalla. The sculpture resembles, in style, that on the triumphal Arch of Severus. Adjoining to this Arch, is the Church of *S. Giorgio in Velabro*, supposed to stand on the site of the *Basilica of Sempronius*.

Arco di Giano Quadrifronte. This building, composed of immense blocks of white Greek marble, was once adorned with columns, which have disappeared. The brick-work above the cornice is of the middle ages. The edifice seems originally to have been either a market-house, or an exchange, of which there were several in ancient Rome, almost every Forum being provided with one of them.²

To the left of the Arch of Janus Quadrifrons is a small stream of limpid water; which discharges itself into the Cloaca-Maxima; and which tradition reports to be *the Lake of Juturna*, where Castor and Pollux were seen to water their horses after the battle at the *Lacus-Regillus*.

Cloaca-Maxima. This great common sewer was constructed, by Tarquinius Priscus, of rude stones, regularly placed, but without cement, and forming three rows of arches: it entered the Tiber between the *Pons-Senatorius* and the Temple of Vesta; and its mouth may be discovered when the river is low. Part of this building lies close to the Arch of Janus.³

Near to the Palatine, or Senatorian Bridge, now called the *Ponte-Rotto*, are remains of an edifice, denominated *the House of Pilate*, but really that of Nicholas Crescens, supposed to have been the son of Pope John x.

Chiesa di S. Maria in Cosmedin, conjectured to be the Temple of Modesty, erected by Virginia, the wife of Volumnius. This edifice stands a little to the left of the Temple of Jupiter Stator: in the portico is an ancient mask; probably intended as the ornament of a fountain; but, in consequence of an idea once prevalent among the populace, that oracles issued from it, called *Bocca della Verità.* Judging by the fine antique marble columns,

---

¹ Venuti says, the Temple of Romulus was preserved a great while in its original state of simplicity; by way of recalling to the remembrance of the Romans the simple manners of their ancestors.

² There were, in this quarter, beside the *Forum Boarium*, the Forums *Olitorium* and *Piscatorium*.

³ Pliny says, that the *Cloacæ*, or Common Sewers, were the most surprising public works at Rome; being cut through hills, and under the very foundations of the city; and, moreover, so spacious that a cart loaded with hay might pass through them. Common sewers were unknown in Greece, and invented by the Romans. The smaller *Cloacæ* all communicated with the *Cloaca Maxima*: these *Cloacæ* were continually cleansed, by streams of water resembling rivers.

discoverable in the walls of this church, the edifice must have been originally large and handsome; the pavement consists of porphyry and other precious marbles; the high altar is adorned with an ancient bath or sarcophagus of red Egyptian granite; and in the tribuna is an ancient pontifical chair.

The first *Custode* of Arcadia, Giovanni Mario Crescimbeni, was buried in this church; his monument is near the great door.

Tempio di Vesta, now *Chiesa di S. Maria del Sole*. When this Temple was erected is uncertain; but it is said to have been repaired by Domitian. Here are nineteen beautiful Corinthian fluted columns of Parian marble, which stand on several steps, and form a circular portico round a Cella, likewise circular; the wall of which is also composed of blocks of Parian marble; and so exquisitely are these materials joined, that they appear to be only one piece. The ancient roof was bronze; but this, together with the entablature, and one of the columns (for there were twenty,) can no longer be found. Here, according to some opinions, the Vestal Virgins kept the celebrated Palladium and the sacred fire. [1]

Tempio della Fortuna Virile, now *Chiesa di S. Maria Egiziaca*. This Temple is supposed to have been erected by Servius Tullius; but the elegant fluted columns with which it is adorned prove that it must have been repaired at a later period. It seems, like many of the ancient Roman edifices, to have suffered from fire; in order to conceal the effects of which, perhaps, the fine stucco that covers the columns and entablature might be employed. The form of this temple is Grecian; the columns are Ionic; and the ornaments of the entablature, though injured by time, are still visible.

Palazzo de' Cesari. On the *Mons Palatinus*, where Romulus founded Rome, Augustus began, and Domitian finished, the splendid Palace of her Emperors; which, like a little city, covered the hill. The form of this palace nearly a parallelogram, may still be traced; and ruins of one half are discoverable in the Orti Farnesiani; and of the other half in the Garden belonging to the English College, the Convent of S. Bonaventura, and the Garden of the Villa-Spada. The entrance seems to have been from the *Via Sacra*. The Gardens of Adonis, on each side of which was a Hippodrome, belonged to this imperial residence; and the Claudian Aqueduct supplied it with water.

In order to see every thing now remaining, the best way is to drive nearly up to the Arch of Titus, then turn to the right, and, a little way on, is a gate, which opens into the Orto Farnesiani. After entering this garden, and ascending some steps that lead to three small dilapidated modern edifices, one of which surmounted by a turret, contains frescos, which, though much injured, merit notice, you are presented with a beautiful view of the Temple of Peace: and, further on, is the

---

[1] Vestal Virgins were so called from their goddess Vesta, or fire: Vesta being derived from the Hebrew root אש fire; whence the Greek Εστα, fire, and the Latin Vesta.

The Vestal Virgins were bound to keep the sacred fire unextinguished; and likewise to reconcile persons who quarrelled with each other.

The temples of Vesta were always circular; perhaps in allusion to the sun.

spot where the Arcadian Academy originally assembled,¹ amidst ever-green oaks, wood-laurels, and fragments of the entablature, frieze, cornices, and capitals of columns, which seem to have once belonged to the Temple of Apollo, built by Augustus, after the victory of Actium: for, among the decorations of the frieze and cornice, are griffins and tridents interlaced with dolphins; symbols of a naval triumph: and moreover, griffins were consecrated to Apollo. These finely executed fragments are now overgrown by the acanthus; which flourishes here so luxuriantly that one might fancy it planted on purpose to point out the source of Corinthian architectural ornaments. Here lies neglected, on the grass, the original medallion of the arms of Arcadia, the Syrinx of Pan encircled with pine and laurel; which medallion once adorned the place of meeting. This garden likewise contains two small subterranean apartments, commonly called *the Baths of Livia;* in which, by the aid of torches, remains may be discovered of beautiful arabesques, and a considerable quantity of gilding, bright as if just done: here also are small *bassi-rilievi,* in stucco. Beyond the baths of Livia is a dilapidated villa of modern date, adorned with frescos,² probably by Raphael's scholars: and from a terrace here, the view of Rome, and its environs, is magnificent. Returning hence, and going round that part of the garden which fronts the Capitol, you find a considerable number of subterranean buildings; some of which resemble the Sette Salle belonging to Titus's Baths; and might probably, like them, have served as reservoirs for water. This garden also contains ruins of the Theatre built by Caligula; and a spacious Hall, the roof of which is well preserved.

On quitting the Orti Farnesiani, and continuing to ascend the Palatine hill, you find, on the left, the Chiesa di S. Bonaventura; previous to reaching which, turn through a gate-way, on the right, that leads to the Villa-Spada, a modern edifice, built on the foundations of some part of the imperial residence; and, probably, that called Nero's Golden House.³ On entering this Villa, you find a portico adorned with frescos, all of which, except one that represents Venus, and is attributed to Raphael, are by Giulio Romano,

---

1 The Arcadian Academy, one of the most celebrated in Europe, was founded in the year 1690, and warmly patronised by Christina of Sweden and the Literati of her time. Its members, at the commencement of the institution, met in the Farnese Garden; and, afterward, at the Bosco Parrasio, on the Janiculum hill: but, at present, they assemble in a house provided for them by the Roman Government; and in which resides their *Custode Generale,* the learned and venerable Abate Godart.

2 Among the frescos are two medallions representing the story of Hercules and Cacus. The Cave of this famous robber, according to the fable, stood between the Tiber and the Temple of Hercules (now, according to some writers, the Church of S. Alexius), on the Aventine Hill.

3 Nero's Golden House (*Domus Aurea*) joined the Imperial Palace of Augustus; and is supposed to have extended over the whole of the Celian Hill. Under the steeple of the Church of S. John and S. Paul are Ruins of a noble Portico, which is said to have belonged to this golden house: and foundations of other buildings, which probably belonged to it likewise, may be traced the whole way from the Villa Spada to the Esquiline Hill. It had a triple portico, supported by a thousand columns: it contained accommodations for animals, both wild and tame; and in the vaulted roofs of the banqueting rooms were machines of ivory that turned round, and, from pipes, scattered flowers and perfumes. The principal eating room was a rotunda, so constructed that it turned round night and day, in imitation of the motion of the earth; and the baths were supplied with sea-water, and the sulphureous waters of Albulæ.

who has painted, on the roof, two small pictures, representing Hercules, some of the Muses, and other heathen divinities. The garden of the Villa contains three ancient subterranean Apartments, which are beautiful in point of architecture, and well preserved: they seem originally to have been adorned with arabesques, judging from the remains now distinguishable: and, here was found the superb basin of red porphyry which adorns the circular hall in the Vatican Museum. Beyond these subterranean apartments, and quite at the end of the garden, are a few balustrades; said, by some authors, to mark the spot where the signal for commencing the games in the Circus Maximus was given. To the left of this spot is a large oblong Court, supposed to have been a Hippodrome; and a magnificent Hall, the roof of which is entire, and decorated with medallions in stucco. [1]

The Garden of the Convent of S. Bonaventura contains ruins of the Aqueduct, erected by Nero, as a continuation of the Claudian aqueduct, to supply his golden house with water.

From the Villa-Spada go back to the Arch of Titus, pass that of Constantine; and, when nearly parallel with the Church of S. Gregorio sul Monte-Celio, turn to the right toward the Forum-Boarium, and you will find a door, leading, by a narrow flight of steps, to what is now called the *Palazzo de' Cesari*, in the Garden of the English College. Here are considerable vestiges of stately porticos, spacious halls, and numberless arches, interspersed with ever-green oaks, laurels, flowering shrubs, aloes, and Indian figs; forming altogether a most picturesque and impressive scene. One part of these ruins completely overlooks the Circus Maximus, which lies immediately below it; and here is a terrace, probably the site of the banqueting hall of the Emperors, whence Nero threw down his napkin, as the signal for beginning the games, when the populace were clamorous for their commencement; and where Caligula, on being roused from sleep, by a similar clamour, ordered the Gladiators to drive away the people; in consequence of which cruel command, several were killed. The ancient pavement of the terrace still remains entire: and, from this spot, the continuation of the Claudian Aqueduct, by Nero, may be seen to great advantage. Fragments of ancient paintings are discoverable throughout all the ruins of the Palazzo de' Cesari.

Circus Maximus, made, by Tarquinius Priscus, between the Palatine and Aventine hills. The length of this Circus is computed to have been four stadia, or furlongs; and its breadth the same: it contained a trench ten feet deep, and as many broad, to receive water; together with seats for one hundred and fifty thousand spectators: it was much beautified by succeeding princes; and particularly by Julius Cæsar, Augustus,

---

[1] The Villa Spada was shown to me, with great civility and patience, by a man in appearance poverty-stricken; who, when I offered him the usual fee, and indeed strongly pressed him to accept it, answered (while the blood mounted to his cheeks), "I take no money: I am placed here as a penance for my sins, which are manifold. I have continued here three years; how much longer I may be doomed to remain, I know not: but I can accept no gratuity whatsoever."

Caligula, Domitian, Trajan, and Heliogabalus; and enlarged to so vast an extent, as to receive, in their respective seats, two hundred and sixty thousand spectators: its form, with the trench and water running through its centre, may still be traced.

Chiesa di S. Gregoria sul Monte-celio, said to be built on the foundations of a Patrician house, and to retain its ancient shape. This church is finely situated; and in the adjoining Garden are three Chapels, built by S. Gregorio. The first, dedicated to his mother, S. Silvia, contains her statue, by Niccolo Cordieri; frescos on the ceiling, by Guido; and four saints in *chiaro scuro*, by the same master. The second Chapel contains two celebrated frescos; the one painted by Domenichino, the other by Guido, in order to prove which was the better artist. That done by Domenichino represents the flagellation of S. Andrew!! that by Guido represents the same Saint going to suffer martyrdom!! The figures of S. Peter and S. Paul, near the altar, are by Guido. The third Chapel contains a statue of S. Gregorio, begun by Buonaroti, and finished by Cordieri. This garden commands a beautiful view of the Palace of the Cæsars.[1]

Terme di Tito. These Baths, which, twenty years since, were completely choked up with rubbish and vegetable earth, apparently thrown in to destroy them, are now open to the light of day; and exhibit beautiful frescos in as perfect preservation as they could have been when first produced by the artist's pencil near two thousand years ago. The Romans learnt the use of baths from the Greeks; and though, at first, employed merely for the purposes of health; they in time became an object of luxury and magnificence. The Baths of Titus were smaller than those of Diocletian and Caracalla: but superior in point of architecture, and more elegantly ornamented: the lower part of the edifice served for bathing; the upper part for academies and gymnastic exercises. Communicating with the Baths are ruins called the Palace of Titus, where the group of Laocoon and his children was found; and, not far hence, the Belvedere-Antinous, or, according to Visconti, Mercury, was found likewise. Near this spot were the gardens of Mecænas; in a building belonging to which Nero stood to see Rome in flames: and near this spot also were the houses of Horace and Virgil. The Baths of Titus are damp.

To the east of the Palace and Baths of Titus, and enclosed within a garden, are immense reservoirs, called *Sette Salle*, which evidently belonged to the Baths, and are in tolerable preservation.

Chiesa di S. Martine in Monte. This beautiful church, not far distant from the Sette Salle, is erected upon that part of the Baths of Titus which was added by Domitian and Trajan: such, at least, seems to be the opinion of antiquaries; because the brickwork in these Baths is very inferior to that in the Baths built by Titus.

The modern edifice is adorned with twenty-four magnificent co-

---

[1] By entering the quadrangle, and ringing a bell on the right, you may always gain admittance to the Church and Chapels of S. Gregorio: they are, during winter, damp and cold.

lumns, brought from Adrian's Villa at Tivoli. The Vase for holy water is ancient. The high-altar, erected about twenty years ago, is peculiarly rich in precious marbles; the paintings which adorn its vicinity were done by Antonio Cavalluccio, who lies buried here. The side aisles are embellished with landscapes, by Gasparo Poussin; the figures in which are by Niccolo Poussin; and the upper landscapes are remarkably well preserved. The Chapel of the Madonna, at the end of the left side aisle, is ornamented with paintings by Cavalluccio, and very fine marbles. The steps leading down to the Burial-Place under the high-altar, and the burial-place itself, were designed by Pietro di Cortona: and here are other stairs, leading to the ancient subterranean Church, which is a part of the Baths, called those of Titus, and famous for being the spot where Pope S. Silvestro held a council, assisted by Constantine and his mother. The mosaic pavement, and matted roof of the baths (on which perhaps were paintings), still remain perfect; as do the walls; and here you encounter no very damp air; therefore invalids may go down with safety.

Chiesa di S. Pietro in Vincoli. This fine Church, which owes its present form to Antonio Sangallo, has a double cupola, like that of S. Peter's. The three aisles are divided by twenty magnificent Doric columns of Grecian marble taken from Diocletian's Baths: the circular wall behind the high-altar made a part of Titus's Baths; whence the pavement of the Sacristy likewise was taken. Here is a picture of S. Margherita, by Guercino. Here also is the Monument of Julius II., designed by Buonaroti, who died soon after he had finished the much-admired figure of Moses; in consequence of which the other figures were done by Montelupo. The Monuments of Cardinals Margotti and Agucci were executed after the designs of Domenichino: and at the end of the tribuna is an ancient pontifical Chair in high preservation. The Sacristy contains a picture, by Domenichino, of S. Peter delivered from prison.

Chiesa di S. Maria della Navicella, so called from the model of an ancient galley, said to have been a votive offering, and placed before it, by Leo X. This Church, designed by Raphael, and supposed to stand on the site of the ancient *Castra Peregrina,* or barracks for auxiliary soldiers, is embellished with fine columns of porphyry and granite, and a frieze beautifully painted in *chiaroscuro,* by Giulio Romano and Pierino del Vaga. The Presbytery, likewise, was painted by the same artists; as were two Altar-Pieces of the Chapels, one representing part of the Transfiguration, the other the Baptism of our Saviour.

Near this spot is the Arch of the Consul Dolabella, over which Nero erected the Aqueduct that supplied his Golden House with water.

Chiesa di S. Stefano Rotondo. formerly the Temple of Claudius. This beautiful and interesting edifice was built by Agrippina, in honour of her husband Claudius; destroyed by Nero, and rebuilt by Vespasian; which accounts for the columns not being uniform. It seems to have had two entrances. The interior part still retains the precise form, together with all the majesty of an ancient temple; and is embellished with a double row of columns, fifty-eight in number, and chiefly granite. The roof is modern. This edifice was converted into a Christian Church by Pope S. Simplicius: it is, during winter, damp and cold.[1]

Obelisk of the Piazza del Popolo; said to have been made at Heliopolis, 522 years before the Christian era. It was brought to Rome by Augustus; found in the Circus Maximus; and placed in its present situation by Sixtus v. Its height, from the ground to the top of the cross, is 112 feet.

To record the exploits of heroes, and to decorate their temples and their tombs, seems to have been the origin of Egyptian obelisks: and most of those which now adorn Rome are engraved with hieroglyphics; which, could we understand them, might throw important lights on the history of past ages.

Obelisk of the Trinità de' Monti. This Obelisk formerly stood in the Circus of Sallust, and was placed in its present situation by Pius VI.: it is forty-four feet and a half in height, without the pedestal, and of Egyptian granite.[2]

Villa-Medici, now the French Academy. On the back-front of this Villa is a fine *basso-rilievo* of Hercules strangling the Nemean lion. The Garden of the Villa-Medici is always open to the public.

Statues, and Obelisk, in the Piazza di Monte-Cavallo; so called, from the admirable sculpture with which it is embellished; namely, two colossal figures, supposed to represent Castor and Pollux, each holding a horse. These twin-gods, the works of Phidias and Praxiteles, are esteemed the finest things of their description at Rome; especially that done by the first-mentioned artist. They once adorned Athens; and are generally supposed to have been brought to Rome, from Alexandria, by Constantine, in whose Baths they were found; though some authors tell us they were sent to Nero, as a present, from Tiridates, king of Armenia. The horses are ill executed, and chiefly modern. The Obelisk, which stands between the statues, was erected by Pius VI.: it is composed of red granite; measures forty-five feet, without the pedestal; and originally adorned the Mausoleum of Augustus.[3]

Chiesa di S. Bernardo. This edifice, the ancient form and roof of which are quite perfect, merits notice, as belonging to Diocletian's Baths. Some persons suppose it to have been a *Calidarium balneum*, or hot bath; but the more general opinion is, that this rotunda, and the one opposite to it, near the Villa-Negroni, were temples dedicated to Apollo and Æsculapius. The convent and garden of the Monks of S. Bernardo, the church, convent, and garden of the Carthusians, the public granaries, together with a large space, called Piazza di Ter-

---

[1] The churches of La Navicella and S. Stefano Rotondo are generally shut: but the Sacristan of the former lives in the vicinity; and the Sacristan of the latter may be found daily, at the new Academy of S. Luke.

[2] The Promenade on the Trinità de' Monti, begun by the French, and now nearly finished by the present Pope, is the pleasantest walk and drive at Rome.

[3] The circular Basin belonging to the Fountain of Monte-Cavallo is said to be the largest piece of granite of this description, in Rome.

mini, a corruption of the word *Thermæ*, all likewise belonged to Diocletian's Baths; which building seems to have been nearly of a square form, enclosing halls, where the youth were instructed, and where men of learning assembled to read their compositions; an open theatre, where shows were exhibited in fine weather; the *Natatio*, the *Sphæristerium*; the *Xystum*; the *Apodyterium*; the *Hypocaustum*; and the different baths, namely, *frigidarium, tepidarium, caldarium*, and *laconicum*. Three sides of the *Natatio*, where people swam in the open air, were bounded by porticos (it occupied what is now the cloister of the Carthusians); on each side of these porticos were *Basilicæ* and *Diætæ*, where public assemblies were held, and sumptuous entertainments given: adjoining to these apartments was an oblong room, probably the place for playing at ball;[1] and, immediately behind the *Natatio*, was the *Xystum*, where the gladiators and wrestlers exhibited in bad weather; this is now the Church of S. Maria degli Angeli. The baths, properly so named, extended in a straight line opposite to the *Theatridium* and *Bibliothecæ* : the *Apodyterium*, or great hall, where the bathers undressed and dressed themselves, was in the centre of the baths. In the centre of the baths likewise was the *Hypocaustum*, or great stove; whence hot water was conveyed, in pipes, and hot air, in flues, to the different chambers: and this part of the building, which is still preserved, serves as an *Atrium* to the Carthusian church. In the Villa Negroni are remains of the great reservoir; and round the exterior of the Baths were walks shaded with plane-trees.[2]

Chiesa di S. Maria degli Angeli. Pius IV. dedicated Diocletian's Baths to sacred uses; because the Christians who built them suffered martyrdom: and Buonaroti, who was employed to erect the church, finding, among the ruins of these baths, an immense apartment, supported by stupendous columns of oriental granite (the *Xystum* already mentioned), formed it into the present Church of S. Maria degli Angeli. The entrance to this majestic edifice, which may vie with S. Peter's in beauty, was a *Caldarium* belonging to the baths, and contains the Monuments of Carlo Maratta and Salvator Rosa. The church itself is in the shape of a Greek cross: the nave is 179 feet long; its height 105 feet; and the antique columns, already mentioned, are sixteen feet in circumference by forty-three high. The pavement is beautiful, and contains a celebrated meridian by Monsignore Bianchini. Near the high

---

[1] The ancient Romans played with several kinds of balls: namely, the *Harpastum*, or foot-ball, which, being placed between two companies of young men, they strove who should drive it through the others' goal: the *Pila*, so called from being stuffed with hair: the *Follis*, so called from being made of a bladder; and with this old men and young children played: the *Paganica*, a ball stuffed with feathers; which derived its name from villages, where it was chiefly seen: and the *Trigonalis*, an appellation common to the *Pila* and *Follis*, and allusive to the form of the tennis-courts where these balls were used.

[2] The expense of bathing in a public bath at Rome was equivalent to about one halfpenny for an adult; but, for a child, nothing: the rich, however, had their persons rubbed with oils and ointments of great value. Hot baths were only used at a stated hour of the evening. Each man stopped at the bath which he judged proper for himself: and if he made use of the *Laconicum*, he returned through the different hot baths; and was thus cooled gradually, before he reached the *apodyterium*.

altar is a picture, by Carlo Maratta, of the Baptism of Our Saviour, much injured by time; and another of the Martyrdom of S. Sebastian, by Domenichino, in good preservation!! This church also contains a fine picture of the Fall of Simon Magus, by Pompeio Battoni; and another of S. Peter raising Tabitha, by Placido Costanza.

The Pope's Oil-Cellar, near S. Maria degli Angeli, merits notice, as it is a well-preserved part of Diocletian's Baths.

Obelisk of S. Maria Maggiore. This obelisk is of red Egyptian granite, and forty-three feet in height, without the pedestal: it was brought to Rome by the Emperor Claudius; and served as one of the ornaments to the Mausoleum of Augustus; whence it was taken, by Sixtus v., and placed in its present situation.

Column in the Piazza di S. Maria Maggiore. This Corinthian fluted column, of Parian marble, was taken from the Temple of Peace; and measures fifty-eight feet in height, without its pedestal.

Basilica di S. Maria Maggiore.[1] This Church, which stands on the summit of the Esquiline Hill, was erected upon the foundations of an ancient temple of Juno-Lucina, about the year 352; and afterward enlarged by Sixtus III. It was likewise repaired by Benedict XIV.; who found, about eight palms below the pavement of the church, a black and white mosaic marble pavement, which is of that kind invented by Alexander Severus.[2] The nave is supported by antique Ionic columns, thirty-six of which are white marble, and four granite. The Baldacchino is supported by antique columns of porphyry. The arch which separates the choir from the nave is adorned with mosaics of the fifth century. The chapel of Sextus V., built after the designs of Fontana, is incrusted with fine marbles, and adorned with Corinthian pilasters, *bassi-rilievi*, and paintings. On the right stand the tomb and statue of Sixtus V.: in the middle is the altar of the Holy Sacrament, decorated with a magnificent tabernacle, supported by four angels of bronze gilt; and on the left, the tomb of Pius V. Among the paintings those most admired are, the Annunciation, by Pompeio Battoni, and the Holy Family, by Agostino Masucci. The Borghese-Chapel, built by Paul V., is peculiarly rich in marbles, paintings, and sculpture. On the right stands the tomb of the above-named Pontiff, surmounted by his statue: here, likewise, are statues of S. Basil and David, by Niccolo Cordieri; and the tomb and statue of Clement VIII.; with statues of Aaron and S. Bernardo, by Cordieri of Lorrain. The paintings between the windows, and on the arches above the tombs, are by Guido!! The altar of the Madonna is magnificently adorned with oriental jasper, agate, and lapis lazuli; and on its entablature is a fine *basso-rilievi*. The frescos above, and round the altar,

---

[1] Several of these ancient Courts of Justice, called *Basilicæ*, were converted into churches, and still retain their original appellation.

[2] These Mosaic Pavements of the middle ages were called *Opus Alexandrinum*, from the inventor. Mosaics, however, seem to have been originally invented by the Persians: for they were used in Persia during the reign of Artaxerxes; thence carried into Assyria, thence to Greece, and, some ages after, to Rome.

and in the vault and angles of the cupola, are by the Cav. d'Arpino. The Sforza-Chapel was designed by Buonaroti. This Basilica is so loaded with gilding and other ornaments, that it resembles a place of public diversion more than a Christian temple.

Obelisk of S. Giovanni in Laterano. This obelisk is the largest at Rome; and supposed to have been even more lofty once, than it is a present. It was originally placed in the Temple of the Sun, at Thebes, by Rameses King of Egypt, transported to Rome by the son of Constantine, and erected, in its present situation, by Sixtus v.: its height, without base or pedestal, is one hundred and fifteen feet, and its diameter nine.

Battisterio di Costantino. This edifice was built by Constantine, and repaired by Gregory XIII. and Urban VIII.: its form is octagon; and three steps lead down to the font, which is an ancient tomb of marble of Ponsevero. The dome is supported by fine porphyry columns, with an antique entablature; and adorned with paintings representing the life of S. John Baptist, by Andrea Sacchi. Other paintings, on the walls, represent the vision of Constantine; his battle with Maxentius; and the destruction of the Idols; which last is by Carlo Maratta. In one of the Chapels are two curious fluted pillars of verde antique; in the other, two columns of oriental alabaster; and the original entrance to this Baptistery is adorned with two noble pillars of porphyry and an antique entablature.

Basilica di S. Giovanni in Laterano.[1] This stately edifice was erected by Constantine; and called the mother church of Rome; though the church of S. Martin and S. Luke is really so. The great portico is adorned with a colossal statue of Constantine, found in his baths; the front of the building, toward the Naples-gate, is beautiful; and the bronze-door, ornamented with *bassi-rilievi*, was taken from the Temple of Saturn. The interior of the church is divided, by four rows of pilasters, into one large, and four small aisles; and the centre aisle, or nave, is adorned with statues of the Apostles; among which are Saints Thomas and Bartholomew, by Le Gros; and S. Andrew, S. James minor, and S. John, by Rusconi. The pavement is mosaic. The altar of the Holy Sacrament is adorned with four magnificent fluted columns of bronze gilt, supposed to have been taken from the Temple of Jupiter Capitolinus; and, above these columns, is a fresco, by the Cav. d'Arpino, representing the ascension of our Saviour into Heaven! The tabernacle, formed of precious marbles, is placed between two Angels of bronze gilt, and four columns of verde antique. At the top of the centre-aisle, near the high-altar, are two noble columns of red granite; and, near the door leading to the Baptistery, two fluted columns of giallo antico, deemed the finest specimens extant of that marble.

---

[1] The name of *Laterano* is supposed to be derived from Plautius Lateranus, Consul elect, who engaged with Seneca and others in the great conspiracy against Nero, and thereby lost his life: hence his palace, having been confiscated, probably remained in possession of the Emperors, till Constantine gave it to the Church, and built the Basilica of S. Giovanni, properly the Pope's Cathedral.

In this church are the Tombs of the Cav. d'Arpino, Andrea Sacchi, and Boniface VIII.; the last of which is ornamented with a fresco, supposed to have been done by Giotto, and representing Boniface, between two Cardinals, publishing the first jubilee of the holy year, in 1300. The Corsini-Chapel (to the left of the great door) is particularly elegant; and was erected by Clement XII., in honour of his ancestor S. Andrea Corsini. Over the altar, between two verde antique columns, is a portrait, in mosaic, beautifully copied from a painting by Guido, of S. Andrea Corsini. On one side of the chapel is the monument of Clement XII.; said to have been once the tomb of Agrippa: it was taken from the Pantheon; and is, in point of shape, the most beautiful sarcophagus extant. On the opposite side stands the tomb of Cardinal Neri Corsini. In this chapel, likewise, are four statues, representing the four cardinal virtues; one of which, Fortitude, is by Rusconi, and much admired; as are the four *bassi-rilievi* in the upper part of the chapel. The pavement is beautiful; and the subterranean part of this building merits notice; as it is simple and appropriate, and contains a fine *Pietà*. In the Sacristy of S. Giovanni in Laterano is an Annunciation, designed, if not executed, by Buonaroti.

Scala Santa. This Edifice is celebrated for containing twenty-seven steps of white marble, reputed to have belonged to the Palace of Pilate.

Not far hence is an Arch, or Tribune, adorned with the famous *Triclinium* of S. Leo; a mosaic originally placed in the eating room of the palace of that Pope, to perpetuate the event of his having crowned Charlemagne Emperor of the west.

Anfiteatro Castrense. This building now makes part of the wall of Rome, near the Naples-gate; though it formerly stood on the outside of the city: it was called *Castrensis,* because appropriated to military games, and combats between soldiers and wild beasts. The interior of the building may be seen in a garden on the right of the Church of S. Croce in Gerusalemme; nothing, however, remains, except a few arches. The exterior part, which was adorned with two rows of columns, should be viewed from the outside of the Naples-gate.

Basilica di Santa Croce in Gerusalemme. This Church, one of the seven *Basilicæ* of Rome, was erected by Constantine near an ancient *Sessorium;* which seems to have been converted into the entrance of the church; and makes a magnificent vestibule. The approach from S. Giovanni in Laterano to S. Croce in Gerusalemme, is particularly handsome; and exhibits fine remains of the Aurelian Wall of Rome: the latter church derives its name from part of the Cross which S. Helena brought from Jerusalem, and deposited here. On each side of the great door is a Vase for holy water, very similar to those in the Cathedral at Siena; and, like them, containing marble fishes beautifully executed. The nave is supported by eight fine columns of Egyptian granite; and its ceiling adorned with a fresco by Conrad Giaquinto; who likewise painted that part of the ceiling of the Tribuna which is over the high-altar: the other part was done by Pinturicchio, and represents the finding of the Cross. The high-altar is adorned with four rare columns of breccia corallina, and an ancient sarcophagus of basalt. The pavement of the church is antique. This edifice contains the subterranean Chapel of S. Helena, adorned with curious ancient mosaics, and an inscription in her honour.

On the right, coming out of the church, is a Garden, which exhibits considerable remains of a building, called *the Temple of Venus and Cupid*; but, more probably, one of the halls, or temples, which adorned the Baths of S. Helena. This Garden likewise exhibits magnificent remains of the *Claudian Aqueduct*: and, not far hence, was an Altar consecrated to bad Fortune.

Chiesa di S. Bibiana.[1] Here are eight antique columns; and a fine antique sarcophagus of oriental alabaster, with a leopard's head in its centre: and here, likewise, is a celebrated statue of S. Bibiana, by Bernini!

Tempio di Minerva-Medica. This picturesque ruin stands in a garden, the door of which is generally open. The temple is round without, but decagon within; and seems to have had six windows and nine niches for statues. Here was found a celebrated statue of Minerva, with a serpent at her feet: but, whether this building was dedicated to Minerva-Medica or not, seems uncertain. In the same garden is *the Aruntian Sepulchre;* together with *subterranean vaulted Apartments*, supposed to have been the receptacles of the Plebeian Dead; whose ashes were consigned to small earthenware urns, simply inscribed with a name, and an exclamation of sorrow.

Arco di Gallieno, commonly called *Arco di S. Vito*. According to the inscription on this arch, it was erected in honour of the Emperor whose name it bears. It is Doric; and proves the decline of architecture in the days of Gallienus.

Remains of *five Aqueducts* are discoverable in this quarter of the city; namely, the *Marcian, Tepulan, Julian, Claudian,* and the *Anio-novus;* and near the church of S. Eusebio is a considerable ruin of a *Castellum* of one of these aqueducts.

Chiesa di S. Prassede. The high-altar of this ancient edifice is adorned with a handsome baldacchino, supported by four fine columns of porphyry; the tribuna is adorned with ancient mosaics; and leading to it are magnificent steps of rosso antico, composed of the largest blocks extant of that rare marble, the fauns of the Capitol and Vatican excepted. In this church is a column, supposed to be that Our Saviour was fastened to when scourged. In the Sacristy is a painting of the Flagellation, by Giulio Romano; and in one of the Chapels are three paintings relative to the life of S. Carlo Borromeo, by an English Painter, named Sterne: they are finely executed, and dated 1741. This church leads to the Catacombs.

Campidoglio. This hill, originally called *Mons Saturnius*, and afterward *Tarpeius,* from Tarpeia, who admitted the Sabines

---

[1] It is difficult to gain admission to this church, unless it be very early in the morning.

into the fortress erected here, was, according to tradition, denominated *Capitole*, or *Capitolium*, because, when Tarquin the elder ordered the foundations of a temple of Jupiter to be laid on this spot, the workmen, while digging, found a human head: in consequence of which the augurs predicted that Rome would become mistress of the world.

When we recollect the number of splendid edifices which adorned the ancient Capitol, we are led to think its extent must have been immense: but, when we view the spot, and see how circumscribed it is, we can only account for the number of its temples by concluding, that here, as in various parts of the city, one edifice was frequently destroyed to make room for another. The square of the ancient Capitol was adorned with porticos by Scipio Nasica; and in its centre was the triumphal arch of Nero. The most ancient temple was that of *Jupiter Feretrius*, erected by Romulus; and its dimensions were only ten feet in length, and five in breadth.[1] The temple of *Jupiter-Capitolinus*, finished by the younger Tarquin, was much larger; and when consumed by lightning, which happened more than once, seems to have increased in magnitude every time it rose from its ashes. The last person who rebuilt this temple was Domitian; and he is said to have expended twelve thousand talents in gilding it. Here were deposited the spoils of conquered nations, as offerings to the gods from the Senate, Consuls, and Emperors of Rome. The statue of Jupiter was gold; and so, likewise, was that of Victory; which is said to have weighed three hundred and twenty pounds. Here, also, were the temples of *Jupiter-Moneta, Fortuna-Primogenita, Fortuna-Privata, Fortuna-Viscola, Vejovis, Isis, Serapis,* etc. embellished by statues without and within; so that the Capitol was denominated The Hall of the Gods. Of these magnificent edifices, however, scarcely a wreck remains: so that the modern Capitol bears no resemblance to the ancient. The present steps, and two side buildings of the latter, were planned by Buonaroti, at the command of Paul III.: and the front of the Senator's house was likewise rebuilt, after the design of Buonaroti. At the bottom of the steps are two Lionesses in basalt, of Egyptian workmanship; and, on the left side, two arches, under which are large stones, supposed to have made part of the foundation of the Temple of Jupiter Feretrius. On the top of the steps are two colossal Statues, reputed to be Greek sculpture; but more probably Roman; one represents Castor and the other Pollux, with their respective horses. On a line with these statues are beautiful Trophies, called those of Marius, but rather supposed to have been done in honour of Trajan's victory over the Dacians: they once adorned a *Castellum* of the Julian Aqueduct; and Piranesi calls them trophies of Augustus. On the same line, likewise, are Statues of the two Sons of Constantine; together with two Roman mile-stones; that numbered "I," and standing on the right, being the column which

---

[1] The statues of the gods, placed in the temples of Rome, during the days of Romulus, were made of potters' clay; and the sacred statues of the Capitol, when injured by time or accident, were not destroyed, but placed in subterraneous depositories, called *Favissæ*.

anciently marked the first mile of the Via-Appia; that on the left, modern. In the centre of the square is a bronze equestrian Statue of Marcus Aurelius, once gilt!!![1] This is the only antique bronze equestrian statue extant. Fronting the steps is the Senator's House, which stands on the ruins of the ancient *Tabularium*, and under the entrance door, is a Statue of Rome triumphant, in Parian marble draped with porphyry: a recumbent statue of the Nile; and another of the Tiber, both in Greek marble. On the right side of the square is the Palazzo de' Conservatori; and on the left the Museo-Capitolino. Beyond the former, on the south side of the hill, are steps which lead to the spot where stood the temple of Jupiter Capitolinus; near which, in a Garden, belonging to a house numbered 139, is that part of the *Tarpeian Rock* whence, it is supposed, criminals were thrown down into the Forum.[2] The garden fronts Caracalla's Baths; and the rock, in this place, may, perhaps, be sixty feet high at the present moment; and formerly it must evidently have been much more; as the level of the Forum is full twenty feet higher now than it was originally.

Chiesa di S. Maria d'Aracœli, anciently *the Temple of Jupiter Feretrius.* The steps leading up to this church, from the side of the Campus Martius, are an hundred and twenty-four in number, and the marble of which they are made was taken from the temple of Jupiter Quirinus, on the Quirinal hill. The interior of the edifice is supported by twenty-two antique columns, chiefly Egyptian granite; and the third column on the left (entering by the great door), bears this inscription: "*A Cubiculo Augustorum.*"[3] It is said that Augustus, about the time of our Saviour's birth, erected here an altar, under the name of *Ara Primogeniti Dei*, now corrupted into *Aracœli*; and an altar, said to be that above-mentioned, is still preserved in this church, and stands between the high-altar and sacristy. The choir behind the high-altar contains a picture, by Raphael, of the Holy Family, which was injured, and has been ill restored. The Chapel of S. Francesco is finely painted, by Trevisani; and here, likewise, is a Chapel painted by Pinturicchio and Luca Signorelli.

Chiesa di S. Pietro in Carcere, or, more properly, *S. Giuseppe.* On the right, going down from the Capitoline hill to this church, are large stones, belonging probably to the ancient *Tabularium*. Under the church is an ancient Prison, built by Ancus Martius, and called Il Carcere Mamertino: it is quite perfect, and well worth seeing, though cold and damp. Here S. Peter was confined; and, in the lowest part of this prison, near a small column to which the Apostle was bound, is a spring of water, said to have issued forth miraculously, that he might baptize the two gaolers, and forty-seven other persons, all of whom afterward suffered martyrdom.

Palazzo del Senatore di Roma.

---

[1] It was found near the Scala Santa, on the spot where the house of his grandfather, Annius Verus, is said to have stood. Winckelmann supposes the statue of the horse to be more ancient than that of the Emperor; and particularly praises the head of the horse.

[2] Dionysius of Halicarnassus says, that criminals were thrown down from the Tarpeian Rock into the Forum.

[3] The *Cubicularii* were officers of the bedchamber belonging to the Imperial Court.

The view from the Tower which crowns this building is particularly worth notice, as it exhibits all the ancient edifices of the city, and shows their respective situations.

Palazzo de' Conservatori. In the quadrangle, beyond the arcade, are statues of Rome triumphant, and the weeping Province! two Dacian Kings, and two Egyptian Divinities, all in the same line. The quadrangle likewise contains a Group of a Lion devouring a Horse! the Bust, and one Hand, of a colossal statue of Commodus; the Bust of Domitian; and immense Feet, and one Hand of a mutilated colossal statue of Apollo. The arcade contains a Statue of Julius Cæsar—Ditto of Augustus, done apparently after the battle of Actium, by the prow of a galley with which it is adorned—a Bacchante—a rostral Column—and a Lion on a pedestal, which bears an inscription of the time of Adrian. To the right of the arcade are eight rooms, recently adorned with Busts, many of which were taken from the Pantheon; and on the staircase, opposite to these rooms, are four *bassi-rilievi*, which originally belonged to the triumphal Arch of Marcus Aurelius on the Corso; here likewise is a *basso-rilievo* (found in the forum), of Curtius leaping into the gulf; and, on the landing-place, are two more *bassi-rilievi*, taken from the Arch of Aurelius.

On this landing-place is a door which leads to the apartments not open to the public, but which the *Custode* is happy to show for a trifling gratuity.

The first room contains Paintings by the Cav. d'Arpino; namely, the battle of the Horatii and Curiatii—the battle of Tullus Hostilius with the army of Veii!—the discovery of Romulus and Remus—Romulus founding Rome—the sacrifice of Numa Pompilius, and institution of the Vestal Virgins; and the rape of the Sabines.

The second room contains Paintings by Laurenti; namely, Junius Brutus condemning his sons to death for having conspired against the Republic—Horatius Cocles, on the Sublician bridge, opposing the Etrurians—Mutius Scævola burning his own hand in presence of Porsenna, after having killed one of the Etrurian Officers, whom he mistook for the King—and the battle in which the Tarquins were defeated.

The third room contains a Frieze representing the triumph of Marius, by Daniello da Volterra!—a Picture of S. Francesca Romana, by Romanelli; and a dead Christ, by Cosimo Piezza—the Statue of the bronze wolf, said to have been struck with lightning when Cæsar fell! This statue is evidently of high antiquity, and perhaps the work of an Etruscan artist[1]—a bronze Bust of Junius Brutus!!—two mosaic tables taken from Adrian's Villa—a Bust of Julius Cæsar—ditto of Apollo—a triform-Diana[2]—a Bust of Adrian—and a *basso-rilievo* representing the temple of Janus, or, according to some opinions, the gate of Eternity.

The fourth room contains a bronze Statue of a Youth, said to be the shepherd Martius taking a

---

[1] Cicero tells us that, in his time, the turrets of the Capitol, the statues of the gods, and the image of the infant Romulus sucking the Wolf, were struck down by lightning.

[2] Emblematical of her sovereignty over Hell, Earth, and Heaven.

thorn out of his foot!!—a Bust in *basso-rilievo* of Mithridates! and the *Fasti Consulares*!![1]

The fifth room contains a Bust, in rosso antico, called Appius Claudius—a bust of Buonaroti—a bust of Medusa, by Bernini—and a bust of Tiberius; together with two Geese, in bronze, said to have been found in the Tarpeian Rock, and to be the representation of those geese which saved the Capitol. Here, likewise, are the following Paintings; a Holy Family, by Giulio Romano; and the Olympic games, attributed to Zuccari.

The fifth room contains a Frieze painted by Annibale Caracci, and representing the military achievements of Scipio Africanus—Tapestry, taken from the designs of Rubens—Busts of Sappho! Socrates! Ariadne! and Sabina Poppæa! the second wife of Nero.

The sixth room contains Frescos by Pietro Perugino, who has represented Hannibal in Capua—Rome triumphant over Sicily, etc, Here, likewise, are Statues of Virgil, Cicero, and Cybele.

The seventh apartment is a Chapel, on the ceiling of which M. A. Caravaggio has represented the Deity. Here, also, are paintings of S. Cecilia, by Romanelli! and the four Evangelists, by Caravaggio, together with an altarpiece, by Nucci.

The eighth room has a door finely carved by Algardy.

The next story of this building contains the Picture Gallery, which is open to the public every Sunday and Thursday morning, from eleven till four o'clock. Some of the most striking pictures in *the first room* are: No. 2, the Madonna, our Saviour, and Saints, copied by Bonatti, from Paolo Peronese—4, the sacrifice of Iphigenia, by Pietro da Cortona—5, the portrait of a lady, by Bronzino—6, S. Lucia, by Benvenuto Garofolo!—9, Vanity, by Titian!—15, the rape of the Sabines, by Pietro da Cortona!—18, a portrait, by Velasquez—33, Hagar driven from the house of Abraham, by Francesco Mola—36, Charity, by Annibale Caracci!—37, Bacchus and Ariadne, school of Guido—38, the Sibyl Persica, by Guercino!!!—39, the Madonna, our Saviour, S. Cecilia, and other Saints, by Annibale Caracci!—49, the Madonna, our Saviour, and S. Francesco, by Annibale Caracci—41, the Holy Family, by Benvenuto Garofolo—42, Mary Magdalene washing our Saviour's feet; a miniature, by M. F. Zibaldi Subleras, copied from the original of her husband!—13, the marriage of S. Caterina, by Correggio—44, the Madonna and our Saviour, by Albano!—45, S. Maria Maddalena, by Tintoretto!—46, David with the head of Goliath by Romanelli—48, the communion of S. Girolamo, by Agostino Caracci!—51, S. John Baptist, by Daniello da Volterra!—52, Christ disputing with the Doctors, by Valentino!—53, the Cumæan Sibyl, by Domenichino!!—60, S. John Baptist, by Guercino—63, a landscape, with the figure of the Magdalene, Caracci school—64, the Magdalene, by Albano—65, the triumph of Bacchus, by Pietro da Cortona—67, S. Cecilia, by Ro-

---

[1] These precious remains of antiquity were found during the Pontificate of Paul III., near the church of S. Maria Liberatrice, in the Forum Romanum, and probably in that part which belonged to the Comitium.

manelli—70, the beatified Spirit, by Guido!—76, Romulus and Remus discovered with the wolf, attributed to Rubens—86, the Madonna adoring our Saviour, by Pietro da Cortona—89, a portrait, by Titian—90, Meleager in *chiaroscuro*, by Polidoro da Caravaggio.

Some of the most striking Pictures *in the second room* are—No. 2, a copy of Raphael's Galatea, by Pietro da Cortona—6, the Adoration of the Magi, by Garofolo—11, a landscape, by Claude Lorrain—12, Ditto, by ditto—25, Love, by Guido—33, an *Ecce Homo*, by Baroccio—37, the Woman detected in Adultery, by Titian—40, Europa, by Guido!—41, Alexander's victory over Darius, by Pietro da Cortona!—43, a head, by Titian—44, Polyphemus, by Guido—47, the Presentation in the Temple, supposed to be by Fra Bartolomeo—48, the Holy Family, by Andrea Sacchi—57, the Pool of Silome, by Domenichino; (parts of this small picture are beautiful)—58, a landscape, by Claude Lorrain—60, a *Presepio*,[1] by Garofolo—62, the Madonna, Our Saviour, and S. John, by ditto—63, the Judgment of Solomon, by Giacomo Bassano—65, the raising of S. Petronilla's Body from the Grave, and the Ascension of her Spirit into Heaven, by Guercino!!!—72, a Gipsy telling a youth his fortune, by Caravaggio!—73, the Madonna, Our Saviour, and Angels, by Perugino—76, a Soldier seated, by Salvator Rosa—77, a half-length figure of S. Girolamo, by Pietro Facini—78, a portrait of Petrarca, by Giovanni Bellino—79, a landscape, by Domenichino—80, a portrait of Buonaroti, by himself!—82, a portrait of Giovanni Bellino, by himself—86, a Witch, by Salvator Rosa—89, S. Sebastiano, by Lodovico Caracci—93, Augustus and Cleopatra, by Guercino—109, S. Barbara, a half-length figure, by Domenichino—111, the Holy Family, by Parmigiano—113, S. Cristoforo, by Tintoretto—114, S. Cecilia, by Lodovico Caracci!—116, two Philosophers, by Calabrese—120, the Graces, by Palma Giovane—123, Europa, by Paolo Veronese!

Museo Capitolino, open to the public every Sunday and Thursday morning, from twelve till four o'clock.[2]

Some of the most striking ef-

---

[1] This is a representation of Our Saviour in the Manger, attended by the Blessed Virgin, Joseph, etc. There is another kind of Presepio exhibited in Roman Catholic countries at Christmas; and consisting of Our Saviour as an Infant, the Blessed Virgin, Joseph, the Wise Men of the East, camels, etc.; all wrought in wax, and sometimes well executed. The best of these exhibitions at Rome is in the Church of S. Maria d'Aracœli.

[2] Those persons who wish to see the Museums of the Capitol and Vatican to advantage should visit them by torch-light, as the torch, like Promethean fire, makes every statue live; in consequence of which, perhaps, the most stupendous efforts of the Grecian chisel were originally placed in subterranean baths.

For seeing the Vatican Museum, four large wax torches, weighing about three pounds and a half each, and costing altogether about six scudi, are requisite. For seeing the Museum of the Capitol, two small wax torches, costing about twenty pauls the two, are sufficient. Admission, however, cannot be obtained to either Museum, for the purpose of viewing the statues by torch-light, without an order from the Pope's Maggiordomo; which order never extends to more than fifteen persons at the same time, and but seldom to so many.

It is expected that every party shall come furnished with wax torches: and it is likewise expected that each party shall give, at the Capitol, to the Custode who shows the statues, and his attendants, from four to five scudi, provided there be fires in one or two of the apartments; and, at the Vatican, from seven to eight scudi, according to the number of fires in the apartments.

forts of the chisel, in this magnificent collection, are:

Quadrangle. No. I, a colossal Statue of the Ocean!

Arcade. No. 1, Endymion and his Dog, the pedestal fine—3, a colossal Statue of Minerva—4, fragment of a Statue of Hercules!—5, Apollo—7, a Bacchante, semi-colossal.

Over the door of the Director's Apartment, four Consular Fasces. No. 9, the Dacian Province—10, a colossal head of Cybele—12, the Capital of a Doric column, taken from Caracalla's Baths—17, Isis, in rare basalt—20, Diana—21, Hercules—22, Isis, in red oriental granite—23, a colossal Statue of Diana—25, Polyphemus—26, Mercury—27, a sepulchral Urn—28, Adrian in a sacerdotal habit—30, Jove armed with thunder—31, a Statue of Mars, the head and armour antique, the rest restored—32, Hercules killing the Hydra.

Canopo. The statues contained in this apartment are said to have been found in the Canopus of Adrian's Villa: it is supposed, however, that not more than three of them are really Egyptian; the rest being productions of the time of Adrian. No. 1, Isis and Apis—3, Canopus—9, Isis—10, Anubis with the Sistrum and Caduceus—12, Isis—13, Isis.

First room, added to the Museum by Pius VII. No. 13, is a square Altar, supposed to be an Etruscan work, representing the labours of Hercules.

Second room. No. 1, the Sarcophagus of Alexander Severus and his mother. Some of the *bassi-rilievi* which adorn this immense monument are fine.[1]—3, a Disk, with *bassi-rilievi,* representing the life of Achilles!—4, an ancient Mosaic, found near Antium, and representing Hercules vanquished by Love!—5, a Satyr with a pipe—11, Pluto and Cerberus!—13, a *basso-rilievo* of Poppæa, second wife of Nero—14, Nero.

Staircase. No. 1, a statue of Modesty, or a Vestal—2, the Top of an ancient Well[2]—5, a Lion devouring a Goat. Fastened into the wall is the Plan of ancient Rome, found in the church of Saints Cosimo and Damiano.

Gallery up stairs. No. 2, Bust of Faustina the elder, wife of Antoninus Pius—5, Euterpe—10, a *basso-rilievo,* representing a man making his will—12, Faunus—14, bust of Silenus—15, bust of Pompey.

Apartment of the Vase. No. 1, a large Vase with Bacchanalian ornaments, found near the sepulchre of Cecilia Metella; and placed on a Pedestal, apparently Etruscan, and originally, perhaps, the parapet which encircled a well: it is adorned with a *basso-rilievo,* representing the twelve principal deities of the heathen world; and was found at Nettuno!—2, (near the window) a bronze Vase, found in the port of Antium; and once the property of Mithridates Eupator, King of Pontus, according to the inscription it bears; which inscription exhibits the most ancient Greek characters extant!—9, Mercury—36, a triform Diana

---

[1] Some writers suppose the monument in question to have been that of Genesius Marcianus, the father of Alexander Severus, and his wife, Julia Mammæa.

[2] Or perhaps a receptacle for sacrificial ashes.

—37, a *basso-rilievo* representing circumstances recorded by Homer—39, a sacrificial tripod—40, ancient Roman weights, scales, and a candelabrum—41, the triumph of Bacchus for the conquest of India—47, Diana of Ephesus—59, Isis—68, the Foot of a tripod of flowered alabaster!—69, a sepulchral Urn, representing the fable of Diana and Endymion—77, Diana of Ephesus—83, a Herma—84, a Herma, representing Bacchus—96, a cinerary Urn supposed to have contained the ashes of a youth—100, a Sarcophagus, with *bassi-rilievi*, representing the fable of Prometheus—101, a Mosaic, in *pietre dure*, of four pigeons, described by Pliny, and found in Adrian's Villa!![1]

Continuation of the Gallery. No. 17, bust supposed to represent Cecrops, first King of Athens—18, Cato the Censor!—19, Group of Agrippina and Nero—21, Marcus Aurelius—23, bust of a laughing Bacchus—26, a young Hercules!—27, Paris—28, a Sarcophagus representing the Rape of Proserpine—29, a cinerary Urn—30, a bust, supposed to represent Marcus Brutus—32, Psyche, with the wings of a butterfly—34, bust of Marcus Vespasian Agrippa!—35, colossal bust of the mother of Niobe—36, a wounded Gladiator; or, more probably, a Discobolus—37, a Wine-vase—41, one of the daughters of Niobe—42, head of Jupiter!—44, Diana-Lucifera—48, a Sarcophagus, with *bassi-rilievi*, relative to the history of Bacchus—49, a cinerary Urn, with a pineapple, the emblem of mourning, at the top—50, bust of Scipio Africanus!—51, bust of Phocion—52, statue of a Consul—54, a semi-colossal head of Antinous—55, bust of Venus—56, a small Pallas—57, a small Isis—58, semi-colossal bust of Jupiter-Ammon!—60, statue of Ceres—62, bust of the mother of Niobe—63, bust of Tiberius—64, Bacchus with a panther at his feet—65, Jove with the eagle at his feet—66, bust of Jupiter Serapis—67, head of Augustus—68, bust of Adrian—70, bust of Caligula—72, statue of Marcus Aurelius—73, bust of Trajan—74, bust of Silenus crowned with ivy—75, bust of Domitius Enobarbus, the father of Nero—76, bust of Caracalla.

Apartment of the Emperors. On the walls are the following *bassi-rilievi*, numbered alphabetically—*A.* Genii in cars—*B.* Bacchus on a tiger, with Fauns, satyrs, etc.—*C.* the chase of the Calydon boar—*E.* the nine Muses!—*F.* Perseus liberating Andromeda!—*G.* Socrates with History, and Homer with Poetry—*H.* Endymion and his dog—*I.* The fable of Hylas; three of the figures in this *basso-rilievo* exactly resemble the three Graces of Siena. In the middle of the room is a statue of Agrippina, the mother of Germanicus, seated in a curule chair! and round the apartment, on two shelves of marble, are busts of the Roman emperors and their relatives, beginning with Julius Cæsar; whose bust, numbered 1,—that of Drusus, numbered 5,—that of Germanicus, numbered 7,—that of Caligula, numbered 9,—that of Messalina, numbered 11,—that of Galba, numbered 16,—that of Julia, the

---

[1] This Mosaic made part of a pavement; and is supposed to have been brought by Adrian from Pergamus, and to have been the work of Sosus.

daughter of Titus, numbered 21, —that of Nerva, numbered 24,— that of Plotina, numbered 26,— those of Adrian, numbered 29 and 30, —that of Julia-Sabina, numbered 31,—that of Marcus Aurelius, numbered 35,—that of Lucilla, numbered 40,—that of Commodus, numbered 41,—that of Clodius Albinus, numbered 47, —those of Septimius Severus, numbered 48 and 49,—that of Macrinus, numbered 53,—that of Maximus, numbered 59,—that of Tribonianus Gallus, numbered 68,—and that of Salonina, numbered 73, are among the most striking.

Apartment of the Philosophers. Among the *bassi-rilievi* on the walls are, G. a funeral procession—I. Victory in a triumphal car—L. a sacrifice to Hygeia, in rosso antico—M. Faunus followed by Spartan ladies: this work bears the name of Callimachos, and is described by Pliny.[1] In the centre of the room is one of the twelve *Camillæ*, instituted by Romulus for the service of the gods. On two marble shelves round the room are busts of Poets, Philosophers, and other distinguished characters of antiquity: those of Virgil, marked 1,—Socrates, marked 4, 5, and 6,—Carneades, marked 8,—Seneca, marked 10,—Plato, marked 11,—Diogenes, marked 21,—Archimedes, marked 22,—Asclepiades, marked 24,—Demosthenes, marked 31,—Pindar, marked 33,—Aratus, marked 38,—Democritus, marked 39 and 40,—Homer, marked 44, 45, 46, and 47,—Aspasia, marked 48,—Cleopatra, marked 49,—Sappho, marked 51, —Lysias, marked 54,—Epicurus, marked 62,—Metrodorus, marked 63,—Epicurus, marked 64,—Aristotle, marked 66,—Massinissa, marked 68 and 69,—Julian, the apostate, marked 72,—Cicero, marked 74,—and Gabrielle Faerno, marked 79, and done by Buonaroti, are among the most striking.

Saloon. The two columns of giallo antico, which ornament the large niche of this apartment, where stands the Hercules of bronze gilt, once belonged to the tomb of Cecilia Metella; and the two figures of Victory, which support the arms of Clement xii., once belonged to the triumphal Arch of Marcus Aurelius. Among the statues are, No. 1, Jove armed with lightning, of nero antico, and found (as likewise was the Altar which serves for its Pedestal) in the Port of Antium!—2, a Centaur, of nero antico, found at Adrian's Villa!!—3, Hercules, in basalt, found on the Aventine hill; the Pedestal is adorned with *bassi-rilievi*, representing the birth, education, and coronation of Jove!!—4, another Centaur, similar to that numbered "2"!! —5, Æsculapius, in nero antico, placed on a circular altar representing a sacrifice, and found, as was the Altar, at Antium—7, Ptolemy-Apion, in the character of Apollo—8, Venus rising from the bath—9, a wounded Amazon —10, an Amazon—11, a wounded Amazon—13, a Muse—14, Minerva!—15, a Faun—16, Apollo, semi-colossal—18, a colossal bust of Trajan!—21, Antinous—22, Adrian—23, Caius Marius, in consular robes!!—24, Julia, consort of Septimius Severus—25, Hercules in bronze gilt, semi-co-

---

[1] Winckelmann seems to think this work Etruscan; and supposes it to represent three Priestesses of Bacchus and a Faun.

lossal, found in the Forum Boarium; and the only antique statue in Rome in which the gilding remains!! This statue is placed upon an altar consecrated to Fortune—26, Isis, with the lotus on her head!—28, a Master of one of the schools for gymnastic exercises, found in Adrian's Villa—29, one of the *Præficæ*, hired to weep at funerals—31, the Goddess of Clemency with a patera and a lance, found on the Aventine hill—32, a colossal bust of Antoninus Pius!—33, Diana, as a huntress; from the Albani collection—34, a Cacciatore, found near the Porta Latina—35, Harpocrates, the god of silence, found in Adrian's Villa.

Apartment of the Faun.—Among the *bassi-rilievi* which adorn the walls of this room, is the triumph of the Nereides over marine Monsters. In the centre of the apartment is the Faun, in rosso antico, found at Adrian's Villa!!!—No. 3, colossal head of Hercules placed on a rostral altar dedicated to Neptune—6, colossal head of Bacchus, placed on a rostral altar, dedicated to Tranquillity—10, an incognito-bust—13, a Sarcophagus, the *bassi-rilievi* on which represent the fable of Diana and Endymion—14, an incognito-bust standing on an altar dedicated to Isis, and found in Adrian's Villa—15, a child playing with a mask—17, Innocence playing with a dove—19, Alexander the Great—21, a child playing with a Swan, and placed on an altar dedicated to the sun!—22, an incognito-bust—26, a Sarcophagus adorned with *bassi-rilievi* representing the battle of Theseus and the Amazons.

Apartment of the dying Gladiator. This super-excellent statue, found in the gardens of Sallust, has been so well restored, by Buonaroti, that the arm he made is deemed nearly equal in merit with the other parts of the figure!!!!![1]—2, Zeno, the founder of the Stoics; this statue stands upon an ancient altar, and was discovered at Lavinium, in the Villa of Antoninus Pius—3, a group of Cupid and Psyche, found on the Aventine hill, and placed on an altar dedicated to Apollo!—4, the Faun of Praxiteles found at Tivoli, in the Villa d'Este!!!—6, Antinous!!! —7, Flora, found in Adrian's Villa!—8, Venus coming from the bath!!!—9, Juno, semi-colossal!!! —10, bust of Alexander the Great! —11, the Egyptian Antinous deified by Adrian, demi-colossal, and found in Adrian's Villa!—12, bust of Ariadne, crowned with ivy—13, Pandora, semi-colossal, placed on an Altar dedicated to Hercules! —14, Apollo, semi-colossal, found in the Zolfatara, near Tivoli!!!— B, bust of Marcus Brutus!

Tempio di Pallade, erected by Domitian in his Forum. This magnificent ruin is half buried in the earth; but that part which appears above-ground of two beautiful fluted Corinthian columns now standing, measures twenty-nine feet in height, each column being nine feet and a half in circumference. The entablature and frieze are rich in well-executed ornaments, especially the latter, which represents the Arts, patronised by Pallas. On the entablature is a

---

[1] Winckelmann supposes the statue called The Dying Gladiator to represent a herald; other antiquaries think it more like a shield-bearer: it seems, however, to be generally considered as a copy of that masterpiece in bronze, by Ctesilaus, which represented a wounded man in the agonies of death.

large figure of the Goddess in *alto-rilievo*.

Tempio e Foro di Nerva. The Emperor Nerva, after the death of Domitian, finished his Forum, which was enlarged and embellished by Trajan, who erected there one of the finest edifices of ancient Rome, a Temple, or Basilica, in honour of Nerva. Contiguous to the entrance into the Forum of Nerva (now called Arco de' Pantani) are the remains of this edifice; namely, part of what seems to have been a cella, and part of a side portico, consisting of three magnificent columns and a pilaster of Parian marble, fluted, and of the Corinthian order, which support an architrave much ornamented and finely worked. The height of these columns is fifty-one feet, and their circumference sixteen feet and a half.[1] The wall now remaining of the Forum of Nerva (supposed to have been originally a part of the city-wall, erected by Tarquin), is equally extraordinary on account of its immense height, and the enormous blocks of stone that compose it, which are cramped together without the assistance of lime, by pieces of hard wood.

Foro e Colona Trajana. The Forum of Trajan, built by Apollodorus of Athens, was, according to the records of antiquity, more splendid than any other Forum at Rome, and contained porticos, statues, a basilica, with a bronze equestrian statue of Trajan in its vestibule; a temple dedicated to that Emperor after his death; a triumphal arch with four fronts, the celebrated Ulpian Library, and a beautiful historic column, the last of which alone remains entire. The column is supposed to have stood in the centre of the Forum, and under this supposition, we may conclude that not much more than half of the latter has been excavated, and that the other part must still remain entombed beneath the churches of S. Maria, and S. Maria di Loretto. The excavations lately made have brought to light a considerable number of columns of grey granite, all broken, but which seem, judging from the situation of their bases, to have belonged to the Basilica. Several fragments of sculpture, inscriptions, etc., have likewise been found, and are now placed in the Forum. Trajan's column, the most beautiful work extant of its kind, was erected at the beginning of the second century, by the senate and people of Rome, in honour of his victories over the Daci, Sarmati, etc. It is of the Doric order, and composed of thirty-four blocks of Greek marble, fastened together with bronze cramps: its circumference, at the bottom, being eleven feet two inches, and at the top ten feet, and its height from the pavement, including the statue on its summit, 133 feet. The *bassi-rilievi* with which it is adorned, represent the Dacian wars, and are supposed to have been designed, and in great measure executed, by Apollodorus. The statue of Trajan, in bronze gilt, originally stood on the top of this column, but the existing statue is that of S. Peter, placed there by Sixtus V. The pedestal of the column exhibits trophies, eagles, wreathes of oak, etc., most beautifully sculptured,[1] and origi-

---

[1] According to some opinions, this edifice was the Temple of Mars.
[2] The shields and arms are those of the Daci, the Sarmati, and their allies, copied from the originals brought to Rome by Trajan.

nally contained the ashes of Trajan in a golden urn.

Dogana Pontificia. This edifice stands on the ruins of a large oblong building, each side of which seems to have been originally decorated with an open portico. Eleven magnificent fluted Corinthian columns of Greek marble still remain, and support a noble cornice, likewise of Greek marble: these columns are above thirty-nine feet high, and particularly well proportioned; their base is attic, and their capitals are adorned with olive-leaves: they have suffered cruelly from fire. The quadrangle of the edifice contains fragments of a fine entablature, and a portico. Some antiquaries believe this splendid ruin to have been the Temple of Neptune, but more probably it was the *Basilica of Antoninus Pius.*

Obelisk of Monte-Citorio. — This obelisk, made, it is supposed, in the time of Sesostris, about a thousand years before Christ, was brought to Rome by Augustus, who used it as the gnomon, or stile, of his meridian line, which was traced on the pavement by means of a bronze dial, near the temple of Juno-Lucina, now the Church of S. Lorenzo in Lucina.[1] The obelisk is of red granite, covered with hieroglyphics, and its height, from the pedestal to the bronze globe on its summit, is ninety feet. Pius VI. placed it on Monte Citorio.[2]

Colonna-Antonina. This stately historic column, erected by the Roman senate to Marcus Aurelius Antoninus, was dedicated by him to his father-in-law, Antoninus Pius, whose statue he placed on its summit. It records the Marcomannic war, in a series of *bassirilievi*, which seem to have been imitated from those on Trajan's column, though inferior in point of workmanship. It is of the Doric order, and composed of twenty-eight blocks of white marble; its diameter being fifteen feet, and its height, from the base to the top of the statue, one hundred and forty-two feet. As this column was extremely injured by lightning, Sixtus V. restored it, at the same time placing on its summit the statue of S. Paul, which, like that of Antoninus Pius, is of bronze gilt.[3]

Mausoleo d'Augusto. Augustus, during his sixth consulate, erected, in the Campus Martius, this superb Mausoleum for himself and family: it was incrusted with white marble, and, being raised to a great height, formed a stately dome. The building seems to have been divided into three stories, round which were broad belts, whereon evergreens were planted: the summit was adorned with a statue of Augustus, and two Egyptian Obelisks stood at the entrance. One story alone remains: here, however, are several sepulchral chambers tolerably perfect. The *Bustum*, where the bodies of the Emperor and his family were burnt, is supposed to have been in the vicinity of his mausoleum, near the church of S. Carlo al Corso. So extraordinary are the changes in this world, that the

---

1 See PLINY's *Nat. Hist.* 1. 36. c. 10.
2 *Mons Citorius*; here formerly stood an Amphitheatre, supposed to have been that of Statilius Taurus.
3 The Base of the Colonna Antonina is modern; and if the Street recently discovered, eighteen feet below the foundation of the Palazzo-Piombino, be, as antiquaries suppose, part of the *Via-Flaminia*, the Colonna Antonina must, when first erected, have stood on a considerable hill.

tomb of Augustus is now converted into a sort of amphitheatre for bull-fights and fire-works!

Campo Marzo. The Campus Martius, consecrated, by Romulus, to the god of war, comprehended an immense tract of ground; extending, in the days of Augustus, from his Mausoleum to the Theatre of Marcellus; and from the base of the Pincian, Quirinal, and Capitoline hills, to the Tiber. In Nero's reign, it is said to have reached to the Ponte Molle.

Mausoleo-Adriano, now *Castel di S. Angelo.* This magnificent edifice was erected by the Emperor Adrian, nearly opposite to the Mausoleum of Augustus, and in the garden of Domitian. It consisted of two stories, with a dome on the top; was incrusted with Parian marble, surrounded with stately columns, and adorned with statues. Some persons imagine the bronze pine, now in the Belvedere-Garden of the Vatican, to have been originally placed on the summit of the dome, and to have contained the ashes of Adrian: while others conjecture that his statue was on the summit, and that his ashes were deposited beneath, in a porphyry sarcophagus. After the fall of the Roman empire, this building became the citadel of Rome; and acquired the appellation of Castello di S. Angelo, from a statue of the Archangel Michael placed there, to commemorate a vision of S. Gregorio; who, being on the top of the edifice, thought he saw an angel announcing to him the cessation of a plague which, at that period, ravaged Rome. Considerable remains of the ancient building may still be discovered within the walls of the modern Fortress; the large hall of which merits notice; as it is painted, in fresco, by Raphael's scholars.

Foreigners, in general, are not allowed to see the interior of the Fortress of S. Angelo above one or two days in the year; when the Soldiers of the Garrison have permission to open the gates, and show the Mausoleum, etc.

Tempio del Sole nel Giardino Colonnese. In Via della Pilotta, near the church of Santi Apostoli, is a door leading up a flight of narrow steps into the Colonna Garden, where lie immense fragments of what is supposed to have been the Temple of the Sun, erected by Aurelian. This edifice, finely situated on the Quirinal hill, was one of the largest temples of ancient Rome, if we may judge by the enormous magnitude of the ruins of the frieze and entablature,[1] which still remain: they are of white marble, beautifully sculptured. The columns which supported the entablature are supposed to have been seventy feet in height. Here was found a votive table of marble, on which the worship of Mithras is represented: and as the worship of Mithras, brought to Rome from Persia, was certainly connected with that of the sun, such a votive offering is an indication that the Temple of the Sun stood here.

This Garden likewise contains ruins of *the Baths of Constantine.*

Obelisk of the Piazza di Santa

---

[1] One of these blocks of marble is twelve feet in length, thirteen in breadth, and eleven in height. Another block is seventeen feet in length, ten in breadth, and six in height. But prodigious to modern eyes as these blocks appear, they are pigmies compared with those mentioned by Josephus as having composed part of the Temple at Jerusalem, after its restoration by Herod. The last-named blocks, according to the Jewish historian, were upwards of sixty-seven feet in length, above seven in height, and about nine in breadth.

Maria sopra Minerva. This little Obelisk, covered with hieroglyphics, was found near the spot where it now stands; in consequence of excavations which were made to lay the foundations of the Convent of the Minerva. The Obelisk which now stands opposite to the Pantheon was found in the same place: and it is conjectured that the Temples of Isis and Serapis stood in this part of Rome; and that these little Obelisks stood before them. A fine statue of Minerva, an Isis, a Serapis, an Isiaic Altar, and other Egyptian antiquities, were found in this vicinity; as were the celebrated statues of the Nile and Tiber; the former of which is now in the Vatican-Museum, the latter at Paris. The obelisk of the Piazza della Minerva was placed there by Alexander VII.; and the elephant, on whose back it rests, was designed by Bernini, and executed by Ferrata.

Chiesa di S. Maria sopra Minerva. This church is supposed to stand on the foundations of a Temple of Minerva, erected by Pompey the Great, in gratitude for his victories: the interior of the edifice, however, though spacious and handsome, exhibits no remains of the ancient temple. Behind the high-altar are the tombs of Leo X. and Clement VII., by Bandinelli; the statue of the former being by Rafaello da Montelupo, and that of the latter by Bacciobigio. Near the side door is the monument of Cardinal Alessandrino, designed by Giacomo della Porta; and that of Cardinal Pimentelli, executed by Bernini: but the most celebrated piece of sculpture in this church is a statue of Our Saviour holding his cross, by Buonaroti! It is near the high-altar. The Altieri-Chapel contains an altar-piece, by Carlo Maratta and Baciccio: and the Chapel of the Annunziata is painted in fresco, by Filippino Lippi, Rafaellino del Garbo, and Fra Giovanni Angelico da Fiesole, who was buried in this church. The adjoining Convent contains *the Casanatense Library*, deemed the best at Rome, with respect to printed books, and adorned with a statue of Cardinal Casanatta, by Le Gros.[1]

Pantheon. The Piazza in which this magnificent Temple stands was completely filled with ruins of ancient edifices, till the Pontificate of Eugenius IV., who, on having these ruins cleared away, discovered, before the portico of the Pantheon, the two Lions of basalt which now adorn the Fontana di Termine; a Head of Agrippa, in bronze; and some ornaments, supposed to have belonged to the pediment. Gregory XIII. erected the Fountain in this Piazza; and Clement XI. embellished it with the Egyptian Obelisk before-mentioned. The Pantheon, which has in great measure defied the injuries of time, seems as if preserved to latter ages for the purpose of furnishing a just idea of ancient Roman taste and splendour. The general opinion appears to be that it was erected by Agrippa, the son-in-law of Augustus; and repaired by Septimius Severus and Caracalla; but that Agrippa did not build the portico at the same time with the rest of the edifice. The Pantheon, judging from its name, was dedicated to all the gods: though Agrippa particular-

---

[1] On the twenty-third of April, from five till seven in the evening, there is fine music in this church.

ly consecrated it to Jupiter the Avenger: and, according to Dion Cassius, wished to have placed the statue of Augustus there, and to have inscribed his name as author of the Temple; which honour the Emperor modestly declined. Agrippa, therefore, placed the statue of Julius Cæsar in the rotunda, among the deities, and the statues of Augustus and himself in the large niches on the outside near the great door: and probably the portico might have been added for the purpose of containing these statues. What strengthens this conjecture is, that immediately over the portico are traces of the original pediment. Formerly there were seven steps leading up to the portico; now, two only are above ground. This stately vestibule is sixty-nine feet long by forty-one wide, and supported with sixteen magnificent columns, each being one entire piece of red oriental granite, the circumference of which is fourteen feet, and the height forty-two. The bases and capitals are of the most beautiful white marble yet discovered among the treasures of antiquity. The portico is surmounted by an entablature and pediment finely proportioned; and in the tympan of the latter are holes that served, no doubt, to fix a *basso-rilievo*, now, alas, taken away. The original bronze doors, embellished with *bassi-rilievi*, became the spoil of Genseric, King of the Vandals, who lost them in the Sicilian sea: the door-case, which is magnificent, still remains; and the present doors appear to have been taken from an ancient edifice. The inside of the temple is circular, and its diameter is a hundred and forty-nine feet, exclusive of the walls, which are eighteen feet thick: the height seems to have been the same as the breadth, till the interior pavement was raised to a level with that of the portico: for originally there was a descent of seven or eight feet into the Pantheon; a construction not unusual in ancient temples. The walls were incrusted with precious marbles, which still remain, as do the ancient cornices and frieze; and it is supposed that the inside of the dome was originally covered with silver *bassi-rilievi*: the outside was bronze gilt. The beams of the ceiling of the dome and portico were cased with thick plates of bronze, which Urban VIII. took away to make the Baldacchino in S. Peter's, and the cannon of the Castle of S. Angelo; thereby drawing upon himself the following pasquinade: "*Quod non fecerunt Barbari Romæ, fecit Barberini.*" All the gods had their respective statues here, in bronze, silver, gold, or precious marble: that of Jupiter the Avenger is supposed to have been in the centre of the tribuna; the infernal deities on the pavement, the terrestrial in the lower niches of the walls, and the celestial in the upper niches. The pavement is composed of porphyry and giallo antico, bordered with other rare marbles; and the aperture in the roof for light is twenty-five feet in diameter. Pliny mentions, among the ornaments, columns with capitals of a metal called *Syracusian*; but none of these are preserved; neither do any of the Caryatides, nor the other statues executed by Diogenes the Athenian, now remain. Pliny

¹likewise mentions, among the statues, a Venus with ear-rings, made of a pearl cut asunder; being the fellow of that which Cleopatra dissolved in vinegar, and drank to the health of Mark Antony. Fourteen beautiful columns of the Corinthian order still adorn the interior of this edifice: and it is said that the two which stand on each side of the high-altar were placed there by Adrian. The small altars are adorned with columns of porphyry, giallo antico and granite, paintings and statues; among the latter of which is a group of a Vestal and a Child found in the subterranean part of the building; this Vestal is now, I believe, called S. Anna. Busts, monuments, and inscriptions, to the memory of distinguished characters whose talents have shed lustre upon Italy, once clothed the walls of the Pantheon; but are now removed to the Capitol; except the inscriptions in memory of Raphael, Annibale Caracci, and two or three other persons.

Bagni d'Agrippa. Immediately behind the Pantheon were Agrippa's Baths, of which scarce any vestige remains; except a semicircular building, now called *Arco della Ciambella.*

Piazza Navona. This was anciently the *Circus Agonalis;* so called, perhaps, from having been the spot where the Agonal games, instituted by Numa in honour of Janus, were celebrated. It is one of the largest Piazzas in Rome, and seems to have retained its original shape. Gregory XIII. adorned it with two Fountains; one of which is ornamented with a Triton, by Bernini; and other sculpture by various artists: and Innocent X. erected the centre Fountain after the design of Bernini. It consists of a circular basin seventy-three feet in diameter; in the middle of which rises a rock, adorned on one side with a sea-horse, and on another with a lion: on the summit of this rock, is an Obelisk of red granite, covered with hieroglyphics, and fifty-five feet in height; it was found in the circus of Caracalla, who brought it to Rome. The four sides of the rock are likewise embellished with four colossal statues, representing four of the principal rivers of the world; namely, the Ganges, the Nile, the Plata, and the Danube. This fountain does honour to the taste of Bernini.

Chiesa di S. Agnese, in Piazza-Navona. This church stands on the *Lupanarium* of the Circus Agonalis, whither S. Agnes was dragged, in order to be defiled. A staircase near the Chapel of S. Agnes leads into the *Lupanarium,* where are considerable remains of antiquity, together with a *basso-rilievo* of S. Agnes miraculously covered with her own hair; and said to be one of the best works of Algardi!

The Church of S. Agnes is built in the form of a Greek cross; and adorned with stately columns of Granite, a beautiful pavement, a cupola finely painted by Ciro Ferri, Corbellini, and Baciccio; a statue of S. Agnes in the flames, by Ercole Ferrata; an antique statue, now called S. Sebastiano; several fine *bassi-rilievi* (the most striking of which is S. Eustachio among the wild beasts, by Ercole Ferrata); the Mausoleum

---

1 The statue of the Nile has its head covered, to signify that its source was unknown to the ancients.

of Innocent x.; and a high-altar incrusted with flowered alabaster, and adorned with columns of verde antique; and a group in marble of the Holy Family, by Domenichino Guido.

The Lupanarium is damp and cold.

Teatro di Marcello, Piazza Montanara. This Theatre, said to have been the second built at Rome for public exhibitions, was erected by Augustus in honour of his nephew Marcellus; and the architecture is so fine as to have served as a model to all succeeding ages. This edifice was four stories high; but the two upper ones are quite destroyed; and have buried, in their ruins, the seats, orchestra, and stage. Almost half, however, of the wall of the first and second story may be traced. The portico of the first story is Doric; the second story Ionic. This theatre was composed of large blocks of Travertino, and held about twenty-five thousand spectators; the Orsina-Palace stands upon its ruins.

Near the Theatre of Marcellus stood *the Prison of the Decemviri;* in which a woman (according to Pliny and Valerius Maximus) was condemned to be starved to death, and saved by her daughter, who had not long been brought to bed, and who got access to her, and supported her with her milk: till, at length, when this circumstance was discovered, the mother received pardon for the daughter's sake; a pension, likewise, was bestowed upon them; and a temple erected on the spot to filial piety.

Portico d'Octavia. This magnificent edifice, which stands in the Pescheria, or fish-market, was erected by Augustus in honour of his sister Octavia, chiefly for the purpose of sheltering the people from rain. It seems to have enclosed a temple of Jupiter, and another of Juno; the latter of which suffered from fire, and was repaired by Septimius Severus and Caracalla. The portico was of a square form, supported by nearly three hundred columns, and adorned with statues of the most exquisite workmanship: it served as an exhibition-hall for painters on certain days of the year. The present remains seem to have been one of the principal entrances: its form is square, with two fronts, similar to each other, and adorned with fluted Corinthian columns of white marble, supporting an entablature and pediment, all finely executed. The Venus de' Medici was found here.

Tempio d'Esculapio, now *Chiesa di S. Bartolomeo.* This Church stands on what is called the Island of the Tiber; being precisely the space between the *Pons Cestius* and the *Pons Fabricius.* The Romans have a tradition that this island was formed by the corn belonging to Tarquin the Proud, in the Campus Martius, having been cut down, and, by order of the consuls, thrown into the river. About the year of Rome 462, when the city suffered from a pestilence, the Sibylline books were consulted; and an embassy sent, in consequence, to bring Æsculapius of Epidaurus to Rome; when the serpent worshipped by the Epidaurians, under the name of Æsculapius, followed the ambassadors into their ship, remained with them during their voyage home, and then quitted the vessel and swam to the island of the Tiber, where a temple was built for him: and to perpetuate the memory of this event, the figure of a serpent is cut in one of the stones that served for the foundation of this temple. The serpent, however, is in the garden of the Convent belonging to the church; and ladies are not allowed to see the garden without an order from the Cardinal. The columns in the church appear to be antique, and are supposed to have belonged to the Temple of Æsculapius; the Sarcophagus, which forms the altar, is handsome.

Chiesa di S. Cecilia in Trastevere. This edifice is erected on the foundations of the house of S. Cecilia; and contains the Bath wherein she suffered martyrdom.

The Court leading to the church is adorned with a fine antique marble Vase; and the Portico is embellished with antique columns, two of which are granite. The high-altar of the church is adorned with four columns of nero and bianco antico supporting a baldacchino of Parian marble; under which rest the ashes of S. Cecilia, in a tomb composed of alabaster, lapis lazuli, jasper, verde antique, agate, and bronze gilt. Here likewise is the statue of S. Cecilia, by Stefano Maderno, in the position in which she was found after her martyrdom! The pavement encircling the altar is of alabaster and various precious marbles; and the ceiling is adorned with ancient mosaics. Here, also, are a small round picture of the Caracci school, and an ancient pontifical chair. On the right of the great door of the church is an ancient Vapour Bath, quite perfect; whose walls exhibit earthen pipes to convey hot air. This is supposed to be the spot where S. Cecilia was killed; it is now converted into a Chapel, and contains two pictures in the style of Guido; the one representing the decapitation of the Saint, the other her coronation.

Basilica di S. Maria in Trastevere, supposed to stand on the foundations of the *Taberna Meritoria,* which was a hospital for invalid-soldiers. The portico of this edifice is supported by antique granite columns, and adorned with ancient mosaics: it likewise contains several ancient inscriptions. The church is a noble structure, divided into three naves by twenty-two magnificent antique columns of red and grey granite: four columns of the same description support a fine architrave; and some of the capitals are adorned with heads of Jupiter and Juno. The pavement is that kind of mosaic which was invented by the Emperor Alexander Severus, and consists of porphyry, verde antique, etc. In the centre of the roof of the middle aisle is an Assumption of the Virgin, by Domenichino!!! and the Chapel to the left, on approaching the high-altar, is embellished with frescos attributed to the same great artist. The baldacchino of the high-altar is supported by four columns of porphyry, and the tribuna adorned with mosaics of the twelfth century. Here, likewise, are two still more ancient mosaics; the one representing birds, the other a sea-port. This Basilica also contains an ancient pontifical Chair; together with the Tombs of two celebrated painters, the Cav. Lanfranco, and Ciro Ferri.

In the Piazza, before the church, is a Fountain, made during the Pontificate of Adrian I., and the most ancient of modern Rome.

Chiesa di S. Prisca, Monte

Aventino. On the left, in ascending the Aventine hill from Rome, is this church; supposed to have been originally a Temple of Diana. Twenty-four antique columns yet remain; and an Isiaic table was found near the church; which circumstance leads some persons to imagine it was a temple of Isis; especially as Isis had a temple on the Aventine hill.

Chiesa di S. Sabina. Further, to the right, is this noble edifice, supposed to stand on the foundations of the Temple of Diana, built by Servius Tullus for the common use of the cities of Latium; and therefore called *Templum commune Latium*: or, else, on the site of the temple of Juno, built by Camillus. But all we know to a certainty on this subject is, that the portico exhibits four antique columns, two of which are rare granite; that the interior of the church is supported by twenty-four particularly beautiful antique fluted shafts of Parian marble, with Corinthian bases and capitals; and that the shape of the church resembles an ancient temple. In the last chapel on the right of the high-altar is a picture, by Sassoferato, representing the Madonna, S. Domenico, S. Caterina, and Angels!! The small paintings round this fine work are good: they represent the life of our Saviour.

Chiesa di S. Alessio. Still further to the right is this edifice, supposed, by some persons, to have been erected on the foundations of the Temple of Hercules. Here are an ancient Pavement and an ancient Well. The high-altar is adorned with fine columns of verde antique; the tabernacle is handsome; and adjoining to the church is the villa of the deceased King of Spain, said to stand on, or near, the site of the Temple of the *Dea Bona*.[1] The Garden belonging to this Villa commands a fine view. Behind the Aventine hill is *Monte Testaccio*, anciently *Mons Testaceus*; which, though one hundred and sixty-three feet in height, and above five hundred feet in circumference, is composed, almost entirely, of potsherds; conjectured to have been heaped upon this spot, in former ages, by workmen belonging to the potteries of the neighbourhood.

Sepolcro di Cajo Cestio. This Pyramid, erected in memory of Caius Cestius, *Septemvir Epulonum*, or provider for the feasts of the gods, measures a hundred and thirteen feet in height; and each of its four sides is, at the base, sixty-nine feet in length. It was built in three hundred and thirty days, and adorned with paintings, now almost totally effaced. It stands near the Porta S Paolo, called *Ostiense*, by Aurelian.

Terme di Caracalla. On the plain below the Aventine, and opposite to the Celian hill, are the magnificent ruins of Caracalla's Baths; which contained sixteen hundred *Sellæ*, or bathing places; and were ornamented with the Farnese Hercules of Glycon, the group of the Toro Farnese, and the celebrated Farnese Flora. The building seems to have been nearly square; and consisted of subterranean apartments, with two stories above them. In order to see what remains, drive toward the Porta S. Sebastiano, till, on the right, you find a green lane (called

---

[1] The Earth.

Via Antonina), leading to a door,[1] through which you enter a vast pile of ruins, once part of the Baths. Here may be traced two immense Courts, which appear to have been open, with niches for statues, and perhaps for baths likewise. Here, also, are two staircases, and almost innumerable apartments of various dimensions.[2] The height of the walls is great; and the whole exhibits one of the best specimens of ancient Roman architecture now existing. After having examined these ruins, return down the Via Antonina; and enter a Garden on the right, which exhibits remains of the subterranean apartments.

Sepolcro de' Scipioni. This Tomb is situated in a Vineyard, on the Via-Appia, still nearer to the Porto S. Sebastiano than are the Baths of Caracalla: it is on the left side of the way, and the words, "*Sepulchra Scipionum*," are inscribed over the door. This was the tomb of Lucius Cornelius Scipio Barbatus, great grandfather of Asiaticus and Africanus; it is a handsome piece of Doric architecture, very perfect, very extensive, and extremely interesting, though now robbed of its most valuable treasures. The candles provided by the Custode of this subterranean repository are so few in number, that persons who wish to see it distinctly, should carry lights of their own: it is excessively damp.

Porta di S. Sebastiano. This is the Appian Gate, sometimes called *Capena*, though that gate appears to have stood below the Villa Mattei, between the Celian and Aventine hills. Immediately within the gate of S. Sebastiano is an Arch, called *that of Drusus*, though it probably belonged to an aqueduct.

Basilica di S. Sebastiano alle Catacombe. This Church is about two miles distant from the gate: it has a portico supported by antique columns, and is supposed to have been erected by Constantine. The high-altar is adorned with four antique columns of green marble; and over the three doors of ingress are paintings, by Antonio Caracci. Under this church are Catacombs, originally formed, no doubt, by the ancient Romans, and whence they took the pozzolana of which their buildings were made. The Christians enlarged these Catacombs, and, in times of persecution, used them as hiding-places and cemeteries; they are said to extend several miles. It is often necessary to stoop in going through these caverns, but, generally speaking, they are neither damp nor difficult of access. The passages are from two to three feet wide; the chambers (of which there are several) from four to six feet broad, and from six to eight in length, some of them being still larger; and here it is said the primitive Christians performed their religious exercises. In the walls are cavities about a span and a half high, and between four and five long, many of which are open and empty; others closed with a piece of marble, sometimes containing an inscription. Few of these cavities appear large enough to contain a full-grown person, though the skeletons of children have frequently been found in them; and this circumstance makes

---

[1] The person who keeps the key of the door lives in a Garden near at hand.
[2] By ascending one of these staircases, which is, however, a service of danger, you see the whole extent of the Baths.

the conjecture, that children, among the ancients, were oftener buried than burnt, very plausible. Here have been discovered several small vases, called lachrymatories, though more probably incense-bottles; and here likewise are places for cinerary urns. When this mark, "☧" is found upon a monument, it is deemed a sure indication of a martyr's sepulchre, being a composition, from the Latin and Greek alphabets, to denote *Pro Christo*.[1] The cross on a monument is also considered as a sign that a Christian lies buried there; but it should be remembered that a cross was the Egyptian emblem of eternal life, and many crosses have been discovered upon Egyptian tombs, and likewise in the temples of Serapis. The churches of S. Lorenzo and S. Agnes also lead to ancient Catacombs, whose extent cannot be accurately known, because it is impossible to explore every part of them, as their communications with each other are so intricate, that several persons have lost themselves in these subterranean labyrinths; which are, however, supposed to be the *Puticuli* mentioned by Horace, Varro, and Festus Pompeius, where the bodies of slaves only, or persons whose circumstances would not allow of their being burnt on funeral piles, were deposited: but, in process of time, persons of a higher rank might probably be interred here, for the Romans, before Christianity prevailed, often buried their dead, as is evident from monumental inscriptions beginning with the words *Diis Manibus*. The Chapel of the Catacombs of S. Sebastiano contains a bust of that Saint, by Bernini. It is necessary to carry lights, in order to see these Catacombs well.

Circo di Caracalla. On the left side of the road, and at the foot of the hill on which stands the tomb of Cecilia Metella, is the Circus of Caracalla, together with ruins of various edifices belonging to it. The first of these that presents itself is a large Rotunda, supposed to have been the quarters of the Pretorian Guard, while the Emperor attended the Circus; and, enclosing this Rotunda, whose second story was a Serapeon, are remains of a double row of lofty walls, between which, it is supposed, were the stables of the horses used for the chariot-races; while the open inner-space, or quadrangle, where stood the before named Serapeon, contained the cars. Near this building is an ancient sepulchre, leading to the Circus of Caracalla, which is more perfect than any other of the whole fifteen that once adorned Rome; for here, the *Metæ*, the *Spina*, the situation of the Obelisk, the seats, and the porticos whither the spectators retired in case of rain, are all discoverable. The Emperor's seat, or *Podium*, seems to have been opposite to the first *Meta*, and from the *Podium* he gave the signal to begin the race. The Spina was raised above the level of the Arena, that the cars might not break in upon the obelisk, altars, and statues which adorned it. The *Meta* was broader than the *Spina*, and along the sides of the Circus, between the seats and the *arena*, was a ditch filled with water, to prevent the cars from aproaching too near the spectators. There was a space of ebout twelve feet

---

[1] Χριστος is the Greek word for Christ.

between the *Metæ* and *Spina*, serving as a passage to the latter, and to the cells where, it is supposed, the altars of Consus were concealed; he seems to have been the God of Counsel; and hence the Romans called a consultation, *Consilium*, and their chief magistrates, *Consules*: they hid the altar underground, to signify that counsels ought to be kept secret. In the great area, between the first *Meta* and the *Carceres*, combats of gladiators and wild beasts were exhibited; and sometimes water was introduced, and *Naumachiæ* represented. In the walls of this Circus, and likewise in those which surround Rome, are earthen pots, whose spherical shape, operating like arches, diminished the perpendicular weight of the fabric, and contributed to strengthen it. The triumphal gate, through which the victors drove, is still nearly perfect, and precisely opposite to the gate of the Via-Appia: the water, likewise, still remains in the Circus, which is supposed to have contained about twenty thousand spectators. To the north of this Circus, in a neighbouring Vineyard, are considerable remains of the Temples of Honour and Virtue, built by Marcellus, after his Sicilian conquests, in the year of Rome 544, and so constructed that it was impossible to enter the former, without passing through the latter.

Sepolcro di Cecilia Metella. Had not the Roman Barons, during the middle ages, converted this beautiful edifice into a fortress, and built a parapet and port-holes round its summit, it might have lasted to eternity, so durable is the manner of its construction. The monument was erected by Crassus, to enclose the remains of his wife, Cecilia Metella; and notwithstanding the above-named ugly parapet, is one of the best preserved sepulchral fabrics of ancient Rome.

About two miles from this monument is an ancient *public Ustrina*, where the dead were burnt: and near the *Fossæ Cluiliæ*, in this neighbourhood, about five miles from Rome, and on a spot now called *Casale Rotondo*, is the scene of combat between the Horatii and Curiatii.

Basilica di S. Paolo, fuori delle Mura. This vast edifice was erected by Constantine over the grave of S. Paul; enlarged by Theodosius, and finished by Honorius. The length of the edifice, exclusive of the tribuna, is two hundred and forty feet, and its breadth one hundred and thirty-eight feet. Antique columns, a hundred and twenty in number, divide it into five aisles; and twenty-four of these columns, placed in the middle-aisle, were taken from Adrian's Mausoleum: they are of rare marble, called pavonazzo, beautifully fluted in a peculiar manner, and of the Corinthian order: each shaft being one entire piece. The pillars which support the great arch of the tribuna are forty-two feet in height, and fifteen in circumference: and behind the shrine of S. Paul is a column, with an equilateral Parian marble base of seven feet, finely worked. The pillars that adorn the altars are porphyry; and under the high-altar, which is rich in precious marbles, rest the ashes of S. Paul. The arch of the great nave is ornamented with mosaics of the year 440; and on the walls, above the columns, are portraits of all the Popes, two hundred and fifty-three in number, beginning with S. Peter and ending with Pius VII. The pavement abounds with fragments of ancient sepulchral inscriptions; and the centre entrance-door, consisting of bronze embellished with *bassi-rilievi*, was cast at Constantinople in 1070. The outside of this church is adorned with mosaics; and under the portico of the adjoining Cloister are antique marbles, and inscriptions.[1]

Chiesa di S. Paolo alle tre Fontane. Near two miles beyond the Basilica of S. Paul is the spot where this great Apostle suffered; and where considerable numbers of Christians were executed, by command of the Emperor Diocletian, after he had employed them in erecting his Baths. On this spot are three Churches: the first, *S. Maria Scala Cœli*, was built by Vignola, and is deemed a good piece of architecture: the inside, an octagon, contains a mosaic, by Francesco Zucca, of the school of Vasari; said to be the first thing of its kind executed in good taste, after the revival of the arts. The second Church, that of *Saints Vincenzo and Anastasio*, contains frescos of the twelve Apostles, a *Noli me tangere*, and the Baptism of our Saviour; all executed after the designs of Raphael, but much injured, except the two last. The third Church, that of *S. Paul*, was built by Giacomo della Porta, and does honour to his taste. The interior of the edifice contains two altars, and three Fountains, called miraculous; together with ten columns of rare marble,[2] which adorn the fountains and altars. Here is a White Stone, on which the head of S. Paul is supposed to have been cut off: and here, likewise, is a picture of the Crucifixion of S. Peter, by Guido; which appears to have been finely executed, but is now much spoiled.

Excavations on the estate of the Duchess of Chablais. Returning from S. Paolo alle tre Fontana, you see, on the right, not far distant from the Tomb of Cecilia Metella, two excavations, which have recently disclosed the lower part of two ancient Roman Villas. That nearest to the tomb of Cecilia Metella is supposed to have belonged to the Consul Marcus Procus, or his daughter; and exhibits the shape and walls of several rooms, where *bassi-rilievi* and a statue have been found; and also some beautiful pavements. The rooms seem to have been painted like those at Pompeii. The plan of this Villa is discoverable, so far as to prove that the apartments were small, though numerous. Here I found ancient glass, some pieces being very thick, others very thin, and in a state of decay. The Villa on the hill to the left exhibits subterranean arches, above which are the foundations of a square portico, once supported, as it seems, by forty stuccoed pillars. The centre of this portico is not excavated: the walls appear to have been adorned with paintings; and the floors paved, like those of the opposite Villa. The first-mentioned Villa was discovered in consequence of a piece of tessellated pavement being worked out of a mole-hill.

Chiesa di S. Urbano alla Caffarella. On the eminence

---

[1] The Kings of England were the protectors of the Basilica of S. Paul before the Reformation.

[2] Two of these columns are green porphyry.

above the Fountain of Egeria is a Church dedicated to S. Urbano; and originally an ancient Temple; supposed, by some writers, to have been consecrated to Bacchus, because it contains an altar dedicated to him. According to other opinions, however, this was originally the Temple of the Muses. Four fluted Corinthian columns of white marble, which once supported the portico, now adorn the outside of the church: the inside is ornamented with a fine frieze of stucco, and medallions of the same on the roof.

Fontana della Dea, Egeria. This Grotto, according to Flaminius Vacca, was consecrated, by Numa Pompilius, to the Wood-Nymphs; and the wather which supplies its Fountain is the Ovidian Almo. At the upper end of the Grotto are remains of a recumbent statue, called Egeria; and round the walls are niches, apparently made for the reception of other statues. It seems probable that there were several of these Nymphæa in the Egerian valley.[1]

Tempio di Redicolo, or more properly *Redeundo*. This Temple, erected when Hannibal raised the siege of Rome, and returned toward Naples, was, therefore, called *the Temple of the Return*, as the word expresses. It is a beautiful brick edifice, adorned with pilasters; and once had a portico, now quite destroyed.

Porta-Pia. This Gate, built by Pius IV., was anciently called *Porta-Nomentana*; because it led to Nomentum.

Chiesa di S. Agnese fuori di Porta-Pia. This Edifice, which is about one mile from Rome, was erected by Constantine over the grave of S. Agnes, at the desire of his daughter Constantia. A corridor, containing forty-eight steps of fine marble, leads down into the church; and on the walls of this corridor are ancient inscriptions. The nave is supported by sixteen antique columns; two of which are beautifully fluted; and the only specimen of the kind now to be met with at Rome. Four other columns, near the high-altar, are of rare marble; and those which support the baldacchino are of the finest porphyry. The high altar is composed of precious marbles, and adorned with two antique Candelabra of bronze gilt; under it lie the ashes of S. Agnes. The Chapel of the Madonna contains a beautiful antique Candelabrum, and a head of our Saviour, by Buonaroti.

Chiesa di S. Costanza. Near the church of S. Agnes is that of S. Costanza; dedicated, by Constantine, to Christian worship, that it might serve as a burial-place for his daughter. This elegant rotunda, supposed to have been originally a temple consecrated to Bacchus, still retains its ancient form. The cupola is supported by twenty-four granite co-

---

[1] The lower classes of the Roman people go annually, on the first Sunday in May, to the Valley of Egeria; where they carouse, and crown themselves with flowers; thence returning to Rome, like Bacchanals, dancing and singing to various instruments of music. This festival commences with the dawn, and ends about mid-day.

Near half a mile beyond the Porta S. Sebastiano, on the left, is a small rivulet, which, being impeded in its course, has formed a marsh: beyond this rivulet is a gradual ascent to the Chapel of *Domine, quo vadis;* where the road divides into two branches; that on the left leading to the Tempio di Redeundo: and from the commencement of the marsh to this temple, and perhaps beyond it, appears to have been the site of Hannibal's Camp.

lumns, placed in a double circle; and in the middle of the church is an elevated square, on which the pagan altar seems formerly to have stood, and where the remains of S. Costanza afterward rested. That part of the roof nearest to the circular wall is adorned with beautiful ancient mosaics, representing a vintage, birds, and arabesques; and apparently executed when the arts were in their highest perfection. The porphyry sarcophagus, ornamented with boys and grapes, which is now in the Vatican Museum, was taken from this temple.

Adjoining to the church of S. Costanza are considerable remains of *a Hippodrome*, built by Constantine, where horses were trained and exercised.[1]

A little further on, is the *Villa-Faonte*, where Nero was supposed to kill himself; and, about one mile from this villa, is the *Ponte Lamentano*, anciently *Pons Nomentanus*, near which are remains of two Sepulchres; that on the left seems to have been *the tomb of Menenius Agrippa*, and now serves as a shelter for oxen; the other is nearly destroyed. Immediately behind these tombs rises, in an amphitheatrical form, the *Mons Sacer;* whither the Plebeians retired, in the year of Rome 260, by the advice of Sicinius; till persuaded to return, by the eloquence of the above-named Menenius Agrippa: and whither they again retired, in the year of Rome 305, in consequence of the tyranny of Appius Claudius.

Porta di S. Lorenzo. This edifice, originally one of the arches of the Martian,[2] Tepulan, and Julian, aqueduct, was made into a City Gate by Aurelian; who called it *Porta-Collatina*, because it leads to Collatia, where Lucretia killed herself.

Basilica di S. Lorenzo. About one mile from the gate of S. Lorenzo is this church; which was erected by Constantine on the foundations of a temple consecrated to Neptune, of which there are considerable and beautiful remains; namely, the six pillars of the portico, four of which are fluted; two pillars of green porphyry at the extremity of the tribuna behind the high-altar; four of red porphyry, which support the baldacchino; a fine antique cornice round the tribuna; ten fluted columns of pavonazzo, partly buried in the earth, two of them having military capitals, the other eight Corinthian capitals beautifully executed: twenty-two columns of oriental granite, which support the nave; together with some very ancient pavement, and some of the time of Constantine. To the right, on enterinng the church, is a Sarcophagus, adorned with *bassi-rilievi* representing an ancient marriage ceremony! and, behind the high-altar is another Sarcophagus with Bacchanalian emblems. The ashes of S. Lorenzo, and other Christian Martyrs, rest here.

Porta Maggiore. This gate, formerly called *Prænestina*, is one of the arches of the *Castellum* of the Claudian aqueduct, which conveyed three streams of water to Rome;

---

1 Beyond the Church of S. Costanza, on the right, in the Garden of the Villa Ruffini, is a Columbarium, recently discovered, and containing a large number of cinerary urns, human bones, and inscriptions. It appears to have been a public burial-place.

2 The Martian Aqueduct, an Etruscan work, merits notice, on account of its great antiquity; as the *Aqua Martia* is supposed to have been conveyed to Rome from the Lake Fucinus (above thirty miles distant), by Ancus Martius.

two coming forty-five miles, and the third above sixty. It is practicable, by the aid of a ladder, to ascend into this Aqueduct at the Gate of S. Lorenzo. The ancient *Porta-Prænestina*, seems to have been so called because it led to Præneste; and the modern name might, probably, have been given because the gate stands in the road to S. Maria Maggiore.

About two miles distant from the Porta-Maggiore, and parallel with the ancient Via-Præneste, is a spot called *Tor de' Schiavi;* where, among other ruins of an ancient Roman Village, are the remains of three Temples, one of which is well preserved, and the subterranean part particularly merits notice.

Porta S. Giovanni. This Gate, anciently called *Celimontana*, from being placed on the *Mons Cælius,* was restored by Gregory XIII., according to the designs of Giacomo della Porta.

The road beyond the Porta S. Giovanni exhibits magnificent remains of the Claudian, Tepulan, and Marcian aqueducts; together with several ancient tombs : and previous to passing the Acqua Santa, formerly called *Salutare*, you see a small, square, brick edifice, adorned with Doric columns, and supposed to have been the Temple of *Fortuna Muliebris* erected by the Roman Senate, in honour of the ladies, on the spot where Veturia and Volumnia overcame the determination of Coriolanus. This Temple was restored by Faustina the younger.[1] Further on to the right, and about five miles from Rome, is a large farm, belonging to the Torlonia family, and called *Roma Vecchia;* but, probably, nothing more than an ancient Roman village (as the suburbs of the city could scarcely have extended so far); where, among other ruins, are the remains of a Theatre, and Reservoirs of Baths, one of them being full of water : they precisely resemble the Sette Salle of the Baths of Titus. Beyond these reservoirs, and still further to the right, is a peculiarly shaped Tomb, which belonged to the family of Cecilia Metella.

GATES OF ROME, NOT ALREADY MENTIONED.

Porta-Angelica, built by Pius IV. Near this gate passed the *Via Triumphalis*, which came down from the *Clivus Cinnæ*, a part of the Janiculum, and now called Monte Mario.

Porta-Latina, supposed to have been the *Porta-Firentina*.

Porta-Pinciana, said to have taken its name from the palace of the Pincian family which stood near it, and from whom the whole hill was called *Mons Pincius*.

Porta-Portense, so denominated from the magnificent harbour of Porto, constructed by Claudius. The gardens, which Julius Cæsar bequeathed to the people, are supposed to have been near this gate.

Porta di S. Pancrazio, anciently called *Aurelia*. By this Gate Trajan's Aqueduct enters Rome : its course is thirty-five miles; and in consequence of having been renewed and augmented by Paul V., it is now called Acqua-Paolo.

---

[1] Between Rome and Torre di Mezza-via, on the left, are three of these square brick edifices; all of which appear to have been ancient Temples : and that nearest to Torre di Mezza-via seems to answer the description given of the Temple of Fortuna Muliebris, better than does any other edifice of this kind on the road to Albano.

BRIDGES OF ROME.

Pons Ælius, now *Ponte S. Angelo.* This fine bridge was constructed by the Emperor Adrian, and repaired by Clement IX.; who, under the direction of Bernini, adorned it with balustrades and statues, which still remain.

Pons Triumphalis, so called, because the Roman generals passed over this bridge when they obtained the honour of a triumph. It is now destroyed; but its remains may be discovered between the Castle of S. Angelo and the Church of S. Giovanni de' Fiorentini when the Tiber is low.

Ponte Sisto, formerly called *Pons Janiculensis*, on account of its proximity to the Janiculum hill. According to some opinions this bridge was built by Trajan; and, according to others, by Antoninus Pius. It was repaired by Sextus IV., and, in consequence, called by his name.

Pons Fabricius, now *Ponte Dei Quattro Capi.* This bridge was constructed, in the year of Rome 738, by Fabricius, *Curator Viarum* (inspector of roads), and called Quattro Capi from two Hermæ of Janus Quadrifrons, with which it was ornamented.

Pons Cestius, now *Ponte di S. Bartolomeo.* This bridge was constructed by Cestius, in the time of the Republic, and repaired about the year 375 of the Christian æra.

Pons Palatinus, or *Senatorius*, broken down, and now called *Ponte Rotto.* This was the first edifice of its kind which the ancient Romans built of stone. The Censor Fulvius is supposed to have begun, and Scipio Africanus and L. Mummius to have finished it. Julius III. and Gregory XIII. repaired this bridge; but the extraordinary inundations of 1598 totally destroyed it.

Pons Sublicius. This bridge, the first thrown over the Tiber, was the work of Ancus Martius; and acquired the name of *Sublicius* from the wooden piles which supported it. On this bridge Horatius Cocles stopped the army of Porsenna, till the Romans had broken down that part which was behind their gallant leader, who then threw himself into the river, and swam to Rome. After that event the planks were laid across, without being fixed with nails, that they might be removed, in case of sudden danger. This bridge was repaired, under Augustus, by M. Æmilius Lepidus; and afterward by Antoninus Pius: but an inundation, in the year 780, broke it down; and, under Nicolas V., it was wholly destroyed. From this bridge the bodies of Commodus and Heliogabolus were thrown into the Tiber; and when that river is low, the remains of the foundations of the bridge may be seen from Ripagrande.

CHAPTER VIII.

ROME.

Basilica di S. Pietro—Obelisk—Fountains—Colonnades—Covered Galleries—Exterior decorations of the Church—Interior dimensions, etc.—Subterranean Church—Ascent to the Cupola and the top of S. Peter's—Old Sacristy—New Sacristy—Vaticano—Museo-Chiaramonti—Museo-Pio-Clementino—Libreria-Vaticano—Chiesa dei P. P. Cappuccini—Palazzi Barberini and Albani—Chiesa di S. Maria della Vittoria—Fontana di Termine—Chiesa di S. Andrea—Palazzo-Pontificio—Palazzo-Rospigliosi—Garden of ditto—Villa Aldobrandini—Fontana di Trevi—Chiese di S. Maria del Popolo—S. Carlo al Corso—S. Lorenzo in Lucina—S. Ignazio—de' S. S. Apostoli—di S. Maria di Loretto—Gesù—S. Andrea della Valle—della Trinità de' Pelegrini—di S. Carlo a Catenari—S. Giovanni de' Fiorentini—S. Maria in Vallicella—S. Maria della Pace—S. Agostino—Palazzi Borghese—Sciarra—Doria—Bracciano—Colonna—Giustiniani—Massimi—Braschi—Farnese—Spada—Mattei—Costaguti—Falconieri—Farnesina—Corsini—Accademia di S. Luca—Villa Olgiati—Borghese—Ludovisia—Albani—Mattei—Church of S. Onofrio—Fontana-Paolina—Villa-Doria-Pamfili—Madama—Mellini—Hospitals—Mosaic Manufacture—Artists—Bankers—Theatres—Carnival—Festival on the Monte Testaccio—Amusements during Lent—Ceremonies of the Holy Week—Illumination of S. Peter's—Fireworks—Days on which the Pope officiates in public—Funeral of the exiled Queen of Spain—Entertainments given to the Emperor of Austria—Kindness of the present Pope to the British Nation—Promenades—Hotels—List of Objects best worth notice, as they lie contiguous to each other.

BASILICA *di S. Pietro.* S. PETER's is placed on the summit of a gentle acclivity, in an immense Piazza of an oval form, once the Circus of Nero. Its centre is adorned with an Obelisk of red Egyptian Granite; the only one which has been preserved entire; it was transported from Heliopolis to Rome by order of Caligula; and afterward placed, by Nero, in his Circus:[1] it measures one hundred and twenty-four feet from the ground to the top of the cross; and was erected by Sixtus V., under the direction of Fontana; who, in order to raise it out of the earth in which it lay buried, contrived forty-one machines with strong ropes and iron rollers; and though all the powers of these machines were applied at once, by means of eight hundred men and one hundred and sixty horses, the work was not accomplished under eight days: and to transport the Obelisk to the place where it now stands, though only three hundred paces from the spot where it lay, cost four months' labour. But the greatest proof of Fontana's skill in mechanics was displayed when he elevated this stupendous mass, and fixed it in its present situation, by the aid of machines consisting of fifty-two powers, all of which were applied at the same moment, in obedience to pre-concerted signals. Being raised to a proper height, it was placed, amidst the acclamations of the people and the discharge of cannon from the Castle of S. Angelo, on the backs of four lions,

[1] The dimensions of the vessel which conveyed this Obelisk to Rome are given by PLINY, lib. xvi. cap. 40.

without any cement; its own ponderosity being sufficient to ensure it from falling. Report says, however, that Fontana nearly miscarried in this last operation; the ropes having stretched so much more than he expected, that the Obelisk could not have been raised high enough to rest on its pedestal, if an English sailor, at a time when every spectator was restricted from speaking, lest the signals should not be heard by the workmen, had not, in defiance to this order, called out—"Wet the ropes;" which being accordingly done, the Obelisk was raised immediately to its destined height. One of the beautiful Fountains that adorn this Piazza was erected by Innocent VIII.; the other by Clement X.; and the Colonnades (deemed a master-piece of architecture) were built by Bernini, during the Pontificate of Alexander VII. Their form is semi-circular; and they consist of two hundred and eighty-four large Doric columns of Travertino, intermixed with eighty-eight pilasters, and forming, on each side of the Piazza, a triple portico, that in the centre being sufficiently spacious for two carriages to pass each other. The height of these colonnades is sixty-one feet, the breadth fifty-six feet, and on the entablature is a balustrade adorned with one hundred and ninety-two statues, each being eleven feet and a half in height. The Fountains were made after the designs of Carlo Maderno; they throw a considerable body of water nine feet high; and the circular basins which receive this water are entire pieces of oriental granite, fifty feet in circumference. Beyond the colonnades are two magnificent covered Galleries, or Cloisters, each being three hundred and sixty feet long, and leading to the Vestibule of the Basilica, which stands on the summit of a noble flight of steps, adorned with statues of S. Peter and S. Paul, by Mino di Fiesole. The Vestibule (which is four hundred and thirty-nine feet long, by thirty-seven wide and sixty-two feet high,) contains equestrian statues of Constantine and Charlemagne;[1] together with a celebrated Mosaic, by Giotto, called *La Navicella di S. Pietro*. The front of the Basilica, which was built according to the designs of Carlo Maderno, is adorned with immense Corinthian columns and pilasters of Travertino; and terminated by a balustrade surmounted by thirteen colossal statues, seventeen feet in height, and representing our Saviour and the Apostles. The *basso-rilievo*, under the balcony in the centre of the building, is by Buonvicino, and represents our Saviour giving the keys to S. Peter. The centre door of the church is bronze, adorned with *bassi-rilievi*; and was made during the Pontificate of Eugenius IV.; and over this door is a *basso-rilievo*, by Bernini, representing our Saviour intrusting the care of his flock to S. Peter. The circumstance of that Apostle having been buried in the Circus of Nero induced Constantine to erect, over his remains, a spacious church; which, having stood eleven centuries, and, at length, falling into decay, Nicholas V. began to rebuild, about the year 1450, after

---

[1] The statue of Charlemagne was done by Agostino Cornacchini, and that of Constantine by Bernini.

the plans of Rosellini and Alberti: his successors, however, discontinued the work, till the Pontificate of Paul II., under whom it went on. Julius II., who was elected Pope about thirty years after the death of Paul, chose the famous Bramante as his architect; and this artist formed the design of erecting a cupola in the centre of the edifice. On the demise of Julius and Bramante, Leo X. intrusted the work to Raphael, and other artists; after whose death Paul III. chose Sangallo as his architect; and, upon the decease of this artist, the last-mentioned Pope committed the work to Buonaroti, who made a new design for the cupola: he likewise intended to have erected a portico, resembling that of the Pantheon; but death frustrated his purpose. Succeeding artists, however, were directed to go on with his cupola; which was completed during the Pontificate of Sixtus V. Carlo Maderno finished the other part of the church, in the Pontificate of Paul V.; and Pius VI. erected the new Sacristy. Buonaroti intended to have built S. Peter's in the form of a Greek cross; but Carlo Maderno followed the plan of Bramante, and made a Latin one. In the year 1694. this edifice was supposed to have cost 47,000,000 Roman crowns; and much more has been since expended for the Mosaics, the new sacristy, etc.

The interior length of S. Peter's from the entrance-door to the end of the tribuna, is six hundred and thirteen English feet; the breadth of the nave two hundred and seven, the breadth of the cross seventy-eight, the diameter of the cupola one hundred and thirty-nine, the height, from the pavement to the first gallery, one hundred and seventy-four, to the second gallery, two hundred and forty, to the representation of the Deity in the lantern, three hundred and ninety-three, and to the summit of the exterior cross, four hundred and fifty-eight feet.[1] So admirably proportioned is this church, that, notwithstanding its immense size, no person, at first sight, perceives the dimensions to be remarkably large: and the statues of children, which support the vases for holy water, do not appear more than three feet in height, though they are really gigantic. The interior of this master-piece of human genius is incrusted with rare and beautiful marbles, adorned with the finest pictures in mosaic existing, and supported by an immense number of magnificent columns, the greater part of which are antique; and seven, if report speak true, were taken from Solomon's Temple. The pavement is marble, and very handsome.

The Sacra Confessione was designed by Carlo Maderno, and is superbly decorated with costly lamps and precious marbles. The Baldacchino was erected by Urban VIII., after the designs of Bernini; and is made of bronze gilt, and nearly ninety feet high. The designs for the mosaics in the Cupola under which the Baldacchino stands, were drawn by Giuseppe d'Arpino; and the Evangelists particulary merit notice; as does the statue of S. Andrew near the high altar, by Du Quesnoy, and that of S. Domenico, by Le Gros. The bronze statue of S. Peter is said to have been cast during the

---

[1] These dimensions are taken from a table in manuscript, hung up in the lower gallery of the Cupola.

Pontificate of Gregory the Great, from the fragments of a demolished statue of Jupiter Capitolinus. At the upper end of the middle nave is the Tribuna, decorated according to the designs of Buonaroti; and containing the Chair of S. Peter; above which the Holy Ghost is represented in painted glass, in the form of a dove. On each side of the Tribuna is a magnificent Monument; that on the right, by Bernini, being in memory of Urban VIII. (whose statue is finely executed in bronze); and that on the left designed by Buonaroti, and executed by Guglielmo della Porta, in memory of Paul III.!! it represents Prudence as an old woman, and Justice as a girl, so beautiful that a Spaniard, Pygmalion-like, is said to have fallen in love with this statue; in consequence of which it was clothed with a bronze garment. Near the tribuna is the tomb of Alexander VIII., adorned with a beautiful *basso-rilievo*, by Angelo Rossi; and over the altar of S. Leo the Great, between columns of red oriental granite, is an *alto-rilievo* of that Pope threatening Attila, King of the Huns, with the vengeance of S. Peter and S. Paul, by Algardi!! Near this altar are two fine Mosaics;[1] the one representing the crucifixion of S. Paul, being a copy from a celebrated picture, by Guido, the other representing the fall of Simon Magus, was copied from a celebrated picture by Francesco Vanni. Further on is a Mosaic of Raphael's Transfiguration; and near it the Tomb of Leo XI., by Algardi. On this side of the church is the Capella del Coro, where the Cardinals, Canons, etc., assemble daily, to attend divine worship; and where there frequently is particularly good music. Not far hence, in an unornamented tomb, rest the remains of Pius VI.; illustrious for the patience and resignation he displayed in adversity;[2] and over the door which leads to the Cupola is a monument to the memory of Maria Clementina Sobieski, with her picture copied in mosaic by the Cav. Cristofari, from a painting by Sterne. The last Chapel on this side contains the baptismal Font, originally the tomb of the Emperor Otho II.; it consists of porphyry, with bronze ornaments, executed by Fontana. Over the altar in this Chapel is a fine Mosaic, copied from a celebrated picture by Carlo Maratta, representing the baptism of our Saviour. On the opposite side of the church is a Chapel containing a *Pietà* by Buonaroti, which appears to disadvantage from not being equally colossal with almost every other surrounding object; the Frescos here are by Lanfranco: on this side, likewise, is a Chapel containing a Column said to be that against which our Saviour leaned when he disputed with the Doctors; and a Sarcophagus which once enclosed the ashes of Probus Anicius, Prefect of Rome. The Braschi-Chapel contains a Crucifix, by Ghirlandajo. Further on,

---

1 These Mosaics, called *Roman*, consist of small pieces of glass (some of them being scarcely larger than pins' heads) tinctured with all the different degrees of colour necessary to form a picture: and when the Mosaics are finished, they are polished in the same manner as mirrors. The ground on which these vitreous particles are placed consists of calcined marble, fine sand, gum-tragacanth, whites of eggs, and oil; which composition continues, for some time, so soft that there is no difficulty either in arranging the pieces, or altering any which may have been improperly placed: but, by degrees, it grows as hard as marble; so that no impression can be made on the work.

2 A monument to the memory of this unfortunate Pontiff is now erected.

toward the high-altar, is the tomb of Christina of Sweden, by Fontana; and over the altar of the Chapel of S. Sebastiano is a fine Mosaic of the martyrdom of that Saint, copied from a celebrated picture, by Domenichino. Beyond this Chapel is the tomb of the Countess Matilda (who died in 1115), by Bernini; and opposite to the Cappella del Coro is the Cappella del Sacramento, which contains a rich Tabernacle, made after the designs of Bernini, and an Altar-Piece painted in fresco by Pietro di Cortona; here, likewise, is the tomb of Sixtus IV., in bronze, adorned with *bassi-rilievi* by Antonio Pollajuolo. Further on is the tomb of Gregory XIII., adorned with statues of Religion and Energy, the latter of which is much admired; and near this monument is a beautiful copy, in mosaic, of Domenichino's *chef-d'œuvre*, the communion of S. Girolamo; for which picture he received only three crowns. Further on, is a copy, in mosaic, of the martyrdom of S. Erasmus, by Niccolo Poussin. Nearer still to the tribuna is a copy, in mosaic, of S. Peter sinking, by Lanfranco: and opposite to this Mosaic is the monument of Clement XIII., by Canova, who has adorned it with recumbent statues of two lions, both excellently executed, and especially that which sleeps. Further on is a copy, in mosaic, of Guido's *chef-d'œuvre*, the Arch-Angel Michael, and likewise a copy, in mosaic, of Guercino's celebrated picture, representing the story of S. Petronilla. This is deemed the finest Mosaic in S. Peter's; and was executed by the Cav. Cristofari. Beyond the altar of S. Petronilla is the monument of Clement X., whose statue was done by Ercole Ferrata: and opposite to this tomb is a copy, in mosaic, of S. Peter raising Tabitha, by Placido Costanzi. The Mosaics which adorn the small cupolas, ten in number, are executed after the designs of celebrated painters.

Under S. Peter's is a subterranean Church, built by Constantine, into which ladies are not usually allowed to descend without permission from the Pope; this permission, however, may easily be obtained.

At the entrance of the circular corridor of the subterranean Church is the Cappella della Confessione, built in the form of a Latin cross; and immediately under the high-altar of the new church. Clement VIII. adorned this chapel with precious marbles, and twenty-four bronze *bassi-rilievi*, representing memorable events in the lives of S. Peter and S. Paul, whose portraits, painted on silver, adorn the altar which covers S. Peter's ashes. Opposite to this Chapel is the Sarcophagus of Junius Bassus, Prefect of Rome; who died in the year 359. Here, likewise, are several other tombs; namely, that of Charlotte, Queen of Jerusalem and Cyprus; that of the Stuarts; and those of Adrian IV., Boniface VIII., Nicolas V., Urban VI., and Pius II. Here, also, are a considerable number of Statues; and among them one of S. Peter; together with *bassi-rilievi*, ancient Mosaics, and interesting Inscriptions. The height of the subterranean church is between eleven and twelve English feet; and the pavement the same as in the days of Constantine.

The door under the monument of Maria-Clementina Sobieski

leads to a staircase, consisting of one hundred and forty-two steps, by which mules might mount nearly to the top of S. Peter's — so easy is the ascent—and on one of the landing-places the Custode of the Cupola may usually be found. It is impossible to form a just idea of the size of this wonderful church, without seeing the upper part; and equally impossible to appreciate the architectural merit of the great cupola without examining its construction. This stupendous fabric is double; and by means of staircases, between the exterior and interior walls, it is not difficult to ascend into the lantern; the ball on the top of which measures twenty-four feet in circumference.

The old Sacristy of S. Peter's (a rotunda), is supposed to have been a Temple of Apollo, which stood at the side of Nero's Circus; the *new Sacristy* was built after the designs of Carlo Marchioni; and communicates with the Basilica by means of two corridors: it is divided into nearly equal parts; one serving for a Sacristy, the other being appropriated to the Canons. In the Vestibule is a statue of S. Andrew, together with columns and pilasters of red oriental granite. This apartment leads to three galleries, adorned with fine columns of African marble pilasters and busts. Opposite to the door of the great Sacristy is a staircase, whose landing-place is adorned with a statue of Pius VI. The great Sacristy is an octagon, fifty feet in diameter, adorned with antique columns and pilasters, which support a cupola; and its chapel contains four columns of bardiglio di Carrara. The Sacristy of the Canons is furnished with presses of Brazil-wood; and contains a picture, by Francesco Penni, of S. Anne, etc.; ditto by Giulio Romano, of the Madonna, our Saviour, and S. John; and two paintings by Cavallucci. Another apartment contains pictures of the ancient Florentine school; two paintings, by Ghezzi; a dead Christ, attributed to Buonaroti; a picture, by Muziani; and two paintings by Cavalucci.

Vaticano. Some writers suppose this Palace to have been erected by Nero, and afterward bestowed, by Constantine, upon the Roman Pontiffs; while others are of opinion that is was built by Constantine on the site of the Gardens of Nero: it seems to have received augmentations from almost every succeeding Sovereign; insomuch that its present circumference is computed to be near seventy thousand feet. *The Scala Regia*, or great Staircase, at whose foot stands the statue of Constantine, was constructed by Bernini; and leads to *the Sala Regia*, built by Sangallo, and containing Frescos, with Latin inscriptions, explanatory of the subjects. The first painting over the staircase-door represents Charlemagne signing the donation of the Church, and is by Taddeo Zuccari; another represents the entry of Gregory XI., into Rome, accompanied by S. Catherine of Siena, and is by Vasari; another, over the door leading to the Cappella-Paolina, is divided into three parts: that to the right representing Gregory VII. withdrawing the censures cast on Henry IV., in the fortress of Canossa; that on the left representing the city of Tunis reconquered under Charles V.; the third represents Victory and Glory. These paintings are by Taddeo and Federico Zuccari.

The Cappella-Sistina, adjoining to the Sala Regia, was built by Sixtus IV., according to the designs of Baccio Pintelli of Florence, and its ceiling painted by Buonaroti in twenty months, so entirely without assistance, that even the colours he used were prepared by himself. The Prophets and Sibyls, the figure of the Deity, and those of Adam and Eve, are particularly admired!!! The Last Judgment, likewise by Buonaroti, occupies the whole wall behind the altar; he was three years in doing it: and parts of this immense fresco are wonderfully fine.[1] The other walls are adorned with Frescos, representing scripture-histories, by Pietro Perugino, and his Florentine contemporaries. The heads, by Perugino, are fine.

Opposite to the Cappella-Sistina is *the Cappella-Paolina*, erected by Paul III. after the designs of Sangallo. The two columns of porphyry, on the sides of the altar, were found in the Temple of Romulus; and toward the end of each are two infants in *basso-rilievo*. The statues in the angles are by Prospero Bresciano. The paintings, which represent the Conversion of S. Paul, and the Crucifixion of S. Peter, are by Buonaroti; and the fall of Simon Magus, friezes, and ornaments of the ceiling, are by Federico Zuccari.

The Sacristy, near the Cappella-Sistina, contains magnificent plate and jewels.

The *Ceiling of the Sala Ducale* is decorated with arabesques, by Lorenzino da Bologna, and Raphaellino da Reggio.

The Loggia, or open Gallery, above the *Sala Ducale*, leads to the *Stanze di Rafaello;* and is embellished with Arabesques, interspersed with Scripture-Histories, by that great artist and his scholars. Some of the finest of these frescos are, God dividing the light from the darkness, by Raphael; Joseph explaining his dreams, by Giulio Romana; Joseph sold to the Ishmaelites; Joseph explaining the dreams of Pharaoh; and the baptism of the Saviour; by Raphael. The greater part of the small *bassi-rilievi* in this gallery are antique, and supposed to have been taken from the Colisæum, the Baths of Caracalla, and the Villa of Adrian.

The Stanze di Rafaello contain some of the very finest frescos existing; but the injuries these apartments have received from time, and still more from the smoke made in them by German soldiers, when Rome was taken by assault, A.D. 1528, has rendered the paintings with which they are adorned less striking, at first sight, than many other frescos: indeed Cignani, a celebrated artist, admired them so little, on a cursory review, that Carlo Maratta, provoked by his want of penetration, requested him to copy one of the heads in the fire of the Borgo. Cignani began; rub-

---

1 The following lines contain a fair comment on this picture:—
 "Good Michael Angelo, I do not jest,
  Thy pencil *a great Judgment* hath exprest;
  But in that judgment thou, alas, hast shown
  A *very little judgment* of thy own!"

bed out; began again; and again rubbed out; till, at length, after several fruitless attempts, he threw away his pencil, exclaiming, "Raphael is inimitable!"

The *Stanze di Rafaello* are four in number; namely, the *Sala di Costantino;* the *Sala d' Eliodoro;* the *Sala della Scuola de Atene;* and the *Sala di l'Incendio.* The apartment leading to them is adorned with frescos by Raphael, representing the Apostles; and also contains the Chapel of Nicholas v., painted by Angelo di Fiesole, the pupil of Masaccio.

The Hall of Constantine was designed by Raphael, and coloured, after his death, by his scholars. The first picture, on the right, represents Constantine addressing his troops before the battle with Maxentius, and was coloured by Giulio Romano. Raphael has represented the moment when the cross appears in the air supported by Angels, who are supposed to be saying to Constantine, "Conquer by this." The dwarf of Julius II., putting on a helmet, forms an absurd episode in the picture. The next painting represents the battle of Constantine, fought against Maxentius, near the Ponte Molle, A. D. 312: it was coloured by Giulio Romano, Pierino del Vaga, Rafaello del Colle, and Polidoro da Caravaggio; and is, according to some opinions, the first picture in the first class of great works. The most striking groups are, an old soldier raising his dying son; two soldiers fighting, in the same part of the picture; and in the opposite part, Maxentius in the Tiber, vainly struggling to extricate himself. The third picture represents the baptism of Constantine by Pope Silvester; and was coloured by Francesco Penni. Raphael has chosen, for the scene of action, the Baptistery, built by Constantine after he had embraced Christianity, and supposed to be that of S. Giovanni in Laterano. The fourth picture, which was coloured by Rafaello del Colle, represents the donation of the patrimony of the church, by Constantine. The composition is admired; but the figures of Constantine and the Pope are said to want majesty. This picture is full of episodes; namely, soldiers driving the spectators back between the columns; a beggar imploring charity; and a father and son answering him; a woman with her back only visible, who leans upon two other women, in order to see the ceremony; and a child mounted on a dog. *In the second room* is a picture, coloured by Raphael, which represents Heliodorus (Treasurer of Seleucus, King of Asia), who came to pillage the Temple at Jerusalem, thrown down and vanquished by two Angels and a Warrior on horseback, whom God sent to the aid of his High Priest Onias; a circumstance recorded in the second Book of Maccabees. This picture is extremely admired; especially the Angels, who are pursuing Heliodorus with such rapidity that they seem to fly. The Warrior on horseback is strikingly fine: the Temple appears swept of the people in a moment; while, in the back-ground, Onias is discovered, at the altar, invoking Heaven. The episode of Julius II. coming into the Temple on men's shoulders appears to have been a foolish whim of his, with which Raphael was unfortunately obliged to comply, by way of representing that Julius, like Onias, delivered the Church from its oppressors. The Pope's chair-bearer, on the left, is a portrait of Giulio Romano. In the same room is another picture, called the Miracle of Bolsena: it was coloured by Raphael; and represents a priest who doubted the real presence of Our Saviour in the Eucharist; till, being on the point of consecrating the wafer, he saw blood drop from it. This picture is much admired; and was extremely difficult to compose, from being painted round a window, which cuts it nearly in half. Julius II. is again brought forward in an episode, and supposed to be hearing mass; but as the head of the Church is not to question the real presence in the Eucharist, he testifies no surprise at the miracle, though the people, in general, express great astonishment, in which the Swiss guards coldly participate. The heads of the Cardinals, the Pope, and the Priests saying mass, are deemed very beautiful, as is the colouring of the picture. The third painting in this room, celebrated for its composition and groups of figures, represents Attila, King of the Huns, advancing against Rome, and discovering, in the air, S. Peter and S. Paul descending to arrest his progress. Raphael has chosen the moment when the apostles are not discovered by the army in general, but by Attila alone. Pope S. Leo appears on a mule, followed by Cardinals; but Attila attends only to the Apostles. The figure which represents S. Leo is a portrait of Leo x.; and the Mace-bearer, on the white horse before the Pope, is a portrait of Raphael's master, Pietro Perugino. The two Sarmatian horsemen, near Attila, are copied from Trajan's column. The fourth picture in this room was coloured by Raphael, and represents S. Peter delivered from prison by an Angel: it contains a double action, first S. Peter, in prison, waked by the Angel; and secondly, S. Peter, going out of prison, conducted by the Angel. The Apostle's figure is not admired, but that of the Angel is charming; and the manner in which the lights are managed is inimitable. *The third room* contains a picture, coloured by Raphael, which represents the School of Athens; and is, in point of expression, a wonderful work; for every Philosopher, by his posture and gestures, characterizes his doctrines and opinions. The scene is laid in a magnificent building, imitated from the original designs which Bramante and Buonaroti made for the church of S. Pietro in Vaticano. In the centre of the picture are Plato and Aristotle, the masters of the school, standing on the top of a flight of steps, and apparently debating on some philosophical subject: near them is Socrates, counting with his fingers, and speaking to a fine martial figure, who represents Alcibiades. Next to Socrates, and distinguished by a venerable beard, is Nicomachus; and below this group is a young man in white, with his hand upon his breast, said to be the portrait of Francesco, Duke of Urbino, nephew to Julius II. Next to Francesco stands Terpander, the Greek musician, with his eyes fixed on Pythagoras, who is writing; and, before whom, a youth holds a tablet, which contains the harmonic consonances. Next to Nicomachus is Alexander the Great; and, near Aristotle, stands a corpulent bald-headed figure, said to be the portrait of Cardinal Bembo. At the feet of Alcibiades, and clothed in the oriental garb, is Averroes, an Arabian philosopher; and immediately behind him is the profile of Aspasia. On a line with Pythagoras, seated at a table, and apparently in deep meditation, is Epictetus; and beyond him, sitting alone, on the second step, is Diogenes, with a cup by his side, and a scroll in his hand. Raphael has pictured the great architect, Bramante, under the character of Archimedes; who is tracing an hexagonal figure. The youth who stands behind Archimedes, in an attitude of admiration, is said to represent Federigo Gonzaga, first Duke of Mantua. The philosopher who wears a crown, and holds a globe in his hand, is Zoroaster; at whose side stand two persons, the younger of whom, with a black cap, is a portrait of Raphael, the elder, of Pietro Perugino. Talking with Zoroaster, and also holding a globe, is a figure said to represent Giovanni, of the House of Antistes. On the opposite side of the school, and next to the base of a column, is Empedocles seated, and attending to Pythagoras. The old head, which appears just above the book placed on the base of the column, is Epicharmus; and the Child with fine hair, just above Aspasia, is Archytas. Connoisseurs deem the composition of this picture admirable; the colouring soft and good; and the figures elegant and well draped: and as the episodes relate to the subject, they add materially to the interest excited by this piece. In the same room is a painting, the upper part of which represents the three virtues which ought to accompany Justice; namely, Prudence, Temperance, and Fortitude. The lower part represents, on the left, Justinian giving the Digests to Trebonian; and, on the right, Gregory ix., under the figure of Julius ii., presenting his Decretals to an advocate. Opposite to the school of Athens is a painting, called Theology, which represents the dispute relative to the Holy Sacrament; and was coloured by Raphael. The composition of the lower part of this picture, and especially the group of S. Augustine dictating to a youth, is extremely admired; but the upper part, namely, the Blessed Trinity, the Madonna, and S. John the Baptist, is said to be too much in the Gothic style. The heads of S. Gregorio, S. Ambrosio, S. Augustine, S. Domenico, S. Bonaventura, and S. Jerome, are deemed particularly fine. Raphael has represented the four first as Fathers of the Church, seated on each side of an altar, upon which the Host is exposed. The place of assembly represents the foundations of a church, with part of the superstructure begun. The fourth picture in this room was coloured by Raphael; and represents Parnassus. Homer is pictured standing at the summit of the mountain, as an *Improvvisatore*, whom Apollo accompanies on the violin; Dante is placed at the right hand of Homer, and Virgil at the left; the Muses surround Apollo, and the lower regions of the mountain contain groups of celebrated Greek, Latin, and Italian poets. Sappho sits in the fore-ground, holding a scroll with one hand, and a lyre with the other; and apparently listening to Laura, who stands with Petrarca behind a tree. On the opposite side of the mountain, and next to one of the Muses, whose back is toward the spectator, stands Tibullus; and next to him Boccaccio: lower down, with a medallion round his neck, is Ovid; and immediately behind him, Sannazaro; while lower still stands Horace, in an attitude of admiration, listening to Pindar, who, like Sappho, is seated. Raphael has placed himself in the group with Homer and Virgil. *In the fourth room* is a painting which represents the victory gained by Leo IV. over the Saracens at Ostia: it is finely executed. In this room, likewise, is one of Raphael's most celebrated works, finished by himself, and representing the Fire in Borgo S. Spirito, near the Vatican; which happened during the Pontificate of Leo IV. The tumult and high wind, raised by the fire are wonderfully expressed; and the young man carrying his father, the figure sliding down a wall, and the woman carrying water on her head, are particularly admired. In the foreground is another woman, quite frantic, raising her hands toward Leo IV., who appears in a tribune; below which is a fine group of people invoking his assistance. The third picture in this room represents the coronation of Charlemagne, by Leo III. The composition is said to be confused; but the young man in armour in the foreground is much admired. The fourth picture represents Leo III., swearing, before Charlemagne, upon the Gospels, that he was not guilty of the crimes laid to his charge by the party who wished to depose him. The composition of this picture is admired; as are several of the heads.

The surbases of these rooms are finely painted in *chiaro-scuro*, by Polidoro di Caravaggio, and retouched by Carlo Maratta.

The *Loggia*, or open gallery, above the Stanze di Raffaello, leads to *an Apartment containing some of the most celebrated easel-paintings extant.*

First Room. Fortune, by Guido!—the three theological Virtues, by Raphael—religious Mysteries, by ditto—the Madonna, the Saviour, and S. Catherine, by Garofalo—Saints, by Perugino—and two pictures, by Beato da Fiesole, relative to the life of S. Nicolo di Bari.

Second Room. The Transfiguration, by Raphael!!!—the Madonna and Saints by Titian!!—and the Communion of S. Girolamo, by Domenichino!!

Third Room. A *Pietà*, by M. A. Caravaggio!!—S. Helena, by Paolo Veronese—the Resurrection of our Saviour, by Perugino—the Madonna with four Saints, by ditto!—and the assumption of the Madonna, designed by Raphael, and painted by Giulio Romano, and Francesco Penni!

Fourth Room. The Madonna, and two Saints, by Guido—the Nativity of the Madonna, by Albano—S. Gregorio, by Andrea Sacchi—S. Romualdo's Vision, by ditto!!—and the crucifixion of S. Peter, by Guido!

Fifth Room. The Martyrdom of S. Erasmus, by Niccolo Poussin—the Annunciation, by Baroccio—the Incredulity of S. Thomas, by Guercino!—a *Pietà*, by Andrea Mantegna—S. Michelina, by Baroccio!—and the Martyrdom of two Saints, by Valentin.

Sixth Room. The Coronation of the Madonna, by Raphael!—the Madonna di Foligno, by ditto!!!—and the Magdalene, by Guercino!

These rooms are open to the public every Sunday and Thursday morning, from twelve o'clock till four.

Museo-Chiaramonti. Appartamento-Borgia. These rooms, four in number, contain Fragments of statues and *Bassi-rilievi*; fine Capitals of pillars, marble columns—a Statue of Æsculapius—a well-preserved ancient fresco, found on the Esquiline Hill, near the Gardens of Mæcenas, and commonly called, The Aldobrandini Marriage; it is supposed to represent the union of Thetis with Peleus!—six other very inferior Frescos, said to be ancient—an ancient Car, found near the Circus of Caracalla, and supposed to have consisted of wood sheathed with bronze—twelve Etruscan Sarcophagi!—*terra-cotta* Lamps, etc.

One of these rooms is adorned with a beautiful ceiling, by Giovanni da Udine, and Pierino del Vaga; it represents the planets, and the Signs of the Zodiac.

Galleria-Lapidaria.[1] This Gallery contains a very large and valuable collection of ancient Inscriptions; several of which were found in the Catacombs: it likewise contains cinerary Urns, and other sepulchral monuments; together with an immense vase, similar to the Receptacles for the ashes of victims offered to the gods, and ornamented with lions devouring weaker animals, one of the ancient emblems of death.

The second division of the Gallery contains, on the right side, a Sarcophagus adorned with a recumbent female figure, surrounded by little Bacchanalians; and three demi-figures in *alto-rilievo* below; supposed to represent a father, mother and son: it was found near the *Via-Flaminia*—the statue of Venus between two Muses—bust of a female Faun—Herma of Plato—statue of Mercury! between Minerva and Ceres—statue of a Muse, seated—small statue of Diana—fragment, supposed to have represented either Minerva, or victory—colossal bust of Rome—statue of Britannicus—ditto of Demosthenes, or Lysias, seated—statue of Apollo—ditto of Jupiter Serapis, very small—statue of Hercules—bust of Augustus when a youth; found at Ostia!—statue of Marcellus seated! between two fragments—statue of Mercury—small statues representing a wild boar, Mithras, and a Swan!—demi-colossal statue of Tiberius seated! well preserved, and found at Piperno, the ancient Privernum[2]—Group of Silenus and a Tiger between two half-length statues—bust, supposed to represent Pompey—bust, called the

---

[1] Whenever I was permitted to see the Vatican Museum by torch-light, I had four torches (each containing four wicks) placed within a reflector, fastened to a long pole; and the light, thus arranged, was most judiciously thrown on all the finest statues, so as to display and magnify their beauties, while their imperfections were left in shadow. Laocoon, thus viewed, appeared fine beyond conception; because his figure only was exhibited, without the rest of the group.

[2] The fourteen cities of Asia Minor, thrown down either by the earthquake which happened at Our Saviour's crucifixion, or (according to some records) in the year 17, and which cities the Emperor assisted the inhabitants to rebuild, erected a statue to him in consequence. On the same occasion there were two medals stamped of Tiberius; in both of which he is represented sitting, with a patera in one hand, and a spear in the other; in short, precisely in the posture of this statue found at Piperno.

Father of Trajan—bust of Augustus when young!—statues of Ceres, Venus, and Mercury—bust of Neptune, found at Ostia—statues of Ceres, Minerva, and Hygeia—and a colossal recumbent statue of Hercules, found at Tivoli, in Adrian's Villa.

The left side of this division of the Gallery contains a Bust, in *terra-cotta*—statues of Æsculapius—Venus rising from the bath, and a Vestal—colossal statue of Alexander—statue of an Emperor, with the globe in his hand—colossal bust of Trajan—ditto of Isis, found in the Garden of the Quirinal Palace—statue of Atropos, found in Adrian's Villa at Tivoli—statue of an Emperor with Victory in his hand—demi-figure of a Dacian Warrior—small statue of Diana-Luna—statue of Augustus—colossal head of a River-God—statue of Marcus Aurelius, placed on a Sarcophagus—statues of a triform Diana—Septimius Severus—a Faun—Apollo—and Paris—and a Sarcophagus, adorned with a recumbent female figure, surrounded by Genii, who are playing with Tortoises, and other emblems of death.

Hall of the Nile, just beyond the entrance to the second division of the Gallery. This new and splendid apartment is paved with fine marbles, and well-restored ancient mosaics; and likewise embellished with a beautiful modern Frieze, copied from antique *bassi-rilievi* too much injured for use. The centre of the apartment exhibits a magnificent ancient Vase of bronze—the celebrated group of the Nile!!—and a group of the Graces, from the Ruspoli gallery; they are supposed to be Grecian sculpture; but the head of the middle figure is modern. Among the sculpture on the right side of this Hall, are statues of Apollino!—Silenus nursing the Infant Bacchus!!—Augustus's Physician (probably Antonius Musa), in the character of Æsculapius!—Minerva—Ganymedes, found at Ostia—the piping Faun!—an Amazon, probably copied from the famous Amazon of Ctesilaus!—and a Canephoro-bust of Trajan; excellent both with respect to likeness and execution!!-statue supposed to represent Diana in an attitude expressive of pity; the hands and arms are restored—statue called Euripides. On the left side of this Hall are, the statue of a Priestess—ditto of Juno!—a demi-colossal statue of Antinous in the character of Vertumnus: it was found at Ostia; but the head is modern!—statue of Diana—a demi-colossal statue of Fortune, found at Ostia!—bust of Sallust, the Historian!—statues of Pindar—Venus—the celebrated Minerva Medica, from the Giustiniani gallery!!—a Faun—Lucius Verus holding Victory in his hand!—and a Discobolus—bust of a Dacian Chief—and the statue of Titus.

At the end of the second division of the *Galleria Lapidaria, and leading to the Museo Pio-Clementino,* is a *Staircase* adorned with two columns of granite and some arabesques, by Daniello da Volterra: and *to the left of the Staircase, are Apartments* containing Statues, Busts, Egyptian Divinities recently discovered near the first Cataract of the Nile, and deemed some of the most ancient specimens extant of Egyptian sculpture; a Mummy found in the burial-place of the Egyptian

R

princes, and wonderfully well preserved, even to the linen which fills the coffin; Mummies of Cats; several other Egyptian Antiquities, and several plaster Casts, from the British Museum, of Statues and *Bassi-rilievi* found at Athens.

Museo Pio-Clementino. Square Vestibule. This apartment contains arabesques, by Daniello da Volterra—the celebrated Belvedere-Torso, supposed to be the remains of a group representing Hercules and Hebe, after the deification of the former; and executed, according to the inscription it bears, by Apollonius, the son of Nestor of Athens!!!![1]— The Sarcophagus of Lucius Cornelius Scipio Barbatus, with his bust, both found in the Tomb of the Scipio family, and made of stone, called peperino [2] — several Inscriptions relative to the Scipio family (all found in their tomb)—and, opposite to the Sarcophagus, a recumbent statue.

The second Apartment contains a Vase of Greek marble!! and four Fragments of Statues; that of a Female seated being much admired on account of the drapery.

In the Balcony is an ancient Dial.

The third Apartment contains a Statue of Meleager!!—and, fixed into the wall on the right, a *Basso-rilievo* representing the Apotheosis of Homer; and, on the left, two *Bassi-rilievi*, the one representing a sea-port, the other an ancient Roman Galley with soldiers fighting.

Portico of the Court. To the right of the entrance door stands a Column of granite, and another of white marble adorned with foliage—an ancient Bath, of Black basalt, found in Caracalla's Baths —a *Basso-rilievo* fixed in the wall, representing Fauns and Griffons, under which stands a fine Sarcophagus adorned with lions' heads, fauns, and Bacchantes, and found under the new Sacristy of S. Peter's—here, likewise, is the Sarcophagus of Sixtus Varius Marcellus.

First Cabinet. Perseus, by Canova—Wrestlers, by ditto— and, in the niches on the sides of the arch, Statues of Mercury and Pallas.

Continuation of the Portico. On the right, a Sarcophagus representing Bacchus and Ariadne in the island of Naxos — another representing Prisoners imploring clemency from their conqueror— in the large niche, a Statue of Sallustia Barbia Orbiana, wife of Alexander Severus, in the character of Venus accompanied by Cupid—a Sarcophagus representing Achilles slaying the Queen of the Amazons; and, opposite to these, two beautiful Half Columns of rare marble.

Second Cabinet. In the centre is the celebrated statue of Meleager, once called the Belvedere Antinous!!! It was found on a spot, named Adrianello, near the church of S. Martino in Monte; with one of the arms and the left hand wanting.—On the right, fixed in the wall, is a *Basso-rilievo* of Achilles killing the Queen of

---

[1] This Torso is said to have been found in the Campo de' Fiori; and if so, it probably was one of the ornaments of Pompey's Theatre.

[2] It would seem extraordinary that the bust and sarcophagus of one of the greatest men of the age in which he flourished should be made of so common a stone as peperino, if we did not collect from Pliny that marble was not used at Rome, for the purposes of sculpture, till about the fiftieth Olympiad.

the Amazons—opposite to this, another *Basso-rilievo*, representing Isiaic Ceremonies—and in the niches under the arch, Priapus and a young Hercules.

Continuation of the Portico. On the right is a Sarcophagus representing the Seasons—another, representing Nereides with the armour of Achilles—opposite to these, a magnificent Bath of red granite—and, fixed in the wall, a *Basso-rilievo*, supposed, according to some opinions, to represent one of the gates of the Temple of Janus; and, according to others, the gate of Eternity. On each side of the entrance to the Hall of Animals is a fine Column of verde antique, and the Statue of a Shepherd's Dog!—Further on are, a Sarcophagus, representing the battle of the Athenians with the Amazons—another, representing Genii and Bacchanalian figures—and, opposite to this, a magnificent Bath of red granite.

Third Cabinet. Here is the inimitable group of Laocoon, son of Priam and Hecuba, and high-priest of Apollo-Thymbræus. Laocoon endeavoured to prevent the reception of the wooden horse into Troy; in consequence of which, he and his two sons are supposed to have been killed by serpents!!!! This is the group mentioned by Pliny, as having been placed in the palace of Titus, and as being the joint work of Agesander, Apollodorus, and Athenodorus of Rhodes: it was found, during the Pontificate of Julius II., in the Baths of Titus.[1] The statue of Laocoon is universally deemed a *chef-d'œuvre* of antiquity; and exhibits the picture of human nature struggling with grief, and trying to oppose the stroke of fate, with all the force of intellect. The left side of this wonderful statue, where the serpent's teeth have penetrated, is that part of the body which seems to suffer most, from its proximity to the heart; and is considered as the finest production of the Grecian chisel now in existence. The right arm was wanting, and Buonaroti attempted to restore it in marble; but not pleasing himself sufficiently to continue the work, it was afterward done in plaster by Bernini. The sons are said to be too much formed for children of nine or ten years of age. Winckelmann supposes this group to have been executed in the time of Alexander the Great; but Pliny does not name the period when Agesander and his associates so eminently distinguished themselves. This Cabinet also contains a *Basso-rilievo*, fixed in the wall, and representing the triumph of Bacchus after his victory over the Indians; and another, representing Bacchanalians. In the niches, on the sides of the arch, are Statues of Polymnia, and a Nymph, found near the Temple of Peace.

Continuation of the Portico. On the right side, fixed into the wall, is a *Basso-rilievo* of Hercules and Bacchus, with their respective attributes — and, below this, a Sarcophagus representing Genii carrying arms. Here, likewise, is a Bath of gigantic magnitude. Fixed in the wall is another fine *Basso-rilievo* of Augustus sacrificing. In the large niche is a Statue of Hygeia; and, fixed in

---

[1] Some persons doubt whether the Laocoon of the Vatican be that mentioned by Pliny; because he says the group was made with one single block of marble, and the Laocoon of the Vatican is composed of two pieces. Winckelmann, however, tells us that, in all probability, the joint, easily discoverable now, was not to be perceived in Pliny's time.

the wall, a *Basso-rilievo* representing Rome with a victorious Emperor—here, also, is another gigantic Bath of granite; and a Sarcophagus adorned with Tritons and Nereides.

Fourth Cabinet. This room contains the Belvedere Apollo!!!! a statue equally celebrated with the group of Laocoon, and found at Antium, toward the close of the fifteenth century. The foot on which the figure stands was broken, and the pieces are not well put together; the two hands are finely restored, especially the left. This statue is supposed to have been brought from Greece by Nero; it is rather taller than the common height of man, appears to tread on air, and exhibits all the masculine beauty, grace, and dignity with which we may suppose Adam to have been adorned before the fall. Two *Bassi-rilievi* are fixed in the walls: that on the right, representing a Chase; that on the left, Pasiphaë with the bull; and in the niches, under the arch, are Statues of Pallas, and Venus triumphant.

Continuation of the Portico. Here are two Sarcophagi: in the centre of the first is Ganymedes; and in the centre of the other, Bacchus between a Faun and a Bacchante: opposite to these is a magnificent Bath of green basalt, found in Caracalla's Baths—close to the door of entrance is a beautiful Column of porphyry; and opposite to the door, a Column of white marble, adorned with sculpture in the arabesque style.

Hall of Animals. This apartment is divided by a vestibule adorned with columns and pilasters of granite. The pavement near the entrance exhibits an ancient Mosaic of a Wolf; and, further on, are other ancient Mosaics, some of which were found at Palestrina. Here is an unique, numerous, and most valuable collection of animals sculptured in every kind of precious marble, and several of them beautifully executed.

Right Side of the Hall. Some of the most striking things here are—a Dog on the back of a Stag – three Greyhounds—two Staghounds—Mithras stabbing the bull!—an Ibis—a *Basso-rilievo* representing the Triumph of Bacchus—a Table of verde antique—Europa—a small Bull—the Lion killed by Hercules—Diomedes destroyed by Hercules—a Centaur and a Love—a Stag in flowered alabaster—and a Lobster.

Gallery of Statues. The most remarkable pieces of sculpture on the right side of this apartment are—a Statue of Claudius Albinus—a half-length Figure of Love, supposed to have been executed by a Grecian artist—a Statue of Paris with the apple of discord—Hercules—Minerva with the olive branch in her hand—a Statue, apparently Etruscan, of a Woman seated—Caligula—a Satyr and a Nymph—an Amazon!—a Faun just waking from sleep!—Juno!—a seated Figure bearing the name of Posidipos!!—a small Isis—heads of Augustus, Julius Cæsar, Balbinus, Marcus Aurelius, Titus, Ajax, Caracalla, Septimius Severus, Antoninus Pius, Claudius Drusus, Nero, Socrates, and Jupiter Serapis; the last in black basalt. At the bottom of the apartment is a Statue of Jove seated, with the lightning in his hand!! (the *Basso-rilievo* on the pedestal represents Silenus and a Faun!)—a Statue of Livia, and a bust of Antinous. The other side of the apartment contains a colossal Bust of Minerva—a Group representing Cato and Portia—four Busts of Plato—a Bust of Socrates—a sitting statue bearing the name of Menander!!—Nero in the character of Apollo—a Statue of Septimius Severus—a sitting Statue of Dido—Neptune with his trident—Narcissus!—Bacchus as a River-God—the Emperor Macrinus—Æsculapius and Hygeia—Venus—Seneca in a consular habit—a Female sleeping—one of the Danaides, with a vase in her hand!—a Faun leaning against a tree—and a Statue of Diana!!

Cabinet of mosaic Masks. The ceiling of this elegant room was painted by Domenico di Angelis, and represents the marriage of Bacchus and Ariadne—Paris giving the apple to Venus—Diana and Endymion—Venus and Adonis—and Paris and Minerva. Here are eight Columns and eight Pilasters of oriental alabaster—a beautiful ancient Frieze—a *Basso-rilievo*, representing the apotheosis of Adrian—with others allusive to the labours of Hercules. Here, also, are Seats of porphyry—a Basin and a Chair of rosso antico—a beautiful antique mosaic Pavement, found in Adrian's villa—a Statue of a Bacchante!!—Ditto of Venus coming out of the bath!!—Ditto of one of Diana's Nymphs with a torch!!—a Faun in rosso antico, found in Adrian's villa!!!—Paris with the apple—Minerva—Ganymedes with the eagle!—and Adonis, or Antinous!!!

Continuation of the Gallery of Statues. A Priestess—a female Figure, marked 727!!!—a recumbent demi-colossal Statue, called Cleopatra, but supposed to represent Ariadne!!!—Mercury, and Lucius Verus!

Continuation of the Hall of Animals. Right side, going out of the Gallery—an equestrian Statue of Commodus—Hercules—an Eagle—Goats with a Bacchus—two Tigers—two Lions, one of which holds in his claws the head of a bull—two *Bassi-rilievi* fixed in the wall, the one represents a cow sucking a calf, the other two wild Boars driven by a Love—a Sphinx of flowered alabaster—the head of an Ass—three small Horses—two Cows—a Sow with her Pigs—a wild Boar—Hercules killing Gerion—a Cow, in grey marble—a Statue of Meleager—a Horse—Hercules and Cerberus—a Stork with a serpent in its mouth—several Heads of horses, oxen, and mules—a group of a marine Monster and a Nymph—a Vase—two Goats—the Head of a Cow—a Lion devouring a Horse—and a Table of verde antique.

Hall of the Muses. This apartment is adorned with sixteen Columns of Carrara marble, whose Capitals were taken from Adrian's Villa. On the right is a Statue of Silenus, and another of Bacchus in female attire. Here, likewise, are Statues of the Muses, found at Tivoli, in the Villa of Cassius—Apollo in his theatrical habit—Hermæ of Sophocles—Epicurus—Hippocrates—Æschines—Demosthenes—Antisthenes—Aspasia—and Pericles—a Statue of Sappho!—a Herma of Bias—a Statue of Lycurgus, or Lysias—a Herma of Periander—a Bust of Alcibiades—Hermæ of Socrates—Zeno—Euripides—and Aratus. The Pavement exhibits a Mosaic (found at Lorium) representing comic and tragic Actors—and another Mosaic, in the arabesque style, found near S. Maria Maggiore. The ceiling was painted by the Cav. Conca, and represents Apollo and Marsyas — the seven sages of Greece — Homer singing to Minerva — Apollo and some of the Muses, with Homer, Virgil, Ariosto, and Tasso, in the angles. Here likewise are *Bassi-rilievi* representing Pluto and Proserpine — the combat of the Lapithæ with the Centaurs, and the birth of Bacchus.

The entrance to the large circular hall contains, on the arch of the door to the right, a medallion of Juno — in the niche a Statue of Pallas — and, below, a medallion with a festoon and a Medusa — in the opposite niche a Statue of Mnemosyne — and below, a *Basso-rilievo* of three poets.

Circular Hall. The Pavement of this apartment is an ancient Mosaic (found at Otricoli) representing Medusa's head, and the battle of the Lapithæ with the Centaurs, encircled by another ancient Mosaic, representing marine Monsters, and found in the environs of Scrofano — a magnificent porphyry Basin, forty-one feet in circumference, adorns the centre of this apartment, which is seventy feet in diameter, and contains a colossal Bust of Jupiter!!! — ditto of Faustina the elder! — ditto of Adrian (formerly in his Mausoleum) — ditto of Antinous — a Herma representing the Ocean — a Bust of Jupiter Serapis — ditto of the Emperor Claudius — ditto of Plotina — ditto of Julia Pia — ditto of Pertinax! — two Hermæ (one on each side of the entrance door) found in Adrian's Villa, and representing Bacchantes! colossal Statues of Commodus in the character of Hercules — Augustus in a sacrificial habit — Ceres, or Melpomene restored as Ceres!!! — Antoninus Pius — Nerva!! — Juno, as queen of heaven!!! — the same heathen divinity as the goddess of health, with the dart, shield,[1] etc.; and a Group representing Bacchus, a Tiger and a Satyr. The busts are placed on columns of porphyry and other rare marbles.

Vestibule in the form of a Greek cross. The door of this apartment is magnificently ornamented with two Egyptian Idols of red granite, under the form of Caryatides, taken from Adrian's Villa, and bearing the likeness of Antinous — two vases of red granite, and a fine antique *Basso-rilievo* representing a combat between gladiators and wild beasts. The Pavement is adorned with an ancient Mosaic, representing arabesques, and a head of Minerva found at Tusculum; and the apartment also contains a half-draped Statue of Augustus; and, fixed into the wall, a *Basso-rilievo* of a Griffon — an Egyptian Idol of nero antico, found at Tivoli, and placed upon a bracket ornamented with two swans — a Statue on a pedestal of Lucius Verus, when young, found at Otricoli — and near the window a large sepulchral Monument of porphyry, in which the remains of S. Costanza were deposited, and which was taken from the church that bears her name — a Statue of a Muse seated, and holding a scroll, supposed to have once adorned the theatre at Otricoli — another Egyp-

---

[1] Juno was worshipped at Lanuvium (where this statue was found) under the title of *Sospita*, and represented as clothed in a goat's skin, and armed with a spear and shield, her feet being protected by sandals.

tian Idol of nero antico, found at Tivoli, and placed on a bracket—below this, a Sphinx, in red granite—a Statue of Venus on a pedestal—and, fixed into the wall above, a *Basso-rilievo* representing three of the Muses. Before the stairs two large Sphinxes of granite—and, fixed into the wall near the arch, supported by columns of granite, a *Basso-rilievo* representing children and lions' heads—on the other side, a *Basso-rilievo*, with Bacchanalian figures—and, below this, another Sphinx—in the niche, a statue of Erato—and, fixed to the wall, another *Basso-rilievo* representing three of the Muses—another Egyptian Idol of nero antico, found at Tivoli—and, below it, a Sphinx—a Statue, placed on a pedestal, of a Muse seated; and, near this, another Statue of a female veiled—above, fixed in the wall, a Figure of Victory, which once adorned the Baths of S. Helena—and, opposite to this, another Figure of Victory—here, likewise, is the sepulchral monument of S. Helena, found at Tor Pignattara—it contained her remains, and is of porphyry—near it is a Statue undraped, and another in the *toga*, both found at Otricoli—on a bracket, an Egyptian Idol, found at Tivoli—and, on a pedestal, a Statue found at Otricoli, of a youth veiled, holding a patera. The bottom of the staircase is adorned with a recumbent Statue of the Tigris in white marble;[1] and another of the Nile, in grey marble. The staircase, which is magnificent, leads to a rotunda, called,

The Apartment of the Car. In the centre of this rotunda is an ancient and elegantly sculptured Car of marble, with two horses, the one ancient, the other modern. On the right of the entrance door is a Statue of Perseus; and, in the niche, a Statue with a long beard, called Sardanapalus; but more probably Bacchus. The apartment likewise contains a Statue which decidedly represents Bacchus!—a Warrior (with one foot on his helmet) called Alcibiades—a Statue veiled, and in the act of sacrificing—ditto of Apollo with the lyre—a Discobolus—statue called Ajax, or Phocion!! probably the former, if we may judge by the cloak; for Phocion always appeared barefooted, and without a cloak, both in his rural retreat, and at the head of the Athenian armies—another Discobolus, imitated from that of Myron—an Auriga of the Circus—a Grecian Philosopher, holding a scroll—an Apollo with the Lizard—and four small, but beautiful, Sarcophagi.

Gallery of Candelabra, etc. The vestibule of this immense Gallery, contains a considerable number of Egyptian Antiquities.

First Division. A Faun, in green basalt!—Diana of Ephesus—small statues of Children—two sepulchral Urns standing on Pedestals adorned with *Bassi-rilievi*.

Second Division. Two Tripods—two fine Vases—small statues of Children—Diana-Lucifera—Ganymedes and the Eagle—and a statue of a female, immediately opposite!

Third Division. A Sarcophagus adorned with *Bassi-rilievi*, representing Diana killing the children of Niobe—a singular Candelabrum, representing lilies!—the Pescatore!—Diana and a

---

[1] The head of the Tigris was restored by Buonaroti.

greyhound—small statues of children.

Fourth Division. A female Figure draped—a Youth draped—a Priestess with the patera—Ceres.

Fifth Division. A Sarcophagus, with a Gladiator on the top—another, with a female Figure, resembling Sappho, on the top.

Sixth Division. Two of the largest and most beautiful Candelabra in Rome!!—other Candelabra!—cinerary Urns, etc.[1]

Seventh Division. Cinerary and other Urns of rare marble—four Candelabra!

Eighth Division. Two Candelabra, one being particularly beautiful!—cinerary and other Urns of rare marble—two handsome basins.

Geographical Gallery. This apartment is adorned with ancient Maps of the Papal territories, Hermæ of distinguished Characters; and, on the ceiling, Frescos by the scholars of Raphael.

Beyond the Geographical Gallery (on the right), is a Room hung with tapestry, and containing, on its ceiling, the descent of the Holy Ghost, finely painted by Guido.

The Stanze di Rafaello, and Vatican Museum, are open to the Public every Sunday and Thursday morning, from twelve o'clock till four.

Libraria Vaticano. The usual entrance to this magnificent apartment is from the Museo-Chiaramonti: the rooms are open to the public on the same days and at the same hours, with the rest of the Vatican-Museum; but the books can only be seen from nine till twelve in the forenoon.[2]

The Vatican Library was commenced, during the fifth century, by Pope S. Hilarius; and the princely apartment which now contains forty thousand manuscripts, and a choice collection of books printed in the fifteenth century, was erected by Sixtus v., after the designs of Domenico Fontana.

The Vestibule contains Chinese works, relative to anatomy, geography, and astronomy; together with two Columns, bearing ancient inscriptions. *The ante-room* is adorned with a ceiling painted by Marco di Firenze, and Paul Brill.

The great Hall of the Library is one hundred and ninety-eight feet long, by forty-nine broad: its ceiling was painted by Zuccari. Round this hall are presses that enclose the manuscripts; any of which, on being asked for, are immediately shown. Here are—a fine fluted Column of transparent alabaster—a Sarcophagus of white marble, with a winding-sheet of Asbestos, nine Roman palms in length and seven broad—

---

[1] The Candelabra of Mars, Mercury, Minerva, and Isis, are deemed the most valuable in the Vatican-Museum, both with respect to their form, and the elegance of their ornaments.

[2] The Custode who shows the Manuscripts, and attends Strangers round the apartment, expects from two to five pauls, according to the size of the party.

The Librarian here has recently discovered that some of the most valuable ancient Manuscripts have been used, in latter days, for other writings, merely to save parchment: the ancient characters, however, are frequently visible below those of modern date;—on ascertaining which, he has already been able to rescue from oblivion some missing books of Cicero's Republica; the Correspondence between Fronto and Marcus Aurelius, before and after the latter became Emperor; a Fragment of an Oration by Q. Aurelius Symmachus, with the Supplement of two other Orations; and the Supplement to the Gothic Ulpian Commentaries. A sight of these Manuscripts may be obtained by any Foreigner who is acquainted with the Librarian.

Etruscan and Grecian Vases — cinerary Urns — and two superb Tables of granite, supported by bronze figures finely executed. Among the rare manuscripts are several Hebrew, Syriac, Arabic, and Armenian Bibles — a Greek Bible of the sixth century in capital letters, written according to the Version of the Septuagint; and from which all the subsequent copies have been taken — a very large Hebrew Bible, presented to the library by the Dukes of Urbino, and for which the Venetian Jews offered its weight in gold a Greek Manuscript, containing the Acts of the Apostles in letters of gold: (this was given to Innocent VIII., by Charlotte, Queen of Cyprus,) — a missal, written in 1118 — another adorned with Miniatures by Giulio Clovio, the scholar of Giulio Romano, and the finest miniature painter of his time — a large Breviary, adorned with fine Miniatures, and presented to the library by Matthias Corvinus, King of Hungary — the Annals of Baronius, written with his own hand in twelve volumes — several volumes of ecclesiastical History, by the learned Onofrio Panvinio, Augustine — a Martyrology, curious on account of its antiquity, and its Miniatures — Manuscripts relative to S. Carlo Borromeo — a manuscript Pliny, with beautiful Miniatures of animals — a Virgil of the fifth century, written in capital letters, and adorned with miniatures representing the Trojans and Latians in the dress of their own times[1] — a Terence equally ancient — another Terence, of the ninth century, illuminated with ancient masks — a beautiful Tasso — a Dante adorned with exquisite Paintings, begun by the Florentine school, and finished by Giulio Clovio — a Treatise on the seven Sacraments, composed by Henry VIII. of England — original Letters between that Prince and Anna Bullen — several Papers written by Luther — the Lives of Frederico di Monte Feltre, and Francesco Maria della Povera, Dukes of Urbino, adorned with exquisite Miniatures by Giulio Clovio — several Manuscripts written on Egyptian papyrus — and the Gospels of S. Luke and S. John, written in the tenth century, and bound in ivory.[2] From the upper part of this Hall branch two Galleries, forming, altogether, a length of nearly half a mile.

The Gallery on the right is supported by fine Columns of porphyry; two of which, with figures on the top, were taken from the Arch of Constantine. Here are modern Paintings — Presses filled with books Etruscan and Grecian Vases — and, at the extremity of the Gallery, *a Cabinet* containing beautiful Cammei of Jupiter, Æsculapius, etc. — Etruscan Antiquities (among which is the recumbent figure of a Child!) — the finest Bust extant of Augustus!! — a Bust of Nero — ditto of Septimius Severus — an ancient silver Salver or Shield — Human Hair found in a sarcophagus — ancient Seals, Rings, etc.

The commencement of the Gallery on the left, contains very fine Etruscan and Grecian Vases

---

[1] These paintings are not good; but they have been excellently engraved by Santi Bartoli, and may be purchased at the Calcografia Camerale.

[2] It seems extraordinary that there are no ancient Rituals here, to show the alterations supposed to have taken place in Church-ceremonies since the time of the primitive Christians.

—Presses filled with books—a Statue of S. Hippolito,[1] found in the Cemetery of S. Lorenzo—and a statue of Aristides of Smyrna. *The second division* contains a Ceiling, by Pozzi, which represents the Church and Religion—ancient lamps—Instruments of torture, and other antiques, relative to the primitive Christians—and an original Portrait of Charlemagne, in Stucco. Near the end of this Gallery is a *Cabinet* superbly adorned with porphyry and other precious marbles; hung round with specimens of the Egyptian Papyrus; and exhibiting, on its Ceiling, the *chef-d'œuvre* of Mengs; who has represented, over the doors, Moses and S. Peter, beautifully painted, though less worthy of admiration than the four Genii, and the four Children, on the coves of the ceiling!! In the centre of this ceiling is History resting upon the wings of Time a tablet supposed to record the works of Clement XIV.; while a Genius presents scrolls of papyrus, by means of which the Pontiff's fame may be transmitted to posterity. Janus is introduced into the picture, as indicative of the present and the past: he appears to be dictating to History. This Cabinet also contains two Candelabra, given by Napoleon to Pius VII. Beyond the cabinet of Mengs are two Rooms in a direct line; and two others on the right; one of which contains a celebrated Collection of Engravings; beautiful Etruscan and Grecian Vases, and a Ceiling painted by Guido; the other contains magnificent Vases, and ancient Inscriptions fixed in the walls. Returning from the cabinet of Mengs, you see, on the left, *two rooms; the first of which* contains paintings, on the Ceiling, by Guido; together with some fine Grecian Vases: *the second* contains Grecian Vases; together with ancient Inscriptions fixed in the wall.

Chiesa dei P. P. Cappuccini, in Piazza Barberini. This Piazza is supposed to have made part of the ancient Circus of Flora; where, according to Suetonius, elephants danced on ropes. The Chiesa dei Cappuccini is rich in paintings. The first picture on the right represents the Arch-Angel Michael; and is deemed Guido's finest easel production!!! S. Paul receiving his sight, in the Chapel opposite to that which contains the Arch-Angel, is by Pietro da Cortona!! and over the door of the church is a cartoon, by Giotto, from which the mosaic, called The Navicella, and placed in the portico of S. Peter's, was taken!

Palazzo - Barberini. A fine *Basso-rilievo* at the foot of the stairs—a fine *Alto-rilievo* of a Lion (taken from Palestrina), on the first landing place.

First floor. The ceiling of the principal Hall of entrance was painted by Pietro da Cortona!! The subjects are allusive to Urban VIII. The centre exhibits the Barberini arms carried to Heaven by the Virtues, in presence of Providence, who is surrounded by Time, Eternity, and the Fates. On one side is Minerva vanquishing the Titans; on another are Religion and Faith, with Voluptuousness beneath on the left, and Silanus on the right. On the third side are figures of Justice

---

[1] This is the most ancient marble statue extant of a Christian; it was executed in the time of Alexander Severus.

and Abundance in the air; and, below them, Charity on the right, and Hercules killing the Harpies on the left. On the fourth side is a figure which represents the Church, accompanied by Prudence, sending Peace to shut the Temple of Janus, chasing the Eumenides, and ordering Vulcan to forge arms for the defence of Rome. Another Hall of entrance contains statues of Commodus, Juno, Dido, and Tiberius; together with Sarcophagi, etc., found at Palestrina; and the statue of a Faun by Buonaroti.

The Apartments on the second floor contain, S. Matthew, by Guercino—S. Luke, by ditto—S. Carlo Borommeo, by Pietro da Cortona—S. Girolamo, by Spagnoletto—the Guitar Player, by M. A. Caravaggio—S. Andrea Corsini, by Guido—the death of Germanicus, by Nicolo Poussin!—a small Landscape, by Claude, between two small paintings, by Albano—Raphael's Fornarina, by himself!—the portrait of a Lady, by Titian!—and a picture by Albert Durer. The following celebrated paintings have recently been added to this collection. Adam and Eve driven from Paradise, by Domenichino—an Angel announcing to the Shepherds the birth of the Messiah, by Bergamo—a large Landscape, by Claude—the Holy Family, by Andrea del Sarto—David with the head of Goliah, by Guercino—the Cenci, by Guido—the Madonna and our Saviour, by Raphael—and Leda, by Correggio.[1]

Chiesa di S. Maria della Vittoria. The front of this edifice was built after the designs of Giovanni Battista Soria; and the interior part after those of Carlo Maderno: stands on the site of the gardens of Sallust; and is deemed, in point of architecture, one of the most beautiful churches at Rome. The inside is adorned with pilasters of Sicilian jasper, a well painted ceiling, a handsome marble pavement, good altarpieces, and fine sculpture. The paintings in the second Chapel, on the right, are by Domenichino! The last Chapel, in the cross-aisle, contains a group, in marble, of Joseph and an Angel, by Domenico Guido: the opposite Chapel, on the left, contains a group of S. Teresa and an Angel, by Bernini. Here, likewise, are two sarcophagi adorned with fine Busts, by Bernini; and an *Alto-rilievo*, in bronze, representing the last supper, by the same artist. The next Chapel is embellished with fine marbles; and contains an altar-piece, by Guercino; with a picture, on each side, by Guido.

Fontana di Termine. This Fountain, which is opposite to the church of S. Maria della Vittoria, was erected by Fontana, at the command of Sixtus v. In the centre of the edifice is a Statue of Moses; and on each side a *Basso-rilievo*; the one representing Aaron conducting the Israelites to quench their thirst; the other Gideon encouraging them to pass the river Jordan, and directing his soldiers to lead the way. This fountain is likewise ornamented with four Lions, two of which are white porphyry, and two basalt; the latter being Egyptian sculpture, and highly estimated.

Chiesa di S. Andrea a Monte-Cavallo. This beautiful little Church was built by Bernini, in

---

[1] The Barberini-Palace is shown from ten in the morning till two.

the form of an ancient temple; it is adorned with fine marble; and contains, in the first Chapel on the right, a picture of S. Francesco Saverio, by Baciccio; by whom likewise are the paintings on each side. The Crucifixion of S. Andrew, over the high-altar, is by Bourguignone; and the next Chapel, dedicated to S. Stanislas, is ornamented with a picture of that Saint, by Carlo Maratta; and a Sarcophagus of lapis lazuli. In the conventual edifice adjoining to this church is a Chapel, once the chamber of S. Stanislas, which contains his Statue, by Le Gros!

Palazzo - Pontificio. This princely edifice is situated on the Quirinal hill; and supposed to stand on the ruins of the Baths of Constantine. It was begun by Paul III., continued by Gregory XIII., and finished by succeeding Pontiffs. The Court-yard, or open Quadrangle of the palace, is three hundred feet long, by one hundred and sixty-five wide; three parts bing surrounded with porticos. The large staircase on the right, leads to the public Chapel, which has been recently fitted up with great elegance by the present Pope. Contiguous to this chapel is a magnificent suite of apartments splendidly furnished in the French style, and enriched with a good collection of pictures; among which are, in *the first room*, Saul and David, by Guercino — S. Agnes, by Annibale Caracci — an *Ecce Homo*, by Domenichino—a sketch of the Transfiguration, by Raphael! The martyrdom of the Jesuits, by Bassano—the Madonna and our Saviour, by Guido— S. Catherine, by Annibale Caracci —Ditto by the Cav. d'Arpino— S. John, by Giulio Romano—the Madonna and our Saviour, by Rubens—the same subject, by Baroccio—the Madonna, our Saviour, S. John, etc., by Palma Vecchio. The small Chapel, adjoining to this room, is beautifully painted, by Guido: the subject being the life of the Madonna, and the Annunciation, over the altar, is particularly admired. *The second room* contains pictures of Animals by Petri, a living artist. *The third room* is adorned with a fine Ceiling. *The fourth* with a Frieze, by Thorwaldsen, representing the triumph of Alexander, and a fine Ceiling. *The fifth room* contains an elegant Bed, and a fine Frieze, representing the triumph of Trajan, by Finetti. *In the sixth room* are copies of Raphael's Arabesques, and a fine Frieze: *in the seventh room* a beautiful Chimney-piece, and a Ceiling by Palagi. *The ninth room* contains a picture of S. Peter, by Fra Bartolomeo!!—S. Paul by the same great artist!! —S. Girolamo, by Spagnoletto— S. Cecilia, by Vanni—S. George, by Pordenone—our Saviour disputing with the doctors, by M. A. Caravaggio!!—the adoration of the Magi, by Guercino—the marriage of S. Catharine, by Battoni —S. Cecilia, S. Agnes, etc., by Caraccioli — S. Sebastiano, by Paolo Veronese—the Ascension of our Saviour, by Vandyck—and a picture by Annibale Caracci, representing a Legend.

These Apartments cannot be seen without an order from the Cardinal Secretary of State.

Palazzo Rospigliosi. This edifice was erected on the ruins of Constantine's Baths; and its Garden contains a Pavilion, the outside of which is adorned with four large *Bassi-rilievi*, found in Trajan's Forum, and three small ones, found in the Baths of Constantine. On the Ceiling of the principal room of the Pavilion is the celebrated Aurora of Guido, according to many opinions, the finest Fresco at Rome!!! Here likewise are two Loves, by the same artist; two Landscapes, by Paul Brill; two Paintings, by Tempesta, both taken from Petrarca; the one represents the Triumph of Fame, and the other the Triumph of Love: two Colums of rosso antico; a bronze Horse, and a statue of Minerva: the four last were found in Constantine's Baths.

Room on the right. Death of Sampson, by Lodovico Caracci—head of Guido, by himself. Garden of Eden, by Domenichino—and Sophonisba, after having swallowed poison, by Calabrese.

Room on the left. The Triumph of David, by Domenichino!—the Saviour, and the twelve Apostles (each being a separate picture), by Rubens—the Saviour bearing his Cross, by Daniello da Volterra—Matrimony, by Giorgione—Andromeda, by Guido—a Love, by Niccolo Poussin—head of Ditto, by himself—the 'five Senses, by Carlo Cigniani!—and an *Ecce Homo*, by Guido. Busts of Adrian, Septimius Severus, Cicero, and Seneca, found in the Baths of Constantine; and the celebrated busts, in basalt, of Scipio Africanus, found, according to Fulvius Ursinus, at Liternum; and bearing, on the right side of the head, a mark which resembles a scar. This mark may be seen on the marble bust of Scipio, in the Capitol; and likewise on his bust in the Villa Albani.

Fontana di Trevi. The water which supplies this beautiful Fountain was brought to Rome by Agrippa, for the use of his baths; and derives its name of *Acqua Vergine* from a young female Peasant, who discovered the source, and showed it to some famishing soldiers. It is deemed the best water at Rome. The decorations of this Fountain were designed by Niccolo Salvi, at the command of Clement XII. The Statues represent Ocean, Salubrity, and Abundance; and the *Bassi-rilievi* over the two last, represent Agrippa and the Peasant-Girl.

Chiesa di S. Maria del Popolo. This church, which stands on the site of a sepulchral Monument that, according to the best authorities, belonged to the Family of Domitian, contains, in the first and third Chapels, to the right, paintings by Pinturicchio; the intermediate Chapel contains an oil-painting, on the wall, by Carlo Maratta. The paintings in the tribuna are by Pinturicchio: and the Chapel to the right of the high-altar contains a picture of the Assumption, by Annibale Caracci! The Chigi-Chapel was decorated according to the designs of Raphael; and contains a statue of Jonas, designed by him, and executed under his immediate orders, by Lorenzetto!! The statue of Elias, also, is supposed to have been designed by Raphael; the other statues were done by Bernini. Near this chapel is the singular Monument of the Princess Odescalchi Chigi.

Chiesa di S. Carlo al Corso. This Church was begun according to the designs of Onorio and Martino Lunghi, and finished by Pietro da Cortona; who erected the cupola. The picture which adorns the high-altar is by Carlo Maratta, and represents the Apotheosis of S. Carlo! The Tribuna, the angles of the cupola, and the

s

ceiling of the nave, were painted by Brandi. The Chapel in the cross, on the right, was designed by the Cav. Paolo Posi; and the picture in mosaic, with which it is adorned, is a copy of that painted by Carlo Maratta in the church of the Madonna del Popolo: the statue of Judith is by Le Brun; and that of David by Pietro Pacilli. The third Chapel on the right contains a picture of S. Barnaba, by Mola!

Chiesa di S. Lorenzo in Lucina. The high-altar of this Church is adorned with a celebrated picture of the Saviour on the Cross, by Guido.

Chiesa di S. Ignazio. This magnificent edifice was erected by Cardinal Lodovico Lodovisio, chiefly after the designs of Domenichino; it is ornamented with fine antique columns of marble; and contains two beautiful Chapels made after the designs of the celebrated Father Pozzi, a Jesuit. That on the right is adorned with an *alto-rilievo*, by Le Gros, representing S. Luigi Gonzaga, whose body is deposited here in a tomb incrusted with lapis lazuli. The other Chapel contains a *basso-rilievo*, by Filippo Valle, representing the Annunciation. Here, likewise, is the Monument of Gregory XV., by Le Gros; and a Picture of S. Giuseppe dying, by Trevisani! The Ceilings of the nave and tribuna are painted by Pozzi; and the former represents the Apotheosis of S. Ignatius; from whose head issue rays, emblematical of his having enlightened the four quarters of the world.

Chiesa de S. S. Apostoli. This noble structure was erected by Constantine; and afterward rebuilt by Fontana. The Portico of the old edifice is still entire; and contains an antique *basso-rilievo* of an Eagle at one end; and, at the other, a *basso-rilievo* of Friendship deploring the death of Volpato, by Canova. The church is divided into three aisles by pilasters of the Corinthian order. The Ceiling of the nave was painted by Baciccio; and represents the Triumph of S. Francesco. The Ceiling of the tribuna was painted by Odazzi, and represents the Fall of the Angels!! The high altar-piece is by Domenichino Muratori. The first Chapel on the right, near the great door, and the Chapel in the cross, on the right, are particularly rich in marbles: and, adjoining to the latter, is another Chapel, which contains eight beautiful antique fluted Columns of white marble. The second Chapel on the left near the great door, is adorned with particularly fine columns of verde antique and other marbles: and over the door of the sacristy is the Monument of Clement XIV. by Canova; who has placed the statue of the Pope between two female figures, namely, Temperance and Meekness!

Chiesa di S. Maria di Loretto. This little Church, which is deemed a fine piece of architecture, was built by Sangallo; and has a double cupola, like S. Peter's: it contains a celebrated statue of S. Susanna, by Fiamingo.

Chiesa di Gesù. This magnificent edifice was erected by Cardinal Alessandro Farnese, after the plan of Vignola; and finished by Giacomo della Porta. The Frescos on the ceiling of the nave, tribuna, and cupola, are by Baciccio; who has represented S. Francesco Saverio ascending to

Heaven!! The angles of the cupola are particularly beautiful. The Chapel in the cross, on the right, was made after the designs of Pietro da Cortona; and contains a picture by Carlo Maratta, representing the death of S. Francesco Saverio. The high altar is decorated with fine columns of giallo antico, and a picture of the Circumcision, by Muziano! The Chapel of S. Ignatius, executed after the designs of Father Pozzi, is peculiarly magnificent; the columns which adorn the altar being lapis lazuli fluted with bronze gilt; and the globe held by the Deity the largest piece of lapis lazuli ever seen. Above the altar, in a niche incrusted with lapis lazuli, is a demi-colossal Statue of S. Ignatius accompanied by three Angels, and done after the designs of Le Gros. The remains of the Saint repose under the altar, in a tomb of bronze gilt, adorned with *bassi-rilievi* and precious stones: and on one side of the altar is a celebrated group of Religion vanquishing Heresy, by Le Gros; and on the other side a group, by Teudone, which represents idolatrous nations embracing Christianity. The Ceiling was painted by Baciccio. This church contains one of the best organs at Rome.[1]

Chiesa di S. Andrea della Valle. This noble edifice stands, according to some opinions, on the site of the *Curia* of Pompey, where Cæsar was assassinated: its Cupola, by Lanfranco, is deemed a master-piece!! the four Evangelists in the angles are by Domenichino; and the S. John is called his *chef-d'œuvre* in this description of painting. The Ceiling of the tribuna was done by the same great artist, and represents the life of S. Andrew: the three large frescos on the walls of the tribuna are by Calabrese, and represent the martyrdom of S. Andrew. The Strozzi-Chapel was designed by Buonaroti; and the Barberini-Chapel is rich in marbles and sculpture, and in paintings, by Passignani.

Chiesa della Trinità, de Pelegrini. This Church contains a High Altar-Piece by Guido, representing the Trinity. Our Saviour is on the cross accompanied by two kneeling Angels; his figure and countenance are particularly fine; over the cross hovers a dove; and higher up, is God the Father!!! The representation of the Deity in the lantern is likewise by Guido.

Chiesa di S. Carlo a Catenari. This is a noble edifice, adorned with one of the most beautiful cupolas in Rome. The Ceiling of the tribuna was painted by Lanfranco; and the cardinal Virtues, in the angles of the cupola, by Domenichino: they are strikingly fine; particularly the figure of Fortitude!!! The Annunciation in the first Chapel, on the right of the entrance-door, is by Lanfranco; and the death of S. Anna, in one of the Chapels of the cross, by Andrea Sacchi! The high altar is decorated with four columns of porphyry, and a picture by Pietro da Cortona. The Ceiling of the Sacristy was painted by Lanfranco, and represents the Assumption; and an adjoining room contains a portrait of S. Carlo, by Guido![2]

---

[1] There frequently is fine music here; and especially on the Festival of Corpus Domini, and for some days after.

[2] The Church of S. Carlo a Catenari contains a Monument to the memory of Lorenzo Sperandi; with an epitaph, which records

Chiesa di S. Giovanni de Fiorentini. This fine Church, erected according to the designs of Giacomo della Porta, contains a Picture of the martyrdom of Saints Cosimo and Damiano, by Salvator Rosa! a Chapel painted by Lanfranco! a Picture of S. Girolamo by Cigoli; and the Monument of one of the Corsini family, by Algardi.

Chiesa di S. Maria in Vallicella, commonly called *Chiesa Nuova.* This splendid Church was built by S. Filippo Neri, after the designs of Martino Lunghi and Pietro da Cortona; the latter of whom painted the Ceiling of the Nave, the Cupola, and the upper part of the Tribuna; which last represents the Assumption. The Altar-Piece of the first Chapel on the right was done by Scipio Gaetano — the dead Christ, in the next Chapel, is a copy from M. A. Caravaggio's celebrated picture in the *Vatican.* The high-altar is adorned with four fine columns of Porta-Santa, and a superb Ciborio. The Tribuna contains Paintings, by Guido; but they are considerably damaged. The Chapel of S. Filippo Neri, (under one of the organs), contains his ashes, and his portrait in mosaic, copied from the original of Guido; the Chapel under the other organ contains a picture, by Carlo Maratta. The next Chapel to that of S. Filippo Neri contains a picture, by Baroccio, of the Presentation of the Madonna in the Temple! The following Altar-Piece is by the same artist, and represents the Visitation: and the Paintings in the last Chapel are by the Cav. d'Arpino. The Sacristy is adorned with a statue of S. Filippo Neri, by Algardi! a picture of the Madonna contemplating the crown of thorns, by Trevisanni; and a Ceiling finely painted by Pietro da Cortona! *The apartments above-stairs* contain a Ceiling which represents S. Filippo Neri, by Pietro da Cortona; the portrait of the Saint from which the mosaic in the church was taken, and a head of our Saviour, by Pietro Perugino!

Chiesa di S. Maria della Pace. This Church contains, on the right of the great door, Raphael's celebrated Sibyls, supposed to be predicting the birth of our Saviour!!![a] This inestimable fresco was almost obliterated, and would soon have been totally extinct, had not a living artist restored it; and so well has he executed this difficult task, that every lover of the art of painting would wish to see him employed in restoring those frescos of the *Stanze di Raf-*

---

that he was famous for terminating amicably the differences which occurred amongst his friends and relations; an uncommon panegyric, though one of the greatest, perhaps, that can be bestowed on any man.

[1] If the Etrurians were, as some authors suppose, originally Cananeans, probably they might bring the Old Testament into Italy: — and as the Romans borrowed many of their religious ceremonies from the Etrurians, it seems fair to infer that the Sibylline Oracles might be derived from the Bible. Libyca prophesied, " That the day would come when all men would see the King of all living things." Cumæa, a Babylonian, prophesied, " That God would be born of a Virgin, and converse among sinners." Delphica prophesied, " That a Prophet would be born of a Virgin." Erythræa, a Babylonian, foretold a great part of the Christian religion, in verses recorded by Eusebius; the first letters of which, being put together, make the words, "*Jesus Christ, Son of God, Saviour:* " and Persica foretold, " That the womb of the Virgin would prove the salvation of the Gentiles."

The word Sibylla is Oriental, and signifies " a Gleaner of ears of corn."

faello, which are hastening rapidly to decay. Above the sibyls are four Prophets, likewise by Raphael. The Frescos on the left of the great door are attributed to Timoteo d'Urbino. The second Chapel, on the right, is embellished with good sculpture; and this church also contains a picture of the Visitation, by Carlo Maratta.

Chiesa di S. Agostino. Here is a celebrated Fresco of the Prophet Isaiah, by Raphael, placed to the left of the great door, and on the third pilaster of the nave!!

Palazzo-Borghese. This is one of the most splendid edifices at Rome; and particularly rich in Pictures. *The Quadrangle* contains statues of Giulia Faustina, an Amazon, etc. The paintings usually shown to Strangers are *in the apartments on the ground floor; the first room* of which contains—the Saviour taken into custody, by Vanderweck—S. Catherine, and other figures, by Parmegianino—a fine painting, by Bassano—S. Peter, by Spagnoletto—the Saviour, by Valentin—a sketch, by Giorgione!—S. Francesco, by the Cav. d'Arpino—Holy Family, School of Titian—S. Domenico, by Andrea Sacchi—Holy Family, by Benvenuto Garofolo!—and the same subject, by Sasso-Ferrato. *The second room* contains—a dead Christ, by Federico Zuccari!—head of Christ, by Agostino Caracci!—head of the Magdalene, by ditto!—Christ dead, by Garofalo!—Diana shooting, by Domenichino!!—Holy Family, by Carlo Dolci—Christ bearing his cross, by Muziano—Christ on the cross, with the two Marys standing near, by Giulio Romano—head of S. Antonio, by Agostino Caracci—head of S. Francesco, by the same artist!—a Landscape, by the Caracci School—head of the Saviour, by Garofalo—and the Saviour, the Apostles, etc., School of Titian!—This room likewise contains a Sarcophagus of porphyry, found in Adrian's Mausoleum. *Third room*—A Madonna and Child, by Garofalo—the same subject, by Giovanni Bellino——head of an old man, by Giulio Romano—ditto of Raphael, by himself!—ditto of Petrarca, by Holbens!—two paintings, by Gentilisca—a story from Ariosto, by Lanfranco!—Holy Family, by Titian—Pordenone and his Family, by himself!—the Last Supper, School of Titian—S. Antonio preaching to the Fishes, by Paolo Veronese—the Madonna and Our Saviour, by Francesco Frangi—S. John Baptist in the Desert, by Paolo Veronese—and S. Francesco, by Annibale Caracci. *Fourth room*—S. Cecilia, by Domenichino!—S. John, by Giulio Romano—S. Sebastiano, by Rustichino—the Descent from the Cross, by Raphael!!—a Mother in bed, surrounded with her Children, School of Titian—the Flagellation, by Sebastiano del Piombo!—a group of Figures eating, by Fiamingo. *Fifth room*—The Woman taken in Adultery, by Titian!—Holy Family, by Andrea del Sarto—Holy Family, by the School of Raphael—four oval pictures, by Albano!!—the battle of Constantine, by the Cav. d'Arpino—two landscapes, by the Caracci School—and the Madonna and Our Saviour, by Pietro Perugino. *Sixth room*—Leda, attributed to Leonardo da Vinci—Venus, by Paolo Veronese—the Graces, by Giulio Romano—Venus, by Andrea del Sarto—ditto, by Giulio Romano—Cupid and Psyche, by Dossi—and Venus, by Annibale Caracci. *Seventh room*—Holy Family, by Giorgione—ancient Mosaics—Descent from the Cross, by Marcello Venuschi—Orpheus, by Paul Brill, and a Picture Gallery, by Fiamingo. *Eighth room*—sacred and profane Love, by Titian!!—Portrait of Cæsar Borgia, by Raphael!—a portrait, by Pordenone—a Cardinal, by Raphael! *Ninth room*—the Graces, by Titian!!—the Prodigal Son, by Guercino!—the Saviour on the Cross, by Vandyck!—a Boy with Flowers, by Annibale Caracci—Holy Family, by Andrea del Sarto—Marriage of Cana, with two small pictures on the sides, by Garofolo—Adoration of the Magi, by Bassano!!—a sketch of Sampson, by Titian—and a Portrait of Cosimo de' Medici, by Bronzino. *Tenth room*—Holy Family, by Venuschi—the same subject, by Scipio Gaetano!—the same, by Andrea del Sarto!—the same, by Giovanni Bellino—and the same, by Garofalo—Lot and his Daughters, by Gherardo delle Notti—the Madonna, Our Saviour, and S. John, by Andrea del Sarto—a portrait, by Titian—the Ascension, by Federico Zuccari—the Madonna and Our Saviour, by Francesco Frangi—a small head of Our Saviour, and another of the Madonna, by Carlo Dolci—and a Concert, by Leonello Spada.

Palazzo-Sciarra. The second story of this edifice contains a small, but choice, collection of Pictures; the greater part of which once adorned the Palazzo-Barberini. *First room*—the Saviour bearing his Cross, by the Cav. d'Arpino—S. Barbara, by Pietro da Cortona—*Noli me tangere*, by Garofalo!—the Madonna and Our Saviour, by Giovanni Bellino—a fine copy of the Transfiguration—S. Sebastiano, by Pietro Perugino!—Our Saviour and the Woman of Samaria, by Garofalo!—S. Francesca and an Angel, by Carlo Venetiano—Abraham's Sacrifice, by Gherardo delle Notti—Raphael's *Fornarina*, by Giulio Romano—a small picture of the Madonna and Our Saviour, by Titian—ditto of the Holy Family, by Bassano—ditto of the Descent from the Cross, by Bassano—a large antique painting, subject unknown. *Second room*—a small Landscape, by Paul Brill—two Landscapes, by Claude Lorrain!—two ditto, by Fiamingo—two of a larger size, by Both!—Cupid, by the Cav. Landi—two small Landscapes, by Breughel!—and, between them, a little Claude—a Landscape, by Niccolo Poussin. *Third room*—the Holy Family, by Francesco Frangi—Noah intoxicated, by Andrea Sacchi—the Saviour bound to the column, by Leonella Spada—Cleopatra, by Lanfranco!—the Descent from the Cross, by Baroccio—the Saviour between Angels, by Fiamingo—Sampson, supposed to have been painted either by Caroselli, or Guercino!!—Moses, by Guido!!—Holy Family, by Albano!!—and Our Saviour, the Madonna, and other Saints, by Albert Durer. *Fourth room*—Vanity and Modesty, by Leonardo da Vinci!!!—Gamblers cheating a Youth, by M. A. Caravaggio!!!—Matrimony, by Agostino Caracci—the Magdalene, by Guido!—S. James, by Guercino—the Death of the Virgin, by Albert Durer—the Adoration of the Magi, by Garofalo!—Titian and his family, by himself!—portrait of a Lady, by Titian!—Martyrdom of S. Erasmus, by Niccolo Poussin!—the *Maddalena delle radici*, by Guido!!—S. Girolamo, by Guercino!—S. Mark, by ditto!—S. John, by ditto!—two Shepherds of Arcadia contemplating a human skull, by Schidone[1]—portrait of a Youth, by Raphael!—head of S. John after decapitation, by Giorgione—the Madonna, our Saviour, and S. John, by Fra Bartolomeo; together with small pictures by Breughel, Albano, etc.

Palazzo Doria. This magnificent palace contains a numerous and fine collection of Pictures.—*The first room*, shown to strangers, is adorned with a painting, by Pietro di Cortona, of Noah's sacrifice; in *the second room*, are Landscapes, by Gasparo Poussin, and Ciccio, Neapolitano: *other ante-rooms* to the Gallery, contain, a Turk on horseback, by Castiglione!—the marriage of S. Catherine, by Scipio Gaetano—two small Landscapes, by Both—our Saviour bearing his cross, by Andrea Mantegna—a large Landscape, with figures of Nymphs and Loves, by Albano—Endymion, School of Rubens—portrait of Macchiavello, by Bronzino!—portraits of Bartoli and Baldo, in the same picture, by Raphael!!—Jansenius, by Titian—Cain slaying Abel, by Salvator Rosa!!—portrait of a Lady, by Rubens—a *Pietà*, by Annibale Caracci!!—the Descent from the Cross, by Vasari: and a small Picture, attributed to Giulio Romano—Semiramis, by Paolo Veronese—Time plucking Cupid's wings, by Albano!—Bathsheba, by Bronca—a *Presepe*, by Bassano—and Grecian Charity, by Simone da Pesaro. *Gallery; first division, left side*. The Visitation, by Garofalo—two small oval Landscapes, by Domenichino!—The blessed Virgin in contemplation, by Sasso-Ferratto!—the Confessor of Rubens, by the latter!—a large Landscape, called *Il Molino*, by Claude Lorrain!!!—six Lunettes by Annibale Caracci; namely, the flight into Egypt!—the Visitation!—the Assumption!—the Saviour borne to the Sepulchre!—the Nativity!—and the Adoration of the Magi!—S. John Baptist, by Valentin—a Head, by Guido—ditto, by Baroccio—S. Francesco, by Domenichino!—Lot and Daughters, by Gherardo delle Notti!—S. Rocco with his dog, attributed to M. A. Caravaggio, and likewise to Schidone—a landscape, by Claude!!! (immediately above Domenichino's lunette of the adoration of the Magi); it represents a sacrifice to the Delphic Apollo—Sketch, by Correggio, of Virtue, and other figures—Holy Family, by Andrea del Sarto. *The second division of the Gallery* contains no pictures. *Third division*. The Magdalene, by Murillo!—a landscape, by Claude, called *Il Riposo in Egitto*!!!—the Madonna adorning our Saviour while asleep, by Guido!—the Prodigal Son, by Guercino!!—a small Landscape, by Annibale Caracci, between two smaller Landscapes, by Claude—a large Landscape, by ditto—Pope Pamfili, by Velasquez!—Judith and Holofernes, by Guido—a large Landscape, by Salvator Rosa, called his *Belisario!!!!*—S. Agnes, by Guercino—Satyr and a Youth, by Agostino Caracci—another Claude!—Holy Family,

[1] The skull rests upon a tomb bearing this inscription: "I too was of Arcadia."

by Sasso-Ferratto!—a Landscape, by Both—four Misers, by Albert Durer!—a Shepherd with Pan's pipe, by Rembrandt. *Fourth division of the Gallery.* Pomona and other figures, by Paolo Veronese—the Madonna, our Saviour, etc., by Garofalo—several Pictures, by Breughel—Animals going into the ark, by Bassano—Susanna, by Annibale Caracci—two Landscapes, by Domenichino!!—Sampson, by Guercino—an Angel visiting S. Peter in Prison, by Lanfranco—Abraham's offering of his son, by Titian!!—a small picture of the Saviour on the Cross, by Buonaroti!—the *Maddalena sedente*, by M. A. Caravaggio—a Sibyl, by Guercino!—Queen Giovanna of Arragon, by Leonardo da Vinci—Simon Magus, S. Peter, and S. Paul, by Tiarino—a Village feast, by Teniers!—a copy of the Aldobrandini marriage, by Niccolo Poussin!—a Woman catching fleas, by Gherardo delle Notti—the Nativity, by Sasso-Ferratto—two Portraits, by Titian!—and the Descent from the Cross, by Padovanino.

Palazzo-Bracciano. This spacious edifice was erected by the Chigi family, and has recently been fitted up with great magnificence by its present possessor, the Duke di Bracciano. *The Quadrangle* and *Staircase* contain some antique and some modern sculpture. The Ceiling of the *Gallery on the right*, up stairs, was painted by Domenico del Frati and the Cav. Landi: the oval near the statue of Hercules is by the latter. The pavement is mosaic, and beautifully copied from that which adorns the circular hall of the Vatican. Here are several pieces of modern sculpture, and at the end of the Gallery four antique Statues, together with the Hercules of Canova represented in the act of throwing Lichias into the sea! *The first room* on this side of the palace contains a Ceiling painted by Camuccini, which represents the fable of Cupid and Psyche! the pavement is a beautiful copy from antique mosaic. *The second room* contains the statue of a Philosopher seated—ditto of an Infant Hercules—and ditto of two Children. *The second division of the Gallery* is adorned with a Ceiling by Pozzi, and a picture of the Madonna and our Saviour, by Rubens. *The third division of the Gallery* leads to a room adorned with a beautiful mosaic pavement, copied from that which represents the arrival of Menelaus in Egypt, and which was found in the Temple of Fortune at Palestrina. *The next room* is ornamented with a mosaic pavement; and *the third room* with a statue of Paris—a picture of the Holy Family, by Gherardo delle Notti—the same subject, by M. A. Caravaggio—the Madonna and our Saviour, by Rubens—the Magdalene, by Gherardo delle Notti—a *Pietà*, by Bassano—a small Landscape, by Fiamingo—the Adoration of the Magi, by Bassano, and a Magdalene, by Guido. *The fourth room* contains several interesting portraits (one of which is by Raphael, and another by Vandyck), and a beautiful miniature *Pietà*, by Annibale Caracci! *The fifth room* contains a Cleopatra, by Guido—the Madonna, and our Saviour, by Sasso-Ferratto—a picture, by Guercino, which represents Painting and Sculpture!—Children, by Giulio Romano!—S. Gregorio, by M. A. Caravaggio—S. Girolamo, by Titian—the marriage of S. Catherine, by Parmegiano; and the Holy Family, by Giulio Romano. *The sixth room* is adorned with two Landscapes by Claude, one of which is beautiful; and, between them, a Holy Family, by Giovanni Bellino—a Magdalene, by Murillo—and our Saviour with the Woman of Samaria, by Pietro da Cortona. *The last division of the Gallery* is adorned with a Ceiling by Palagi—a beautiful modern Urn—and an antique statue of a Canephora.

Palazzo Colonna. This immense edifice stands on the site of the *Domus Cornelii*. The staircase is adorned with a statue representing a Captive (probably taken from the Forum of Trajan); and fixed in the wall, opposite to the door of entrance, is a *Basso-rilievo* of porphyry, representing the head of Medusa, and supposed to be a likeness of Nero. *The ante-room to the Gallery* contains several pictures; among which are, Calvin, by Titian—Luther, by the same artist—Cain and Abel, by Andrea Sacchi—Europa, by Albano—a Peasant eating, attributed to Annibale Caracci—and a Portrait, by Paolo Veronese. *The Colonna Gallery* (with respect to size and architecture, the finest apartment at Rome), measures, in length, two hundred and nine feet; and, in breadth, thirty-five: at each extremity is a Vestibule, separated from the rest of the Gallery by columns and pilasters of giallo antico. The ceiling is well painted; and represents the sanguinary battle of Lepanto, fought in the Gulf of Patras; and among the pictures and statues which embellish this apartment are the following. A Landscape, by Niccolo Poussin—ditto by Vander-Werf—ditto by Gasparo Poussin, Orizonte, Paul Brill, Breughel, Berghem, etc.—the Madonna, the Saviour, and S. John, by Romanelli—S. Peter with the Angel, by Lanfranco—the Magdalene in glory, by Annibale Caracci—S. Sebastiano, by Guercino—S. John in the Desert, by Salvator Rosa—Cæsar sacrificing, by Carlo Maratta—and a Sketch by Titian, of himself and his family at their devotions. Statues of Venus, Germanicus, Trajan, and Flora; together with that of a recumbent Female, supposed to be Grecian sculptures.

This Palace likewise contains a small Column of rosso antico, called, The *Colonna Bellica*: it once stood before the Temple of Bellona; and was found in its vicinity.[1]

Palazzo-Giustiniani. This edifice stands on the site of Nero's Baths; whence several of the antiquities of its museum were taken; but as the major part has been sold, little now remains worth notice, except a group in the hall of entrance, representing two warriors fighting; and, in the other apartments, a Grecian Statue with the arms elevated—a group called Matrimony—a bust of Scipio—a statue called Paris—ditto of a Goat—a group representing Hercules and Cerberus—and the statue of a sleeping Female.

Palazzo-Massimi. This edifice contains a statue of a Discobolus, in white marble; copied from that, in bronze, by the celebrated Myron; and deemed one of the finest pieces of sculpture in

---

[1] When Rome declared war against a foreign enemy, an arrow was shot from the top of the column which stood before the Temple of Bellona.

Rome!!! Here, likewise, are two small statues of Loves!—a fine picture of S. Girolamo reading, with an Angel looking over him, by Niccolo Poussin!—and, on the Back-Front of the palace, are Frescos, by M. A. Caravaggio!

Palazzo-Braschi. This palace, built after the designs of the Cav. Morelli, and one of the most magnificent edifices at Rome, is adorned by a Staircase particularly beautiful, both with respect to its construction and its decorations; among the latter of which are sixteen Columns of red oriental granite; pilasters of the same; and four antique statues, namely, Commodus, Ceres, Achilles, and Pallas. *In the Apartments upstairs* are the following pictures. The Madonna and our Saviour, by Guido—the Madonna, our Saviour, and Saints, by Garofalo—Dalida and Sampson, by M. A. Caravaggio—Miracle of the loaves and fishes, by Garofalo!—the Woman detected in adultery, by Titian!—the Madonna and Angels, by Murillo!!—the marriage of S. Catherine, by Fra Bartolomeo—the marriage of Cana in Galilee, by Garofalo!—S. Sebastiano, by Fiamingo—Copy, by one of the Caracci school, of a Holy Family painted by Raphael—Lucretia, by Paolo Veronese—and the Crucifixion, by Tintoretto.

An unfinished apartment of this Palace contains a celebrated colossal statue of Antinous, in the character of Osiris, the Indian Bacchus: it was found at Palestrina, during the Pontificate of Pius VI.; is of beautiful Greek marble, and about eleven English feet in height. The left hand once held a thyrsus of bronze; and close to the left leg stands the mystic basket of Bacchus. The bronze drapery, which originally covered part of this figure, is, like the thyrsus, lost: the face and hair precisely resemble the *alto-rilievo* of Antinous in the Villa Albani; the character is beautiful; the position grand and imposing; the execution delicate; the preservation of the marble perfect; in short, this is deemed, according to the opinion of Flaxman (our British Phidias), the finest of all the existing statues of Antinous.

Palazzo-Farnese. This immense palace, commenced by Sangallo, and finished by Buonaroti and Giacomo della Porta, is deemed a fine piece of architecture.[1] *Before it* stand two magnificent oval Basins of Egyptian granite (above seventeen feet in length, and in depth between four and five), which were found in Caracalla's Baths: and in *the Quadrangle* is the Sarcophagus of Cecilia Metella, made of Parian marble, and found in her monument. *The Gallery above stairs* is adorned with some of the most admired Frescos in Rome, executed by Annibale Caracci and his scholars. The centre piece on the Ceiling represents the Triumph of Bacchus and Ariadne! Other paintings represent Paris receiving the golden apple from Mercury—Pan offering goat-skins to Diana—Galatea with Tritons, Nymphs, and Loves—Jupiter and Juno—Apollo flaying Marsyas—Boreas carrying off Orythia—Diana and Endymion—Eurydice recalled to the Shades Below—

---

[1] Most of the materials for building the Farnese Palace were taken from the Coliseum and the Theatre of Marcellus: indeed, the Coliseum, during many years, seems to have been considered merely as a stone quarry.

Europa on the bull—Aurora and Cephalus in a chariot, Titan asleep, and Cupid flying with a basket of roses—Venus and Anchises—Hercules and Iole—Cupid binding a Satyr—Salmacis and Hermaphroditus — Syrinx turned into reeds by Pan—Leander, conducted by Cupid, swimming to visit Hero—Perseus and Andromeda — combat between Perseus and Phineas— Polyphemus playing on the syringa, to charm Galatea — Polyphemus hurling the fragment of a rock at Acis—Jupiter and Ganymedes—and Hyacinthus and Apollo. Another apartment, called *Il Gabinetto*, contains fine Frescos, by Annibale Caracci; namely, Hercules supporting the celestial Globe — Ulysses delivering his Companions from Circe — the same Hero passing the Islands of the Syrens—Anapus and Amphinomus saving their Parents from death, during an eruption of Ætna—Perseus beheading Medusa—and Hercules wrestling with the Nemæan Lion. The ornaments in *chiaro-scuro,* which divide these paintings, are beautifully executed.

Palazzo-Spada. The ground-floor of this edifice contains two rooms adorned with fine Sculpture. *In the first*, is a copy of the head of Laocoon, and a statue of Antisthenes seated!! *In the second*, are eight *Bassi-rilievi* found in the Temple of Bacchus!! and a colossal statue of a Warrior holding a globe, supposed (though without good authority) to represent Pompey the Great, and to be the figure at whose base Cæsar fell!! This statue, if report speak truth, was found in a vault, under the Strada de Leutari, near the Piazza di Pasquino. Among the pictures *up-stairs,* the following are some of the most striking. *First room,* David with the head of Goliah, by Guercino; and Roman Charity, by M. A. Caravaggio. *Second room.* Judith with the head of Holofernes, by Guido—Lucretia, by ditto—the head of Seneca, by Salvator Rosa—a Landscape, by Teniers—Jacob at the Well, by Niccolo Poussin—and Time unveiling Truth, by Albano. *Third room.* S. Anna teaching the Madonna to work, by M. A. Caravaggio!!—the Saviour before Pilate, by Gherardo delle Notti—Judith with the head of Holofernes, by M. A. Caravaggio—Beatrice Cenci, by Paolo Veronese—and Dido on the funeral Pile, by Guercino. *Fourth room.* Portrait of Paul III., by Titian—ditto of Cardinal Spada, by Guido—a Snow Piece, attributed to Teniers—the heads of two Boys, attributed to Correggio!!—The Magdalene, by Guercino; and a female Musician, by M. A. Caravaggio.

Palazzo-Mattei. This palace was built after the designs of Ammannati, on the site of the Circus Flaminius. *The Quadrangle* exhibits an ancient and valuable *Basso-rilievo* of green basalt, representing an Egyptian sacrificial procession! and on the stairs are two antique Seats of marble, and two fine *Bassi-rilievi. The corridor above* is likewise ornamented with *bassi-rilievi;* and in the rooms usually shown to strangers are the following paintings: Fish, Poultry, and Butcher's meat, four pictures, all by Passeri—Charles I., and Charles II., of England, by Vandyck—two Landscapes, attributed to Passeri—Holy Family, of the Caracci-school—Abraham's sacrifice, by Guido—the Nativity, by Pietro da Cortona; and the Cavalcade of Clement VIII., and the Entry of Charles V., into Bologna, by Tempesta. *The gallery* contains a bust of Cicero; and its Ceiling is finely painted by Pietro da Cortona, Paul Brill, etc.

Palazzo-Costaguti. This palace contains six Ceilings finely painted in fresco: the first, by Albano, represents Hercules wounding the Centaur—The second, by Domenichino, represents Apollo in his car; Time bringing Truth to light; and Boys with lions' skins, Hercules's club, etc.!!— The third, by Guercino, represents Rinaldo and Armida!—The fourth, by the Cav. d'Arpino, represents Juno nursing Hercules. This room likewise contains portraits of a Duke and Duchess of Ferrara, by Titian; and an interesting picture of a Gipsy, by M. A. Caravaggio.—The fifth ceiling by Lanfranco, represents Justice embracing Peace—and the sixth, by Romanelli, represents Arion thrown into the sea, and preserved by a dolphin.

Palazzo-Falconieri. The pictures here, collected by Cardinal Fesche, are very numerous, and several of them very fine; those of the Flemish school especially. *The first floor* contains, the Visitation, by Daniello da Volterra—Christ supping with the Pilgrims, by Paolo Veronese, who has introduced portraits of his own family into the picture—the last Judgment, by Tintoretto—the Assumption, by Guido!—a Madonna and Child, by Andrea di Salerno—a fine Bassano—the Daughter of Herodias with the head of S. John (the latter finely executed), by Guercino—the Holy Sepulchre, by Albano!—the Madonna, the Saviour and S. John, by Murillo!—Peace and Justice, author doubtful—a fine portrait, by Titian—S. Carlo Borommeo, by Domenichino—Semiramis, at her toilet, receiving intelligence of a revolt, by Mengs—two portraits, by Paris Bordone—a Landscape, by Salvator Rosa—ditto, attributed to Titian—ditto, attributed to Annibale Caracci—ditto, by Gasparo Poussin—the Saviour borne by Angels after the Crucifixion, by Correggio!—two Children, by ditto!—Holy Family, by ditto!—a Madonna and Child, by Annibale Caracci—S. John, by Leonardo da Vinci—a picture in the style of Murillo, author unknown—a picture painted by Raphael when he was only eighteen, and before he quitted the school of Perugino—and another, painted afterward, when he was five-and-twenty—the Holy Sepulchre, by Annibale Caracci! —Sketch, by Correggio—Holy Family, by Andrea del Sarto—Madonna and Child, by Schidone! —Cupid mounted on an Eagle, by Domenichino!—Holy Family, by Correggio! three Frescos, sketched by Buonaroti, and finished by Sebastiano del Piombo—S. John preaching, by Rembrandt! —four Heads, by ditto, one being his own likeness—a Landscape with Cattle, by Cuyp!—another, with Fishermen, by ditto!—a Landscape, by Paul Potter—a Philosopher, by Gerard Dow!— a Battle, by Wouvermans!—the Caravan, by Adrian Vanderwelde! —a Landscape, by Paul Potter— the Saviour in prison, by Teniers! —a Landscape, by Isaac Van Ostade!—the inside of a Cottage, or Stable, by Teniers!—Peter denying the Saviour, by Gherardo delle Notti—the Magdalene, by

Vandyck!—insides of Churches, by Peter Neff—an *Ecce Homo*, by Rembrandt—the Ascension, by Vandyck, etc. etc. *The second floor* has not lately been shown to Foreigners; but contained, when last exhibited to public view, a picture of Diana and other Figures, by Le Sueur—the Saviour, Mary, and Martha, by ditto—the following pictures by Niccolo Poussin: Holy Family with Angels—Human Life, represented by the four Seasons!—the Deluge!—and a Landscape, called *Les Chartreux !*—Landscapes, by Claude, etc. etc.[1]

Palazzo Farnesina. The Entrance-Hall of this edifice is finely painted in fresco, by Raphael and his Scholars; who have represented the History of Psyche. On the Ceiling are the Council and Banquet of the Gods—in one of the Angles are the Graces; and she whose back only is seen was executed entirely by Raphael. *In an adjoining room* is his Galatea, together with a fine colossal Head (in one of the Lunettes), sketched by Buonaroti.[2] On the Ceiling of this room is Diana in her car—and the Fable of Medusa—together with several other ornaments, by Daniello da Volterra, Sebastiano del Piombo, and Baldassar Peruzzi. *The Hall above stairs* is adorned with a painting of Vulcan's Forge, by Peruzzi: and a Frieze, executed by the Scholars of Raphael.[3]

Palazzo-Corsini. This noble palace, once the residence of Christina of Sweden, contains a magnificent double Staircase, which leads to a suite of apartments enriched with some good sculpture, and several fine pictures. *First room*. A Sarcophagus found at Antium!—an ancient Mosaic—a Head, copied from Guido, in modern Mosaic—Bust, in nero antico. *Second room*. Marriage of S. Catherine, by Carlo Maratta—and two Landscapes, by Orizonte. *Third room*, An *Ecce Homo*, by Guercino!!—a Head, by Rubens—S. Peter and S. Agata, by Lanfranco—Holy Family, by Baroccio—S. Girolamo, by Guercino—the Madonna and our Saviour, by M. A. Caravaggio!—the same subject, by Vandyck—two small Landscapes, by Salvator Rosa—two Heads (supposed to represent Luther and his Wife), by Holbein—Holy Family, by Fra Bartolomeo!—ditto, by Garofolo—the Saviour and the Woman of Samaria, by Guercino—Heathen Divinities, by Albano—portrait of Julius II., attributed to Raphael—portrait of Philip II., attributed to Titian—a Drawing, by Lanfranco—and an ancient consular Chair of Parian marble. *Third room*. The Madonna and our Saviour, by Andrea del Sarto—a Vestal, by Carlo Maratta—Holy Family, by ditto—Raphael's *Fornarina*, attributed to Giulio Romano—S. Girolamo, attributed to Titian—Paul III., attributed to Raphael—the Magdalene, by Barroccio—S. John, by Guercino—Holy Family, by Bassano—Crucifixion of S. Peter, by Guido!—a wild beast

---

[1] In order to see Cardinal Fesche's pictures, it is requisite to apply to his Secretary for permission; and likewise to mention the names of the persons who wish to be admitted.

[2] We are told that Buonaroti, thinking the figures in this room too diminutive for the situations in which they are placed, drew the above-named Head, in order to make Raphael sensible of his error: and Raphael is supposed to have felt the criticism so poignantly that he was disgusted with his work, and left it unfinished.

[3] Unless the Custode be apprized beforehand, it is not always possible to gain admittance to the Palazzo-Farnesina.

Hunt, by Rubens!—a Rabbit, by Alber Durer!—The Decapitation of S. John, by Guido!!—and a small statue of the Saviour, by Buonaroti. *Fourth room.* The Madonna, by Carlo Maratta—an *Ecce Homo*, by Carlo Dolci—and ditto, by Guido. *Fifth room.* Portrait of a Lady, by Leonardo da Vinci—the Sons of Charles v., by Titian—and Pope Pamfili, by Velasquez. *Sixth room.* The Woman detected in Adultery, by Titian!—a large Landscape, by Gas. Poussin!—two Landscapes, by Orizonte—the Saviour disputing with the Doctors, by Luca Giordano—a Madonna and Child, by Murillo; and S. Sebastiano, by Rubens. *Seventh room.* A *Pietà*, by Lodovico Caracci—S. John Baptist, by M. A. Caravaggio—two oval pictures, by Albano—Judith with the head of Holofernes, by Gherardo delle Notti!—Love, sleeping, by Guido—Seneca in the Bath, by M. A. Caravaggio—Landscapes, by Gas. Poussin—Peter denying our Saviour, by Valentin—a Sketch for a Frieze, by Polidoro da Caravaggio!—and Susanna, by Domenichino. *Ninth room.* Sheep, etc., by Teniers!—Holy Family, by Niccolo Poussin!—Prometheus, by Salvator Rosa!—the Plague at Milan, by Muratori—a Landscape by Niccolo Poussin—and two oval pictures of Angels, by Sebastiano del Piombo.

Accademia di S. Luca. This Academy, and the adjoining Church of Saints Luca e Martina, stand near the Forum of Augustus; and the latter is supposed to have been built on the foundations of the *Secretarium Senatús*. The Academy contains the Skull of Raphael—a celebrated picture by that Artist, of S. Luke, painting the portraits of the Madonna and our Saviour, and Raphael himself looking on![1]—a picture of our Saviour with the Pharisee, by Salvator Rosa—ditto, by Gas. Titian!—two Landscapes, by Poussin—two Heads, by Angelica, one being her own portrait—Models, by Buonaroti, of some of his figures in the Cappella de' Principi at Florence; and several other interesting pieces of Sculpture and Painting. The Church of Saints Luca e Martina, contains a recumbent statue of the latter Saint, under the high-altar, by Niccolo Menghino: and here likewise is a subterranean Chapel, made by Pietro da Cortona, at his own expense.

VILLAS NEAR ROME.

Villa-Olgiati, fuori la Porta del Populo. This Casina, likewise called Villetta-Nelli, was once inhabited by Raphael and his scholars; who have embellished it with Arabesques, and other Frescos: some of which are in tolerably good preservation: and one of these paintings, namely, the Marriage of Alexander and Roxana, is deemed well worth notice.

Villa Borghese. The Paddock in which this magnificent Villa stands, is near three miles in circumference, and contains a handsome Fountain, and a Temple, called that of Æsculapius, from an antique statue of Æsculapius placed there. The Portico of the Villa leads to a splendid *Hall*, the Ceiling of which was painted by Mariano Rossi, and represents

---

[1] This picture has been so much restored, that very little now remains of the original painting by Raphael.

the Combat between Furius Camillus and the Gauls. Here, likewise, placed most advantageously, near the ceiling, is an *Alto-rilievo* of Curtius leaping into the Gulf!!! The horse (than which nothing can be finer) is certainly antique; but, according to some opinions, the figure of Curtius is modern. *Another room on the ground floor*, is embellished with a Fresco on the Ceiling, by Caccaniga; it represents the Fall of Phaëton; and among the statues, are Ceres — a Persian Soldier — Domitian, and a Vestal; all recently found at Frascati — an Hermaphrodite (supposed to be Grecian sculpture) resting on a Mattress, excellently executed by Bernini — and another statue, supposed to be Grecian sculpture, and called The faithful Shepherd. The Ceiling of *the Gallery up stairs* was painted by Pietro Angeletti, and represents the fable of Acis and Galatea. Over the chimney-piece of *another apartment* is a *Basso-rilievo*, in rosso antico, by Agostino Penna. Here, likewise, is *a room* painted by Hamilton; who has represented the story of Paris and Helen; and in the same room is a superb modern Vase, made of oriental marble. The most striking easel pictures are : S. John, by Mengs — a Bacchanalian Scene, by Niccolo Poussin — Holy Family, by Luca Giordano — a Hen and Chickens, by Petra! — two Snow-pieces, by Foschi! — and the portrait of Paul v., by M. H. Caravaggio. This villa also contains two Ceilings painted by Conca (the one representing Anthony and Cleopatra; the other a Bacchanalian Sacrifice); and likewise a ceiling painted by Lanfranco, and retouched by Corvi, which represents Hercules, Antæus, and heathen Divinities.[1]

Villa-Ludovisia, near the Porta-Salara.[2] One of the buildings in the Garden belonging to this Villa contains Guercino's Aurora; a Fresco equally famous with, though totally different from, that of Guido; the one representing Day-break, the other Sun-rise. The Ceiling of the room immediately over Guercino's Aurora is adorned with a beautiful figure of Fame, accompanied by War and Peace, all by Guercino. Another building contains a celebrated statue of Mars seated, with Love at his feet!! — a beautiful group, supposed to represent Phædra and Hippolitus, by Menelaus, a Grecian sculptor!!! — a group, called Pætus and Aria!! — and a *basso-rilievo* of Pyrrhus!! Near the garden-gate is an admirable head of Juno: and this garden likewise contains a statue of a Senator, with " Zeno" (the name of a Grecian sculptor), on the drapery.[3] It is necessary to choose a fine day for seeing the Villa Ludovisia, every thing worth notice being in the garden.

Villa-Albani. This is one of the most magnificent Villas in the environs of Rome; and contains a large collection of Statues, Busts, *Bassi-rilievi*, etc. *Staircase*. A *basso-rilievo* representing Hercules and the Hesperides — dito of three of the Children of Niobe — ditto of Juno Lucina, or

---

[1] The Custode of the Villa-Borghese lives at the Borghese-Palace, in Rome; but is always ready to show the Villa, when desired; and is generally there from two o'clock till four in the afternoon, during winter and spring.

[2] The Villa-Ludovisia, though beyond the streets, is within the walls of Rome.

[3] It is impossible to obtain admission to the Villa-Ludovisia without an order from the Prince of Piombino.

the goddess Rumilia, supposed to protect infants: this *Basso-rilievo* is Etruscan, and the most ancient work of its kind at Rome. *Rooms leading to the Gallery.* Group of a Faun and a Bear — head of a young Faun! — small statue of Pallas, in bronze! — Apollo Sauroctonon, in bronze! — an Egyptian statue of Canopus, in green basalt! — ditto of Osiris — a deified Hercules! — and the celebrated *Alto-rilievo* of Antinous!!! *Gallery.* This apartment is incrusted with rare marbles, and its ceiling painted by Mengs; who has represented Apollo and Mnemosyne encircled by the Muses! Here are *bassi-rilievi* representing Hercules between two of the Hesperides — Icarus and Dædalus[1] — Bellerophon and Pegasus — and Marcus Aurelius seated, with Faustina in the character of Peace. Here, likewise, is a statue of Jupiter, and a statue of Pallas! *Galleries of sculpture below stairs.* The Satyr Marsyas; (the limbs of this statue are modern) — a beautiful column of flowered alabaster — a *basso-rilievo* representing the history of Alcestis — ditto representing Phædra and Hippolitus — Agrippina seated — Basin, ten feet in diameter, adorned with *bassi-rilievi* representing the labours of Hercules! — an Etruscan Minerva — two Vases adorned with *bassi-rilievi* — head of Jupiter Serapis in basalt! — small statue of a Comedian — Apollo seated and draped — a Child hiding itself under a mask — a small antique Fountain; and several Urns in basalt. These galleries likewise contain Hermæ of the most distinguished Characters of Antiquity, etc. etc.

At the end of each Gallery, below stairs, is a small *Peristyle:* that on the left side contains an ancient mosaic Pavement, and a statue of Diana of Ephesus — and here, likewise, is an Etruscan Altar, embellished with *Bassi-rilievi.* The opposite *Peristyle* is adorned with Canephoræ,[2] and one of the Statues called Caryatides, which were found on the Via-Appia, and are supposed to be Grecian sculpture!!

Another Building, adorned with a circular Portico, contains Busts and Statues; among which are those of Æsop, Bacchus, two Canephoræ, and another of the statues called Caryatides. This Portico leads to a small *Apartment* containing an Egyptian statue, in oriental alabaster, of Isis, found at Rome, near the site of her temple in the Campus Martius — other statues of Egyptian Deities; and an Owl in basalt, with the Phallus on its head. Near this apartment is *another,* adorned with a *basso-rilievo* representing Trimalcion followed by Comedians, entering a banqueting-room.

The statue of Domitian, discovered between Frascati and Palestrina in the year 1758, and placed under the large Portico of the Villa Albani, is noticed by Winckelmann both on account of the excellence of the sculpture, and likewise because almost every statue of Domitian was destroyed by the Romans after his death: this statue was found with the arms and head broken off, and the trunk injured by strokes of a mattock; the head, however, escaped injury.

---

1 Found at the foot of the Palatine-hill.
2 Noble Roman Ladies, Priestesses of Minerva, who carried on their heads, in baskets, various things destined for sacrifice.

Villa Mattei. This villa is situated beyond the Arch of Dolabella, though within the walls of Rome. The garden is adorned with an Egyptian obelisk; and commands a particularly good view of Caracalla's Baths. *The first room* shown to strangers, in the Villa, contains a copy of the Demoniac Boy. *The second room* is ornamented with the statue of a sleeping Love—ditto of Venus, by Canova—and a group, called Filial Affection, by a Spanish Artist. *The third room* contains a copy of Raphael's Galatea—a picture of the Salutation—and another of the Saviour dead. *The fourth room* contains a picture of Horatius Cocles on the Sublician Bridge, copied by Camuccini from that in the Capitol—a Landscape—and the rape of the Sabines. *The fifth room* contains a striking picture of a Saint blessing a dying person—another picture of the martyrdom of a Saint, and a bust of Nero, by Canova. *The sixth room* is adorned with an ancient Pavement, found near the Villa.

Villa Doria-Pamfili, fuori la Porta S. Pancrazio. On the Janiculum hill, and in the way to this Villa, is *the Church of S. Onofrio;* which contains, under its portico, three Lunettes, painted by Domenichino. The Madonna and Our Saviour, over the door, were likewise done by the same great master; and, in the Church, are the Tombs of Torquato Tasso and Alessandro Guido; the former of whom died in the adjoining convent, which contains a Bust, moulded from his face.

Beyond the church of S. Onofrio is the *Fontana-Paolina*, constructed at the command of Paul v., by Fontana, with materials taken from the Forum of Nerva. This magnificent Fountain is adorned with six Ionic columns of red granite, that support an entablature, upon which rest the armorial bearings of the Pontiff. From three niches, between the columns, rush three torrents of water, and precipitate themselves into a vast basin of marble: while from two smaller niches rush smaller streams, out of the mouths of dragons. The water is supplied from Trajan's Aqueduct. About three quarters of a mile beyond the Porta S. Pancrazio, on the *Via Aurelia*, is the *Villa Doria-Pamfili;* of which Algardi was the architect. The Paddock belonging to this Villa is nearly four miles in circumference; and, according to some opinions, the site of the Gardens of Galba. The Villa contains several pieces of Sculpture, among which are the famous Olympia—Faustina!—Vespasian—Marcus Brutus—and a Sibyl. Here, likewise, is a Sketch, by Raphael—ditto, by Giulio Romano—a bust of Demosthenes!—ditto of another Philosopher—a group of Cybele seated on a lion!—Groups of Children at play—Clodius in female attire—an Hermaphrodite—Bacchus, in rosso antico—a *Basso-rilievo* of a famous Gladiator, who lived during the reign of Caracalla—and two beautiful Sarcophagi, one representing the story of Meleager, the other Diana descending from the celestial Regions to visit Endymion. In a room above stairs is a portrait of the Cenci; and in the attic story a small Museum. The roof of this Villa commands a fine view of Rome; and in the Garden, near the gate of entrance, is *an ancient public Burial-place* well worth observation!

Villa-Madama, fuori la Porta-Angelica. This edifice, which stands near the base of the Monte Mario (anciently *Clivus Cinnæ*), was designed by Raphael, and finished, after his death, by Giulio Romano, who painted the portico, and designed the ornaments in stucco, with which it is embellished. The interior of the villa, though in a ruinous state, exhibits a beautiful Frieze, and a Ceiling, both painted by Giulio Romano, who has represented, on the latter, the Cars of Diana and Apollo, Birds, Beasts, etc.; among which are a sleeping Lion, and a Goat going to be sacrificed, both finely executed. This room likewise contains most valuable Cartoons; which are so totally neglected, that they must very soon be quite spoiled. Two other rooms exhibit Friezes and Cartoons, cruelly injured, but once very beautiful. The view from this villa is charming; and the Ponte Molle, Tiber, city of Rome, and mountains of the Apennine, appear to more advantage here than from any other spot.

A winding path leads from the Villa-Madama to the upper part of the Monte Mario, where stands the *Villa - Mellina*, whence the Mediterranean sea may be discovered.[1]

There are several Hospitals at Rome: *that of S. Spirito* is a noble edifice, and receives Foundlings, and sick persons of all descriptions.[2] *The Hospital of S. Michele* likewise is a spacious building, and receives Invalids, aged Persons, and Orphans; the last of whom are taught the arts of Painting, making Tapestry, etc.

The Mosaic Manufacture near S. Peter's, under the direction of the Cav. Camuccini, is highly worth notice; as are the *Studii* of that distinguished artist,[3] and the Cav. Landi. Keiserman, No. 31, Piazza di Spagna, is a celebrated Landscape Painter in water colours. The Cav. Fidanza is a good Landscape Painter in oils; and especially successful in imitating Salvator Rosa. Rebell is a fine Painter, and particularly successful in sea-views: but Voogd and Reinhards appear to be considered as the best Landscape Painters at Rome. Granet represents the insides of Churches in a wonderful manner. Metz

---

1 Basilicæ are, generally speaking, open from sun-rise till sun-set. Persons wishing to be sure of admittance, at any given hour, to Palaces or Villas, should apply a day before-hand. Admittance to the Museums of the Capitol and Vatican may usually be obtained on days when they are not open to the public, by an application to the Custode of each Museum; who, when thus called upon, expects a fee of five or six pauls; and perhaps more, if the party he attends be very numerous. At S. Peter's it is advisable to appoint the Sacristan a day before-hand; and likewise at small unfrequented churches.

The expense of seeing the whole of S. Peter's, including the subterranean Church, amounts to several pauls; as there are three or four Sacristans, each of whom expects a fee. In other churches there is but one Sacristan; and he does not expect more than two pauls. At a Palace it is usual to give at Rome, as at other cities of Italy, from three to five pauls, according to the size of the party: and in subterranean apartments, where the Custode provides wax lights, it is usual to give from three to four pauls.

Late in the spring, when the weather at Rome becomes hot, parties frequently go to the Villa-Madama, taking with them a cold dinner, which they eat on the terrace there, and then proceed to the shady walks which surround the Villa—Mellini, ordering their carriages to meet them at the foot of the hill behind that Villa.

2 The want of cleanliness in this Hospital makes it a dangerous place to visit.

3 The Cav. Camuccini has, at his private house, a collection of pictures by the most distinguished masters, and likewise some fine statues and *bassi-rilievi*, which he allows to be seen by Travellers every Sunday morning, from ten o'clock till two.

draws beautifully; and has published fine Engravings of the Last Judgment, and other frescos in the Vatican.

The greatest Sculptor of the present day is the Cav. Thorwaldsen, whose chisel produces *Bassirilievi* which, like the Frescos of Raphael, may be called inimitable.[1]

One of the most celebrated Cameo-cutters is Girometti; and the best Artist of this description, who works in shells, is Dies, at No. 76, Via della Croce.

Rome is usually frequented during winter by several English medical men; among whom is Dr. Clark, who resides in the Piazza di Spagna.

Messrs. Torlonia and Co., the principal Bankers in this city, are particularly obliging and useful to the British Nation.

Rome contains six Theatres: all of which are open during Carnival, and some at other seasons.

The Carnival usually begins eight days previous to Ash Wednesday; and finishes with Shrovetide. During this period of general festivity the Corso, a fine street extending from the Porto del Popolo to the foot of the Capitol, is decorated with tapestry and silk hangings from every window and balcony;[2] enlivened with military bands of music, and crowded with Masqueraders, in carriages and on foot, from two in the afternoon till sunset; during the latter part of which time, horse races, like those at Florence, are exhibited. At night the Teatro Aliberti, a large and handsome edifice, is open for masked balls: and though, during the three last days of Carnival, the crowd of Masks on the Corso, and in other parts of the city, is great beyond conception, and though the number of persons at the masked balls often exceeds five thousand, not a single word is spoken that can hurt the most delicate ears, nor a single thing done that can tend to disturb public tranquillity.

Another Festival, little known to Travellers, but well worth observation, from being a remnant of the ancient *Saturnalia*, is that celebrated on Sundays and Thursdays, during the month of October, on the Monte Testaccio. This hill contains the public wine vaults of the city, and from being composed of large fragments of pottery, between which the air constantly penetrates, is peculiarly fitted for its present use, as an invariable coolness is preserved beneath its surface. On this hill, during the days already mentioned, tables are spread with refreshment: and hither, on these days, flock the whole population of Rome and its environs, to drink wine fresh drawn from the vaults beneath their feet. It is impossible to conceive a more enlivening picture than the summit of Monte Testaccio exhibits on this occasion. Groups of peasants, arrayed in their gayest costume, are seen dancing the *Santarella;* others are seated in jovial parties round the tables; and others mingle with the upper ranks of Romans, who leave their car-

---

[1] A studio near the Via-Babuino contained, in 1822, thirteen statues, recently discovered in the Greek Island of Ægina: they are finely executed in the Etruscan style, of high antiquity, and originally adorned the pediment of a temple:—they now belong to the King of Bavaria.

[2] When Triumphs and other public Processions took place in ancient Rome, the streets were decorated, as at this day, with veils or hangings.

riages at the foot of the hill, and stroll about to enjoy this festive scene. Bodies of cavalry and infantry parade to and fro, to preserve order; while the pyramid of Caius Cestius, and the adjoining Tombs of the Protestants, by forming a strong contrast to these Saturnalian rites, add interest to the picture.[1]

During Lent the principal amusements are Church Ceremonies, the Academy of the Arcadians; the Academy Tiberina; the music (which begins about three o'clock every afternoon, and is especially good on Fridays), at S. Peter's; and Serletti's Concert, which consists of a pianoforte and about twenty singers, who manage so as to give their voices the effect of a full band of instrumental music. They chiefly perform the Marcello Psalms; so called from a noble Venetian who composed this music, which is particularly fine. In the Church of Gesù, likewise, there frequently is fine music during Lent.

The Ceremonies of the Holy Week commence on Palm Sunday, in the Chapel of the Pontifical Palace at Monte Cavallo; where the Pope officiates, and blesses the Palms; after which, *The Passion* is beautifully chanted. In order to see this function, which represents the entry of our Saviour into Jerusalem, it is necessary for Foreigners to go at half-past nine in the morning.[2]

On Wednesday, in the Holy Week, at four in the afternoon, the *Tenebræ* and the *Miserere* are sung by the Pope's Choir in the Cappella-Sistina,[3] and likewise in S. Peter's.

On Holy Thursday, Foreigners should be in the Cappella-Sistina by half-past eight in the morning, to see the Ceremony of carrying the Host to the Cappella-Paolina; the illumination of that Chapel, and the representation of the Holy Sepulchre. They should then endeavour to obtain front seats in the Loggia, near the Court leading to the Museo-Chiaramonti; but if unable to accomplish this, they should station themselves near the steps leading to S. Peter's, in the covered Gallery not exposed to the sun, in order to see the Benediction; which takes place about noon, and is a peculiarly fine sight.[4] After the benediction, the Pope washes the feet of thirteen Pilgrims; and then waits upon them while they dine. To see both these Ceremonies is attended with so much difficulty that Foreigners would do well to relinquish the former, and witness the latter, which is generally considered the most interesting of the two: and in order to accomplish this, they should ascend the stairs opposite to those leading to the Museo-Chiaramonti; and instead of entering the Pilgrims' Hall, on the top of the stairs, turn into the Loggia on the left, which leads to the Dinner-room. At four in the afternoon the *Tenebræ* and

---

[1] Pinelli constantly attends the Festival at Monte Testaccio, to study subjects for his characteristic pencil; and late in the spring parties frequently go to dine here, taking a cold dinner with them.

[2] It is not deemed proper, during the Holy Week, to appear in public without wearing mourning; and wherever the Pope officiates, Ladies are directed to appear in Veils.

[3] Allegri's *Miserere* is that usually sung in the Cappella Sistina.

[4] On quitting the Cappella Sistina, to obtain front seats in the Loggia, the best way is *to descend the first Staircase on the left.*

Miserere are again sung by the Pope's Choir in the Cappella-Sistina; after which, the inside of S. Peter's is illuminated by an immense Cross, thickly studded with brilliant lamps, and suspended from the centre of the cupola.

On Good Friday, at ten in the morning, Foreigners should go to the Cappella-Sistina, in order to see the Host taken by the Pope from the Cappella-Paolina. At four in the afternoon the *Tenebræ* and *Miserere* are again repeated in the Cappella-Sistina; while the illuminated Cross is again displayed in S. Peter's; and about half-past seven in the evening of this day there is a particularly good Arcadia.

On Saturday morning, at eight o'clock, Jews and Turks receive baptism in the Church of S. Giovanni in Laterano; where, during the morning, there usually is fine vocal music; and about nine o'clock the resurrection service is performed in the Pontifical Chapel at Monte Cavallo, by the Pope, Cardinals, etc.

On Easter Day, at nine in the morning, Foreigners should be at S. Peter's, in order to procure good places for seeing the Pope enter that Church in state: and after having witnessed this splendid procession, they should once more place themselves either in the Loggia near the Court leading to the Museo-Chiaramonti, or opposite to the Loggia, in one of the Arches of the covered Gallery below, to see the second Benediction, and obtain a good view of the Piazza di S. Pietro, which, on Easter-day, seldom contains less than a hundred and fifty thousand persons, soldiers inclusive. Between twelve and one o'clock, the Pope returns in state from the interior of S. Peter's, and immediately ascends to the Loggia on the outside of the church; where he no sooner appears than all the troops kneel; and, when he has pronounced the blessing, the drums beat, the cannon of S. Angelo fire, and the bells ring in every direction; while the superb costume of the Pontifical Court, the picturesque dresses of the peasantry, and the splendid equipages of the Cardinals, foreign Princes, etc. render this scene equally magnificent and impressive.[1] About half an hour after sunset commences the first illumination of the outside of S. Peter's; which is effected by means of four thousand four hundred paper lanterns, lighted by men suspended on the outside of the edifice by ropes, and drawn up and down by persons stationed within: but the service is so imminently dangerous, that these lamp-lighters receive the sacrament before they begin their labour. The lamps which compose this first illumination cast a light somewhat resembling that of the moon; but, at seven o'clock, literally in one moment, the whole scene changes, and presents the most brilliant spectacle imaginable; as every part of the Church, to the very summit of the cross on the cupola, appears one blaze of fire. The materials which compose this second Illumination are pitch, wood-shav-

---

[1] Persons who wish to have a particularly fine view of the Pontifical Court on Easter-day, should stand near the foot of the *Scala Regia*, or great Staircase of the Vatican, about half-past nine in the morning, and see the Pope and his Attendants descend the stairs on their way to S. Peter's.

ings, and eighty-four flambeaux, so wonderfully managed that the effect is perfection. About eight o'clock commence the Fireworks of the Castle of S. Angelo. This magnificent sight begins with an explosion, called the *Girandola;* and produced by four thousand five hundred rockets, so arranged as to represent an eruption of Vesuvius. A variety of beautiful changes then take place; and the whole closes with a second *Girandola*, that appears to convert the very Tiber into flames; and throws reflected light upon the majestic dome of S. Peter's, which shines brilliantly amidst the seeming conflagration.[1]

These fireworks, and the illumination of the church, are repeated on S. Peter's day.

On Ascension day the Pope usually officiates at S. Giovanni in Laterano; and gives the Benediction from the great Loggia on the outside of that church; he likewise officiates on the Festival of Corpus Domini, when there is a magnificent Procession in the Piazzo di S. Pietro, together with fine Music; the latter being repeated for several days in S. Peter's and the Church of Gesù. On the first Sunday in Advent he usually officiates in the Capella-Sistina; on Christmas-day at S. Maria Maggiore, whither he goes in state;[2] on the eighteenth of January, at S. Peter's, whither, likewise, he goes in state (that being the anniversary of the day when S. Peter's Chair was placed in the church);[3] on the second of February, in the Pontifical Chapel of Monte Cavallo, in order to bless the Candles, which is a splendid ceremony; and again on Ash Wednesday, in the Pontifical Chapel of Monte Cavallo, in order to throw Cinders on the heads of the Cardinals, etc.

The magnificence displayed at Rome in church-ceremonies, and indeed on every public occasion, is unparalleled; but during the winter and spring of 1819, it could not be witnessed without astonishment. The first event which called forth this spirit of magnificence was the death of the exiled Queen of Spain, whose funeral is said to have cost thirty thousand scudi. After lying in state several days at her own residence, the Barberini Palace (where, in conformity to Spanish customs, her Ladies waited round her as if she had been still living; and her Gentlemen attended daily to ask what she would choose to eat for dinner, and whether she would like to go out in her carriage); she was removed, in an elegant open sarcophagus, drawn by a pair of her own horses, to the Basilica of S. Maria Maggiore; and placed on a sumptuous bier in the centre of that church; which, being hung

---

1 Persons desirous of seeing both the Illumination and the Fireworks to advantage, should go in an open carriage to the Piazza di S. Pietro half an hour after sun-set; remaining in the Piazza till the second Illumination of the Church has taken place, and then driving *quickly* to their station for seeing the Fireworks,—passing over the Ponte Sisto, instead of the Ponte S. Angelo.

The best Station for seeing the Fireworks is the Loggia of the Palazzo-Altovite, in the Piazza di S. Angelo, No. 15; and the front places in this Loggia are usually let at a scudo each.

2 There is an interesting Function, on Christmas-day, at the Church of S. Maria Maggiore, from four in the morning till seven: persons, however, who go at half-past five, or even an hour later, see the most interesting part of this Function; which consists of a Procession, with the Cradle, etc.

3 On the eighteenth of January, at three in the afternoon, there is beautiful Music in S. Peter's.

with black and silver ornaments in a manner assimilating perfectly with the style of the edifice, gave it the appearance of a vast public assembly-room arrayed in gorgeous mourning attire. Here all the Ladies and Gentlemen belonging to the Court of the deceased, the Cardinals, and other Roman Princes and Nobles, together with all the Foreigners of distinction, and legions of inferior persons, were assembled to hear the service for the Dead, and to take a last look at her Majesty; who, dressed with regal splendour, and resembling a large doll more than a corse, was placed in so exalted a situation as to be universally seen. After this ceremony, she was carried for interment to S. Peter's, preceded by all the Confraternities in Rome, and attended by a considerable number of Dignitaries of the Church, and likewise by the Representatives of the Apostolic Chamber; the former walking bare-headed, the latter on horseback, and wearing their ancient costume. The queen was carried on a large open bier by thirty bearers, followed by the sarcophagus, already mentioned, which conveyed her to S. Maria Maggiore; and, after this, came the deposed King of Spain's state carriages, sixteen in number, each being drawn empty by a set of fine horses, and attended by livery servants. The procession amounted to three thousand persons; most of whom held large wax torches; and when their light (piercing through the veil of evening) was thrown on the castle of S. Angelo, where minute guns were fired as the Body passed; when the same light glanced on the magnificent colonnades of the Piazza di S. Pietro, and at length illuminated the façade of the church itself, this scene, combined with the death-like quietude of every spectator, the sonorous and solemn sound of the great bell at S. Peter's, and the roll on the muffled drums with which the body was received into the church, produced, altogether, the most impressive effect imaginable.

The scenes which took place, in consequence of the Emperor of Austria's visit to Rome, were of a very different description. No sooner was it known that he intended to honour the ancient Mistress of the world with his presence than those hinges of papal government, the Cardinals,[1] worked incessantly to prepare for his reception; insomuch that every weed was removed from the streets and squares, every museum put into the nicest order, and almost every apartment of the immense pontifical palace on the Quirinal hill (except a few rooms occupied by the Pope), new painted and new furnished; while three hundred cooks were hired for the Emperor and his suite, thirty carriages, besides those which followed the funeral of the Queen of Spain, put into requisition for his service; and three hundred coachmen and footmen clothed in sumptuous liveries, and engaged to wait on him, his companions, and attendants: and from the moment when he arrived to that on which he departed, a fête of some description was daily proposed for his amusement, to fill up the time not occupied by church ceremonies. The most striking

---

[1] The word *Cardinal* is derived from *Cardo*, a hinge; and no council has been so long established in Europe as that of the Cardinals; for, though at times debarred from exercising its authority, it never, since first constituted, was, even for one moment, abolished.

of these entertainments was the illumination of S. Peter's, and the display of fire-works at the Castle of S. Angelo; the former being lighted according to Buonaroti's plan, the latter exhibiting the Mausoleum of Adrian in its original form, superadded to the *girandola*, and other customary changes. The Fête gievn at the Capitol was likewise particularly splendid. The two museums of sculpture and painting, and the Senator's palace, which fronts the steps leading to the capitol, were all united by temporary galleries, and their façades completely covered with fire-works, so contrived that the Emperor let them off in due succession, merely by lighting the touch-paper of one rocket. The interior of the three united buildings was hung with white silk spotted with silver stars, like the drapery used by the Greeks in very ancient times; the ceilings were adorned with paintings, and the floors covered with green cloth; while some of the finest sculpture now in existence added dignity and interest to every apartment. An ode, written in honour of the Emperor, was sung by the best vocal performers, supported by the best orchestra Italy could produce; while sixteen rooms were thrown open containing supper-tables, exhibiting, among other decorations, highly-finished miniature paintings on wax; and loaded with every luxury of the Roman market; such indeed was the quantity of eatables provided for this entertainment, that no sooner had one dish been emptied than another appeared, as if brought by magic, to fill its place. One of these supper-tables encircled the bronze statue of the wolf which was struck with lightning when Cæsar fell; and this statue made a beautiful ornament; other tables were adorned with equal taste; in short nothing was wanted, but the presence of Rosa Taddei and Sgricci in the Arcadian hall, to add, by the wonderful notes of their incomparable lyres, to the various enchantments of the evening.[1]

It is necessary that English Ladies should have tickets for the ceremonies of the Holy Week, etc. which tickets may be procured by an application to the British Consul: and so particularly kind is the present Pope to the British Nation, that every possible civility is shown them, when they attend the functions of the Roman Catholic Church. He likewise allows English Ladies to be introduced to him either in his garden, or a small room adjoining; and, when received in the latter, he seats them by his side, and converses with much graciousness. His countenance beams with benevolence, and his manners are gentlemanlike: but from stooping excessively, he appears infirm.[2]

British Travellers have lately been allowed to hire an apartment in the Foro Trajano, for the celebration of divine service accord-

---

[1] The hall where the Arcadian Academy assemble, when they present the laurel crown to any one of their Members, is in the Palace of the Senator at the Capitol.

Rosa Taddei (called, in Arcadia, Licora Parthenopia) is a celebrated *Improvvisatrice*: and Sig. Tommaso Sgricci's powers, as an *Improvvisatore*, are such that, on being given the most difficult subject for a tragedy which his audience can suggest, he never fails, after considering about ten minutes, to speak, on the given subject, a tragic drama, divided into five acts, so well constructed, and so beautiful with respect to versification and sentiments, that it is scarcely possible for those who listen not to think him inspired.

[2] Ladies cannot be introduced to the Pope without wearing veils, and dresses which come up to the throat. He does not like to speak French himself, but permits Foreigners to answer him in that language.

ing to the rites of the Protestant Church.

The *Corso, the Paddock of the Villa Borghese, the road between the Porta Pia and the Mons Sacer*, and *the drive*, already mentioned, *on the Trinità de' Monti*, are the Promenades most frequented at Rome. This city contains several Hotels, and a very considerable number of private lodgings. Among the former are *L'Hôtel de Londres*, Piazza di Spagna—*L'Hôtel d'Europe*, Piazza di Spagna—*L'Hôtel de la Ville de Paris*, and *L'Hôtel des Russies*, Via della Croce—*L'Hôtel de la Grande-Bretagne*, Via Babuino—*L'Hôtel de S. Carlo*, and *L'Hôtel de la Sibylle*, in the Corso.

I will now close my account of Rome with a List of the Objects best worth notice, as they lie contiguous to each other; beginning with the Antiquities.

Foro Romano—Tempio di Giove Tonante—Tempio della Concordia—Arco di Settimio Severo—Tempio di Saturno—Colonna di Phocas—Tempio di Antonino e Faustina—Tempio di Giove Statore—Chiesa di S. Maria Liberatrice—Tempio di Remo—Tempio della Pace—Tempio di Venere e Roma—Arco di Tito—Colosseo—Arco di Costantino—Chiesa di S. Teodoro—Arco di Settimio Severo in Velabro—Arco di Giano Quadrifronte—Cloaca Massima—Chiesa di S. Maria in Cosmedin—Tempio di Vesta—Tempio della Fortuna Virile—Palazzo de' Cesari—Circus Maximus—Chiesa di S. Grigorio sul Monte Celio—Terme di Tito—Sette Sale—Chiesa di S. Martino in Monte—Chiesa di S. Pietro in Vincoli—Chiesa di S. Maria della Navicella—Chiesa di S. Stefano Rotondo.

Obelisk of the Piazza del Popolo—Obelisk of the Trinità de' Monti,—Villa Medici—Statues, Horses, and Obelisk in the Piazza di Monte Cavallo—Chiesa di S. Bernardo—Chiesa di S. Maria degli Angeli—Obelisk of S. Maria Maggiore—Column in the Piazza di S. Maria Maggiore—Basilica di S. Maria Maggiore—Obelisk of S. Giovanni in Laterano—Battisterio di Costantino—Basilica di S. Giovanni in Laterano—Scala Santa—Anfiteatro Castrense—Basilica di Santa Croce in Gerusalemme—Temple of Venus and Cupid—Claudian Aqueduct—Chiesa di S. Bibiana—Tempio di Minerva Medica—Arco di Gallieno—Chiesa di S. Prassede.

Campidoglio—Tempio di Pallade—Tempio e Foro di Nerva—Foro e Colonna Trajana—Dogana Pontificia—Obelisk of Monte Citorio—Colonna Antonina—Mausoleo d'Augusto—Campo Marzo—Mausoleo Adriano.

Tempio del Sole, nel Giardino Colonnese—Obelisk of the Piazza di S. Maria sopra Minerva—Chiesa di S. Maria sopra Minerva—Pantheon—Bagni d'Agrippa—Piazza Navona—Chiesa di S. Agnese—Teatro di Marcello—Portico d'Octavia—Tempio d'Esculapio—Chiesa di S. Cecilia in Trastevere—Basilica di S. Maria in Trastevere.

Chiesa di S. Prisca, Monte Aventino—Chiesa di S. Sabina—Chiesa di S. Alessio—Villa of the late King of Spain—Sepolcro di Cajo Cestio—Terme di Caracalla—Sepolcro degli Scipioni.

Churches and Palaces. *Basilica di S. Pietro—Vaticano.*

Chiesa dei P. P. Cappuccini, in Piazza Barberini — Palazzo-Barberini — Chiesa di S. Maria della Vittoria — Fontano di Termini — Chiesa di S. Andrea, à Monte Cavallo — Palazzo-Pontificio — Palazzo - Rospigliosi — Garden containing Guido's Aurora — Fontana di Trevi.

Chiese di S. Maria del Popolo — di S. Carlo al Corso — di S. Lorenzo in Lucina — di S. Ignazio — de' S. S. Apostoli — di S. Maria di Loretto — di Gesù — di S. Andrea della Valle — della Trinità de' Pelegrini — di S. Carlo à Catenari — di S. Giovanni de' Fiorentini — di S. Maria in Vallicella — di S. Maria della Pace — di S. Agostino.

Palazzi Borghese — Sciarra — Doria — Bracciano — Colonna — Giustiniani — Massimi — Braschi — Farnese — Spada — Mattei — Costaguti — Falconieri — Farnisina — Corsini — Accademia di S. Lucca.

CHAPTER IX.

TIVOLI, FRASCATI, PALESTRINA, AND ALBANO.

Excursion from Rome to Tivoli — Pons Mammeus — Monument of Julia Stemma — Lago de' Tartari — Bridge of the Solfatara — Ponte Lucano — Adrian's Villa — Villa of Cassius — Inns at Tivoli — Temple of the Tiburtine Sibyl — Temple of Vesta — Grotto of Neptune — Grotto of the Sirens — Circular Terrace — Villa of Varus — Ponte del Aquoria — Tempio della Tossa — Mæcenas's Villa — Site of the Villa of Sallust — Site of the Temple of Hercules — Garden of the Villa d'Este — Claudian Aqueduct near the Convent of S. Cosimato — Horace's Villa and Sabine Farm — Excursion from Rome to Frascati — Sepulchres — Grotto-Ferrata — Villas Belvedere and Ruffinella — Ruins of Tusculum — Excursion to Palestrina — Temple of Fortune — Excursion to Albano — Tomb of Clodius — Amphitheatre — Reservoir — Prætorian Camp — Museum — Lago Castello — Castel-Gandolfo — Emissario — Domitian's Villa — Tomb of the Curiatii — Climate of Albano and Aricia — Lodging-houses, etc. — Character of the Romans.

As British Travellers seldom visit Rome without making excursions thence to Tivoli, Frascati, Palestrina, and Albano, it may not, perhaps, be superfluous to mention what I found the most convenient way of seeing those places.

TIVOLI.

This excursion ought to be made in dry and temperate weather; and persons who wish to view the scenery to advantage should go in May or October.

I hired an open carriage, with six seats and four horses, paying ten scudi for going and returning the same day; and giving to my driver, for *buona-mano*, one scudo.[1] The distance from Rome to Tivoli is about eighteen miles, and the road, generally speaking, good, though now and then, in the an-

---

[1] The common price, per day, for a light open carriage with two horses, from Rome to Tivoli and back, *buona-mano* not included, is four scudi.

cient *Via Tiburtina* (great part of which still remains), there are large loose blocks of basalt, which, if not avoided, might break a carriage.

After passing the Gate and Church of S. Lorenzo, the first interesting object I discovered was the *Ponte-Mammolo (Pons Mammeus)*, thrown over the Teverone, anciently called the Anio, from King Anius, who precipitated himself into it. This bridge is about four miles distant from Rome, and derives its present appellation from Mammea (the mother of Alexander Severus,) by whom it was repaired. Further on, I observed *a small Monument* erected to the memory of Giulia Stemma, by her children: and beyond this, on the left of the high-road, and very near it, is *the Lago de' Tartari*, anciently a volcano. The water of this lake petrifies every vegetable substance with which it comes in contact, and is curiously hedged round with stalactites. I proceeded next to *the Bridge of the Solfatara*, thrown over a stream anciently denominated *Aquæ Albulæ*, which smells offensively, and is so white as to resemble milk: then, driving about two miles further, I was presented with a beautiful Landscape, formed by the Ponte Lucano, the Anio and the Plautian Tomb. *The Ponte Lucano* is supposed to derive its name from M. Plautius Lucanus, which seems probable, as close to this bridge stands the above-mentioned Burial-place of his family, a remarkably handsome edifice of its kind, constructed with travertino, taken from quarries on the side of the Apennine, near Tivoli. After crossing the Ponte Lucano, I observed two roads, the one leading to Tivoli, which is about two miles distant; the other leading to Adrian's Villa, which is about one mile and a half distant from the bridge, and nearly twice as much from the town. I took the latter road; and after having been precisely three hours and a half in my carriage, from the time I left Rome, arrived at *Adrian's Villa*, where, ordering the drivers to wait, I walked through the Ruins with a Cicerone who is always on the spot to attend Travellers. Adrian himself was the architect of this celebrated Villa, which extended three miles in length, and one in breadth, and contained Temples, Theatres, Baths, and Porticos, adorned with *chefs-d'œuvre* of sculpture and painting; to which buildings he gave the names of the most remarkable edifices in the world, calling one the Lycæum of Aristotle, another the Academia of Plato, a third the Prytaneum of Athens, a fourth the Serapeon of Canopus, a fifth the Pœcile of the Stoics, etc. etc. I was conducted first to the *Greek Theatre*, of which the Proscenium, and seats for the spectators, may still be traced: hence I proceeded to examine three ruins, called, *the Temple of the Stoics, the Maritime Theatre*, and *the Library;* the two first of which exhibit considerable remains. I then visited a ruin, called *the Temple of Diana and Venus*, on my way to the *Imperial Apartments*, the vaults of which are, in some places, nearly perfect: hence I went to *the Barracks of the Prætorian Guards;* and *a Hall* destined, it is supposed, for philosophical studies; part of the Ceiling still remains. Hence I proceeded to *the Baths*, observing *traces of the Naumachia;* and lastly visited *the Serapeon*, where some of the paintings are tolerably well preserved.[1]

Having spent an hour and a half in this Villa, I got into my carriage and ascended the hill to Tivoli; passing through a fine wood of olives, and observing Ruins on the right, supposed to be *remains of the Villa of Cassius*. Tivoli, the ancient *Tibur*, a place of high antiquity, is built upon rocks formed of a deposition from the water in this neighbourhood, united with roots and branches of petrified trees. The Anio descends from a great height at the east end of the town; where it forms a large and beautiful cascade: and, after a second fall, under a lofty bridge, loses itself among rocks, which are worn into fantastic shapes by the force of the water. A branch of the same river is carried through Tivoli; and forms small Cascades, which should be viewed from the opposite bank. The best inn at Tivoli in some respects is *La Regina*; though in point of situation, that called *La Sibilla* is preferable. After breakfasting at the former, I visited *the Temple of the Tiburtine Sibyl*, now converted into a Church: it is the most ancient Temple remaining at Tivoli; and appears to have been built in the form of a parallelogram, with an open portico, adorned by four Ionic columns, and terminated with a pediment. The Columns on the outside of this edifice are still discoverable; but there is nothing worth notice within. Adjoining to the above-named Temple is a shabby modern building, which extends to *the Temple of Vesta*. This beautiful specimen of ancient architecture, proudly situated on a rock which hangs over one of the cascades, is a small Rotunda, surrounded by an open portico of fluted Corinthian columns, whose capitals are adorned with lilies, (emblematical, perhaps, of Vestal purity), and support an entablature decorated with heads of oxen and festoons.[2] Hence I proceeded through an excellent path, made by General Miollis, to the *Grotto of Neptune*. Nothing can be more delightful, both to the painter and the naturalist, than this walk; the views it presents being remarkably picturesque; and the petrifactions in the rocks extremely curious. I observed, in one place, a petrified carriage-wheel; and in another the hoof of a quadruped. The Grotto of Neptune, into which the Anio precipitates itself with such violence as to form a spray resembling rain, combines the sublime and beautiful so wonderfully, that even Salvator Rosa's magic pencil could not do justice to the scene; and at the entrance of the Grotto is a rock which, with very little aid from Imagination, might be figured as the Genius of the Anio sculptured by the nervous hand of Buonaroti. Returning hence, and then descending a narrow flight of steps into a deep ravine, I reached *the Grotto of the Sirens*: somewhat similar to that of Neptune; and beheld the third fall of the Anio.[1] I then re-as-

---

[1] Scarce any windows can be traced in the remaining buildings of Adrian's Villa. Persons who bring a cold dinner from Rome, and spend the day here, find a tolerable apartment to dine in, furnished by the Custode; who expects, for the use of this apartment, and his attendance, one scudo.

[2] The door of entrance, and the only window which remains perfect, are narrower at top than at bottom; and, thus far, the Temple resembles an Egyptian edifice.

[3] The steps and path leading to the Grotto of the Sirens are dirty and unfit for Ladies.

cended to the Temple of Vesta; and having ordered a donkey to attend, in case any one of the party should be tired with walking, I set out for *the circular Terrace,* which exhibits the small Cascades to great advantage, and makes a round of about four miles. While pursuing this tract I passed, on the right, *the Villa of Quintilius Varus;* observing *Reservoirs* which probably belonged to the Baths of the Villa; while, on the left, I had a distant prospect of *the Cathedral*, which is only remarkable for standing on the site of *the Temple of Hercules*. Having crossed the *Ponte del Aquoria,* an ancient Bridge in high preservation, I visited an edifice similar in shape to the Temple of Minerva Medica at Rome, and equally well preserved. It is called *Tempio della Tossa;* but whether because originally consecrated to Tussis, the coughing God, or because it was the sepulchre of the Tossie Family, seems uncertain. Hence I proceeded, on *the ancient Via Valeria,* to *Mæcenas's Villa;* the ruins of which prove that it must have been vast and magnificent: and the part through which the *Via Valeria* passes, is well preserved and very interesting. Near this Villa are curious rocks consisting of petrifactions: and opposite to it is *the site of the Villa of Sallust,* called, by some persons, *that of Horace;* but his Villa was ten miles distant.

Having passed *the site of the temple of Hercules,* to which Mæcenas's domain extended, I walked through *the Garden of the Villa d'Este,* which contains Water-Works, called *the Girandola,* a Fountain embellished with a colossal statue of the Tiburtine Sibyl, and another Figure representing Tivoli. *The Villa* contains Ceilings painted by Zuccari, Muziano, etc.; but they have suffered cruelly from neglect. Hence I returned to the inn; dined there; and afterward drove back to Rome in four hours.

Persons who wish to see the remains of *the Claudian Aqueduct near the Convent of S. Cosimato,* should sleep at Tivoli; and then set out early next morning, upon donkeys, or mules, for the above-named Convent; which stands on a cliff, overhanging a deep and narrow valley, through which flows a stream that, from being considerably obstructed in its course by fragments of rocks apparently fallen from the surrounding precipices, is broken into beautiful cascades. Here, where the Claudian Aqueduct crossed the river, one arch remains: and some of *the subterranean part of this Aqueduct,* which was carried through the centre of several mountains, may be seen buried *under the Convent Garden,* and as perfect as if just finished; not even the plaster having suffered from time. The mountains of S. Cosimato are formed of the same tartareous deposition with those of Tivoli. *Horace's Villa,* and *Sabine farm*, are three miles distant from the Convent; but so little now remains of the Villa that its foundations cannot easily be traced.[1]

FRASCATI.

I hired, at the latter end of

---

[1] Travellers usually pay at La Sibilla, at Tivoli, for dinner, per head, seven pauls—tea, two pauls—breakfast, two pauls—beds, each three pauls—servants each, per day, three pauls—and donkeys each, three pauls. It is impossible to procure good wine or good water at either of the inns.

April, an open carriage with six places and four horses, paying eight scudi; and was enabled, by setting out early, to accomplish this excursion with great ease in one day.

Twelve miles distant from Rome, and near the site of the ancient *Tusculum*, stands Frascati; and the most interesting objects in the direct road thither (which is a tolerably good one), are *the Sepulchres of Genesius Marcianus*, and *Lucius Valerius Corvinus*.

On my way to Frascati I visited *Oretto-Ferrata;* which lies but little out of the direct road; and whence to Frascati, about one mile and a half in distance, the drive is delightful. On turning off for Grotto-Ferrata I found the road rough at the commencement, but not dangerous; and after proceeding about a quarter of a mile I found it perfectly good. Grotto-Ferrata, usually denominated, the site of Cicero's *Tusculanum*, was, in times past, a celebrated Convent, founded by S. Nilus of the Order of S. Basil, and subsequently fortified with high walls, and gates of iron, from the latter of which its present name is derived. The Church contains *a Chapel* consecrated to S. Nilus, and adorned, by Domenichino, with beautiful Frescos, uncommonly well preserved. The most celebrated of these Frescos are, S. Nilus praying for rain—Rain descending—S. Nilus meeting the Emperor Otho III.—(In this picture Domenichino has represented himself, clothed in green, and holding the bridle of the Emperor's horse; with Guido leaning on the horse, and Guercino behind Guido). The demoniac Boy, deemed one of the finest pictures existing!!!—Saints Nilus and Bartolomeo praying to the Madonna — and an Architect showing the plan of the Convent to S. Nilus. The altar-piece is by Annibale Caracci—the Salutation, and all the other Frescos on the walls, and in the cupola, are by Domenichino.

An apartment up stairs contains part of a Frieze, said to have been found in Cicero's Villa, and representing a Grecian General speaking to an Officer and a Soldier who are bringing a wounded Man into his presence.

From Grotto-Ferratà, where my carriage waited while I saw the Chapel of S. Nilus, etc., I drove to *the Belvedere*, at Frascati, a handsome Villa, beautifully situated, and embellished with water-works. In this Villa, I was permitted to eat a cold dinner which I had brought from Rome; and here I dismissed my carriage, ordering it to return for me in four hours. After dinner I procured a Cicerone, to show me the way to Tusculum; and under his guidance took a delightful, and, generally speaking, a shady walk, through the Belvedere-domain, to *the Villa Rufinella* (supposed, by some antiquaries, to have been the site of Cicero's Villa), thence proceeding to Tusculum, where I discovered remains of a small Theatre; a small Amphitheatre, quite perfect, so far as it has been excavated (for, owing perhaps to an earthquake, the arena is buried in vegetable mould); Reservoirs for water; remains of what appears to have been the ancient Road from the Villa Ruffinella to Tusculum; together with Inscriptions, etc., etc. The distance from the Belvedere to Tusculum is about two miles and a half; the ascent continual, but not steep. From Tusculum I walked back to the Belvedere; thence proceeding, in my carriage, through Frascati to Rome.[1]

PALESTRINA.

Palestrina, the ancient Præneste, about twenty-five miles distant from Rome, is well worth notice; both on account of its *Cyclopian Walls*, and *the Temple of Fortune*, erected here by Sylla, and afterward repaired and embellished by Adrian; and of which, considerable remains may be traced, though the modern town is built on its foundations.

The road to Palestrina is, generally speaking, ancient pavement, remarkably well preserved; especially the latter part. Specimens of Cyclopian Walls[2] present themselves just within the town of Palestrina, and likewise on the ascent leading toward the Citadel. The Temple of Fortune seems to have consisted of two parts; the lower being called *Fortuna Primigenia;* and the higher, *Fortuna Prænestina;* and, judging by its remains (the most interesting of which may be traced at the Seminario, near the Cathedral), it must have been very large and magnificent. Some parts of the Walls, belonging to the first and second Terrace of this Temple, display specimens, quite perfect, of ancient Roman stone-work, called *Opus Incertum;* while other parts resemble the Etruscan walls of Fiesole; and others exhibit specimens of reticulated brick-work. There are three Terraces; and, under the lowest, magnificent Reservoirs for water. The lower Temple, which stood on the middle Terrace, was embellished with a celebrated Mosaic Pavement, supposed by Winckelmann, to represent the arrival of Menelaus in Egypt. Ruins of an ancient Lighthouse may be discovered on the middle Terrace; and, on the uppermost, is the Palazzo-Barberini, whither the Mosaic Pavement has been removed, and where it may now be seen. On the summit of the hill, above the Temple, was the Citadel of Præneste, encompassed by Cyclopian Walls, still in high preservation, and commanding a very extensive prospect. In the environs of the modern town are remains of *the Villa of Antoninus Pius* (where the Braschi-Antinous was found); and a picturesque Ruin, called *the Temple of Vesta*, and probably erected by Adrian; as its shape, in some parts, resembles a known production of his, the Temple (near the Colosseo) dedicated to Venus and Rome.

A pair of strong horses would take a light calash from Rome to Palestrina in about five hours and a half; and return in five hours: and the usual price charged by Voiturins for going in this manner, is four scudi a day.

The Inn at Palestrina contains four small bed-rooms, with tolerably clean beds; and likewise fur-

---

[1] I gave, to the Custode of the Villa-Belvedere, five pauls for the use of an apartment to dine in, and two pauls for exhibiting the water-works: and to the Cicerone who accompanied me to Tusculum, I gave four pauls.

[2] These Walls, composed of smooth angular stones, skilfully joined together without cement, are by some authors attributed to the Pelasgi: but, be this as it may, they are evidently the most ancient kind of stonework used for surrounding towns and citadels of Italy and Magna Græcia. Why they are called Cyclopian, seems doubtful: perhaps from κυκλεω, to surround.

nishes good wine, pigeons, eggs, coffee, and milk. The Cicerone is very intelligent; and Travellers who dislike walking may procure donkeys.

ALBANO.

The distance from Rome to Albano is fourteen miles; and the road, generally speaking, excellent.[1] Having already given some account of this road, I shall now content myself with saying, that, on the left, just before entering Albano, I passed what is denominated the Tomb of Ascanius; though supposed, by antiquaries, to be that of Clodius.

Albano, situated between Castel-Gandolfo and Aricia, stands on the site of Pompey's Villa, named *Albanum Pompeii*. Remains of *an Amphitheatre, a Reservoir*, and *a Prætorian Camp*, erected, perhaps, by Domitian, may be traced here: but the object best worth notice in this town is a small *Museum*, belonging to Sig. Guiseppe Carnevali; which consists of sepulchral Monuments, found under a bed of lava in the vicinity of the ancient *Alba-Longa*. The shape of each of these sepulchral Monuments is that of a vase; and within each of the Vases was found a small cinerary Urn of *terra-cotta*, containing ashes and bones, and made (as is conjectured) in the precise shape of the huts of the aboriginal inhabitants of the spot.[2] Each cinerary Urn exhibits unknown characters; and these sepulchral Monuments likewise have Doors, with curious Fastenings. The cinerary Urn was placed in the centre of each Monument; and encircled with small *terra-cotta* Vessels (one to hold the sop for Cerberus, others for the purifying water, wine, oil, bread, incense, etc.); a Lamp, like those of pottery used now in cottages; a Stile passed through a Canceller; Knives, and a Lance. After seeing this Museum, Travellers, who have three hours to spare, should proceed, through a beautiful and shady path, to the hill which commands the *Lago-Castello,* or Lake of Albano; which is the crater of an extinct volcano, nearly six miles in circumference, and famous for particularly large and fine eels. *Castel-Gandolfo* stands on the top of the hill; and a beautiful Walk leads down to the Lake, where, in the water, remains may be seen of the ancient *Alba-Longa*. Here, likewise, is a subterraneous Canal, called the *Emissario,* one of the most extraordinary works of the ancient Romans, and said to have been made during the siege of Veii, in obedience to the Delphic Oracle. It measures about one mile and a half in length, and appears quite perfect. Another path, to the left of Castel-Gandolfo, leads back to Albano; and the Ilexes which shade this walk are some of the largest in Italy.[3] The Garden of the Villa-Barberini, at Castel-Gandolfo, comprises *the Ruins of Domitian's Villa;* and on the outside of the Gate of Albano, leading to Aricia, is *an ancient Tomb,* on the left,

---

[1] The best inn at Albano—namely, *La Villa di Londra*—furnishes good dinners and tolerable beds, at reasonable prices.

[2] The Urns are shaped by hand, instead of being cast in a mould, like Grecian vases.

[3] Persons who do not choose to walk may hire a donkey for three pauls, including the *buona-mano* of the man who leads it. The Albano Cicerone expects four or five pauls; and the Cicerone at the Emissario two, if he find lights.

called *that of the Curiatii;* though there does not seem to be any ground for this assertion.¹

The air, both at Albano and Aricia (one mile distant), is less oppressive during summer, though perhaps not more salubrious, than that of Rome; and the country is beautiful: private lodging-houses may be procured at each place; and a public carriage goes three times a week, during summer, from Rome to Albano; the fare, for going, being five pauls, and the same for returning.

I will now close this Chapter with what seems to me the present character of the Romans.

This people, taken collectively, neither possess the mildness of the Tuscans, nor the good-humoured buffoonery of the Neapolitans. The nobility seldom trouble themselves to attain deep erudition; but are polite and very kind to Foreigners. Gentlemen belonging to the Church and Law are usually well-informed: it is, however, remarkable, that the most learned of these are not, generally speaking, Romans by birth. Tradesmen of the first class seldom impose on foreigners; but the populace are frequently prone to exaction, passionate, and sometimes revengeful: they likewise retain much of their former haughty character; and the inhabitants of Trastevere, said to descend from the ancient Romans, are not only brave to ferocity, but so proud of their ancestors, that nothing can induce them to match with a person who does not boast the same origin.

A gentleman told me, he lodged in the house of one of these Trasteverini, a barber by trade, and wretchedly poor, when his daughter was addressed by a wealthy and respectable German: but, notwithstanding these advantages, the lover received a rude and positive refusal from the mother of the girl. My acquaintance, surprised at this behaviour, asked the mother why she acted so imprudently? — " Your daughter (continued he) is wholly unprovided for; surely, then, you ought to rejoice in an opportunity of uniting her to a rich and worthy man." " Rejoice in uniting her to a Foreigner — a Barbarian!" (exclaimed the woman). " No:— and were my daughter capable of cherishing so disgraceful an idea, I should not scruple to plunge a dagger into her heart."

---

1 According to some opinions, the pyramids upon the top of the monument in question are allusive to Egypt, and indicate that the edifice was erected in honour of Pompey.

The Curiatii had monuments erected to their memory near the Fossæ Cleliæ, where they fell.

CHAPTER X.

NAPLES.

Country between Rome and Naples—Genzano—Velletri—Cora—Pontine Marshes—Terracina—Fondi—Itri—Cenotaph of Cicero—Mola—Gaëta—Minturnum—Garigliano—S. Agata—Capua—Naples—Situation of that city—Bay—Ancient Light-houses—Size and population of Naples—Villa-Reale—Studii Publici—Quadrangle—Gallery of ancient Sculpture—Apartments up-stairs—Palazzo-Reale—Chiesa di S. Ferdinando—Castel Nuovo—Castello dell' Uovo—Chiese di S. Maria del Parto—di S. Brigida—di S. Giovanni de' Fiorentini—di l'Incoronata—della Pietà de' Torchini—di S. Maria Nuova di Monte-Oliveto—di Gesù Nuovo—di S. Chiara—di S. Giovanni Maggiore—del Salvatore—di S. Domenico Maggiore—dello Spirito Santo—di S. Maria della Sanità—di S. Giovanni a Carbonara—de' S. S. Apostoli—Arcivescovado—Liquefaction of the blood of S. Gennaro—Chiese di S. Filippo Neri—di S. Paolo Maggiore—di S. Maria Maggiore—di S. Pietro a Majella—Cappella di S. Severo—Chiese di S. M. Annunziata—di S. Maria del Carmine—di S. Martino de' Certosini—Castello di S. Elmo—Palazzo-Berio—Albergo de' Poveri—Theatres—Promenades—Market built by the French—Monument to the memory of Eustace—Water—Climate—Society—Hotels and Lodging-houses—Character of the Neapolitans—List of Objects best worth notice, as they lie contiguous to each other.

BEFORE I enter upon a description of Naples, I will give a short account of the country through which we passed, on our way thither.

The road to Albano has been already described; I shall therefore say nothing on this subject, but merely observe that Travellers, going to Naples, might easily see every thing worth notice at Albano, by making a stop of three hours and a half at the last-named town, which they must necessarily pass through on their way.

Aricia, one mile distant from Albano (as has been already mentioned), is beautifully situated on the *Via Appia,* and contains a handsome Church. Four miles hence is *Genzano,* pleasantly placed near the Lake of Nemi, in a country which produces good wine. The Festival of Flora, which takes place during the month of June, at Genzano, merits notice; the ground, at this festival, being covered, for a considerable extent, with a beautiful mosaic work of flowers; many of which are gathered several weeks before; and yet so exquisitely preserved as to appear unfaded. In the neighbourhood of Genzano is the site of the ancient *Lavinium;* and not far distant, on the seashore, lies Pratica, the ancient *Laurentum,* where Æneas is said to have landed when he came to Italy. Six miles from Genzano is *Velletri,* once a considerable town belonging to the Volsci, and celebrated for being the country of Augustus, whose family resided here, though it is supposed that he was born at Rome. The *Palazzo-Lancellotti* is now converted into an inn,[1] which contains thirty beds, and particularly fine water.[2] The situation of this

---

[1] *The Albergo Reale.*
[2] Wholesome water cannot be procured between Velletri and Terracina; and therefore Travellers usually take a supply from the former town.

Palazzo is delightful; and its marble staircase merits notice; but the Posthouse is a much more comfortable Inn. Nine miles hence, though not in the high road, lies *Cora*, an ancient town of Latium, which contains ruins of *two Temples*, the one consecrated to Hercules, the other to Castor and Pollux: and persons who have leisure would do well to visit them. From Velletri to *Torre de' tre Ponti*, on the Pontine Marshes, the country is pretty; and on a height, not very distant from the road, stands Piperno, anciently *Privernum*, a Volscian city.[2]

Between Tre Ponti (anciently *Tripontium*) and Terracina lie the Pontine Marshes (*Palus Pomptina*), computed to be about twenty-four miles in length, and varying from six to twelve miles in breadth. Appius Claudius seems to have been the first person who undertook to drain them: Cethegus and Cæsar continued the work; which, during the middle ages, was repaired by Cecilius Decius, at the command of Theodoric. Boniface VIII. was the first Pope who began to drain these noxious swamps. Martin V., before his accession to the pontifical Chair, was employed to carry on the business; and succeeded wonderfully, by making a Canal, called Rio-Martino. The Princes of the House of Medicis, and, after them, Sixtus V., made new Canals: succeeding Popes followed a similar plan; till, at length, Pius VI. nearly accomplished this benevolent work; forming on the foundations of the Via Appia, which were long hidden under water, a road justly esteemed one of the best in Europe; and draining the swamps so judiciously as to render them capable of being cultivated. French Engineers pursued the same wise measures; and Pius VII. is at length putting the finishing stroke to this Herculean labour; which has so essentially purified a tract of country, whose gales, in former times, were fraught with death, that but little danger is to be apprehended from travelling through it now, except during the prevalence of the dog-star.

I would, nevertheless, advise Travellers in general, and particularly Invalids, neither to pass the Pontine Marshes with an empty stomach, nor till after the sun has been up an hour. The dew which immediately precedes sunset should likewise be avoided; and the inclination to sleep, which almost every Traveller feels while breathing this air, should be *strenuously resisted*.

At one of the western extremities of the Pontine Marshes is the mouth of the river Astura; and, beyond that, Capo d'Anzio, the ancient *Antium:* while at the other western extremity rises Monte Circello, the Headland of Circæum, immortalized by Homer. Beyond the Marshes, in a beautiful situation, stands *Terracina*, the approach to which is particularly fine: it was originally built by the Volsci; and called by them *Anxur;* but the Greeks afterward called it *Traxina;* whence comes the modern name of Ter-

---

[1] There is a post-road from Velletri to Sermonetta (the spot, according to some opinions, called by S. Paul, *Tres Tabernæ*), Case-Nuove, Piperno, Maruti, and Terracina.

[2] *Tre Ponti* is a very bad inn; where, however, it might be possible to dine better, perhaps, than at Mesa, the ancient Station *Ad Medias*, or half-way house; and where, on each side of the entrance to the inn, if such it may be called, is an ancient Milliary.

racina. Here are considerable remains of antiquity; and persons who have two leisure hours should inquire for the Cicerone, who is always in attendance at the Inn, and accompanied by him visit *the Cathedral*, supposed to have been built on, or near, the site of a Temple dedicated to Apollo. The portico of this Church contains a Sarcophagus with an Inscription in honour of Theodoric, first King of Italy; and the Baldacchino is supported by four Corinthian Columns of Parian marble, taken from the Temple of Apollo; considerable remains of which may still be traced, near the Cathedral. On the brow of a high hill above the Cathedral are ruins called by some persons *Theodoric's Palace*, and by others, who judge from Virgil's description, *the Temple of Jupiter Anxur*: but be this as it may, the only vestiges discernible now, are *the subterranean part*, with *a low square building* above it.[1] The temple of Jupiter Anxur was erected by order of the Consul Posthumius, after the designs of Vitruvius Pollio. On the way to this spot stand *the ancient Walls of Anxur, remains of Reservoirs, Tombs*, etc.; and here likewise is a magnificent view of Monte Circello, and the Bay of Naples. The Inn at Terracina[2] stands beyond the town, and near *the ancient Port*, made by Antoninus Pius; which, though now choked up with mud, is well worth notice. An endless variety of beautiful flowers and shrubs adorn the rocks beyond Terracina; between which town and a building called Torre de' Confini, the road passes near a pestiferous Lake. Torre de' Confini divides the patrimony of S. Peter from the kingdom of Naples; and five miles beyond the entrance to the Neapolitan territories is *Fondi*, a small town on the Via Appia, which constitutes its principal street: it once belonged to the Aurunci, a people of Latium; and, in the year 1534, suffered cruelly in consequence of an attempt made, one night, by Hariaden Barbarossa to seize the beautiful Julia Gonzaga, Countess of Fondi, with a view of presenting her to the Grand Signior. Julia, however, being roused from sleep by the clamours of her people at the approach of the Turks, sprang from her bed, leaped out of window, and escaped to the neighbouring mountains: while Barbarossa, being thus disappointed of his prize, revenged himself by pillaging and destroying the town, and carrying many of its inhabitants into slavery. Fondi exhibits considerable remains of Cyclopian walls. The air here is deemed unwholesome, owing to the above named Lake. Eight miles from Fondi stands *Itri*, a large village also built on the Via Appia, in a country abounding with vines, figs, and lentisks, which last produce gum-mastic. Here are remains of a Cyclopian tower. On the right, about a quarter of a mile from Mola, is an ancient edifice, in good preservation, supposed to be *the Cenotaph of Cicero*, placed on the spot where he was murdered,

---

[1] Antiquaries assert that the ruins of Theodoric's Palace, and the Temple of Jupiter Anxur, may both be traced on this height above Terracina.

[2] This inn may be called good, in point of size and accommodations; but when its master is absent, which frequently occurs during the prevalence of *mal' aria*, the waiters are uncivil and imposing.

while endeavouring to escape from his enemies. *Mola*, the ancient *Formiæ*, eight miles from Itri, is approached by a road commanding beautiful scenery; and contains an inn, called *La Villa di Cicerone*, which is large, and charmingly situated;[1] and exhibits in its Garden Ruins of what is denominated *Villa-Formianum;* but probably that Villa was further removed from the sea, and near the Cenotaph of Cicero. Mola commands a fine view of Gaëta, five miles distant, and, according to tradition, founded by Æneas in honour of his Nurse, Caieta. Persons who have leisure would do well to employ a few hours in seeing this town; which contains ten thousand inhabitants, and some antiquities that merit notice. Its Port was either constructed, or repaired, by Antoninus Pius: and the Baptistery of its Cathedral is adorned with a *basso-rilievo* bearing the name of Salpion, an Athenian sculptor, and representing Ino, consort of Athamas, King of Thebes, sitting on a rock and hiding one of her Children in her bosom, to save it from its Father's fury. Here likewise, on the summit of the hill, above the town, is a building called *Torre d'Orlando*, and supposed to be the Mausoleum of Munatius Plancus, the Founder of Lyons. But to return to the high road. Six miles from Mola, are *considerable remains of an Aqueduct*, a *Theatre*, etc.;[2] which probably belonged to the ancient town of *Minturnum*: and close to these ruins flows the Garigliano, anciently the *Liris;* and, in former times, the boundary of *Latium;* which is now called the Campagna di Roma.[3] A marsh in this neighbourhood was the spot to which Marius fled, when he fell into the power of the Magistrates of Minturnum. Crossing the Garigliano on a bridge of boats, we proceeded to *S. Agate;* where the Inn, though not large, is rendered comfortable by the civility of its master. S. Agate is pleasantly situated near Sessa, a small town supposed to be the ancient *Suessa Auruncorum*, to which there is a beautiful Walk, over a magnificent Bridge, from the inn at S. Agata. The Via Appia passed through Suessa, where there are other antiquities. The road from S. Agata to Capua, sixteen miles distant, traverses rich vineyards and corn-fields. The approach to Capua is handsome; but the modern town, built on the banks of the Volturno, anciently *Volturnus*, and about one mile and a half distant from the Ruins called ancient Capua, is, judging by the report of Strabo and Florus,[4] very unlike the latter; as, instead of being one of the most splendid cities of Europe, it is ill-built, dirty, and devoid of any object particularly worth notice. The road from Capua to Naples, a distance of fifteen miles, is one continued garden, but exhibits no view of

---

[1] There are two other inns at Mola,—*The Post-house*, and *The Albergo Reale;* both of which, though inferior to *The Cicerone* with respect to situation, are, in accommodations, superior.

[2] In order to obtain a good view of this Theatre, it is necessary to get out of your carriage, and walk round to the back part of the building.

[3] The whole of what is now denominated *Italy*, between the Liris and the extremity of Calabria, appears to have been, during the reign of Nero, called *Magna Græcia*.

[4] These Authors describe Capua as particularly magnificent. Strabo says, it derived its name from *Caput*, because it was one of the capitals of the world; and Florus ranks it with Rome and Carthage.

the bay, and scarce any of the city.¹

The Via Appia is kept in excellent condition throughout the Ecclesiastical territories: but, near S. Agata, and within a few miles of Capua, proper care has not lately been taken to replace loose stones. Between Capua and Naples the road is excellent.

Naples, in Italian Napoli, seems, at first sight, to be universally considered as the most captivating city of Italy; owing to its immense number of inhabitants, magnificent quay, and beautiful situation: this first impression, however, sometimes wears off; while the bad taste which pervades almost every building, induces scientific Travellers to prefer Rome, even in her present mutilated state, to all the gaiety of Naples. This latter city is so ancient that it seems scarce possible to pierce through the clouds of obscurity which envelope its origin: Tradition, however, reports that it was founded by an Argonaut, thirteen hundred years before the Christian æra; and afterward peopled and enriched by Greek colonies from Rhodes, Athens, and Chalcis. It anciently bore the name of *Parthenope;* an apellation bestowed by the Phœnicians, in consequence of its charming situation. Near Parthenope stood another city, called *Paleopolis*, from being so old that its origin was ascribed to Hercules: and when Parthenope was destroyed by her jealous neighbours, the people of Cumæ, and afterward rebuilt in obedience to an oracle, the new city was called Neapolis, to distinguish it from the old one, called Paleopolis, till, at length, both were joined together by Augustus. Naples, however, still retained her Grecian manners, customs, and language; and even to the present day retains them, in several parts of her territories. This city is built on the acclivity of a tufo mountain, at the extremity of a Bay nearly thirty miles in diameter (called, by the ancients, *Crater Sinus*). and sheltered on the right by the Promontory of Miseno, and on the left by that of Sorrento: while the lofty island of Capri, rising in its centre, acts like an enormous Mole to break the force of its waves. Nothing can be more magnificent than the city of Naples when viewed from this bay, whence all its buildings present themselves to view, rising amphitheatrically, till crowned by the sombre Castle of S. Elmo. Stretching to the Promontory of Sorrento, on one side, lie Portici, Resina, Torre del Greco, Torre del Annunziata, Vesuvius, Pompeii, Castel-a-mare, and Vico; and extending to the Promontory of Miseno, on the other, Pozzuoli, Nisida, and Baia. The bay of Naples was once much larger than it is at present; as appears from the situation of two ancient Lighthouses; both of which now are actually in the heart of the city. Ruins of the most ancient may be seen behind the church of S. Onofrio de' Vecchi; the other

---

¹ Between Capua and Naples, in the town of Aversa, there is an excellent Lunatic Asylum, called *The Maddalena*. This edifice, which is spacious and elegantly clean, has belonging to it a large garden and a handsome church: and that persons who are sent to this Asylum may be pleased with its outward appearance, the grates of every window are shaped and painted to represent flower-pots filled with flowers. The attendance here is particularly good, and the utmost gentleness and indulgence are practised toward the patients, each of whom pays fifteen ducats per month; for which sum they live comfortably. The Maddalena accommodates five hundred patients.

stood on the site of Gesù-Nuovo. Naples is nine miles in circumference; and contains nearly three hundred and eighty-two thousand inhabitants: but the only parts of this city calculated to arrest the attention of Foreigners are the Strada-Toledo, the Largo del Palazzo, and the Chiaja, which comprehends a public Garden, called the Villa Reale, and considerably more than half a mile in length; extending, on the margin of the bay, from the Chiatamone toward the Grotto of Posolipo. This garden is adorned with luxuriant trees, shrubs, flowers, and modern statues; and in its centre stands the celebrated antique Group, called *Il Toro Farnese;* which was originally brought from Rhodes to Rome, and removed thence to Naples: it represents Amphion and Zethus, the sons of Lycus, King of Thebes, tying Dirce by the hair of her head to the horns of a Bull; and is supposed to have been formed from one solid block of marble, by Apollonius and Tauriscus, about two hundred years before the Christian æra. This group was found, cruelly mutilated, in Caracalla's Baths, and restored by Battista Bianchi of Milan. The head of the bull, and the upper part of the figure of Dirce, are modern: the trunks alone of the figures of Amphion and Zethus (one leg excepted) are antique; but the statues of Antiope, and the young man seated, are nearly in their original state.[1]

Among other objects of interest at Naples are the following.

Studii Publici. This University was erected by the Viceroy Ferdinando Ruiz de Castro, Count de Lemos, according to the designs of M. G. Fontana; and opened in 1616, by Don Pedro de Castro, son and successor to the Count. During 1790, Ferdinando I. removed the University to the Convent of Gesù-Vecchio; and converted the edifice built by the Count de Lemos, into a royal Museum; which is now enriched with the antiquities found at Minturnum, ancient Capua, Herculaneum, Pompeii, Stabiæ, Nuceria, and Pæstum; together with the collection of paintings that once adorned the Palace of Capo di Monte: and this Museum, to which his Neapolitan Majesty has given the name of *Borbonico,* may now be considered as the finest in Europe, with respect to Grecian antiquities.

The *Quadrangle* contains a colossal statue of Alexander Severus—ditto of Flora—ditto of the Genius of Rome—and ditto of Urania: and *the Staircase* is adorned with a Lion in Carrara marble, and two statues in Greek marble, taken from Herculaneum. Surrounding the Quadrangle are the Academies of Sculpture, Painting, and Architecture, and the apartments appropriated to antique Statues, etc.

First division of the Gallery of ancient Sculpture. No. 14, a lustral Basin from Herculaneum—15, bust of Ptolemy-Soter—16, a Warrior seated—18, a Gladiator!—20, equestrian statue of a Roman Warrior—22 a Sportsman—24, Pyrrhus, from Herculaneum—26, group of two Men cutting

---

[1] According to some opinions, Amphion and Zethus were represented by the Rhodian artists as endeavouring, by command of Antiope, their mother, to seize the bull, and set Dirce free.

up a Pig—27, bust of a Female—28, an Amazon on horseback—30, a wounded Gladiator!—32, a Wrestler, from Herculaneum—34, a Wrestler, restored as a Gladiator!!—35, a Gladiator—36, another Wrestler, restored as a Gladiator—37, a Gladiator!—38, bust of Gallienus!—39, Jove, in *terra-cotta*, from Pompeii!—42, a young Roman Lady, from Herculaneum—44, Marcus Nonius Balbus, Proconsul and Patron of Herculaneum—45, a dead Amazon—47, a Daughter of M. N. Balbus, from Herculaneum!—49, the Mother of Balbus, from Herculaneum—52, another of the Balbi-family!—and 54, M. N. Balbus, both from Herculaneum—56, a Bust!—57, a young Lady, probably one of the Balbi-family, from Herculaneum—58, bust of a Philosopher—59, Juno, in *terra-cotta*, from Pompeii!

Second division of the Gallery.
62, equestrian statue of Marcus Nonius Balbus, jun., in Greek marble, from Herculaneum!!!!—63, ditto of Marcus Nonius Balbus, sen., likewise taken from Herculaneum; but, being found in a mutilated state, it has been restored!!!—67, group of Apollo with a Swan!!—68, small statue of Jupiter-Serapis, found in his temple at Pozzuoli!—70, group of Ganymedes and the Eagle!—77, bust of the Indian Bacchus—79, ditto, from Herculaneum—81, small statue of a Priestess, from Herculaneum—82, Minerva—83, small statue of a Priestess of Diana, from Herculaneum—84, bust of Minerva!—86, Ceres—87, bust of Minerva, from Herculaneum—92, Apollino, from ditto—94, small statue of Æsculapius—96, group of Bacchus and Cupid!!—97, the celebrated colossal Hercules of Glycon, found at Rome, in Caracalla's Baths, and demed one of the finest statues extant; it represents Hercules previous to his deification!!!—98, group of Venus victorious and Cupid, from ancient Capua!—99, bust of Cybele, from Herculaneum—100, Juno—101, bust of Minerva, from Herculaneum—102, Minerva, a fine Etruscan work, from Herculaneum!!—103, group of Faunus and the Infant Bacchus!!—107, bust of the Indian Bacchus—109, bust of Jove—110, Diana-Lucifera—118, Minerva!!—120, Bacchus—122, Euterpe.

Third division of the Gallery.
123, a lustral Basin, found in the Temple of Isis, at Pompeii!—124, Agrippina, the mother of Nero, seated!!![1]—125, another lustral Basin, found in the Temple of Isis, at Pompeii!—127, bust of Nerva—128, ditto of Antoninus Pius—130, Trajan, sen.—131, bust of Septimius Severus—132, Antonio the younger—133, bust of Galba—134, colossal bust of Titus!—138, Trajan's Sister—139, bust of Tiberius—142, colossal bust of Antoninus Pius!—144, Lucilla—148, Tiberius—149, a Bust!—150, bust of Caracalla—151, Tiberius—153, colossal statue of Claudius seated, from Herculaneum!—155, Trajan, from Minturnum!!—156, bust of Lucius Verus—157, Statue of ditto!—159, Caligula, from Minturnum!—161, a magnificent porphyry Basin, supposed to have been used as the lustral Vase in a Temple,

---

[1] Agrippina seems to be represented at the moment when told that her unnatural son dooms her to death. The mild, pathetic, deep despair, expressed throughout the whole of this charming statue, proves that Sculpture, when carried to its utmost height of excellence, can move the passions even more than does the finest poetry.

dedicated to Æsculapius—162, colossal bust of Cæsar!—163, statue of ditto—164, bust of Marcus Aurelius—165, statue of ditto!—166, bust of Adrian—167, Lucius Verus!—169, colossal statue of Augustus, seated, from Herculaneum!—170, bust of Caracalla!—172, bust of Adrian!

The open Court, adjoining to the Gallery of ancient Sculpture, contains various Antiquities: among which are several statues found in Herculaneum; Cornmills of lava, which were brought from Pompeii; a Machine for bruising olives, in order to make oil (also of lava, and brought from Pompeii), together with Diotæ of *creta-cotta* and *terracotta*.

Hall of Flora. No. 200, colossal statue of Flora, found in Caracalla's Baths at Rome!!!! (According to some opinions this *chef-d'œuvre* of the Grecian chisel does not represent Flora, but Hope, or one of the Muses.)—201, the *Torso Farnese*, attributed to Phidias, and supposed to have represented Bacchus!!!—202, a *Basso-rilievo* representing Bacchus intoxicated!—203, Fragment, from ancient Capua, supposed to have been a Psyche; and attributed to Praxiteles!!!—206, a *Basso-rilievo* representing Orpheus, Eurydice, and Mercury; and supposed to be very ancient Grecian sculpture—207, a *Basso-rilievo* from Herculaneum!—208, *Bassi-rilievi*, one of which represents Scylla, the famous Promontory of Calabria—209, *Torso* of a Boy!—210, a *Basso-rilievo* representing Helen, Venus, Cupid, Paris, etc.!

Hall of Apollo. No. 212, a colossal porphyry statue of Apollo in his theatrical dress!—214, Isis—218, a Phrygian Slave—222, Apollo—225, a Phrygian Slave—228, a Goat, in rosso antico, from Pompeii—229, bust of Marcus Aurelius!—230, Ceres—231, bust of Annius Verus—235, Diana of Ephesus, in oriental alabaster and bronze!—238, a small Egyptian statue of Isis in basalt, from Pompeii—243, an Egyptian Priest, in basalt!—247 and 248, another Basin, with its Stand, from Pompeii—251, bust of L. Junius Brutus, from Herculaneum—252, small statue of Meleager, in rosso antico!

Hall of the Muses. No. 256, a large and beautiful Vase of Greek marble, adorned with *bassi-rilievi* relative to the education of Bacchus, and according to the inscription it bears, executed by Salpion, an Athenian sculptor—260, Clio, from Herculaneum—261, small statue in *terra-cotta,* representing an Actor masked, and dressed for the stage, from Pompeii!—262, Terpsichore, from Herculaneum!—263, Mnemosyne, from ditto!—264, Apollo seated—265, Minerva!—266, Melpomene, from Herculaneum!—267, small statue, in *terra-cotta,* of an Actress, masked and dressed for the stage, from Pompeii!—268, Erato, from Herculaneum—273, Urania, from ditto!—275, *Basso-rilievo,* representing seven female Figures, from Herculaneum—276, Calliope!—277, Euterpe!—and 281, Thalia; all three from Herculaneum—282, a small statue of Apollo, from Pompeii!—283, *Rilievo,* representing four Figures!!—284, Polyhymnia!

Hall of the Venuses. No. 287, Adonis!—288, Venus, attributed to Praxiteles, and called " *Venere Callipiga,*" the rival of the Venus de' Medici: there is, however, an unpleasant expression in the countenance of the former, from which the latter is exempt!!!—289, statue called "*Venere genetrice!!*" —295, Cupid, supposed to be an ancient copy of the celebrated Cupid of Praxiteles—296, Statue called "*Venere accovacciata!*" —299, the marine Venus!—304, a small statue of Venus seated, from Pompeii!—307, Bacchus, in the character of an Hermaphrodite!

Hall of Hercules. No. 311, a Herma, from Herculaneum—312, herma, of Euripides, from ditto— 314, bust of Marius—318, Jupiter-Stator seated, from Cuma!— 323, bust of Marcus Brutus—324, herma, representing Homer—325, herma of Socrates!

Hall of Atlas. No. 326, Atlas supporting the celestial globe— 327 and 328, lustral Basins, from Pompeii!—331, bust of Antisthenes!—332, Homer, from Herculaneum—333, bust of Æschines, from ditto!—334, bust of Periander, from ditto—335, bust of Socrates—336, bust of Euripides— 337, bust of Lycurgus—338, Sylla, from Herculaneum—340, bust of Solon—342, bust of Zeno, from Herculaneum—343, bust of Anacreon—344, a Philosopher, from Herculaneum!!—345, bust of Demosthenes, from ditto—350, bust of Zeno—351, statue supposed to represent Niobe—352, bust of Herodotus—353, bust of Lysias—354, same subject!— 355, bust of Euripides—356, bust of Sophocles—357, small statue of Cicero, from Herculaneum—358, bust of Carneades! —359, bust of Plato, from Herculaneum—360, bust of Posidonius!!—363, Aristides, found in Herculaneum, and deemed one of the choicest master-pieces of the Grecian chisel!!!!—364, bust of Socrates, from Herculaneum.

Hall of Antinous. No. 367, Antinous!—368, Vase, from Herculaneum—370 and 371, Candelabra—372, herma of Herodotus and Thucydides—373, a large Vase—377, a Consul, from Pompeii—378, bust of a Vestal!— 381, a Bust!—382, bust supposed to represent the Indian Bacchus! —383, bust of Seneca—385, bust of Cicero, from Herculaneum— 386, statue of Plenty, from Pompeii—387, bust of Claudius Marcellus—388, bust of Juba—389, bust of a laughing Faun—391, ditto!—392, bust of a Philosopher!—393, bust of Vespasian— 394, colossal bust of a young Hercules—399, ditto of Alexander!— 400, group of Electra and Orestes, from Herculaneum—401, colossal bust of Juno!—406, ditto!— 412, bust of L. C. Lentulus— 413, bust of Agrippina the elder —415, bust of a Female—417, bust, supposed to represent Terence, from Herculaneum—418, bust of Plato, from ditto—422, bust of Varro—423, a Sibyl!— 424, bust of Homer!

Cabinet. No. 427, Hermaphrodite-Faun!!—428, group of a Love and a Dolphin—429, small statue of Diana, from Herculaneum!—432, small statue of Bacchus, found in the Temple of Isis at Pompeii—433, Venus, from ditto—434, small statue of Isis, from ditto—442, small statue of a Faun, from Pompeii—444, small statue of Silenus seated, from Herculaneum!—454, bust of a Lady, from Pompeii—456, bust of a Faun, from ditto—459, bust of a Lady, from Herculaneum—465, small statue of a Faun, from ditto—467, small statue of a Philosopher seated—473, small statue of a Youth, from Herculaneum—475, small statue of a Female.

The Gallery of ancient Sculpture likewise contains columns of precious marbles, found in Herculaneum, Pompeii, and other parts of Magna-Græcia.

Apartment on the ground-floor, containing Egyptian Antiquities. Among the most interesting things in this collection are, the statue of Isis, found in her Temple at Pompeii—an Isiac Table, and two Salvers on stands, also found there—a small statue of Pluto, found in the Temple of Serapis at Pozzuoli—beautiful small vases, Lachrymatories, and Incense-bottles—a Wine-cup—Egyptian Divinities and Mummies.

Apartment on the ground-floor containing bronze Statues and Busts, chiefly found in Herculaneum. Left side. Statue of Mammius Maximus—statue of an Infant Hercules!—bust of Ptolemy-Apion!—statue of M. Calatorius—bust of Seneca—half-length statue of Diana, from Pompeii—bust of a young Hercules—statue of Augustus!—small group of a Faun and a Youth, from Pompeii. (The eyes in both these statues are of silver; and the stand, which supports them, is beautifully inlaid with the same metal.) *Recess.* Head of Virgil's Horse, and several small Bronzes; among which is a group supposed to represent Alexander and Bucephalus! *Left side continued.* Small statue, from Pompeii, of Apollo, with silver eyes—statue of Claudius Drusus—bust of Archytas—statue of a Satyr!—bust, called Plato!—statue of Nero Drusus—busts of Lucius Cæsar, Sappho, and Scipio Africanus—statue, called Antonia. *Right side.* Bust of Antinous in the character of Bacchus—busts of Commodus, Sylla, Caracalla, Ptolemy-Alexander, Augustus, Democritus, Ptolemy-Philadelphus, and Ptolemy-Soter—statue of a Discobolus!—statue of Piety—statue of a Discobolus!—busts of Berenice, Heraclitus, Tiberius, Livia, and Lepidus—statue of an Actress—busts of Caius Cæsar, Ptolemy-Philometor, and Annius Verus. *Centre of the Apartment.* Statues of two Deer—statue of a drunken Faun reposing on a skin of wine!—statue of a horse, supposed to have adorned the Theatre at Herculaneum!—statue of Mercury seated!!—statue of Apollo, from Pompeii.

Another Apartment, usually locked up, though always opened when Travellers wish to see it, contains a beautiful little statue of Bacchus, found in Pompeii; a small Etruscan Diana, with a coloured border to her robe, found in Herculaneum; and a small Venus, lately found in Pompeii.

Apartment up stairs. On the landing-place there are three doors; that on the left leads to the rooms where the Papyri, brought from Herculaneum, are unrolled. Though all these scrolls are so much scorched as to resemble tinder, yet some of them (about four hundred) have, by a most tedious process, been opened; and about ninety were found in a legible state. Among these are, fragments of a Latin poem, relative to the war between Anthony and Octavius—Epicurus upon Nature—a work by Polystratus—fragments of a work by Colotes—Philodemus upon Music and Rhetoric—and works which bear the names of Demetrius, Carniscus, Chrysippus, etc. The number of scrolls brought to the Museum is said to amount to about seventeen hundred; but, of those not yet operated upon, about one hundred only seem sufficiently perfect to be capable of expansion. Thirty-nine years after the discovery of Herculaneum a considerable number of scrolls of Papyrus, owing to an excavation made in a garden at Resina, were discovered in a house supposed to have belonged to Lucius Piso.

The middle-door leads to the Library, which contains nearly an hundred and fifty thousand printed volumes, including several of the fifteenth century; and a large collection of precious manuscripts; among which are those of S. Thomas Aquinas, and the Aminta of Tasso. Here likewise is the *Uffizio* of the Madonna, illuminated by Giulio Clovio, bound in gold, and decorated with *bassi-rilievi*, and another book, called the *Flora!* which likewise contains *chefs-d'œuvre* in miniature painting!

Antiquities found in Herculaneum, Pompeii, Stabiæ, Capri, etc. *First room. Cabinet of Gems.* Here are Necklaces, Earrings, Brooches, and Gold ornaments of almost every description. Camei and Intagli, among which is the celebrated Cameo, said to be the most precious work of its kind in existence; and representing the Apotheosis of the first Ptolemy on one side, and the head of Medusa on the other—two ancient Mosaics, one of which exhibits a *tympanum*, or tambarine, like those now used at Naples—four monochromatic Paintings on marble—a beautiful flying figure of Victory, and several other Paintings, from Herculaneum and Pompeii—a collection of ancient Colours, used in fresco-painting—two Loaves—a Honey-comb—Fruits—Grain—and other Eatables, all burnt to cinders. *Second room. Ancient Glass.* Good Glass for windows—vases of various shapes—Rummers, not unlike those in present use—small Dishes, some of which are painted—Incense-bottles, supposed to have been Lachrymatories, till lately found with odoriferous gums remaining in them—large Bottles for medicines, found in an apothecary's shop at Pompeii, etc., etc. A glass Vessel, not yet (I believe) placed in this room, contains Rouge, similar to that worn at present. *Third room.* Kitchen-Furniture, consisting of Bronze Utensils, many of them lined and inlaid with Silver—marble Mortars—a Gridiron—a variety of elegantly shaped bronze Moulds for pastry—a portable bronze Stove—Boilers—Stewing-pans—Frying-pans, etc. *Fourth room.* Scales and Weights;[1] the latter elegantly ornamented—a great variety of Lamps—a Lantern, glazed with horn instead of glass—Candelabra; some of which are particularly elegant—beautiful Steelyards—and a Basin of bronze inlaid with silver. *Fifth room,* Sacrificial Vases—a Wine-cup, shaped like a horse's head—sacrificial Knives—a Brush, supposed to have been used in sprinkling the purifying water,[2] and like

---

[1] The pound weight of Magna Græcia appears to have been like the present pound weight of Naples, between ten and eleven ounces: and the ancient steelyards, if I may so call balances made of bronze, resemble those now used at Naples in shape, though far superior in beauty.

[2] Every ancient Temple contained a vase filled with purifying water, and placed, it is supposed, near the entrance: and with this water every person who came to solemn sacrifices was sprinkled.

what Roman Catholic priests now use for a similar purpose — two Couches for the gods, exhibited at festivals called *Lectisternia*, and composed of bronze inlaid with silver!—a bronze Altar—two Chairs for the Priests—bronze Tripods; one of which is particularly elegant—Vessels for incense—a variety of other Vessels used in heathen temples; and a beautiful Vase lately found at Pompeii. *Sixth room. Right side.* Several pieces of furniture employed in ancient Baths; among which are Scrapers for the skin, and elegant Essence-bottles — a child's toy, representing a Carriage — ancient Greek Armour—two Bells, for marking time—and another toy representing a Car. *Seventh room. Right side.* Inkstands, with remains of ink—Styles—Pens of cedar—a Case for Styles—Tablets—Letters for stamping bread; which letters appear to have been used in a manner so like printing, that one wonders such an invention should have escaped the Ancients—Mirrors of metal—chirurgical Instruments, but no lancets—Opera-tickets for the boxes and benches; the latter tickets being numbered to correspond with the numbers of the seats at the theatres—musical Instruments; namely, the Sistrum, Cymbal, etc.—Bells for cattle, precisely like those used at the present day—Dice—Household-gods—an elegant portable Stove—bronze Door-cases—Nails — Screws — Locks — Keys — Latches — Bolts —Hinges, etc.— The two last-named rooms likewise contain Bridles—Stirrups—a Mosaic Table with beautiful Feet, from Pompeii—Rings—Necklaces — Ear-rings —Bracelets —Pins for the hair—ornaments called *Bullæ*, worn by young Patricians till they were allowed to assume the *Toga*—Silver Cups, Saucers, and Spoons; but no Forks.[1]

Apartments containing sepulchral Grecian Vases, etc. The Pavements of these rooms were taken from Herculaneum, Pompeii, Stabiæ, etc.; and are particularly beautiful. The collection of Vases is highly interesting. Those found in the tombs of the Rich are light-coloured, and exhibit paintings which usually represent mythological subjects: those found in the tombs of the Poor are dark-coloured, and quite plain.[2] *The first room* contains a Table from Pompeii with beautiful Feet; and a Vase, the painting on which represents Orestes tormented by the Furies. Some of the most interesting paintings on the Vases *in the second room* are, the Sepulchre of Agamemnon—Hercules stealing the Tripod of Apollo—and an ancient Repast. A Widow

---

[1] The Mirrors, Combs, Rouge, and other personal ornaments belonging to this collection, were found in the tombs of females; the Arms, Armour, Papyri, and Styles, in the tombs of men; the Toys in the tombs of children (I saw Tops and a jointed Doll, found in a tomb); and Kitchen-furniture was found in every tomb, as were Vases for wine, oil, etc.: so that, by examining the abodes of the Dead, we have been taught the domestic economy of the Living who inhabited this earth from two to three thousand years ago. Dice, likewise, are continually found in ancient tombs.

[2] This distinction, however, could not have subsisted in very remote ages, when pottery appears to have been made of materials black as jet, and beautifully polished,—but not adorned with paintings. In a tomb, thirty feet under ground, at S. Agnello, a village situated in the Piano di Sorrento, a skeleton was lately discovered of a warrior, cased in armour, and supposed to have been one of the Phœnicians who colonised there. The armour is of a kind which announces no common person: but, nevertheless, the skeleton was surrounded with plain black vases, and incense-bottles of plain red pottery. This tomb likewise contained a lachrymatory of Oriental alabaster, and apparently of Egyptian workmanship.

bewailing the death of her husband is likewise a common subject on these urns. The Vases *in the third room* exhibit paintings of Hercules killing the Centaur—an Egyptian Ceremony, etc. *The fourth room* contains models, in cork, representing the inside of two ancient Sepulchres; one of which exhibits a corse in the centre (with a piece of money in its mouth, and an incense-bottle on its breast[1]) surrounded by lamps, vases for the purifying water, oil, wine, incense, etc.; and a dish for Cerberus's sop. The other, which is the precise representation of the inside of a Tomb found at Pæstum, contains a painting (the subject of which is a Combat); four vases, a dish for Cerberus's sop, and the corse placed in the centre, with arms and armour by its side. This room likewise contains the model of an ancient public Cemetery at Naples. *In the fifth room* are several Vases embellished with paintings, which appear to represent Widows sacrificing; and two others, on the first of which is the story of Cadmus; and on the second the tomb of Agamemnon; Electra and Orestes being on one side, near the tomb; and on the reverse side Ægisthus and Clytemnæstra in the act of marrying. The subjects of some of the paintings on the Vases *in the sixth room* are, Hercules slaying the Sicilian King; with a beautiful ancient car on the reverse side of the Vase —Achilles dragging Hector round the walls of Troy—the Olympic games—the same subject repeated —an ancient Repast, particularly curious, because it exhibits the manner in which the Ancients drank—Hercules in the garden of the Hesperides, with a tree, and a serpent twined round it, very much like the modern representation of the Garden of Eden—Penelope in a car, and the gods looking down upon her; together with a painting of *Pulcinella,* dressed as he now dresses on the Neapolitan Stage, except that instead of a half-mask, he has one which entirely covers his face. Here likewise are two ancient drinking cups; together with a small, but extremely beautiful Vase, on which is written, "The Lucretia." *In the seventh room* are several particularly fine Vases, brought from Nola.[2]

Apartments containing Easel-Pictures.[3] Among the most admired paintings in these rooms are, the Magdalene!—a portrait of Paul III.—another picture representing Paul III., etc., but unfinished—Danaë!!—and a portrait of Philip II., all by Titian. A Guardian Angel protecting a Child, by Domenichino!—the Magdalene, by Guercino!—S. Peter, by ditto.—A Pietà!—Rinaldo and Armida—Hercules between Vice and Virtue—Venus, a Faun, etc. all by Annibale Caracci. A Pietà, by Agostino Caracci!—The Saviour dead!—an *Ecce Homo!*—the Marriage of S. Catherine—the Madonna and our Saviour with a Rabbit!—two colossal Paintings —and two small pictures (one a Holy Family, the other a Ma-

---

[1] It is not uncommon to find the breast of a corse surrounded by six or eight incense-bottles.

[2] The earthen Vases of the Ancients were not consecrated to the Dead alone, but frequently used in sacrifices (especially those made to Vesta); and likewise given, in very early ages, as prizes to the victors at Grecian festivals. Earthen vases filled with oil were bestowed on the conquerors at the Panathenæa; and probably this sort of ware served also for domestic purposes.

[3] One of these rooms contains excellent Models, in cork, of the Temples, Basilica, etc. at Pæstum; and likewise of other ancient edifices in Magna Græcia.

donna and Child), all by Correggio. Portrait of the Mother of Raphael—portrait of a Fencing Master!—the Holy Family—Leo x. between Cardinals Passerini and Bembo!—the Madonna and the Saviour—the Madonna, the Saviour, Elizabeth, and S. John!! all by Raphael. The adoration of the Magi, by Andrea da Salerno—Copy of the *Madonna della seggiola,* by Giulio Romano—portrait of Giulio Clovio, by himself—Alexander vi., by Sebastiano del Piombo—Holy Family, by ditto—Holy Family, by Andrea del Sarto — Bramante, and the Duke of Urbino, by ditto—the Assumption, by Fra Bartolomeo—the Madonna and our Saviour, by Leonardo da Vinci—S. John, by ditto!!—a large Landscape, by Claude!!—an Angel, by Schidone!—Charity, by ditto!!—a Head, by Vandyck—Lucretia—Vespucio—Columbus—and two laughing Children, all by Parmegianino.—The last Judgment, designed by Buonaroti, and coloured by one of his Scholars—two Heads, by Rembrandt— the Fall of Simon Magus, by Lodovico Caracci—and the Crucifixion, by Marco da Siena.

The Museo-Borbonico is usually open to the public every day, festivals excepted, from eight in the morning till two in the afternoon; and Foreigners usually give, to each Custode, from two to six carlini, according to the size of the party he attends, and the trouble he takes in explaining things: Foreigners, however, are not expected to repeat these fees every time they visit the Museum.[1]

Palazzo-Reale.[2] This edifice, erected by the Count de Lemos, according to the designs of the Cav. Fontana, to whose taste it does honour, contains magnificent apartments handsomely furnished, and enriched with fine pictures; namely, Tobias, his Son, and the Angel, by Guercino—Susanna in the Bath, by Lodovico Caracci—the Descent from the Cross, by Daniello da Volterra!—the same subject, by Annibale Caracci—Atlas, by Guido—Charity, by ditto—Cupid and Psyche, by Gherardo delle Notti—Charity, by Schidone—an *Ecce Homo,* by Correggio—the Madonna of Monte-Casino, by Raphael—and S. Peter and S. Paul, by ditto. This palace likewise contains *a Hall* hung round with portraits of the Viceroys of Naples, by Massimo and Paolo Matteis; and a handsome Chapel, with an Altar of agate, lapis lazuli, and other precious marbles. *The Residence of Prince Leopoldo,* which is nearly opposite to the Palazzo-Reale, contains the finest Collection of Pictures in Naples.

Chiesa di S. Ferdinando. This church is richly adorned with marbles: and the Ceiling of the Nave, the Cupola, and its Angles, are embellished with the best frescos of Paolo Matteis. The Statues of David and Moses, in one of the Chapels, are by Vac-

---

1 Persons who purchase FINATI's excellent account of the Gallery of Sculpture are not expected to give any fee below stairs, except two carlini to the Custode of the rooms which contain the Egyptian Antiquities and the Bronzes: and Travellers who wish to dive deep into the Antiquities of Magna Græcia should endeavour to obtain an introduction to the Canonico Don Andrea di Jorio, who is not only a distinguished antiquary, but likewise a most gentlemanly and agreeable companion.

2 It is necessary to have an order for seeing the Palazzo-Reale at Naples, and the other Regal residences. These orders must be signed by the Lord High Steward; and Foreigners who apply for them pay one piastre. None of the Regal residences, however, are worth seeing, except the Palace at Naples, and that at Caserta.

caro; and the Picture which adorns the High-Altar is by Solimena.

Castel Nuovo. This fortress, begun in 1283, according to the designs of Giovanni Pisano, but not completed till 1546, contains the Arsenal, and a triumphal Arch, erected in honour of Alphonso of Arragon.

Castella dell' Uovo. This was once a Villa belonging to Lucullus; but an earthquake separated it from the main land; and William I. second King of Naples, built a palace here. It derives its name from its shape.

Chiesa di S. Maria del Parto. The ground on which this edifice stands was given by Frederic II. of Aragon, to his Secretary, Sannazaro: and behind the high-altar is the Tomb of that great Poet, by Poggibonzi, one of Buonaroti's scholars. The ornaments are too numerous, but the composition is good, and the *Bassi-rilievi,* allusive to the Piscatory Eclogues, and other writings of Sannazaro, are finely executed. On the sides of the Monument are statues of Apollo and Minerva, now called David and Judith; and on the top is the bust of Sannazaro, with his Arcadian name, *Actius Sincerus,* placed between two weeping Genii. The inscription,

"*Da sacro cineri flores. Hic ille Maroni Sincerus musâ proximus ut tumulo,*"

is by Cardinal Bembo.

Chiesa di S. Brigida. Here is the Tomb of Giordano, and a Cupola painted by that distinguished artist.

Chiesa di S. Giovanni de' Fiorentini. This edifice, built by a scholar of Buonaroti's, is said to be a fine specimen of architecture.

Chiesa di l'Incoronata. Here are remains of Paintings by Giotto.

Chiesa della Pietà de' Torchini. This church is adorned with a fine Altar-Piece, by Solimena, and a beautiful Painting in the Lantern of its Cupola, by Giordano!

Chiesa di S. Maria Nuova. Here are good paintings, by Marco di Siena.

Chiesa di Monte-Oliveto. Here are curious statues, in *crettacotta,* by Modanino di Modena, representing illustrious characters of the fifteenth century: and that called Joseph of Arimathea is, in fact, the portrait of Sannazaro. This church also contains a picture of the Purification, by Vassari (who likewise painted the Sacristy), an Assumption, by Pinturicchio; and one of the best organs in Italy.

Chiesa di Gesù Nuovo, or *Trinità Maggiore.* This church, one of the finest in Naples, was built according to the designs of Novello di S. Lucano: it has suffered considerably from earthquakes; by one of which the Cupola, painted by Lanfranco, was destroyed, the four Evangelists excepted. The other Paintings in the present Cupola are by Paolo Matteis. Over the great door is a large Fresco, by Solimena, representing Heliodorus driven out of the Temple! The Chapel of the Madonna was likewise painted by Solimena. The Chapel of S. Ignazio is adorned with fine marbles, and the whole edifice incrusted and paved with the same. The Chapel of the Trinity contains a Picture by Guercino.

Chiesa di S. Chiara. This was originally a Gothic structure, commenced in 1310, according to the designs of Masuccio, who likewise built the Campanile, which, though not completed as he purposed, is much admired in point of architecture. The interior of the church was adorned with paintings by Giotto, till the Regent, Bario Nuovo, not understanding their merit, ordered them to be covered with white-wash. During the year 1744, Vaccaro modernized the nave, which was, at the same time, beautifully paved with rare marbles, and embellished with a Ceiling, painted by Sebastiano Conca and Francesco Mura: that part which represents S. Chiara putting the Saracens to flight, is by the last-named artist, and a work of great merit: he likewise painted the picture that adorns the High-Altar, near which are two fluted Columns; and, according to tradition, that on the left was brought from Solomon's Temple.

One of the Chapels contains a Picture by Lanfranco; and, in another, some Paintings by Giotto are still remaining. The *Bassirilievi* over the great door deserve attention.[1]

Chiesa di S. Giovanni Maggiore. This edifice is built upon the ruins of a Temple which was erected by Adrian to his Favourite, Antinous. It was consecrated by Constantine and S. Helena to S. John Baptist; and, in consequence of its great antiquity, a Tomb which it contains has been dignified with the appellation of Parthenope's Sarcophagus.

Chiesa del Salvatore, or Gesù Vecchio. Here are Paintings by Marco di Siena, Francesco Mura, Solimena, etc.

Chiesa di S. Domenico Maggiore. This church contains an Annunciation, attributed to Titian; and a Flagellation, attributed to M. A. Caravaggio. The Ceiling of the Sacristy is adorned with a painting of S. Domenico in glory, by Solimena! The Convent belonging to this church formerly comprised the University; whose Professors taught their Scholars in vaults underground.

Chiesa dello Spirito Santo. This is a fine edifice in point of architecture, and contains a painting, by Giordano, of the Madonna presenting a rosary to S. Domenico.

Chiesa di S. Maria della Sanità. Here are good Pictures, by Giordano, Bernardino Siciliano, Andrea Vaccaro, and Agostino Beltrano. This Church leads to the Catacombs; as likewise do the Churches of S. Severo, and S. Gennaro de' Poveri. The Catacombs of Naples are said to be much larger than those of Rome: it is not easy, however, to ascertain this; it being impossible to penetrate far into them. The general opinion seems to be, that they were, like the Roman Catacombs, public burial-places, formed originally by excavations made in search of pozzolana.[2]

Chiesa di S. Giovanni a Carbonara. This church merits notice on account of containing a Gothic Tomb, immensely large, of Ladislaus, King of Naples; another of Giovanni Caracciolo, and some fine Sculpture in the Vico-Chapel.

Chiesa de S. S. Apostoli. This church, erected on the site of a Temple of Mercury, and conse-

---

[1] This church likewise contains an elegant Latin Epitaph, in memory of a young Lady who expired on the day destined for her nuptials.

[2] No invalid should attempt to visit these subterraneous repositories, the investigation of which cannot be wholesome even for persons in health,—all the unhappy sufferers during the last Plague having been thrown in here.

crated to the Apostles, by Constantine, was rebuilt during the seventeenth century, and adorned with particularly fine Frescos. The Ceiling of the great Nave, and Choir, the five Pictures on the walls of the latter, and the Angles of the Cupola, are by Lanfranco! as likewise are the Ceilings of the small Chapels, and the large and beautiful Fresco over the great door. The Cupola was painted by Benasca, and the Lunettes are the work of Solimena and Giordano; the latter of whom has likewise adorned the Cross with four paintings representing the Annunciation! the Nativity! the Birth of the Madonna! and the presentation in the Temple! The High Altar is richly embellished with precious marbles; and the Filomarini-Chapel (great part of which was executed after the designs of Guido, by Calandra da Vercelli), is adorned with a beautiful *Basso-rilievo*, by Fiamingo, representing a Concert of Children!! Opposite to this Chapel is that of the Conception, richly adorned with precious marbles, and embellished with Paintings by Solimena and Marco di Siena.

Arcivescovado. This cathedral, commonly called La Chiesa di S. Gennaro, the Patron-Saint of Naples, is a Gothic edifice, built by Niccolo Pisano: but the ancient Cathedral, dedicated to Santa Restituta, was erected, during the reign of Constantine, upon the site of a Temple of Apollo. Charles I. of Anjou began the new Cathedral, which was finished in 1299; but, being destroyed by an earthquake, it was rebuilt by Alphonso I. The outside is incrusted with white marble and ornamented with two columns of porphyry. The inside is not splendid; though supported by nearly a hundred columns of Egyptian granite, African marble. etc., taken from the Temples of Neptune and Apollo. The Font, placed near the great door on the left, is an ancient Vase of Basalt, adorned with the attributes of Bacchus; (decorations not very appropriate to a Christian Temple.) The High Altar, made according to the designs of Cav. Posi, is composed of precious marbles and adorned with two antique Candelabra of jasper. Under the high altar is a subterranean Chapel, called *Il Soccorpo*, which contains the body of S. Gennaro; and is supposed to be a remaining part of the Temple of Apollo. This Chapel is incrusted with white marble adorned with columns of the same; and likewise embellished with *bassi-rilievi* in the arabesque style. Behind the tomb of S. Gennaro is a statue of the Constructor of this Chapel, Cardinal Caraffa,[2] attributed to Buonaroti. Adjoining to the present cathedral is the ancient *Church of S. Restituta;* which, though in part destroyed, still contains Columns probably taken from the Temple of Apollo; an Assumption, by Pietro Perugino; and some Mosaics of the time of Constantine. In the modern Cathedral, and situated opposite to the Church of S. Restituta, is the

---

[1] Cardinal Caraffa, Archbishop of Naples, is celebrated for having melted Virgil's horse. The arms of Naples being a horse, there formerly stood one of bronze near the Cathedral: the vulgar said it was cast by Virgil (whom they believe to have been a Magician); and they entertained such superstitious notions of the great efficacy of this statue in all distempers of horses, that, when these animals were ill, they were brought from every part of the kingdom, however remote, to be led round the statue. Therefore, in order to abolish so silly a custom, the Archbishop melted down the whole of Virgil's horse, the head excepted.

Chapel of S. Gennaro, called *Il Tesoro*, and built in consequence of a vow, made by the city of Naples during the Plague of 1526. The entrance to this Chapel is through a magnificent bronze door adorned with fine Columns of rare marble, and Statues of S. Peter and S. Paul. The interior of the edifice is a rotunda, embellished with a Cupola, painted by Lanfranco!![1] and supported by forty-two Corinthian Columns of brocatello; betwen which, on festivals, are placed thirty-five silver Busts of Saints, executed by Finelli; and eighteen Busts, in bronze, by other artists. The high altar is adorned with a Statue of S. Gennaro in the act of blessing the people; and likewise with a silver Tabernacle, containing the head of the Saint, and two small Vessels filled with his Blood, supposed to have been collected by a Neapolitan Lady during his martyrdom. Here also is a picture of S. Gennaro coming out of the furnace, by Spagnoletto. The Painting in the large Chapel, to the right of the high altar, is by Domenichino! as are the Arches and Angles of the roof, and the Pictures in three of the small Chapels.

The Ceremony of liquefying the blood of S. Gennaro takes place three times a year; namely, in May, September, and December, and is an interesting sight to Foreigners: if it liquefy quickly, the joy expressed by the Neapolitans is great; but if there be any unexpected delay, the tears, prayers, and cries, are excessive; as the non-performance of this miracle is supposed to announce some dreadful impending calamity.

Chiesa di S. Filippo Neri de' P. P. Gerolimini. This is one of the handsomest churches at Naples: the outside being cased with marble; the inside lined with the same, and divided into three aisles by twelve magnificent Columns of granite. The pavement is marble, and very elegant; and the High-Altar is composed of agate, sardonyx, jasper, lapis lazuli, mother of pearl, etc. Here also are fine Paintings in the Angles of the Cupola; a celebrated, though much damaged Fresco, above the great door, by Giordano, representing our Saviour chasing the Buyers and Sellers from the Temple; over the fifth Altar, on the right, S. Teresa with her Carmelites at the foot of a crucifix, by the same artist; and, on the opposite side, S. Francesco, by Guido. The Chapel of S. Filippo Neri is richly decorated; and contains, in its Cupola, a painting by Solimena, which represents the Saint in glory; and on the opposite side of the high-altar is another Chapel, the Cupola of which was painted by Simonelli, the subject being Judith showing the head of Holofernes to his army. The Chapel of S. Alessio contains a Picture by Pietro da Cortona; and in the Sacristy are Paintings attributed to Guido, Domenichino, Spagnoletto, etc. The Ceiling is by Giordano.

Chiesa di S. Paolo Maggiore. This stately edifice stands on the site of an ancient Temple, supposed to have been erected by Julius Tarsus, Tiberius's Freedman; who consecrated it to Castor and

---

[1] Domenichino began to paint the cupola, but died soon after the commencement of his work; which, from motives of envy, was obliterated by Lanfranco.

Pollux. A considerable part of the portico of this Temple remained till the earthquake of 1688; but, now, only two Columns and the Entablature are entire. These noble vestiges of antiquity, two Bases of other columns, and the Trunks of the statues of Castor and Pollux (recumbent figures half buried in the wall), are on the outside of the church; the interior of which is elegantly incrusted with marble, and adorned with paintings by Solimena, Massimo, etc. The Frescos on the ceiling, by Corenzio, were originally fine; though now much injured; but that above the great door is in good preservation. The Sacristy contains the *Chefs-d'œuvre* of Solimena: and the Cloisters of the adjoining Convent are adorned with antique Columns, and built upon the site of *an ancient Theatre*, where Nero first exhibited in public; because he deemed it less derogatory to imperial grandeur to act with the awkwardness of a beginner in one of the Grecian cities, than in his own Capital.

Chiesa di S. Maria Maggiore. This church is said to have been erected on the ruins of a Temple of Diana; and has a well-painted Ceiling.

Chiesa di S. Pietro à Majella. The Ceiling of the Nave is finely painted by Calabrese!

Cappella di S. Severo. This chapel, the Mausoleum of the Sangro-family, and called S. Maria della Pietà, is a singular edifice, adorned with rare marbles, and surrounded with arches; each of which contains a Sarcophagus, and a Statue of one of the Princes of Sangro: while attached to every adjoining pilaster is the tomb of the Princess who was wife to the Prince in the arch, each of the last named tombs being ornamented with a Statue representing the most conspicuous virtue of the lady in the tomb. One of the most remarkable statues is that of Modesty, covered from head to foot with a veil; through which, however, the features are clearly discernible. The sculptor was Corradini. Vice undeceived is likewise a remarkable work; it represents a Man caught in a net, and struggling to extricate himself, by aid of the Genius of Good-Sense! the sculptor was Queirolo. Here, likewise, is a dead Christ covered with a veil, which seems damped by the sweat of Death! The sculptor was Giuseppe San Martino; and all these works peculiarly merit notice from being original; as neither Greeks nor Romans seem to have attempted showing the face and form with distinctness through a veil. This chapel has suffered severely from earthquakes.

Chiesa di S. M. Annunziata. This edifice, which was destroyed by fire, and rebuilt in 1782, according to the designs of the Cav. Vanvitelli, is one of the most chaste and beautiful specimens of architecture at Naples. The columns by which it is supported, forty-four in number, are all composed of white marble. The Prophets in the Angles of the Cupola are by Fischietti; to whose pencil they do honour. Pictures which adorn the High-Altar, and those of the Cross, are by Francesco Mura. A Chapel on the right, near the high-altar, is adorned with a beautiful *Pietà;* and another chapel, near the great door, contains a picture of the

Madonna and our Saviour, and little Angels, the last of which are finely executed. The Ceiling of the Sacristy and Tesoro are painted by Corenzio; and the Presses exhibit the life of our Saviour curiously sculptured in wood (some parts being gilt), by Giovanni di Nola.

Chiesa di S. Maria del Carmine. This church is richly ornamented with rare marbles; and contains Paintings by Solimena, Giordano, and Paolo Matteis.

Chiesa di S. Martino de' Certosini.[1] This church, which once belonged to the magnificent Certosini convent, now the Asylum of military Invalids, was built after the designs of the Cav. Fansaga, and is more splendid and beautiful than any other sacred edifice at Naples: indeed it may vie with every church existing, in the excellence of its paintings, and the value of its marbles and precious stones. Above the principal entrance is a picture, by Massimo, representing our Saviour dead, and attended by the Madonna, the Magdalene, and S. John. The Ceiling and upper part of the walls of the Nave were painted by Lanfranco, except the twelve Prophets, by Spagnoletto, which are particularly fine!! and the figures of Moses and Elias by the same artist. The Choir is beautiful; and exhibits Paintings on the Ceiling, begun by the Cav. d'Arpino, and finished by Berardino. The unfinished picture of the Nativity, immediately behind the high-altar, is by Guido, who did not live to complete it: the other Pictures are by Massimo, Lanfranco, and Spagnoletto; that of our Saviour administering the Communion (by Spagnoletto), and that of the Crucifixion (by Lanfranco), are much admired. The High-Altar, made after the designs of Solimena, is splendidly adorned with rare marbles, and precious stones; as likewise are the Altars of the Chapels. That consecrated to S. Bruno, contains a fine Altar-Piece, etc., by Massimo—another Chapel is finely painted by Matteis—another, by Solimena—another is embellished with three good pictures; namely, S. John baptizing our Saviour, by Carlo Maratta! S. John preaching, by Matteis; and the decapitation of the Saint, by Massimo. These chapels are likewise rich in sculpture; and one of them contains a strikingly-fine Bust, by Giuseppe San-Martino. *The Sacristy* contains a Ceiling, beautifully painted by the Cav. d'Arpino—Presses ornamented with mosaics made of wood, and executed in a masterly style by a German Monk, in 1620—a fine picture of our Saviour on the Cross, the Madonna, the Magdalene and S. John, by the Cav. d'Arpino—S. Peter denying our Saviour, by M. A. Caravaggio!!—and our Saviour carried up the holy Stairs to the house of Pilate, by Massimo and Viviani. The Ceiling and Arches of *the Tesoro* are by Giordano! and above the altar, which exhibits magnificent precious stones, is a painting of our Saviour dead, with the Madonna, the Magdalene, S. John, etc., a highly-celebrated work, deemed the master-piece of Spa-

---

[1] The Church of S. Martino stands near the Castle of S. Elmo, on the hill called Monte Vomero, which rises above the city of Naples. To persons who walk, the distance is inconsiderable; though, from the steepness of the ascent, and the almost innumerable steps which compose the foot-way, this walk is fatiguing. The coach-road is circuitous, but good.

gnoletto!!! *The Council Hall* contains a Ceiling painted by Corenzio—the Doctors of the Church, ten in number, by Paolo Fignolio—and the Flagellation, by the Cav. d'Arpino! *The next apartment* contains the history of S. Bruno round the Walls; with sacred subjects on the Ceiling, by Corenzio! The Corridors of the adjoining Convent are composed of marble supported by columns of the same; and the view from the interior of this proudly-situated edifice is enchanting. Immediately below the conventual Garden lies the large flat-roofed city of Naples; whose streets appear like narrow foot-paths; while the buzz of its inhabitants, who look like pigmies, and the noise of the carriages, which seem no larger than children's toys, are with difficulty distinguishable. On one side is Capo di Monte, and the rich Neapolitan Campania; on another rise the majestic mountains of the Apennine, with Vesuvius in their front; while on another lies the wide-stretching Bay of Naples, bordered by Portici, etc., on the left, and Pozzuoli, etc., on the right. This stupendous view is seen to the greatest advantage from that part of the conventual Garden called *The Belvedere*.[1]

Castello di S. Elmo. This fortress, formerly denominated S. Ermo, and, according to some writers, S. Erasmo, was begun by the Normans; and is chiefly formed out of an immense rock, said to be hewn into subterranean apartments which extend to the Castello Nuovo. Charles v. erected the citadel.

Palazzo-Berio. This noble edifice contains a fine collection of Pictures, a good library, and, in the Garden, a celebrated Group of Venus and Adonis, by Canova.[2]

Albergo de' Poveri. This immense and magnificent building (not yet finished) is an Asylum for Orphans and Children whose parents cannot afford to give them the advantage of education. Here the boys are instructed in reading, writing, drawing, engraving, the elements of the mathematics, etc.; and the Girls in sewing, spinning, weaving linen, knitting, and other things useful to the poor.

Naples contains several Theatres. The *Teatro Reàle di San Carlo*, one of the largest and finest opera-houses in Italy, was so nearly destroyed by fire, during the year 1816, that nothing but the party-walls, and front of the building, remained: eleven months afterward, however, this Theatre rose from its ashes, adorned with even more than its original splendour; and exhibiting six rows of boxes (thirty-two in each row), a *parterre* capable of accommodating six hundred and seventy-four persons seated, and above one hundred and fifty standing; a stage, the dimensions of which are immense: spacious corridors; excellent stairs; and an adjoining edifice, called *the Ridotto*, which comprises ball-rooms, eating-rooms, and apartments of gaming; the last being constantly

---

1 The abominable Neapolitan custom of throwing dead bodies, without coffins, into burial-places under the churches, renders those which are most used as receptacles for the Dead, dangerous to the Living.

Travellers who wish to visit the Churches least objectionable on the above-mentioned account, should confine themselves to S. Maria del Parto—S. Martino—Trinità Maggiore—S. Chiara—S. Domenico Maggiore—S. Maria della Pietà—S. Paolo Maggiore—S. Filippo Neri—S. Gennaro—the Annunziata, and the S. S. Apostoli.

2 Here the servants are interdicted from receiving fees.

open, night and day. The *Teatro Reale del Fondo* is another opera-house, smaller than San Carlo, but handsome. The *Teatro de' Fiorentini* exhibits buffa operas and plays. The *Teatro Nuovo* is appropriated to the same purpose. The *Teatro di San Ferdinando* is larger than any other, except San Carlo. The *Teatro della Fenice* is very small, and exhibits musical pieces and plays: and the *Teatro di San Carlino*, likewise very small, is much frequented on account of *Pulcinella*,[1] who exhibits there, and is a character peculiar now to the Kingdom of Naples, and, apparently of Grecian origin; his performances are highly interesting to persons acquainted with the Neapolitan dialect. The *Teatro della Fenice*, and the *Teatro di San Carlino*, are usually open twice during twenty four hours, namely, at five in the afternoon; and again at ten at night. The Theatres Royal are opened alternately; because the same singers, dancers, and musicians, belong to both.

The principal Promenades are, the *Villa Reale;* the *Chiaja;* the *Giardino Bottanico*, made by the French, and lying in the way to the *Campo Marzo*, also made by the same nation; who likewise constructed a Road called, by them, *Strada-Napoleon*, which extends from Naples to Capo di Monte; and is a magnificent and particularly beneficial work; as carriages which could not formerly be drawn up the hill without the aid of four horses, now go constantly with a pair; so that this beautiful drive is become, during summer, the favourite airing of the Neapolitans. The Road begun by Murat, but not finished, from Naples to Pozzuoli, is also a delightful Promenade.

Persons who have time to spare would do well to visit *the Market built by the French* in imitation of an ancient *Forum Nundinarium;* and adorned by a figure of abundance in its centre. (This market communicates with the Strada Toledo.) British Travellers should likewise visit *the Chapel of the Crocelle*, in the Chiatamone; there a Monument has been lately erected to the memory of the Rev. John Chetwode Eustace, the eloquent and animated Author of " *The Classical Tour through Italy.* " This monument is placed behind the altar; and consists of a plain tablet of white marble; on which, between two pillars, a female figure (perhaps representing Italy) stands in relief, leaning, in a pensive attitude, on a tomb; and by her is a stork, in the act of devouring a serpent. The inscription is in Latin, and ends with the following lines:

" *Care, vale! Patriæ manet, æternumque manebit*
Te genuisse decus, non tumulasse dolor. "

Great care should be taken by Foreigners in order to procure good water, a scarce commodity at Naples; that of the Fontana-Medina, near the Largo del Castello, and that of the Fontana di S. Pietro Martire, and its environs, is wholesome; but persons who do not contrive to procure water from one of these Fountains, which are supplied by an aqueduct, incur the risk of being attacked with a dysentery, or some other putrid disease.

The climate of Naples differs materially in different parts of the

---

[1] In Neapolitan, *Polecenella*.

city. Persons who wish for a situation congenial to weak lungs, should reside in the Fouria. In the Largo del Castello and its environs the air is tolerably soft: but in the quarter of S. Lucia the vicinity of the sea, united with the dampness occasioned by a tufo mountain, directly under which the houses are built, renders the air dangerous to invalids, and not very wholesome even for persons in health. The houses on the Chiaja are less dangerous than those in the quarter of S. Lucia, because further removed from the tufo mountain; but their situation is too bleak for persons afflicted with tender lungs. Pizzo-Falcone is wholesome, and not noisy; a peculiar advantage at Naples.

The society in this city is not deemed so good as at Rome; neither is the Carnival so brilliant: but the Festival of S. Maria Piedigrotto, on the 8th of September, is a sight worth seeing.[1]

Here are several Hotels: and a considerable number of private lodging-houses; among the former of which are: *The Grand-Bretagna—The Crocelle—The Villa di Londra—The Albergo Reale—The Albergo di Venezia, and The Hôtel des Iles Britanniques.*

The character of the Neapolitans appears to have been mistaken by Travellers; who seem inclined to think the lower classes of people cunning, rapacious, profligate, and cruel; and the more exalted ignorant, licentious, and revengeful; this, however, is not, generally speaking, true; for the common people are open-hearted, industrious, and, though passionate, so fond of drollery, that a man in the greatet rage will suffer himself to be appeased by a joke; and though a Neapolitan sometimes does an injury, from the first impulse of anger, he is not malicious. Those among the common people who have mixed much with Foreigners are expert in making bargains, and eager to extort money; but those who have lived chiefly among each other display no such propensities; and what seems to indicate a good disposition is, that they all may be governed by kind words; while a contrary language never fails to frustrate its own purpose. Gentlemen of the church, law, and army, are tolerably well educated; and in this middle rank may be found as much true friendship, as much sterling worth, and as many amiable Characters, as in any nation whatsoever: neither are examples wanting, among the nobility, of talents, erudition, and moral virtue, though such for a length of years has been the nature of the Neapolitan Government, that persons gifted with power to distinguish themselves, have seldom ventured to exert it.

I cannot dismiss this subject without mentioning a peculiar trait of charity we met with among the common people. Our cook, by birth a Neapolitan, was married to a young woman whom we hired, one summer, as our housemaid; and, after having been with us a few weeks, she requested per-

---

[1] On the eve of the Festival of Corpus Christi, the Magistrates of Naples give a concert of vocal and instrumental music to the common people, in a long and wide street, which is fitted up for the occasion, with Galleries on each side; a Fountain in the centre, adorned with evergreens and statues; and, at the upper end, a handsome Temple, in which the musicians are placed. The street is brilliantly illuminated; and all these preparations are made within the space of six hours. The concert begins at eight in the evening, and ends at ten; and this entertainment is called the *Festa di Chiatamone*.

mission to go and see her adopted child, who was (she said) very ill. The word "adopted," surprised us so much, that we inquired why a man and woman who worked hard for their bread, and were both young enough to expect a family of their own, had been induced to adopt a child? They replied, that the child was a foundling, and therefore belonged to the Madonna; consequently, by such an adoption, they ensured her blessing on themselves and their own offspring; and, afterward, when we mentioned this circumstance to our Neapolitan friends, they informed us, that such instances of charity were by no means rare among the common people.[1]

I will now close my account of Naples with a List of the objects best worth notice, as they lie contiguous to each other.

Studii Publici—Palazzo Reale—Chiesa di S. Ferdinando—Castel Nuovo—Castello dell' Uovo—Chiesa di S. Maria del Porto—di S. Brigida—di S. Giovanni de' Fiorentini—dell' Incoronata—della Pietà de Torchini—di S. Maria della Nuova—di Monte-Oliveto—di Trinità Maggiore—di S. Chiara—di S. Giovanni Maggiore—di Gesù Vecchio—di S. Domenico Maggiore—dello Spirito Santo—di S. Maria della Sanità—di S. Giovanni à Carbonara—de' S. S. Apostoli—Arcivescovado—Chiesa de Gerolimini—di S. Paolo Maggiore—di S. Maria Maggiore—di S. Pietro à Majella—Capella di S. Severo—Chiesa di S. M. Annunziata—di S. Maria del Carmine—di S. Martino de Gertosini—Castello di S. Elmo—Palazzo-Berio—Albergo de' Poveri.

[1] Some writers have said that, among the common people of Naples, there are forty thousand termed *Lazzaroni*, from having no home, and being consequently obliged to make the streets their sleeping-place. This, however, is a mistake; it being quite as rare to see the indigent without a bed at Naples, as in any other city of Italy. The fact is, that the Lazzaroni sleep three or four in one bed, paying a grain each to their landlord.

CHAPTER XI.

ENVIRONS OF NAPLES.

Excursion to Baiæ—Virgil's Tomb—Grotto of Posilipo—Island of Nisida—Pozzuoli—Cathedral—Pedestal adorned with bassi-rilievi—Temple of Jupiter Serapis—Piers of the ancient Mole—Monte Nuovo—Lucrine Lake—Lake Avernus—Temple of Proserpine—Grotto of the Cumæan Sibyl—Nero's Villa and Vapour-baths—Cæsar's Villa—Baiæ—Temple of Venus—Camere di Venere—Public Baths—Temples of Mercury and Diana Baiana—Villa of Marius—Piscinæ of Hortensius—Villa of Lucullus—Piscina Mirabile—Cape and Port of Misenum—Cento Camerelle—Sepolcro d'Agrippina—Amphitheatre of Pozzuoli—Excursion to Cumæ—Sulfatara—Sepulchral Monuments of Puteoli—Cicero's Villa—Arco Felice—Ancient Cumæ—Grotto of the Sibyls Cumea and Cumana—Tempio de' Giganti—Excursion to the Lake d'Agnano—Villa of Lucullus—Baths of S. Germano—Grotto del Cane—Pisciarelli—Astroni—Excursion to Caserta—Aqueduct—Palace—Ancient Capua—Excursion by night to Vesuvius—best Cicerone—Expense attending this Excursion—Herculaneum, how discovered—Description of that city—descent into the Theatre—Museum at Portici—Excursion to Pompeii—Destruction of Torre del Greco, etc. in 1794—Least fatiguing method of seeing Pompeii—Discovery of that city—Excavations made by the French—Present appearance of Pompeii—Objects best worth notice there—Customs and manners of the Moderns similar to those of the Ancients—Excursion to Pæstum—time employed in going—expense—Cross road—great road—Nocera—Cava—Vietri—Salerno—Pæstum; its supposed origin—Walls, Gates, Temples, etc.—Sonnet—Eboli—Convent of La Trinità—Excursion by water to Sorrento—Situation of that town—Accommodations—Antiquities—Climate—Description of the Plain of Sorrento, etc.—Character of the Sorrentines—Provisions—Lodging-houses—Massa—Amalfi—Castel-a-Mare—Capri—Excursion to the Islands of Procida and Ischia.

I WILL now endeavour to give an account of the Environs of this City, which are particularly beautiful, and as peculiarly interesting.

EXCURSION TO BAIÆ.

We set out from Naples at nine in the morning, in a close carriage, which we hired for eight hours, to convey us to Pozzuoli, and wait there, till we had taken the usual round. We then drove to the end of the Riviera di Chiaja, got out of our carriage, and ascended from the Mergellina quarter to a Garden, where, situated on the summit of the arch of that entry to the Grotto of Posilipo which fronts the city, stands *Virgil's Tomb*: its shape appears to have been a cylinder, with a dome, supported by a square base, and ten niches for cinerary urns: these, however, have disappeared; as likewise has the bay-tree by which this sepulchre was once overshadowed. Virgil's tomb gave birth to four lines so beautiful that I cannot forbear inserting them: their author was asked, "whether he would prefer Fame during life, or Renown after death?" to which question he answered thus:

"*Virgilii ad tumulum divini præmia Vatis,*
Extendit viridem laurea densa comam.
Quid tibi defuncto hæc prosit? felicior olim
Sub patulæ fagi tegmine vivus eras."[1]

---
[1] I was favoured by a friend with the following imitation of these lines:—
    The glorious plant that crowns the Poet's head,
    Still throws its fragrant leaves o'er Virgil dead;
    But to the lifeless eye, th' unconscious heart,
    What pleasure can its fragrant leaves impart?
    Far happier He, when 'neath the beechen shade,
    At ease outstretch'd, his living form was laid.

The garden which contains this tomb commands a magnificent view; and in an arbour here, immediately above the English burial-ground, Travellers frequently dine.

Returning to our carriage, we drove through the *Grotto of Posilipo*;[1] drawing up the glasses while we passed that part which is near Pozzuoli, and, at times, damp and unwholesome. Mention is made of this Grotto by Strabo, Seneca, Pliny, etc.; but by whom it was formed seems uncertain. At the entrance is a chapel; in the centre are two large funnels cut through the roof to admit light and air; and suspended over the road are lamps always kept burning. The length of the Grotto is computed to be two thousand three hundred and sixteen feet, its breadth twenty-two, and its height in the most lofty part eighty-nine feet. After emerging from this singular cavern we passed *the Island of Nisida*, formerly *Nesis*, where Marcus Brutus had a villa; and where now is the Lazaretto; and then, on arriving at *Pozzuoli* (called, by the Greeks, *Dicæarchia*,[2] and, by the Romans, *Puteoli*), we engaged a guide, ordered a boat for Baiæ, etc.; and a donkey to go round by land to the Lucrine Lake: we likewise ordered the guide to purchase a couple of torches for the subterranean part of our intended excursion; and, while the boat was preparing, visited the objects best worth notice at Pozzuoli. *The Cathedral*, once a Temple consecrated to Augustus, exhibits large square stones joined together without cement, and some remains of Corinthian columns, all of which appear to have belonged to the ancient edifice. In the principal Piazza stands *a Pedestal of white marble*, found in 1693; on which are represented figures, in *basso-rilievo*, personifying the fourteen cities of Asia Minor, that were, during one night, destroyed by an earthquake, in the reign of Tiberius, and rebuilt by that Emperor. In the same Piazza is an antique Statue, bearing the name of Q. Flavio Maesio Egnatio Lolliano: and not far distant is the Temple dedicated to *the Sun*, under the name of *Jupiter Serapis*,[3] a magnificent edifice erected during the sixth century of Rome; but partly thrown down and completely buried by an earthquake, till the year 1750 of the Christian era, when it was fortunately discovered by a peasant, who espied the top of one of the columns a few inches above ground; in consequence of which, an excavation was begun, and the temple displayed to view, almost entire: indeed, had those parts which were thrown down by the earthquake been restored to their proper places, this building would have exhibited the most perfect, and one of the noblest vestiges of antiquity yet discovered — but, alas, the Kings of Spain and Naples, instead of restoring, or even leaving things in the state wherein they were found, have taken away columns, statues, all, in short, that they deemed worth

---

[1] Παυσις της λυπης, the ancient appellation given to this part of the environs of Naples, means *a cessation from sorrow*: and no spot can exhibit more cheerful beauty than does the hill of Posilipo.

[2] Δικαιαρχια.

[3] This name is probably derived from two Hebrew words denoting *the burning fire, or substance.* — See PARKHURST's *Hebrew Lexicon*, 7th edit. 8vo. p. 346.

The Temple of Jupiter Serapis is seen to peculiar advantage by torch-light.

removal: neither have they excavated sufficiently, as the front of the principal entrance does not appear to be yet unburied: enough, however, meets the eye, to form one of the most interesting objects imaginable. This temple is a hundred and thirty-four feet long, by a hundred and fifteen feet wide, its form being quadrangular. Its pavement consists of beautiful marbles, with which the whole edifice appears to have been lined: three of its columns alone remain standing; and these have been robbed of their capitals: each shaft is one solid piece of cipollino. Four flights of marble steps led to the middle part of the Temple; which part was sixty-five feet in diameter, and of a circular form; and near the site of one of the flights of steps are two rings of Corinthian brass, to which the victims destined for slaughter were probably fastened: the receptacles for their blood and ashes still remain; as do the bathing rooms for the priests, which are nearly perfect. The quantity of water in and about this Temple, added to the circumstance of there being, within its walls, upward of thirty small apartments, several of which resemble baths, induce a belief that the Sick and Infirm resorted hither, to bathe in consecrated water, which the priests provided; obtaining, no doubt, thereby, a considerable revenue.[1]

Not having time to visit the Amphitheatre of Pozzuoli, we embarked in our little vessel, and examined *the Piers of the ancient Mole,* a magnificent work, supposed to have been constructed by the Greeks, and repaired by the Roman Emperors, and to which Caligula joined his bridge of boats. Then leaving, on the right, Monte Nuovo (formed A.D. 1538, in thirty-six hours, by a volcanic explosion,)[2] we landed at the *Lucrine Lake,*[3] between which and the Lake Avernus,[4] Agrippa opened a Canal of communication, forming of both *the Julian Port.* Hence we proceeded to the Lake Avernus, the Tartarus of Virgil, described in the sixth book of the Æneid; and once so noxious, that if birds attempted to fly over it, they dropped down dead.[5] We observed on its banks *the ruins of a Temple,* supposed to have been dedicated either to Proserpine or Pluto; and then walked, through a shady and beautiful path, to *the Grotto of the Cumæan Sibyl,* which led from Virgil's Tartarus to the Cocytus, Acheron,[6] Styx, Elysium, etc. Through this Cavern (the Grotto of Posilippo in miniature), we walked, preceded by men carrying lighted torches, till we came to what are called

---

1 The water adjoining to this temple is now used for medicinal purposes.

2 The earthquake which produced Monte Nuovo ingulphed the village of Tripergole, filled up great part of the Lucrine Lake, and probably destroyed the oyster-beds for which it was celebrated by the Latin poets.

3 According to Pliny, a dolphin, during the reign of Augustus, frequented this Lake; and was rendered so tame by a boy, that he would sit upon the fish's back, and actually cross the Lake in this manner.

4 Supposed to be the crater of an extinct volcano.

5 Ancient historians assert that no fish could exist in this Lake: at present, however, it abounds with fish; and many aquatic birds not only fly over it, but repose unhurt upon its bosom. It was originally called *Aornos;* a Greek word, which means *without birds.*—See LUCRET. lib. vi.

6 The Acheron was the *Palus Acherusia* of the ancients; called by Virgil, from the blackness of its water, *Palus Tenebrosa.* The Lake of Fusaro is situated on the *Palude Acherusia;* and, at certain seasons, a Traiteur resides near the Lake, and supplies Travellers with dinner.

the Sibyl's Baths, which consist of three small Chambers adorned with Mosaics, but now nearly filled two feet deep with water, so that we were obliged to mount our donkey by turns, in order to penetrate them: having accomplished this, we sent the donkey by land to Bauli; re-embarking ourselves, and rowing to *Nero's Villa*, where we landed again, to visit the *Vapour Baths*, which are, however, so intensely hot, that it is imprudent to examine them from motives of mere curiosity. They are used by the Neapolitans during summer; and the water here boils an egg in two minutes. On re-embarking for Baiæ, we observed *other Hot Baths*, which belonged to Nero's Villa; and *the steps* which led from that edifice to the sea; together with the *Ruins of Cæsar's Villa*, situated upon the north point of the Bay of Baiæ. Here we again quitted our boat, and walked to *the Temple of Venus Genitrix*, a beautiful ruin, the outside of which is octagonal, the inside circular. The Garden immediately behind this temple contains chambers, called *La Camere di Venere*, which exhibit remains of stucco Ornaments finely executed; and adjoining to these chambers are *Ruins of Public Baths*. Hence we proceeded to *the temples of Mercury and Diana Baïana*; the first of which is a circular edifice, nearly perfect, with an aperture in its dome similar to that of the Pantheon: the second is a fine ruin; and appears to have been hexagonal without; but, like the temple of Venus, circular within. Some writers imagine these three temples, as they are now called, made part of the public Baths. Getting again into our boat, we saw *the Villa of Marius, and the Piscinæ of Hortensius*; the foundations of which may still be discerned under water; and then, re-landing at Bauli, ascended to *the Villa of Lucullus*, where Tiberius expired. The substructions of this Villa, and the celebrated *Reservoir*, called *Piscina Mirabile*,[1] consisting of forty-eight piers, merit observation; as does the neighbouring *Cape of Misenum*, whose harbour contained the Roman Fleet, commanded by Pliny the Elder, at the time of that eruption of Vesuvius which buried Herculaneum, Pompeii, and Stabiæ. Misenum was the principal Port of the Romans in the Tyrrhene sea, as Ravenna was in the Adriatic; and from the summit of the hill on which stand the ruins of the Villa of Lucullus, we had a fine view of the former Port, the Stygian Lake (for such, according to Virgil, is the Mare morto, or third basin of this harbour), and the Elysian Fields,[2] situated on the banks of the Mare morto. Returning from the summit of the hill, we visited the *Cento Camerelle*, supposed to have been a prison; and consisting of a large number of small subterranean apartments vaulted, and lined with plaster. After seeing what appears to have been the Guard-rooms, we descended into the Vaults, by the aid of torches; and then walked back to the Ma-

---

[1] This building contained Reservoirs of purified water, for the use of the Roman Fleet: which water, from being purified ere it entered the reservoirs, was not liable to become putrid when kept in barrels.

[2] The Elysian Fields are supposed to have been a Roman burial-ground for persons of opulence.

rina di Bauli; observing, on our way, a double row of *Columbaria;* and visiting, lastly, what is called *Il Sepolcro d'Agrippina;* though, probably, it was a Corridor of the Theatre which belonged to her Villa, for, according to Tacitus, she was privately buried, after having been killed by order of Nero; and the identical spot which enclosed her remains is unknown.[1]

Having refreshed ourselves with a cold dinner, which we brought from Naples, we embarked for Pozzuoli; and, on arriving there, ordered our carriage to be got ready, while we visited *the Amphitheatre*. This edifice has suffered considerably from earthquakes; but is, nevertheless, better preserved than any other ancient structure at Pozzuoli. Its form is an oval of two storeys high; its arena is about a hundred and ninety feet long, by a hundred and thirty feet wide; the walls of the building are composed of large square stones; and the number of spectators it contained was forty-five thousand. Near this spot is a subterranean Ruin, called *Il Laberinto di Dedalo;* but, more probably, a Reservoir for the water used in the amphitheatre.[2]

EXCURSION TO CUMÆ, ETC.

Again we left Naples at nine in the morning, in a carriage hired for six hours: and, on arriving at the gate of Pozzuoli, engaged a Cicerone, with whom we proceeded to *the Solfatara;* in order to see the process of making alum, vitriol, and sal-ammoniac, from the volcanic substances found in the crater. We then visited *Cicero's Villa,* of which a Wine-Cellar alone remains; the stately porticos and spacious gardens described by Pliny, being all swept away by the hand of Oblivion. Cicero called this Villa *The Academia,* from having composed his Academic Questions here; and in this Villa died the Emperor Adrian; to whose memory Antoninus Pius erected a stately Temple to serve the purpose of a tomb. Proceeding toward the Arco Felice, we were presented with an interesting and picturesque view from the banks of the Lake Avernus, comprehending Monte Nuovo, the Temple supposed to have been dedicated either to Proserpine, or Pluto; the Lucrine Lake, with part of Baiæ, Misenum, Capri, etc., and previous to arriving at the Arco Felice we discovered traces of *the Aqueduct* which conveyed water to Cumæ, and the neighbouring Villas. *The Arco Felice,* or *Gate of Cumæ,* served also for a Citadel and an Aqueduct; and its summit, if the day be clear, exhibits a fine view of the Circeau Promontory, and the Islands of Ischia, Ponza, and

---

[1] Many persons extend this excursion by visiting *the Theatre of Misenum,* of which part of the Proscenium, the Declivity for Seats, and the Corridors remain; and by likewise visiting the *Grotta Traconara,* a vast reservoir under the Promontory, and *the Fish-ponds of Lucullus* under its western side. Pliny says, the fishes in these Reservoirs, belonging to the Roman Villas at Baiæ, were so tame that they fed out of the hand, and when called by their feeders leaped out of the water; that each fish knew its name; and that several of them were adorned with necklaces and ear-rings.

[2] Our expenses during this excursion were as follow:—
Carriage, piastres, 3. Buona-mano to coachman, carlini, 3. Boat with four oars, piastres, 3. Cicerone, piastre, 1. Temple of Jupiter Serapis, carlini, 2. Baths of Nero, ditto, 4. Camere di Venere, ditto, 2. Cento Camerelle, ditto, 2. Piscina Mirabile, ditto, 2. Donkey and Guide, ditto, 10.
It is not necessary to have a boat with four oars, unless the party be large.

Vandolena; the last of which was the ancient *Pandataria*, whither Julia was banished. Remains of *the Via Consularis,* leading from Pozzuoli to Cumæ, are discoverable on each side of the Arco Felice; after passing through which, and turning to the right, we observed a Ruin, called *the Temple of the Giants*, because some colossal statues were found within its walls; here likewise are considerable remains of the Cumæan Aqueduct. We proceeded next through what appears to have been *one of the Streets of Cumæ,* to *the Castle;* which, judging from the large stones that compose it, was a Grecian work; and which, during the fifth century, when Alaric, King of the Westragoths, subdued this country, was in such good condition that he deposited the spoils of his conquests here, as a place of strength. After examining this Ruin, we ascended the Hill above it; where, according to Virgil, Dædalus alighted, after his flight from Crete, consecrated his wings to Apollo, and built a temple to that god: but the only antiquities now remaining here are *Baths* and *Reservoirs* for water. From the summit of this hill the Acheron is discoverable toward the south; and about four miles northward stands *the Torre di Patria,* on the site of the ancient *Liternum*, whither Scipio Africanus retired, and where he died. After descending from the height which exhibits this prospect, we visited a Grotto, called that of the *Sibyls Cumea and Cumana;* and then returned to Naples by the Lake of Fusaro. The last-named Grotto is supposed to communicate with that on the margin of the Lake Avernus; and contains *an ancient Staircase*, leading to several *ancient Baths*.[1]

EXCURSION TO THE LAKE D'AGNANO, ETC.

We hired a carriage for four hours; drove to the village immediately beyond the Grotto of Posilipo; inquired for the keeper of the Grotto del Cane; and told him we were going thither; first, however, stopping at *the Lago d'Agnano*, once the crater of a volcano, as appears by its form; and likewise by the volcanic substances that compose its environs. On the bank of this Lake are *some remains of a Villa which belonged to Lucullus,* who opened a communication between the sea and this lake; converting the latter into a Reservoir for fish. Contiguous to the ruins of this Villa are *the Vapour Baths of S. Germano,* frequented, during summer, by persons afflicted with the rheumatism. Hence we proceeded to *the Grotto del Cane*, the mephitical air of which throws a dog into convulsions, extinguishes a lighted torch, and prevents a pistol from going off: but the first being a cruel experiment, we contented ourselves with witnessing the two last. Our next object was the *Pisciarelli;* a rivulet of boiling water, issuing from the base of the cone of the Solfatara, and, in distance, about a mile from the Lago d'Agnano. This water boils an egg in eight minutes, and is strongly impregnated with alum and vitriol; the latter of which preponderates to such a degree as to produce ink, when mixed with

---

[1] To the Cicerone who attended us during this excursion we gave ten carlini; he furnishing torches for the Grotto of the Sibyls.

galls. Every little aperture in the earth round this hill exhibits sulphur crystallized, sal-ammoniac, vitriol, etc. Having satisfied our curiosity here, we proceeded to *Astroni*, a romantic crater of an extinct volcano, now converted into a royal hunting park. The crater is walled round at its summit (to prevent the game it contains from escaping), and computed to be about four miles and a half in circumference. The interior part exhibits solid lava, scoriæ, tufo, pumice, and other productions usually found in active volcanos.[1]

EXCURSION TO CASERTA, ETC.[2]

Caserta is about sixteen miles from Naples, and so near to modern Capua that, by sleeping at the latter town, we made this excursion on our way from Naples to Rome. On arriving at Caserta we ordered a pair of fresh horses to take us to *the Aqueduct*, which is about five miles further off; and near three hours must be employed in order to see it well, and return to Caserta. The hill we ascended on our way, exhibits an extensive and beautiful prospect of the Campania Felice. On arriving at *the Aqueduct*, the Keeper conducted us along the top of part of that structure; showing us the course of the water at one of the turrets. Hence we descended through the passages of the two loftiest rows of arches, and proceeded to the centre-arch, to read the inscriptions; afterward taking a more distant view of this magnificent work, which extends twelve miles in a straight line, and twenty-six computing its sinuosities. Charles III. erected it, employing as his architect the Cav. Vanvitelli. On our return to Caserta we visited *the Palace*, built likewise by Vanvitelli, at the command of Charles III.; and deemed, in point of size and architecture, the most splendid royal residence existing: its form is rectangular; its length seven hundred and forty-six feet, its breadth five hundred and seventy-six, and its height one hundred and thirteen feet. The great Court or entrance to this edifice is five hundred and seven feet in length, and particularly magnificent; so likewise is the great Staircase. The Vestibule to the chapel, and the Chapel itself, highly merit notice; and the latter contains, in the royal gallery, a fine picture by Mengs. The large Theatre is adorned with twelve columns of basalt, taken from the Temple of Jupiter Serapis, and may vie, in point of size and splendour, with several of the public theatres of Europe: but the royal apartments in this palace, though vast, and beautifully proportioned, are so ill furnished as to be little worth attention. On our way to modern Capua we passed through what is supposed to have been *the ancient town*, and observed a *sepulchral Monument* on the left, and another on the right; the latter being low, and of a circular form, with niches for cinerary urns.[3] *The remains of the Amphitheatre* likewise lie on the right, close to the road; and the exterior Wall, the colossal Busts in the key-stones of the arches, the three Corridors, the

---

1 To the Keeper of the Grotto del Cane and Vapour-baths we gave six carlini; and to the Keeper at Astroni two carlini.

2 It is not necessary to carry a cold dinner to Caserta, the inn there being tolerably good.

3 Remains of a *Crypto-Porticus* are supposed to be discoverable on this side of the road.

four principal Entrances, the declivity for the Seats, the Staircases and Arena, are all discoverable. Between this Amphitheatre and modern Capua are *remains of an Arch*, supposed to have been one of the Gates of the ancient town; which, if this be its site, was situated four miles from Caserta, and one mile and a half from modern Capua, between the rivers Volturno and Clanio.

EXCURSION TO VESUVIUS.

Wishing to see a slight eruption of Vesuvius, which happened in November 1818, we hired a carriage to go to Resina (five miles distant from Naples); took with us a basket of cold meat, bread, and wine, together with six torches;[1] and set out five hours before sun-set. When arrived at Resina, we drove to the house of Salvatore, the best Cicerone of the mountain; and after dismissing our carriage, and giving directions that it should be ready again in seven hours at the same place, to convey us home, we requested Salvatore to provide us with mules, guides, and one *chaise-à-porteur*, and likewise to undertake to pay the guides himself; that we might not be importuned for more than the proper price, namely, each donkey and guide one ducat, and each *chaise-à-porteur*, with eight men, six ducats. To the Cicerone it is customary to give from twelve to fifteen carlini.[2] From Resina to the Hermitage on Vesuvius our mules conveyed us in two hours; and, after resting a short time, proceeded with us for about half an hour longer; when we dismounted, and were either carried in the *chaise-à-porteur*, or walked up toward the crater. This walk was extremely fatiguing, and occupied a full hour: but when we reached the little plain on Vesuvius, our labours were richly recompensed by the sight of five distinct streams of fire issuing from two mouths, and tumbling wave after wave, slowly down the mountain, with the same noise, and in the same manner, as the melting Glaciers roll into the Valley of Chamouni: indeed, while I contemplated this awful and extraordinary scene, I could have fancied myself transported to the base of the Montanvert, had it not been for the crimson glare and excessive heat of the surrounding scoriæ.

After resting ourselves some time, we descended, by a path knee deep in ashes, to the spot

---

[1] These torches are eighteen grani each, if bought at Naples; and three carlini each, if bought at Resina.

[2] Persons who ascend and descend Vesuvius by daylight usually give, for each donkey and guide, eight carlini; for each *chaise-à-porteur*, with six men, four ducats; and to the Cicerone twelve carlini. Sometimes, however, six piastres are demanded for a *chaise-à-porteur* during the night, and four piastres during the day.

Persons who wish to see what is called *The Grotto*, on Vesuvius, should provide themselves with a cold dinner, and set out from Naples about nine in the morning for the house of Salvatore, at Resina; thence proceeding on donkeys to the Hermitage; and, after dining there, proceeding again on donkeys to the Grotto, about an hour's ride, on a good road. Donkeys cannot go nearer than the foot of the hillock on which the Grotto is situated: persons, therefore, who resolve to examine this curious production of Vesuvius, must walk about a quarter of a mile up a very steep ascent. When I made this excursion, I returned, after examining the Grotto, to the Hermitage; where I remained, till it became quite dark, viewing the eruptions of the mountain, and then walked down to Resina by torch-light. I paid for my donkey and guide twelve carlini; for wine, and the use of a room with a fire, twelve carlini; and to the Cicerone twelve carlini for himself, and six for the use of his torches.

where we had left our mules; thence proceeding, on foot, till within a short distance of the Hermitage; when we mounted the mules, and returned to Resina.

It is advisable for persons who ascend Vesuvius to provide themselves with strong boots, and stout walking sticks; unless they resolve to be carried the whole way in chairs; which, though practicable, is expensive.

EXCURSION TO HERCULANEUM, AND THE MUSEUM AT PORTICI.

Herculaneum was situated about five miles from Naples: and the present descent into this entombed city is at Resina. We took wax torches with us; because the Cicerone seldom provides a sufficient number: and we likewise put on thick shoes, and wrapped ourselves up; because the air of Herculaneum is damp, and the pavement wet in several places. This city, according to Dionysius of Halicarnassus, was founded by Hercules.[1] The Alexandrian Chronicle mentions it as having been built sixty years before the siege of Troy; Pliny and Florus speak of it as a great and flourishing city; and some authors conjecture that it was the Capua whose luxuries ruined Hannibal's army.[2] Dion Cassius gives the following account of its destruction, which happened on the twenty-fourth of August, in the year seventy-nine. "An incredible quantity of ashes, carried by the wind, filled air, earth, and sea; suffocating men, cattle, birds, and fishes, and burying two entire cities, namely, Herculaneum and Pompeii, while their inhabitants were seated in the theatres." The people of Herculaneum, however, must have found time to escape; as very few skeletons, and very little portable wealth, have been discovered in those parts already excavated. Some quarters of the city are buried sixty-eight feet deep in ashes and lava; others above a hundred. This seems, from Dion Cassius, to have been the first great eruption of Vesuvius that the Romans witnessed; though there undoubtedly were volcanos in the adjoining country, from ages immemorial. The last named author says, that the ashes and dust ejected by Vesuvius darkened the sun at Rome; and were carried by the wind to Egypt: and Giuliani asserts, that during the eruption of 1631, the ashes were carried to Constantinople in such quantities as to terrify the Turks. The spot where Herculaneum stood was not ascertained till the beginning of the last century; but, about the year 1713, a peasant, while sinking a well at Portici, found several pieces of ancient mosaic, which happened to be at that time sought for by the Prince d'Elbeuf, who was building a house in the neighbourhood. The Prince, wanting these fragments of marble to compose a stucco in imitation of that used by the Ancients,[3] purchased, of the peasant, a right to search for them; on doing which, he was recompensed with a statue of Hercules, and another

---

[1] Perhaps founded in honour of the Sun; as the word *Hercules* appears to be derived from a Hebrew compound, meaning *universal fire*, and allusive to the attributes of the sun.

[2] The Via Appia having passed through it, is, I believe, one reason for this conjecture.

[3] The first coat of ancient stucco appears to have been made of small pieces of brick, or marble, mixed with pozzolana and lime.

of Cleopatra: this success encouraged him to proceed with ardour, when the architrave of a marble gate, seven Grecian statues, resembling Vestals, and a circular Temple, encompassed by twenty-four columns of oriental alabaster on the outside, the same number within, and likewise embellished by statues, were the reward of his labour: in short, the produce of these excavations became considerable enough to attract the attention of the Neapolitan Government: in consequence of which, the Prince d'Elbeuf was commanded to desist; and all researches were given up, till the year 1736; when Don Carlos, on becoming King of Naples, wished to build a palace at Portici; and purchased, of the Prince d'Elbeuf, his lately erected house, together with the ground whence he had taken so many valuable antiquities. The King now made an excavation eighty feet deep, and discovered buried in the earth an entire city; together with the bed of a river which ran through it, and even part of the water: he also discovered the Temple of Jupiter, containing a statue reputed to be gold; and afterward laid open the Theatre, directly over which the peasant's well was found to have been sunk. The inscriptions on the doors of this Theatre, fragments of bronze horses gilt, and of the car to which they belonged (decorations probably of the grand entrance), together with a considerable number of statues, columns, and pictures, were now brought to light: but, nevertheless, in the year 1765, not more than fifty labourers were employed in making these valuable excavations; in 1769, the number was reduced to ten; and, in 1776, to three or four. Resina (anciently *Retina*) and Portici being built immediately over Herculaneum, the workmen could not venture to excavate as they would have done had the surface of the earth been less encumbered; consequently the plans of Herculaneum and its edifices are not accurate: it is, however, ascertained that the streets were wide, straight, paved with lava, and bordered with raised footways; that the buildings are composed of tufo and other volcanic substances; the interior walls adorned with frescos, or stained with a deep and beautiful red colour; the architecture Grecian, and, generally speaking, uniform. The rooms in private houses were small, and either paved with mosaics, or bricks three feet long, and six inches thick. It does not appear that the generality of the people had glazed windows; though some excellent plate glass has been found in Herculaneum; but almost every window seems to have been provided with wooden shutters, pierced so as to admit light and air. The most considerable edifice yet discovered is a Forum, or Chalcidicum. This building seems to have been a rectangular court, two hundred and twenty-eight feet long, and encompassed with a portico supported by forty-two columns: it was paved with marble, and adorned with paintings. The portico of entrance was composed of five arcades, ornamented with equestrian statues of marble; two of which, the celebrated Balbi, have been already described. Opposite to the entrance, and elevated upon three steps, was a statue of the Emperor Vespasian; and on each side a figure in a curule chair: in the wall were niches adorned with paintings, and bronze statues of Nero and Germanicus: there likewise were other statues in the portico. This Forum was connected, by means of a colonnade, with two Temples, in form rectangular; and one of them a hundred and fifty feet long; the interior part being ornamented with columns, frescos and inscriptions in bronze; and near these edifices was *an open Theatre*, capable of containing ten thousand spectators, and the only building now discoverable; all the other excavations having been filled up. By a passage close to the Peasant's Well we descended into *this Theatre*. The front of the stage seems to have been decorated with columns, statues, etc., all of which are taken away, two inscriptions excepted. The Proscenium was found entire; and is a hundred and thirty feet long. Part of the stage, and the base of one of the columns of flowered alabaster, with which it was adorned, were likewise discovered; and in front of the stage, according to De la Lande, were bronze statues of the Muses. Fragments also were found of bronze horses, supposed to have decorated the top of the wall which terminated the seats. All, however, which we were able to discern was the Stage, the Orchestra, the Consular Seats, and Proscenium; together with the Corridors or lobbies; some parts of which exhibit beautiful Arabesques, and Stucco stained with the dark red colour already mentioned: we likewise saw the impression of a human Face on the ceiling of one of the lobbies. This theatre appears to have been lined with Parian marble, and built about the same time with that at Verona, after the designs of Numisius.

Persons who are fearful of encountering a damp and oppressive atmosphere, should not venture down into Herculaneum; especially as there is, in the Studii, a model of this city; which, in its present state, apeared to us more calculated to appal than please; particularly when we heard the carriages at Portici rolling over our heads like thunder, and felt conscious of being buried ourselves eighty feet deep in lava.[1]

From Herculaneum we proceeded to *the Museum at Portici;* which, being a part of the royal Palace, cannot be seen without an order from the Lord High Steward. This Museum consists chiefly of Paintings found in Herculaneum and Pompeii: and judging from the beauty of the composition, and the unskilfulness of the execution, many persons think that several of them are copies, done by common house-painters, from the most renowned pictures of antiquity. The composition of Apollo and the Muses (now, I believe, in Paris), is said to be so exquisite, that were an artist to study for years he could not change any one fold in the drapery to advantage; and the execution is said to be so bad, that more than an hour could not have been employed upon each figure.[2] The subjects of the most celebrated

---

[1] We gave six carlini between the two Guides who accompanied us down into Herculaneum.

[2] The pictures found in Herculaneum and Pompeii, except those done on marble, and now in the Studii at Naples, were all painted on the walls of private houses and public edifices; and, according to the opinion of

Paintings are supposed to be—Dido abandoned by Æneas!—the seven days of the week, represented by the seven planets—Theseus with the Minotaur dead at his feet—Hercules and Telephus—Telephus suckled by a deer, or Latinus, son of Faunus, King of the Aborigines, an allegorical painting relative to the origin of the Romans—the Centaur, Chiron, teaching Achilles to strike the lyre, ascribed to Parrhasius; though, more probably, copied from a work by that artist!—Hercules strangling the serpents sent by Juno to destroy him—Iphigenia discovering Orestes—Orestes and Pylades chained, and conducted, by the soldiers of King Thoas, before the statue of Diana—a Parrot drawing a car, and a Grasshopper driving; supposed to be a copy from Zeuxis, who was famous for these whimsical subjects!—a Faun and a Bacchante—small pictures of Rope-dancers, Bacchantes, etc., one of whom holds a musical instrument used by the Neapolitans to this day—a Bacchante carried off by a Centaur—another Centaur carrying off a Youth—small paintings representing Children engaged in various occupations—quadrupeds, birds, fishes, fruits, etc.—a female Centaur with a Nymph (Zeuxis is supposed to have invented female Centaurs)—a female Centaur and a Youth; she holds a cymbal of gilt bronze; the thrones of Mars and Venus, with their attributes, are in the same picture!—Boys making wine; this painting exhibits an ancient wine-press—Boys engaged in other occupations—a Naval Combat, ill done, but curious, because it exhibits ancient galleys, and the mode of fighting them—a Landscape with trees, and a temple; in the centre of which last is a buckler ornamented with the head of Medusa; it being an ancient custom to suspend votive bucklers in public edifices—an Egyptian landscape—a Crocodile hunt—Crocodiles and Hippopotami—(from the latter, says Pliny, man learnt the art of bleeding himself, as this animal, when too full of blood, presses its foot against pointed reeds, by which means the operation is performed)—The education of Bacchus, supposed to be the copy of a fine original!—Iphigenia ready for sacrifice, supposed likewise to be the copy of a fine original!—a Bacchanalian ceremony, in which three figs are offered to the god; the number three being sacred, and typical among the heathens—a garden;

Winckelmann, not much more ancient than the Augustan age—at which period Painting was in its wane. This art, though the offspring of Sculpture, did not take birth till after its parent had reached maturity; for the Jupiter of Phidias, and the Juno of Polycletes, deemed *chefs-d'œuvre* of Sculpture, existed before the invention of Painting. Apollodorus and his disciple Zeuxis, who flourished in the fifteenth Olympiad, were the first painters who distinguished themselves in the style called *clair-obscur:* and Euphranor, the contemporary of Praxiteles, and consequently posterior to Zeuxis, is supposed to have enriched the growing art by the introduction of symmetry, shading, and perspective. Painting, nevertheless, made a much slower advance toward perfection than did Sculpture: because the latter, from its birth, became a necessary appendage to heathen worship; whereas the former did not acquire the privilege of entering consecrated edifices till after it had reached its meridian. In course of time, however, some of the Grecian temples became Pinacothecæ; and, at Rome, the works of celebrated painters were exhibited in the Temple of Peace: but it does not appear that the pictures of heathen deities were ever adored like their statues; and, consequently, there is reason to suppose that Painting, from want of the same encouragement, did not arrive, in ancient days, at the same height of perfection with Sculpture.

(it is curious to observe in this and other pictures that the ancient Roman gardens were precisely what Italian gardens are now.)—Four pictures in one, namely, a hare and a fowl, a pheasant and two apples, three birds and some mushrooms, two partridges and three fishes: (the hare, by ancient epicures, was deemed the best quadruped, and the thrush the best bird)—Diana! —a Citharist, supposed to be Sappho, near whose left ear is a flower, the sign of a lady of pleasure—Hylas and Ganymede, the latter of whom holds a fan of peacock's feathers, which fans were used by the great people of antiquity to chase away flies; and are still carried in grand processions at Rome, to hinder those troublesome insects from annoying the Pope—a Woman looking at herself in a mirror of yellow metal (Pliny, however, mentions mirrors of green glass, the first of which was made at Sidon: Nero had an emerald mirror. The Roman ladies are said to have carried these mirrors always about them; it likewise appears that they used false hair, false teeth, false eye-brows and eye-lashes, pomatum, rouge, and white paint; and they frequently stained their hair.)—A young Female with light hair, the sign of a lady of pleasure—Bacchus—the Grecian horse brought into Troy—markets, shops, and schools, situated under porticos, as was the custom in Greece and Rome—a two-wheeled carriage, for the conveyance of baggage, with a postilion on one of the horses, a mule saddled, and a blind man conducted by a dog—a man riding one, and guiding three horses—(the Romans frequently used to ride two, and even four horses at once, leaping from one to the other with extraordinary agility.)—Five Etruscan Priests, three of whom are crowned with tiaras, the High Priest's being gold—Peace or Peleus, supposed to have invented the poniard—a Female seated, with two lyres and a garland, the lyre being significant of harmony, union, and conjugal love, perhaps because the Muse Erato is said to have instituted marriage—a theatrical representation of a Man in a scoffing mask making horns, and showing them to a woman who hides her face; this was the custom of the Greeks—two paintings of theatrical representations, in one of which is a Youth in a *half-mask;* the only thing of the kind yet discovered—a Poet, supposed to be Æschylus, dictating a drama to the tragic Muse— Psyche and a winged Genius, with a shoe on his head and another in his hand, both resembling ours of the present day—an Egyptian temple—the worship of Osiris— a caricature of the Cæsars, representing Æneas, his father and son, as impure deities with dogs' heads. Drawing in caricature seems to have been common among the ancients, who frequently compared men to, and represented them under the forms of, beasts.[1]

Several of these paintings have lately been removed to the Studii at Naples; whither, according to report, it is the intention of the Neapolitan Government to remove the whole.

---

[1] The Custode of this Museum expects from three to six carlini, according to the size of the party he attends.

EXCURSION TO POMPEII.

We made the same bargain with respect to our carriage as when we went to Caserta; for though Pompeii is only thirteen miles and a half distant from Naples, the latter excursion requires more time than the former. We took with us a cold dinner, wine, plates, knives, forks, glasses, etc. as nothing, except water, can be procured at Pompeii. The road lies through Portici, Torre-del-Greco, and Torre del Annunziata; in the way to the first of which, is the Ponte Maddalena, under whose arches passes the Sebeto, anciently *Sebethus*. The commencement of this drive exhibits gardens and vineyards of the most luxuriant description: but, near Torre-del-Greco, almost the whole country has been laid waste by streams of lava, which, during the summer of 1794, destroyed that town and its vicinity. Vesuvius had for some time ceased to vomit fire and smoke as usual; a circumstance that generally presages mischief: and late in the evening of Thursday, June the 12th, the inhabitants were alarmed by a sudden and violent shock of an earthquake, which was thrice repeated, continuing each time about three minutes and as many seconds. This first calamity produced a general consternation; insomuch that the people fled from their houses into their gardens, and thence to the seaside, where they passed the night in dreadful alarm. Next morning processions of men, women, and children were seen barefooted in the streets of Naples, proceeding to the Cathedral, to implore the protection of S. Gennaro. From Thursday till Sunday the weather was tempestuous, the air hot, loaded with vapours, and, at intervals, suddenly darkened for some minutes; during which period there were several slight shocks of an earthquake, attended by a rumbling sound, like distant thunder. On Sunday evening the inhabitants were again alarmed by a noise so violent that it resembled a continual discharge of cannon; when, in a moment, burst forth a volcano, not in the crater on the summit of Vesuvius, but toward the middle of the mountain on the western side. The explosion made every edifice tremble in Torre-del-Greco, which is only five horizontal miles from this new volcano, at whose mouth issued a column of smoke, that continually mounted, and increased in magnitude, till it formed itself into the shape of an immense pine. This column was sometimes clearly distinguished; and at others obscured by ashes: it continued augmenting rapidly in circumference, till at length it began to decline downward; when, from the quantity of dense matter which composed the column being much heavier than the air, the former, of course, fell to the ground. Torrents of flaming lava, of a portentous magnitude, now poured down the mountain, principally in two directions; one stream, of about a mile in breadth, bending its destructive course toward Torre-del-Greco, a town said to contain eighteen thousand persons, the other taking the direction of Resina; while several small rivulets of liquid fire were observed in divers places. Torre-del-Greco soon fell a prey to the lava; which, in its progress, desolated the whole hill leading down from Vesuvius, sweeping away every house, so that the terrified inhabitants were compelled to abandon their all, and take refuge in Naples. At length, the lava, after three hours' devastation, ran into the sea; on whose banks, for one-third of a square mile, it raised itself a bed from fifteen to twenty Neapolitan *palmi*[1] above the level of the water, and as much, if not more, above the level of the streets of Torre-del-Greco. The reflection from this torrent of lava illuminated the whole city of Naples, and filled its inhabitants with dread; while the other torrent, which flowed toward Resina, on arriving at the gate, divided itself into three streams, one running between the gate and the Convent de' Padri Francescani; the second to the Piazza; and the third to the Convent del Carmine, near Torre del Annunziata. Wherever the lava ran it covered the country with a crust from twenty to thirty *palmi* deep: in and about Resina it left, for a short time, some few isolated buildings, namely, the Palazzo-Brancaccia, the Chiesa de' Marinari, and the Convent de' Francescani; but these soon caught fire; and five women, with one old man, after vainly ringing the church and convent-bells for assistance, saved themselves by flight. The Palazzo-Caracciolo now fell a prey to the flames, as did every other building in the neighbourhood of Resina, till the whole surrounding plain exhibited one vast sheet of lava. The town of Torre-del-Greco likewise was completely buried; some few tops of the loftiest buildings excepted; while every part of the country through which the lava ran became a desert; the trees being thrown down, the houses razed, and the ground, for many miles distant, covered with cinders and ashes; which last lay about one finger deep in Naples. On the sixteenth of June the air was so dense as nearly to obscure the mountain; but, next day, the fire made itself new channels; which circumstance might, probably, be the preservation of several fine buildings near Resina.[2]

The approach from Torre del Annunziata to Pompeii is through the Suburb anciently called *Pagus Augustus Felix*, and built on each side of the Via-Appia, which, from the commencement of this Suburb to the Herculaneum-Gate, is flanked by a double row of Tombs.

Pompeii appears to have been

---

1 A Neapolitan *palmo* is rather more than ten English inches.

2 I cannot dismiss this subject without mentioning an extraordinary circumstance which occurred at Pienza, near Siena, just before the destruction of Torre-del-Greco. Professor Santi of Pisa (a gentleman whose name I have already mentioned) resided at Pienza when this circumstance happened; and to him I was obliged for the following particulars, which may serve to rescue many ancient historians from the reproach of credulity.

On the 16th of June a dark and dense cloud was discovered at a great height above the horizon, coming from the south-east, that is, in the direction of Vesuvius, which may be about two hundred horizontal miles distant from Pienza. At this height the cloud was heard to issue noises like the discharge of several batteries of cannon; it then burst into flames; at which moment fell a shower of stones for seven or eight miles round; while the cloud gradually vanished. These stones are volcanic, being composed of grey lava, resembling what is found on Vesuvius; and Mr. Santi, who took infinite pains to investigate this phenomenon, felt confident that the cloud rose from Vesuvius, which was at that moment disgorging fires whose force and effects cannot be calculated: it could not have arisen from Radicofani; because, though this mountain is one continued mass of volcanic rocks, which bespeak it the offspring of subterranean fire, and though it has been sometimes visited by dreadful earthquakes, still neither history nor even tradition records that it ejected flames, smoke, or vapour, at any period whatsoever.

populous and handsome: it was situated near the mouth of the Sarnus (now called Sarno), and the walls which surrounded the city were above three miles in circumference, and are supposed to have been originally washed by the sea, though now about one mile distant from its margin. Pompeii (as already mentioned), was buried under ashes and pumice-stones, and at the same time deluged with boiling water, during the year 79, and accidentally discovered by some peasants in 1750, while they were employed in cultivating a vineyard near the Sarno. The excavation of Herculaneum was attended with much more expense than that of Pompeii, because the ashes and pumice-stones which entombed the latter were not above fifteen feet deep, and so easy was it to remove them, that the Pompeians who survived the eruption of the year 79, evidently disinterred and took away a large portion of their moveable wealth; though, generally speaking, they seem to have made no efforts toward repairing the mischief done to their houses; an extraordinary circumstance, as the roofs only were destroyed.[1] The most interesting parts, hitherto restored to light, of this ill-fated city, have been disinterred by the French, who uncovered its Walls, Amphitheatre, Forum-Civile, Basilica, and adjoining Temples, together with the double row of Mausolea, on the outside of the Herculaneum-Gate. Still, however, several streets remain buried, but excavations are going on daily; and, were a thousand labourers employed, it is supposed that the whole town might be uncovered in a twelvemonth.

The streets are straight, and paved with lava, having on each side a raised footway, usually composed of pozzolana and small pieces of brick or marble. The Via Appia (which traverses the town, and extends to Brundusium,) is broad, but the other streets are narrow; carriage-wheels have worn traces in their pavement, and judging from these traces, it appears that the distance between the wheels of ancient carriages was not four feet. The houses hitherto excavated are, generally speaking, small; most of them, however, were evidently the habitations of shopkeepers: but those few which belonged to persons of a higher class, were usually adorned with a vestibule, supported by columns of brick, each house possessing an open quadrangle, with a supply of water for domestic purposes in its centre; and on the sides of the quadrangle, and behind it, were baths and dressing-rooms, sitting-rooms, bed-chambers, the chapel which contained the Lares, the kitchen, larder, wine-cellar, etc., none of which appear to have had much light, except what the quadrangle afforded, there being, toward the streets, no windows. The walls of every room are composed of tufo and lava, stuccoed, painted, and polished, but the paintings in the large houses are seldom superior in merit to those in the shops; perhaps, however, the ancient mode of painting houses, like that now practised in Italy, was with machines called *stampi*; which enable the common house-painter

---

[1] Suetonius says, that Titus endeavoured to repair the devastation made by Vesuvius at Pompeii: but, if he succeeded, subsequent eruptions demolished his work.

to execute almost any figure or pattern upon fresco walls. The ceilings are arched, the roofs flat, and but few houses have two stories. The windows, like those in Herculaneum, appear to have been provided with wooden shutters, and some of them were furnished with glass, which seems to have been thick and not transparent, while others are supposed to have been glazed either with horn or talc. Every apartment is paved with mosaics; and on the outside of the houses, written with red paint, are the names of the inhabitants, with their occupations, including magistrates, and other persons of rank: so that if the stucco on which these names were written had been well preserved, we should, at the present moment, have known to whom each house in Pompeii originally belonged. All the private houses are numbered: and on the exterior walls of public edifices are proclamations, advertisements, and notices with respect to festivals, gladiatorial shows, etc. The public edifices were spacious and elegant, and the whole town was watered by the Sarno, which seems to have been carried through it by means of subterranean canals.

I will now mention the objects best worth notice, as they lie contiguous to each other.

Villa of Diomedes. The first building disentombed at Pompeii was this Villa, the skeleton of whose master, Marcus Arrius Diomedes, was found here, with a key in one hand, and gold ornaments and coins in the other. Behind him was found another skeleton, probably that of his servant, with vases of silver and bronze; and in three subterranean Corridors, which appear to have been used as cellars, seventeen skeletons were discovered, one of which, adorned with gold ornaments, is conjectured to have been the mistress of the Villa, and the others her family. This edifice has two stories. On the ground-floor are several rooms nearly in their original state, as are the Garden and the Cellars, the first of which is surrounded with Colonnades, and has a Pergola and a reservoir for water in its centre; the latter, wherein the seventeen skeletons were found, contain wine-jars, filled with, and cemented to the walls by ashes. The upper story exhibits Paintings, mosaic pavements, hot and cold Baths, with Furnaces for heating water. Part of the ancient Roof of this Villa is likewise preserved: and, on the opposite side of the Via Appia, are the Tombs of the Family of Diomedes.[1]

Building appropriated to the Silicernium after funerals. This is a small Structure (on the right, between the Villa of Diomedes and the Herculaneum-Gate); its interior was stuccoed and adorned with paintings (now obliterated) of birds, deer, and other ancient emblems of death; it contains a Triclinium, or eating table, whereon the Silicernium, or funeral repast, was served.[2] There are places for three mattresses round this table, and in the wall was a recess, where probably the bust

---

[1] One of the apartments in the Villa of Diomedes has windows looking toward the garden.

[2] A Triclinium means the place where the Greeks and Romans reposed on mattresses while they ate; and was so called because it held three mattresses only.

of the deceased might be exhibited to the guests. The recess is now destroyed.

Repository for the ashes of the dead. This edifice, wherein the ashes of persons who had not private tombs are supposed to have been deposited, has, on its summit, an ornament shaped like an altar, and adorned with *bassirilievi* emblematical of death.

Semicircular roofed Seat. On the left side of the Via Appia is a deep Recess, decorated with stucco ornaments: it seems to have been a covered seat for foot-passengers; and here were found the skeletons of a mother with her infant in her arms, and two other children near her. Three gold rings (one being in the form of a serpent), and two pair of ear-rings, enriched with fine pearls, were found among these skeletons. Opposite to this semicircular seat, and at a small distance from the Via Appia, are ruins of a Villa supposed to have belonged to Cicero.

Inn. This appears to have been a large building, provided with horses, carriages, etc.; and situated on the outside of the city, because Strangers were not permitted to sleep within its walls. Remains of the wheels of carriages, the skeleton of a donkey, and a piece of bronze, resembling a horse's bit, were found here.

Columbarium, called the Tomb of the Gladiators. This Sepulchre, which stands on the right of the Via Appia, particularly merits notice; because its interior is perfect, and contains a considerable number of places (shaped like pigeon-holes) for cinerary urns.

Semicircular Seat, not roofed. On the back of this Seat is the following inscription, in capital letters; as, indeed, are all the inscriptions at Pompeii: " MAMMIÆ P. F. SACERDOTI PVBLICAE LOCVS SEPVLTVRAE DATVS DECVRIONVM DECRETO." Behind the Seat stands the Tomb of Mammia, which appears to have been handsomely built, and elegantly ornamented. Further on, near the Herculaneum-Gate, is another semicircular Bench; and to the left of the Via Appia, on the outside of the Gate, is a Path leading to a Sally-Port; by the steps of which it is easy to ascend to the top of the Ramparts.

Herculaneum-Gate. There were four entrances to Pompeii, namely, the Herculaneum-Gate; the Sarno, or Sea-Gate; the Isiac-Gate, (so called because near the Temple of Isis); and the Nola-Gate: all of which entrances were apparently devoid of architectural decorations, and composed of bricks, stuccoed. The Herculaneum-Gate is divided into three parts: the middle division, through which passes the Via Appia, is supposed to have been for carriages; and one of the side entrances, for foot-passengers coming into the city; while the other was appropriated to foot-passengers going out of it. The Via Appia is about twelve feet wide, and composed of large volcanic stones of various shapes and sizes, fixed deep into a particularly strong cement. The footways on either side of this street are between two and three feet in width.

Post-House. This is the first Building on the right, within the Gate: and as Augustus established posts, or what was tantamount, on all the Consular roads, making Pompeii one of the stations, this building probably was a Post-House: several pieces of iron, shaped like the tire of wheels, were found here. In a House on the opposite side of the way are a Triclinium, and some Paintings which merit notice.

Building commonly called a Coffee-House;[1] *but more probably a Thermopolium, or Shop, for hot medicated potions.* Here we find a Stove; and likewise a marble Dresser, with marks upon it, evidently made either by cups or glasses; and consequently the contents of these cups, or glasses, when spilt, must have been (as medicated draughts frequently are) *corrosive.* On the opposite side of the Street is a House which, according to an inscription nearly obliterated, belonged to a person named Albinus: and several amulets, representing birds, tortoises, dolphins, and other fishes, in gold, silver, coral, and bronze, were found here.[2] Adjoining is another Thermopolium.

House of Caius Ceius. This Edifice, which stands opposite to a Fountain, and is now occupied by Soldiers, appears to have contained public Baths. Not far distant is an Edifice, adorned with a Pavement of fine marble, and a good Mosaic, representing a Lion. This quarter of the town likewise contains subterranean Structures, wherein the citizens of Pompeii are supposed to have assembled, during very hot or rainy weather, to transact business. This description of building was called a Crypto-Porticus; and usually adorned with columns; and furnished with baths and reservoirs for water.

House called the Habitation of the Vestals. Here, according to appearance, were Three Habitations under the same roof; and likewise a Chapel, with a place for the sacred fire in its centre; and, in its walls, three Recesses for the Lares. On the Door-sill of one of the apartments is the word, "SALVE" *(Welcome)*, wrought in mosaic: another Door-sill is adorned with two Serpents, also wrought in mosaic. A room of very small dimensions has, in the centre of its pavement, a Labyrinth, or table for playing at an ancient game; and the pavement of another room exhibits a Cornucopia. The skeletons of a man and a little dog were found here: and in the apartment called the *Toletta,* several gold ornaments for ladies were discovered. Not far distant is an edifice which appears to have been an Anatomical Theatre; as upwards of forty chirurgical instruments, some resembling those of the present day, and others quite different, were found within its walls.

Ponderarium, or *Custom-House.* Here were found a considerable number of weights, scales, and steelyards, similar to those now in

---

1 Coffee is a native of Africa, supposed to have been unknown to the Greeks and Romans; and not being mentioned by any European writers engaged in the Crusades, it seems to have been equally unknown in Syria, during the thirteenth and fourteenth centuries. It is found wild, from Caffa, the south province of Narea, in Africa, to the banks of the Nile; and was first brought from Arabia into Europe about the middle of the fifteenth century. It was used at Grand Cairo early in the sixteenth century; and first mentioned in the West of Europe by a German traveller, who returned from Syria in 1573. Pietro della Valle, a Venetian, says, in a letter of his, that he intended bringing some of it to Venice, where he thought it was unknown. This berry, which has now made its way through the whole civilized world, was first brought into France during the year 1644; and in 1671 a coffee-house was opened at Marseilles. In 1652, Daniel Edwards, an English merchant, brought with him, from Turkey, a Greek servant who understood the method of roasting and making coffee; and this servant was the first person who sold it publicly in London.

2 The Ancients wore amulets round their necks, to preserve themselves from witchcraft.

use at Naples; together with one weight of twenty-two ounces, representing the figure of Mercury. Near the Ponderarium is an Edifice which, judging by the materials discovered there, seems to have been a Soap-Manufactory; and not far distant are two Shops for hot medicated potions.

Public Baking-House. This Building contains an Oven; together with Mills for pulverizing corn. Shops of a similar description abound in Pompeii.

Wine and Oil Shop. The Vessels which contained wine and oil may still be seen here, and in many other Shops of the same kind. Here likewise are Stoves; with which these Shops seem usually to have been furnished; perhaps for the purpose of boiling wine.[1]

House of Caius Sallust. Contiguous to the Wine and Oil Shop is one of the largest Houses yet discovered at Pompeii; and, according to the Inscription on its outside-wall, once the abode of Caius Sallust. Here is a Triclinium, with places where mattresses appear to have been spread for the family to lie down while they ate. This Triclinium is in the back part of the House; and, in another part, is a tolerably well preserved picture of Diana and Actæon; and likewise a small room, paved with African marbles, and adorned with a picture of Mars, Venus, and Cupid, well preserved, and executed in a style much superior to the generality of frescos found at Pompeii. In the Lararium, or Chapel for the Lares, a small statue was discovered; as were some coins, and a gold vase, weighing three ounces: bronze vases likewise were found in this house: and four skeletons, five armlets, two rings, two ear-rings, a small siver dish, a candelabrum, several bronze vases, and thirty-two coins, were found in its vicinity.

Academy of Music. This Edifice appears to have been spacious; and its Quadrangle is ornamented with a painting of two Serpents twined round an Altar, above which is a Lararium. The large rooms exhibit paintings representing musical instruments; and a piece of iron, which apparently belonged to a musical instrument, was discovered here.

House of Pansa. This is a good house, handsomely decorated with marbles and mosaics. In the centre of its Quadrangle are a Well and a small Reservoir for fish; and in its Kitchen a Fire-Place, resembling what we find in modern Italian kitchens, and Paintings representing a spit, a ham, an eel, and other eatables. Here were found several culinary utensils, both of earthenware and bronze; and not far hence is a Shop, wherein a variety of colours, prepared for fresco-painting, were discovered.[2]

Forum Civile. This is a very large oblong Piazza, which appears to have been bordered with magnificent Porticos, supported by a double row of tufo and travertino columns, and paved with marble. One entrance to this Forum is through two Archways, the use of which is not apparent. Beyond the second Archway on the left, are remains of a Temple, supposed to have been consecrated to Jupiter, because a fine head of that heathen deity was found

---

[1] The Ancients, according to Claverius, were in the habit of boiling their wines.

[2] These Colours are now placed in the Studii at Naples.

there. Several steps, now shaken to pieces by earthquakes, lead to the Vestibule of this Temple, which seems to have been quadrilateral, spacious, and handsome, and its Cella is elegantly paved with mosaics.¹ On the right of these Ruins stands the Temple of Venus, exhibiting beautiful remains of its original splendour. The shape of the edifice is quadrilateral; its dimensions are large, and its walls adorned with paintings. The Cella, which stands on fifteen steps, is paved with mosaics; and in a contiguous apartment is a well-preserved painting of Bacchus and Silenus. Here likewise is a small Recess, supposed to have been a Lararium. The lower part of the Temple contains a Herma, resembling a Vestal, together with an Altar (or perhaps the basis of the statue of Venus), which seems to have slid from its proper place, in consequence of an earthquake. The steps leading to the Cella have the same appearance, and all the edifices in this part of Pompeii must have suffered more from the earthquake which preceded the eruption of the year 79, than from that eruption itself, as the repairs going on at the very moment of that eruption evidently prove. Beyond the Temple of Venus, and fronting the Via Appia, stands the Basilica, or principal Court of Justice, a majestic structure, of a quadrilateral form, in length a hundred and ninety feet, and in breadth seventy-two. The walls are adorned with Corinthian pilasters; and the centre of the building exhibits a double row of Corinthian columns, twenty-eight in number. The Tribunal for the judges, which stands at the upper end of the Court, is considerably elevated, and has, immediately beneath it, a subterranean apartment, supposed to have been a prison. In the court, and fronting the Tribunal, is a large Pedestal, evidently intended to support an equestrian statue: and on an outside wall of this structure (that wall which fronts the house of Championet), the word "BASILICA" may be discovered, in two places, written with red paint. Beyond the Basilica, and fronting the Temple of Jupiter, are three large edifices, supposed to have been dedicated to public uses, and that in the centre was evidently unfinished, or repairing, when buried by the eruption of 79. On the side of the Forum, and opposite to the Basilica, are edifices resembling Temples; one of which, supposed to have been consecrated to Mercury, contains a beautiful Altar, adorned with *bassi-rilievi* representing a sacrifice. Marbles of various sorts, apparently prepared for new buildings, together with a Pedestal which seems, from the inscription it bears, to have supported the statue of Q. Sallust, and another Pedestal, inscribed with the letters " C. CVSPIO C. F. PANSÆ," occupy the centre of the Piazza: and, judging, from marks in the pavement, the entrance to this Forum was occasionally closed with gates of bronze or iron.²

House of Championet, so called because excavated by a French

---

1 Behind the Archways near this Temple are paintings representative of Mars and Juno; a circumstance which induces some persons to suppose it was consecrated to the latter.

2 Antiquaries conjecture, that immediately after the eruption of the year 79, the inhabitants of Pompeii disentombed the Forum Civile, and took away all its best statues and other decorations; a circumstance which would easily account for the small number of moveable treasures found there by modern excavators.

General of that name. This Habitation appears to have suffered considerably from the earthquake of the year 63: it has a Vestibule paved with mosaics, and, in the centre of its quadrangle, a Reservoir for the rain-water which fell on its roof; this Reservoir appears to have had a covering. At the back of the house is another Vestibule: and under the sitting-rooms and bed-chambers (all of which are paved with mosaics, and more or less decorated with paintings), are subterranean Offices, a rare thing at Pompeii. Skeletons of females, with rings, bracelets, and a considerable number of coins, were found in this house.

Crypto-Porticus, and Chalcidicum, built by Eumachia. In the Via Appia, and near the Forum Civile, over the entrance to what seems to have been a covered passage, is the following inscription:

" Eumachia. L. F. Sacerd. Publ. Nomine Suo et M. Numistr. I Frontonis. Fili. Chalcidicum Cryptam Porticus Concordiæ Augustæ Pietati sua Pecunia Fecit Eademaque Dedicavit."

Just beyond this Passage, and leading to what appears to have been a Chalcidicum, is the Statue of a Female in a Vestal's dress, with the following inscription on the pedestal:

" Eumachiæ. L. F.
Sacerd. Publ.
Fullones."

This statue still remains on the spot where it was discovered in the summer of 1820; and, judging from the inscription, it seems that Eumachia, a public Priestess, built, at her own expense, in her own name, and that of another person, a Chalcidicum and Crypto-Porticus, and likewise paid for having them consecrated to the use of the Pompeian washerwomen, by whom, as a token of gratitude, her statue was erected. The Chalcidicum (a spacious Piazza), was adorned with Colonnades elevated on steps, some parts of which are cased with white marble, and other parts unfinished: but the marble slabs, prepared for casing the unfinished parts, were discovered on an adjacent spot, where they may still be seen. The centre of the Chalcidicum evidently contained a large sheet of water, in which were several Washing-Blocks, cased with white marble; these Blocks, and the Channel through which the water was conveyed into this spacious basin, still remain, as does a small Temple, fronting the Forum Civile, from which there seems to have been an entrance into the Chalcidicum.[1]

Continuation of the Via Appia. On each side of this Street are Shops and other buildings, which exhibit the names and occupations of the persons by whom they were once inhabited: these names, etc., written with red paint; and the Wall, fronting the Via Appia, and belonging to the Chalcidicum, displays the ordinances of the magistrates, the days appointed for festivals, etc., likewise written with red paint. Here are Bakers' Shops, containing Mills for pulverizing corn; Oil and Wine Shops; a House adorned with pictures of heathen divinities; and another House elegantly painted, and supposed to have belonged to a Jeweller. In this Street, and likewise in other

---

[1] The Tomb of Eumachia stands just beyond the Walls of Pompeii, near the Herculaneum Gate, and appears to have been erected by the public.

parts of the town, are several Fountains, which were supplied by water brought in a canal from the Sarno: and at the lower end of the Street, near the Portico leading to the Tragic Theatre, was found, in 1812, a skeleton, supposed to be the remains of a Priest of Isis, with a large quantity of coins, namely, three hundred and sixty pieces of silver, forty-two of bronze, and eight of gold, wrapped up in cloth so strong as not to have perished during more than seventeen centuries. Here likewise were found several silver vases, some of them evidently sacrificial, and belonging to the Temple of Isis; small silver spoons, cups of gold and silver, a valuable cameo, rings, silver *bassi-rilievi*, etc.

Portico ornamented with six Columns of Tufo. The Capitals of the Columns which supported this Portico appear to have been handsome, and its front, according to an inscription on a Pedestal that still remains, was adorned with the statue of Marcus Claudius Marcellus, son of Caius, Patron of Pompeii. The statue, however, has not been found. Beyond this Portico is a long Colonnade, leading to the Tragic Theatre.

Temple of Hercules. This Edifice, apparently more ancient than any other Temple at Pompeii, is said to have been thrown down by the earthquake of the year 63,¹ rebuilt, but again demolished in 79. The ruins prove, however, that it was once a stately Doric structure, which stood on a quadrilateral platform, with three steps on every side leading up to it. The platform still remains, and is ninety feet long, by about sixty feet wide. Traces of gigantic Columns also remain; and beyond the Platform, and nearly fronting the east, are three Altars: that in the centre is small, and probably held the sacred fire; those on the sides are large, low, and shaped like sarcophagi: the latter kind of altar, called *Ara*, being, when sacrifices were made to the terrestrial deities, the place on which the victim was burnt.² Behind these Altars is a Receptacle for the sacred ashes; near the Temple is a Burial-place, and on the left, a semicircular Bench, decorated with lions' claws carved in tufo: it resembles the seats near the Herculaneum Gate.

Upper entrance to the Tragic Theatre. This wall has been restored, and, beyond it, are steps leading down to the Postscenium of the Tragic Theatre; and likewise to the Forum Nundinarium; so called because a market was held there every ninth day. Not far hence was the great Reservoir of the water of the Sarno, which supplied the lower part of the city, and particularly the Forum Nundinarium.

Tribunal, or *Curia of Pompeii.* This is an oblong Court, surrounded by Porticos; and containing a Rostrum, built of peperino, with steps ascending to it. Tribunals were usually placed near Forums and Theatres: and this Tribunal is supposed to have been erected by a family who likewise built at their own expense the Tragic Theatre, and a Crypto-Porticus, in order to adorn the Colony.

---

1 This earthquake is mentioned by Seneca.
2 The Altare, so called because *high*, was the place where sacrifices were offered to the celestial deities.

Temple of Isis. It appears, from an inscription found here, that this edifice was thrown down by the earthquake of 63, and rebuilt by Numerius Popidius Celsinus. It is sixty-eight feet long by sixty feet wide; in good preservation, and peculiarly well worth notice: for to contemplate the altar whence so many oracles have issued, to discern the identical spot where the priests concealed themselves, when they spoke for the statue of their goddess, to view the secret stairs by which they ascended into the Sanctum Sanctorum; in short, to examine the construction of a Temple more Egyptian than Greek, excites no common degree of interest.[1] This Temple is a Doric edifice, composed of bricks, stuccoed, painted, and polished. The Sanctum Sanctorum stands on seven steps (once cased with Parian marble), its form being nearly a square: its Walls, which are provided with niches for statues, display, among other ornaments in stucco, the pomegranate, called, in Greek, *Roia*, and one of the emblems of Isis. The pavement is Mosaic. Here, on two altars, were suspended the Isiac Tables: and two quadrangular basins of Parian marble, to contain the purifying water, were likewise found here; each standing on one foot of elegant workmanship, and bearing this inscription: "Longinus ii Vir." On the high altar stood the statue of Isis; and immediately beneath this altar are apertures to the hiding-place for the priests; contiguous to which are the secret Stairs. The lower end of the Temple, fronting the Sanctum Sanctorum, contains the Altars whereon victims were burnt; together with the Receptacles for their ashes, and the Reservoir for the purifying water. A figure of Harpocrates was found in a niche opposite to the high-altar.[2] Other parts of the Temple contain small altars, a Kitchen, in which were found culinary utensils of *cretacotta* (containing ham-bones and remains of fishes), together with the skeleton of a priest leaning against the wall, and holding in his hand a hatchet. Here also is a Refectory, where the priests were dining at the moment of the eruption which entombed their city; and where chickens' bones, eggs, and earthen vessels were discovered: burnt bread was likewise found here; together with the skeletons of priests who either had not time to make their escape, or felt it a duty not to abandon their goddess. When this Temple was excavated, its walls exhibited paintings of Isis with the sistrum, Anubis with a dog's head, priests with palm-branches and ears of corn, and one priest holding a lamp;[3] the Hippopotamus, the Ibis, the lotus, dolphins, birds, and arabesques. Most of these, however, have been removed to Naples; as have the statues of Isis, Venus, Bacchus, Priapus, and two Egyptian idols, in basalt, which were likewise found here. Sacrificial vessels of every description, candelabra, tripods, and couches for

---

[1] The traffic between the Pompeians and Alexandrians is supposed to have given rise to the worship of Isis at Pompeii.
[2] A profound silence was observed during Egyptian sacrifices.
[3] The priests in these paintings are represented with heads shaved, garments of white linen, and woven shoes, through which the feet were seen. History, however, tells us that the priests of Isis were obliged to walk barefooted.

the gods, were also discovered in this Temple.¹

Not far hence is an Edifice, which, judging by the rings of iron found in its walls, was probably the Receptacle for beasts destined to be slain on the Isiac altars.

Temple of Æsculapius. The centre of this little building contains a large low Altar, made with tufo, and shaped like a sarcophagus. The Cella is placed on nine steps; and seems, if we may judge by the traces of columns still discernible, to have been covered with a roof. Here were found statues of Æsculapius, Hygeia, and Priapus, all in *creta-cotta.*

Sculptor's Shop. Several statues were discovered here; some being finished, others half finished, and others only just begun. Several blocks of marble, and various tools, now preserved in the Neapolitan Academy of Sculpture,² were likewise discovered here.

Comic Theatre. This Edifice, built of tufo, and supposed to have been the Odeum for music, is small, but nearly perfect; and was covered with a roof resting upon columns, between which were apertures for light. Here are the places for the Proconsul, and Vestals; the Orchestra,³ the Proscenium, the Scenium, and the Postscenium; together with all the Benches and Staircases leading to them, for male spectators; and another Staircase, leading to the Portico, or Gallery, round the top of the Theatre; in which Gallery the females were placed. The Orchestra is paved with marble, and exhibits the following Inscription in bronze capitals:

"M. OCVLATIVS M. F. VERVS II VIR PRO LVDIS."

and on the outside of the edifice is another Inscription, mentioning the names of the persons at whose expense it was roofed.⁴

Two admission tickets for theatrical representations have been found at Pompeii: these tickets are circular, and made of bone; on one of them is written "ΑΙΣΧΥΛΟΥ;" and above this word is marked the Roman number, XII., with the Greek corresponding numerical letters, IB, beneath it. The other ticket is numbered in a similar manner, and likewise marked with the name of a Greek poet; both tickets having, on the reverse side, a drawing, which represents a theatre.⁵ The Odeum seems to

---

1 One of these couches was made of ivory, and too much injured to admit of reparation: the other, made of bronze, has been restored; and is now placed in the Museo-Borbonico, at Naples.

2 This Academy is under the same roof with the Museo-Borbonico.

3 The orchestra (ορχεισθαι) of the Greeks is supposed to have been what, in modern Continental theatres, we call the parterre; the Proscenium seems to have been what we denominate the orchestra; the Scenium was the stage; and the Postscenium the place where the machinery of the theatre was prepared for exhibition, and where the actors dressed.

4 Roofed theatres were not common among the Ancients, whose theatrical representations appear to have been exhibited by daylight.

5 Augustus, in order to prevent confusion with regard to places for the audience in theatres, decreed that all the different ranks of persons, in the respective cities of the Roman empire, should be provided with tickets, specifying the part of the theatre, and the number of the seat they were entitled to occupy. This circumstance is related by Suetonius. The arrangement of the audience was as follows:—Persons of Consular rank and Vestals, being few in number, occupied the two shortest lines of seats, close to the orchestra, and sat on portable chairs: Knights, being likewise few in number, compared with Plebeians, occupied the shortest lines of stone benches (these were immediately behind the portable chairs); Plebeian men occupied the uppermost, and consequently the longest, lines of stone benches; while the Female part of the audience, Vestals excepted, were commanded by Augustus to occupy the portico, or gallery; near which stood the Officers appointed to keep order.

have suffered from the earthquake of 63.

Tragic Theatre. This edifice, which stands upon a stratum of very ancient lava, is much larger than the Odeum; and, in point of architecture, one of the most beautiful buildings in Pompeii. It was composed of tufo, lined throughout with Parian marble; and still exhibits the Orchestra, the Proscenium, the Stage; the Marks where Scenes, or a Curtain were fixed; the Podium on the right of the Orchestra for the chief magistrate, where a curule chair was found; the Podium on the left, for the Vestals, the benches for patricians and knights, in the lower part of the Cavea, and those for plebeians, in the upper part; the Entrance for patricians and knights; the Entrance and Stairs for plebeians; the Gallery round the top of the Theatre, for ladies; which Gallery appears to have been fenced with bars of iron (as the holes in the marble, and the remains of lead, used for fixing the bars, may still be discovered); the Stairs of entrance to this Gallery, and the Blocks of Marble projecting from its Wall, so as to support the wood-work, to which, in case of rain or intense heat, an awning was fastened.[1] The Stage, judging by the niches that still remain, appears to have been adorned with statues;[2] the Proscenium is enclosed by dwarf walls, and divides the stage from the Orchestra and seats appropriated to the audience. This stage, like those of modern days, is more elevated at the upper than the lower end; very wide, but so shallow, that much scenery could not have been used; although the ancients changed their scenes by aid of engines with which they turned the partition, called the *scena,* round at pleasure. There are three entrances for the actors, all in front; and behind the stage are remains of the Postscenium.

This Theatre stands on the side of a hill, according to the custom of the Greeks; and on the summit of this hill was an extensive Colonnade (already mentioned), destined, perhaps, to shelter the spectators in wet weather; and likewise to serve as a public walk; the view it commands being delightful.

The Comic and Tragic Theatres stand near each other, and contiguous to a public Building surrounded with Colonnades, and supposed to have been

The Forum Nundinarium. This Forum is of an oblong shape, and bordered by Columns of the Doric order, without bases; the materials of which they are composed being tufo stuccoed, and painted either red or yellow, as was the general practice at Pompeii. These Columns still exhibit figures in armour, and names of persons, traced, no doubt, by the ancient inhabitants of this Forum to while away their vacant hours. Within the Colonnades are Rooms of various dimensions, supposed to have served as Shops and Magazines for merchandize; some of the largest being about fifteen feet square: and above these rooms was a second story, which appears

---

[1] The Campanians invented awnings for theatres, to shelter the audience from the rays of the sun: but were, in consequence, called effeminate; a character which still seems appropriate to them.

[2] The partition between the dressing-rooms and the stage was called the *Scena;* and decorated with statues, columns, etc. for a tragedy; and, for a comedy, with cottages, and other pastoral objects.

to have been surrounded with wooden balconies. In one room was found an apparatus for making soap; in another a mill for pulverizing corn; and in another an apparatus for expressing oil. On the eastern side of this Forum were stalls for cattle; and in the Prison, or Guard-house, were found skeletons in the stocks, armour, and the crest of a helmet adorned with a representation of the siege of Troy.[1] The square contains a Fountain of excellent water, a small ancient Table, and likewise a large modern Table, shaded by weeping willows, so as to make a pleasant dining-place in warm weather.[2]

Amphitheatre. In the centre of a spacious Piazza (probably a Circus for chariot-races), stands this colossean Edifice; which, when disentombed, was so perfect that the paintings on the stuccoed wall surrounding the Arena appeared as fresh as if only just finished: but, on being too suddenly exposed to the air, the stucco cracked, and fell off; so that very few paintings now remain. The form of this Amphitheatre is oval; the architecture particularly fine; and a handsome Arcade, once embellished with statues, the niches and inscriptions belonging to which still remain, leads down to the principal entrance. This Arcade is paved with lava, and the statues it contained were those of C. Cuspius Pansa, and his Son. The Amphitheatre rests upon a circular subterranean Corridor of incredible strength, as it supports all the seats. An iron railing seems to have defended the spectators who sat in the first row: and the entrances of the Arena appear to have been defended by iron grates. The walls of the Podium, when first unburied, displayed beautiful paintings; but, on being exposed to the air, they were destroyed, like those in the Arena. Above a flight of steps leading to the upper seats is a *basso-rilievo* (in marble), which represents a charioteer driving over his opponent; and above the seats is a Gallery, which was appropriated to female spectators: it encircles the top of the edifice; and commands a magnificent prospect of Vesuvius, Castel-a-mare, the site of Stabiæ, the mouth of the Sarno, and the beautiful Bay of Naples: and in the upper part of the circular Wall of this Gallery are Blocks of Stone, pierced to receive the Poles which supported the awning.[3]

Near the northern entrance to the Amphitheatre are remains of a Building furnished with a Triclinium; and therefore supposed to have been the Silicernium belonging to the edifice.

City Walls. Pompeii was fortified by double Walls built with large pieces of Tufo; one Wall encompassing the city, the other passing through the centre of a ditch, made to strengthen the fortification: and between these Walls is the broad Platform of

---

[1] Ancient Forums were always guarded by soldiers; and therefore the place wherein the stocks and armour were found most probably was the Guard-house.

[2] The model of the Stocks, the Skulls of the persons whose skeletons were found in them, and some of the half-finished Sculpture discovered in the Statuary's Shop, are kept here.

[3] Skeletons of eight lions, and one man, supposed to have been their keeper, were, according to report, discovered in this Amphitheatre.

the Ancients, which, at Pompeii, seems to have been twenty feet in breadth. The Walls were about twenty feet high; some parts consisting of smooth stones, from four to five feet square, and apparently not joined by any cement; though placed with such skill as to resemble one entire mass: while other parts are ill built, with rough stones of various shapes and sizes; and were, perhaps, hastily piled together after the destructive earthquake of the year 63. Curious Characters are engraved on some of those stones. The Walls were fortified with low square Towers; and the four Gates of the City stood at right angles.[1]

No Traveller should neglect an opportunity of visiting Pompeii; which exhibits, even now, one of the most interesting objects in the known world: and when first disentombed, when skeletons were seen in the houses; when lamps, candelabra, glass of various kinds and shapes, ornamental vases, culinary utensils, and even the very bread of the suffocated inhabitants were discernible; when the Temples were filled with statues of heathen deities, and adorned with all the elegant and costly embellishments of heathen worship, what a speculation must this city have furnished to a thinking mind!—and though the greater part of its moveable wealth now enriches the royal Neapolitan Museums, still to visit it, even now, is absolutely to live with the Ancients: and when we see houses, shops, furniture, implements of husbandry, etc. etc., exactly similar to those of the present day, we are apt to conclude that customs and manners have undergone but little variation for the last two thousand years. The practice of consulting augurs, and that of hiring persons to weep at funerals, are still kept up in the mountainous and secluded parts of Tuscany; and the Tuscan cattle, when destined for slaughter, are frequently adorned with chaplets of flowers, precisely as the Ancients used to adorn their victims for sacrifice. The Roman butchers, likewise, still wear the dress, and use the knife, of heathen sacrificing priests. The old Roman custom of not eating above one regular meal a day, and that about the ninth hour of Italy (three o'clock with us), is kept up by many of the Italians; and, during the month of May, it is common to see peasants dressed, as in former times, like Pan, satyrs, etc.[2] I do not, however, mean to infer, from what I have said, that the modern Greeks and Italians equal the Ancients in works of art; there being, in this respect, a considerable difference between the present race and their forefathers.[3]

---

[1] The number of skeletons hitherto found in Pompeii and its suburbs is said to be less than three hundred; a small proportion of its inhabitants, if we may judge from an advertisement found on the outside of a large private house, and importing that it was to be let for five years, together with nine hundred shops, all belonging to the same person: and, supposing no mistake to have arisen with respect to the import of this advertisement, how great must have been the trade, and consequent population, of a city where one individual possessed nine hundred shops!

[2] In Tuscany the ancient practice of placing herbs, eggs, and what we call *a whet*, upon the table before dinner, is still kept up at hotels.

[3] Persons who intend to enter Pompeii by the Herculaneum Gate, should, on arriving at the Villa of Diomedes, send their carriage and dinner to the Forum Nundinarium; ordering their driver to be in waiting there an hour before sunset, to convey them to the Amphitheatre, and thence back to Naples. But persons who drive in the first place to the Amphitheatre, and then enter Pompeii by

EXCURSION TO PÆSTUM.

The distance from Naples to Pæstum is computed to be fifty-four miles; and the time employed in going, with a light four-wheeled carriage and four horses, is as follows:—

	Hours.
From Naples to Pompeii	2¾
Salerno	3
Eboli	3½
Pæstum	3

Persons who are restricted for time may accomplish this excursion in two days, by ordering their Voiturin to send forward a relay of horses to take them from Salerno to Pæstum: but the more eligible plan is to sleep the first night at *Eboli;* the second at *Salerno;* and to return on the third day to *Naples.* The former mode of going usually costs from thirty-five to forty piastres for the horses; the latter about thirty.[1] From Salerno to Pæstum there is a cross road, six or eight miles shorter than that which goes through Eboli; but not good, even during summer; and, at other seasons, impracticable. The great road from Naples to Eboli is excellent. Wishing to sleep the first night at Eboli, we set out as early as possible from Naples; and, on entering the valley near the Sea Gate of Pompeii, drove through cotton plantations, watered by the Sarno; thence proceeding to *Nocera,* anciently *Nuceria,* a town of high antiquity;[2] but where nothing now remains worth notice, except *the Church of Santa Maria Maggiore,*[3] which is adorned with an antique Font, for the immersion of adults, similar to that in the Baptistery at Pisa. The Church is of an orbicular form; it contains a double circle of Columns of precious marbles; and seems to have been originally a Temple consecrated to all the gods. From Nocera we drove through a rich vale, exhibiting picturesque scenery, to *La Cava,* a large town with porticos on each side of the high street, like those at Bologna. On quitting La Cava we were presented with a sight of *an ancient Aqueduct,* and *a Villa* which stands amidst hanging gardens at the foot of the Apennine, in a very remarkable situation. We then drove to *Vietri,* built on the side of a mountain in the immense and magnificent Bay of Salerno, and exhibiting views of the most beautiful description. Vietri (which has risen from the ashes of the ancient *Marcina*) is not far distant from Amalfi, the Islands of the Sirens, and the Promontory of Minerva; which all lie toward the right; while, on the opposite side of the Bay, rises the celebrated Promontory of Leucosia, anciently called *Promontorium*

---

the Forum Nundinarium, should send their dinner to the Villa of Diomedes; ordering their carriage thither half an hour before sunset, as visitants are not permitted to remain at Pompeii after the close of day. We gave to our Cicerone here one piastre—to the person who provided us with water, a dinner-table, and benches to sit upon, five carlini—to the Custode of the Temple of Venus, two carlini—and to the Custode of the Temple which contains the newly found Altar adorned with *bassi-rilievi,* one carlino.

1 An English family, consisting of six persons, lately paid, for an open carriage and four horses, only twenty-four piastres, *buonamano* inclusive. They slept the first night at Salerno; paying for supper eight carlini a head, and for beds four carlini a head. The next day they visited Pæstum; remaining there five hours, and then returning to sleep at Eboli; whence they proceeded next morning to Amalfi (a water excursion, which takes up three hours), and the same evening reached Naples.

2 Augustus founded a Roman colony here.

3 Some writers call this church the *Madonna della Vittoria.*

Posidium. From Vietri we drove between the sea and the mountains of the Apennine, richly wooded, and embellished with convents, villages, and ruins of ancient edifices, to *Salerno*, formerly *Salernum;* the approach to which is enchanting. This town, situated about twenty-seven miles from Naples, and celebrated by the poets of the Augustan age for its delightful position, was anciently the capital of the Picentes; and is, at the present moment, a handsome sea-port embosomed in the Gulf to which it gives a name. *The Precincts of the Cathedral* here, and the Church itself, contain some antiquities brought from Pæstum; among which are Columns, apparently of Roman workmanship, two or three Sarcophagi, and the Basin of a Fountain, all placed in the Court before the edifice, and the last fixed the wrong side upward in the wall of the Court. Among the antiquities within the Cathedral are two fine Columns of verde antico, a mosaic Pavement, and two Vases for the purifying water; one of which is adorned with *bassirilievi*, representing the history of Alexander's expedition to India; the other with representations of the pleasures of the vintage. The subterranean Church, beneath this Cathedral, is said to contain the bones of S. Matthew. Salerno boasts a tolerably good Inn, where we breakfasted, at the same time providing ourselves with bread, meat, fruit, wine, water, every thing, in short, which we were likely to require at Pæstum; and being anxious to get thither as soon as possible, we ordered our drivers to take the summer road, instead of going round by Eboli: this road, however, we did not reach for above an hour; but kept on the highway, which traverses a rich and beautiful country, to us rendered doubly interesting by little groups of Calabrian farmers, dressed as Salvator Rosa frequently portrays them, and all armed with short swords and fowling-pieces: some of these people were walking; others riding; others regaling themselves in temporary arbours close to the road; and as the harvest was getting in, when we passed this road, we likewise had the pleasure to observe the Calabrian mode of thrashing corn; which operation is accomplished by means of a small vehicle, shaped like an ancient car, placed on a wooden harrow, and drawn by two oxen: in this vehicle sit two children, or one man, to guide the oxen; who walk round and round a circular paved space, enclosed by a dwarf wall, and strewed with the unthrashed grain; which is continually turned by the harrow, while the animals thrash it with their hoofs. Two or three of these vehicles are frequently employed at the some moment, in each of the above-described enclosures.[1] After proceeding from six to eight miles through this luxuriant and populous country, we observed that the farm-houses gradually diminished in number; till, at length, on our turning off to the right, to take the summer road, they totally disappeared; while the face of the country became wild, melancholy, and like the Pontine Marshes twenty years ago. We also found the soil loose and swampy; and the crazy

---

[1] The smooth thrashing-floors, with cattle working in them, in the open fields of Magna Græcia, are described by Homer.

bridges, made with boughs of trees, and thrown over deep ditches, which we were compelled to cross, frequently endangered our carriage and horses, and obliged us to walk. At length, however, we arrived within sight of *Persano*, a hunting-seat belonging to the King of Naples: but, on learning that the bridge in this neighbourhood, thrown across the Silaro by Murat, was not sufficiently finished for carriages to pass over it, we found ourselves under the disagreeable necessity of fording the river; in order to accomplish which we quitted the Persano road, and turned off a second time to the right, proceeding through woods of tamarisk and clumps of myrtle, till we reached the banks of the Silaro, anciently *Silarus*, and famed, from time immemorial, for the petrifying quality of its waters: when, having with difficulty procured a forder to walk at the head of our horses, we dashed down a sharp descent into the stream, which is by no means narrow, and rather deep; though, during dry seasons, not dangerous: our horses, however, seemed inclined to make it so; for, being much heated, and finding their situation very refreshing, they no sooner got midway through this river, than they stopped short; thus subjecting us to be driven out of our course by the current: indeed the poor jaded animals were with such difficulty induced to proceed, that I began to apprehend we might, like other commodities washed by the petrifying Silaro, be all converted into stone. The strong arm of our forder, however, at length compelled the horses to continue their journey; and after having gained the opposite side of the river, we proceeded, amidst wide desolation, through a vast plain unembellished now with roses,¹ vainly seeking for Pæstum; which, from its peculiar situation, is so difficult to find, that I no longer wonder at its having, when abandoned by its citizens, remained for ages undiscovered: after driving four miles without seeing a single habitation, or any living thing, except one eagle, and several herds of that stupid swinish looking animal the buffalo, we at length approached a small patch of cultivation fenced with hedges of wild vines; when, turning toward the sea, we beheld, about a mile distant from its margin, and encompassed with silence and solitude, three stately edifices; which announced themselves as *the remains of Pæstum*; not, however, such remains as seemed to accord with the effeminate, though finished taste of the rich and luxurious Sybarites—on the contrary, I could not help fancying myself transported to India, and placed before the simply majestic specimens of Hindoo architecture represented by the pencil of Daniel. There is a room in a farm-house, near the Temples, where Travellers who wish for shelter may eat the dinner they bring with them; but its wretched inhabitants can supply nothing except water; and even that is extremely unwholesome; for the aqueducts which once conveyed healthy beverage to the town, are now no more.

---

1 This plain is celebrated by Virgil for its roses that bloomed twice a year (in May and December); but the bushes which produced these flowers are said to have been removed while the kingdom of Naples was under French government.

Travellers should neither sleep at Pæstum, nor approach its environs till an hour after sunrise; neither should they remain within its walls long enough to encounter the dew which falls immediately before sunset: and though, taking these precautions, it may be possible to escape the dangerous effects of *Mal' aria*, even during the months when it is most prevalent, (those of July, August, and September), still I would counsel Travellers to prefer visiting Pæstum in April, May, or October.

This city, supposed to be the ancient *Poseidonia* of a colony of Sybarite adventurers, who, on landing here, found a town, drove its inhabitants to the mountains, and established themselves in their stead, appears, from its name, to have been dedicated to Neptune, called Ποσειδων by the Greeks. The Sybarites, however, were supplanted by the Lucanians; and these by the Romans; under whose dominion Poseidonia assumed the name of Pæstum; and, after having survived the Roman empire in the west, was destroyed by the Saracens about the commencement of the tenth century.[1] Previous to describing the ruins of this venerable city, it seems expedient to remark, that some of these ruins appear to be of much higher antiquity than others; probably because the Sybarites, after having banished and succeeded the original inhabitants, supposed to have been Etrurians, repaired the walls, embellished the temples, and erected baths and other edifices, congenial to the taste of an opulent and luxurious nation: and when Poseidonia fell under the yoke of the Romans, it is natural to imagine they might have introduced Roman architecture.

Walls of Pæstum. These Walls, like those of Pompeii, are composed of very large smooth stones, put together with such nicety, that it is difficult to distinguish where they join;[2] they are two miles and a half in circumference, and nearly of an elliptical form; their height seems to have been about fifty English feet, their breadth, or platform, about twenty, and they were fortified by eight low towers, twenty-four feet square within, and at the windows twenty-three inches thick: these Towers are less ancient than the Walls; and some of the stones which compose them measure five feet in length.

Gates. Pæstum had four Gates, placed at right angles; but that which fronts the east alone remains perfect; it consists of one simple arch, about fifty feet high, and built of stones incredibly massive. On the key stone of this Arch it was easy once to discern two *bassi-rilievi;* the one representing the *Sirena Pestana* holding a rose; the other representing a *Dolphin;* ancient symbols of a maritime people: time, however, has so far obliterated these symbols that I could not discover them. Within the Gate was a second Wall; and between the two are remains of Soldiers' Barracks; and likewise of the ancient Pavement of the city, which re-

---

[1] The temples of Pæstum were visited by Augustus as venerable antiquities, even in his days; but appear, during modern times, to have been totally forgotten, till discovered in 1755 by a young painter of Naples, who once more brought them into public notice.

[2] The Etruscan walls of Fiesole appear to have been of the same description in point of architecture.

sembles that of Pompeii. On the outside of the northern Gate are several vestiges of Tombs, some of which appear to have been lined with painted stucco. Grecian armour, and vases of rare beauty, exhibiting Greek inscriptions, were found in many of them.

Temple of Neptune This Edifice, the most majestic, and apparently the most ancient here, or indeed in any other part of the European world, is composed of stone, evidently created by the torpedo touch of the Silaro: for, like the stone of Tivoli, it consists of wood, and various other substances petrified; and though durable as granite, abounds with so many small cavities, that it resembles cork. The shape of this Temple, supposed to have been consecrated to Neptune, is quadrilateral; its length, out and out, a hundred and ninety-seven English feet; its breadth eighty: it has two fronts, both being adorned with a pediment, supported by six enormous fluted columns. Each side is supported by twelve columns (those in the angles not being counted twice); and a Doric Frieze and Cornice encompass the whole building. The above-named exterior columns, generally composed of six, though, in a few instances, of seven blocks of stone, are in height only twenty-seven feet; their circumference, at the bottom, is twenty feet six inches; but considerably less at the top: and the number of flutings to each column is twenty-four. They have no bases; but rest on the third step of the platform on which the edifice is erected. The capitals are quite simple; and more in the style of Hindoo architecture than any other. Two flights of steps lead to the two Vestibules, each of which is supported by two pilasters with two columns between them; the breadth of each vestibule being eleven feet six inches. The Cella, forty-four feet in breadth, is enclosed by four dwarf walls, and adorned with fourteen columns, disposed in the same manner as the exterior row, but less massive, the circumference at the bottom being only thirteen feet ten inches, and much less at the top; and the flutings to each only twenty in number. The situation of the High-Altar, and those on which victims were sacrificed and offerings made, is discoverable; and it appears that these altars fronted the east. The interior columns support an immense architrave; on which rises another set of still smaller columns; destined, perhaps, to support the roof of the portico: five of these columns remain on one side, and three on the other. Gigantic steps about five feet deep, and three in number, lead up to the platform on which the temple stands, and encompass it on every side.[1] The largest stone of this stupendous edifice contains one way thirteen feet eight inches; another way four feet eight inches; and another, two feet three inches; making, altogether, one hundred and four cubic feet.

I have already mentioned that some authors suppose the Etru-

---

[1] There being only three steps seems extraordinary; because they are so inconveniently deep, it is scarcely possible to ascend them. But as the number three was, as I have already observed, sacred and typical among the Ancients, this might perhaps be the cause why the Pæstum temples are surrounded by three steps only.

rians were originally Cananeans; and if this be admitted, it will appear probable that when they emigrated to the European Continent, their first landing place might be Pæstum: and it seems equally probable that, on landing, they might erect the stupendous Temple I have endeavoured to describe.[1]

Basilica, so called, because no appearance is exhibited here, either of altars or a cella. This Edifice, which stands, like the Temple of Neptune, on a quadrilateral platform, is in length, out and out, a hundred and sixty-eight feet six inches; and in breadth eighty feet six inches: it has two fronts, each being adorned by nine fluted columns without bases; and resting on the third step of the platform; which step is five feet two inches deep. Each side is adorned by sixteen columns (the angular columns not being counted twice), resting, likewise, on the first step of the platform: the circumference of the largest columns, at the bottom, is fourteen feet six inches; and, at the top, much less. Both fronts have a Vestibule; and the interior of the building is supposed to have been divided into equal parts by columns placed in a straight line from one entrance to the other; but only three of these columns now remain; and they do not range with the exterior ones. Where these three columns stand, the pavement seems to have been raised; and probably this spot was appropriated to the magistrates. The Portico, which is supposed to have been appropriated to the common people, measures, in breath, fifteen feet; and the Cross Walk fifteen feet six inches. A Doric Frieze and Cornice adorn the outside of the edifice.

Temple of Ceres. This Temple, supposed to have been dedicated to Ceres, though smaller, and consequently less imposing than that of Neptune, exhibits a lighter and more elegant style of architecture: its form is quadrilateral; its length, out and out, a hundred and eight feet; and its breadth forty-eight. There are two fronts; each being adorned with six columns, which support a magnificent entablature and a pediment. Each side presents twelve columns, supporting a similar entablature; and every column is fluted, and rests, without base, on the third step of the platform on which the temple stands: the diameter of each column is four feet at the bottom; less at the top; and the height thirty feet. At the entrance is a Vestibule, supported by six columns with plain round bases; and beyond are four steps leading to the Cella, which is twenty-five feet wide, and encompassed, on the four sides, by a dwarf wall. The situation of the High-Altar, and of those whereon victims were sacrificed and offerings made, is discoverable; these altars fronted the east. Remains of Sarcophagi

---

[1] An ancient inscription at Palermo is written in Chaldæan characters; and therefore some persons suppose the primitive inhabitants of Palermo to have been emigrants from Chaldæa and Damascus: and if this conjecture be well founded, the Etrurians were more probably of Chaldæan than Cananean origin. Another circumstance merits notice: the inside walls of the most ancient sepulchral monuments at Pæstum exhibit paintings; and we learn from the Prophet Isaiah, that the Chaldæans were in the habit of painting the walls of their apartments.

are likewise discoverable within the precints of this temple; the outside of which is adorned with a Doric Frieze and Cornice; and all its columns, together with those of the Basilica, and the Temple of Neptune, appear to have been stuccoed. The Pavement of these buildings was Mosaic.

Theatre. This edifice is almost totally destroyed; but the fragments of griffons and fine *bassi-rilievi*, which have been found here, evince that it was erected at a period when sculpture was rising fast to its zenith of perfection.

Amphitheatre. This Edifice likewise is nearly destroyed: it appears to have been of an oval form, a hundred and seventy feet wide, by a hundred and twenty long. Ten rows of Seats, and some of the Caves for wild beasts, may still be traced: it stood precisely in the centre of the town.

The great antiquity of Pæstum, and the uncertainty as to what its remaining edifices originally were, and to whom they belonged, brought to my recollection a celebrated Italian sonnet, which may be thus imitated.

" Say, Time—whose, *once*, yon stately Pile," I cried,
" Which, *now*, thou crumblest, ruthless, with the soil?"—
He answer'd not—but spread his pinions wide,
And flew, with eager haste, to ampler spoil.

" Say, then, prolific Fame, whose breath supplies
Life to each work of wonder—what were *those?*"—
Abash'd, with blushes only she replies,
Like one whose bosom heaves with secret throes.

Lost in amaze, I turn'd my steps aside;
When round the Pile I saw Oblivion glide,
    And scatter poppies o'er each vacant shrine:—
" Speak!" I exclaim'd—" for once, mute Nymph, reveal—
Yet wherefore from thy lips remove the seal?—
    Whose *once* it was avails not—*now* 'tis Thine!"

Having dined in the temple of Neptune, and at the same time enjoyed the most delicious and impressive mental feast which European scenery can furnish, we set out to return home by way of Eboli; sending our carriage empty to ford the Silaro, while we walked over the new bridge. We were nearly four hours in driving to *Eboli*; and, as it was quite dark, I can give no account of the road, further than that we found it smooth, and apparently excellent, except the first four miles. We slept at Eboli, where the Inn contains several beds, but an ill-provided larder; and next morning pursued our way to *Salerno.*[1] Wishing to visit *the Benedictine Convent of La Trinità*, near *La Cava*, we stopped at the entrance of that town, and sent for a light carriage and two strong horses, to take us up a rocky mountain of the Apennine, on which the Convent is situated, at the distance of two miles from the high road, and in the mule-path to Amalfi. The ascent to La Trinità presents fine scenery; and the Convent, which is partly hewn out of a rock, and partly built upon it, is spacious even to magnificence; but contains nothing particularly worth examination; as the curious re-

[1] There is at Eboli an inn called *La Rosa Petrilla*, which, though not usually resorted to by Travellers, contains good beds and a tolerably plentiful larder.

cords, once kept there, were removed, when the French suppressed this confraternity. After having seen the Convent of La Trinità, we proceeded to Naples; stopping, however, at *Pompeii*; through which town we walked, while our carriage went round the outside of the walls to meet us at *the Villa of Diomedes:* and, during this walk, we were struck with the similitude of shape and architecture between the Temple of Hercules here, and that of Neptune at Pæstum.

EXCURSION, BY WATER, TO SORRENTO.

Sorrento, anciently called *Syrentum,* from its enchanting situation, and supposed to have been a Phœnician colony, is between five and six leagues distant from Naples; and lies on the left side of the bay, beyond Castel-a-mare, and near Capri. Persons who wish to go and return the same day should set out very early in the morning, it being necessary to allow four hours for rowing to Sorrento; three for refreshing the boatmen; and four for returning.[1] This excursion may be made by land through Castel-a-mare and Vico; but, from the former place to the commencement of the Piano di Sorrento, a distance of six miles, there is only a mule-road.

The Inn at Sorrento being a bad one, Travellers should either provide themselves with a cold dinner when they visit this town, or dine about a mile distant, in the Piano, or Plain, at a Lodging-house called *La Cocomella* (originally a Convent belonging to the Jesuits), or at a neighbouring Lodging-house, near S. Pietro-a-Majella; both of which habitations are rented by a civil and intelligent man, named Guarracino, who furnishes dinners, wine, and beds, either by the night, or for a longer period; and, generally speaking, Travellers find it more pleasant to land on the rocks near the Cocomella than at Sorrento; especially as the path to the former lies through picturesque Caves, now a public bathing place; but supposed to have been, in Homer's days, the Temples of the Sirens: and, if we may judge by their present appearance, more probably the scene whence Virgil borrowed images for his Tartarus, than is the Grotto of the Cumæan Sibyl. The upper story of the Cocomella boasts a Terrace which commands one of the most beautiful prospects existing; and under the Quadrangle, which contains a curiously constructed Well of delicious water, is a *Crypto-Porticus.*

The Sorrentine shore exhibits *remains of a Temple supposed to have been dedicated to Neptune; ancient Baths,* two of which are perfect;[2] *considerable vestiges of an edifice supposed to have been*

---

[1] A boat with ten oars, thus hired, usually costs three piastres, beside a few carlini to the boatmen for their dinner.

[2] Contiguous to, and on the left of the great Arch of the Temple of Neptune, is a small Corridor, nearly perfect, though half filled with water; and leading to a large, circular, ancient Bath, which by the aid of a boat may be seen through a chasm in the cliff, and is said to contain paintings. Between this Bath and the Marina grande di Sorrento is an ancient Bath of a quadrilateral form, in perfect preservation, and supposed by antiquaries to have made part of a Temple consecrated to Venus.

the magnificent *Temple of Ceres*, which once adorned this coast; and on the foundations of which a modern Villa now stands;[1] *remains of a quadrilateral edifice of reticulated brick work*, supposed to have been a Temple consecrated to Hercules; *interesting traces of the Villa of Vedius Pollio*, on the ascent behind the Temple;[2] and, in a Cove just beyond the Marina di Puolo,[3] *considerable vestiges of ancient Arches, Corridors*, etc. now called *Portiglione*, perhaps a corruption of the words *Porta Leoni;* for these Arches, according to the present appearance of the Ruin, may probably have been entrances to Caves belonging to a Theatre; and consequently appropriated to lions and other wild beasts.[4] But the Temple of Minerva, erected by Ulysses (if we may credit Seneca),[5] on a height denominated in modern times, *La Punta della Campanella*, the temple of Apollo, which stood on the same promontory, and several other Temples, mentioned by classic writers as having once adorned the Sorrentine shore, are now levelled with the dust, or engulphed by the Tyrrhene Sea, which has made such encroachments, that what formerly was a fine road, extending from the town of Sorrento to the base of the cliff crowned by the Temple of Ceres, is at present deep water.[6]

When Bernardo Tasso came from northern Italy to settle at Sorrento, he found the streets adorned with handsome houses, and their inhabitants so kind and hospitable to foreigners, that he

---

1 The remains of the Temple of Ceres are on the Cliff, in an Orchard, once belonging to the Guardati family, and near the Villa-Correale: and on the Beach, beneath this Temple, pieces of a composition denominated Sorrento stone are frequently found. The colour of the composition is blue; some pieces being opaque, others transparent: and it is supposed they made part of the interior decorations of the Sorrentine temples. Emeralds and white Cornelians are also found in considerable numbers on the Sorrentine shore; and ancient Coins, Lamps, Vases, and personal Ornaments, in the ancient public Burial-ground; which appears to have been situated on the left side of the high road leading from Sorrento to Ponte Maggiore. There likewise are remains of a *Columbarium* on the Cliff near the Capuchin Convent.

2 Considerable masses of the *Opus reticulatum*, some of which have fallen into the sea, a Terrace with its original pavement remaining, and Corridors under it, stuccoed, and in one part painted with the deep red colour so prevalent at Pompeii, is all now discoverable of the Temple of Hercules; the ruins of which edifice form the point of the Promontory of Sorrento, once called the Promontory of Ceres. The Villa of Pollio exhibits remains of a Bridge; two Reservoirs for fishes, in one of which is a spring of fresh water: a Kitchen with its stoves and fire-place quite perfect; several adjoining Rooms, probably offices for servants; Pavements of ancient stucco, and Walls of the *Opus reticulatum*. It is said that when Augustus was feasting with Vedius Pollio in this Villa, a slave broke by accident a crystal vase belonging to a costly set; upon which Pollio condemned him to be thrown into the reservoir, and become food for the fishes: but Augustus, indignant at this cruel order, forbade its execution; likewise commanding the whole set of crystal to be broken, and thrown into the reservoir; and at the same time ordering the reservoir itself to be rendered useless.

3 It seems probable that *Puolo* may be a corruption of the word *Pollio*.

4 The ascent from the Cove to the Ruins above the Arches being steep and dangerous, I would counsel Travellers, after having seen the Arches, etc., to row to the Marina di Puolo, landing there, and then walking to the Cliff (immediately above the Cove); where, in a *Masseria* belonging to Don Salvatore di Turris, are Ruins which evidently communicated with those below called Portiglione. The form of these Ruins, and the Arches still visible in that part nearest to the Cove, seem to announce a Theatre: behind these Ruins are considerable remains of Walls of reticulated brick-work, which, judging from their shape, appear to have enclosed a Circus; and in this enclosure a fine column of marble (probably used instead of an obelisk) was recently discovered.

5 " Alta procelloso speculatur vertice Pallas."—See SENECA, Epist. lxxvii.

6 On the side of this road, now inundated by the sea, stands a mass of ancient brick-work; which, according to tradition, was a Monument erected by the Sorrentines to the memory of Lyparus, a foreign prince, who resided among them, and was a great benefactor to their country.

calls Sorrento "*L'Albergo della Cortesia;*" speaks of the deliciousness of the fruit; the variety and excellence of the animal food; and then adds: "*L'aere è sì sereno, sì temperato, sì salutifero, sì vitale, che gl' uomini che senza provar altro cielo ci vivono sono quasi immortali:*" and most certainly there is no spot in southern Italy so free from reflected heat during summer, or so much calculated at all seasons to promote longevity, as the plain of Sorrento. This plain, which is three miles in length, and one in breadth, appears to be the mouth of an extinct volcano; as it consists of deep and narrow glens, rocks, caverns, and small level spots of tufo: while the surrounding mountains are all composed of lime-stone.[1] Sorrento itself, though reported to have been once a larger city than Naples, is now small; but contains, together with the neighbouring villages, from eighteen to twenty thousand inhabitants. The plain is one continued series of orchards divided from each other by lofty walls, and intersected with houses. These orchards, however, are not of the common sort; for the pomegranate, the aloe, the mimosa, the mulberry, the apple, the pear, the peach, the sorbus, the vine, the olive, the bay, the cypress, the wide-spreading oak, and magnificent maritime stone-pine, which peculiarly marks an Italian landscape, are so beautifully mingled and contrasted with multitudes of oranges and lemons, that persons standing on a height, and looking down upon this plain, might fancy it the garden of the Hesperides. Here is one carriage-road three miles in length, and formed by means of bridges thrown over the ravines; the other public paths are narrow, and all lie between lofty walls,[2] which, though injurious to the beauty of the country, afford shade, even at mid-day during summer; and shelter from storms of wind during winter.

Sorrento has suffered so severely from earthquakes, war, and rapine, that few of its antiquities remain. Its Fortifications are said to have been the first erected in Italy for the purpose of having cannon planted on them; its Streets exhibit ancient pavement, and resemble those of Pompeii, as does the manner in which its houses are constructed. An Inscription, near one of the Gates, in honour of Trajan; another in honour of Antoninus Pius; another, under the Portico of the Church of S. Antonino, mentioning a Temple dedicated to Venus; the Pedestal of an ancient Egyptian Statue, not long since perfect; mutilated *bassi-rilievi;* Columns, Sarcophagi, and Altars, may still be traced in this town: and on the outside of the Cathedral, over the great door, is a beautiful *basso-rilievo,* executed in Parian marble, and taken from the Temple of Apollo, which stood near the Punta della Campanella, originally called the Promontory of Minerva, from having been crowned with a Temple dedicated to that goddess.[3] But the object most interesting to strangers is

---

[1] The tea-tree is said to grow wild on this part of the Apennine.

[2] These walls appear to have been built to preserve the earth on each side from falling into the paths; which were originally ravines, formed by the hand of Nature.

[3] The site of the Temple of Apollo is near the village of Torca (anciently called *Theorica,* from the processions of the gods exhibited there), and not far distant from the village of S. Agata. A church was erected, during the ninth century, on the foundations

the paternal *Mansion of Torquato Tasso,* beautifully situated on a cliff supposed to have been the site of an ancient Temple. On the outside of this mansion is a mutilated Bust, in *terra-cotta,* of the immortal Bard; and, in the Saloon up-stairs, a marble Bust called Torquato Tasso, though it more probably represents his father. Here, likewise, is a fine medallion of Alexander the Great: and beyond this Saloon is a Terrace commanding an extensive view of the Bay of Naples: but the chamber in which Tasso was born is fallen into the sea. The Villa now belongs to the Duca di Laurito, who descends, in the female line, from Tasso's family. Near this Villa (and belonging to the Palazzo-Mastrolili) is a Garden, through which a path leads to *the Corridors of the Temple of Neptune,* terminated by a remaining part of that Temple, which exhibits a magnificent *Grecian Arch.*

Between Sorrento and Meta, and very near the former, are some Antiquities highly worth notice; namely, *the Greek Piscina* (the shape of which, the Crypto-Porticus, and the Wells, apparently intended to ventilate this reservoir, may all be discovered; though the centre has recently been filled with earth, and converted into a garden); and *the Roman Piscinæ,* or rather a part of the ancient Greek Reservoir, repaired by Antoninus Pius, in the year 160, and still quite perfect. Here, likewise, are a considerable number of Wells, apparently designed to ventilate the Reservoir, which still supplies Sorrento and its Piano with excellent purified water. The Arches of this Reservoir are so skilfully constructed as to support a large Garden, which contains the loftiest Orange-trees in the whole Piano. Further on, in the way to Meta, is the site of *an ancient Temple,* supposed to have been dedicated to Venus; and here are two *myrtle-trees,* so uncommonly large, that one could almost fancy them coeval with the Temple. At the extremity of the Plain, and immediately under the lime-stone mountains, is *Meta,* a large Village, containing a handsome Church, beautifully situated, and near which are several very old and fine Olive-trees, of a kind seldom met with in Italy.

The inhabitants of Sorrento and its vicinity still retain the character given of them by Bernardo Tasso, with respect to their attention and kindness to Foreigners. Hospitable, so far as making entertainments goes, they cannot be; having no longer the power; but their fruit, milk, time, and best services are always at the command of a Stranger. Three or four generations of one family often live together, under the same roof, according to the ancient Grecian custom; and it is not uncommon to see grandfathers and grandmothers above ninety years old and perfectly exempt from infirmities: with respect to the healthfulness of the climate, therefore, Bernardo Tasso seems again to have judged right; and with regard to provisions, beef, veal, fish, butter, honey, milk, fruits,

---

of this Temple, and adorned with some of its columns, which still remain; and therefore Travellers who visit S. Agata should endeavour to see these relics of antiquity. In heathen times a procession went yearly from the Pantheon at Sorrento to the Temples of Minerva and Apollo; and the custom is still observed, with this difference,—that the Blessed Virgin, and other Christian Saints, are substituted for the heathen divinities.

and water, are all excellent; hog-meat is so remarkably fine that hogs are denominated The Citizens of Sorrento; and the wine of this district is light and wholesome; though less esteemed by the Moderns than it was by the Ancients.[1] Lodging-houses may easily be procured at reasonable prices in the Plain; but they are generally ill-furnished: *the House of Captain Starace, at S. Agnello*, is, however, comfortably furnished; and, what is more important still, its master unites the wish with the capability of assisting Foreigners; insomuch that, when under his protection, they can never want a friend. He has one or two smaller houses. The Villa Correale, a beautiful specimen of Grecian architecture, situated near the sea, and surrounded by enchanting scenery, is also let as a lodging-house: so likewise are the Villa Spinelli, at Ponte Maggiore; the Villa Marisca, which stands in a Garden, near Carrota; and the Villa Serra-Capriola, at Meta.[2]

The mountains which border the Piano di Sorrento abound with delightful walks and rides.

The spot called *Conti delle Fontanelle, e di Cermenna*, and between two and three miles distant from the town of Sorrento, is well worth seeing; as it presents a magnificent view of the Gulphs of Naples and Salerno, the Islands of the Sirens, immortalised by Homer, and one of which contains ruins of an ancient Temple; the coast near Amalfi, etc.; and during the month of September immense nets for catching quails are erected on this spot, below which is the Tunny fishery. The excursion to the Conti occupies four hours, if it be extended to a stupendous Arch, formed by the hand of nature, on the margin of the Gulph of Salerno, which Arch, and the path leading to it, furnish fine subjects for the pencil.[3]

Camaldoli, a suppressed, but once magnificent Convent, situated on a summit of the Apennine, about two miles from Ponte Maggiore, is likewise worth seeing; and the present possessor allows strangers, who come provided with a cold dinner, to eat it in the refectory.

The ride from Sorrento to Airola, and back, occupies about four hours; and exhibits the most sublime and beautiful prospects in the whole neighbourhood. On reaching the foot of a hillock, crowned by the Church of Airola, the Traveller should turn to the left; passing through a lane; and thence proceeding, through a *pergola* to a cottage; on the left of which are steps leading to a pretty Coppice, composed of arbuti, Mediterranean heaths, and other shrubs; and at the extremity of this Coppice is a Cliff, which commands the whole Piano di Sorrento, the Bay of Naples, Vesuvius, and part of the Gulph of

---

[1] Persons who wish to be enlightened with respect to the history and antiquities of the Sorrentine Republic, should consult a work written upon this subject by Philippo Anastasio, and entitled "*Antiquit. Surrent.;*" and another work, written by his nephew, and entitled "*Agnelli Anastasii Animadversiones.*"

[2] The Cav. Correale has other Villas to let, charmingly situated on a height called Capo di Monte, and very near the town of Sorrento.

[3] In order to see this Arch, pass the wine-house on the summit of the hill between the two Gulphs; then turn into the second path on the left, through a vineyard; and pursue this path till you reach the cliff; down which follow the goat-track, between myrtles and other shrubs, till you arrive at the Arch.

Salerno. About four miles beyond the village of Airola is that of S. Maria del Castello; which commands a fine view of Amalfi, and the whole Gulph of Salerno: but Travellers, who extend their excursion to S. Maria del Castello, should carry a cold dinner with them.

The ride from Sorrento to S. Agata, and back, occupies about four hours; and exhibits fine prospects.

The ride from Sorrento to Massa, a distance of between three and four miles, likewise exhibits fine prospects. This last-mentioned town, if we may credit ancient writers, was the favourite abode of the Sirens; and the place where, during the age of Ulysses, there was an academy, renowned for learning and eloquence; but the students abused their knowledge, to the colouring of wrong, and the corruption of manners; consequently, the Sirens were fabled, by the sweetness of their voices, to draw the unwary into ruin. Massa displays vestiges of an Aqueduct; and appears to have been once a considerable town: it does not, however, furnish an inn capable of accommodating Travellers; though good wine may be procured at the wine-shops.[1]

The excursion from Sorrento to Amalfi is particularly interesting, and may be accomplished, with ease, in the following manner, during a cool and tranquil day. From the Piano to that part of the Conti where begins a descent, called the Scaricatojo, Travellers may be conveyed either in *chaises-à-porteur*, or on mules, in about one hour; thence descending the mountain, on foot, to the Gulph of Salerno, where a boat, ordered over night, and as large as the Marinella affords, should be in attendance.[2] The descent occupies rather more than an hour, and, though steep, is not dangerous. On reaching the Marinella, Travellers should embark, without loss of time, for Amalfi, passing Positano, a romantically situated town, peopled by rich merchants, and adorned with handsome houses. The time occupied in rowing from the Marinella of the Scaricatojo to Amalfi is, generally speaking, about three hours. The whole coast exhibits enchanting scenery, and the situation of Amalfi is picturesque beyond description. This town boasts much of its high antiquity; and here, A. D. 1137, a copy of Justinian's Pandects was accidentally discovered. The Sea-Gate appears to be ancient, and the Cathedral, a spacious and handsome edifice, stands proudly, on the site of a heathen Temple, and contains an antique Vase of porphyry, now the baptismal Font, together with two immense Columns of red oriental granite, similar to those in the church of S. Maria degli Angeli, at Rome. The Columns which adorn the high altar are likewise antique: and, under the

---

[1] A narrow open carriage, similar in width to those the wheels of which have left traces in the streets of Pompeii; *chaises-à-porteur*; donkeys; and excellent mules,—may be hired at Sorrento, and in its environs. For the open carriage the usual demand is one piastre per day—for a *chaise-à-porteur*, from three to ten carlini, according to the distance and time occupied—for a mule and guide to Castel-a-mare and back, from eight to ten carlini—for ditto, to S. Agata, Torca, or Capo-Campanella, six carlini—and for ditto, to Camaldoli, Airola, the Conti, or Massa, four carlini: but if the rider should dismount, and detain the mule and guide at any of the above-named places, the guide would expect at least one carlino an hour for this detention.

[2] Most of these boats are small.

cathedral, is a Crypt, supposed to be part of the heathen Temple, and decorated with excellent Paintings, probably by the Florentine school. Amalfi is built in an amphitheatrical form; and the upper part of the town exhibits magnificent views, and contains some ancient Greek Paintings. No comfortable inn can be found here: but Travellers who bring their dinner with them, are permitted to dine in a Garden belonging to the Capuchin Convent. Large boats and skilful boatmen may be hired on the beach at Amalfi: and in case of a contrary wind for returning to the Scaricatojo, it is advisable to hire one of these large boats, instead of going back in a small one. Cheap and good writing paper may be purchased at Amalfi, as may wine, ice, fruit, vegetables, and fish. Three hours should be allowed for rowing back to the Scaricatojo; one hour and a half for ascending the mountain, and about one hour for returning to the Piano di Sorrento.¹

A pleasant water excursion may be made from Sorrento to Castel-a-mare, whither a Sorrento boat usually goes in one hour and a quarter, and returns in about two hours. Castel-a-mare, situated at the foot of the hill on which stood the ancient Stabiæ, is encircled by a beautiful country, and embellished with a Quay, made by the French. Here are several small Lodging-houses, but no inns fit to sleep at. On the hill above Castel-a-mare is a Villa belonging to the King of Naples, together with two or three large lodging-houses, delightfully situated in the vicinity of shady walks and rides; and on this hill it is possible to trace *the site of Stabiæ*, but nothing more, as the excavations made in that village have been filled up. Sculpture, Paintings, and a considerable number of Papyri were found in Stabiæ, but very few skeletons; therefore it is supposed the inhabitants had time to escape, before their dwelling-place was entombed by the ashes from Vesuvius.

Carriages and donkeys may be hired at Castel-a-mare to convey Travellers to Pompeii, which is not four miles distant.

Another pleasant water excursion may be made to Capri. This island, situated about three leagues and a half from Sorrento, and about eight from Naples, was anciently called *Capreæ*, and is celebrated for having been the retiring-place of Augustus, and the residence, during several years, of Tiberius. It is nine miles in circumference, and contains about nine thousand inhabitants, and two towns, Capri and Ana-Capri, the latter being situated on the summit of a rock, to which there is an ascent of above five hundred steps. The people chiefly consist of mechanics, husbandmen, and sailors; perfect equality reigns among them, every body appears industrious, nobody seems poor, and so salubrious is the climate that scarce any maladies visit the island. The most comfortable way of managing this excursion is to hire a ten-oared boat, taking a cold dinner, bread, salad, fruit, plates, glasses, knives, forks, etc., but no wine; that be-

---

¹ The usual price for a mule from the town of Sorrento to the descent called the Scaricatojo, is four carlini; and for the same mule from the Scaricatojo to Sorrento, four carlini. The usual price for a boat with four oars, and places for four passengers, from the Marinella of the Scaricatojo to Amalfi, is one piastre; and for a boat with six oars, and places for six passengers, from Amalfi to the Marinella, three ducats.

ing excellent at Capri; and setting out very early in the morning, as sixteen hours are required for rowing to the island, seeing every thing worth observation there, and returning. When Travellers land, donkeys are immediately brought down to the beach, for their accommodation;[1] and the best mode of proceeding is to mount these animals, and ride to the Steps leading up to *Ana-Capri;* dismounting at the steps; walking up, and sending the donkeys before. On arriving at the top of the steps, you find a good mulepath, and may therefore remount, and ride round Ana-Capri. On returning to the steps, it is again prudent to dismount, and walk down, sending the animals before. Having reached *the Plain*, ride or walk to *Capri*, and then proceed to a *Villa* above the town, on the way to *the eastern Promontory*, where stood *Tiberius's Palace;* dine in this Villa, the owner of which will give the use of his house and kitchen, and provide a large party with wine, for two ducats. After dinner remount the donkeys, and ride to *the Piscina of Tiberius's Palace,* called Villa Jovis, and supposed to have been erected by Augustus. Near this Villa are ruins of an ancient Lighthouse; beyond which, in consequence of a recent excavation, small Rooms, and a Corridor, with Mosaic Pavements, have been discovered. Among the ruins of the Villa, vestiges of Baths, and a Theatre, may still be found; and after having examined these, and contemplated the magnificent view from the summit of the lofty rock, once crowned by the Villa, return to the Beach.

Tiberius had twelve Villas at Capri, all magnificent, and well fortified: but as persons were sent hither on the death of the tyrant to demolish his works, and not leave one stone upon another, it is difficult to ascertain where all these Villas stood. The Monte di S. Michele, however, exhibits extensive ruins, and a long range of vaulted Apartments, in a semicircular form, together with traces of an ancient Road leading to the summit of the hill. Mosaic Pavements were found on the height where the Fortress is placed; and on the northern coast are remains of a building still called *Il Palazzo,* and supposed to have been one of the imperial winter habitations.

The best water on the Island is to be found at the Villa Jovis. The town of Capri contains no inn, but there is a private house, where Travellers may, in case of necessity, be provided with beds. Immense flights of quails visit this Island during the month of September, and are caught in nets by the inhabitants, to supply the Naples market.

The usual price of a twelve-oared boat by the day, at Sorrento, is from four to five ducats, including a dinner for the boatmen, who are deemed the most skilful mariners in Italy; and these sons of Neptune celebrate annually, at Sorrento, on the first Sunday in August, a marine Festival, particularly interesting to Travellers, because supposed to be now precisely the same as in ages of remote antiquity. It concludes with a dance in the sea, performed by mariners, whose dexterity in leaping out of their boats, diving,

---

[1] *Chaises-à-porteur* may likewise be procured in the town of Capri.

and throwing fountains of water on each other, is admirable.²

EXCURSION TO THE ISLANDS OF PROCIDA AND ISCHIA.

As good accommodations may be procured at Ischia, the most comfortable manner of making this excursion is to hire a boat at Naples for two or three days, visiting *Procida* first, and *Ischia* afterward. We pursued this plan, taking a cold dinner with us, and determining to dine at Procida and sleep at Ischia. As the weather was warm, we set out early, and, after doubling *the Cape of Pausilipo*, passed a picturesque *Hermitage*, together with several ruins of ancient buildings, and, among others, those commonly called *The Schools of Virgil*, but conjectured to have been a *Villa belonging to Lucullus*. We then rowed under *the Promontory of Misenum*, to obtain a good view of this great Harbour of the Romans, and arrived at Procida in two hours and a half, from the time when we left Naples, the distance being about four leagues. Procida (called by the Greeks *Prochyta*), though a small island, is remarkably populous, and its inhabitants are reputed to be rich: the women dress in the Greek style, the men wear Phrygian caps (as do all the mariners in the Bay of Naples), and it is said they retain many of the ancient Grecian customs. The grapes, figs, and wine of Procida are excellent; the houses flat-roofed, with terraces on the top; and the staircases generally on the outside of the walls. We were permitted to dine in a large shooting-seat belonging to the King of Naples, and delightfully situated on the brow of a cliff overhanging the sea. From the landing-place to this royal Villa is a short mile; and after contemplating the beautiful views in its vicinity, we re-embarked, and proceeded to Ischia, anciently called *Inarime*, and *Pithecusa*,² and about six leagues distant from Naples. According to some opinions, Ischia is the offspring of a volcano, and certainly it appears to have suffered severely from volcanic eruptions, though, during the last three hundred years, nothing of this kind has happened. It is eighteen miles in circumference, and famed for hot baths, which, in summer, are much frequented; and likewise for mineral waters, supposed to have been in several cases salutary. The town of Furio contains a Chapel which merits notice. The whole island is beautiful, and from the heights of Monte di Vico, and Monte S. Nicolo, the Epopeus of the Classics, the views are particularly fine.

Ischia produces some of the best wines in the vicinity of Naples, and contains a good Lodging and Boarding House, belonging to a person known by the name of Don Tommaso.

---

1 We paid for each mule and donkey, at Capri, six carlini; to each guide two carlini; to the Cicerone half a piastre; and to the custom-house officer three carlini.

2 Ischia and Procida are supposed to have been originally united under the name of *Pithecusa*.

CHAPTER XII.

RETURN TO ENGLAND, THROUGH GERMANY.

Journey from Rome through Perugia to Florence—Objects best worth notice on that road—Hannibal's route into Italy—Journey from Florence to Dresden—Ferrara—Rovigo—Padua—Baths of Abano—Arqua—Venice—Objects best worthy notice—Basilica of S. Marco—Palazzo Ex-Ducale—Accademia delle Belle Arti—Chiese de' Gesuiti—dei Carmilitani—del Carmine—di S. S. Giovanni e Paolo—di S. Giorgio Maggiore—del Redentore—di S. Maria della Salute—Palazzi Pisani-Moreta—Grimani—Barberigo—Scuola di S. Rocco—Palazzo Manfrini—Arsenal—Promenades—Theatres—Hotels—Water—Conegliano—Pordenone—Tagliamento—S. Tommaso—Ponteba—Custom-house there—Villach—Beds and Provisions in Germany—Table-linen—Peasantry—Country Towns, etc.—Klagenfurt—Friesach—Judenburg—Leoben—Merzhofen—Schottwien—Traskirken—Vienna—Custom-house—Hotels—Imperial Residence—Cathedral—Churches of S. Peter—S. Michael—the Augustines—Capuchins—S. Charles and S. Rupert—Imperial Arsenal, and other public Buildings—Fountain—Imperial Libraries—Jewels—Medals—Cabinet of Natural History—Belvedere Gallery of Paintings—Lichtenstein Gallery—Porcelain Manufacture—Prater—Lau Garten—Schoenbrunn—Coffee-houses—Water—National Dish—Theatres—Population—Distance from Florence—Stockerau—Znaim—Schelletau—Iglau—Stecken—Czaslau—Planian—Prague—Population—Objects best worth notice—Inns—Budin—Lobositz—Aussig—Peterswald—Inns between that town and Dresden—Saxon Peasants—Custom-house—Dresden—Population—Architecture—Religion—Character of the Inhabitants—Inns—Objects best worth a Traveller's attention—Mode of obtaining admittance to the Picture Gallery, etc.—List of some of the most striking Pictures—Treasury—Cabinet of antique Sculpture—Dresden China—Theatres—Distance from Vienna to Dresden—Ditto from Dresden to Hamburgh—Voyage down the Elbe to the last-named city—Population of Hamburgh—Description of the Town and Port—Inns—Private Lodgings—Sagacity of a Stork—Voyage from Hamburgh to Cuxhaven—Harwich Packets—Prices—Days on which these Vessels sail—Inns at Cuxhaven.

WISHING to see the Cascade of Terni, and the celebrated Lake of Trasymenus, we took the Perugia road from Rome to Florence; and found it so very interesting, that I shall give a brief account of the objects best worth attention.

Civita-Castellana, supposed by some writers to be the ancient *Veii,* though, more probably, the ancient *Fescennium,* was the first town which attracted our notice; and is, in point of situation, particularly strong and beautiful.

Narni, the next considerable town in this road, was formerly called *Nequinum,* from the obstinacy of its citizens; who, during a siege, killed their wives and children, in order to save their provisions; and, when all these were consumed, chose rather to lay violent hands upon themselves than surrender. This place gave birth to the Emperor Nerva.

A little beyond Narni, and about a mile out of the road, are remains of a magnificent *Bridge,* supposed to have been thrown, by Augustus, over the river Nera (anciently the *Nar*), for the purpose of uniting two hills. In order to examine this stately ruin, we made our carriages wait in the road to Terni, while we walked down the hill, at whose foot the bridge presents itself. It consists of large stones joined together without any cement or iron cramps, and cut, on their outsides, into the form of diamonds. On the dry land, next to Narni, is one entire arch, the piers of which are above forty common paces asunder. The piers still remaining in the water prove the immense size of the other arches; which were not, however, of an equal diameter. The length of this bridge is supposed to have been 850 Roman *palmi;* and a Roman architectural *palmo* is nearly nine English inches. The distance between the piers of the first arch is computed to be 100 *palmi,* and its height 150; the distance between the piers of the second, 180 *palmi;* that between those of the third, 150; and the last arch, which ends on the other side of the Nera, is 190 *palmi* in breadth.

Terni derives its ancient name, *Interamna,* from the two arms of the Nera, between which it is situated. Cornelius Tacitus, and the Emperors Tacitus and Florianus, were born in this city, which contains the ruins of an Amphitheatre in the Episcopal Garden, and those of a Temple of the Sun, in the church of S. Salvadore. At S. Siro, in the cellars of the College, are the remains of a Temple of Hercules, and in the *Casina* of the *Casa-Spada,* some ruins of ancient Baths.[1]

Four miles from Terni is the famous Cascade called *Caduta delle Marmore,* and formed by the fall of the Velino (anciently the *Velinus*) into the Nera. These cataracts are said to have been made about the year of Rome 671, by Curius Dentatus, who, in order to drain the territory of Rieti of its standing waters, cut channels, through which he discharged them into the Velino, and thence into the Nera, forming, by these means, a cascade, consisting of three leaps, the first computed to be 300 English feet, the two others, united, between 4 and 500. Wishing to see these cataracts in perfection, we set out from Terni about ten o'clock of a clear morning, and ascended the *Monte di Marmore* in calashes, till we approached the Velino, which announces itself at a considerable distance by its thundering noise. We then walked to view the narrow pass through which it rushes down the fall of 300 feet; and afterward proceeded to a temple built on a promontory, for the purpose of contemplating the three leaps together. Here we remained till twelve o'clock, when the effect of the sun upon water, which, from the velocity of its fall, rises into vapours, resembling millions of curled white feathers, is beautiful beyond description; indeed, there are very few celestial rainbows half so brilliant as the terrestrial ones at Terni. After having seen these, we returned to the bottom of the Monte di Marmore, and then dismounted from our calashes, and walked to view the cataract from below. This walk occupied nearly two hours; it lies through a Gentleman's grounds, of which nothing can exceed the beauty, except the stupendous cataracts by which they are terminated.

Spoleti, or *Spoleto* (formerly *Spoletum*), is a very ancient city, situated on the acclivity of a mountain, and watered by the Clitumnus, celebrated in days of yore for the whiteness of the cattle which grazed near it. The citizens of Spoleto repulsed Han-

[1] Near Terni stands Rieti, anciently *Reate,* celebrated for its Vale of Tempe.

nibal immediately after the battle of Trasymenus; and they still preserve a gate, called Porta-Fuga, with an inscription in memory of this event. The Cathedral contains paintings, *bassi-rilievi*, and ancient mosaics. The Aqueduct is a beautiful fabric, supported by stone arches, and, in one part, by a double arcade, said to be 300 feet high.

Between Spoleto and Foligno, and close to the road, is the Temple of Clitumnus, now converted into a chapel, and dedicated to S. Salvadore. The front toward the plain is adorned with four pillars, two pilasters, and a pediment: the edifice is oblong, and exhibits the following words cut in stone: " *T. Septimius Plebeius.*" [1]

Foligno, anciently *Fulginas*, stands on the Via Flaminia; and contains a Cathedral, the altar and frescos in which merit notice.

Between Foligno and Perugia lies *Assisi* (anciently *Assisium*), the birth-place of S. Francesco.[2] It is situated on a hill so near to the great road, that Travellers may visit it with ease. The church of S. Francesco, in this city, contains several pictures of the old school, which are worth notice. The Monastery of Francescan nuns, called the nuns of S. Clare, likewise deserves attention; and the Church of S. Maria, or the *Filipini*, once a temple of Minerva, is a beautiful piece of antiquity.

Perugia (anciently *Augusta Perusia*), the capital of the rich and charming province of Umbria, and once the strongest city of Etruria, displays a handsome modern Gate (the Porta S. Pietro), and contains antiquities, and paintings of the old school, well worth observation; but, exclusive of this, Travellers should sleep here, in order to avoid passing a night at Torricella. Perugia is magnificently situated on the summit of a lofty mountain of the Apennine, and seems by nature almost impregnable: such, indeed, was the strength of this city, and such the valour of its inhabitants, that Hannibal did not venture to attack it, even after having gained the important battle of Trasymenus: and, to this moment, the Perugians are famed for being the most daring and ferocious of the Roman people.

Between Torricella and Camuscia, at five miles' distance from the former, is the miserable village of *Passignano*, rendered famous by the above-named victory gained near this spot by Hannibal, 217 years before Christ.

Six miles further on is the *Ponte-Sanguinetto*, situated below a village of the same name, and both so called from the effusion of Roman blood spilt there.

Between Passignano and the rivulet called Sanguinetto, *the site of the Roman camp*, and *the Pass* through which Hannibal came down from the heights, may be discovered.

Four miles further on is Spilonga, a small hamlet on the confines of Tuscany; and three miles from Spilonga stands *Ossaia*, where, on a house in the street, is the following inscription:—

---

1. It does not appear certain that the present chapel of S. Salvadore was anciently the Temple of Clitumnus. Pliny places this temple near the source of the river; and Suetonius says, that Caligula went to Mevania to see the Temple of Clitumnus. The small town of Bevagna unquestionably stands upon the site of the ancient Mevania, which lies to the west of the river Timia, and at the influx of the Tacarena and Rucciano into the Clitumnus.

2 Metastasio also was born at Assisi.

' Nomen habet locus hic Ossaia, ab ossibus illis
Quæ dolus Annibalis fudit et hasta simul."

"This place bears the name of Ossaia, from the bones of those unfortunate men whom Hannibal slew here."

Ossaia is by many writers supposed to have been the actual field of battle; though, perhaps, it rather was the hill to which the small remains of Flaminius's troops retired: because, thirteen miles, the reputed distance between Passignano and Ossaia, seems too large a space for the contending armies to have occupied. It is impossible to view the country between Passignano and Ossaia, without feeling the highest admiration of the military skill of Hannibal; who contrived, on an enemy's ground, to draw that enemy into a narrow, swampy, and uncommonly foggy plain, where no army, however brave, could long have defended itself; for on three sides are heights, which were possessed by the troops of Carthage; and, on the other, is a large unfordable lake.

On the hill above Camuscia, and within the distance of a walk, stands *Cortona* (formerly *Coritus*), said to be the most ancient of the twelve great cities of Etruria, and famed, in the days of Pythagoras, for the bodily strength of its inhabitants, and the salubrity of its air. In the Cathedral is a large antique Sarcophagus, supposed to be that of the unfortunate Consul Flaminius; and representing the battle of the Lapithæ with the Centaurs. Many of the churches are curious in point of architecture; and most of them contain good pictures, both of the old and new school. Several of the private houses contain valuable paintings. The ancient Etruscan Walls of this city are in some places discoverable; they were formed of immense blocks of marble, without any cement whatsoever; and, in the Museum of the Academy, and in those which belong to the nobles of Cortona, are other Etruscan antiquities.

Arezzo (anciently *Aretium*), is remarkable for the extensive view from its fortress; and remains of the ancient Amphitheatre are still to be seen. Arezzo gave birth to Petrarca.

As the subject of this chapter has led me to speak of Hannibal, I will subjoin a detail of what appears to have been his route into Italy, which I have traced from an ancient map as far as Embrun upon the river Durance in Dauphiné, and afterward founded upon the authority of Polybius, strengthened by the present appearance of the ground.

Hannibal set out in the midst of winter U. C. 535, with an army of fifty thousand foot, and nine thousand horse, beside elephants, from

(Ancient Names.)	(Modern Names.)
Septa	*Ceuta*, in Africa, a sea-port, and crossed to
Fretum Erculeum	*The Straits of Gibraltar;* whence he probably proceeded by sea to
Calpe	*Tarifa, the Pillars of Hercules in Europe;* then passed through the
Country of the Bastuli	*The Kingdom of Granada, in Spain,* to
Malaca	*Malaga;* and thence proceeded through the

(Ancient Names.)	(Modern Names.)
Country of the Bastiani	The Kingdom of Murcia, to the camp of Spartarius, thence going to
Cartago-nova...	Carthagena, and traversing the
Province of Contestanorum	The Kingdom of Valentia, to
Alone[1]	Alicant; at which sea-port it seems probable that he embarked his troops, and passed up the river
Sucro	Segura, or Xucar, to Valencia, thence proceeding along the river
Iberus	Ebro, through the
Country of the Illercaones	The Principality of Catalonia, to
Tarraco, or Tarrago	Tarragona, and
Cartago-Vetus ..	Villa-Franca: he then crossed the
Rubricatus	The River Llobregat, proceeded to, and crossed, the
Gerunda	The River Gerona, and then came to
Rhoda	Rosas: though some authors assert that he followed the course of the Gerona to the Pyrenean mountains, and crossed thence into Gaul. From Rosas, however, according to the map, he went to
Veneris Fanum ..	Port Vendres, thence to
Caucoliberis, or Illiberis	Collioure, in the Province of the Volcæ Teclosages, or Rossiglione; thence he proceeded to
Narbo	Narbonne, the Country of the Bebricas, and thence to
Agatha	Montpellier and
Nemausus	Nismes; when, passing through the country of the Volcæ Arecomii, he proceeded to the banks of the
Rhodanus	The Rhone, down which river he passed to
Avenio	Avignon; thence traversing to
The Country of the Cassuares	Provence, to Dauphiné, the country of the Allobroges; thence he proceeded to
Augusta Tricastrinonum	S. Paul-trois-Châteaux, and then went by the river
Druentia	Durance, to
Embrodunus ...	Embrun; whence he marched to, and crossed
Mons Vesulus, or Visus	Monte Viso, one of the great Alps, said to be 9,997 English feet in height, but not so difficult of access as are many of those mountains; it lies almost in a direct line with Embrun, and the road to it is not strongly guarded

---

[1] Called, by some authors, Lucenium.

(Ancient Names.)	(Modern Names.)
	by narrow defiles, as are many passages into Italy. Thence he went to
Pinarolum	*Pignerol*, a city of Upper Dauphiné, about 20 miles from Turin; thence he followed the course of the
Padus	*Po*, then went to
Alba-Pompeia . .	*Albe*
Dortona	*Tortona*, and
Ticinum	*Pavia*; crossed the river *Trebbia*, subdued *Placenza*, *Parma*,
Regium	*The Kingdom of Modena*, and
Mutina	*Modena* itself; then came to
Fæsulæ	*Fiesole*; thence proceeded to
Aretium	*Arezzo*; and thence to
Trasimene	The Lake of Perugia, or Trasymenus.

Hannibal is supposed to have passed through Gaul, to the foot of the Alps, in ten days. It seems an impossibility that he should have reached the Fenestrelles, Cenis, S. Bernard, or S. Gothard, in so short a time. It likewise seems improbable that he should have rejected the passage of Monte Viso, which lay directly before him, to search for some other at a greater distance; especially as his only route to that other was through narrow and dangerous defiles. He is said, by Polybius, to have passed through the country of the Allobroges, over an immense Alp, whence he saw and pointed out to his soldiers the rich and beautiful plains of Italy; after which he immediately descended into valleys watered by the Po.

All this exactly described Monte Viso, near the Italian side of which lie the plains of Piedmont, and through these plains runs the Po, which rises at the foot of Mount Viso. Polybius likewise says, the first city taken by Hannibal in Italy was Turin; and that, too, might be; for Turin is only twenty miles distant from Pignerol.

When I was at Lausanne, I consulted Gibbon, who resided there, with respect to this route; and he seemed to think it might probably be that pursued by Hannibal: moreover, a friend of mine, who ascended Viso, told me, the plains of Italy were discernible from its summit. On this point, however, I cannot speak from my own knowledge; as I only visited the base of the mountain.

From Florence to Dresden we travelled *en voiturier;* and though our time of setting out was the middle of April, yet, even at that mild season, the wind on the Apennine, between Florence and Bologna, was so piercing, that a lady of our party became, in consequence, alarmingly ill: and likewise, in passing through Germany, she suffered severely from stoves, which are universally substituted for fire-places; from damp beds, for there are no warming-pans, nor any other machine for drying beds in Germany; from the keen air of the Alps between Venice and Vienna; from the severity of the climate in Moravia and Bohemia; and from the excessive roughness of the roads between Prague and Dresden. Nevertheless, we endeavoured to guard against some of these inconveniences, by providing ourselves with fur travelling caps, warm pelisses, shoes and boots lined with fur, and great coats, which we were glad to put upon our beds in Moravia and Bohemia; where there are no coverlids, except small eyder-down quilts, which generally slip off ere the night be half spent. But, notwithstanding every precaution that prudence can suggest, it seems to me impossible for invalids, in general, and especially those who are afflicted with pulmonary complaints, to attempt taking this journey without risk to their lives.

As I have already given an account of the road between Florence and Bologna, I shall only say that, after remaining a short time at the last-named place, we proceeded, in five hours and a half, to *Ferrara;* through a good road, and a remarkably rich country. Midway between this city and Bologna is a neat and pleasant inn, the Albergo della Fenice, called *Il Tè,* where Travellers may dine or sleep.

Ferrara is a fortified town, celebrated for containing, in its public Library, the Tomb of Ariosto, his Chair, Inkstand, and handwriting; together with a bronze Medallion of that great Poet, found in his tomb; where likewise was found an account of his last illness and death. This Library also contains the original Manuscripts of *Tasso's Gerusalemme Liberata,* and Guarini's *Pastor Fido,* with several Volumes of Music, illuminated by Gosmei: and in the Hospital of S. Anna, Travellers are shown the Cell where Tasso was confined. The inn we slept at (*I tre Mori*), is large, but comfortless; the climate of Ferrara is unwholesome, and the water bad.[1]

Our next day's journey was to Monselice; and occupied ten hours and a half; the road being, for some miles, sandy. Soon after quitting Ferrara, we crossed the Po, on a *pont-volant;* and beyond Rovigo passed the Adige in a similar conveyance. The Posthouse at Monselice is a good inn. Next day, we proceeded to Mestre in nine hours and a half, exclusive of the time spent at Padua, in seeing that city.

Padua, the birth-place of Livy, is large, and strongly fortified; but not handsome, its University excepted; which was built by Palladio. This University, founded by the Emperor Frederick II., in opposition to that of Bologna, once contained eighteen thousand students; and still possesses public Schools, a chemical Laboratory, an anatomical Theatre, a Museum of natural history, and a botanic Garden.

The Palazzo della Giustizia contains an immense Town-hall, the ceiling and walls of which were originally painted by Giotto and his scholars; and re-touched, in 1762, by Zannoni: the ceiling, however, was destroyed, in consequence of the roof blowing off; but the paintings on the walls remain. This apartment contains a Monument to the memory of Livy, and two Egyptian Statues.

The Palazzo del Podesta contains a painting, by Palma il Giovane, of our Saviour blessing the city of Padua.

The Duomo contains a modern

---

[1] Boats large enough to accommodate a family may be hired, at Ferrara, to go to Venice; and this voyage occupies about twenty hours.

Monument to the memory of Petrarca; a Madonna, by Giotto, which once belonged to Petrarca; and, in the Sacristy, a portrait of that Poet among the other Canons.

The Church dedicated to S. Antonio di Padova was begun by Niccolo Pisano, in 1255; and finished by Sansovino, in 1307: it contains Statues of Cardinal Bembo, and other eminent Characters; *bassi-rilievi* by T. and A. Lombardo, Sansovino, Campagna, etc., a Crucifix, by Donatello; and Frescos, by Giotto. The adjoining *Scuola* contains Frescos, by Titian: and in the Area, before the Church, is an equestrian Statue, by Donatello, of the famous General, surnamed Gattamelata.

The Church dedicated to S. Giustina, built by Andrea Riccio, after the designs of Palladio, and deemed a fine specimen of architecture, is adorned with a celebrated painting over the high-altar, by Paolo Veronese; together with beautiful *bassi-rilievi,* said to have been executed by Reichard, a French artist: they ornament the Stalls in the Choir.

Padua contains good hotels; the most comfortable of which is the *Stella d'Ora:* and from this city a public Passage-boat sets out every morning, at an early hour, for Venice.[1]

The drive from Monselice to Padua is extremely interesting; as the road runs parallel with the Canal leading to Venice; and is bordered with Villas, built after the designs of Palladio, and embellished with a fine view of the Rhœtian Alps. The road from Padua to Mestrè is likewise interesting; as it exhibits a fine view of Venice.

After sleeping at Mestrè, where there is a comfortable Hotel, and a good remise for carriages, we embarked, next morning, in a gondola; which conveyed us, in about two hours, to Venice, for five francs and a half, *buona-mano* inclusive: we were, however, stopped twice on our voyage, by Austrian custom-house officers, and obliged to present them with a couple of francs.[2]

Venice, one of the most considerable cities in Italy, and supposed to derive its name from the Veneti, who peopled the neighbouring coasts, is built upon piles in the midst of shallows, called *Lagunes,* and reputed to contain about a hundred thousand inhabitants.

It is scarce possible to discover the magnificent edifices of Venice, floating, as it were, on the bosom of the deep, without exclaiming: Singular and beautiful city! of whose appearance imagination can form no idea, because no other work of man is like thee. Enchantment seems to have raised thy

---

[1] The village of *Abano,* anciently *Aponium,* between five and six miles from Padua, is much frequented during summer, on account of the Warm Baths in its neighbourhood; where the Sudatory, and *Bagno di Fango,* or Mud-Bath, are said to have proved in many cases beneficial. It seems doubtful whether Pliny, by the *Fontes Patavini,* means the present Baths of Abano; because he reports the former to have emitted smells from which the latter are exempt. About six miles from Abano is *the Villa Catajo,* celebrated for frescos by Paolo Veronese. One mile from Catajo is the little town of Bataglia, so named from the rapid conflux of two rivulets: and about three miles from Bataglia lies Arqua, or Arquato, imbosomed in the Euganean hills, and famous for having been the residence and burial-place of Petrarca.

[2] Travellers who have no carriage of their own frequently embark at Francolino, which is five miles from Ferrara, and go all the way to Venice by water; a voyage of eighty miles, on the Po, the Adige, the Brenta, and the Lagunes.

walls for the abode of the monarch of the ocean, when he chooses to desert his pearl-paved caves, and emerge above the surface of his watery kingdom!

Venice is seven miles in circumference, and composed of a large number of small islands, separated by canals, and re-united by bridges; the great canal, which is in the form of an S, dividing the city into two nearly equal parts. The Rialto, the Piazza di S. Marco, containing the Church dedicated to that Evangelist, and its Campanile three hundred feet in height, together with all the Churches and Palaces erected by Palladio, Sansovino, Scamozzi, and San Michele, particularly merit notice; as does the Arsenal, though an empty shadow now, of its former self: but what excites most interest at Venice is to observe how amply and conveniently this city is supplied, not only with necessaries but the luxuries of life; though it possesses naturally neither soil nor fresh water.

The Basilica of S. Marco is reputed to be the most ancient Christian temple in Italy. On the outside, above the principal entrance, is a figure of S. Mark finely executed in mosaic. The interior of the edifice is completely lined with Mosaics; and those in the Chapel of the Madonna are particularly well executed: the Pavement is Mosaic; and the Doors, which were brought from Constantinople, are Corinthian brass. The celebrated Horses of bronze gilt, carried to Paris by Napoleon, but now returned, and extremely ill placed on the outside of the church, are four in number; and, according to general opinion, the work of Lysippus: they originally adorned Corinth; where, it is supposed, they belonged to the chariot of the sun: from Corinth they were brought to Rome by the Consul Mummius (surnamed Achaicus, for having sacked the first-mentioned city); thence they were removed to Byzantium, and thence to Venice: Winckelmann calls them the finest bronze horses extant.[1]

The view from the top of the Campanile of S. Marco is particularly well worth seeing; and the ascent particularly easy. This Tower was the place where Galileo made his astronomical observations.

The Palazzo Ex-Ducale contains, in the great Council Chamber, Tintoretto's largest easel-picture; which serves to show how entirely great talents may be thrown away by want of proper attention to methodical arrangement, the whole performance exhibiting a mass of confusion; though it abounds with fine groups, and in some parts is wonderfully well executed. On the Ceiling of this apartment is a Fresco, by Paolo Veronese, representing Venice crowned by Fame! and among the sculpture is a beautiful group, in marble, of Ganymedes and the Eagle, attributed to Phidias. The Hall with four doors, contains a painting, by Titian, of Faith, S. Mark, etc. The Hall of the Inquisition is ornamented with a picture by the Cav. Bassano! and another by the School of Titian. The collegial Hall contains Europa, by Paolo Veronese! and two pictures by Tintoretto. The Cabinet contains a Fresco on its Ceiling, by Paolo Veronese; together with

---

[1] The Treasury of the Church of S. Marco is said to contain the Gospel of S. Mark, written with his own hand; and a Missal adorned with Miniatures, by Giulio Clovio.

easel-pictures; one being by the same master, and others by Tintoretto.

The Accademia delle belle Arti contains several fine pictures; among which are, the Assumption by Titian, originally placed in the Church where he lies buried!!— the same subject by Palma Vecchio—the resurrection of Lazarus, by Bassano! — the marriage of Cana, by Paduanino — Adam and Eve, by Tintoretto—the Holy Family, by Paolo Veronese—and the Miracle of S. Mark, by Tintoretto.

The Chiesa de' Gesuiti (a handsome edifice, elegantly incrusted with Mosaics of verde antique, etc., resembling in their effect green damask hangings), contains a picture of the martyrdom of S. Lorenzo, by Titian; and, in the Sacristy, the Presentation, by Tintoretto.

The Chiesa dei Carmilitani is lined with precious marbles, and very magnificent.

The Chiesa del Carmine contains the best Organ at Venice; and a picture of the Presentation, by Tintoretto.

The Chiesa di S. Giovanni e S. Paolo contains a painting by Titian; another by Perugino; a beautiful window of painted glass; and, in a large Chapel adjoining the Church, some fine *Alti-rilievi*.

The Chiesa di S. Giorgio Maggiore was built by Palladio, in a style of grand simplicity.

Il Redentore was likewise built by Palladio; and is, in point of architecture, a beautiful Church.

The Chiesa di S. Maria della Salute contains the Descent of the Holy Ghost, painted by Titian when he was sixty-four; two pictures by Luca Giordano; and one, by Antonio Treva, which was buried eighteen years, without being materially injured.

The Palazzo-Pisani-Moreta contains a picture of Alexander with the family of Darius, by Paolo Veronese; a work which seems composed in defiance to classical knowledge and good taste; but, nevertheless, so harmonious is the colouring, and so beautiful the painting, that few persons can contemplate this picture without forgetting its faults, and dwelling only on its excellencies.

The Court of the Palazzo-Grimani contains a colossal statue of Marcus Agrippa; which was originally placed in the vestibule of the Pantheon at Rome. This statue is Greek workmanship, and much admired.

The Palazzo-Barberigo, in which Titian died, contains a picture of the Saviour, by that great artist—the Holy Family, by Tintoretto—the portrait of a Venetian Senator, by Titian — the Magdalene, likewise by Titian!— Venus—Paul III.— and S. Sebastiano, all by Titian; who left the last unfinished, in consequence of his death — Susanna and the Elders, by Tintoretto—and the Prodigal Son, by Leandro Bassano.

The Scuola di S. Rocco contains, on the ground floor, a picture of the Annunciation, and other Works, by Tintoretto, who painted in this School for thirty years: and in a room above stairs is a very large and fine picture of the Crucifixion, likewise by Tintoretto.

The Palazzo-Manfrini contains a splendid collection of pictures; which may by seen by Travellers every Monday and Thursday, from ten in the morning till four.

The Arsenal, which occupies

an Island nearly three miles in circumference, is so well defended by lofty walls, turrets, etc., as to resemble a fortress. Its principal entrance is adorned, on the outside, with the winged Lion of Venice; a colossal Lion in white marble, taken from the Piræus at Athens! another Lion, taken from Athens; a Lioness, taken from Corinth; and another, having the word "*Attica*" marked upon it. The object best worth notice, within the walls, is the ancient Armoury.

The Rialto, the Piazza di S. Marco, and the Street and Garden made by Napoleon (a magnificent work), are the only Promenades at Venice. This city contains several Theatres; the largest of which is *the Fenice*: it likewise contains good Hotels; namely, *La Gran-Bretagna* — *Il Lione Bianco* — and *L'Albergo d'Europa*: the first, though the best inn at Venice, is, during winter and the early part of spring, cold and gloomy; the last stands in a much warmer situation.

The gold chains made in this city are particularly beautiful, and the wax-candles remarkably good.

Persons who are anxious to obtain spring-water, may be supplied daily from the terra firma.

On the day of our departure we dined at the Gran-Bretagna; then went in a gondola to Mestrè, slept there; and the next morning early set out for Conegliano, where we arrived in nine hours. About ten miles from Mestrè lies Treviso. Beyond Treviso we passed the Piave; and after crossing the spot where one of Napoleon's great battles was fought, proceeded to Conegliano. The latter town is rather large, and *La Posta* is a good inn.

Our next day's journey was to Pordenon, which we were seven hours and three quarters in reaching; the road between this place and Conegliano being bad at all times, and after rain dangerous, as it lies close to the foot of the Alps, from which mountains torrents of water frequently descend, and inundate the adjacent country. *La Posta*, at Pordenon, is a good inn: here we slept; and next morning proceeded in nine hours to S. Tommaso. Our road, as far as Spilimbergo, lay near the Alps, and through the bed of a torrent, disagreeable at all times, and unsafe after rain. From Spilimbergo we decended into the Tagliamento, a tremendous torrent after rain, but in dry weather fordable. It takes a full hour to travel through this water, with the assistance of oxen and guides;[1] and though the weather, before we crossed, had long been dry, the different streams of which the Tagliamento is composed were wide and rapid, insomuch as to be very disagreeable. Soon after fording this torrent, we passed a town called S. Agnello, a little beyond which is the village of S. Tommaso. The road on this side the Tagliamento is good; the inn at S. Tommaso is bad.

Our next day's journey was to Ponteba, or Pontafel, whither we were twelve hours in going. We took the road by Osoppo, that being deemed the best; though even that, as far as L'Ospedalletto, is rough and dangerous, especially for the first ten miles. At L'Os-

---

[1] Our Voiturier paid, for three guides and two oxen, one sequin.

A fine bridge has been lately thrown over the Tagliamento; but is not, I believe, yet completely finished.

pedaletto, we entered a defile of the Alps, which leads to Venzone, a pretty town, embosomed in these mountains; and hence to Resiuta we found the road, which lies parallel with the bed of the Tagliamento, excellent, the views sublime, and the Alpine plants, which enamel the rocks, particularly beautiful. The inn at Resiuta is clean and comfortable; but the water here, as in most parts of the Alps, is bad; and many inhabitants of this country, especially women, are afflicted with immense goitrous swellings. At Resiuta we began to pass bridges made of wood, and covered at the top; there are five or six of them in this part of the Alps; and in Germany, likewise, all the bridges are made of wood, though not all covered at the top. From Resiuta, which is somewhat above half way to Ponteba, the road lies through defiles of the Alps, near the bed of the Tagliamento, and is good, though too narrow; the views are sublime.

Ponteba, the frontier town of Carinthia, is a miserable-looking place; and here our luggage underwent so rigorous an examination in the open street, before we were suffered to drive to the inn, that it required Argus's eyes not to be plundered of every thing valuable our trunks contained, and Herculean strength to unpack and repack, after the fatigue of a twelve hours' journey: such, indeed, is the inconvenience Travellers must necessarily be exposed to at this custom-house, that I would advise nobody to pass Ponteba who can possibly go another way; it being the great object of the custom-house officers to thieve; for which purpose, they endeavour to throw small parcels on the ground, under the carriages, and even examine coach-seats, writing-boxes, and letters. They seize gold and silver lace, snuff, and tobacco; and for unmade silks, gauzes, etc., they oblige you to deposit double the worth, to be paid back, however, when you quit the Imperial territories.[1] They accept no fees; and are slower in their operations than it is possible to conceive.

After sleeping at Ponteba, where the inn is a bad one, we proceeded in ten hours and a quarter to Villach, through a wide defile of the Alps, and found the road good, and the country beautiful, every mountain being clothed to its summit with noble fir-trees. The German villages, however, at the foot of the mountains, in some measure spoil the beauty of the scene, as nothing can be more uncouth than the wooden buildings which compose them, except the fences, which are, if possible, still worse. The houses are roofed with wood; and the consequence is, that these awkward edifices are continually burnt to the ground. The Germans seldom have a wash-hand basin in any bed-room of their country inns; and even at Villach, a large town, we could not find one. The inn we slept at, however (its sign, *The Crown*), is clean and good; though tall people cannot sleep comfortably, either here or in any part of Germany; the beds, which are very narrow, being placed in wooden frames, or boxes, so short, that any person who happens to be above

---

[1] Your silks, etc. are plumbed; you are asked what road you purpose taking; and you then receive an order for the money you have deposited to be returned at the Custom-house on the confines.

five feet high must absolutely sit up all night, supported by pillows; and this is, in fact, the way in which the Germans sleep.

With respect to provisions, we found no cause for complaint; meat, bread, and wine (somewhat like Hock), beer, soup, and bouillie, sour-crout, stewed prunes, coffee, and milk, being excellent; and water, generally speaking, good. The usual dinner-hour is twelve o'clock; at which time Travellers may always find something to eat at the inns, German cookery being simple and wholesome. One requisite to a comfortable meal it is, however, very difficult to obtain, namely, clean table-linen : we, indeed, were obliged to purchase table-cloths and napkins on our journey; so much were we disgusted by the dirty linen which was produced every where, except in the very large towns.

Women, in this country, seem to work harder than men; and at public-houses female servants not only cook the dinner, and wait at table, but even feed the horses. The peasantry have fine complexions, with a great appearance of health and strength, but their countenances seldom express good-humour, or quickness of apprehension; they dress neatly, and wear high shoes, like those of our English Farmers. The women are said to be depraved in their morals.

Most of the country towns through which we passed consist of straight streets, with a large square in their centre, adorned by an obelisk, statues of the Madonna, our Saviour, etc. The German horses are remarkably strong and handsome; and the whole country, from Ponteba to Vienna, wears the face of wealth, more, perhaps, than any other part of Europe.

The passing through this part of Germany seems like living some hundred years ago in England; as the dresses, customs, and manners, of the people precisely resemble those of our ancestors. Many of their implements of husbandry, also, appear similar to ours; and their kitchens are furnished with plates, dishes, basins, and ewers of pewter, and wooden trenchers, exactly like those which may still be seen among us, in old farm-houses. The herbs and shrubs also resemble those of England, except that barberry-bushes are substituted for blackberries; while the firs grow so luxuriantly, that young plants, a few inches high, literally carpet the woods.

The road from L'Ospedalletto to Villach possesses one great advantage, that of being perhaps the only approach to Italy which does not lie over the summits of the Alps. It is, indeed, remarkable, that although we were surrounded by these "cloud-clapt" mountains the whole of the way, we seldom, if ever, descended a hill steep enough to render a drag-chain necessary; neither did we perceive any fault in the road, its narrowness excepted.

From Villach we proceeded to Klagenfurt, in eight hours and a half, through a good road, and a finely cultivated and beautiful country, adorned wtih a noble sheet of water, called the Lake of Fel. The vallies are variegated with small villages and rustic churches, like those of England; the near mountains clothed to their summits with firs and other trees, while behind them rise Alps covered with eternal snow.

Klagenfurt, is a large and strongly-fortified city; the houses are tolerably neat, and the spires of the churches built in the Turkish style, and covered with white metal. We slept at *The Golden Star,* a tolerable inn, and next day proceeded, in nine hours and a half, to Friesach, through an excellent road, and a bold, finely wooded, and richly cultivated country. In the way to Friesach lies S. Veit, a handsome town. We found *The Wolf* at Friesach a good inn; and after sleeping there, drove in ten hours and a quarter to Judenburg, stopping, however, at Neumark, which is about midway, to dine. We found the road to Neumark smooth, and the country well cultivated, though less beautiful than before; but as we approached Judenburg it became picturesque and finely wooded. We slept at *The Golden Cross and Scythe,* a clean good inn, and went next day, in nine hours and a quarter, to Leoben. Our road continued good, winding near a meandering stream called the Muhr, and the views were beautiful. Travellers usually dine about midway, at Khraubath. *The Imperial Eagle* at Leoben is a comfortable inn, and the town is rather handsome, many of the houses being built with stone or brick.

Our next day's journey was through Bruck to Merzhofen, which we reached in five hours and three quarters, and therefore might easily have gone further; but hearing that the beds at the next Post were engaged, and finding the inn at Merzhofen tolerable, we slept there, and then proceeded, in nine hours and a half, to Schottwien, passing through a good road to Mörzuschlag, where we dined, and then ascended a very lofty mountain, at the foot of which lies Schottwien.¹ The ascent is good, and takes up about one hour; the descent employs more than double that time, and is sharp and dangerous, the road being narrow and ill-kept, insomuch that waggons ascend on the Schottwien side with sixteen and sometimes twenty horses. We found the country from Merzhofen to Schottwien wild, and finely wooded; and previous to our arrival at Mörzuschlag we passed the town of Krieglach.

The *Post House* at Schottwien is a tolerable inn.

Our next day's journey was to Traskirken, whither the drive took up ten hours and a quarter. After quitting Schottwien we entered an extensive plain highly cultivated, and passed through Neukirken and Neustadt, reaching the latter in about six hours and a half. Neukirken is a large town, and contains good inns. Neustadt also is large, contains good inns, and is fortified. We dined here, and afterward proceeded to Traskirken, through a flat and good road, exhibiting, to the right, a prospect of Hungary and the Danube.

We slept at Traskirken (which, though it may be called a large town, does not possess comfortable inns); and then drove, next morning, in four hours and a half, to Vienna, through a flat country,

---

¹ From Mörzuschlag we took extra horses to the summit of this mountain, which Travellers should not descend after it becomes dark.

abounding with game, and thickly spotted with villages, but not well cultivated.

On entering Vienna we were taken to the custom-house, where the officers, though apt to be troublesome to foreigners, were civil to us. The hotels in this city are not so good as might reasonably be expected in the capital of a great empire, and therefore the most comfortable mode of living is to take a private apartment, and employ a *Traiteur*.

Vienna, properly so called, and built at the confluence of the Danube and the Wien, is small, but strongly fortified; its faubourgs, however, are immense, and contain finer buildings than the town itself; in which the palaces are few, and not spacious; and the want of those splendid streets and squares which usually embellish the capital of a great empire, prevents it from appearing, to foreign eyes, a handsome city.

Among the objects best worth notice are, *the Imperial Residence*, the great Chapel belonging to which is adorned with two altar-pieces, by Titian—*the Cathedral of S. Stephen*, a fine Gothic structure, containing an *Ecce Homo*, attributed to Correggio, and a crucifix, by Donner; *the Belfry* of this church, and its *Sacristy*—*the Church dedicated to S. Peter*—*the Front of the Church of S. Michael*, adorned with Statues by L. Mattielli—*the Church of the Augustines*, embellished with an altar-piece by Malbertsch —*the Capuchin Church*, which contains the Burial-place of the House of Austria—*the Church of S. Charles*, on the Bennwegg; and *the Church of S. Rupert*, which is the most ancient in Vienna.—*The Imperial Arsenal*— *the buildings of the university*, and *the Imperial Chancery*—*the Bank*—*the Mint*, once the Palace of Prince Eugene—*the Chancery of Bohemia and Austria*—*the Hôtel de Ville*—*the Fountain*, by Donner, which adorns the Neu-Markt —*the Imperial Library*, said to contain 300,000 printed volumes, and 12,000 manuscripts, and always open to the public from eight in the morning till twelve, during summer; and from nine to twelve, during winter, Sundays and other holidays excepted. This Library is enriched with an ancient Tomb, brought from the vicinity of Ephesus; an Etruscan Vase, celebrated by Winckelmann; and the famous *Senatus Consultum*, mentioned by Livy. *The Imperial Private Library*—*the Jewels of the Crown* —*the Imperial Cabinet of Medals*, which contains a celebrated Cameo of Alexander, by Pyrgoteles; and *the Imperial Cabinet of Natural History*, open every Tuesday morning.

The Imperial Gallery of Paintings at the *Belvédère*, which contains a large work, by Titian, finely executed, though not equal to those at Venice—charming pictures by Rembrandt, especially a portrait of himself, which, for *bravura* and truth, may be denominated his *chef-d'œuvre!*—a fine picture by Rubens, representing an Emperor receiving pardon for some offence against the Holy See—Jupiter and Io, by Correggio!!—Ganymedes, by the same master!! The former of these last named works has been retouched in the back-ground, but is, exclusive of this circumstance, pure from the pencil of Correggio —two heads, by Denner; and some excellent flower-pieces, by Van Huysum. These pictures are on the ground-floor. *The rooms above stairs* likewise contain paintings highly worth notice, from being the works of the very earliest masters of the Flemish and German schools. They are in excellent preservation, possess great merit, and form a most interesting history of the progress of the Art. One of these pictures, an oil-painting, is reputed to have been executed during the year 1292.

The *Belvédère* is open to the public on Mondays, Wednesdays, and Fridays. Many of the pictures once belonged to our unfortunate King, Charles I. It is usual to give two florins for seeing the whole collection.

The Gallery of Paintings in the Lichtenstein Palace contains the story of Decius in seven large pictures, by Rubens—S. Sebastiano, by Vandyck—two portraits, by Holbein—the Guitar-Player, by M. A. Carravaggio—the sacrifice of Iphigenia, by N. Poussin—a Countryman eating, by Beccafumi—a head, by Seybold, being his own portrait—a Madonna and Child, by Teniers—another, by Hanneman — flower-pieces, by Van Huysum, Trechsler, etc.

One florin satisfies the *Custode* above-stairs; and two pauls are sufficient for the Porter below. This Gallery may be seen at all times; but is much inferior to that at the *Belvédère*.

The *Porcelain - manufacture* merits notice.

The *Prater* is one of the most magnificent Promenades in Europe. The usual time of going is after dinner. Coffee, excellent milk, beer, bread, etc., may be procured here.

Lau-Garten is a public place, near the Prater, somewhat like Vauxhall. Here you may dine (under the shade of fine horse-chesnut-trees), in the garden; or in a spacious room, with the rest of the company, every party, however, having its separate table: it is possible, likewise, to get a private room. A band of music, which plays during dinner, receives from each party a paul or two. Dinner (wine excepted) costs one florin per head, and is excellently well served. Here are billiard-tables, a dancing-room, coffee-room, etc. The waiters speak French and Italian.

Schoenbrunn is another public garden, well worth notice, where a good dinner may be had for the above-named price.

These two gardens are open for dinner-company from the first of May to the last of September; and during the rest of the year the same *Traiteur* serves, for the same price, at Vienna, in his own house, where Travellers may board.

There are two remarkably good coffee-houses in this city, the *Café de Kramer*, and the *Café de Milan*.

Water-drinkers would do well, while resident here, to supply themselves either at the Capuchin-Convent, in the *Place-Neuve;* or at the Palace of Prince Schwarzenberg.

The national dish in Germany is small chickens fried very dry, being first cut into pieces, as for a fricassee; and this dish is particularly well served by *Traiteurs*.

There are two Theatres in the city of Vienna, and three in the suburbs; none of them large; but the orchestra at the opera-house is excellent, and the stage-decorations are good. It is difficult, at this theatre, for foreigners to obtain boxes. Ladies, however, may sit in the *parterre*, sending beforehand for seats. There are frequent and beautiful exhibitions of fire-works at Vienna. This city, with its fauxbourgs, is said to contain two hundred and seventy thousand inhabitants.

The distance from Florence hither is about nine hundred Tuscan miles; and the expense of barriers and turnpikes for one carriage from five to six Tuscan sequins.[1]

Our first day's journey from Vienna was to *Stockerau*, a drive of five hours and a half, through a good but sandy road. On quitting Vienna, we had a beautiful view of the Danube, together with several royal parks and gardens, which, all united, form an enchanting scene. The Danube is immensely wide, and at the same time so translucent as to be a great embellisher of every country through which it flows. The road to Stockerau traverses a vast plain, richly cultivated, and adorned with several towns. After sleeping at a comfortable inn (the sign, *Our Saviour and the woman of Samaria*), we proceeded in two hours and a half to *Mallebern*: where, in consequence of one of our party being taken ill, we were compelled to pass the night at a bad inn. The road thither is flat and good, but sandy; the country richly cultivated, and much like the south of France.

From Mallebern we drove in six hours to Jezelsdorf, through a flat and good road, passing a *Château* belonging to the Emperor, and a handsome town called Hollabrunn.[2] The towns on this side Vienna are chiefly built of stone and brick; the villages consist of neat thatched cottages. The country is a rich and extensive plain, planted, near Jezelsdorf, with a large number of vines. The water in the last-named town is bad. After dining here, we proceeded in three hours and a half to *Znaim*, through a good road,[3] and an immense and richly-cultivated plain, abounding with corn and vineyards.

Znaim, the first town of Moravia, is large, handsome, and built somewhat like an Italian city. It contains several inns. We slept at *the Three Crowns*, and found nothing to complain of, except bad water. Next day, we drove in five hours and a quarter to Schinta through a very rough road, and an immense plain abounding with corn. The inn at Schinta is almost too bad even to dine at: we were, however, obliged to stop for a couple of hours, to rest the mules; after which we proceeded in three hours and a half to *Schelletau*, through a very rough road, and an open swampy country, rich in corn and woods of fir. Our inn here was *the Post-House*, which we found tolerably good. Next day we drove in six hours to Iglau, through a good road, and an open corn-country, passing Stannern and other small villages on our way. Iglau, the last city of Moravia, is handsomely built in the

---

1 Better carriages are built at Vienna than in any other city of the Continent; and that sort known by the name of *Bâtarde* is peculiarly safe and convenient for travelling. The usual price for one of these carriages, vache, trunks, and every other requisite inclusive, is from five to six hundred imperial florins.

2 Hollabrunn contains good inns.

3 We had extra horses to ascend the hill beyond Jezelsdorf.

Italian style; and the outsides of some of the houses are embellished with curious old paintings. The square contains good inns. The spires of the churches in this country, like those of Carinthia, are chiefly covered with white metal. The dress of the female peasants is pretty; but, 'what looks odd to foreign eyes, the women wear short petticoats and drawers, while the men's coats reach to their shoes. Fur seems much worn by both sexes. After dining at Iglau, we proceeded in two hours and a half to *Stecken*, through a good road, and a country richly cultivated with corn, and variegated with woods. The inn at Stecken is bad; we were, however, obliged to sleep there, though better accommodations may be obtained at Deutschbrodt, a drive of above two hours and a quarter further. Stecken is the first post in Bohemia.

Our next day's journey was to *Czaslau*, a drive of nine hours and three quarters; we dined, however, by the way, at Hauvre, where the inn is tolerable. Our road to Czaslau (the first part excepted, which traverses a hill¹), was rough; the country abounds in corn and woods of fir.—Czaslau is a handsome town, with a large square and obelisk in its centre; the houses are chiefly white and tiled at the top; the ornaments of the belfries here, and in Moravia, consist of five or six spires beside a cupola, all covered with white metal. We slept at *the Post-House*, a tolerably good inn, where the master was remarkably civil and honest; for we left, at this inn, a pair of pistols, which were sent after us.

Our next day's journey was to *Planian*, a drive of six hours and a quarter, through a tolerable road, and a vast plain of corn. On our way we went near Mollin, a large town, and through Collin, which also seems large. There are two tolerable inns at Planian, where we slept, in consequence of illness: but ought to have proceeded to Boemischbrod, a drive of two hours and a half further. Next day, however, we reached *Prague*, after travelling ten hours in a good road, through a vast plain, richly cultivated, and interspersed with towns and villages, but not pretty. We descended almost constantly for many miles before we entered Prague.

This is one of the handsomest cities in Europe, built in the Italian style, and famous for its bridge; its size, likewise, is considerable, and its fortifications are strong. The inhabitants, however, bear no proportion to the capaciousness of the town, as they do not, according to the best computations, amount to ninety thousand. The *University of Prague* has long been celebrated. *The Cathedral*, a finely situated Gothic structure, and *the Church of the Holy Cross*, are said to be worth notice, but unfortunately we had not time to examine them. The beautiful Bridge of Prague is thrown over the Moldau, which runs into the Elbe.

Here are several inns; we went to that called *The Prince of Prussia*. *The Lion* is much recommended.

---

1 We ascended this hill with extra horses.

The Sclavonian language (a dialect of the German) is spoken in Moravia and Bohemia.

From Prague, we drove in four hours and a half to Schlan, through a good road, generally up hill, and over a vast plain, tolerably cultivated with corn and hops. We dined at Schlan (where, though the town is not small, the inn is indifferent); and thence proceeded, in five hours, to *Budin*, through a very bad road, the soil being loose and boggy: the country, however, is rich in corn and game. Budin contains two inns, neither of which can be called good. Next day we drove, in five hours, to *Lobositz*, through a boggy, and (after rain) an extremely dangerous road. To ascend the hill out of Budin, it is requisite that every carriage should have extra horses: indeed, for the whole post, extra-horses are useful; and heavy carriages should be held up by men. Immediately after quitting Budin, we crossed the Elbe, and generally kept it in sight afterward till our arrival at Dresden. Lobositz contains two tolerable inns; *the Pos.-House*, and *the Free-Masons' Arms* (called *L'Austeria Grande*); we slept at the latter, not being able to obtain extra-horses in order to proceed. Next morning we drove, in five hours and a half, to Aussig,[1] through a road, bad at all times, and excessively dangerous after rain; being rocky, in some places, to a degree that risks breaking heavy carriages to pieces, and so boggy in others, that the lightest vehicle can scarcely escape overturning, unless held up by men. And, to increase the danger of this road, it lies close to the Elbe, on the brink of a precipice.

Travellers, whose carriages are heavy, should put their luggage into a waggon, and themselves either upon horses or into a light calash, between Lobositz and Aussig; and Invalids ought not to attempt going any way but on horseback, the jolts being so violent that it requires considerable bodily strength to bear them; as a proof of which, two persons who went in carriages, at the same time with us, broke blood-vessels; while others were overturned, and nearly killed with fatigue. It seems extraordinary that the Emperor does not have this road mended, as it might be done in a short time, and at a small expense, especially on the banks of the Elbe, where the soil is chiefly a rock. He has, however, made the following road from Prague to Dresden, which is reckoned better than that we took:

	Posts.
From *Schlan* to *Teinitz*	1
Postelberg	1
Toplitz	2
Peterswald	1½
Zehist	1
DRESDEN	1

Perhaps it might be possible to go down the Elbe from Budin to Dresden; from Aussig, it certainly would; though, in either case, Travellers ought to send forward some hours before-hand, in order to have a proper boat provided.

The inn at Aussig is small, but clean; and the country from Lobositz thither very romantic. After dining at Aussig, we set out for Peterswald, which we were seven hours in reaching, as the road is bad, even to be dangerous;

---

[1] Aussig is famous for its strong sweet wine, called Postkaltzky.

it traverses a high mountain, to ascend which either oxen, or extra-horses, are requisite.

Peterswald is the last town in the Imperial dominions, and does not contain one good inn. But a quarter of a mile out of the town, at a hamlet called *Iledorf*, or *Hilesdorf*, there is a clean, comfortable public-house, which stands close to the high-road, on the right, the sign being *the Free-Masons' Arms*. At this house we slept; and next morning, drove in eight hours to Dresden. On quitting Hilesdorf, we ascended a steep hill,[1] and then passed a wood of fir; after which, we descended almost constantly through a rich corn-country, till our arrival at Dresden. We found the road sometimes rough, but, generally speaking, good; the villages neat, the peasantry clean; and, after leaving Peterswald, we did not see one beggar.

There is a comfortable looking inn not far from Hilesdorf, and another at Pirna, about ten English miles from Dresden.

The dress of the Saxon peasants resembles that worn in England some centuries ago; and when we spoke English to these people, they frequently understood us.

The approach to Dresden announces the richness of Saxony; and at the gate of the city we found a custom-house officer, who attended us to our inn; where, on being presented with a couple of florins, he retired without examining our luggage.

Dresden, the capital of Saxony, is supposed to contain about 50,000 inhabitants; though some authors rate the population at double that number.

The architecture of Dresden is simple, light, and elegant; the streets are straight, wide, and clean; the squares spacious; the palaces, churches, and other public edifices, magnificent; and the bridge thrown over the Elbe, which divides the old from the new buildings, is one of the finest in Europe.

Here are, as it were, three cities; the old town, the new town, and Frederickstadt. The fortifications are strong; the environs rich and beautiful; and the Elbe, though not clear, is broad and handsome. Lutheranism is the established religion of the country; but the Calvinists have public meeting-houses, and the Sovereign has one Romish church; he and his family being Roman Catholics.

The inhabitants of Dresden are, generally speaking, well conditioned, and very civil to Foreigners; who live here with comfort, at a moderate expense: and Painters may study with great advantage at Dresden; not only on account of the precious works of art which are submitted to public view, but likewise because there reigns throughout this town a tranquillity peculiarly favourable to the studious.

Here are several good inns; and private lodgings also may be procured without difficulty.

The objects best worth a Traveller's notice are—*The royal Romish Church*, which contains a celebrated organ, by Silbermann; and a fine picture of the Ascension, by Mengs—(the Belfry of this church is 303 feet in height)—*The Picture Gallery—The Treasury*, or *Jewel-Office—The Gallery of Antiques—The*

---

[1] We were drawn up this hill by the aid of oxen.

royal Libraries—and *The Collection of Dresden China*. *The Cabinet of Natural History*, and *The antique Armoury*, should likewise be visited, if Travellers have time to spare.

In order to gain admittance to the Picture Gallery, the Treasury, the Gallery of Antiques, and the Royal Libraries, it is requisite to send, over night, your name, country, and quality, to the respective Directors; together with the number of persons you intend to bring, and the hour at which you mean to come. You may either go from nine till half-past ten in the morning, or from half-past ten till twelve; from two till half-past three in the afternoon, or from half-past three till five. To the Director of the Picture-Gallery each party pays from four florins to one ducat, and to the Sweeper half a florin; which sum once given, you are at liberty to go without expense afterward. To the Master of the Jewel-Office every party pays four florins, and to each of his servants half a florin; which sum once given, you are at liberty to go free of expense afterward. The *Custode* who shows the Collection of Dresden China expects a ducat, provided the party he attends be large.

Picture Gallery. This immense collection, certainly the finest of its kind in Europe, contains *chefs-d'œuvre*, excellently well preserved, of the best masters: so that it is scarcely possible for any person to study the Dresden Gallery, without becoming a real Connoisseur.

Here are, in *the Flemish School*, Adonis and Venus—a Satyr and a Faun—Neptune calming a tempest—Meleager presenting the Boar's head to Atalanta—and S. Jerome meditating; all first-rate productions, by Rubens. Several works by Netscher (particularly a man seated, and writing), which show precisely how small pictures ought to be painted. Admirable works by Teniers, Ostade, Ruysdaal, Wouvermans, Brughel, Berghem, and Paul Potter. The Annunciation—and the judgment of Paris, both by Vander Werf—the Madonna with the Saviour in her arms, and a little naked Boy in the lower part of the picture, by Holbein—and portraits of a Burgomaster and his Wife, by the same artist.

The Italian School contains, the Madonna enthroned with the Saviour, by Correggio, in his first manner—the Madonna enthroned with the Saviour, S. George, etc., by the same great master—his Magdalene, a small recumbent figure, said to be the most faultless picture ever painted—and the Nativity, called Correggio's Night, and by many persons deemed the *chef-d'œuvre* of colouring, though now injured by having been washed—the Madonna, the Saviour, etc., called Correggio's—S. Sebastian—and a portrait, by Correggio, of his Physician—The Tribute Money, by Titian, deemed one of his finest pictures—and the Madonna, the Saviour, Pope Sixtus V., Cherubim, etc., attributed to Raphael.

Other celebrated paintings *in the Flemish School* are, Noah sacrificing after having left the Ark, by N. Poussin—Luther and his wife, by J. Holbein—a Child borne away by an eagle! (This picture, the work of Rembrandt, seems improperly called the rape of Ganymedes)—a portrait of Rembrandt, by himself; and another of his Mother, weighing gold, likewise by Rembrandt—portrait of Salvator Rosa, by himself—Peasants dancing, by Teniers—portrait of Henry VIII., of England, by J. Holbein—a Girl with a lighted candle gathering grapes, by Gerard Dow!—a head of N. Poussin, by himself—Moses found in the Nile, by Poussin—Rembrandt's daughter, by Rembrandt—a small Madonna and Child, by Albert Durer—Fruit and Flowers, by A. Minjon—a Landscape, by Berghem, and a Landscape with Cattle, by Ruysdaal—our Saviour raising the Dead, with other small but highly finished pictures by Dieterich—a Landscape, with Lions, by Rubens!—a Landscape, with a forest and a hunted stag, by Ruysdaal and Vander Velde!—Manoah and his wife sacrificing, and the Angel ascending to heaven, by Rembrandt—the Repose in Egypt, by Ferdinand Bol!—the feast of Ahasuerus, by Rembrandt—a Girl standing at an open window and reading a letter, school of Rembrandt—Narcissus and Nymphs, by N. Poussin—the Martyrdom of S. Erasmus, by ditto—a Landscape with Cattle, by Vander Velde—a Cock and Hen endeavouring to oppose an Eagle who has seized one of their chickens, by Hondekoeter!—a Landscape with a Shepherd playing on his pipe, by Claude—a Landscape, by Berghem—a Battle by Wouvermans!—the Madonna and our Saviour, by Vandyck!—several exquisitely finished Heads, by Denner and Seybold—a Philosopher reading, by Konink!—a Banker conversing with a Peasant who has brought him money, by Quintin-Matsys—a forest, Dogs, and Falcons, by Vander Velde and Paul Potter—Joseph presenting his Father to Pharaoh, by Ferdinand Bol—a head of Seybold, by himself—the Madonna, the Saviour, and S. Anne, by J. Van Eyk, the reputed inventor of oil-colours—S. Jerome penitent, by Vandyck—a Tooth-Drawer, by G. Honthorst—Venus seated, and Cupid playing with a Dove, by Vander Werf—a Banker weighing gold and a Woman looking at him, by Quintin-Matsys—Syrinx and Pan, by N. Poussin—Noah sacrificing after the Deluge, and a Bacchanalian scene, both by Poussin—a Stable, by Wouvermans—and the idolatry of Solomon, by Poussin.

Other celebrated paintings belonging to *the Italian School*, are S. Cecilia, etc., by Giulio Romano—a recumbent Magdalene, by P. Battoni—Parnassus, by Tintoretto—a Concert, by the same master—the Resurrection of our Saviour, by Paolo Veronese—a Woman carried off by a Man, at whose feet lies another man wounded, by J. C. Procaccini—the repose in Egypt, by Trevisani—Head of a man with a cap on, by Titian!—Adam and Eve driven from Paradise, by Albano!—Mars seated, by Benvenuto Garofolo—Samson combating the Philistines, by Giulio Romano—Herodias with the head of S. John, by Leonardo da Vinci—the Genius of Glory, by Annibale Caracci—the Repose in Egypt, by Lodovico Caracci—the Madonna and our Saviour, by Annibale Caracci—the Woman detected in adultery, by Tintoretto—the same subject, by Bartolomeo Biscaino!—a recumbent Venus, by Titian, and another by Guido—Peace, by Dosso Dossi—Justice, by ditto—the Saviour in the stable, with

Angels adoring him, by Albano!—the Saviour crowned with thorns and supported by an Angel, by Annibale Caracci!—a Bacchanalian feast, by Garofolo—a young Bacchus by Guido—the Assumption, by A. Caracci—S. George and the Dragon, by Raphael—an *Ecce Homo*, by Guido—Lot and his Daughters, by Guercino—the Angel and Tobias, by Titian—Titian's Mistress, by himself—the Head of our Saviour, by A. Caracci—a Candle-Light piece, by Rubens!—a Holy Family, called the Madonna with the basin, by Giulio Romano—Loves dancing, and Venus above, in the clouds, by Albano—two pictures of Galatea, by ditto—the Fall of the Angels, by Tintoretto—the good Samaritan, by Paolo Veronese—a Madonna and Child, by Schidone—the portrait of Thomas Parr, when above a hundred years old, by Vandyck—and the Madonna and our Saviour in glory, by Ramenghi called Bagnacavallo.

Cabinet of Drawings in Pastel—Portrait of Raphael Mengs, by himself—of his Father, by the same—and of Cupid, by the same!—several other beautiful drawings, and some small paintings in enamel. *This Gallery is warm.*

Treasury, or Jewel-Office. The most striking things here are—*Second room*—a ship of ivory, and a vase of the same, with *bassi-rilievi* representing a battle. *Third room*—a chimney-piece adorned with all the most valuable productions of Saxony, namely, china, diamonds, and other precious stones, pearls, etc. *Fourth room*—superb pieces of plate, etc. *Fifth room*—(fitted up with peculiar elegance) fine *camei*—a *basso-rilievo* on the shell of a Nautilus—another large *basso-rilievo* representing a youth travelling into foreign countries upon an unbridled horse; but, having Virtue for his guide, Vice flies before him. *Sixth Room*—three pieces of enamel, by Mengs—antique enamel—pearls representing men and women about one finger high, among which a Potter is much admired. *Seventh room*—a pyramid of precious stones, antique *camei*, etc., in the centre of which is the head of Augustus II.; and at the foot of the column are small enamelled figures, in the respective dresses of the several European nations. This pyramid is said to have cost 100,000 crowns. *Eighth room*—an onyx, esteemed the largest in the known world—the Great Mogul seated on his throne, and celebrating his birth-day; a superb toy—an Egyptian temple, likewise a superb toy—the Jewels of the crown; being a dazzling collection of fine brilliants—a large and beautiful green diamond, said to be unique, with several large red and yellow diamonds. *The rooms are paved with marble, and very cold.*

Cabinet of antique Sculpture. The most striking things here are—a young Bacchus eating grapes—Meleager—one of the sons of Niobe, dead—an Etruscan statue of Minerva, the drapery of which is curious—a *basso-rilievo* of Artimesia, in jasper, attributed to Lysippus—statues of two female Fauns—Æsculapius and Venus, the head of the first particularly fine—statues of Vestals, found in Herculaneum by the Prince d'Elbeuf, and by far the finest things in this collection; the drapery being wonderfully executed!!!—a fragment of a Gladiator, or Wrestler, going to anoint himself, attributed to Phidias!— an Etruscan altar — a Grecian altar, with niches in it— a Sarcophagus, with a dog. Here are other valuable pieces of sculpture; but, as most of them have been sadly mutilated and ill-restored, artists only can appreciate their merits. *This Cabinet is cold.*

Under the apartments which contain the above-named antiques is a collection of Dresden china, from its commencement, by J. F. Bottcher, in 1701, to the present period. The inventor of this china was an apothecary's man at Berlin; and finding himself suspected of being able to make gold, he deemed it prudent to retire to Dresden; where, being ordered to prepare a powder for the transmutation of metals, he happened, in the course of his studies on this occasion, to discover the art of making Dresden china. *The rooms which contain this china are damp and cold.*

There are two theatres at Dresden.

The distance from Vienna to this city is about four hundred and fifty English miles; and the expense of ferries and barriers for one carriage about three Tuscan sequins. The distance from Dresden to Hamburgh is about the same; and, in consequence of hearing that the road was execrably bad, and that the inns were very indifferent, we determined to dismiss our mules and go by water, in an excellent boat, with three cabins, four beds, a place behind for men-servants, and another before for baggage. Our beds, fuel, kitchen-utensils, knives, forks, spoons, glasses, cups, saucers, plates, and dishes, were found by the master of the boat, who paid all the port-duties to the princes whose territories lay in our route, and maintained himself and four watermen, we giving him two hundred and fifty-five dollars of Saxony (being florins three hundred eighty-two and a half), an extravagant price, as boats a very little smaller go for one hundred and twenty-five dollars. Indeed, I would advise large families to hire a couple of these smaller boats; by which means, they would be better accommodated, and pay somewhat less than we did.[1]

The Elbe is a remarkably safe river as far as Hamburgh, though in some places so shallow that large boats are apt to touch ground; but this does no harm, as the bottom is a soft sand. We were seven days and a half on our passage, the wind being contrary; but with a favourable breeze, or indeed none at all, this voyage is usually accomplished in less than a week, even though you cast anchor for a few hours every night, in order to avoid the noise which the boatmen make while going on. We continually passed villages where bread, meat, fish, vegetables, eggs, milk, butter, and good wine were to be purchased; and beer we took from Dresden.

The banks of the Elbe are finely wooded. The most remarkable towns we passed near were *Meissen*, where the Dresden china is made, and where there is a covered bridge over the Elbe; *Torgau*, where there is another covered bridge over the Elbe (the

---

[1] It is necessary to have two mattresses for each bed, and curtains to all the cabin-windows.

country from Dresden hither abounds with vineyards);[1] *Wittemberg,* a handsome town, which contains a University, and is famous for having been the abode of Luther, whose Tomb is in the Church belonging to the Castle:[2] here, likewise, is a bridge thrown over the Elbe; and here provisions of all kinds, beer, and wine, may be purchased better and cheaper than in any other place between Dresden and Hamburg; *Coswick,* rather a large town, not far from which are the celebrated *Gardens of Verlitzen;* and by landing at a place where the boatmen pay a tax, and walking to another place where they likewise pay a tax, Travellers may see these gardens without delaying their voyage; *Magdeburg,* a large and strongly-fortified city, belonging to Prussia; where, however, strangers cannot land without having their passports examined. We were detained here some hours, that our boatmen might pay the port-duties, which are heavy. After quitting this city, we passed several villages belonging to Hanover, among which was *Lauenburg,* rather a large place, where, though the people look robust, there is a great appearance of poverty.

The Elbe becomes immensely broad as it approaches Hamburgh, which city, supposed to contain a hundred and twenty thousand inhabitants, is built somewhat in the style of an old English country town. The streets are straight, and planted with trees close to the houses; the quay abounds with people of every nation; the port is crowded with ships; and the whole city exhibits an appearance of being the world's exchange. Here are no duties to pay at the custom-house. The inns at Hamburgh are neither good nor cheap. Private lodgings may be obtained; though, like the inns, they are bad and dear.

There are large numbers of storks on the banks of the Elbe, and in the city of Hamburgh; and, what is remarkable, these birds are held in such veneration by the common people, that they would probably murder any foreigner who attempted shooting a stork.

The filial piety of this fowl has long been celebrated; and its sagacity in other instances seems equally extraordinary, judging from the following circumstance. A wild stork was brought by a farmer into his poultry-yard, to be the companion of a tame one he had long kept there; but the tame stork, disliking the idea of a rival, fell upon the stranger, and beat him so unmercifully, that he was compelled to take wing, and with some difficulty got away. About four months afterward, however, he returned to the poultry-yard, recovered of his wounds, and attended by three other storks, who no sooner alighted than they fell upon the tame stork and killed him!

From Hamburgh to Cuxhaven we went by water in one of the boats which usually convey passengers, each of which is large enough to accommodate five or

---

[1] Of all the excellent wines in this neighbourhood, that of Torgau is deemed the best.
[2] Luther was chosen first to teach philosophy, and afterward theology, in the University founded by Frederick Elector of Saxony, at Wittemberg.

six persons; and contains beds, and a fire-place for cooking provisions. The time of embarkation is regulated by the tide. We were about eighteen hours in going; and paid to our watermen, three in number, seventy marks for the boat, and four for drink-money; finding provisions for ourselves, but not for the watermen.[1]

On arriving at Cuxhaven we luckily met with a packet ready to sail for Harwich.

Every Cabin, or Whole Passenger, pays for going from Cuxhaven to Harwich, in a Post-Office packet . . L.5 5 0

Every Half Passenger L.3 0 0
Every four-wheeled carriage (the charge for shipping it not inclusive) 8 0 0

Female Servants pay as Whole Passengers;—Children, under six years, as Half Passengers;—and above that age as Whole Passengers.[2]

Harwich packets sail to Cuxhaven every Wednesday and Saturday, about two o'clock in the afternoon, weather permitting; and return twice a week, if possible.

Cuxhaven, though a small town, contains clean Inns.

---

[1] Public boats convey Passengers and luggage from Hamburgh to Cuxhaven every Tuesday and Friday, weather permitting. The price paid by a Cabin Passenger is fifteen marks—by a Steerage Passenger eleven marks and four skillings—and by Servants four marks and twelve skillings each.

[2] As the rates of Passengers by Post-office packets are occasionally altered, the best mode of gaining certain intelligence on this subject is by an application at the General Post-office in London.

APPENDIX.

CHAPTER I.

CLIMATES OF THE CONTINENT.—REQUISITES FOR TRAVELLERS, ETC.

Climates of Nice, Massa, and Pisa—Invalids cautioned against exposing themselves to the influence of the sun—Newly-built houses, and houses not built on arches, unwholesome—Ground-floors healthy only in summer—Best winter situation for Invalids—Eligible situations during other seasons of the year—Naples, Genoa, and Lisbon liable to destructive vicissitudes of weather—Barcelona, Valencia, and Alicant recommended during winter—Requisites for Invalids and other Travellers on leaving England—Means of preserving health during a long journey—Bargains with Innkeepers, etc.

My family were advised to travel over-land to Italy; and we therefore passed through France. Nice was recommended as the best winter-climate for pulmonary complaints, and we consequently resided there several months: but experience convinced us that we might have adopted a more eligible plan; as we saw at Nice no instance of recovery from pulmonary consumption; neither did this appear extraordinary in a climate where a fervid sun and an uncommonly sharp wind are perpetually combating with each other. Massa, in point of climate, is the counterpart of Nice; but Pisa, as I have already mentioned, is one of the best winter-climates in Europe, and ought, I am persuaded, in pulmonary complaints, to be decidedly preferred to every other city of Italy, from the commencement of October till the end of April. The marshy ground and standing water about Pisa formerly rendered the air unwholesome; but this evil is now removed; and the consequent increase of population has not only banished grass from the streets, but dispensed cheerfulness and health throughout this elegant city. It seems requisite, however, to give Invalids, who purpose residing here, one caution, namely, never to sit, stand, nor walk in the sun, without being defended by a parasol; and always to prefer walking on the shady side of a street.* Newly-built houses are to be avoided here, and in every other part of Italy; as it is, generally speaking, four or five years ere new walls become dry. Houses, not built on arches, are likewise to be avoided; and ground floors, during winter, spring, and

---

* Persons who are under the necessity of exposing themselves to the influence of the sun in warm climates, ought to line the crowns of their hats with writing-paper several times doubled; and likewise to sponge themselves daily with vinegar: indeed, this wash is not only a preservative against those fevers which result from hot weather or *mal' aria*, but also a most salutary application in consumptive cases.

autumn, are unwholesome; though healthy in summer. That side of the Pisa Quay, called *La parte di mezzo-giorno*, is, as I have already mentioned, the best winter situation for Invalids, because warmer and less damp than any other: for though the climate is uniformly soft (owing to mountains which operate as a screen from every wind, except sea-breezes), it is sometimes complained of for being moist, and wanting elasticity: but this very want frequently proves beneficial to weak lungs: and indeed I am fully convinced, from experience, that the lives of many consumptive persons might be saved, were they sent by sea to Leghorn,* advised to winter at Pisa, cautioned against travelling much by land; and, above all things, interdicted from crossing the Apennine and Alps; which travellers often do, in order to spend the summer months in Switzerland, one of the most unequal climates of Europe. From the beginning of May till midsummer I would counsel consumptive persons either to reside at the Baths of Pisa, or in the city of Florence; and, during the great heats, to seek a villa, the more spacious the more wholesome, on those hills which lie just beneath Fiesole; where there is a constant and sometimes a very fresh breeze from noon till sun-set; insomuch that I have sat out of doors in the shade at mid-day (when the thermometer often rises to 85, and even to 90), without feeling more warmth than is easily supported: and as the wind always abates when the sun declines, and the surrounding higher mountains of the Apennine attract the noxious vapours, this situation is not liable to those dangerous vicissitudes from heat to cold which are particularly baneful to weak lungs. Florence, during the height of summer, though wholesome, is, as I have already mentioned, oppressively hot; in autumn temperate; but in winter foggy and cold. To persons who require a bracing summer-climate, I would recommend the Baths of Lucca; where the thermometer seldom rises higher than from 76 to 78; or the town of Carrara, which, from the loftiness of its position, from its vicinity to the sea, and likewise from the days (owing to the height of the mountains) being shorter there, than in many other parts of Italy, is very cool. Siena, also, from being built on an eminence, and therefore frequently visited by refreshing breezes, is deemed an eligible summer-abode, but owing to that reflected heat from which no large city can be exempt, it is often oppressively hot during the months of July and August. Rome, from the end of October till the end of April, is considered, when the lungs are not ulcerated, as even a better climate, in consumptive cases, than Pisa: and at all seasons that part of Rome not affected by *Mal' aria*, is particularly congenial to old persons; insomuch that there are not, perhaps, half so many instances of longevity, without in-

---

* Rates of Passengers by the Mediterranean Packets, which sail from Falmouth:—

From Falmouth to Gibraltar, Cabin Passenger, 38*l*.—Steerage Passenger, 22*l*.

Do. Malta, Cabin Passenger, 59*l*.—Steerage Passenger, 33*l*.

From Falmouth to Messina, Cabin Passenger, 64*l*.—Steerage Passenger, 34*l*.

Passengers provide their own bedding; and female servants pay as Cabin Passengers.

Packets sail from Falmouth for the Mediterranean every third Tuesday throughout the year, weather permitting.

firmities, in any other populous city of Europe.* Naples, from the quantity of sulphur with which its atmosphere is impregnated, cannot be a good situation in all stages of a decline: at Naples, likewise, the wind is frequently strong and piercing; and the continual vicissitudes from heat to cold, which are common here during winter and spring, render the climate, at those seasons, a bad one. I have already recommended the Plain of Sorrento as the most healthful summer-abode in southern Italy; and during a long residence there, I seldom saw the thermometer rise to 78; never felt the heat of summer oppressive, unless I exposed myself to the mid-day sun, which is always dangerous in warm climates; neither was I ever tormented by musquitoes, which, during the months of July, August, and September, are a serious evil in many parts of the Continent: the Baths of Lucca, however, the city of Siena, and all lofty situations, are, generally speaking, exempt from this pest. I can likewise safely recommend the climate of the town of Sorrento, and that part of its Piano called S. Agnello, as peculiarly salubrious and delightful in winter; though, during the vernal and autumnal equinox, this district, like other countries near the sea, is visited by storms; but they are not sufficiently violent to injure the orange-trees; which, loaded with golden fruit during the months of November, December, and January, conspire with the ever-green olives, ilexes, and pines, to give this favoured spot the semblance of perpetual spring.

The climate of Genoa cannot (as I have already mentioned) be recommended; that of northern Italy is cold during winter, and at other seasons liable to sudden and unwholesome changes. Lisbon, also, is subject to these destructive vicissitudes of weather; insomuch that but few consumptive Invalids have recovered the blessing of health from visiting the banks of the Tagus. Spain, as a place of residence, is on some accounts objectionable; because the water and provisions (fruit and other vegetables excepted) are not, generally speaking, good in that country; but, with respect to climate, Barcelona, Valencia, and Alicant are, during winter, preferable even to Pisa.†

REQUISITES FOR INVALIDS, AND OTHER TRAVELLERS, ON LEAVING ENGLAND.

Travellers, who intend going from London to Paris, should apply for passports to the French Minister in the first-named capital. These passports are obtained without any expense, except a trifling gratuity to the Minister's porter; and they are absolutely needful; because British subjects cannot, at the present moment, enter France without them; neither can Post-Masters at Paris, nor within forty-five miles of that city, supply a foreigner with horses, unless he exhibit a passport; and lately, indeed, passports have been called for, and strictly examined, in every large town throughout the Continent. Persons who intend travelling from France, through Switzer-

* The inhabitants of Rome, however, usually go into the country during the month of October; or take very strong exercise, to preserve themselves from the bilious fever prevalent in the city during that period.

† Persons who wish to preserve health, either in Portugal, Spain, or Southern Italy, during winter, should endeavour to keep themselves warm by means of additional clothing, rather than fires.

land, to northern Italy, should take care to have these important vouchers signed by the Austrian Ambassador at Paris: this, however has been already mentioned.*

Circular Exchange-Notes, from Herries and Co., St. James's-Street, or Hammersley and Co., Pall-Mall, are particularly advantageous to travellers; because payable at sight in all the principal cities of Europe, and likewise exempt from the deduction of one per cent, to which common letters of credit are subject. Letters of recommendation to all the British Ministers on the Continent are also highly advantageous. Letters to respectable Foreigners are useful; and frequently guard Travellers from imposition. The English complain of being pillaged in foreign countries: but if they would procure recommendations to men of respectability, instead of trusting to Innkeepers and *Valets-de-place*, they might find themselves much less imposed upon. The lower class of Italians usually form a league to pillage Travellers. Thus, if a *Valet-de-place* hire your lodging, he receives (from the landlord) a certain stipend during your stay; and this sum never fails to be added on to your rent: if he hire your carriage, he receives a considerable fee from the job-man; while you pay dearer in consequence: nay, every artist or mechanic you employ, and every article you purchase, is, generally speaking, taxed, either by your *Valet-de-place*, or your Courier. Persons who go to Italy by sea, cannot, however, require this latter class of servant: and, indeed, I would counsel those who travel by land, to dispense with so costly a domestic: whose place may always be supplied by a good post-book, and an active man-servant, who understands the management of carriages.

The following articles are useful to Travellers in general; and some of them particularly needful to Invalids.

Leather sheets, made of sheep-skin, or doe-skin—pillows—blankets—calico sheets—pillow-cases—a musquito-net, made of strong gauze or very thin muslin—a travelling chamber-lock—(these locks may always be met with in London; and are easily fixed upon any door in less than five minutes)—Bramah-locks for writing-desks and coach-seats—a tinder-box and matches—a small lantern—towels, table-cloths and napkins, strong but not fine—pistols—a pocket-knife to eat with—table-knives—a carving-knife and fork—a silver tea-pot—or a blocktin tea-pot, tea, and sugar-canister, the three last so made as to fit into the kettle—penknives—Walkden's ink powder—pens—razors, straps, and hones—needles, thread, tape, worsted, and pins—gauze-worsted stockings—flannel—double soled shoes and boots, and elastic soles; which are particularly needful, in order to resist the chill of brick and marble floors—clogs, called *Paraboues*; which are to be purchased of the Patentee, Davis, Tottenham-Court-Road, No. 229—warm pelisses, great-coats and travelling-caps—The London and Edinburgh Dispensatory; or the Universal Dispensatory, by Reece—a thermometer—a medicine-chest, with scales, weights, an ounce, and

---

* See the former part of this Work, Chapter I, page 24, which contains a Note of consequence with respect to Passports.

half-ounce, measure for liquids—a glass pestle and mortar—Shuttleworth's drop measure, an article of great-importance; as the practice of administering active fluids by drops is dangerously inaccurate—tooth and hair-brushes — portable soup — Iceland moss — James's powder — bark — sal-volatile—æther—sulphuric acid—pure opium—liquid laudanum—paregoric elixir — ipecacuanha — emetic tartar — prepared calomel—diluted vitriolic acid—essential oil of lavender — spirit of lavender—sweet spirit of nitre—antimonial wine — super-carbonated kali—court-plaster and lint.* A strong English carriage, hung rather low, with well-seasoned corded jack springs, iron axletrees, and *sous-soupentes* of rope covered with leather † — strong wheels — anti-attrition grease § — strong pole-pieces—a drag-chain, with a very strong iron shoe; and another drag made of leather, with an iron hook ** — a box containing extra linch pins, tools, nails, bolts, etc., for repairing, mounting, and dismounting a carriage — this box should be made in the shape of a trunk, padlocked, and slung to the hind-axletree—one well, if the carriage be crane-necked; two, if it be not—a sword-case—a very light imperial — two moderate-sized trunks, the larger to go before — a patent chain and padlock for every outside package—lamps, and a stock of candles fitted to them — a barouche seat, and a very light leather hat-box, or a wicker basket, with an oil-skin cover suspended under it. The bottom of the carriage should be pitched on the outside; the blinds should be made to bolt securely within-side; and the doors to lock. A second-hand carriage, in good condition, is preferable to a new one; and crane-necks are safer than single perches, though not necessary.†† Wheels made for travelling on the Continent should neither have patent tire nor patent boxes: mail-coach, or common brass boxes, answer best. In those parts of Germany where the roads are bad, it is advisable to cord the wheels of travelling carriages; and the mode of doing this effectually is, to attach the cords to iron cramps fixed on the tire; afterward fastening them round each nave. Every trunk ought to have a cradle; that is, some flat smooth pieces of oak, in length the same as the inside of the trunk, about two inches and a half wide, nearly half an inch thick, and cross-barred by, and quilted into, the kind of material used for saddle-girths; a distance of three inches being left between each piece of wood. This cradle should be strapped very tight upon the top of the trunk (after it has been packed) by means of straps and buckles fastened to its bottom: and thus the contents can never be moved, by jolts, from the situation in which they were originally placed. Every

---

* Families who design to spend any length of time on the Continent, should likewise provide themselves with an ironing-cloth.

† *Sous-soupentes* are not necessary unless a carriage be heavy laden, and its springs weak.

§ This useful article may now be purchased at Paris, Florence, and Naples; though not so cheap as in England.

** On descending steep hills, especially when the road is rough, a shoe may be forced off from the tire of a wheel: and in this case the hook, which careful drivers always put on at the same time with the shoe, keeps the wheel dragged, and prevents danger.

†† Carriages without perches, invented by Elliot and Holbrook, Westminster-Road, are convenient on the Continent.

Savage, in Queen-Street, Long-Acre, fits up travelling-carriages remarkably well.

trunk should have an outside cover of strong sail-cloth painted.

Persons who travel with their own sheets, pillows, and blankets, should double them up of a convenient size, and then place them in their carriage, by way of cushions, making a leather sheet the envelope.

Ten drops of essential oil of lavender, distributed about a bed, will drive away either bugs or fleas: and five drops of sulphuric acid, put into a large decanter of bad water, will make the noxious particles deposit themselves at the bottom, and render the water wholesome: twenty drops of diluted vitriolic acid will produce the same effect.*

Persons who wish to preserve health, during a long journey, should avoid sitting many hours together in a carriage, by alighting and walking on while their horses are changed, provided they travel post; and by walking up all the ascents, provided they travel *en voiturier;* and persons who get wetted through should take off their clothes as soon as possible, rub themselves with *Eau de Cologne*, and then put on dry warm linen, scented with Hungary water.

I will now close this subject by observing, that Travellers should never fail, before they enter an Inn upon the Continent, to make a strict bargain with the Landlord relative to their expenses; and bargains of every description should be made in the currency of the country.†

---

* After the vitriolic acid has been put into the water, it should stand two hours; and then three parts of the water should be poured into another decanter, and the rest thrown away.

† Persons who are going from London to the Continent, and wish, previous to their departure, to exchange Bank-notes for Napoleons, may be provided with the latter, at a few hours' notice, by Fisher and Co., No. 3, Cockspur-Street.

CHAPTER II.

Steam-Packet from London to Calais—Ditto from Dover to Calais—Ditto from Dover to Boulogne—Expense of going from Dover to Calais in a Post-Office Packet—Ditto from Dover to Ostend—Expense of going from Brighthelmstone to Dieppe, and from Southampton to Havre—Vessel from Plymouth to Bordeaux—Diligence from London to Paris—Dejean and Emery good Voiturins—Dover, best inn—Calais, best inns—Expense of hiring carriages—Tax upon English carriages—Sealed letters—Money of France—Expense attendant upon travelling on the Continent—Excursion from Plymouth to Guernsey, S. Malo, Nantes, Tours, and Orleans—Price of Post-horses, etc.—Water-Diligence—Public carriages—Canal of Languedoc—Messagerie à Cheval—Distance from Calais to Paris through Amiens—Ditto through Beauvais—Distance from Ostend to Paris—from Dieppe to ditto—from Havre to ditto—Route from Calais through Amiens to Paris—Ditto from Calais through Beauvais to Paris—Ditto from Ostend through Lille to Paris—Ditto from Dieppe through Rouen to Paris—Ditto from Havre through Rouen to Paris—Hotels in the last-named city—Firewood—Quarters of the town in which apartments at Hotels are most expensive—Quarters in which they are most reasonable—Unfurnished apartments—Eatables and wine—Restaurateurs—Cafés—Véry, a celebrated Restaurateur—Wages of a Valet-de-place—Price of job-coaches and hackney-carriages—Ditto of public carriages which go to Versailles, etc.—Ditto of public boats, provisions, breakfast and dinner at a Restaurateur's—Best shops—Music and Dancing Masters—English Library and Newspapers—Notary Public who transacts business for the British Nation—English Surgeon—Apothecaries and Chemists—Upholsterers—Prices at the Theatres—Messageries Royales—Offices of the Coche-d'eau—Voituriers, where to be found—Their usual prices—General Post—Petite Post—Route from Paris through Dijon to Geneva—Paris through Lyons to Chambery—Paris through Nevers and Moulins to Lyons—Lyons through Avignon and Aix to Nice—Lyons to Avignon by water—Avignon to Nismes and Montpellier—Aix to Marseilles and Toulon—Paris to Bordeaux and Bayonne—Paris to Brest—Paris to Dunkirk—Lille through Ypres to Ostend—Lille to Brussels—Paris through Brussels to Ostend—Paris through Rheims to Liege—Paris through Chalons-sur-Marne to Strasburg—Paris through Troyes to Strasburg—Paris through Langres to Besançon—Paris to Grenoble—Paris through Toulouse to Perpignan—Paris through Chartres to La Rochelle—Paris through Caen to Cherbourg—Paris through Rennes to L'Orient—Paris to Nantes—Nantes through Rennes to S. Malo.

A STEAM-PACKET has been recently established to run, in twelve hours, from her Moorings, off the Tower of London, to Calais direct, every Wednesday and Saturday morning; and she returns from Calais on Mondays and Thursdays.

Fares.—Chief-cabin, 32s.—fore-cabin and fore-deck, 22s.—Children under ten years of age, half-price—four-wheeled carriages, 4l., and two-wheeled carriages, 2l. each.—Refreshments to be had on board—dinner, 2s. 6d.

Every passenger is allowed one hundred weight of baggage, which must be sent to Galley-Quay, Lower Thames-street. Passengers' names, with the keys of their trunks, must be addressed to Mr. Norman, No. 1, Water-Lane, Tower-Street, London, and sent (as must the baggage) not later than one o'clock the day previous to starting.

Steam Packets are likewise established to run from Dover to Calais in about three hours and a half; and *vice versá:* and from

Dover to Boulogne, and *vice versá*.

These Packets are less liable than other vessels to produce sea sickness; carriages, without being dismounted, are safely conveyed in them; and the time in which they reach their destined port, can, during moderate weather, be ascertained to a nicety: but nautical men appear to question the prudence of venturing in a Steam Packet, unless the weather be moderate. The charges in the Steam Vessels which run from Dover to Calais, and Boulogne, and *vice versá*, are the same as in Post-Office Packets.

The expense of going from Dover to Calais in a Post-Office Packet is as follows:

	l.	s.	d.
Ladies, Gentlemen, and female Servants, each	0	10	6
Men Servants, each	0	5	0
Four-wheeled carriages, each	3	3	0
Horses, each	1	1	0
Dismounting and shipping a four-wheeled carriage	0	10	6
Shipping trunks, etc., about	0	5	0
Wharfage	0	4	0
Town and Harbour dues	0	2	0
Commissioner	0	5	0

The duty on every horse is seventeen shillings; which, with other charges, amounts to about three pounds per horse.

The expense of going from Dover to Ostend in a Post-Office Packet is as follows:

	l.	s.	d.
Ladies and Gentlemen, each	1	1	0
Servants, each	0	10	6

Persons who land at Ostend, instead of Calais, save two posts and a half on their way to Paris; beside an extra-charge of half a post, which is paid on leaving Calais.

Families who sail in a Post-Office Packet are expected to give a trifling gratuity to the Mariners.

Post-Office Packets sail from Dover for Calais four times a week, and for Ostend once a week. The passage from Dover to Boulogne is somewhat longer than from Dover to Calais: but persons who land at Boulogne save four posts and a quarter on their way to Paris: it must, however, be acknowledged, that the passage from Dover to Boulogne is, generally speaking, less favourable than from Dover to Calais; though, on returning to England, the Boulogne packets usually have a much shorter and better passage than those which sail from Calais.

The distance between Dover and Calais is twenty-six miles and a half; and between Dover and Ostend rather more.

Passengers find their own provisions.*

The expense of going from Brighthelmstone to Dieppe in a public Packet is as follows:

	l.	s.	d.
Ladies and Gentlemen, each	1	11	6

besides three shillings to the Boatman who takes Passengers on board; and the same to the Boatman who takes them on shore at Dieppe.

	l.	s.	d.
Four-wheeled carriages, each	4	4	0

Passengers find their own provisions; and the common passage, with a fair wind, is from eight to ten hours.

The expense of going from Southampton to Havre in the public Packet is as follows:

---

* Persons who do not cross the Channel in a Steam-packet, should endeavour to reach Calais soon enough to save the tide: by doing which they are enabled to land from their vessel on the Quay, instead of being taken on shore in a French Harbour-boat, and obliged to pay four livres and a half per head for going.

Persons who land in a Harbour-boat at Dover (which is only needful when the tide does not serve to bring deck-vessels close to the Dover Quay) are charged four shillings per head.

	l.	s.	d.
Ladies and Gentlemen, each	2	2	0
Servants, each	1	1	0
Children each, if under twelve years	1	1	0
Four-wheeled carriage	5	5	0

which, with other charges, amounts to between six and seven guineas.

Two-wheeled carriage	3	3	0
Horses, each	4	4	0

Cabin, if a Family take it entirely to themselves, 2*l*.

Provisions during the voyage, half a guinea per head.

The Southampton Packets usually sail twice a week.

A new and fast sailing Cutter of fifty-six tons register, called "The Sarah," goes from Plymouth to Bordeaux every fortnight; and particulars respecting passage-money, etc., may be obtained, by an application to Hawker and Sons, Briton Side, Plymouth.

A Diligence goes periodically from London to Paris; and places may be taken, and parcels booked, at the White Bear, Piccadilly, in the former city; and at the *Messageries Royales de la Rue Notre Dame des Victoires*, in the latter. The whole expense usually incurred by each inside-Passenger, from London to Paris, is about five pounds; and outside-Passengers, of course, pay less: they sit with the *Conducteur*,[*] on a comfortable seat, which holds three persons, in front of the Diligence. Every Passenger is allowed to take, cost-free, as much luggage as weighs fourteen pounds.

Dejean, of Geneva, conveys Passengers from London, through Paris, to Switzerland and Italy, allowing them to remain two days in the last-named city; or longer, provided they agree to pay an extra-price for so doing. Further particulars may be obtained by an application at No. 33, Hay-Market, London.

Emery, an excellent Voiturin, likewise conveys Passengers from London, through Paris, to Switzerland and Italy. Further particulars may be obtained by an application to Recordon, Watchmaker, Cockspur-street, Charing-Cross, No. 33; or to Emery himself, at the White Bear, Piccadilly.

The best Inn at Dover is *Steriker's London Hotel*.

The most comfortable Inns at Calais are *L'Hôtel Dessin* and *Quillacq's. The Hôtel Royal* and *Hôtel Meurice* are likewise good inns. They all furnish travelling carriages, which may be either purchased or hired: and a carriage hired at Calais to go to Paris, remains there, at the disposal of the Hirer, during fifteen days; so that he may, within that period, return in it to Calais without additional expense. A French Cabriolet may usually be hired for about four Napoleons; and a coach for five or six.

Every English carriage, on entering France, is valued at the Custom-House; and one-third of the value deposited there, by the owner; who, on quitting France, by the same route, receives back about two thirds of the deposit: unless he stay beyond three years,

---

[*] The Conducteur has the charge of Passengers and luggage.

[†] Coaches corresponding with the *Messageries Royales, Rue Notre Dame des Victoires*, at Paris, go every morning and evening from The Golden Cross, Charing-Cross; and also from The Cross-Keys, Wood-street, Cheapside. In these Offices places may be secured to Dover, Calais, Paris, and all the great towns of France; and likewise to Brussels, Geneva, and Milan.

The *Directeur des Messageries* in London engages to convey luggage of every description to any part of the Continent, either by *the Diligence* or *the Roulage*.

in which case the whole sum is forfeited. Should he quit France by a route different to that whereby he entered, he must have his Custom-house papers countersigned at the last Frontier-*Bureau;* and then, either send them to the Custom-house where his deposit was made, requesting to have the sum due to him remitted to his Banker; or, should he design passing again through France within the specified three years, he may, by retaining his papers, and producing them at the Custom-house belonging to the Port where he embarks his carriage, recover the two thirds of his deposit. Beside this deposit, a duty of twenty francs is paid upon every English carriage when landed in France; and between thirty and forty francs more are usually charged for clearance, etc.

English Families on arriving at Calais, or Boulogne, generally commission their landlord to clear their luggage; and the great Inns at Calais, and Boulogne, are provided with Commissaries who manage this business; for doing which they expect per carriage and family, ten francs.

Travellers charged with sealed letters should not expose them to the view of Custom-house Officers; and luggage should be plumbed at every Frontier Custom-house.

MONEY OF FRANCE.

Gold coins most in use are the Napoleon, or new Louis, worth twenty francs; the double Napoleon, worth forty francs; and the old Louis, worth twenty-three francs and eleven sous.

Silver coins most in use are, the piece of five francs; the piece of two francs; the piece of one franc; and the piece of fifty centimes, being half a franc. Copper coins most in use are, the piece of two sous, being ten centimes; and the piece of one sou, being five centimes. Twenty sous make one franc, or livre, for they are synonymous.

Accounts are kept in francs and centimes, both by Bankers and other persons: but, as the different Banking-houses at Paris vary in the prices they give for paper drawn on them, it is advisable for Travellers to make inquiries respecting this subject before they leave England.

Napoleons are the most profitable coin a Traveller can take to France: and it is, generally speaking, easy to exchange English money for Napoleons, at Dover, Brighthelmstone, and Southampton.

The expense attendant upon travelling on the Continent greatly depends upon the disposition of the Travellers, and the manner in which they travel. Persons who go post in an English carriage, preceded by a Courier, usually disburse a large sum of money, without living at all more luxuriously than persons who travel in a Diligence. At small provincial Inns, I have often seen better dinners carried to the *Table d'Hôte* than my Family procured by the order of our Courier. We were, indeed, sometimes compelled to wait for the refuse of the *Table d'Hôte,* probably because the larder at a provincial Inn may not always be sufficiently well stored to provide for Travellers who go post, and are therefore accidental Visitors; though Diligence-Passengers, being constant Customers, are certain to find a good meal prepared for

FRANCE—EXPENSE OF TRAVELLING.

them. After this preface, the Reader will not be surprised when I subjoin, that persons who travel post in France, with an *avant-Courier*, seldom pay less, per head, than three francs for breakfast, and ten for supper and beds: but persons who travel without parade (though in their own carriage), seldom pay more, per head, than two francs for breakfast, three for dinner, and from five to six and a half for supper and beds.*

Fees to Servants at public-houses are very moderate; a Porter never expecting more than twelve sous, and a Chambermaid or Waiter, never more than double that sum, from each Traveller. Twenty-four sous are likewise quite sufficient to satisfy the Servant who greases the wheels of a travelling-carriage. French Inns, some years since, were not celebrated for cleanliness, beds and table-linen excepted; but now they are, on all points, much improved.

An English Gentleman, who lately made an excursion from Plymouth to Guernsey, and thence to S. Malo, Rennes, Nantes, Tours, and Orleans, gives the following account of expenses, etc.

Passage from Guernsey to S. Malo, for an Adult, ten shillings English; and for a child under twelve years of age, five shillings English.†

The road from S. Malo to Rennes is rough; from Rennes to Nantes better; and from Nantes to Tours and Orleans excellent.

The banks of the Loire (anciently called the *Ligeris*), between S. Malo and Orleans, are enchanting. Nature, indeed, seems to have borrowed the pencils of Salvator Rosa and Claude Lorrain to unite, in one vast and ever-varying landscape, the boldness and sublimity of the one, with all the placid beauties of the other. Passage-boats may be met with to descend the Loire from Orleans to Nantes, one of the most delightful aquatic excursions in France. The Masters of these boats land their Passengers every evening, that they may eat and sleep on shore; and the fare, from Orleans to Nantes, does not exceed fifteen francs. The latter is a handsome town, pleasantly situated; and containing excellent Inns. Good dinners, table-wine inclusive, are furnished by the Innkeepers here at three francs a head; and a large Family may live very comfortably in this part of France for five hundred pounds per annum. Tours is a handsome town, containing two excellent Inns, The *Boule d'or*, and The *Faisan*; and, likewise, an English Protestant-Chapel. Innkeepers at Tours furnish breakfast, without tea, for one franc a head; dinner, table-wine inclusive, for three francs; and a bed for about thirty sous.

The fruit in this neighbourhood is delicious, and remarkably cheap.

PRICE OF POST-HORSES, etc.

The usual price for every horse is one franc and fifty centimes (thirty sous) a post; and every

---

* Persons who travel in their own carriage are usually charged at the Hotel-Dessin, at Calais, for breakfast, per head, 2 francs—dinner, 6 francs—coffee, 1 franc—bed and sitting-room, 9 francs—and for their servants, per head, three francs and a half for breakfast and dinner: but, at other Hotels, some of the charges are more moderate.

† A Packet sails from Weymouth to Guernsey every Wednesday and Saturday, weather permitting; and the Hotels in both places are good.

French post is, generally speaking, from five to six English miles in length.

A driver cannot demand more than seventy-five centimes (fifteen sous) a post; but expects from thirty to thirty-five sous for a common post, and twice that sum for a post-royal. Postillions, indeed, both in France and Italy, seem to think they have a right to the same sum, per post, for themselves, that the postmasters charge per horse.

Travellers, on arriving in France, ought to purchase the "*Livre de Poste;*" a new edition of which is printed yearly; and as alterations are frequently made in this post-book, it is expedient to enquire for the last edition.

The following regulations are usually found in the "*Livre de Poste.*"

Two-wheeled carriages, called *cabriolets*, must have two horses and one postillion.

Coaches, called *berlines,* and post-chaises with poles, must always have four horses; though never more than six; with two postillions.

Four-wheeled carriages *à limonière* (that is, with shafts, instead of a pole), must have three horses and one postillion.

Post-masters at Paris, and within fifteen leagues of that city, are forbidden to supply a stranger with post-horses, unless the Stranger exhibit a permission to travel post, from the *Directeur Général;* which permission is delivered, gratis, to every person who presents a proper passport.

It is the custom now in France to put shafts to every English post-chaise; lashing the pole under the perch: because an English post-chaise, conveying four persons, is permitted to travel with one postillion and three horses (four being paid for), provided it have shafts; which can always be obtained in post-towns for twenty francs: and this mode of travelling generally costs about fourteen-pence, English, per mile, fees to postillions inclusive.

An English post-chaise, conveying three persons only, is permitted to travel with one postillion and three horses, no fourth horse being paid for, provided the carriage have shafts.

Distances, in this country, are computed by leagues; one French league being equal to about three thousand geometrical paces; and stones are frequently placed half a league from each other, on great roads, to mark distances.*

TARIFF.

CABRIOLETS.

No. of Persons.	No. of Horses.	Price per Horse.	Sum Total.
1	2	1½ Francs.	3 Francs.
2	2	1½	3
3	3	1½	4½
4	3	2	6

LIMONIÈRES.

| 1, 2, or 3 | 3 | 1½ | 4½ |
| 4 | 3 | 2 | 6 |

N. B. For every person exceeding the number of four, there is an extra charge of one franc and fifty centimes.

BERLINES.

| 1, 2, 3, or 4 | 4 | 1½ | 6 |
| 5 or 6 | 6 | 1½ | 9 |

N. B. For every person exceeding the number of six, there is an extra charge of one franc and fifty centimes.

A *berline* is not to be drawn by more than six horses.

One child, if under seven years, pays nothing: and two children, if not above that age, are consi-

---

* As there are no regular toll-gates either in France or Italy, Travellers seldom find themselves called upon to contribute toward the expense of repairing the roads; except it be on crossing some of the new bridges (where a toll of from one to three francs per carriage is paid); and likewise on crossing the Simplon, and the Mont Cenis.

dered equivalent to only one adult.

In cases where permission is granted to post-masters to put on extra-horses, the third, or extra-horse, is charged at one franc and fifty centimes per post. This permission is sometimes granted for the whole year, and sometimes for the six winter months only, commencing on the first of November.

It is customary, in ascending the mountain of Tartare, near Lyons, and the mountain of Echelles, to employ oxen; and to pay for them, per pair, thirty sous a post.

It is likewise customary and advisable, at every post, to pay the post-master for his horses before they set out.

The posts in France are well served; and the roads, generally speaking, good: it has, however, of late years, been much the practice to travel in Diligences; which go, both by land and water, from Paris to all the departments of the empire. The Water-Diligence, called a *Coche-d'eau*, should always be preferred to the Land-Diligence in those provinces where the roads are rough, and where the Traveller can *descend* a river; to ascend being tedious.

USUAL PRICE OF PUBLIC CARRIAGES THROUGHOUT FRANCE.

	Sous
One inside place, per league, in a Diligence	16
One place in the cabriolet, or outside seat of a Diligence	10
One place in a *Fourgon*, or luggage-cart	6
One place in a *Coche-d'eau*	3

Public carriages in France are more convenient and less crowded than in England; and the civility Foreigners generally receive from Conductors of Diligences, Passengers, and Inn-keepers, renders this mode of conveyance pleasant: beside which, luggage of every description is conveyed remarkably safe by French Diligences.*

The Diligence which goes from Paris to Brussels contains eight places; the distance is sixty-six leagues; and every passenger pays three louis-d'or; being, for that sum, provided with dinner, supper, half a bottle of table-wine at each meal, and a good bed at night. Sometimes, indeed, there are several beds in the same chamber; but, for twenty sous extra, a room containing only one bed may usually be procured. The Passengers pay the fees to servants at inns, who do not, however, expect more than ten sous per night from any person travelling in a Diligence.

The Brussels Diligence stops on the first night at Peronne, on the second at Mons, and on the third arrives at Brussels.

CANAL OF LANGUEDOC.

From Bordeaux to Toulouse, against the stream, the Merchant-boat is ten days in going up the Garonne: from Toulouse to Bordeaux, with the stream, three days in going down. The price, per head, in the Merchant-boat, from Bordeaux to Toulouse, is twelve livres. The price per head in the Government packet-boat down the Canal, from Toulouse to Beziers, is nine livres ten sous; and

---

* We experienced this; for, on our arrival at Lyons, we found it necessary to send our imperials by the Diligence to Nice; they contained trinkets, lace, etc. of considerable value; and, owing to inattention on the part of our Courier, were neither locked nor corded; but, nevertheless, arrived at Nice in perfect safety.

the accommodations are good. Luggage, per quintal, costs four livres twelve sous; and the time employed in going is three days. The voyage, on board a Merchant-boat, from Toulouse to Cette, generally occupies a week. Merchant-boats take carriages; but the Government packet boat does not. Between Bordeaux and Toulouse, during summer, the Garonne is occasionally so shallow that boats cannot pass. The canal shuts on the fifteenth of August, that it may be cleansed, and opens again on the first of October.

The towns visited by Travellers who pursue this route are, Bordeaux, Toulouse, Villefranche, Carcassonne, Beziers, and Adge; where Vessels bound for Marseilles may be heard of daily, by an application at the Custom-house.

Travellers may go from Paris to Cette by the inland navigation.

The passage by sea, for one person, from Cette to Leghorn, costs three Napoleons; and from Marseilles to Leghorn, five Napoleons.

MESSAGERIE A CHEVAL.

In the western and southern parts of France, persons who choose to travel on horseback consign their luggage to the *Messager-en-chef*, who conveys it from place to place in a *Fourgon*, or covered cart, setting out himself very early every morning; but previously informing his Passengers where they are to dine, and likewise where they are to sleep. He provides them with good horses; and does not regulate their hour of departure further than to require that they shall reach the dining-place by twelve at noon. On arriving, they always find a good dinner prepared for them, with half a bottle of table-wine allotted to each passenger. After dinner they set out again; and, on reaching the inn where they are to sleep, find a good supper ready to be served; and, generally speaking, every passenger gets a good bed. The *Messager* seldom takes his little troop above six leagues a day: and so economical is this mode of travelling, that, from Nantes to Paris, a journey of ninety leagues, the price is only sixty francs, every expense, except fees to servants at inns, inclusive.*

The distance from Calais to Paris, through Amiens, is computed to be,
English miles 156½
From Calais to Paris, through Beauvais 172
From Ostend to Paris, through Lille . 192¾
From Dieppe to Paris, through Rouen 123
From Havre-de-Grace to Paris, through Rouen 164½

ROUTE FROM CALAIS, THROUGH AMIENS, TO PARIS.

Posts.
1½ Hautbuisson—Road good. An extra half post is paid on quitting Calais.
1 Marquise—Best inn, *Le Cerf*.
1¾ Boulogne—Road paved. When the pavement is not well kept, say to your postillion, "*Allez sur la terre;*" and he will generally take the road on the side of the pavement. Parker's *Hôtel d'Angleterre* and *L'Hôtel de Londres* are good inns.
  A Packet is established to sail from Rye to Boulogne every Monday. Price, for each Cabin Passenger, one guinea.
2 Samer—The *Téte de Bœuf* is a good inn.
1 Cormont—Best inn, *Le Renard*.
1½ Montreuil—The water here is bad. *L'Hôtel de Londres* and *L'Hôtel de l'Europe* are good inns.
1½ Nampont
1 Bernay
1 Nouvoin—The country from Calais hi-

---

* If Travellers find themselves aggrieved, either by an Innkeeper or a Postmaster in France, they should have immediate recourse to the Maire or Sous-Préfet of the district; these Magistrates being bound to redress grievances. Every Postmaster is obliged to keep, under the superintendence of the Maire of the district, a Register, in which Travellers have a right to enter their complaints.

ther is, generally speaking, open, and thinly peopled.

1½ *Abbeville*—A handsome city, seated on the Somme, and supposed to contain 20,000 inhabitants. Best inns, The *Tête de Bœuf, L'Hôtel d'Angleterre, L'Hôtel de l'Europe,* and *L'Hôtel de France.*
1½ Ailly le Haut Clocher
1½ Flixcourt
1 Pecquigny
1½ *Amiens*—anciently *Ambianus.* This is a large and handsome city, and a cheap place for permanent residence. The *Cathedral* here (*particularly its nave*) is deemed the most perfect piece of Gothic architecture in France; and the best inns are, The Post-house, *L'Hôtel du Roi de Prusse, L'Hôtel de l'Abreuvoir,* and *L'Hôtel des Ambassadeurs.* The country from Abbeville hither abounds with corn; and many parts of the road are bordered with fruit-trees. An extra half post is paid on quitting Amiens.
1 Hébercourt
1 Fleurs
1½ Bretouil—The *Hôtel de S. Nicolas* here is a tolerably good inn.
1½ Wavigny
1 S. Juste*—The road from Boulogne hither is good; and hence to Paris paved and in excellent condition.
2 Clermont—*Le Point du Jour* is a tolerable inn.
1¼ Lingueville
1¼ Chantilly
1¼ Luzarches
1¼ Ecouen—The *Hôtel de Lille* is a very good inn.
1½ S. Denis
1 *Paris*—An extra post is paid, both on entering and on quitting this city.
—
31½ posts.

ROUTE FROM CALAIS, THROUGH BEAUVAIS, TO PARIS.

This road is less hilly than that through Amiens, and in all respects equally good.

13¾ *Abbeville*—See the preceding route, from Calais, through Amiens, to Paris.
2¼ Airaines—The Post-house is a good inn; and *Le Lion d'Or* appears good.
1¼ Camps
1½ Poix
1¾ Granvilliers—*L'Hôtel d'Angleterre* is the only tolerable inn.
1¼ Marseille-sur-Oise—Best inns, *Le Grand Cerf,* and *L'Epée Royale.*
2¼ Beauvais—Best inns, *L'Ecu de France,*

Les Trois Fleurs-de-Lis, and *Le Cygne.*
1¾ Noailles
1½ Puisieux
1¾ Beaumont-sur-Oise—Best inns, *Le Paon,* and *Le Grand Cerf.*
1½ Moiselles
1½ S. Denis
1 *Paris.*
—
32½ posts.

ROUTE FROM OSTEND TO PARIS, THROUGH LILLE.

2½ Tourout
1 Rousselart
2 Menin
2 *Lille*—The inhabitants of this city amount to 65,000. † The *Citadel* is one of the strongest in Europe. *The principal Gate, the Theatre,* and *the Exchange,* merit observation. *L'Hôtel de Gand,* near the Diligence Office, is a good inn; so likewise is *L'Hôtel de Bourbon.* An extra quarter of a post is paid on quitting Lille.
1½ Pont-à-Marcq
2½ Douay—This town contains *a fine Arsenal, a Cannon Foundry,* and *an Artillery School.* The *Church, the Hôtel de Ville, the Grande Place,* and *the Ramparts,* deserve notice. *L'Hôtel de Versailles* is one of the best inns. An extra quarter of a post is paid on quitting Douay.
1¾ Bac-Aubencheul
1½ *Cambray*—anciently *Camaracum.* The *Citadel,* though old, is a fine one. The *Hôtel de Ville* and *the Episcopal Palace* merit attention; as does *the pyramidical Belfry* of the large Church.
1½ Bonavy
1½ Fins
2 Péronne—This town is seated on the Somme. The best inn here is The *Hôtel S. Martin.*
1½ Marché-le-Pot
1 Fonches
1 Roye
1½ Conchy-les-Pots
1 Cuvilly
1 Gournay-sur-Aronde
1½ Bois-de-Lihus
1½ Pont S. Maxence
1½ Senlis
1 La Chapelle-en-Serval
1½ Louvres
1½ Bourget
1½ *Paris.*
—
36½ posts.

---

* The Postmaster has a right to put on an extra horse from S. Juste to Clermont.

† Lille contains a good School for young Ladies, kept by persons of high respectability, who teach the French, English, German and Italian languages, together with music, dancing and every kind of fancy work, for thirty-five louis-d'or per annum, board, washing and all expenses inclusive. They likewise pay great attention to the health of their Pupils, and are celebrated for the cleanliness of their Seminary.

ROUTE FROM DIEPPE TO PARIS, THROUGH ROUEN.

Dieppe is a handsome town, supposed to contain 20,000 inhabitants. *The large Church of S. Jacques* merits notice; as does *the view from the Cliffs*. The best inns are, *The Hôtel de Paris*, *The Hôtel Delarue*, and *The Hôtel d'Angleterre*. The master of the last-named excellent inn is an Englishman, by name, Taylor.*

2   Omonville—An extra quarter of a post is paid on quitting Dieppe.
1½   Totes—The inn here is tolerably good.
1½   Cambres
2   *Rouen*—This city, anciently called *Rotomagus*, is supposed to contain 73,000 inhabitants. *The Great Hall of the Palace—the old Castle—the large Church—the ci-devant Benedictine Church of S. Ouen, and its Belfry—and the Church belonging to l'Hôpital Madelaine*, merit notice. The road between Paris and Rouen presents rich and beautiful scenery. An extra half post is paid on quitting Rouen.
1½   Forge-Ferette
1   Bourg-Baudouin
1¼   Ecoüis
2   Tilliers
2   Magny
1½   Bordeau-de-Vigny
2   Pontoise—*The Church of S. Martin* is celebrated for its architecture; and *the Church of S. Mallon* contains a famous Descent from the Cross.
1½   Franconville
1½   S. Denis
1   *Paris*.

22¼ posts.

ROUTE FROM HAVRE-DE-GRACE TO PARIS, THROUGH ROUEN AND S. GERMAIN-EN-LAYE.

Havre, situated at the mouth of the Seine, is a flourishing commercial city, which contains 19,600 inhabitants, and possesses the advantage of a Port accessible during almost every wind: its *Floodgates and Basins*, made by Napoleon, merit notice. The largest inn at Havre is The *Hôtel de S. François*; but *The Hôtel d'Angleterre* is the cheapest and most comfortable. The usual charge for supper and beds at the latter is four francs a head; and for dinner, at the *table d'hôte*, from two to three francs.

2   La Botte—An extra half post is paid on quitting Havre
1½   Bolbec
1¼   Aliquerville
1½   Yvetot
2½   Barentin
2   *Rouen*
1½   Port S. Ouen
2   Louviers
1½   Gaillon
1¾   Vernon
1½   Bonnieres
1½   Mantes
2   Meulan
1   Triel
1½   S. Germain-en-Laye
1½   Nanterre
1½   *Paris*.

27¾ posts.

Paris (as I have already mentioned), is said to contain more than three hundred Hotels, many of which are splendidly furnished: some of them, however, may be with more propriety denominated ready-furnished lodging-houses, than Hotels; as they neither provide eatables nor waiters; though the English custom of doing both has lately gained ground. Hotels provide fire-wood; which is an expensive article, and can only be purchased reasonably at the wood-yards, where it usually costs from thirty to forty francs a load. The *Rue de la Paix*, the *Place Vendôme*, the *Rue de Rivoli*, and the *Rue de Richelieu*, contain the best Hotels; among which are The *Hôtel de Londres, Place Vendome*, The *Hôtel Meurice, Rue S. Honoré*, The *Hôtel d'Hollande, Rue de la Paix*, and The

---

* Persons who go from Dieppe to Paris, and are not anxious to see Rouen, may pursue a shorter route,—namely, through *Bois-Robert, Pommerevel, Forges, Gournay*, *Gisors, Chars, Pontoise*, and *Franconville*. Packets from Dieppe to Brighton sail every evening from the fifteenth of April till the fifteenth of October.

Hôtel de Wagram, Rue de la Paix: but accommodations for a moderate-sized family, in this quarter, usually cost five hundred francs a month; whereas the same accommodations, in the *Faubourg S. Germain*, may be obtained for two-thirds of that sum; and near the *Messageries Royales* for still less.* Ready-furnished apartments may likewise be hired in private houses; and several respectable Parisians take Boarders: but Families who design to remain some time at Paris, and wish to live with economy there, should rent an unfurnished apartment in the Faubourg S. Jacques, hiring furniture of an upholsterer. Persons who travel in a Diligence, may usually procure apartments at the Hotel attached to the Diligence-Office, or some other in the vicinity.

Eatables and wine are good at Paris; and *Restaurateurs* will send plentiful dinners to large families at four or five francs per head, bread, fruit, and wine, not included: but single men are better served by taking their meals at the house of a *Restaurateur*; which is a sort of tavern, where Ladies likewise may dine without the smallest impropriety. Ladies are also in the habit, after dinner, of frequenting the *Cafés*; where tea, coffee, chocolate, capillaire, etc. are served in the morning; and coffee, liqueurs, beer, lemonade, and ices, in the evening. There also are *Cafés* for what is called a *dejeûner à la fourchette*; which consists of sausages, meat, eggs, etc., and excellent wines; and as the Parisians seldom dine before five or six o'clock, they frequently take these meat breakfasts. Véry, in the *Palais-Royal, Galerie de pierre*, is a celebrated *Restaurateur*; but persons who dine at his house should take care to order only such a number of portions of each dish as they are likely to eat; every portion being charged separately. The *carte à manger* is given into your hands the moment you enter these taverns, with the price per portion of every dish, and a list of the wines and their prices.† Grignon, Passage Vivienne, is an excellent Restaurateur.

The *Café des Mille Colonnes* and the *Café de Foy, Palais-Royal*, and *Tortoni*, on the *Boulevard des Italiens*, are celebrated for the excellence of their ices, etc. The *Café Anglais* and *Café-Hardy*, on the *Boulevard des Italiens*, are likewise celebrated for excellent ices, and meat breakfasts.

A good *Valet-de-Place*, who speaks English, may be hired for five francs a day, he finding himself in every thing.

A Job-Coach, coachman's wages inclusive, usually costs from eighteen to twenty francs per day; and from four hundred and fifty to five hundred francs per month: but, if these carriages be taken a few miles into the country, the coachman expects five francs for himself.

Hackney-Coaches, Chariots, and

---

* The Proprietors of great Hotels do not, in general, like to receive Travellers by the day; but at The *Hôtel de Bruxelles*, Rue de Richelieu, The *Hôtel d'Angleterre*, Rue Filles S. Thomas, and The *Hôtel de Montauban*, Rue Git-le-Cœur, this is not the case. The master of the first-named house keeps a good *Table d'Hôte*, at which Ladies may dine without any impropriety: and at all of these Hotels families may be supplied with excellent dinners in their own apartments for four francs a head, with breakfast for two francs a head; with wood, per day, for two francs; and with a saloon, bed-room, and servants' rooms, for about twenty francs a night. For servants' eating, the usual charge is five francs and a half per day.

† The price of ready-furnished apartments, and likewise of provisions, at Paris, are high, owing to the great influx of British Travellers.

Cabriolets, are paid for either by the course or by time. For a coach, or *Fiacre*, the price is thirty sous per course; the driver having a right to demand a fare whenever ordered to stop; but if he be not ordered to stop, he must drive from one extremity of Paris to the other for the above-mentioned price. The fare by time is two francs for the first hour, thirty sous for every subsequent hour, and fifteen for every half-hour, unless it be from midnight till four in the morning, when the price is doubled: and if the clock strike twelve immediately before the dismissal of a hackney-coach, the coachman has a right to demand ten sous extra. Hackney-Coachmen expect drink-money; though they cannot demand it.

The price in public Carriages which go to Versailles, S. Cloud, S. Denis, and other environs of Paris, is from twenty to forty sous each Passenger. The public carriages which go to Versailles, S. Germain, S. Cloud, and all the western environs of Paris, are stationed near the *Pont Louis XVI*. Regular stages start from Rue Rivoli and Rue de Chartres; and those which go to S. Denis, and the other northern environs, in the *Rue d'Enghien*, near the Gate of S. Denis.

Public Boats go almost every day to Meudon, S. Cloud, etc.

The average price of prime joints of butchers' meat is from ten to fourteen sous the pound [*] — of fowls, from thirty-five sous to six francs each — of the best bread, from three to six sous the pound — and of common table wine, from fifteen to twenty-five sous the bottle.

A breakfast *à la fourchette*, usually costs one franc per head; unless tea be required, when the price is three francs; but, in these prices, wine is not included.

A dinner at a *Restaurateur's* may usually be procured for two francs a head, or even less, exclusive of wine.

Corcelet, *Marchand de Comestibles, au Gourmand, Palais-Royal*, sells ortolans, game, poultry, Hamburgh-beef, Bayonne-hams, Bologna sausages, Perigord, and other celebrated meat-pies, grocery, Italian, Swiss, and English cheeses, English ale, porter, mustard, tea, Cayenne-pepper, curry-powder, and fish-sauces; wines, liqueurs, with almost every other article of luxury for a table. He likewise sells *ratafias*; but liquors of this kind, whether in France or Italy, are extremely deleterious.[†]

Meunier, *Rue de S. Pères*, No. 22 — and Duclos, *Faubourg S. Honore*, No. 76, sells good Bordeaux, Champagne, and other wines.

Good chocolate is to be found at No. 91, *Rue Neuve des Petits Champs*.

Berthellemot, in the *Palais*

---

[*] The French pound, called *poids de table*, is about fourteen ounces and a half; and the kilogram about thirty-five ounces.

[†] A melancholy proof of this occurred not long since at Pisa. Two Ladies were living together in that city, when one of them complaining of cramp in her stomach, the other gave her a wine-glass of Ratafia, which happened to be in the house. Shortly after having swallowed it she died, so evidently in consequence of poison, that strong suspicions fell upon her friend; who, to prove her innocence, took the same quantity of Ratafia herself which she had administered to the deceased, and expired within a few hours. Impelled by this circumstance, Professor Santi of Pisa wrote a beautiful little work, to show that Ratafia has of late years been made with Italian laurel-leaves; the extract from which is a deadly poison.

Royal, is a good Confectioner.

The best shops for Lyon-silks, embroidery, etc., are Nourtier's, *au Page, Rue Vivienne* — Gaillard, *Rue de la Paix*, No. 6 — Letourneur, *Rue S. Honoré*, No. 247 — and *au Pauvre Diable, Rue Montesquieu*. French figured silks and satins are from ten to fourteen francs the *aune*, which is an English ell; Levantines, from six to ten francs; and Florence-silks, from four to seven francs.

One of the best shops for lace is Le Sueur's, *Rue de Grammont*.

A celebrated shop for embroidery is that of Mademoiselle le Bœuf, *à la Balayeuse, Rue Neuve des Petits Champs*; and in the same street is a celebrated shop for corsets, kept by Mademoiselle Picard, at No. 52.

Mademoiselle Leroy, *Rue S. Honoré*, No. 345 — and Madame d'Herbault, *Rue Neuve S. Augustin*, are celebrated milliners.

Frogé, *Boulevard des Italiens*, No. 15, is an excellent Tailor.

MM. Prarond, *Rue de la Barillerie*, No. 1, sell good silk stockings.

Melinotte, in the *Rue de la Paix*, is an excellent Ladies' Shoemaker; and charges, whether for silk or leather shoes, six francs the pair; for thin boots, from twelve to fifteen francs; and for thick boots lined with fur, twenty-four francs: Ladies' shoes and boots ready-made, may, in other shops, be purchased cheaper; and excellent men's shoes and boots, together with Ladies' shoes, called *Piquées* (and calculated to resist the chill of brick floors), may likewise be met with at Paris.*

Ashley, *Rue Vivienne*, No. 16, is one of the best Boot and Shoemakers in Paris.

Morton, *Rue Duphot*, No. 15, is a good Coach-maker, and repairs carriages remarkably well.

The highest price usually given to music and dancing-masters, is six francs a lesson.

Galignani, Librarian, *Rue Vivienne*, No. 18, sells books in all languages, and publishes two English newspapers, one every morning, Sundays excepted; the price per month, being nine francs and a half — per quarter, twenty-five francs — per half year, forty-six francs — and per year, eighty-eight francs. For one extra franc per quarter the paper is franked throughout Italy, Switzerland, and Germany: — and a Sunday Paper; the price of which is five francs per month, or fourteen francs per quarter. Subscriptions are received by every Bookseller and Director of the Post-Offices throughout France, Italy, Switzerland, and Germany; they must, however, be paid in advance.

M. Narjot, *Rue S. Anne*, No. 77, is a Notary-public, who transacts business for the British nation.

Persons who require medical aid would find skilful Practitioners in Dr. Bury, *Rue de la Paix*, No. 12 bis — Dr. Macloughlin, *Rue de la Paix*, No. 8 — and Dr. Lefevre, *Grande Rue Verte*, No. 42.

Renard, *Rue Vivienne*, No. 19, Apothecary and Chemist, sells English medicines, and prepares prescriptions in the English manner.

Darrac, *Rue Neuve S. Eus-*

---

* These *Piquées* are made sufficiently large to be worn over other shoes, and lined with calico wadding, or cotton, quilted into thin white satin.

tache, No. 7—and Vibert, *Rue Richelieu*, No. 86, are good Upholsterers.

The charges at the French Opera, or *Académie Royale de Musique*, are as follows:—Balcony, each person, ten francs—First row of boxes, second row (front), Amphitheatre and Orchestra, seven francs and a half—Second row of boxes (sides), and third row (front), six francs—Third row of boxes (sides), four francs—Fourth and fifth rows of boxes, and Pit, three francs and a half.*

The charges at the Italian Opera are:—First row of boxes and balcony, and second row of boxes (front), ten francs—Second boxes (sides), orchestra, and ground-floor boxes, seven francs and a half—Third boxes (front), six francs—Third boxes (sides), five francs—Fourth boxes, and gallery of third boxes, four francs—Pit, three francs and twelve sous.†

Prices at the Comic Opera:—First row of boxes, balcony, ground-floor boxes, and orchestra, six francs and twelve sous—First gallery and second boxes, four francs and a half—Third boxes, three francs and twelve sous—Second gallery and fourth boxes, two francs and fifteen sous—Pit, two francs and four sous.

Prices at the Théâtre Français:—First boxes, second boxes (front), orchestra, and balcony, six francs and twelve sous—Second boxes (sides), and first gallery, five francs—Third boxes, three francs and six sous—Pit, two francs and four sous.

Prices at the Odéon, or *Second Théâtre Français*:—Stage boxes, balcony, and orchestra, five francs—First boxes, and inferior places in the orchestra, three francs and a half—First gallery and second boxes, two francs and a half—Third and fourth boxes, second gallery, and pit, one franc and a half.

The Minor theatres in Paris are—Théâtres des Variétés, du Vaudeville, de Madame, de la Porte S. Martin, de l'Ambigu Comique, de la Gaîté, and the Cirque Olympique.

The *Messageries Royales*, or Diligence-Office, is in the *Rue Notre Dame des Victoires*, No. 22: and from this office Diligences go periodically to every town in France situated on the great roads.

An excellent Coach for Boulogne and Calais starts daily from *Rue de la Jussienne*, No. 16.

Return Carriages for all parts of the Continent are always to be had at Meurice's Hotel, *Rue S. Honoré*.

The Offices of the *Coche d'eau de Haute Seine* are situated on the *Quai Dauphin, Ile S. Louis*, No. 6—*Port S. Paul*, No. 8.

Voituriers, returning from Paris to Switzerland and Italy, may frequently be met with at the Hôtel de Toulouse, *Rue Git le Cœur*, No. 6, near the *Pont S. Michel;* and at the Hôtel Montauban, in the same street; and persons going to Switzerland, or Italy, would of course be able to make a better bargain with these men than with a French Voiturin. The Voituriers belonging to Dejean, and those belonging to Emery, may be heard of at the Hôtel de Tou-

---

* Operas are represented here only three times a week; namely, on Sundays, Wednesdays, and Fridays.

† Operas are performed here on Mondays, Tuesdays, Thursdays, and Saturdays.

louse; and their prices usually are as follow:—For each passenger from London to Geneva, dinner, supper, and beds inclusive, twenty Louis-d'or — From London to Florence, thirty-six Louis-d'or — From Paris to Florence, twenty-six Louis-d'or—and from Paris to Milan, twenty-two Louis-d'or. The expense of breakfasts, and the gratuities to the servants at inns, are paid by the passengers. Each Passenger is allowed a cwt. of luggage.

GENERAL POST-OFFICE.

The office where letters are franked is opened at nine in the morning. Letters for foreign Countries must be franked before two o'clock, and letters for France put into the post before five.

The *Poste Restante* is open from eight in the morning till seven in the evening.

Letters from Great Britain arrive late on Mondays, Thursdays, Fridays, and Sundays.

Letters for Great Britain go on Mondays, Tuesdays, Fridays, and Saturdays, and *must be franked to Dover*.

Letters for the hereditary dominions of the Emperor of Austria, and likewise for Austrian Italy, go every day, and *must be franked*.

Letters for Spain and Portugal go on Wednesdays and Sundays, and *must be franked*.

Letters for Switzerland go every day *via* Basle—on Mondays, Wednesdays, and Fridays, *via* Porentruy—and on Tuesdays, Thursdays, Saturdays, and Sundays, to Geneva, Lausanne, the Valais, etc. and *must be franked*.

Letters go daily, *without being franked*, to the Netherlands, Prussia, all the German States not belonging to the Emperor of Austria, Denmark, Sweden, Russia, and Poland—on Mondays, Wednesdays, Fridays, and Sundays, to the Kingdom of Sardinia—and on Mondays, Wednesdays, and Saturdays, to Nice.

Letters for Parma and Piacenza go on Mondays, Wednesdays, Fridays, and Sundays, and *must be franked*—and letters for Southern Italy go on the same days, *without being franked*.

Letters and parcels of particular consequence are ensured, on the payment of double postage. Money likewise may be conveyed with safety per post, on the payment of five per cent.

All letters delivered from the General Post-Office at Paris are charged according to their weight; and a single letter from Great Britain usually costs about twenty-six sous.

Besides the General Post-Office there are other offices where letters are received for Paris, the Departments, and foreign Countries. These are situated as follows:—*Rue Lenoir, S. Honoré*—*Rue des Tournelles*, No. 10—*Rue Grand Chantier*, No. 7—*Rue Bergère*—*Rue Duphot*, No. 24—*Rue Verneuil*, No. 20—*Rue Condé*, No. 8—*Rue des Fossés S. Victor*, No. 35—*Rue Coq Heron*, No. 14.

The *Petite Poste* Offices, where letters are taken in for the Capital and its environs exclusively, are very numerous. The postage, per letter, is three sous in Paris, and four sous in the environs; and the letters are taken out of the bags, and distributed every two hours.

ROUTE FROM PARIS TO GENEVA THROUGH FONTAINEBLEAU AND DIJON.

1 Villejuif
1¼ Fromenteau
1½ Essonne
1¼ Ponthiery
1 Chailly
1¼ Fontainebleau
1½ Moret
1½ Fossard
1 Villeneuve-la-Guyard
1½ Pont-sur-Yonne
1½ *Sens*—A third horse, for the six winter months, both going and returning.
1¼ Villeneuve-sur-Yonne
1 Villevallier
1 Joigny
1½ Bassou
2 *Auxerre*—A third horse, for the six winter months, both going and returning. An extra quarter of a post is paid on quitting Auxerre.
1 S. Bris—A third horse, for the six winter months, both going and returning.
2 Vermanton
2¼ Lucy-le-Bois—A third horse, for the six winter months, both going and returning.
1 Avallon
2 Rouvray—A third horse all the year from Avallon to Rouvray; and *vice versâ*, during the six winter months.
2 Maison-neuve—A third horse all the year from Maison-neuve to Rouvray: but not from Rouvray to Maison-neuve.
2 Vitteaux
1¾ La Chaleur—A third horse all the year from Vitteaux hither, but not returning.
1½ Pont-de-Pany—A third horse all the year from this place to La Chaleur, but not returning.
2½ *Dijon*—An extra quarter of a post is paid on quitting this city.
2 Genlis
1¾ Auxonne—A third horse, for the six winter months, both going and returning.
2 Dole
2½ Mont-sous-Vaudrey—A third horse throughout the year, both going and returning.
2½ Poligny
1½ Montrond—A third horse throughout the year going, but not returning.
1½ Champagnole
1½ Maison-neuve (Jura)—A third horse all the year, both going and returning.
1½ S. Laurent (Jura)—A third horse all the year, both going and returning: a fourth horse going, but not returning.
1½ Morez—A third horse all the year, both going and returning.
1½ Les Rousses—A third and fourth horse all the year going, but not returning.
1¾ La Vattay.
2 Gex—This is the last French post. A third and fourth horse all the year from Gex to La Vattay; but not returning.
2 *Genève*—A third horse throughout the year from Geneva to Gex; but not returning.
———
64¾

The price of post-horses between Geneva and Gex is the same as in France.*

The road through Dijon and Poligny to Geneva having been already described, I shall add nothing further on the subject except this, that Travellers ought not to attempt passing the Jura during winter, nor very early in the spring, lest their progress should be impeded by snow.

ROUTE FROM LYONS TO GENEVA, BY CERDON AND S. GERMAIN-DE-JOUX.

1½ Mirabel
1 Montluel
1¾ Meximieux
1½ S. Denis—Best inn, *Le Lion d'Or*.
1 S. Jean-le-Vieux
1½ Cerdon
1½ S. Martin-du-Fresne
1 Nantua
1½ S. Germain-de-Joux
1 Chatillon
1½ Avanchy
1½ Coulonges
2 S. Genix
1 Genève.
———
19¾ posts.

ROUTE FROM PARIS, THROUGH LYONS, TO CHAMBERY.

29¾ Rouvray—See the route from Paris to Geneva, through Dijon
1 Roche-en-Berny
1½ Saulieu—A third horse for the six winter months, both going and returning.
1¾ Pierre-Ecrite—A third horse all the year, both going and returning.
1½ Chissey—A third horse all the year from Chissey to Pierre-Ecrite; but not returning.
2½ *Autun*—This town contains about 9,000 inhabitants; and is adorned with two gates, *The Porte d'Arroux* and *The Porte S. André*, both of which merit notice. Autun was anciently called *Augustodunum*. Here

---

* See, under APPENDIX, SWITZERLAND, the continuation of this route, from Geneva by the Simplon, to Milan.

are several inns; but *L'Hôtel de la Poste* is that most frequented.

2 S. Emilan—A third horse all the year from Autun to S. Emilan; and *vice versâ* for the six winter months. A high and steep hill. Country beautiful.

1½ S. Leger—A third horse all the year from S. Leger to S. Emilan; but not returning.

1 Bourgneuf—A third horse all the year, both going and returning.

1½ *Chalons-sur-Saône*—called, by Cæsar, *Cabillonum*. This city, situated at the mouth of the Central Canal, which unites the Saône and the Loire, contains 12,000 inhabitants, and was considerably embellished by Napoleon: its Quay is handsome; and *Les Trois Faisans* is a very good hotel. The *Hôtel du Parc* and The *Hôtel de l'Europe* are likewise good inns. A *Coche-d'eau* sets out daily from Chalons for Lyons.

2 Senecey

1½ Tournus—A third horse, both going and returning, for the six winter months. Inn, *Le Sauvage*, and good.

2 S. Albin

2 Mâcon—This city, anciently called *Matisco*, contains 11,000 inhabitants; and is adorned with a fine Bridge, and a beautiful Quay, from which the Alps are discoverable. The wine of Mâcon is particularly celebrated; and *L'Hôtel de l'Europe* is an excellent inn.

2 Maison-Blanche

1½ S. Georges-de-Rognains

1½ S. Georges-à-Anse

1½ Limonest—A third and fourth horse all the year going, but not returning.

1½ *Lyon*—A third and fourth horse all the year from Lyons to Limonest; but not from Limonest to Lyons. This city, anciently called *Lugdunum*, said to contain 100,000 inhabitants, and, in point of riches, the second city of France, is watered by the rivers Rhône and Saône (anciently the *Rhodanus* and *Arar*), and surrounded by a beautiful country. Lyons was considerably embellished by Napoleon, to whom it owes its fine iron bridge. *The Museum* contains celebrated Drawings by Poussin (the subject of which is the Seven Sacraments); together with several Paintings, among which are the Last Supper, by Philippe de Champaigne—an Allegory, by Rubens—a fine Teniers—a Wild Boar Hunt, by Sneyders—and the Resurrection, by Le Brun. Here likewise are several antiquities; namely, three fine Mosaic Pavements (one represents Chariot-races in a Circus)—the Table on which is engraved the speech made by the Emperor Claudius Cæsar in favour of Lyons—the Fragment of a Horse's Leg—Sacrificial Vases, etc., which seem to have belonged to a temple of Isis—ancient Lamps—Lares—and ancient Armour, —all found near the city. *The Hôtel de Ville, the Public Library*, and *the Shops*, merit notice; the Theatre is spacious and handsome, and the Quay of the Rhône magnificent. The best inns at Lyons are *L'Hôtel de l'Europe*, *L'Hôtel de Provence*, and *L'Hôtel du Parc*.* A Diligence goes daily in four days and a half during summer, and in four days during winter, from this city to Turin. A Diligence goes daily to Marseilles; and a *Coche-d'eau* three times a week to Avignon.

The road from Rouvray to Lyons is, generally speaking, good. An extra half post is paid on entering, and a post on quitting Lyons.

1½ Bron—A third horse all the year going, but not returning.

1 S. Laurent-des-Mûres

1½ La Verpillière—This village contains a tolerable inn.

1½ Bourgoin—A fine road from Bron hither.

2 La Tour-du-Pin—This town is seated on the Bourbre

1 Gaz—Immediately beyond La Tour-du-Pin, on the right, lies the route to Grenoble.

1½ Pont-de-Beauvoisin—Frontier of France.† At Guingette, between Gaz and Pont-de-Beauvoisin, the Rhône, the mountains of Bugey, La Chartreuse, and Savoy, are all discoverable. Pont-de-Beauvoisin is situated on the Guières.

2 Echelles—A third horse all the year, both going and returning. The Guières, a torrent over which a fine bridge has been thrown, forms the boundary between France and Savoy;

---

* This is a cheap place for permanent residence: but persons who wish to live economically, either here or in any other provincial town of France, should lodge and board in a private house with a respectable French family. Board and lodging for one person seldom costs more than thirty pounds sterling per annum. House-rent in these towns is cheap; as a comfortable family-residence may sometimes be procured for twenty-five or thirty pounds per annum. Mutton and beef are cheap; the former being from three to five pence English, the pound; the latter somewhat less. Bread is cheap. Fowls and ducks are about two shillings English the couple, and turkeys from two to three shillings each: game also is cheap and plentiful.

† Here Travellers have to encounter a French Frontier Custom-house on one side of the Bridge, and a Savoyard Frontier Custom-house on the other: the latter, however, is not much to be dreaded; but the Inn, under the same roof with the French Custom-house, is a dangerous sleeping-place, the bed-rooms being so situated that all the beds are damp. There is a better Inn near the French Custom-house; and at Echelles, only two posts distant, the Post-house affords good accommodations.

and about six miles from this bridge is the once terrific passage of La Chaille: but the present road being bordered with a dwarf wall, every appearance of danger has vanished.

Echelles is seated on the Guières, whose waters are here seen issuing impetuously from the mountains of La Chartreuse: and about five hundred paces beyond Echelles commences the celebrated *Chemin de la Grotte*, made by Charles Emmanuel, second Duke of Savoy; and so wonderfully improved by the Emperor Napoleon, as to be at this moment one of the safest and most magnificent roads in Europe.

1½ 6. Thibault-de-Coux—A third and fourth horse all the year, both going and returning.

Between the Chemin de la Grotte and S. Thibault-de-Coux the road traverses a lofty mountain; and near S. Thibault-de-Coux, at a short distance from the road, is a fine cascade, formed by a stream of limpid water, which falls perpendicularly from the height of a hundred and twenty feet.

1½ *Chambery*—A third horse all the year, both going and returning.*

7¼ posts.

Chambery, the capital of Savoy, is pleasantly situated in a fertile valley watered by the rivulets Albano and Leisse; and contains about 10,000 inhabitants. The *Academy des Beaux Arts*, and *the Promenade*, merit notice; and the heights which surround this little city are covered with vineyards, pasturages, and forests of firs. Inn, *La Poste*, and very comfortable.

ROUTE FROM PARIS TO LYONS, THROUGH NEVERS AND MOULINS.

8½ Fontainebleau—See the route from Paris to Geneva, through Dijon.
An extra quarter of a post is paid on quitting Fontainebleau every way, the Moret road excepted.

2 Nemours—This little town is well-placed, well-built, and watered by the river Loing, and the Canal of Briare. The new bridge is handsome, and the inns are tolerably good.

1½ La Croisière
1 Fontenay
1 Puis-la-Lande

1 Montargis
1½ La Commodité
1 Nogent-sur-Vernisson
1½ Bussière
1½ Briare—This town has given its name to the Canal which forms a communication between the rivers Seine and Loire; the latter of which is seen, covered with vessels, from the hill above Briare.
2 Neuvy-sur-Loire
1½ Cosne
1½ Pouilly
1½ La Charité—pleasantly situated on the Loire.
1½ Pougues—Here are mineral waters.
1½ *Nevers*—This city (anciently *Nivernum*) is seated at the confluence of the Nievre and the Loire, over the latter of which rivers there is a fine bridge. *The Palace of the Dukes of Nevers* is deemed a beautiful specimen of Gothic architecture. *The choir of the great Church* merits notice. Principal inns, *L'Hôtel Royal*, and *L'Hôtel du Lion d'Or*.
1½ Magny
1½ S. Pierre-le-Moutier
1¼ S. Imbert
1½ Villeneuve
1½ *Moulins*—This town, situated on the Allier, is embellished by a magnificent Bridge; and contains the *Mausoleum of Montmorency*, who was beheaded under Louis XIII. It is deemed a fine piece of sculpture, and stands in the *Collège Royal*. In the environs of Bressol, a village near Moulins, there is a considerable quantity of petrified wood.
2 Bessay
2 Varennes—About noon the famous mountains, called *Puis de Dôme* and *Mont d'Or*, are discoverable from this town.
1½ S. Gérard—The inn here is a good one.
1½ La Palisse
1½ Droiturier
1 S. Martin—A very high situation. The road near this town exhibits fine landscapes.
1 La Pacaudière
1½ S. Germain-l'Epinasse
1½ Roanne—Hence to Lyons the road is very hilly. At Roanne the Loire becomes navigable. Best inns, *L'Hôtel de Flandres*, and *L'Hôtel du Renard*.
1 L'Hôpital
1 S. Symphorien
1½ Pain-Bouchain
1½ Tarare—Peasants usually keep oxen at the foot of the mountain of Tarare, to aid carriages in ascending. Fine views of the Alps between Tarare and Lyons.
1½ Arnas
2 Salvigny
1½ *Lyon*.†

61½ posts.

---

* See, under APPENDIX, ITALY, the continuation of this Route, from Chambery, by the Mont Cenis, to Turin.

† From La Palisse to S. Gérard a third horse all the year going, but not returning.—From La Palisse to Droiturier a third horse

[CH. II.] **FRANCE—AVIGNON, AIX, NICE, ETC.** 345

ROUTE FROM LYONS, THROUGH AVIGNON AND AIX, TO NICE.

1 S. Fons
1 S. Symphorien d'Ozon—A third and fourth horse all the year, both going and returning.
1½ *Vienne*—A third and fourth horse all the year, both going and returning. An extra quarter of a post is paid on entering and on quitting Vienne. This city contains several antiquities; among which are *an Amphitheatre*, almost entire; *the ruins of a triumphal Arch*, erected in honour of Augustus; and *a Temple*, adorned with columns thirty feet in height.*
    The wine called *Côte-rotie* is made near Vienne.
2 Auberive—A third horse all the year, both going and returning.
1 Péage de Roussillon—A third horse for the six winter months, both going and returning.
1½ S. Rambert
1½ S. Vallier—This town, seated at the confluence of the Galaure and the Rhône, contains a good inn.
1¾ Tain—celebrated for red and white wine, called *Hermitage*.
2½ *Valence*—A third horse for the six winter months, both going and returning.
    Valence, called *Valentia* by the Romans, contains a University, and an edifice, now made into a Church, which is supposed to have been originally built by the Romans. Pius VI. died here. Best inn, The Post-house.
1½ La Paillasse
1½ Loriol
1½ Derbières
1½ Montelimart—The Post-house here is one of the best provincial inns on the Continent.
2 Donzère—A third horse all the year, both going and returning. This town contains a good inn; and the wines of the neighbourhood are excellent.
2 La Palud—A third horse throughout the year from La Palud to Donzère.
1½ Mornas—A third horse throughout the year, both going and returning.
1½ Orange—remarkable for *a triumphal Arch*, erected in honour of Marius and Catullus, and almost entire.
2 Sorgues—A third horse throughout the year, both going and returning.
1½ *Avignon*—This city, seated on the left bank of the Rhône, and built in the Italian style, was anciently called *Avenio*: it contains 23,000 inhabitants, and a considerable number of handsome edifices, the most striking of which is *the Cathedral*. The ci-devant *Church of the Cordeliers* contains the Tomb of Laura. The *Hôtel d'Europe* is one of the best inns France can boast; and The *Hôtel de Petrarque et Laura*, between Avignon and Vaucluse, is celebrated by Travellers for its dinners, consisting of excellent trout and other fish.
    The Fountain of Vaucluse is within a few miles of Avignon.
2½ S. Andiol—Between this place and Avignon a fine wooden bridge has been lately thrown over the Durance, anciently *Druentia*; a rapid river, which Travellers were formerly compelled to cross in a ferry, sometimes at the risk of their lives.
1½ Orgon—The inn here is good.
2 Pont-Royal—The country from S. Andiol hither is, generally speaking, flat and uninteresting.
2 S. Canat
2 *Aix*—A third horse throughout the year, both going and returning. The two last stages are hilly.
    Aix, anciently called *Aquæ-Sextiæ*, and the capital of Provence, stands in a spacious plain, watered by the Arc, is handsomely built in the Italian style, and contains 23,700 inhabitants. The Mineral Waters and Hot Baths here have long been celebrated. *The Cathedral* merits notice; as that part called *La Rotondo* is adorned with columns which once belonged to a temple of Vesta; and the *College Chapel* is embellished with an Annunciation and a Visitation, by Puget.
    This is a cheap town for permanent residence: its best inns are, *L'Hôtel du Cours*, *L'Hôtel des Princes*, and *La Mule Blanche*.
    An extra half post is paid on quitting Aix.
1¾ Bannettes
1½ La Grande Pugère
2½ Tourves—A third horse all the year, both going and returning. Between La Grande Pugère and Tourves there is a steep hill; and the whole road from Aix to the last-named Post is at times rough and rotten.
1½ Brignolles—This town is pleasantly situated between the rivers Caranciu and Issole. A third horse, during

all the year going, but not returning.—From Droiturier to S. Martin a third horse all the year, both going and returning.—From Pacaudière to S. Martin a third horse all the year going, but not returning.—From Pacaudière to S. Germain a third horse all the year, both going and returning.—From Roanne to S. Symphorien a third horse all the year, both going and returning.—From S. Symphorien to Pain-Bouchain a third horse all the year going, but not returning.—From Tarare to Pain-Bouchain a third horse all the year going, but not returning.—From Arnas to Salvigny a third horse all the year, both going and returning.

* Pontius Pilate, after having been deprived of the office of Procurator of Judea, on account of his malpractices, and banished to Vienne, died there, by his own hands.

the six winter months, both to go and return.

1½ **Flassans**—A third horse all the year, both going and returning.

1 **Luc**—A third horse all the year, both going and returning. The road from Brignolles hither is good. The country abounds with olives, vineyards, and corn.

1½ **Vidauban**

1½ **Muy**—A third horse all the year, both going and returning.

2 **Frejus**—A third horse all the year, both going and returning.

Frejus, called by the Romans *Forum Julii*, still exhibits vestiges of its ancient splendour; namely, *one Arch of the Port* made by Cæsar, and the Ruins of *an Aqueduct*, etc.: but what must always render this town memorable is, that Napoleon landed here, on his return from Egypt; embarked here, when banished to Elba; and landed again, not far hence, after quitting that island.

The country round Frejus is magnificently wooded.

2 **Lestrelles**—A third horse all the year, both going and returning. The mountains from which the last-mentioned Post derives its name may almost vie in height with the Alps; and are richly clothed with myrtles, arbuti, and a great variety of other flowering shrubs. These mountains exhibit beautiful scenery.

3 **Cannes**—A third horse all the year, both going and returning. This is the precise spot where Napoleon landed in 1815.

2 **Antibes**—A third horse all the year, both going and returning.

Antibes, anciently called *Antipolis*, and celebrated for the elegance of its *Port*, which is adorned with circular arcades, somewhat in the style of the ancient Port of Ostia, likewise contains Ruins of *an Amphitheatre*.

4* A third horse all the year.

66¾ posts.

The country between Antibes and Nice is an extensive plain near the Mediterranean sea, embellished with hedges of pomegranates, myrtles, and aloes; and watered by the Var, which divides France from the dominions of the King of Sardinia. Travellers going to Nice were formerly obliged to ford the Var,—an operation which was always unpleasant, and often dangerous; but a long wooden bridge is now thrown over that torrent.

* The distance, according to the French Post-book, is four posts from Antibes to Nice; but the Italian Post-books call it only 2½ posts.—See, under APPENDIX, ITALY, the continuation of this Route from Nice to Genoa.

ROUTE FROM LYONS TO AVIGNON, BY WATER.†

Families who wish to descend the Rhône from Lyons to Avignon, may either take the *Coche d'eau* to themselves for ten Louis d'or, or perhaps less, the expense of putting a carriage on board, and disembarking it at Avignon inclusive; or they may, for the same price, hire a private boat. We pursued the latter plan; and, quitting Lyons about noon, arrived before six in the evening at *Cordreuil*, where we slept. The views on each side of the river, between Lyons and Cordreuil, are beautiful. The second day we left the last-named place about nine in the morning, and were presented with views even finer than on the preceding day. A magnificent chain of lofty rocks clothed with vineyards, and crowned with ruins of ancient castles, formed the great features of the landscape; while, here and there, a small village, at the water's edge, and sometimes a large town in a valley between the hills, added to the richness of the scenery. Deserted Chateaux, and Convents, placed on the pinnacles of craggy rocks, presented themselves at every turn of the river; while the rocks frequently appeared in such wild and extraordinary shapes, that one might easily have mistaken them for castles with giants striding on their battlements. No words, however, can do justice to this scenery; which is rendered doubly beautiful by the immense breadth, peculiar clearness, and great rapidity of the

† The road from Lyons to Avignon and Marseilles being frequently in bad condition, it is advisable for Travellers to go down the Rhône, if possible.

Rhone. About four o'clock we arrived at *Valence*, which commands a distant view of the Alps, and stands directly opposite to a picturesque rock, crowned by the remains of a castle. We slept at the Post-House, a tolerably good inn, though too far from the water. The third day we quitted Valence at nine in the morning; and found the rocks increase in magnitude, and the prospect of the Alps grow more and more sublime as we proceeded. Early in the afternoon we came in sight of the *Pont S. Esprit;* and passed under the middle arch, without experiencing, in consequence, any disagreeable sensation. This celebrated bridge, three thousand feet in length, is built with consummate skill and beautiful simplicity.

The inn at *S. Esprit* is good. The fourth day we left this town at eight in the morning, and arrived at *Avignon* about twelve. There are two castles, opposite to each other, not far from the Pont S. Esprit, which form a picturesque view. On approaching Avignon we found the country flat, and the prospects less pleasing than before.

ROUTE FROM AVIGNON TO NISMES AND MONTPELLIER.

2¾ La Bègude-de-Saze—A third horse all the year, both going and returning.
2⅜ La Foux—A third horse all the year, both going and returning.
1⅜ S. Gervasy—A third horse all the year, both going and returning.
1⅜ Nismes—This city, anciently called *Nemausus*, and said to contain 40,000 inhabitants, is adorned with handsome modern buildings; but more particularly worth seeing on account of its *Amphitheatre*, and several other monuments of antiquity; one of which, called *La Maison Quarrée*, and supposed to have been a Corinthian Temple, erected by the people of Nismes about the year of Rome 754, in honour of Caius and Lucius, sons of Agrippa, is in high preservation. Here likewise are Remains of an ancient *Pharos*. Best inns, *Le Louvre*, and *Le Luxembourg*.

The Fountain of Nismes has long been celebrated; and the *Pont-de-Garde*, a Roman Aqueduct (attributed to Agrippa), 174 Paris feet in height, and 728 in length, is not quite four leagues distant from this city, and well worth notice.

1¾ Uchau—An extra quarter of a post is paid from Nismes hither.
1¾ Lunel—celebrated for its wines.
1½ Colombières
1¾ *Montpellier*—This town, anciently called *Agathopolis*, and supposed to contain 33,000 inhabitants, has long been famed for its climate; which, though unfavourable to weak lungs, is in other respects salubrious. Rain seldom falls here: snow and fogs are equally uncommon; but the *marin*, or sea-wind, produces damp: and the *vent de bise*, which continually visits Montpellier, is of all winds the most piercing.* The principal hotels are *Le Cheval Blanc*, *L'Hôtel du Midi*, *Le Petit Paris*, and *Le Luxembourg*: but persons who purpose to reside any length of time at Montpellier should hire a ready-furnished apartment, and have their dinner from a *Traiteur*. Here are *a Theatre, an Aqueduct*, and several pleasant promenades. Montpellier and Grasse are famous for the best perfumes in France.

The Mason-Spider is an extraordinary insect, which naturalists report to be found only near Montpellier.

14¾ posts.

ROUTE FROM AIX TO MARSEILLES AND TOULON.

2 Le Grand-Pin—An extra quarter of a post is paid on quitting Aix. A third horse all the year, both going and returning.
2 *Marseille*—Between Le Grand-Pin and Marseilles, and about half a league from the latter, is one of the finest views in France.
Marseilles, anciently called *Massilia*, and one of the largest and safest Ports of the Mediterranean, is supposed to contain 111,150 inhabitants. *The Cathedral*, a very ancient edi-

---

* The *vent de bise* prevails so much in all the southern part of France, as to render the climate prejudicial to consumptive persons: and beside this objection to the above-mentioned country, there is another, of almost equal magnitude; namely, the natives still retain the character given them by Horace:
"*Novisque rebus infidelis Allobrox.*"

fice, is adorned with the works of Puget: and *La Consigne* contains a celebrated representation of the Plague, by the same master. *The Arsenal* merits notice. *The Theatre* is one of the handsomest in France; and *the Lazzaretto* one of the finest in Europe. The principal inns are *L'Hôtel des Ambassadeurs, Rue Beauveau; La Croix de Malte, Rue des Pucelles; L'Hôtel des Empereurs, Rue Suffren; L'Hôtel d'Europe, Rue de Pavillon; L'Hôtel de Franklin, Rue Beauveau; L'Hôtel de Pologne, Rue Thyar;* and *L'Hôtel des Princes, Rue Canebière.* The Quay, and the environs of Marseilles are beautiful; but this town, during summer, is much infested by musquitoes. An extra half post is paid on quitting Marseilles.

2 Aubagne
1½ Cujes
2 Beausset—A third horse all the year, both going and returning.
2 Toulon—A third horse, during the six winter months, from Toulon to Beausset, but not returning.
——
11½ posts.

Toulon is supposed to contain 26,000 inhabitants. *The Ports, the Marine-Arsenal, the Hôtel de Ville,* adorned with two colossal Caryatides, by Puget, *a ceiling* in the house he once occupied, representing the Fates, *the Military Arsenal, the Lazzaretto,* and *the Cathedral,* are the objects best worth notice in this city.

Near Toulon is the small town of *Hyères,* opposite to some Islands of the same name (anciently called the *Stæchades*), and about one league distant from the sea. This town is so much and so justly celebrated for the excellence of its climate during winter, that Valetudinarians are sent hither from all parts of France; but during the summer months it is particularly unwholesome. Oranges, lemons, and pomegranates, grow most luxuriantly at Hyères in the natural ground; and sugar canes are said to do so likewise, when properly cultivated.

ROUTE FROM PARIS TO BORDEAUX AND BAYONNE.

1½ Croix de Bernis
1 Lonjumeau
1½ Arpajon
1½ Estrechy
1 Etampes
1 Montdésir
1½ Angerville
1½ Toury
1½ Artenay
1 Chevilly
1½ Orléans—This city (anciently *Aureliani*) contains about 40,000 inhabitants.* The great Church merits observation, and the environs are delightful. The Fauhourg d'Olivet communicates with the city *by a Bridge* which is much celebrated. Orleans is embellished with a University, an Academy of Sciences, and a public Library. The *Hôtel de Ville* contains a portrait of the Maid of Orleans. An extra half post is paid on quitting Orleans, and on entering, by the way of Ferté S. Aubin.
2½ Ferté S. Aubin
2 Motte-Beuvron
1 Nouan
2 Salbris
1½ La Loge
2 Vierzon—A small, but ancient town.
1½ Massay
2 Vatan
1½ Epine-Fauveau
2 Chateauroux—This town is situated in an extensive and beautiful plain. Best inn, *S. Catherine.*
2 Lottier
1½ Argenton
2 Fay
2½ Ville-au-Brun
2½ Monterol
2 Chanteloube
2 Maison-rouge
1½ Limoges—This city (anciently called *Lemovices*) contains 20,000 inhabitants. *The ci-devant Abbey of S. Martial* is interesting on account of its antiquity. Best inn *L'Hôtel de Perigord.* An extra quarter of a post is paid on quitting Limoges.
1½ Aixé
1½ Gatinaud
1½ Chalus
1½ La Coquille
2 Thiviers
1½ Palissons
1½ Tavernes
1½ Périgueux—This city (anciently called *Pretoricii*) is famed for delicious meat pies. Here are *some Roman Antiquities*—and near the town is a *Fountain,* remarkable for the daily flux and reflux of its waters. Best inn, *L'Hôtel de France.*
2½ Massoulie
2 Mucidan
2 Mont-pont
2 S. Médard

* Orleans is a remarkably cheap town for permanent residence.

2¼ Libourne
1¼ S. Pardoux
2 Carbon-blanc
2 *Bordeaux*—An extra half post is paid from Carbon-blanc hither.

Bordeaux (anciently called *Burdigala*), one of the largest, richest, and handsomest cities in France, is seated on the Garonne, and supposed to contain 99,000 inhabitants. The objects best worth notice are—*the Cathedral*, adorned with two extraordinary *bassi-rilievi*—*the Exchange*—*the Church of the ci-devant Chartreux-Convent*—*the Theatre*—*the Quays*—and *the remains of Roman Antiquities.* The wines of Bordeaux are excellent. Best inn, *Le Maréchal de Richelieu*.

1¾ Bouscant—An extra half post is paid on quitting Bordeaux.
1¾ Castres
1½ Cerons
1½ Langon
2 Bazas
2½ Captieux
2 Poteau
2½ Roquefort
1¼ Caloy
1½ *Mont-de-Marsan*
1¾ Campagne
2 Tartas
1½ Pontons
1¾ S. Paul-les-Dax
2 S. Geours
2 Cantons
2 Ondres
1½ *Bayonne*—This town is finely situated at the confluence of the Nive and the Adour. *The Cathedral* is a venerable edifice. Travelling-beds may be purchased at Bayonne. Best inn, *S. Étienne*.
100¼ posts.*

ROUTE FROM PARIS TO BREST.

2½ Versailles—An extra half post is paid on quitting this town.
2½ Pont-chartrain
1½ La Queue
1½ Houdan
1 Marolle
1½ Dreux—Memorable for the battle of 1552, under Charles IX.
1½ Nonancourt
1½ Tillières
1¼ Verneuil—Memorable for the battle of 1424.
2 S. Maurice
2¼ Mortagne
2 Le Mêle-sur-Sarthe
1¼ Mélinbroust
1½ *Alençon*—An extra quarter of a post is paid on quitting this town.
1¾ S. Denis-sur-Sarton
1¾ Prez-en-Pail
2 Ribay
2¼ Mayenne
2 Martigné
2 *Laval*—This town contains 15,000 inhabitants; there are quarries of jasper in its vicinity. Best inn, *Le Louvre*.
2½ Gravelle
2 *Vitré*—This is a considerable town.
2 Chateau-bourg
1½ Noyal
1½ *Rennes*—This city (anciently called *Redones*) is supposed to contain about 29,000 inhabitants. *The Place-Royale*—*The Palais de Justice*—and *The Hôtel de Ville* merit notice. Best inns, *Le Tour d'Argent*, and *L'Hôtel de France*.
1½ Pacé
1½ Bedée
1½ Montaubani
1½ S. Jean
1 Broons
1½ Langouèdre
2 Lamballe
2½ *S. Brieux*—This town has a good Port
2 Chatelaudren
1½ Guingamp
1½ Bois-mormant
1 Bellisle-en-Terre
2¼ Pontou
2 Morlaix—*The Church of N. D. des Mers* is a singular edifice; *the Hospital* is a fine one, and the Port considerable. *L'Hôtel d'Europe* is a good inn.
1½ S. Egonec
1 Landivisiau
2 Landerneau
1½ Guipava
1 *Brest* †—An extra half post is paid on entering this town, and on quitting it.
75¼ posts.

* Third horse throughout the year at every post, both going and returning, between Orleans and Argenton.
A third horse throughout the year from Argenton to Fay, but not returning.
A third horse all the year between Fay and S. Pardoux, both going and returning.
A third horse for the six winter months, both going and returning, between Bordeaux and Langon.
A third horse all the year, both going and returning, between Langon and Captieux.
A third and fourth horse all the year, both going and returning, between Captieux and Poteau.
A third horse all the year, both going and returning, between Poteau and Roquefort.
A third horse all the year, both going and returning, and a fourth horse going, but not returning, from Caloy to Mont-de-Marsan.
A third and fourth horse throughout the year, both going and returning, between Mont-de-Marsan and Bayonne.
† Postmasters are allowed to put on a third horse at almost every stage between Mortagne and Brest.

Brest, anciently called *Brivates*, is supposed to contain 27,000 inhabitants; and its Harbour, one of the safest in Europe, is sufficiently capacious to admit five hundred ships of war. *The Quays*, *the Arsenal*, and *the Theatre* particularly merit notice. The principal hotels are, *La grande Maison*; *Le grand Monarque*; *La Tour d'Argent*; and *Le grand Turc*.

Another road from Brest to Paris, through *Lamballe*, *Dol*, *Maienne*, and *Alençon*, is five posts shorter than the road already described.

ROUTE FROM PARIS TO DUNKIRK.

1½ Bourget
1½ Louvres
1½ Chapelle-en-Serval
1 Senlis
1½ Pont S. Maxence
1½ Bois-de-Lihus
1½ Gournay
1 Cuvilly
1 Couchy-les-Pots
1½ Roye
1 Fonches
1 Marché-le-Pot
1½ Péronne
2 Fins
1½ Bon-Avis
1½ *Cambray*
1½ Bac-Aubencheul
1¾ *Douay*
2½ Pont-à-Marcq
1½ *Lille*
2 Armentières
1½ Bailleul
2½ Cassel
2½ Berg-S.-Winox
1 *Dunkerque*.

38½ posts.

Dunkirk, so called from originally containing the Kirk of the Duns, is supposed to have 21,200 inhabitants. The houses are built with uniformity; *the front of the church of S. Éloi* merits notice, and *the Quay* is a fine one. The best inns are, The *Post-house*; The *Hôtel d'Angleterre*; The *Hôtel du Sauvage*, and The *Hôtel du Nord*.*

* From Dunkerque to Paris, through *Calais, Boulogne*, and *Amiens*, is 39 posts;

ROUTE FROM LILLE TO OSTEND, THROUGH YPRES.

2 Warneton
2 Ypres—*The Church of S. Martin*—and *The Canal of Boesingen*, merit notice.
2½ Dixmude
3 *Ostende*—See (under APPENDIX, GERMANY) the route from Vienna, through Ratisbon and Brussels, to Ostend.

9½ posts.

ROUTE FROM LILLE TO BRUSSELS.

1½ Pont-à-Tressain
1½ Tournay
2 Leuse
1½ Ath
1½ Enghien
1½ Hall
1½ *Bruxelles*—See (under APPENDIX, GERMANY) the route from Vienna, through Ratisbon and Brussels, to Ostend.

11 posts.

ROUTE FROM PARIS TO OSTEND, THROUGH BRUSSELS.

1½ Bourget
2 Mesnil-Amelot
1 Dammartin—This place commands a fine view, and the Ruins of the Castle are picturesque.
1¾ Nanteuil-Haudouin
1½ Lévignen
2 Villers-Cotteretz
1½ Verte-Feuille
1½ *Soissons*—Anciently called *Suessiones*. The great Church, and the ci-devant Abbey of S. Medard, where *Louis le Débonnaire* was confined by his children, merit notice. The environs of this city are charming. An extra half post is paid on quitting Soissons.
2 Vourains
2 Laon—Prettily situated on the summit of a hill.
2½ Marle
1½ Verrins
2 La Capelle
2 Avesnes
2 Maubeuge—When Travellers are obliged to send for horses to Donzies, they pay, in consequence, an extra half post.
2 Mons—The famous battle of Genappe, which took place in 1792, was fought near Mons—*The Castle*—and *the Abbey de Wautru*, merit notice.
1 Casteau
1½ Braine-le-Comte
2 Halle
1½ *Bruxelles*—There is another road, in distance 34½ posts, from Brussels to

and through *S. Omer, Arras*, and *Péronne*, 37 posts.

Paris, through *Valenciennes*. Both roads are chiefly paved, and tolerably good; though in some places they want repair.*

1½ Asche
1½ Alost
1½ Quadregt
1 Gand
2 Alteren
2 Bruges
2 *Ostende.*

46½ posts.

ROUTE FROM PARIS, THROUGH RHEIMS AND SEDAN, TO LIEGE.

12½ *Soissons*—See the route from Paris, through Brussels to Ostend.
2½ Braine
1½ Fismes
1½ Jonchery
2 *Reims*—This town is said to have 30,000 inhabitants. *The great Church is a fine Gothic structure, with a beautiful front. The Church of S. Nicholas, the Place Royale,* and some remains of *Roman Antiquities,* merit notice. At *Courtagnon* and *Méri,* in the neighbourhood of Rheims, a large number of fossils are continually discovered. An extra quarter of a post is paid on quitting Rheims.
2 Isle
2½ Rethel
1½ Vauxelles
1½ Launoy
2½ *Mezières*—An extra quarter of a post is paid on quitting this town. A third horse all the year between Rethel and Launoy, and Launoy and Mezières.
2½ *Sedan*—Here is a good Arsenal and a Cannon Foundery. The great Turenne was born at Sedan. Best inns, *La Croix d'Or,* and *Le Palais Royal.*
3 Paliseux
2½ Telin
2 Marche
2 Bouzin
2 Nandrin
2 *Liege*—See (under APPENDIX. GERMANY) the route from Brussels, through Aix-la-Chapelle and Liege, to Spa.

45

ROUTE FROM PARIS TO STRASBURGH, THROUGH CHALONS-SUR-MARNE, S. DIZIER, BAR-LE-DUC,

NANCY, LUNEVILLE, PHALZBOURG, AND SAVERNE.

1½ Bondy—This town gives its name to the neighbouring forest.
1 Vert-Galand
1 Claye—Between Paris and Meaux is a plain, famed for the retreat of the Swiss, in 1567, under Pfyffer, who escorted Charles IX., Catherine de Medicis, and the ladies of her court in safety to Paris, by cutting his way through the army of their enemies.
2 Meaux—This town stands in a beautiful plain, watered by the Marne, and was the first place which deserted the party of the League, and submitted to Henry IV. Over one of the gates are these words: *Henricum prima agnovi.* Good cheeses are made at Meaux. Best inns, *La Sirene* and *La Croix d'Or.*
1½ S. Jean
1 La Ferté-sous-Jouarre—A small town embellished with pretty walks.
2 La Ferme-de-Paris
1½ Château Thiery—The birth-place of La Fontaine.
1 Paroy
1½ Dormans
1 Port-à-Binson
1 La Cave
1 Epernay—Famed for its wines.
2 Jaalons
1 Mastogne
1 *Chalons-sur-Marne*—*The Hôtel de Ville, the Great Church,* and *the Jard,* are the objects best worth notice. Near this city Attila was defeated by the Franks and Romans. Best inns, *La Pomme d'Or; Le Palais Royal; La Croix d'Or;* and *La Ville de Nancy.* An extra quarter of a post is paid on quitting this town.
1 Chépi
1 La Chaussée
1 S. Amand
1 Vitry-le-Français—Built by Francis I.
2 Lonchamp
1½ S. Dizier—Here the Marne becomes navigable.
1½ Saudrupt
1½ *Bar-le-Duc*—Famous for sweetmeats, trout, and excellent wine.
2 Ligny
1 S. Aubin
1½ Void
1½ Laye
1½ Toul—*The principal Church* merits notice. The wines of Toul are good.

* Persons who go from Brussels to Paris, through *Genappe, Valenciennes, Mons, Cambray,* and *S. Quentin,* should visit, at the last-named town, the *Tunnel* cut through solid rocks, and passing three miles under ground, to facilitate the inland navigation from Cambray to the capital. This Tunnel, one of the most patriotic works of Napoleon, is well ventilated, lighted by means of lamps, and usually provided with water about six feet deep. It admits one barge only at a time, towed by men, who have a commodious gallery to walk in.

1½ Velaine
1½ *Nancy*—This fine city suffered cruelly from a battalion of Republicans, who passed through it in 1792, and destroyed all the *chefs-d'œuvre* of art they unfortunately met with. *The Place-Royale* merits notice, as do *the Tombs of the ancient Dukes of Lorraine, in the ci-devant Franciscan Church. The Cloister of the Franciscans au bon secours* contains *the grave of king Stanislaus,* the great embellisher of this city. The Theatre is pretty, and the *Hôtel de petit Paris* and the *Hôtel Royal* are the principal inns. An extra quarter of a post is paid on quitting Nancy.
2 Dombasle
1½ Luneville
1¾ Benamenil
2 Blamont
2 Heming
1 Sarrebourg—Here the Sarre becomes navigable.
1 Hommartin
1 Phalsbourg
1½ Saverne—The road over the mountain of Saverne is much celebrated, and does honour to human industry.
1¾ Wasselonne
1½ Ittenheim
1½ *Strasbourg.*

60¾ posts.*

Strasbourg (anciently called *Argentoratum*), contains 50,000 inhabitants. The objects best worth notice in this city are— *The Munster*, and its famous *Tower* — the *Church of S. Thomas,* which contains *the Mausoleum of Marshal Saxe,* by Pigale — *the Arsenal and Cannon-Foundry* — the *public Granaries* — the *Foundling-Hospital* — *the Hospital Bourgeois* — the *Observatory* — the *Maison de Ville* — the *Citadel* — the *Bridge over the Rhine* — and *the Public Library*, which is open on Tuesdays, Thursdays, and Saturdays. Here is an *Académie de musique*, a French, and a German Theatre. *The Ville de Lyon* is a good inn; as are the *Hôtels de l'Esprit, de la Fleur, la Maison Rouge,* etc.

ROUTE FROM PARIS TO STRASBURGH, THROUGH TROYES, LANGRES, VEZOUL, BEFORT, AND BASLE.

1 Charenton
1½ Grosbois
1 Brie-Comte-Robert
2 Guignes
1 Mormant
1½ Nangis
1½ Maison-rouge
1½ Provins
2 Nogent-sur-Seine
1 Pont-sur-Seine
1½ Granges
1½ Grèz
2½ *Troyes*—This city is supposed to contain about 27,000 inhabitants. *The Cathedral, the Church of S. Etienne,* and *the Château* (once the residence of the Counts of Champagne), are the objects best worth a Traveller's attention. The water here is scarcely drinkable. An extra half post is paid on quitting Troyes.
2½ Montiérame
1½ Vandœuvre
2½ Bar-sur-Aube—Celebrated for its wines.
1¾ Colombey
1 Suzennecourt
2 *Chaumont*—The *front of the College Church* is admired. Best inn, *La Fontaine.*
2 Vesaignes
2 Langres—This is the highest situated town in France. Several Roman Antiquities have been found here. *The mineral waters of Bourbonne-les-Bains* are only seven leagues distant from Langres.
1½ Griffonottes
1½ Fay-Billot
1½ Cintrey
1½ Combeau-Fontaine
1½ Pont-sur-Saone
1½ *Vezoul*—Celebrated for its wines. Principal inns, *Les Diligences, L'Aigle Noir, La Tête d'Or.* At Leugne, a village to the east of Vezoul, there is a famous *Grotto.* The *mineral waters of Luxeul* are only six leagues from Vezoul.
1½ Calmoutier
2 Lure—This town is peculiarly situated on an island formed by a pond, and surrounded with woods and mountains.
2½ Champagney
2 Befort—A strong town. Principal inns, *Le Luxembourg, La Ville de Versailles, Le Sauvage.*
2 Chavanes
2 Altkirk
2 Trois-Maisons

* A third horse all the year between Epernay and Jâlons.
Do. between S. Dizier and Sandrupt.
Do. between Sandrupt and Bar-le-Duc.
Do. between Ligny and S. Aubin.
Do. between Velaine and Nancy.
Do. between Blamont and Heming.
Do. between Saverne and Wasselonne.
A third horse, during the six winter months, between Ittemheim and Strasburgh.

2 Basle*—Frontier-town of Switzerland. See (under APPENDIX, GERMANY) the route from Augsburg to Constance, Schaffhausen and Basle. Travellers ought to avoid arriving late at night here, lest the gates of the town should be shut.
1 S. Louis-sous-Huningue
1½ Gros-Kempt
2 Bantzenheim
1½ Fessenheim
1½ Neuf-Brisack—Built by Louis XIV. The Post-house is out of the town.
2 Markolsheim
2¼ Friesenheim
1½ Kraft
2 *Strasbourg*—You drive through the beautiful plains of Alsace, and discover, at a great distance, the Munster-Tower of Strasburgh.

74¼ posts.

ROUTE FROM PARIS TO BESANÇON, THROUGH LANGRES.

34½ to Langres—See "Route from Paris to Strasburgh, through Troyes."
1½ Lonjeau
3 Champlitte
2¼ Gray—A pretty town. Principal inns, *La Ville de Lyon*, and *Le Chapeau rouge*.
1½ Bonboillon
1½ Recologne
2 *Besançon*.

47 posts.

Besançon, anciently called *Vesontio*, is a large and handsome town, seated on the Doubs, and possessing a strong Citadel, erected on a rock by Louis XIV. Here are several remains of antiquity; the most interesting of which are, an *Amphitheatre* of a hundred and twenty feet in diameter; a *triumphal Arch*, and *the ruins of a Temple*. Principal inns, *L'Hôtel National*, and *L'Hôtel des Anciens Sauvages*. The environs of this town are picturesque; and contain celebrated *warm Baths*.

ROUTE FROM PARIS TO GRENOBLE.

60½ To *Lyon*—See the route from Paris to Lyons, by Auxerre and Autun.
1½ Bron †
1 S. Laurent-des-Mûres
1½ Verpillière
1½ Bourgoin
1½ Eclosse
2 La Frête
1½ Rives
1½ Voreppe
2 *Grenoble*.

74 posts.

This city, seated on the Isère, and anciently called *Gratianopolis*, is supposed to contain 30,000 inhabitants. The objects best worth notice are—*the General-Hospital*—*the great Church*—*the Arsenal*—and *a bronze Hercules*, which adorns one of the Promenades. The seven Wonders in the environs of Grenoble, (which, by the by, do not quite deserve their name), are—*La Tour sans venin*—*La Fontaine-ardente*—*La Montagne inaccessible*—*Les Cuves de Sassenage*—*Les Pierres ophtalmiques de Sassenage*— *La Manne de Briançon*—and *La Grotte de N. D. de la Balme*.§

---

* Persons who like water-parties should, if possible, go down the Rhine to Strasburgh.

† A third horse all the year from Lyons to Bron; but not returning.
Do. from Bourgoin to Eclosse; but not returning.
Between Eclosse and La Frête, a third horse during the six winter months, both going and returning.
A third and fourth horse throughout the year from Voreppe to Rives; but not returning.

§ ROUTE FROM GRENOBLE TO GAP, LEADING TO MONT-GENÈVRE; AND THENCE TO TURIN; BY WAY OF EMBRUN, MONT-DAUPHIN, AND BRIANÇON.

2 Vizille*—It is much to be lamented that there are no relays of post-horses on the direct road from Vizille to Briançon and Mont-Genèvre; as a fine road has been lately made over this Alp, which is considerably lower than Cenis, and provided with a Convent for the accommodation of Travellers.
A third horse all the year between Grenoble and Vizille.
1 La Frey—A third and fourth horse all the year going, but not returning.
1½ La Mure—A third horse all the year, both going and returning.
1¾ Souchons—A third horse all the year, both going and returning.
1¾ Corps—A third horse all the year, both going and returning.

2 La

ROUTE FROM PARIS TO PERPIGNAN, THROUGH TOULOUSE.

40½ Limoges—See the route from Paris to Bordeaux.
3 Pierre-Buffière
1½ Magnac
1½ Massère
2½ Uzerche
2 S. Pardoux
1½ Donzenac
1½ Brives
2½ Cressensac
2 Souillac
2½ Peyrac
2¾ Pont-de-Rhodez
2½ Pélacoy
2½ *Cahors*—anciently called *Cadurci*. Here are some Remains of a *Roman Amphitheatre*.
3 Madeleine
2 Caussade
2¾ *Montauban*—A handsome town, beautifully situated, on a hill; and containing above 23,000 inhabitants. The best inns are, *Le Tapis Verd*, *L'Hôtel des Ambassadeurs*, and *Le Grand Soleil*. An extra quarter of a post is paid on quitting Montauban.
2½ Canals
1¾ S. Jorry
2½ *Toulouse.*

82½ posts.

This city, watered by the Garonne, and anciently called *Tolosa*, contains 55,500 inhabitants. The *front of the Hôtel de Ville* and *the Bridge* merit attention; the latter being one of the finest in Europe. Toulouse is embellished with a variety of pleasant Promenades. Principal inns, *L'Hôtels du Nord*, and *de France*.

1½ Castanet—An extra quarter of a post is paid from Toulouse to Castanet.
1½ Bassiège
1½ Villefranche
2½ Castelnaudary—This town is near the great Canal of Languedoc.
1½ Villepinte
1 Alzonne
2½ *Carcassonne*—In the upper town is a Castle which contains *some old Law-deeds*, written in a very peculiar manner upon the bark of trees. The ci-devant *Capuchin Church* merits notice. Principal inns, *L'Hôtel de l'Ange*, *L'Hôtel de S. Jean*, and *L'Hôtel de petit Paris*.
2 Barbeirac
1½ Moux—A plain covered with olives, vines, corn, and mulberry-trees, and encircled by barren rocks.
2 Cruscades
2½ Narbonne—Here are Ruins of several *Roman edifices*, and *in the Cathedral* is *the tomb of Philip the Bold*. Principal inns, *L'Hôtel de la Daurade*, and *L'Hôtel de France*. This city was anciently called *Narbonensis*.
2½ Sigean
2 Fitou
1 Salces
2 *Perpignan*—The great *Church* deserves notice.

109½ posts.*

ROUTE FROM PARIS TO LA ROCHELLE, THROUGH CHARTRES, TOURS, AND POITIERS.

2½ Versailles
2 Connières
1¾ Rambouillet—Here is a strong Castle, in which Francis I. expired.
1½ Epernon
1 Maintenon
2½ *Chartres*—anciently called *Carnutes*. The great *Church* and its *Belfry* are worth seeing.
2 La Bourdinière
2 Bonneval
2 Chateaudun
1½ Cloye
2 Pezou
1½ Vendôme
1¾ Neuve S. Amand
1¾ Chateau-Regnault
2 Monnoye
1¾ *Tours*—anciently called *Turones*. This town, pleasantly situated on the Loire, contains 21,000 inhabitants. The *Mall*, the *Cathedral*, and the *Church of S. Martin*, merit notice. The *Cathedral Library* contains valuable manuscripts. Tours is one of the most eligible situations in France for a permanent residence; the society being good, the surrounding country beautiful, and the climate particularly salubrious, and very

2 La Guingette-de-Boyer
1½ Brutinet
1½ *Gap*—The last Post-house established on this road is at Gap. Principal inns, *Hôtel de Laval*, *Hôtel de Marchand*.

11 posts.

* Postmasters are authorised to put on a third horse at every stage between Limoges and Grizolles: and, at Souillac, the Postmaster is authorised to add a pair of oxen to every four-wheeled carriage, going either to Peyrac or Cressensac; charging three francs, drink-money for the driver inclusive.

A third horse all the year between Villefranche and Castelnaudary; for the six winter months between Castelnaudary and Villepinte; Do. between Carcassonne and Barbeirac; and all the year between Narbonne and Perpignan.

FRANCE—CAEN, CHERBOURG, NANTES.

seldom visited by the *vent de bise;* added to which, provisions and house-rent are cheap. An extra quarter of a post is paid on quitting Tours, except by way of Monnoye.

1½ Carrés—This country is watered by the Loire and the Cher, and famed for excellent fruits.
1 Montbazon
1 Sorigny
2 S. Maure
2 Ormes
1½ Ingrande
1 Chatellerault
1 Barres-de-Nintré
1 La Tricherie
1 Clan
2 Poitiers—This town, formerly called *Pictavi*, is built at the confluence of the Clain and the Boivre, and said to contain 21,000 inhabitants. Here are the Remains of *an ancient Theatre*, and *a triumphal Arch*, or *Aqueduct*, the latter of which is now converted into a gate.
1 Croutelle
2½ Lusignan
1½ Villedieu-du-Perron
2 S. Maixent
1½ La Crèche
1½ Niort—This town contains *a Gothic Church*, which was built by the English. Principal inns, *Le Raisin de Bourgogne*, *Les Trois Pigeons*, *L'Hôtel de la Paix*, etc. Niort is said to have 15,000 inhabitants.
1½ Frontenay
1½ Mauzé
1 Laigne
1¾ Nuaillé
1½ Grolaud
1 La Rochelle—Here are the Remains of a celebrated *Dike*, which was constructed by Cardinal Richelieu. La Rochelle contains 18,000 inhabitants: its harbour is safe and commodious; and its principal inns are, *L'Hôtel des Ambassadeurs*, and *L'Hôtel des Princes*. The road through *Tours* and *Orleans* to Rochelle is 61 posts; and that through *Vendôme, Tours, Poitiers, Niort,* and *Saintes,* 69 posts and a half.*
—— 61¾ posts.

ROUTE FROM PARIS TO CHERBOURG, THROUGH CAEN.

1½ Nanterre
1½ S. Germain-en-Laye
1½ Triel

1 Meulan
2 Mantes
1½ Bonnières
2 Pacy
2 *Evreux*
2¼ La Commanderie
2 La Rivière-Thibouville
1½ Le Marché-Neuf
1¾ L'Hôtellerie
1½ Lisieux
2 Estréez
1¾ Moult
2 Caen—A large city, remarkable for being the burial-place of William, the Conqueror of England. Principal inns, The *Hôtels d'Angleterre, de Londres, d'Espagne,* etc. An extra quarter of a post is paid on quitting Caen.
1½ Bretteville l'Orgueilleuse
2 Bayeux
1½ Vaubadon
2½ S. Lo
1¾ S. Jean-Day
1½ Carentan
1½ Sainte Mère-Eglise
2 Valognes
2½ Cherbourg—The improvements made in this Harbour by Napoleon highly merit notice. Inns, *L'Hôtel d'Angleterre, Le Grave Turc,* etc.
—— 44½ posts.

ROUTE FROM PARIS TO L'ORIENT, THROUGH RENNES.

4¼ Rennes—See the route from Paris to Brest.
2 Mordelles
2½ Plélan
2 Campénéac
1 Ploërmel
1 Roc S. André
2 Pont-Guillemet
2½ *Vannes*—Inns, *Le Dauphin, Le Lion d'Or,* and *L'Hôtel de France.*
2 Auray—Near this town is a *ci-devant Chartreuse,* which merits notice.
2 Landevant
1½ Hennebon
1½ L'Orient—This is one of the prettiest towns in France. Inns, *L'Hôtel du Commerce,* and *L'Hôtel des Etrangers.*
—— 64 posts.†

ROUTE FROM PARIS TO NANTES.

10½ Dreux—See the route from Paris to Brest.
1½ Morvillette

---

* A third horse all the year between Monnoye and Tours.
Do. for six months between Tours and Ormes.
Do. all the year between Poitiers and Lusignan.
Do. all the year between La Crèche and La Laigne.
Do. during the six winter months between La Laigne and Nuaillé.

† A third horse, during the six winter months, between Rennes and Plélan.
Do. the whole year between Plélan and Ploërmel.
Do. during the six winter months between Ploërmel and S. André.
Do. the whole year between S. André and Vannes.

1	Châteauneuf
1	Digny
1½	La Louppe
2	Regmalard
2	Bellesme
2	S. Cosme-de-Vair
1½	Bonnetable
2	Savigné
1½	*Le Mans*—This town, watered by the Sarte, contains above 18,000 inhabitants: its *Cathedral* merits notice. Its principal inns are, *Le Croissant*, *Le Dauphin*, and *La Boule d'Or*.
2	Guesselard
1	Foulletourte
2½	La Flêche
1½	Durtal
2	Suette
2½	*Angers*—A large and populous town, seated on the Mayenne.
2½	S. Georges
1	Champtoce
1½	Varades
1¾	Ancenis
1½	Oudon
1¾	La Sailleraye
1½	*Nantes*.

48¾ posts.

Nantes, the *Condivicum* of the Romans, and one of the most considerable cities in France, contains 75,000 inhabitants. It is built at the confluence of the rivers Erdre and Sèvre with the Loire, and adorned by twelve bridges; most of which are handsome. Among the best hotels are *L'Hôtel de France*, and *L'Hôtel des Etrangers*. An extra quarter of a post is paid on quitting this city.

ROUTE FROM NANTES, THROUGH RENNES, TO SAINT-MALO.

1½	Gesvres
1½	La Croix-Blanche
2	Nozay
1½	Derval
1½	Breharaye
2	Roudun
2	Bout-de-Lande
2	*Rennes*
2½	Hedé
2½	S. Pierre-de-Plesguen
1½	Châteauneuf
1½	S. Malo—An extra half post is paid if the tide be high.

22 posts.*

S. Malo is built on a rock, surrounded by sea, and communicating with the land by a causey, called the *Silon*. The *Ramparts* merit notice. The best inns are *L'Hôtel du Commerce*; *L'Hôtel de la Paix*; *L'Hôtel de France*; and *L'Hôtel des Voyageurs*.

---

* A third horse, all the year, between Nantes and Gesvres.
Do. during the six winter months between La Croix Blanche and Nozay.
Do. during the six winter months between Bout-de-Lande and Rennes.
Do. all the year between Rennes and Hedé.
Do. during the six winter months between Hedé and Châteauneuf; and all the year between Châteauneuf and S. Malo.

CHAPTER III.

SWITZERLAND.

Post-horses, etc.—Most advantageous way of seeing Switzerland—Money of that country—Geneva—Arrival and departure of Letter-Couriers—Expense of living at Geneva—Diligences—Hotels—Route, going post, from Geneva by the Simplon to Milan, and *vice-versâ*—Price of post-horses on that road—Passage of S. Gothard—Passage of the Grand S. Bernard—Passage of Splugen.

Post-horses are only to be met with in particular parts of this country; but draught-horses may always be hired of Swiss Voiturins: as may saddle-horses and mules.* Persons, however, who wish to see Switzerland to advantage, should travel on foot; a mode so commonly adopted, that the Foot-passenger is as well received, even at the best inns, as if he came in a splendid equipage. The expense incurred by travelling on foot through Switzerland seldom exceeds five shillings, English money, per day, for each Traveller: half a crown being, on an average, the price of a *table-d'hôte* supper, wine, and lodging inclusive; and Pedestrians should make supper their principal meal.

Accounts are kept in livres and batz; one Swiss livre being ten batz, or thirty French sous. The old Louis-d'or, the Napoleon, the French écu, and demi-écu, are the coins which pass best throughout Switzerland.

GENEVA.

ARRIVAL AND DEPARTURE OF LETTER-COURIERS.

Letters from Great Britain *arrive* on Tuesdays, Wednesdays, Fridays, and Sundays, at six in the afternoon, by the French Courier.

Letters for Great Britain *go* on Mondays, Wednesdays, Fridays, and Saturdays, at eight in the morning, by the French Courier.

Geneva is not a cheap place for permanent residence; but, nevertheless, there are Genevese Families who take Boarders at four louis-d'or a month; whereas a person who hires a private lodging, and dines daily at a *table-d'hôte*, cannot spend less than double that sum.

This town is famous for watches, and gold trinkets of all descriptions.

Diligences go several times a week from Geneva to Lausanne, Neuchâtel, Lyons, Grenoble, and Turin, by way of the Mont-Cenis.

ROUTE, GOING POST, FROM GENEVA, BY THE SIMPLON, TO MILAN: BEING A CONTINUATION OF THE MILITARY ROUTE MADE BY NAPOLEON.

The price of post-horses from Geneva, by the Simplon, to the Frontier of Switzerland, is the same as in France; unless (which sometimes happens) Travellers be

---

* The price, per day, of a pair of draught-horses, is from twelve to sixteen florins, beside half a florin to the driver. The price, per day, of a saddle-horse, or mule, is an écu-neuf.

imposed upon, and made to pay in Swiss livres.

2½ Dovaine
2 Thonon
1½ Evian
2½ S. Gingoux
2½ Vionnaz
2½ S. Maurice
2½ Martigny
2½ Riddes
2½ Sion
2½ Sierre
2½ Tourtemagne
2½ Viège
1½ Brigge
2½ Barisello
3½ Sempione (village so called)
2½ Isella
2½ Domo-d'Ossola
2 Vogogna
3 Fariolo, *or* Baven
2½ Arona
1½ Sesto-Calende
2 Cascina
1½ Ro
1½ *Milan.*

52½ posts.

ROUTE FROM MILAN, BY THE SIMPLON, TO GENEVA, ACCORDING TO THE ITINERARIO ITALIANO, PUBLISHED AT MILAN, IN THE YEAR 1820.

1½ Ro
1½ Cascina
2 Sesto-Calende
1 Arona
1½ Belgirate
1½ Baveno
2 Vogogna
2 Domo-d'Ossola
2½ Isella
2½ Sempione (village so called)
4½ Brigge
1½ Viège
2 Tourtemagne
2 Sierre
2 Sion
2 Riddes
2 Martigny
2 S. Maurice
2 Vionnaz
2 S. Gingoux
2½ Evian
1½ Thonon
2 Dovaine
2½ *Geneva.*

47½ posts.

PASSAGE OF S. GOTHARD.

Previous to the existence of the new roads over the Simplon and Cenis, this was one of the most frequented routes from Switzerland into Italy: and the journey from Fluelen to Bellinzone is easily accomplished in four days, whether on foot or on horseback: neither can this passage be called dangerous at any season, except while the snow is melting. Between Fluelen and L'Hôpital, the *Pfaffen-Sprung, the Cascade, the Devil's Bridge, the Schollenen, the Urner-lock,* and the beautiful prospect presented by the Valley of Urseline, are the objects best worth a Traveller's attention. A little beyond the village of L'Hôpital is *L'Hospice des Capucins,* where Travellers meet with clean beds, good wine, and a hospitable reception; in return for which they are expected, on going away, to leave a trifling present for the support of this useful establishment. The summit of S. Gothard is a small plain, encompassed by lofty rocks; and the height of this plain is supposed to be 6,790 English feet above the level of the Mediterranean sea. Between L'Hospice and Bellinzone the views are beautiful; and the whole route is much embellished by the river Tesino, the forests of firs, the pasturages, the pretty hamlets placed in elevated situations; and the vines, poplars, chesnuts, walnuts, and fig-trees, which continually present themselves to view.

Travellers who pass S. Gothard on foot, or on horseback, usually sleep the first night at *Ursern;* the second at *Airolo,* where the inn is good; the third at *Giornico;* and the fourth at *Bellinzone.* Carriages may pass, by being dismounted, from Altorf to Giornico; but the expense of conveying a carriage over S. Gothard is seldom less than twenty-four louis-d'or.

Travellers may either proceed from Bellinzone to Milan, by the Lago Maggiore, or the Lago di Como.*

PASSAGE OF THE GRAND SAINT BERNARD.

Persons who wish to go the shortest way from French Switzerland into Italy, usually cross the Grand S. Bernard; there is, however, no carriage-road beyond Branchier; though English carriages have occasionally been dismounted at Martigny, and carried over the mountain to Aoste, at the expense of eighteen or twenty Napoleons per carriage, according to its size; the transport of trunks not included. The price, per day, for every porter-mule employed on S. Bernard is twenty-six batz; guide and tax for the Commissary inclusive; though Foreigners pay more.

From Martigny to L'Hospice is about nine leagues. At *Liddes*, where the ascent begins to grow steep, Travellers commonly pause to see the collection of minerals and antique medals belonging to the *Curé* of Arbeley. These medals were chiefly found on S. Bernard. From Liddes to *S. Pierre* is one league; and the latter village contains an Inn: here, likewise, is the *military Column*, placed by the Romans on what they deemed the highest part of the Maritime Alps.† This country is remarkable for deep hollows bordered with rocks, into which hollows the Drance precipitates itself with such violence as to exhibit a scene by many persons preferred to the fall of the Rhine at Schaffhausen. From S. Pierre to L'Hospice is three leagues; and every step toward the summit of the mountain increases the steepness of the path, and the wildness of the prospects. White partridges are seen here in large numbers.

About one league beyond S. Pierre the road consists of snow, frozen so hard that a horse's hoof scarcely makes any impression on it: this road traverses two valleys; the first being called *Les Enfers des Foireuses*, and the second *La Vallée de la Combe;* between which spot and L'Hospice the quantity of snow decreases.— *L'Hospice* is supposed to be the most elevated of all human habitations in the old world; and some benevolent Monks of the Augustine order live here constantly, for the purpose of accommodating and succouring Travellers, several of whom owe their preservation to these humane ecclesiastics; who make a practice of searching out every unfortunate person lost in the snow-storms, or buried by the avalanches: and in this search they are aided by large dogs, who scent Travellers at a considerable distance; and, in spite of impe-

* The Lake of Como, anciently called *Lacus Larius*, is said to be fifty miles in length, from three to six miles in breadth, and from forty to six hundred feet in depth. This Lake, combined with the town of Como, anciently *Comum*, presents a beautiful landscape. Pliny the younger was born at Como; and in the front of the Cathedral is his Statue. The distance from Como through Barlassina to Milan is three posts.

† The most elevated point of the Grand S. Bernard, namely, Mont-Velan, is supposed to be (as I have already mentioned) more than ten thousand English feet above the level of the Mediterranean sea: and l'Hospice, according to Saussure, is eight thousand and seventy-four Paris feet (though subsequent computations make it only six thousand one hundred and fifty Paris feet) above the level of the Mediterranean sea.

netrable fogs and clouds of snow, are always able to discover and pursue the right road. These useful animals (who seldom bark, and never bite a stranger), carry in baskets, fastened to their necks, cordials and eatables calculated to revive those persons who are nearly frozen to death: and, notwithstanding all that has been lately written relative to the extinction of this race of dogs, they are, at the present moment, more numerous than heretofore. Every Traveller is courteously received at L'Hospice; and the Sick are provided with good medical and chirurgical assistance, without distinction of rank, sex, country, or religion; neither is any recompense expected for all this hospitality; though persons who possess the means seldom fail to leave a testimony of their gratitude in the Poor's box belonging to the Church. Travellers should, if possible, find time to ascend the Col de Tenèbres (which is not a very fatiguing excursion), in order to see a fine view of that part of Mont-Blanc which cannot be discovered from Chamouni. The valley in which L'Hospice stands is long, narrow, and terminated by a small Lake, on the extremity of which the Convent is erected. Near this spot there formerly was a temple consecrated to Jupiter; and, according to some opinions, the Convent stands precisely on the site of this Temple, from which S. Bernard derives its ancient name of *Mons-Jovis*. The conventual Chapel here contains a Monument to the memory of the French General Dessaix, who is represented as being in the act of falling from his horse into the arms of a Grenadier, and uttering the words " *Allez, dire au Premier Consul,*" etc. On the Monument is the following inscription: " *A Dessaix; mort à la bataille de Marengo.*" The body was brought hither from Milan by order of Napoleon, who erected this interesting piece of sculpture to commemorate the heroic death of his Friend. The descent from L'Hospice to Aoste occupies between six and seven hours: and at Aoste there are remains of a *triumphal Arch*, built in the time of Augustus; *the ruins of a Circus*, etc. From the last-named town Travellers may proceed either to Turin or Milan. The road to the former city passes through a beautiful country, and the time employed in going need not exceed twenty hours.*

PASSAGE OF SPLUGEN.

Persons travelling from Suabia, or the country of the Grisons, to Venice or Milan, will find this the shortest route: though nobody should attempt to cross the mountain of Splugen at the season of the avalanches: and, indeed, at all seasons, great caution should be used in dangerous places not to agitate the air, even by speaking in a loud voice. When there is such an accumulation of snow that the pointed rocks on the summits of the Alps are covered, *avalanches* may be expected hourly. The road, so far as *Coire*, is good; but carriages can proceed no further: from Coire, therefore, Travellers must either walk or ride, or be conveyed in a *traineau,* or a

* See this route, under APPENDIX, ITALY.

chaise-à-porteur: and the safest and pleasantest mode of passing this Alp is under the guidance of the *Messager*, who goes every week from Lindau to Milan, and undertakes, for a certain price, to defray all the expenses of the passage, board and lodging inclusive. It is a much greater fatigue to cross Splugen than Saint Gothard: but the wildness and sublimity of the prospects compensate for every difficulty. The road between Coire and the village of *Splugen* is called *Via-Mala*, not, however, from being a particularly bad road, but in consequence of the terrific aspect of the country through which it passes. One of the most striking objects in this route is *the Paten-Brücke*; where, by leaning over the wall of a bridge, the Traveller discovers an abyss which the rays of the sun never enlightened, and at the same time hears the tremendous roaring of the Rhine, which forms, in this place, a circular basin, whence it issues, like a silver thread, out of a narrow passage in the rocks. Beyond the Paten-Brücke is *Schamserthal*, one of the most romantic valleys of the Alps; and in *the Rheinwald*, or forest of the Rhine, are firs of so uncommon a magnitude, that one of them is said to measure twenty-five ells round the trunk. *The fall of the Rhine*, in this forest, exhibits one of the sublimest objects in nature, which, while it fills spectators with awe, affords them the pleasure of contemplating scenes in the creation that no pencil could imitate. The road here is frequently so narrow, that a Guide should be sent a-head, in order to stop the beasts of burden (coming from the opposite side of the mountain), in places where it is possible to pass them; and to avoid these unpleasant rencounters, and at the same time escape the wind, which rises about mid-day, Travellers should leave Splugen between two and three in the morning. The generality of persons, when they ascend this mountain, lie down at full length in a traineau, drawn by an ox, with their heads next to the pole; because the ascent is so steep, that their feet would otherwise be considerably higher than the rest of their bodies. It takes a couple of hours to reach the summit, where there is a good inn. The descent on the opposite side, called *the Cardinal*, exhibits terrific precipices, at the bottom of which runs the Lyra, with an impetuosity that seems momentarily to increase. The Traveller is then presented with a view of the melancholy *valley of S. Jacques*; and proceeds amidst broken rocks and fallen mountains, in rude confusion piled upon each other, like the disjointed fragments of a demolished world; till at length, the hills of *Chiavenna*, covered with peach and almond-trees, gradually present themselves to view; and unite with the balmy zephyrs of Italy to banish fatigue, by exhilarating the spirits.

Travellers usually embark at *La Riva*, and continue their journey, either by *Como* or *Bergamo*.

CHAPTER IV.

ITALY.

LEGHORN, PISA, AND FLORENCE.

Italian Posts—Italian Miles—Price of Post-horses in northern Italy—Do. in Tuscany—Do. in the Principality of Lucca—Do. in the Ecclesiastical Territories—Do. in the Kingdom of Naples—Other particulars relative to travelling post in Italy—Particulars relative to travelling *en voiturier*—Tuscany—Current coins—Bankers' accounts—Pound-weight—Tuscan measure called a braccio—Prices at the principal Hotels—Buona-mano to Attendants—Wages of a Valet-de-Place—Leghorn—Price of carriages—Entrance paid by English Travellers at the Theatre—Articles best worth purchasing—Provisions—Asses' milk—Fruit—Beccafichi—Ortolans—Size of a Tuscan barrel of wine—Do. of oil—Do. of a catastre of wood—Public carriage from Leghorn to Pisa—Boats—Diligence from Leghorn to Florence—Environs of Leghorn unwholesome—Arrival and departure of Letter-Couriers—Pisa—Fees to Custom-house Officers and Musicians—Winter price of Lodging-houses—Boxes at the Theatre—Entrance-money—Expense of Job-carriages—Servants' wages—Dinner at a Restaurateur's—Mode in which dinners should be ordered from a Traiteur—Firewood—Mats—Eatables—Milk, cream, oil, and wine—Scales and weights for kitchen-use recommended—Music, drawing, and language-masters—Fees to Medical Men—Banking-house—Prices for making wearing apparel—Bookseller—Tuscany recommended as a cheap country for permanent residence—Arrival and departure of Letter-Couriers at Pisa—Price for franking letters—Price of a seat in the Diligence from Pisa to Florence—Persons going this journey advised not to have their baggage plumbed—Hotels and private Lodging-houses at Florence—Winter price of the latter; and where to apply for information respecting them—Price of board and lodging in an Italian family—Further particulars relative to prices at Inns—Coffee-houses—Restaurateurs—Table d'Hôte—Price, per month, for a carriage and horses—Do. per day—Provisions in general—Asses' milk, wine, oil, ice, medicines—Price of Butchers' meat, bread, poultry, etc.—Price of table-wine—Best Bookseller—Shops for foreign wine, English porter, tea, medicines, etc.—Grocer—Silk-mercer—Linen-drapers—Shoes and boots—Tailors—Ladies' dress-makers—Coach-makers—Money-changer—Firewood—Fees to Medical Men and Notaries Public—Prices at the Theatres—Music-masters, etc.—Sculptors—Painters—Bankers—Arrival and departure of Letter-Couriers—Country-houses near Florence.

LENGTH OF AN ITALIAN POST.

The length of an Italian post is from seven to eight miles: but the miles of Italy differ in extent; that of Piedmont and Genoa being about one English mile and a half; that of Lombardy, about sixty yards less than an English mile; that of Tuscany, a thousand geometrical paces; that of the Ecclesiastical State, the same length (which is about one hundred and fifty yards short of an English mile); and that of the Kingdom of Naples, longer than the English mile, by about two hundred and fifty yards.

PRICE OF POST-HORSES IN THE SARDINIAN TERRITORIES.

Every draught horse, per post, one French livre and fifty centimes.

Every carriage furnished by a post-master, one livre and fifty centimes.

ITALY—PRICE OF POST-HORSES, ETC.

Every postillion, one livre and fifty centimes.

TARIFF.

CABRIOLETS.

No. of Persons.	Horses.	Price for each Horse.
1, or 2	2	1 liv. 50 cent.
3	3	1 50
4	3	2

LIMONIERES.

1, 2, or 3	3	1 50
4	3	2

BERLINES.

1, 2, or 3	4	1 50
4, or 5	6	1 50
6	6	1 75

A child, if under six years of age, is not paid for.

If a *Limonière* contain above four persons, and if a *Berline* contain above six, an additional charge is made of one livre and fifty centimes per post.

PASSAGE OF CENIS.

From the first of November to the first of April the price of every draught-horse, from Molaret to Lanslebourg, and from Lanslebourg to Susa, is two livres per post: and from the fifteenth of September to the fifteenth of May, the same price is charged for every additional horse and mule, from Susa to Molaret, from Molaret to Mont Cenis, and from Lanslebourg to Mont Cenis; but not *vice versâ*. To every *Cabriolet*, containing one or two persons, one additional horse is added—to every *Cabriolet*, containing three persons, two additional horses and a postillion—to every *Cabriolet*, containing four persons, three horses and a postillion — to every *Limonière*, containing two persons, two horses and a postillion—to every *Limonière*, containing three or four persons, three horses and a postillion — and to every *Berline*, containing three or four persons, two horses and a postillion.

PASSAGE OF THE ECHELLES.

The Post-master here is obliged to furnish, in addition to his horses, draught-oxen, at one livre and fifty centimes the pair, per post. To every *Cabriolet à glaces*, drawn by two horses, one pair of oxen must be added — to every *Limonière*, drawn by three or four horses, one pair of oxen in summer, and two pair in winter — to every *Berline*, drawn by four horses, two pair of oxen—and to every *Berline*, drawn by six horses, two pair of oxen in summer, and three pair in winter. To an open *Cabriolet*, containing only one person, no oxen are added; but the post-master at Echelles is authorised to add an extra-horse to S. Thibault-du-Coux.

ASCENT OF THE SIMPLON.

The Post-masters at Domo d'Ossola and Yeselles are authorised to put one additional horse to carriages drawn by two or three horses; and two additional horses to carriages drawn by four horses: but they are not authorised to put more than six horses to any carriage whatever.

PASSAGE OF THE BOCCHETTA.

From Novi to Voltaggio, and from Voltaggio to Campo-Maronee, and *vice versâ*, twenty-five centimes per post are added to the charge for every draught-horse.

At Turin it is advisable that persons who intend to travel post should apply to the *Direzione generale delle Poste*, for an order respecting post-horses; which order, called a *Bulleton*, saves trouble, and prevents imposition.

PRICE OF POST-HORSES IN THE LOMBARDO-VENETIAN REALM.

Every pair of draught-horses, per post, five French livres and fifty centimes.

Every *Calesse*, furnished by a post-master, forty centimes; and every close carriage, furnished by a post-master, eighty centimes.

Every postillion, one livre and fifty centimes: postillions, however, are seldom satisfied with less than double that sum.*

PRICE OF POST-HORSES IN TUSCANY.

Every pair of draught-horses, ten pauls a post; except on quitting Florence, when the price is six pauls per horse.

The third horse, four pauls.

Every saddle-horse, five pauls.

Every postillion, three pauls.

Hostler, at every post, half a paul for every pair of horses.

Every *Calesse*, furnished by a post-master, three pauls; and every carriage, with four places, six pauls.

A postillion expects five pauls for every common post, and six pauls on quitting Florence.

PRICE OF POST-HORSES IN THE PRINCIPALITY OF LUCCA.

Every pair of draught-horses, ten pauls a post.

The third horse, four pauls.

Hostler, at every post, half a paul for every pair of horses.

Every saddle-horse, five pauls.

Every postillion, three pauls.

Every *Calesse*, furnished by a post-master, three pauls; and every carriage, with four places, six pauls.

Travellers, on quitting Lucca, are charged fifteen pauls for every pair of draught-horses.

PRICE OF POST-HORSES IN THE ECCLESIASTICAL TERRITORIES.

Every pair of draught-horses, ten pauls a post.

The third horse, four pauls.

Every saddle-horse, four pauls.

Every postillion, three pauls and a half.

Hostler, at every post, half a paul for every pair of horses.

Every *Calesse*, furnished by a post-master, three pauls; and every carriage with four inside places (furnished by a post-master), six pauls per post.

A postillion expects five pauls per post.

Travellers are charged an extra half-post on quitting Rome.

PRICE OF POST-HORSES IN THE KINGDOM OF NAPLES.

Great Roads. Every draught-horse, and every saddle-horse, six carlini and a half per post.

Every postillion one carlino and a half per post for each horse.

Hostler, at provincial post-houses, half a carlino for every pair of horses—hostler, at the Naples post-house, one carlino for every pair of horses.

Cross Roads. Every draught-horse, nine carlini per post.

Every postillion, two carlini per post.

Every carriage with two inside places, furnished by a post-master, five carlini; and every car-

---

* The price of Post-horses in the Duchies of Parma and Modena is the same as in the Lombardo-Venetian realm; except from Fiorenzuola to Cremona, and from Castel San Giovanni to Pavia, at which places the price is seven livres and fifty centimes for every pair of draught-horses.

riage with four inside places (furnished by a post-master), ten carlini per post.

A postillion expects six carlini a post.

For a post-royal, in the Neapolitan territories, an extra half-post is charged.

Hostlers in Italy are seldom contented with less than twice their due: and the person who throws water over the wheels of travelling carriages (a necessary operation in hot weather), expects half a paul for his trouble.

An English post-chaise, with shafts, conveying two or three persons only, and not heavily laden, is allowed to travel with two, or, at most, three horses, in those parts of northern Italy which are not mountainous: but, if the carriage convey four persons, it is not allowed to travel with less than four horses. A *Calesse*, conveying three persons, and only one trunk, is allowed to travel with two horses.

In Tuscany, if the road be not mountainous, an English post-chaise, with a pole, conveying three persons, and no trunk, is allowed to travel with two horses only: but English carriages conveying four persons and trunks, are not allowed to travel with less than four horses. In the Ecclesiastical territories, a two-wheeled carriage, conveying three persons, and only one trunk, is allowed to travel with two horses; but, if it convey more than one trunk, three horses are indispensable: and persons who travel with more than two large trunks, are subject to a tax of two pauls per post for every extra-trunk, vache, or portmanteau. A four-wheeled carriage, with a pole, conveying six persons and one trunk, is allowed to travel with only four horses; but if it convey seven persons, or six persons and two large trunks, six horses are indispensable. A four-wheeled carriage, half open, in the German fashion, and conveying only two persons, and one small trunk, is allowed to travel with only two horses.

To the driver of every extra draught-horse, it is customary to give two pauls, though he cannot demand any remuneration.

In the Neapolitan Territories, a four-wheeled carriage, conveying four persons and one large trunk, is allowed to travel with four horses only; but if it convey six persons, and two large trunks, six horses are indispensable. A two-wheeled carriage, conveying two persons and one large trunk, is allowed to travel with two horses; but, if it convey three persons and a large trunk, three horses are indispensable.

Every post-master should be paid for his horses before they set out.

Shafts are not used either in the Tuscan, Roman, or Neapolitan Territories.

The average price paid in Italy for accommodations at Inns, by persons who travel post, is as follows:

	Pauls.
Breakfast, per head, in large towns	3
————— in small towns	2
Dinner, per head, in large towns	10
————— in small towns	8
Beds, from three to five pauls each.	

It is more economical, and less troublesome in Italy, to travel *en voiturier,* than to travel post, but it is more fatiguing; because persons who accomplish a long journey with the same horses must, generally speaking, travel slower than if they changed horses at every post; and, therefore, persons who follow the latter plan, need not rise so early as those who follow the former. If a Voiturin have good horses, they will go from forty to fifty Roman miles a day; arriving, in due time, at the destined sleeping-places. Mules are less expeditious, because they seldom trot.

A Voiturin usually expects for conveying Travellers, in their own carriage, from one part of the Continent to another, twelve francs a day per draught-horse: six francs a day for each master; three francs a day for each child; and four francs and a half a day for each servant: and for this price he furnishes good horses, or mules, together with breakfast, supper, and beds; or dinner, supper, and beds: but, if he convey Travellers in a carriage belonging to himself, he seldom expects more than three-quarters of the above-named price, because he can make a considerable profit by filling the carriage with passengers on his return.

The *buona-mano* usually given to a Voiturier, if he behave well, is about half a Spanish dollar per day.

The fare, in a public carriage, from Florence to Rome, and likewise from Rome to Naples, suppers and beds inclusive, is from ten to twelve scudi; unless it be a *voiture de retour,* in which case the fare is about eight scudi.

If passengers, merely to accommodate themselves, require a Voiturier to stop one or more days on the road, he expects them to pay six francs per night, for the sustenance of each of his horses.

A Voiturin commonly pays in Italy, for his Passengers, the following prices at inns:—

Breakfast, per head, from a paul and a half to two pauls—dinner, three pauls—supper and bed, five pauls: but Foreigners who pay for themselves at inns can seldom, if ever, make so good a bargain.

Italian and Swiss Voiturins usually pay for their passengers, in France, four francs a head for supper and beds; and about two francs for dinner. Italian and Swiss voiturins likewise pay, for permission to travel in France, a tax of five sous a horse per post, unless it be at those post-houses where they dine or sleep.

As Neapolitan Voiturins are deemed the worst in Italy, because notorious for breaking their engagements, Travellers should avoid going *en voiturier*, from Naples to Rome; unless it be with the Post-master's horses.

TUSCANY.

CURRENT COINS.

	English.
	l. s. d.
Ruspone, equal to about	1 11 6
Zecchino	0 10 6
Francescone, or *Scudo**	0 5 0
Half ditto	0 2 6
Piece of three *paoli*, or pauls	0 1 6
Piece of two *paoli*	0 1 0
Lira	0 0 9
Paolo	0 0 6
Mezzo-Paolo	0 0 3

Piece of two *crazie*, four of which make one *paolo*, or *paul*.

Crazia, eight of which make one paul.

Quattrino, five of which make one *crazia*.

Soldo, one of which makes three *quattrini*.

The one-paul piece of Rome

---

* Ten pauls make one Francescone, or scudo; which is five francs and sixty centimes of France.

An Old Louis-d'or is usually current in Tuscany for about forty-two pauls, and a Napoleon for about thirty-six pauls: but the value of French gold is fluctuating.

is current for one paul of Tuscany.

The two-paul piece of Rome is current for two pauls of Tuscany, wanting four *quattrini*.

The Spanish dollar is usually current for about nine pauls and a half. This coin is frequently called a *pezzo-duro*.

The real value of the *ruspone* is only sixty pauls; but it can seldom be purchased under sixty-three; owing to the *agio* on gold: and, from the same cause, the *zecchino*, which is worth only twenty pauls, can seldom be purchased under twenty-one.

Bankers' accounts throughout Tuscany, are kept in *pezze, soldi,* and *danari;* or *lire, soldi,* and *danari.*

Twelve *danari* make one *soldo;* twenty *soldi* make one *lira;** five *lire* and fifteen *soldi*, or, at most, six *lire*, make the imaginary coin called a *pezze*, or piece of eight; and for each of these, a Banker charges so many English pence, according to the exchange, when he gives cash for a bill upon London.† Bankers, according to the Tuscan law, are obliged either to pay in gold, or to allow an *agio* if they pay in silver: the *agio* varies from week to week according to the demand for gold.

The pound weight of Tuscany is divided into twelve ounces; the ounce into twenty-four deniers; and the denier into twenty-four grains. The Tuscan ounce is somewhat less than the English.

The common Tuscan measure, called a *braccio*, is about twenty-two English inches and a half; two *braccia* making one ell.

Prices at the principal Hotels are much the same in Leghorn, Pisa, and Florence; namely, for a large apartment from twenty to thirty pauls a day; and for smaller apartments, from ten to fifteen pauls a day. For breakfast, from two to three pauls a head; for dinner, from eight to ten pauls a head; for servants, from four to five pauls a head per day; and with regard to *buona-mano* to attendants at inns, the waiter usually expects about one paul per day, and the chamber-maid still less; that is, if Travellers reside at an inn by the week or month; but, if they come for a few nights only, they are expected to pay more liberally.

The wages of a *valet-de-place* is four pauls per day throughout Tuscany, he finding himself in board, lodging, and clothes.

LEGHORN.

The price of close carriages here is rather exorbitant; but open carriages, called *Timonelli*, ply in the High Street, like our Hackney coaches, and may be hired on reasonable terms.

The price of a box at the Theatre varies according to the merit of the Performers; but is usually high. The entrance-money paid by English Travellers, exclusive of the price of a box, is three pauls for an opera, and two for a play.

Tea, coffee, sugar, English mustard, foreign wines, brandy, rum, arrack, porter, Bristol-beer, and Gorgona anchovies, may all be purchased cheaper at Leghorn than in any other city of Italy; so likewise may soap, starch, and hair-powder.

---

* A *lira* of Tuscany is one paul and a half.
† If the exchange be, as it usually is, in favour of England, every paul costs about five pence.

Mecali, in Via-Grande, has a magnificent shop, containing a great variety of sculpture in alabaster and Carrara marble, jewels, trinkets, silks, linens, muslins, etc.; but the persons who serve in this shop usually ask much more than they take.

Silks, linens, and muslins, may be purchased very cheap of the Jews, by the expert in making bargains.

Persons who wear flannel should provide themselves with a stock at Leghorn; it being sometimes difficult to find this useful article of clothing in other parts of Italy. Townley, in Via Grande, sells flannel, and other English goods.

Provisions at Leghorn are, generally speaking, good; butter and oil, however, must be excepted; as both are very indifferent; but it is easy to obviate this inconvenience, by having *Cascina* butter from Pisa, and oil from Lari. Carriers, called *Procaccini*, go daily to the former place; and from the latter the Peasants come to sell poultry, fruit, etc., at Leghorn, three or four times a week.

Invalids may be regularly supplied with good asses' milk at one crazia the ounce; (the usual price throughout Tuscany); goats' and cows' milk may likewise be procured with ease; but persons who make a point of having the last quite genuine, should send into the country for it; and with respect to asses' milk, it is requisite for some trusty person to watch the milking of the ass, in order to prevent the infusion of hot water.*

Malta and Genoa oranges, fine dates, and English potatoes, may frequently be purchased at Leghorn. There is an oyster-house near this city, and the oysters are good, but extremely dear. Figs and grapes, in their season, are abundant and excellent; particularly the white fig, and small transparent white grape; the last of which, if gathered dry, put into paper bags, and hung up in an airy room, may be preserved all the winter. The best sort of dried figs is generally sold in small baskets of about one foot long and four or five inches wide. Levant figs and Spanish raisins may be purchased at Leghorn; and about the month of September large numbers of small birds, resembling the English wheatear, and called in Italian *Beccafichi*, are caught daily on the plain near this town. Ortolans also abound in southern Italy.

A Tuscan barrel of wine contains twenty flasks, and a barrel of oil sixteen flasks. Wood is sold by the *catastre*, the dimensions of which should be these: length, *braccia* six; breadth, *braccia* one and a half; height, *braccia* two.

A public carriage goes daily from Leghorn to Pisa.

Public boats likewise go daily by means of the Canal, and the passage-money in these vessels is six *crazie*, or at most one paul for each person. The price of a private boat is from from ten to twelve livres; and the price of one place in the Diligence, from Leghorn to Florence, thirty pauls.

It is not advisable for Travellers

---

* The man who milks the ass usually carries, under his cloak, a bottle filled with hot water; some of which he contrives to mix with the milk so expertly that it is difficult to detect him.

to hire a country-residence near Leghorn, its environs being reckoned unwholesome.

ARRIVAL AND DEPARTURE OF LETTER-COURIERS.

Sunday, at eight in the morning, arrive letters from all parts of Tuscany, Elba, Lucca, Naples, Sicily, Rome, Lombardy, Venice, Switzerland, Germany, and Trieste, and all northern Europe.

Monday afternoon from Pisa, Pietrasanta, Lucca, Massa, Piedmont, Genoa, France, Spain and Portugal.

Wednesday, at seven in the morning, from the same places as on Sunday, Elba excepted.

Wednesday afternoon, from the same places as on Monday; and likewise from Great Britain.

Friday, at seven in the morning, from all parts of Tuscany, Elba, Lucca, Rome, Naples, Lombardy, Venice, and Trieste.

Friday afternoon, from France, Great Britain, Spain, and Portugal, Piedmont, Genoa, Lucca, Pisa, and Pietrasanta.

Monday, at half past six in the evening, go letters for all parts of Tuscany, Elba, Lucca, Naples, and Sicily, Rome, Lombardy, Venice, Switzerland, Germany, and all northern Europe.

Tuesday, at half past seven in the evening, go letters for Pisa, Pietrasanta, Massa, Lucca, Piedmont, Genoa, France, Great Britain (*via* France), Spain, and Portugal.

Wednesday, at half past seven in the evening, go letters for all parts of Tuscany, Lucca, and Rome.

Thursday, at half past seven in the evening, go letters to the same places as on Tuesday.

Friday, at half past seven in the evening, go letters to the same places as on Monday.

Saturday, at half past seven in the evening, go letters to Pisa, Lucca, Pietrasanta, Massa, Piedmont, Genoa, France, Great Britain, Spain, and Portugal, *via* France.

Letters are usually delivered about nine in the morning; and must be put into the post-office before five in the evening, and franked for every place beyond Tuscany.

PISA.

A custom-house officer follows Travellers to their inn, or lodging, when they enter Pisa, and expects a fee of five pauls. A band of musicians likewise waits upon Strangers at their arrival, and expects from three to five pauls.

BEST LODGING-HOUSES. AVERAGE PRICE IN WINTER.

Casa-Agostini, Lung' Arno, No. 722, about twenty sequins per month. — Casa-Bertoli, Lung' Arno, No. 721, large and handsome apartments, a third floor, about thirteen sequins a month.— No. 742, Via-Coraia; rooms small, but neat, and sufficient in number for two persons; price moderate.—Casa-Lenzi, Lung' Arno, about twenty sequins a month. —No. 951, Via di Sapienza, two suites of handsome apartments.— No. 694, Lung' Arno, one suite of good apartments; thirty sequins a month.—Marble Palace, Lung' Arno, fine apartments.—Casa-Chiesa, a good apartment.—Casa-Rau, fine apartments.—Casa-Panichi, Lung' Arno, No. 716, a neat apartment on the first floor, large enough for three persons. —No. 887, Via S. Maria, fourteen well-furnished rooms, and a small garden; twenty sequins a month, if taken for half a year. All these lodging-houses are well situated for Invalids: other apartments, which have not this advantage, let at a much lower price. Rooms sufficient to accommodate a moderate sized family may usually be hired at the *Tre Donzelle* for about twenty sequins a month. The price of every lodging, however, varies from year to year, according to the number of Foreigners. The hire of linen per month is generally about five sequins for a large family; but linen and plate are commonly found by the owners of lodging-houses.

Boxes at the Theatre may be procured on very moderate terms; except it be during the last week of Carnival, when the price is considerably augmented. The entrance-money paid by English Travellers, exclusive of the hire of a box, is two pauls.

The hire of a carriage and horses, coachman's wages inclusive, is from eighteen to twenty sequins a month; and the price for an airing, *buona-mano* inclusive, is ten pauls.

The wages of a Housemaid, throughout southern Italy, is about three crowns a month and a dinner; she finding herself in lodging, bread and wine—the wages of a Footman from four to eight crowns and a dinner; he finding himself in bread and wine—the wages of a Housemaid who finds herself in bed and board, and fetches Fountain-water, is at Pisa one lira per day *—and the wages of a good Cook, throughout southern Italy, is from ten to twelve crowns per month and a dinner; he finding himself in lodging, bread and wine, and an Assistant to wash saucepans, dishes, etc. †

The price of dinner, per head, at a *Restaurateur's*, table-wine and bread inclusive, is from three to five pauls.

Families who have their dinner daily from a *Traiteur* should not order it per head, but per dish; specifying the kind of dinner they wish for, and the price they choose to give.

There are various sorts of firewood at Pisa: that called *legna dolce* is the most wholesome; though it consumes very quick: that called *legna forte* is usually burnt in kitchens; but may be mixed with the other, for parlour-consumption; though I would not advise the burning it in bed-rooms. Vendors of wood frequently cheat in the measure, either by bringing a *braccio* to measure with not so long as the law directs, or by placing the wood hollow, and thus making it appear more than it is.

The husks of olives serve for fuel, and are an excellent substitute for charcoal, and in olive-countries very cheap.

Invalids always find it necessary to mat their rooms during winter, in order to avoid the

---

* By Fountain-water is meant that conveyed to Pisa through the Aqueduct.

† It is an excellent general rule, either not to let your cook market for you, or to limit him to a certain sum for dinner, charcoal, and kitchen fire-wood: but English Travellers who are accompanied by honest English Servants, always find it answer to let those Servants market for them.

chill which strikes to the soles of the feet from brick and marble floors. Mats of all lengths may be purchased on the Quay; the price is half a paul the *braccio*; and every mat ought to be two *braccia* and a half wide.

The Pisa market is, generally speaking, a good one; though fresh fish can never be absolutely depended upon but on Fridays, unless it be in Lent. The best fishes are the dory, called *pesce di S. Pietro;* the grey and the red mullet, called *triglia;* the turbot, called *rombo;* the tunny, called *tonno;* the lamprey, called *lampredo;* sturgeon, called *storione; ombrina, pescecavallo, spada, dentici, parago,* (all five peculiar, I believe, to the Mediterranean); the sole, called *sogliola;* the Mediterranean lobster, called *gambero del mare;* prawns and shrimps. The fish which comes from Via Reggio is generally excellent. The tench and carp at Pisa are remarkably fine; so likewise are the pike, and other fishes, of the Arno and Serchio.* The mutton of Pistoja, which may frequently be purchased at Pisa, is excellent in point of flavour, and particularly light of digestion. The Lucca-veal, frequently sold at Pisa, is excellent. Beef and pork are very fine; turkeys good; capons and fowls indifferent; hares excellent; other game plentiful, but not always so well flavoured as in England. Wild-fowl good and plentiful. Venison may be purchased both in spring and autumn, but is reckoned best during the latter season. Wild-boar may be purchased during winter and spring. With respect to vegetables, the broccoli and salads are particularly good; but vegetables in Italy, salad excepted, should, generally speaking, be stewed, or they may probably disagree with weak stomachs. Pisa is well supplied with grapes, figs, pears, apples, and other winter-fruits, the best of which come from Florence and Pistoja. The butter made at the royal *Cascina* is excellent.†
Good cows' milk and cream may be purchased at the above-named *Cascina*. Good oil may be bought at some of the palaces; as every Tuscan nobleman sells the produce of his olive-gardens and vineyards. With respect to table-wine, that of Pisa is unwholesome; but that of Florence may easily be procured by water-carriage, and is not only pleasant to the taste, but salutary to most constitutions.—There are several kinds of Florence-wine; and that usually drank as common table-beverage, costs from a paul and a half to two pauls the flask.

Scales and weights are necessary articles of kitchen-furniture in Italy.

Persons who wish to be instructed in music, drawing, and the Italian and French languages, may procure good masters, upon moderate terms, at Pisa.

The common fee to medical men is a scudo from Foreigners; though the natives give much less. Some of the English Travellers give a sequin a visit to Italian physicians.

Caso-Mecherini, the principal banking-house at Pisa, will supply

---

* What Italians deem the best fishes are distinguished by the appellation of *Pesce Nobile*. The taste of Englishmen, however, does not exactly agree with that of the Italians in this particular.

† This butter supplies the Roman markets, and suffers very little from its journey.

Foreigners with money; but it is more advantageous to procure it at Leghorn.

The price of common shoes is eight pauls the pair, whether for men or women.

The price for making a man's suit of clothes about twenty pauls, all charges inclusive.

The price for making a Lady's dress nine or ten pauls, beside body lining.

Sig. Antonio Peverata, Bookseller, No. 694, Lung' Arno, is an honest man, and very useful to Foreigners.

Pisa may be called a cheap place for permanent residence; as may Pistoja, Florence, and Siena; because, supposing the exchange in favour of England (which it commonly is throughout Tuscany), a moderate sized family might, in any of the above-named cities, live handsomely for six hundred pounds sterling per annum; and even large families who visit Italy, either for the purpose of educating their children, or of travelling from place to place in search of amusement, will not, if they know how to avoid imposition, find their disbursements exceed one thousand pounds sterling per annum. For the purpose of education, better masters may usually be procured at Florence than in any other Italian city.

Sunday morning arrive letters from Florence, and other parts of Tuscany, Rome, Naples, Sicily, Bologna, northern Italy, Switzerland, Germany, the kingdom of the Netherlands, Denmark, Sweden, Poland and Russia.

Monday evening from Genoa, France, Spain, Piedmont, Massa, Carrara, Lucca, and Leghorn.

Tuesday evening from Piombino, Porto Ferrajo, Lucca, and Leghorn.

Wednesday morning from Florence, and other parts of Tuscany, Rome, Naples, Bologna, northern Italy, Switzerland, Germany, the Netherlands, Denmark, Sweden, Poland, and Russia.

Wednesday evening from Lucca, and Leghorn, Genoa, France, and Great Britain.

Thursday evening from Lucca.

Friday morning from Florence, and other parts of Tuscany; Rome, Bologna, Ferrara, Ancona, Venice, etc., Genoa, France, Spain, Great Britain, Piedmont, Massa, and Carrara.

Friday evening from Piombino, Portoferrajo, Lucca, and Leghorn.

Saturday evening from Lucca and Leghorn.

Monday evening go letters for Florence, and other parts of Tuscany, Rome, Naples, Sicily, Bologna, northern Italy, Switzerland, Germany, the Netherlands, Denmark, Sweden, Poland, Russia, Piombino, Portoferrajo, Leghorn, and Lucca.

Tuesday evening go letters for Genoa, France, Spain, Great Britain, Piedmont, Massa, Carrara, Lucca, and Leghorn.

Wednesday evening go letters for Florence, and other parts of Tuscany; Rome, Naples, Bologna, Ferrara, Ancona, Venice, and Lucca.

Thursday evening go letters for Leghorn, Lucca, Genoa, France, and Great Britain.

Friday evening go letters for Florence, and other parts of Tuscany; Rome, Naples, and Sicily, Bologna, northern Italy, Switzerland, Germany, the Netherlands, Denmark, Sweden, Poland, Russia, Piombino, Portoferrajo, and Lucca.

ITALY—FLORENCE.

Saturday evening go letters for Genoa, France, Spain, Great Britain, Piedmont, Massa, Carrara, Lucca, and Leghorn.

Letters must be put into the Post-office before five in the afternoon, and franked for every place, except Florence and Leghorn. The price for franking a single letter to England is six crazie.

The price of one place in the Diligence from Pisa to Florence is one sequin.

Persons going from Pisa to Florence had better not have their baggage plumbed, it being necessary either to undergo an examination, or present the custom-house officers in the latter city with five or ten pauls, according to the quantity and quality of the luggage.

FLORENCE.

The best Hotels, and some of the best private Lodging-houses in Italy are to be found at Florence; and the price of good apartments, compared with the prices at Rome and Naples, is not exorbitant.

LODGING-HOUSES. AVERAGE PRICE IN WINTER.

Palazzo S. Clemente, Via S. Bastiano, two suites of handsome apartments, each thirty sequins a month; a good garden; and the warmest situation in Florence—Palazzo-Strozzi, Via della Scala, a fine house, and beautiful garden; sixty sequins a month—Palazzo-Corsi, Via Ghibellina, two suites of apartments, each thirty sequins for one month only; but less if taken for a longer term—Palazzo-Quaratesi, Via d'ogni Santi, one set of apartments, forty-five sequins a month; another set, twenty-eight ditto—Casa-Pucci, opposite the Teatro-Goldoni, is a good lodging—The Palazzo-Acciaioli, Lung' Arno, contains several apartments—Casa-Riccasoli, Lung' Arno, is a pretty house for a small family: and in the Piazza S. Maria Novella, and several other parts of the city, small apartments may be easily met with.

Plate and linen are generally found in the lodgings at Florence; but, if not found, the hire of linen for a large family is about five sequins a month. Noble apartments unfurnished may be hired by the year for, comparatively speaking, nothing.

As the Tuscans take no pains to advertise their vacant apartments, and it is consequently difficult to discover them, Travellers would do well to apply for information at the shops of Molini, Meggit, and Townley.

Board and lodging for a Lady, or Gentleman, in an Italian family, tea and foreign wine not inclusive, usually costs about fifteen sequins a month: and at the house of Madame Merveilleux du Plantis, which contains good apartments, comfortably furnished, board and lodging, tea and common table wine inclusive, costs, for a Lady, or Gentleman, by the year, fifty pounds sterling; by the half year, thirty pounds; by the quarter, twenty pounds; per month, seven pounds; and per week, two pounds. Since the first part of this work was printed, Madame du Plantis has removed from No. 4380, to No. 4245, Piazza S. Maria Novella. Featherstonhaugh's *Hôtel de l'Europe*, Piazza S. Gaetano, is excellent.

At the *Hôtel des Armes d'Angleterre*, kept by Gasperini, a Family, consisting of four masters and four servants, may have a good apartment, breakfast, excellent dinners, tea, wax-lights, and night-lamps, for eighty francesconi a week : * and the master of the *Locanda di S. Luigi* (by name Luigi Falugi), will supply four masters and four servants with breakfast, dinner, a good dessert, and two bottles of table-wine, together with milk and butter for tea, at five scudi a day.

The price, per head, for breakfast, at a Coffee-house, is about one paul; † and the price, per head, for dinner, at the house of a *Restaurateur,* or at a *Table d'Hôte,* is from three to five pauls, table-wine inclusive.

The price, per month, for a good carriage and horses, coachman's wages inclusive, is from twenty to twenty-five sequins, according to the expense of provender.

Innkeepers usually charge for their carriages, by the day, about twenty pauls.

Provisions, in general, are good; though fresh fish can only be procured on Fridays and Saturdays. Figs, peaches, water-melons, and grapes are, in their repective seasons, excellent. Good cows' milk and good butter are not to be obtained without difficulty; asses' milk is excellent; and the wine made in the neighbourhood of Florence is palatable and wholesome: the best sorts, called *Vino Santo, Leatico,* and *Artiminio,* come from the vicinity of Fiesole, where the oil, likewise, is particularly good. Ice (or, more properly speaking, frozen snow) costs two pauls and a half per every hundred pounds.

The best medicines are sold at the Farmacia Formini, in the Piazza del Granduca; and by the Grand Duke's Apothecary.

The usual price of butchers' meat is from five to six crazie the pound — the usual price of the best bread about four crazie the pound — a turkey costs from five to ten pauls, according to its size; a fowl from one lira to three pauls —partridges from four to six pauls the brace—a beccafico from three to five crazie—an ortolan from six crazie to a paul—and the best table wine from a lira to two pauls per flask.

Sig. Giuseppe Molini, Bookseller, has an English Reading Room, and a shop containing English books, paper, pens, pencils, etc., in Via Archibusieri; and a much better Library at No. 823, Piazza di S. Maria in Campo; where he likewise has a Printing Office. Meggit, in the Piazza del Duomo, sells good Foreign wine, porter, tea, English medicines, etc. His black tea is twelve pauls a pound; his green tea sixteen pauls. Townley, in the Palazzo-Ferroni, S. Trinità, likewise sells English goods. One of the best Grocers is Caroli, Via della Croce: his Levant-coffee is from twenty-two crazie to three pauls the pound; his West-Indian coffee two pauls the pound. The best Silk-mercer is Borgogni, near the Piazza del Granduca. Florence silks are of various qualities; one sort being from nine to ten pauls the braccio; another from six to seven; and the slightest from three to five pauls, according to the weight. The best linen-drapers' shops are

---

* Anti-attrition grease may be purchased of Gasperini for five pauls a pot.

† Every cup of coffee usually costs two crazie; every cup of chocolate something more.

kept by Jews, near the Mercato Nuovo. Shoes and boots are, generally speaking, better made at Florence than in any other part of Italy: the usual price charged for the former is eight pauls the pair; and for the latter from thirty to forty pauls. Florentine Tailors charge for making a man's suit of clothes from twenty to twenty-five pauls. Ladies Dress-makers usually charge twelve pauls for making a trimmed dress, and nine for making a plain one. There are several good Coach-makers at Florence. Pestellini, Money-changer, near the Piazza del Duomo, will supply Travellers who are going to Rome with dollars and Roman scudi at a lower price than they are current for in the Ecclesiastical State. Fire-wood at Florence is from thirty-five to thirty-eight pauls the catastre; and charcoal from three to four pauls a sack.

Fees to medical Men are much the same as at Pisa: and the sum given to a Notary-public, for his seal and attestation, is ten pauls.

A box at the Pergola may generally be obtained for fifteen, or, at most, twenty pauls; but every British Traveller pays three pauls for admission, beside the expense of the box. At the Cocomero, and the Teatro-Nuovo, boxes usually cost from eight to twelve pauls; and every British Traveller pays, for admission at these theatres, two pauls over and above the price of a box.

The best Music-Masters charge ten pauls a lesson; other Masters do not charge more than five. Sig. Morani teaches Italian remarkably well.

The most distinguished Sculptors are Ricci, Bartolini, and the Brothers Pisani.*

Gulflocher, in Borgo-Ogni Santi, No. 3951, sells alabaster.

Ermini is a good Painter; and may usually be found at the Royal Academy.

Bankers at Florence give the same exchange, and nearly the same *agio*, as at Leghorn. Messrs. Donat Orsi and Co., in the Piazza del Granduca, are honourable in their dealings, and very obliging to Foreigners; as is Sig. Sebastiano Kleiber, in Via-Larga.

The best *Padrone di vetture* at Florence is Balzani, who may always be heard of at the Aquila Nera: his horses and mules are good, and his drivers remarkably civil.†

ARRIVAL AND DEPARTURE OF LETTER-COURIERS.

Monday, at nine in the morning, arrive letters from Arezzo, Cortona, and Castiglion Fiorentino.

---

* Travellers who purchase alabaster for the purpose of having it sent to Great Britain by sea, should deal with the Brothers Pisani, as their punctuality may be relied on.

† Washerwomen in Tuscany commonly charge for washing and ironing as follows:—

Sheets, per pair	crazie 12
Pillowcases, each	1
Tablecloth, if large	6
Napkin	1
Towel	1
Shirt, if plain, crazie 6; if frilled	7
Shift	4
Drawers	4
Pantaloons	8
Corset	5
Pocket-handkerchief	1
Neckcloth	1
Kitchen-apron	2
Pockets, per pair	2
Sleeping waistcoat	4
Nightcap, if not trimmed	2
Silk-stockings, per pair	4
Cotton-stockings, per pair	2
Plain white dresses, each	16
Petticoats, each	8

Persons who wish to be economical in Italy should have their linen washed out of the house, and ironed at home.

Francesca Lambardi, in the Piazza San-Spirito, No. 2079, is a good laundress.

Tuesday, about the same time, arrive letters from Great Britain, France, Piedmont, Switzerland, Genoa, Spain, Sarzana, Pietrasanta, Pisa, Leghorn, Lucca, Massa, Piombino, Portoferrajo, Perugia, Cortona, Arezzo, etc., Rome, Viterbo, Siena, Poggibonsi, Prato, Pistoja, Peschia, and Volterra:

And *Tuesday, about noon, arrive letters* from Germany, Russia, Prussia, Holland, Trieste, Venice, Upper Italy, and Bologna.

Thursday, at nine in the morning, arrive letters from Great Britain, France, Piedmont, Switzerland, Genoa, Spain, Sarzana, Pietrasanta, Pisa, Leghorn, Lucca, Massa, Piombino, Portoferrajo, the Kingdom of Naples, Rome, Perugia, Cortona, Arezzo, etc., Siena, Poggibonsi, Prato, Pistoja, and Peschia:

And, *about noon, arrive letters* from Bologna, Ferrara, and Ancona.

Saturday, at nine in the morning, arrive letters from Great Britain, France, Piedmont, Switzerland, Genoa, Spain, Sarzana, Pietrasanta, Pisa, Leghorn, Lucca, Massa, Piombino, Portoferrajo, the Kingdom of Naples, Rome, Viterbo, Siena, Poggibonsi, Prato, Pistoja, and Pescia:

And, *about noon, arrive letters* from Germany, Russia, Prussia, Holland, Switzerland, Trieste, Venice, Upper Italy, and Bologna.

Tuesday, at one o'clock post-meridian, go letters for Germany, Russia, Prussia, Holland, Switzerland, Trieste, Upper Italy, and Bologna:

And, *at five o'clock post-meridian, go letters* for Poggibonsi, Siena, Viterbo, Rome, and the Kingdom of Naples, Great Britain, France, Spain, Piedmont, Genoa, Sarzana, Massa, Lucca, Pietrasanta, Pisa, Leghorn, Arezzo, Cortona, Castiglion Fiorentino, Prato, Pistoja, Pescia, and Volterra.

Thursday, at one o'clock post-meridian, go letters for Great Britain, France, Spain, Piedmont, Genoa, Sarzana, Massa, and Pietrasanta:

And, *at five o'clock post-meridian,* for Bologna, Ferrara, Ancona, Portoferrajo, Lucca, Pisa, Leghorn, Arezzo, Cortona, etc., Perugia, Rome, the Kingdom of Naples, Siena, Pistoja, Prato, and Volterra.

Saturday, at one o'clock, post-meridian, go letters for Germany, Russia, Prussia, Holland, Switzerland, Trieste, Upper Italy, Bologna, Great Britain, France, Spain, Piedmont, Genoa, Sarzana, Massa, and Pietrasanta:

And, *at five o'clock, post-meridian,* for Poggibonsi, Siena, Viterbo, Rome, the Kingdom of Naples, Arezzo, Cortona, etc., Perugia, Leghorn, Pisa, Piombino, Portoferrajo, Lucca, Pistoja, Prato, and Pescia.

Letters for every country, Tuscany excepted, must be franked, and put into the Post-Office before noon every day, except Saturday, when they are received till three o'clock.

COUNTRY-HOUSES NEAR FLORENCE.

Villa Mattei, near the Porta S. Gallo, a large house.

Villa del Cav. Gerini, on the Bologna-road; a good house, well furnished, and delightfully situated.

Villa-Vitelli, at Fiesole, healthy and cool.

Villa-Baroni, at Fiesole, ditto,

but in too elevated a situation for weak lungs.

Palazzo - Bruciarto, near the Porta S. Gallo, an excellent house, in rather too warm a situation for summer.

Villa Careggi de' Medici, a most excellent house, in a cool, dry, and healthy situation.

Villa del Nero, at Majano, a most excellent house, equally well situated.

There are, in the neighbourhood of Fiesole, several other Villas, which might be hired from Midsummer till the commencement of the vintage: as the Tuscans seldom occupy their country-houses till the end of September, when the vintage begins. From twenty to thirty sequins a month, plate and linen inclusive, is the highest price demanded for the best Tuscan Villas.

CHAPTER V.

ROME, NAPLES, AND ITS ENVIRONS.

Money of Rome—Bankers' accounts—Pound-weight—Measures—Hotels and other Lodging-houses—Best water—Best air—Prices of the best Lodgings—Prices charged by Traiteurs—Price of dinner per head at the houses of Restaurateurs—of breakfast at a Coffee-house—of Job-carriages and horses—Expense of keeping your own carriage—Hackney-coaches—Wages of a Valet-de-place—Fire-wood—Butchers' meat, wild fowl, poultry, fish, and other eatables—Tallow-candles—Charcoal—Best markets for fruit and vegetables—Wines of the country—Foreign wines—Best Confectioner—Oil—Honey—Tea—Grocers—Rum—Best wax-candles—Medicines—Woollen cloth—Furs—Roman pearls—Silk-mercer—Milliner—Language-master—Music-masters—Dancing-masters—Drawing-masters—Ancient bronzes, etc.—Sulphurs—Roman Mosaics—Scajuola, and paintings all' Encausto—Bronze lamps and silver plate—Stationer—Manuscript music—Prints and drawings—English writing paper, and English books—Circulating Library—Calcografia Camerale—Fees to Medical Men—Theatres—price of boxes—Unfurnished apartments—Procaccio from Rome to Naples—Best Roman Vetturino—Post-Office—Neapolitan territories—Passports—Fees to Custom-house Officers—Money of Naples—Exchange—Common Neapolitan measure, pound-weight, and rotolo—Hotels and other Lodging-houses at Naples—Job-carriages—Expense of keeping your own carriage—of keeping a saddle-horse—Hackney-carriages—Wages of a Valet-de-place—of a Cook—Mode in which persons who keep their own Cook should order dinner—Price of unfurnished apartments—Price usually paid by Families who have their dinner from a Traiteur—Price per head for dinner at a Restaurateur's—of breakfast at a Coffee-house—of Butchers' meat, fish, poultry and cheese, bread, oil, butter, Sorrento hams, tea, coffee, sugar, ice, and wines made in the Neapolitan territories—Fire-wood, charcoal, wax and tallow-candles—English Warehouses—Naples silks, gauzes, ribands, etc.—Sorrento silk-stockings—Musical instrument strings—Circulating Library—Borel's Library—Stationer—Coachmaker—English Medical Men—Music-master—Dancing-master—Price of boxes at the Theatres—Arrival and departure of Letter-Couriers and Procacci—Expense of franking letters, etc.—Piano di Sorrento—Price of Lodging-houses—Provisions—Oil, milk, wine of Sorrento and Capri—Charcoal and fire-wood—Clotted cream—Quails—Articles not found at Sorrento—Boats which go daily from Sorrento to Naples and return the same evening—Passage-money—Meta-boats—Best method of conveying a large Family from Naples to Sorrento—Post-Office—Sorrento recommended as a cheap place for permanent residence—Physician there—Comparative view of Family-expenses in various parts of the Continent.

ROME.

MONEY OF ROME.

Doppia . . worth thirty-two *paoli* and one *baioccho*.
Scudo . . . . . ten *paoli*.
Mezzo-Scudo . . five *paoli*.
Piece of three *paoli*.
Piece of two *paoli*.
Piece of one *paolo*.
Mezzo-paolo.
Baioccho, worth the tenth part of a *paolo*.

The old Louis-d'or is current at Rome for forty-four pauls—the Napoleon for thirty-seven pauls—and the Spanish dollar for ten pauls.

Bankers' accounts are kept in pauls.

The Roman pound-weight is twelve ounces; the Roman *canna* is about two yards and a quarter English measure; and the Roman mercantile *palmo* is between nine and ten English inches.

HOTELS AND OTHER LODGING-HOUSES.

I have already mentioned the names of the principal Hotels at Rome. The Masters of these Hotels, however, will seldom receive Travellers for less than a week: but at the *Gran Vascello*, in Via-Condotti, accommodations may be obtained by the night. The price of large apartments at the principal Hotels is seldom less than a Louis-d'or per day. The charges for breakfast, dinner, and servants' board, are much the same as at Florence.

Almost every house in the Piazza di Spagna contains apartments which are let to Foreigners; and the best of these apartments are in the Casa-Rinaldini. Via-San-Bastianello contains good lodgings; as does the house called Margariti's, and situated on the ascent to the Trinità de' Monti. The Palazzo-Negroni is an excellent lodging-house. Via-Babuino, Via della Croce, Via-Condotti, Via-Frattina, and Via de' due Macelli, contain several lodgings; as do Via-Vittoria, Via-Pontefici, Via-Condotti, and Via-Bocca di Lione: the Palazzo-Canino, in the last-named street, is one of the best lodging-houses at Rome. The Palazzo-Gavotti, the Palazzo-Fiano, and the new part of the Palazzo-Sciarra (all on the Corso), contain good accommodations; as do the Piazza-Colonna, and the Palazzo-Cardella, near Via di Ripetta; in which street, likewise, several lodgings may be met with. The Piazza de' Santi Apostoli contains good apartments. The Palazzo-Sceva, and the Palazzo-Collicola, near the Forum of Trajan, contain good apartments; as does the Palazzo-Maggi, near the Capitol. No. 152, Via-Rasella, is a large well situated house; as is Casa-Giorgio, in the Lavatore del Papa. The Palazetto-Albani, and the Villa-Miollis, are good houses; but unwholesomely situated; especially the latter.

The best water at Rome is that of the Fontana di Trevi, and the Piazza di Spagna; the best air, that of the centre of the Corso, the Piazza di Spagna, the Trinità de' Monti, the environs of the Fontana di Trevi, and the Foro-Trajano, and its environs. The price lately given for the best apartments at Rome, plate and linen inclusive, has been from thirty to fifty Louis-d'or a month. Large and well-situated lodgings may, however, be procured for about eighty scudi a month; and small apartments for half that sum.* The best *Traiteurs* usually charge English Families ten pauls a head for dinner, bread and wine not inclusive; and this dinner usually furnishes the servants with more than they can eat: but (as I have already mentioned) persons who get their dinner from a *Traiteur*, should not order it per head, but per dish.† The *Traiteur* near the Palazzo-Sciarra, on the Corso, will supply one person with dinner for five pauls: and at the houses of *Restaurateurs* in general, a gentleman may be found in

---

* Persons who are not anxious to live in that part of Rome which the English usually prefer, would do well to seek apartments in the Strada-Giulia; where the rent of two or three good rooms is not more than from ten to twelve scudi a month.

† Four or five dishes, sufficiently large to supply four Masters and four Servants with a plentiful dinner, bread and dessert not inclusive, usually cost from twenty-five to thirty pauls.

dinner, bread, and table-wine, for five pauls.* Breakfast at a Coffee-house usually costs about one paul, and the charge for every cup of coffee is two baiocchi.

The price, per month, for a good carriage and horses, coachman's wages inclusive, is from sixty to seventy scudi, according to the expense of provender. The price per day, from twenty-four to twenty-five pauls—and for four hours, either morning or evening, twelve pauls. A good carriage and horses may frequently be purchased for about one hundred pounds sterling; and the expense of keeping them, coachman's and footman's wages, with grease for wheels inclusive, is about twenty-six scudi per month. A coachman's wages is eight scudi per month, he finding grease and oil; and a footman's wages six scudi per month. They expect liveries once a year.

Hackney carriages may usually be hired for four pauls an hour, in the Piazza di Monte Citorio.

The wages of a *Valet-de-place* are from four to five pauls a day, he finding himself in every thing.

Fire-wood is sold by the cart-load, which, during winter, usually costs about twenty-eight pauls, without carriage and porterage, and this amounts to from five to eight pauls more, according to where the wood is taken. The best wood may generally be obtained at the Ripetta.

Rome is better supplied with eatables than any other city in Italy. The average price of the best beef is from seven to eight baiocchi a pound—gravy-beef, from five to six baiocchi—mutton, from six to eight baiocchi—lamb, six baiocchi—veal, from ten to twenty baiocchi—kid, ten baiocchi—excellent pork, from six to six and a half baiocchi—excellent wild-boar, from five to six baiocchi—woodcocks, from twenty to twenty-five baiocchi each—a wild goose, from four to five pauls—wild ducks, ditto, per brace—widgeons each, about fifteen baiocchi—and teale, about one paul—partridges, from twenty-five baiocchi to four pauls each—small chickens, two pauls each—large fowls, three pauls each—hares, from three to four pauls each—rabbits, twenty-five baiocchi each—capons, forty-five baiocchi each—turkies (the best poultry in Italy) ten baiocchi a pound, and sometimes less—tame ducks, each two pauls—pigeons, ditto—quails, each, four baiocchi—beccafichi, from three to four baiocchi each — ortolans, twelve baiocchi each. Soles, turbots, carp,† and other prime fishes, are seldom sold for less than from fifteen baiocchi to two pauls the pound: though common fish rarely costs more than ten baiocchi. Dried salmon is twelve baiocchi a pound—salted cod, three baiocchi. Good butter two pauls a pound, generally speaking, though it may sometimes be procured for fourteen or fifteen baiocchi. Cows' milk, per foglietta, five baiocchi—goats' milk, three baiocchi. Parmesan cheese, twenty-two baioc-

---

* At the Palazzo-Fiano, in the Corso, there is a Restaurateur who serves at a fixed price per portion, as is done at Paris; his charge for a plate of good soup being, baiocchi 2½; a plate of bouilli, with vegetables, baiocchi 7½; a plate of roasted meat, ditto; a plate of common fruit, 2 or 3 baiocchi; and a foglietta of good table-wine, from 8 to 10 baiocchi.

† The carp brought from the Lake of Albano to the Roman fish-market sometimes weigh twenty pounds each, and are particularly delicious.

chi the pound—Dutch cheese, seventeen baiocchi—Brinzi, eighteen baiocchi. Household bread, two baiocchi and a half—a panetto, or roll, always one baioccho; at present, three of these weigh eleven ounces. Spanish rolls, two baiocchi and a half each. Grapes, apples, pears, peaches, and apricots, from two to four baiocchi the pound. Sweet oranges, three or four for one baioccho—Seville oranges, six or seven for ditto—lemons, each from one to two baiocchi—best chesnuts, twelve for one baioccho—potatoes, one baioccho the pound—beans, one baioccho and a half the pound. Eggs per dozen, from ten to twenty baiocchi. Wax candles, from forty-four to forty-five baiocchi the pound—Spoletto-tallow candles, twelve baiocchi the pound—Roman ditto, ten baiocchi. Charcoal, per sack, containing about 130lb. sixty baiocchi. The best markets for fruit and vegetables are those of the Piazza-Navona and the Pantheon; the melons of Perugia are remarkably good, as is the Roman brocoli.

The wine of Orvietto usually sold at fifteen or sixteen baiocchi the small flask, is good, but seldom genuine: indeed, the Romans are accused of adulterating their white wines with a poisonous metallic substance. The wines of Albano and Gensano, however, may usually be purchased at the Scotch College for two scudi and a half, or at most, three scudi the barrel; and are wholesome, because genuine. A barrel contains fourteen large flasks, and every large flask five fogliette. The foglietta is nearly an English pint. Spanish table-wine, which, if genuine, is good and wholesome, may be purchased in the magazines at Ripa-Grande, and usually costs from sixteen to eighteen scudi the barrel. Spanish white wines may likewise be purchased of Don Rafaele Anglada, No. 26, at Ripa-Grande; as may a remarkably good sweet wine of Portugal, called Setubal. Good Marsala, together with French wines, spirits, tea, groceries, English patent medicines, fish-sauces, mustard, etc., are sold by Lowe, No. 420, Corso. Foreign wines and spirits are likewise sold by Freeborn, No. 7, Via-Condotti; and by Townley, No. 58, Via-Condotti. Townley sells flannel also, and other English goods. French wines are sold at No. 40, Piazza di Spagna. Spillman, No. 81, Via della Croce, sells good foreign wines and spirits; but his prices are high: he is the best Confectioner at Rome, and remarkably honourable in his mode of dealing: the average price of his ices (which are excellent) is twelve baiocchi the square cake; ices in the shape of fruit cost more. Oil varies in price from eight to twenty-four baiocchi the foglietta, according to its quality; but good salad oil is not easily obtained. Roman honey is good, and seldom costs more than seven or eight baiocchi the pound. Tea may be purchased of all the principal grocers. Black tea usually costs, per pound, about twelve pauls—green tea, from fifteen to eighteen pauls, according to its quality—Levant coffee, unburnt, about thirty-two baiocchi—Martinique coffee, unburnt, from twenty-four to thirty baiocchi—good lump-sugar, about two pauls—the best powder-sugar, about fourteen baiocchi—wax candles, from forty-three to forty-five baiocchi—and wax torches, forty-two baiocchi. The above-named groceries and wax lights may be purchased better and cheaper at No. 90, in the Piazza di Trevi, than at any other shop. Good sugar, wax lights, and brandy (the last four pauls a bottle), are sold at No. 111, Piazza di Monte Citorio. Faiella, in the Piazza di Spagna, sells good groceries. The brothers Cogorni, grocers, in the Piazza Rondonini, sell good rum at six pauls the bottle; or, five and a half, provided the empty bottles be returned: they likewise sell good Bordeaux, Cyprus, and Malaga. Genuine wine of Nice may sometimes be purchased at the Palazzo-Borromeo, for four pauls a bottle. The average price of Bordeaux Laffitte is eight pauls, and of the inferior sort six pauls, the bottle. The average price of good Marsala is five pauls; and of good Malaga four pauls, the bottle. Wine-merchants, in general, allow from three to five baiocchi for every empty bottle, when returned.

The best medicines are to be purchased at the Farmacia Marini Borioni, Via del Babuino, No. 98; and this shop contains excellent castor oil, Epsom salts, pearl barley, oatmeal, and sago, and tolerably good bark. The Spezieria del Collegio Romano likewise furnishes tolerably good bark: but if medicines be wanted during the night, they can only be procured at the Spezieria in the Via del Gambero.

Furs are very good and not dear. Roman pearls, if made and sold by Pozzi, No. 101, in Via-Pasquino, are well worth purchasing: but those made and sold in Via-Padella, and other places, are of a very inferior quality, and liable to turn yellow. The best Silk-mercer is Ciampi, No. 471, on the Corso. The best Milliner resides in Via de' due Macelli, at No. 106.

The best Language Master at Rome is Sig. Giuntotardi: the best Music-Masters are Signori Sirletti, Doria, Moroni, and Confidate. Sig. Giuntotardi's price is one zecchino for three lessons. Eminent Music Masters ask ten pauls a lesson. Dancing-Masters charge from five to seven pauls a lesson; and Drawing-Masters about five pauls an hour. Sig. Santarelli, (who may be heard of at Monaldini's, in the Piazza di Spagna,) is an excellent Drawing-Master, and very moderate in his charges: and the Cav. Fidanza (already mentioned as an eminent Artist), teaches landscape painting at his own house; though he does not go from home to give lessons.

Vescovali, at No. 20, in the Piazza di Spagna, has a large collection of ancient bronzes, Vases, Medals, etc., for sale. Sulphurs are sold at No. 31, Via-Capo-le-Case, for three scudi per hundred: they are likewise sold at No. 53, on the Corso; and in the Piazzo di Spagna, by Pavoletti, who is deemed particularly skilful in the art of making pastes and sulphurs. Small and beautiful specimens of Roman Mosaics may be found in the Piazza di Spagna, and its environs. Specimens of *Scajuola* and Paintings *all' Encausto*, may be found at No. 3, in the Forum Romanum, near the arch of Severus. One of the bests shops for bronze Lamps, and silver Plate, is that of Sig. Belli, No. 63, in Via-Valle. One of the best Stationers' shops is in the Piazza Colonna, and opposite to the Post-Office. Manuscript Music, both ancient and modern, is sold by the Abbate Santini, at No. 49, Via-Vittoria. Bouchard, Bookseller, at No. 69, in the Piazza di Spagna (a very fair dealer), sells coloured Drawings, Prints, and English Books. Monaldini, Bookseller, in the Piazza di Spagna, sells English Books, English writing and drawing Paper, etc., and Piale, at No. 428, on the Corso, has a small circulating Library, which contains a few English Books. The subscription to this Library is seven pauls for one month only; and fifteen pauls per quarter. Large assortments of Prints, and coloured Drawings, are to be found on the Corso; and likewise at No. 49, Via-Condotti, a fair dealing shop. The Calcografia Camerale also contains a considerable collection of Prints; the prices of which are specified in the catalogue; and from ten to fifteen per cent. is deducted, if a large number of prints be purchased.

The usual fee given, by the Romans, to their Physicians, is three pauls a visit; but Foreigners are expected to pay more liberally.

Rome (as has been already mentioned) contains six Theatres; namely, *The Aliberti*, which is opened for masked Balls during Carnival; *The Argentina*, where operas are performed between Christmas and Lent; *The Valle*, where operas and plays are performed at the same season; *The Apollo*, or *Tordinoni*, likewise an opera-house; *The Pace;* and *The Pallacorda*. The price of a good box at the Teatro-Aliberti, during Carnival, is from fifteen to twenty pauls; besides which, every person pays three pauls for admission. At the other Theatres, the price of boxes varies according to the merit of the performers; but nothing is paid for admission, except by those persons who go into the *parterre*.

Persons who intend to make a long stay, and to live economically in this city, should endeavour to hire an unfurnished apartment, and furnish it themselves; furniture being very cheap, and the rent of unfurnished apartments very low.

A Procaccio goes every week from Rome to Naples, and conveys luggage.*

The best Roman *Padrone di Vetture* is Balzani, who may always be found, or heard of, at the Locanda del Orso; and is the brother and partner of Balzani, the *Padrone di Vetture*, at Florence.†

POST-OFFICE.

Letters for Great Britain and France go on Mondays, Thursdays, and Saturdays; and may be franked, on Mondays, from nine

---

* Persons who wish to convey luggage by water from Rome to Naples, should apply to the Masters of the vessels at Ripa-Grande: but as luggage going either by the Procaccio or by water must be taken to the Customhouse at Naples, it is not advisable to send books, or any thing contraband, by these conveyances.

† Washerwomen at Rome commonly charge for washing and ironing as follows:—

Sheets, per pair	baiocchi 8
Pillowcases, each	1
Tablecloth	5
Napkins, per dozen	12
Towels, per dozen	12
Shirt, if plain, 6; if frilled	7
Shift	4
Drawers	4
Corset	5
Pocket-handkerchiefs, per dozen	12
Kitchen-aprons, per dozen	12
Neckcloth	1
Pockets, per pair	2
Sleeping waistcoat	4
Neckerchief, if frilled	7
Nightcap, if frilled	2
Plain white dresses, each	20
Petticoats, each	5
Cotton stockings, per pair	2
Silk ditto	4

in the morning till four in the afternoon; on Thursdays, from nine in the morning till twelve; and on Saturdays, from nine in the morning till half-past eight in the evening.

Letters for the kingdom of Naples go on Tuesdays and Fridays; and letters for Tuscany on Mondays, Thursdays, and Saturdays.

Letters for Tuscany, and the kingdom of Naples, may be franked either before noon, or between five and seven in the evening. The expense for franking a single letter to Great-Britain is fifteen baiocchi; and for franking a single letter, either to Florence or Naples, two baiocchi and a half.

The Post-office is usually open from nine till twelve in the morning, and from three till seven in the evening.

Letters from Great Britain may be expected on Mondays and Thursdays.

NEAPOLITAN TERRITORIES.

In order to enter the kingdom of Naples, it is necessary to procure a passport either from the Neapolitan Government, or one of its Ambassadors.

Travellers, on quitting Rome for Naples, derive no advantage from having their luggage plumbed; as, at Terracina, the last town in the Papal territories, and also at the frontier, Custom-house officers have a right to examine trunks, etc.; but a fee of from five to ten pauls, according to the quantity of luggage, always prevents the exercise of this right. At Fondi, the first town in the Neapolitan dominions, six carlini per carriage, given at the Custom-house, will generally secure luggage from examination.

MONEY OF NAPLES.

Gold. Piece worth thirty *ducati,* or ducats — ditto, worth fifteen ducats—ditto, worth four ducats—ditto, worth three ducats—ditto, worth two ducats.

Silver. Scudo, worth *grani,* or grains, 132—*Pezzo-duro,* worth grains from 123 to 124—Piastre, worth grains 120—Piece, worth grains 66—ditto, worth grains 60—ditto, worth grains 50—ditto, worth grains 40—ditto, worth grains 30—ditto, worth grains 26—ditto, worth grains 24—ditto, worth grains 20—ditto, worth grains 13—ditto, worth grains 12—ditto, worth grains 10—ditto, worth grains 5.

Copper. Piece worth four grains—ditto, worth 3 grains—ditto, worth 2½ grains—ditto, worth 2 grains—ditto, worth 1 grain—ditto, worth half a grain.

One *ducato* is worth ten *carlini,* and one *carlino* is worth ten *grani.*

Accounts are kept in ducats and grains. The exchange upon London is fixed every Monday and Thursday afternoon; and Neapolitan Bankers give so many grains, according to the exchange, for every pound sterling.

The value of French gold varies from time to time; but an old Louis d'or is usually worth from five hundred and forty to five hundred and sixty grains; and a Napoleon, from four hundred and sixty to four hundred and eighty-five grains.

Messrs. Falconnet and Co., the most eminent Bankers at Naples, are very obliging to Travellers: and Messrs. Reynolds and Co., Bankers, are honourable in their dealings, and particularly obliging to Travellers.

The common Neapolitan measure, called a *canna*, is equal to about two yards and a quarter English;* the Neapolitan pound to about eleven English ounces; and the *rotolo* to about thirty-one English ounces.

HOTELS AND OTHER LODGING-HOUSES AT NAPLES.

From two hundred to three hundred ducats a month have, during the last few years, been demanded in winter and spring, for the best ready-furnished apartments in this city: now, however, handsome lodgings, large enough to accommodate a moderate-sized Family, may be obtained for a hundred or, at the utmost, a hundred and fifty ducats a month, in those parts of Naples usually frequented by Foreigners, namely, the Chiaja, the Chiatamone, and the Strada di S. Lucia: in other situations lodgings are much cheaper. I have already mentioned the names of the best hotels: it may not, however, be superfluous to add, that the situation of the *Gran-Bretagna* is bleak during winter and spring; and that the back rooms in the *Crocele*, and other hotels near the tufo-rock, are damp and unwholesome. The price of apartments at the principal hotels is, generally speaking, higher than in any other part of Italy. Dinner usually costs ten carlini per head for masters; breakfast, twenty-five grains; and servants' board, per day, from four to six carlini a head. Job-men, who supply strangers with carriages, usually charge three ducats per day; and not much less by the month: but a good carriage and horses may frequently be purchased here for less than one hundred pounds sterling: and the expense of keeping them amounts to about fifty ducats a month, including twelve ducats for the coachman's wages. Provender for a coach-horse costs about four carlini per day—a stable and coach-house four ducats a month, and shoeing each horse one ducat a month. Provender for a saddle-horse costs about three carlini per day. Hackney-carriages of all descriptions are to be met with in every quarter of Naples, at the following prices: Carriage with four places, a *course*, four carlini; and if taken by the hour, first hour, five carlini, and every subsequent hour three carlini. Carriage with two places, a *course*, twenty-six grains; and if taken per hour, first hour three carlini, and every subsequent hour twenty grains. The drivers of these carriages cannot demand any thing more than the fare, though they expect a trifling gratuity. The wages of a *valet-de-place,* is from five to six carlini a day, he finding himself in every thing: and it is difficult to meet with a good Cook, who finds his own Assistant, under twelve ducats a month. Neapolitan Servants expect neither board nor lodging. Persons who keep their own cook should order dinner at so much per head, fire-wood and charcoal inclusive: and persons who mean to reside long at Naples, and wish to live economically, should endeavour to procure an unfurnished apartment; and either purchase or hire furniture themselves. Good apartments unfurnished may be obtained for four, or at the utmost, five hundred ducats per annum. Families who have their dinner from a

---

* One canna contains eight Neapolitan palmi; and one palmo is about 10¾ English inches.

Traiteur, are seldom well-served under five or six carlini a head, Servants inclusive: but a well-cooked dish, sufficient for two persons, may be procured, at a Cook's shop, for five carlini. Persons who dine at the houses of *Restaurateurs,* are presented when they enter with the *carte à manger;* and the expense of dining at these taverns, bread and table-wine inclusive, is, generally speaking, from three to six carlini a head. One cup of coffee at a coffee-house usually costs five grains; one cup of chocolate, eight grains; and breakfast altogether, butter inclusive, two carlini. Provisions at Naples are good and plentiful. Beef on an average costs from twenty-four to twenty-six grains the rotolo—mutton about twenty grains—veal from thirty to forty grains—pork about twenty grains —and fish, from three to eight carlini. Naples oysters are good; though perhaps not so well fattened as in the days of Lucullus. Turkies are cheap and remarkably good; a small turkey costs from six to eight carlini; a fowl from three to four carlini; and a small chicken from fifteen to twenty grains. Parmesan cheese costs about nine carlini the rotolo; and English cheese, about ten carlini. Bread of the best quality usually costs from six to eight grains the rotolo. Oil varies in price; but the best usually costs from four to five carlini the rotolo. Milk is scarce and dear. The only good butter comes from Sorrento, and is six carlini the rotolo. The best veal, pork, and hams, likewise come from Sorrento; and the last usually cost four carlini the rotolo. Green tea on an average is twenty carlini the English pound; and black tea sixteen carlini—coffee from eleven to thirteen carlini the rotolo—loaf-sugar eight carlini— and other sorts, from six carlini to forty-five grains. Fruit is cheap and excellent. (It is supposed that in Magna Græcia the ancients iced their cherries, figs, water-melons and many other fruits; and the moderns would do wisely by adopting the same plan.) Ice, or rather frozen snow, is four grains the rotolo; iced water, two grains per quart; ices, in glasses, are eight grains each; and ices in cakes, twelve grains each. The wines of Posilipo, Capri, and Ischia, are palatable and wholesome; and cost about three ducats and a half the barrel, which holds fifty-six caraffi, or pints. The wines of Proceda and Calabria are good and wholesome; and cost about four ducats and a half per barrel. The Sicilian wines likewise are good.* Fire-wood usually costs from twenty to twenty-two ducats the large canna;† and charcoal fifteen carlini the quintal. Wax-lights of the best quality, called Venice-candles, are about six carlini the pound; and tallow candles twelve grains the pound in the shops, and eleven grains at the *Fabbrica.* Sig. Graindorges has, in the Largo del Castello, an English Warehouse, which contains porter, ale; French, Spanish, and Portugal wines; excellent Lachrymæ both white and red, Marsala, brandy, rum, Hollands, liqueurs, gunpowder, hyson, and black tea; Durham mus-

---

* Some of the best Calabrian and Sicilian wines are those of Piedimonte, Mongibello, S. Eufemia, Marsala, and Siraguse. Good Malaga may frequently be met with; and is sold by the *rubbio*, which contains about sixteen English quarts.

† The large canna contains sixty-four palmi; it being a rule to have the canna square every way.

tard; English writing-paper, pens, and pencils; fish sauces; court-plaster; English cheese; curry-powder; anti-attrition grease; English razors, saddles and bridles; James's powder, Epsom and Cheltenham salts, soda-powders, spirit of hartshorn, and spirit of lavender. Strong's British Warehouse, No. 1, Strada-Molo, near the Fontana-Medina, contains several of the same articles; and Terry, in the Strada-Toledo, sells English writing-paper, pens, elastic soles, and a considerable variety of other English goods. Paturle and Co. at No. 329, Strada-Toledo, have a large assortment of French silks, velvets, gauzes, lace, shawls, ribands, and almost every article manufactured at Lyons. Toro, at No. 12, Strada S. Francesco di Paola, is an excellent Shoemaker. Cardon and Co. at No. 209, Strada di Chiaja, are good Milliners and Dress-Makers, as likewise is Mademoiselle Houlemont, at No. 29, Vico Lungo San Matteo, dirempetto La Trinità de Spagnuoli. Naples is celebrated for its silks, gauzes, ribands, coral and tortoise-shell manufactures, soap, essences; and especially for its silk stockings, made at Sorrento, which are remarkably strong. Silks for Ladies' dresses are usually sold according to their weight: common silks are of various qualities; that called *Battavia* (two palmi and a quarter wide), is twenty-four carlini the canna—that called *Ormisino* (four palmi wide), is from twenty-four to twenty-eight carlini the canna — that called *Cattivella* (seven palmi wide), is from thirty-two to forty carlini the canna. Richer silks, called the King's, and sold at the *Fabbrica reale,* in the Strada-Toledo, are more costly. Thin ell-wide silk, called *Tafita,* is also sold at this shop for about twenty carlini the canna. *Cottone e setta* is strong, warm, cheap, and said to wash well. Silk stockings cost from sixteen to twenty-five carlini the pair, according to their weight and quality. Common silks, and *Cottone e setta,* are sold in the streets near the Largo del Castello, and in the Strada Sedile di Porto. Naples is likewise famous for musical instrument strings in general, and harp strings in particular. There is a circulating Library and Reading Room in Strada S. Giacomo, No. 19, near the Strada Toledo, and Sig. Borel has a large collection of books for sale, near the Church of Trinità Maggiore. Sig. Angelo Trani has an excellent Stationer's Shop in the Largo del Palazzo; and Sig. Luigi Tisi Pascuzzi, opposite to the Fontana di Monte Oliveto, is a good Coachmaker, and an honest man.

Dr. Kissock, an English Physician, resides at Naples; as do Mr. Roskilly, an English Surgeon, and Mr. Reilly, an English Apothecary, who sells English medicines. One of the most celebrated Music Masters is Sig. Lanza, who charges a piastre an hour; and the most celebrated Dancing Master is Sig. Formichi, who charges the same.

For boxes at the Theatres there is a fixed price; beyond which nothing can be demanded for admission. A box, in the third row, at the Teatro di S. Carlo, usually costs five piastres; in the fourth row, four piastres; and in the fifth row, three piastres; and seats in the *parterre,* where Ladies may go without the smallest impropriety, cost six carlini each.

A box in the third row, at the Teatro del Fondo, usually costs three piastres; and in the fourth row, two piastres, or, at most, two and a half. Seats in the *parterre* are five carlini each. The Fondo is better calculated, both for seeing and hearing, than is S. Carlo.

A good box at the Teatro de' Fiorentini may be procured for fifteen carlini—at the Teatro della Fenice, for twelve carlini — and at the Teatro di S. Carlino, for ten carlini.*

The Victory Hotel, kept by Martinzer, is a very good one.

ARRIVAL AND DEPARTURE OF LETTER-COURIERS AND PROCACCI.

Sunday, arrive letters from France, Italy, and Germany. *In the afternoon goes* the Courier of Cilento.

Monday and every other day, Sunday excepted, arrive and go the Courier and Procaccio of Salerno, and the Courier of Palermo.

Tuesday, arrive letters from Bari, Lecce, Foggia, Lucera, and Manfredonia: likewise the Procaccio of Melfi, Nocera, Materdomini, and Sanseverino. *In the evening go letters* to Italy, Germany, and Great Britain.

Wednesday, arrive the Procacci of Rome and Cilento: *and on Wednesday go* the Procaccio of Melfi, and the Courier of Palermo.

Thursday, arrive letters from Spain, Italy, France, Germany, Great Britain, Messina, Palermo, Malta, and Calabria; Basilicata, Sora, and Campo-basso: likewise the Procaccio of Bari, Lecce, Foggia, Lucera, Abruzzi, Calabria, Basilicata, Sora, and Campobasso.

Friday night goes the Procaccio to Rome.

Saturday morning arrives the Procaccio of Nocera, Materdomini, and Sanseverino; and *Saturday go* the Procacci of Bari, Lecce, Abruzzi, Foggia, Basilicata, Sora, and Campo-basso; and the letters for Sora and Campo-basso. *At night go* the Procacci of Calabria and Nocera, Materdomini and Sanseverino, Bari, Lecce, Abruzzi, Foggia, Basilicata, Sora, and Campo-basso; and the letters for Sora and Campo-basso. *At night go* the Procacci of Calabria and Nocera, Materdomini, Sanseverino, and Monte-Sarchio. *At night likewise go* letters for Italy, Messina, Calabria, Palermo, and Malta, Bari, Tarento, Lecce, Lucera, Foggia, Basilicata, and Abruzzi.

During summer the Procacci *set out on the Friday night* instead of the Saturday morning. On the first Saturday in every month go letters for Ragusa and Constantinople.

---

* Washerwomen at Naples commonly charge for washing and ironing as follows:—

Sheets, per pair	grains 12
Pillowcase	2
Tablecloth	6
Napkin and Towel, each	1
Kitchen-apron	1
Shirt	6
Shift	5
Drawers	4
Sleeping waistcoat	4
Nightcap	3
Petticoat	6
Corset	5
Neckcloth	2
Pocket-handkerchiefs, per dozen	12
Stockings per pair, if silk	4
A plain white dress	25
A frill	5
A muslin cap, if bordered with lace	5
Stockings per pair, if cotton	2

In the Strada-Vittoria, No. 38, there is a good Laundress, by name Lastrucci: but her charges are high. She speaks English and French.

Letters for Great Britain must be franked; and the price is fifteen grains for every single letter. Letters for France must be franked; and the price is ten grains for every single letter.

The office for franking letters is open every day, Sunday excepted, from nine till twelve in the morning, and from four till five in the afternoon.

Tuesday and Friday are the best days for franking letters addressed to Great Britain; and Thursday is the only day on which letters from Great Britain are received.

PIANO DI SORRENTO.

Price of Lodging-houses.

The price of Lodging-houses depends on the term for which they are taken, and also on the season of the year. During summer, from eighty to a hundred ducats per month are demanded for the large Villa-Marisca—from sixty to seventy ducats per month for the large apartment in the Villa-Spinelli—sixty ducats per month for the Villa-Starace—from sixty to eighty ducats per month for the large apartment in the Palazzo-Cocomella; and from forty to fifty ducats for the small apartment—sixty ducats per month for the upper apartment in the Villa Correale; and more for the lower apartment, if a considerable number of beds be required. Small apartments, calculated to accommodate a Lady and her Servant, or a single Man, may always be procured for fifteen ducats per month; and sometimes for two-thirds of that sum. Plate and linen are included in these prices.

AVERAGE PRICE OF PROVISIONS, ETC.

Excellent beef (prime pieces), from twenty to twenty-four grains the rotolo — excellent veal, from twenty-four to thirty grains—delicious pork, from fourteen to sixteen grains - excellent hams, pigs' cheeks, and bacon, from twenty-four to thirty grains — excellent butter, sixty grains—bread of the best quality (which is brought daily from Castel-a-mare), seven grains — macaroni, from ten to twelve grains—fish, from ten to forty grains, according to its quality—fruit from two to four grains — clean ice, or, properly speaking, frozen snow, to mix with wine, two grains—and snow for icing liquors, one grain and a half —excellent salad-oil, about thirty grains the measure — excellent milk, three grains the measure, which is nearly an English quart — wine of Sorrento, per caraffa, three grains — wine of Capri, if it come direct from that Island, about thirty carlini the barrel—charcoal, from twelve to fifteen carlini the quintal—and fire-wood, seventy carlini the small canna.

Sorrento and its Piano are famous for delicious honey, clotted cream, and a dish called, in Devonshire, *junket:* and (what seems extraordinary) the Sorrentines give it a similar name. Quails, during the month of September, are particularly good, plentiful, and cheap in this country; but poultry is always scarce, and seldom good; fine fish is likewise scarce in the Piano di Sorrento; though attainable almost every evening at S. Agata, whither it is brought from the Gulph of Salerno during the day, in order to be sent to Naples at midnight.*

Families who remove from Naples to the Sorrentine shore, would do well to take with them tea, sugar, wax candles, soap, and cheese. Neither brandy nor rum, nor the wines of Spain, Portugal, and France, can be purchased at Sorrento: but boats go daily thence, and also from the Piano to Naples; and every Master of a boat may be trusted to execute commissions, and even to bring letters and money, for Foreigners. The Sorrento boats, and those belonging to the Marina Grande of the Piano, set out soon after day-break, and return between three and four o'clock every afternoon, weather permitting. The Meta boats go more irregularly; there being, at times, a dangerous surf upon that beach. The price paid by the Sorrentines for going to Naples in a public boat, is six grains per head; and the best method of conveying a Family from Naples to Sorrento, is to hire one of these public boats, and embark about midday; at which time the wind is usually favourable. A Mariner, by name Epifanio, who frequently commands the boats belonging to the Marina of the Piano, is remarkably well-behaved, and an excellent Pilot: and a boat, commanded by him, may be hired for three or four ducats, according to its size; and he may generally be met with at the Molo at Naples, from ten in the morning till twelve, every day, Sundays excepted.

Letters put into the Sorrento Post-Office go perfectly safe to Naples: and letters addressed either to Sorrento, or any of the Villas in the Plain, are delivered with punctuality. A large Family, if economical, might live comfortably at Sorrento for four hundred pounds per annum.†

Doctor Cangiani, a well-educated Neapolitan Physician, resides in this town; and occupies the house once inhabited by the Sister of Torquato Tasso.

I will now close my account of the average prices of necessaries and luxuries in France and Southern Italy, by the following comparative view of Family-expenses in various parts of the Continent.

Generally speaking, a French franc (usually worth about tenpence) will go as far in France as does a shilling in England: a Tuscan paul (usually worth about five-pence) will go as far in Tuscany as does a franc in France: a Roman paul (usually worth about four-pence) will go as far in the Ecclesiastical territories as does a Tuscan paul in Tuscany: and a carlino of the Kingdom of Naples (usually worth about three-pence) will go as far in the Neapolitan dominions as does a Roman Paul at Rome.

---

* A fish called by the Sorrentines *Morena* may frequently be procured at S. Agata. This fish was highly prized by the ancient Romans; some of whom, in order to augment its bulk and flavour, fed it with the flesh of their Slaves.

Particularly strong Silk Stockings may be purchased, for a moderate price, at the manufactory of Don Filippo Castellano, in the Piano di Sorrento: and excellent Gauze, for Mosquito-nets, may be purchased very cheap at Sorrento.

† Washerwomen here are particularly moderate in their charges.

CHAPTER VI.

Route from Geneva to Chambery—from Chambery over the Mont Cenis to Turin—New Road made by Napoleon—Passage of Mont Genèvre—Route from Nice through Genoa to Pisa—from Leghorn through Pisa to Florence—from Pisa through Lucca and Pistoja to Florence—from Pisa to Modena—Expense of travelling *en voiturier* from Lucca through Pistoja to Florence—Price charged by Voiturins for conveying luggage from Florence to Rome—Lascia-Passare—Route from Florence through Siena to Rome—from Florence through Perugia to Rome—from Genoa through Bologna, Rimini, Sinagalia, Ancona, Loretto, and Terni, to Rome—from Milan through Bergamo, Verona, Vicenza, and Padua, to Venice, Bologna, and Florence—from Milan to Bologna, through Piacenza, Parma, Reggio, and Modena—from Milan to Turin—from Aoste to Turin—from Turin over the Maritime Alps to Nice—from Turin over the Bochetta to Genoa—from Rome to Naples—Passports—Modes of dividing this journey—Buona-mano usually given to a Voiturier—Route *en voiturier* from Pisa to Massa and Carrara—from Rome to Florence through Perugia—Caution against travelling through Perugia to Rome during the great heats—Route *en voiturier* from Calais to Rome, during winter—from Florence through Siena to Rome—from Rome to Naples—Passports—Route from Florence through Bologna, Venice, Vienna, Prague, and Dresden, to Hamburgh—from Florence through Mantua, and by the Tyrol to Augsburg and Wurtzburgh—and, during summer, from Rome through Florence and Milan by the Simplon to Geneva, and over the Jura Alps to Poligny, Dijon, Melun, Paris, and Boulogne—and likewise, during summer, from Florence to Venice, Milan, Turin, and over Mont Cenis to Pont-de-Beauvoisin—Passports.

ROUTE FROM GENEVA TO CHAMBERY.

2 Eluiset
2 Frangy—Two good inns.
1½ Mionas
1½ Rumilly—A small village, placed at the junction of the Seran and the Nephe. Inn, *Les Trois Rois*.
1½ Albens
1½ Aix-les-Bains—formerly called *Aquæ Gratianæ*. The mineral waters of Aix are in high repute; and its Baths (supposed to have been constructed by the ancient Romans) were repaired by the Emperor Gratian. Best inn, *La Cité de Genève*.
2 Chambery.
——
11½ posts.

ROUTE FROM CHAMBERY, OVER THE MONT-CENIS, TO TURIN.

2 Montmeillant—The country from Chambery hither is well cultivated; and the vineyards near Montmeillant produce good wine. The latter town is finely situated on the Isère. Two bad Inns; but that on the Hill is the best.
1½ Maltaverne
1½ Aiguebelle—The country between Maltaverne and this village is barren: but the situation of Aiguebelle is pleasant; the inhabitants, compared with their neighbouring compatriots, are wealthy; the Post-house, though destitute of a Remise, is in other respects a tolerably good inn; and *L'Hôtel de l'Union* (an equally good inn) possesses an excellent Remise.
2½ La Grande Maison—The new Road, constructed by order of the Emperor Napoleon, commences just beyond Aiguebelle, and passes through the Maurienne, a narrow valley, bordered by some of the most gigantic of the Maritime Alps, parts of which display barren scenery, while other parts are embellished with pasturages, and clothed with woods.
2 S. Jean de Maurienne—Between Aiguebelle and S. Jean de Maurienne are several bridges, thrown over a brawling torrent, called the Arc, and one of the tributary streams to the Isère. The villages of Epierre, La Chapelle, and La Chambre, all situated in the Maurienne, once exhibited a striking picture of poverty and disease. *Crétins* were seen at almost every door; and the inhabitants were universally afflicted with *Goîtres*. But Napoleon, to secure his new road, drained the marshes, and confined within its proper channel the destructive torrent which continually flooded the valley: and by these means he rendered the air salubrious, prevented the increase of *Crétins*, exterminated

	Goîtres, and changed a glen of misery into a line of prosperous towns and hamlets.
2	S. Michel—Beyond S. Jean de Maurienne the road crosses the Arvan on a stone bridge, and then traverses the Arc on another bridge; facing which is a rivulet of water that petrifies every substance it touches, and has consequently made for itself a natural aqueduct. Mid-way between S. Jean de Maurienne and S. Michel is the hamlet of S. Julien, celebrated for its wines. The *Hôtel de Londres*, at S. Michel, is a good inn.
2½	Modane—Two inns, *L'Hôtel de la Poste* and *L'Hôtel des Voyageurs*, both tolerably good.
2	La Verney
2	Lans-le-Bourg—Not far distant from La Verney is the double Cascade of S. Benoît, one of the finest waterfalls in the Alps; but, though near the road, not close to it: and between La Verney and Lans-le-Bourg is Termignon, situated on the Arc, not far from its confluence with the Leisse. Between Modane and Lans-le-Bourg the Emperor of Austria is building a strong Fortress, to command the passage of Mount Cenis.

Lans-le-Bourg, situated at the base of Cenis, contains a considerable number of inhabitants, most of whom are employed in facilitating the passage of the mountain; by removing the new-fallen snow, during eight or nine months of the year, from those places where, if suffered to accumulate, it might block up the road; and by affording Travellers every assistance they require.

L'Hôtel Royal, at Lans-le-Bourg, is an excellent inn, built by order of Napoleon for the accommodation of his officers, but now kept by an English woman. *L'Hôtel de la Poste*, likewise, is a good inn, though inferior to the other.

After heavy falls of snow, carriages are sometimes from six to seven hours in ascending Cenis on the Savoy side; and from four to five hours in descending on the side of Piedmont; and when the snow is particularly deep, carriages are dismounted, and put into *traineaux*; this, however, rarely happens; and the only dangerous part of the passage of Cenis during winter, namely, the gallery situated at the base of an avalanche, which falls annually, is now avoided, by means of a road lately made practicable for carriages, from the Italian Barrier to the wild and almost terrific Plain of S. Nicolo; and through the centre of that Plain to Molaret. This new part of the passage, though an excellent road, and perfectly exempt from danger respecting the avalanche, requires fences; and should on no account be passed without a guide, either in the dark, or after sudden and heavy snow-storms, as it lies close to the brink of precipices till it enters the Plain.

Few scenes can be more astonishing or more truly sublime, than that presented to Travellers who cross Cenis. Pompey is supposed to have been the first person who attempted making a passage over this Alp, which, from his days till the year 1811, could only be crossed on foot, on a mule, or in a *chaise-à-porteur*. Napoleon, however, determined to make a carriage-road; and, to accomplish his purpose, employed the Cav. Giovanni Fabbroni; who, in five months, with the aid of three thousand workmen, formed a new route, practicable for carriages at all seasons of the year; and not only practicable but perfectly safe (the circumstance of the avalanche excepted), although it traverses a part of Cenis, which is five thousand eight hundred and ninety-eight English feet above the level of the Mediterranean sea. This excellent and wonderful road unites the Valley of the Arc, in Savoy, with that of the Doria-Riparia, in Piedmont; passing, at Lans-le-Bourg, over a fine bridge thrown across the Arc; thence winding up the side of Cenis, by means of six galleries, cut through pasturages and forests, to La Ramasse; whence, during winter, venturous Travellers, when coming from Piedmont, used, previous to the formation of the carriage-road, to descend to Lans-le-Bourg (a distance of two leagues), in seven minutes; each Traveller being seated in a traineau, guided by one man only; who, if careless or unskilful, risked the loss of his own life, together with that of the person he conducted: at present, however, these vehicles may be used on the carriage-road with perfect safety, though not with their former celerity; the descent being so gradual, that it is needless for a light carriage to have a drag-chain. The most elevated part of the route is a plain, two leagues in length, encircled by the loftiest peaks of Cenis, and leading to the Post-House (a small inn), the Barracks, and La Grande Croix, another small inn. The Plain of Cenis is embellished with a beautiful and, according to report, an unfathomable Lake, whose limpid waters reflect the surrounding heights, and contain some of the most delicious trout in Europe.

Fronting this Lake stands a hamlet called Tavernettes, because every house receives Travellers: and at the extremity of the Lake, on the Piedmontese side, and to the left of La Grande Croix, stands L'Hospice, which was founded by the Emperor Charlemagne, for the accommodation of Travellers; suppressed at the commencement of the French Republic, but restored, and rendered more than usually flourishing, by the Emperor Napoleon.

One of the best dinners I ever saw, consisting of all the eatables Cenis produces, was served at L'Hospice; and what is still more important to Alpine Travellers, we had excellent wine, likewise the produce of the Mountain, and large fires. With our dessert came children, carrying salvers filled with the various flowers which enamel Cenis; and the only return we were allowed to make for this hospitality was a small contribution toward the maintenance of the establishment.

The descent from the Italian Barrier into Piedmont displays much more stupendous scenery than does the ascent from Savoy; and the difficulty of constructing the carriage-road was much greater on the Piedmontese side than on the other. The first gallery which presents itself, on this side, is six hundred and fifty feet in length, and cut, in several places, through solid rocks of granite. The Plain of S. Niccolo is adorned with fine Cascades; and, opposite to the hamlet of La Ferrière, is another gallery, above two thousand feet in length, and cut through a remarkably hard and precipitous rock of solid granite. Here, a wall, nine feet in height, and six hundred in extent, defends the gallery from earth and loose stones, which might otherwise fall into and destroy it. The scenery in this part of the route is enchanting. Near Molaret rise the fruitful hills of Chaumont, watered by the Doria-Riparia, which descends from Mont Genèvre; and on the left is the beautiful Valley of Cenis, extending to Susa. From the Post-House at Molaret, to the extremity of the pass of Gaiglione, the road, generally speaking, is cut through rocks at the brink of a precipice flanked by a strong dwarf wall; and then traverses a hill (covered with rich vegetation, and exhibiting a distant view of the Valley of the Doria, and the mountains near Turin), till it enters the Faubourg of Susa.

As travellers who pass Cenis are liable to encounter fogs, snow-storms, and dangerous gusts of wind, Napoleon established, in the most elevated and exposed parts of the route, twenty-six small Inns, or *Refuges*, provided with bells, which, during the prevalence of thick fogs, are rung, to guide Travellers from one Refuge to another: and these inns are tenanted by *Cantonniers*, whose business it is to keep the road in good condition.

The number of *Cantonniers* instituted by Napoleon has been reduced by the King of Sardinia; who still, however, preserves two companies, amounting to about fifty men: and to assist in defraying the expense of keeping the new route in repair, and maintaining the establishment at L'Hospice, there is a tax, amounting to two livres, for every horse or mule who passes Cenis; three livres for every carriage not on springs, and six livres for every carriage with springs—small expenses these compared with what was formerly paid for conveying Travellers, baggage, and carriages over this Alp.* The new road is safe and good at every season.

The *Cantonniers* of Lans-le-Bourg are robust, intelligent, and honest: neither *Crétins* nor goitrous swellings of any description are seen here: and, what seems extraordinary, the Savoyard Peasants speak better French than do the Peasantry of France.

3 Post-house on the plain of Mont Cenis
3 Molaret
2 Susa—This town, anciently called *Segusium*, is watered by the Doria; and was once defended by the strong Fortress of La Brunetta, which is now destroyed; but there still remains near the town, *a triumphal Arch*, erected by Cotns, the monarch of the Cottian Alps who resigned his sceptre to Augustus,
In the valleys, between the base of Cenis and Susa, the inhabitants are afflicted with goîtres; which they attribute to the chill the throat continually receives in consequence of the excessive coldness of the water; which is, generally speaking, the only beverage they can command: neither can they afford to purchase clothes sufficient to defend them from the rigours of their climate; nor any sustenance, except bread, chesnuts, and the fish of the lakes and torrents; nay, even salt, the only cordial within their reach, cannot be universally attained, on account of the heavy tax laid upon it.
1½ S. Georgio
1 S. Antonino
1½ Avigliano
1½ Rivoli
1¾ Turin—The road between Susa and Turin is, generally speaking, a descent; and, in its approach to the latter town, passes through a rich country, fertilized by canals, which distribute the waters of the Doria. Near Turin this road is heavy. The approach to Turin, by way of Rivoli, is handsome.†

33½ posts.

PASSAGE OF MONT GENEVRE.

The distance from Briançon to Mont Genèvre is three leagues; and the road recently made under the direction of the Cav. Giovanni Fabbroni, over this moun-

---

* The last time I passed Cenis, before the new road was made, the expense of conveying four persons and an English coach was ten louis-d'or, from Lans-le-Bourg to Novalesa.
† An extra half post is paid on entering and on quitting Turin.

tain, traverses a forest of pines, firs, and larches; not, however, by means of long and beautiful winding galleries, like those of the Simplon and Cenis, but by short and numerous turns, resembling a corkscrew, like those of the Col di Tenda. Forests of larches crown the heights above the plain of Mont Genèvre, which exhibits an extraordinary sight in the Alps, namely, fields of rye and oats, seldom unproductive, though frequently injured by the severity of the climate; and here, during the month of May, when Cenis still wears his winter mantle, spring puts on her gayest dress, and exerts her utmost activity: Travellers, however, who pass the Mont Genèvre, should recollect that Bears are more common here than on Cenis. The plain is not so extensive as that of the last-named mountain; but contains a village, and a Convent for the reception of Travellers. From *Mont Genèvre* to *Cesanne* is two leagues—from *Cesanne* to *Sestrières*, four leagues—the descent from *Sestrières* to *Fenestrelles*, four leagues —and at the latter village there is a tolerable Inn. The double Fort of Fenestrelles merits notice, both with respect to its construction and its situation. Hence to *Pignerol* is eight leagues—from *Pignerol* to *Nonè*, four leagues and a half—and from *Nonè* to *Turin* the same distance. Nonè contains a tolerable Inn.

ROUTE FROM NICE, THROUGH GENOA, TO PISA.

Should the carriage-road ever be finished from Nice to Genoa, it will enable Travellers to go in carriages through France to Italy without crossing the great Alps: and it will likewise be a less circuitous route than those hitherto frequented. I have already mentioned in the former part of this work (page 105), the present state of the new road between Genoa and Pisa: and I will now add, that from Nice to Mentone, and again from Savona to Genoa, there is a passable road for carriages: but the intermediate spaces are only practicable for mules. Inns may be found at Mentone, San Remo, Oneglia, Albenga, and Savona; and it is a very short day's journey for a mule from each of these towns to the other.

6	Mentone
1½	Ventimiglia
3	*San Remo*
5	*Oneglia*
4	Alassio
4½	*Finale*
3¾	*Savona*
4½	Voltri
3½	Genoa—The Gates of this city are always shut one hour after sunset.*
3	Recco
1½	*Rapallo*
1¾	Chiavari
2¾	Bracco
1½	Mattarana
1½	Borghetto
3	Spezia
2¼	*Sarzana*
1½	Lavenza
1	*Massa*
1	Pietra-Santa
1	Via Reggio
1	Torretta
1	Pisa—Between Torretta and Pisa Travellers cross the Serchio in a ferry.
69½ posts.	

ROUTE FROM LEGHORN, THROUGH PISA, TO FLORENCE.

2	*Pisa*
1	La Fornacette
1	Castel del Bosco
1	La Scala—Inn, *La Posta*, and very uncomfortable.
1	Ambrogiana—Inn, *La Posta*, and very uncomfortable.
1	La Lastra
1	*Firenze*—The whole road from Leghorn to Florence is excellent, and

---

* An extra half post is paid on entering and on quitting Genoa.

almost totally exempt from hills: the inns are bad: but this is of little consequence to persons who go post; as the journey does not occupy more than ten hours with post horses. Persons who travel *en voiturier*, and sleep upon the road, generally stop at Capretta; which is about mid-way between Pisa and Florence; and where the Inn is better than those at La Scala and Ambrogiana.*

—— 8 posts.

ROUTE FROM PISA, THROUGH LUCCA AND PISTOJA TO FLORENCE.

1½ *Lucca*—An extra half post is paid on going from Pisa to Lucca; and an extra half post on quitting Lucca.
2 Borgo-a-Buggiano
1½ *Pistoja*
1½ Prato
1½ *Firenze*.

8 posts.

ROUTE FROM PISA TO MODENA.

5 *Pistoja*
1 Piastre
1 S. Marcello—The Inn here is tolerably good, and pleasantly situated on a hill.
1 Piano-Asinatico.
½ Bosco-Lungo—Last post of Tuscany.
1 Pieve di Pelago—First post of the Modenese.
1 Batigazzo
1 Monte-Cenere
½ Paullo
½ Serra de' Mazzoni
1 S. Venanzio
½ Formigine
½ Modena—Travellers are frequently charged one post from S. Venanzio to Formigine, and the same from Formigine to Modena.

15½ posts.

The journey from Pistoja to Modena was performed with ease by an English Gentleman during the month of November, and without an avant-courier to order horses, within twenty-four hours: or, to speak more precisely, he was on the road travelling seventeen hours and a half, and stopped for changing horses, etc., three hours. The ascents are judiciously formed; the road is good, and well defended from danger; but the accommodations are bad.

The distance from Modena to Mantua is five posts and a half.

Voiturins will take an English post-chaise, carrying three or four persons, from Lucca through Pistoja to Florence, in one day and a half, for nine scudi, *buonamano* not inclusive, and they will likewise convey luggage from Florence to Rome for two pezzi-duri the hundred weight.

ROUTE FROM FLORENCE, THROUGH SIENA, TO ROME.

Previous to undertaking this journey, it is advisable for British subjects, if they travel in their own carriage, to apply to the British Consul-General at Rome for a *Lascia-passare* for Ponte-Centino, and another for the Porta del Popolo at Rome.

1 S. Casciano—A post-royal. A third horse.
1 Tavernelle—A third horse.
1 Poggibonsi—Best inn, *Il Lione Rosso*. The road from Florence hither is hilly, and, in general, paved.
1 Castiglioncello—A third horse. Road good.
1 *Siena*—Best inn, *L'Aquila Nera*, already mentioned. Road hilly, but good.†
1 Montarone

---

* Persons who wish to go either from Leghorn or Pisa to Rome, without passing through Florence, may save three posts by taking the direct road through Poggibonsi to Siena. This journey *en voiturier* occupies about six days and a half; and *Voiturins* usually convey an English carriage, containing four persons, from Leghorn to Rome, for about sixteen louis-d'or.

The direct road from Leghorn, through Pisa, to Poggibonsi, is as follows:

Posts 5, to La Scala.
  2, to Poggibonsi.

† Travellers would do wisely to take wine and water from Siena, for the rest of their journey, both being excellent here, and unwholesome in most of the succeeding towns. It is likewise advisable to take fruit from Siena. On entering this city Travellers are obliged to leave the keys of their trunks at the Gate, and pay one lira; for which sum the keys are brought to the opposite gate, and delivered up when their owners quit Siena.

1 Buonconvento—Road from Siena hither excellent; though, near Buonconvento, there is a very steep hill. The *Albergo del Cavalletto*, in the last-named town, contains good beds; but the rooms are dirty.
1 Torrenieri—A third horse to Poderina, and the same returning.
1 Poderina
1 Ricorsi—A third horse to Radicofani.
1 Radicofani—A large and good Inn, already mentioned. Road from Buonconvento hither excellent, but hilly.
1 Ponte-Centino—This is the first Custom-house in the Ecclesiastical territories: and Travellers who are not provided with a *Lascia passare* for Ponte-Centino meet with an unpleasant detention here, and pay for having their baggage plumbed. The road from the Post-house on Radicofani to the torrent at the base of the mountain is excellent; but thence it traverses six or seven times the bed of the torrent; which bed consists of large loose stones occasioning continual jolts; and beyond Toricelli, this torrent (as has been already mentioned), is, after rain, sometimes dangerous: but, in case of necessity, Travellers may sleep at Toricelli.*
1 Aquapendente—The road beyond the torrent, to this town, is excellent; and the Inn here tolerably good.
½ San-Lorenzo Nuovo—A good inn, already mentioned. Road excellent.
1 Bolsena—Road excellent. A third horse to Montefiascone.
1 Montefiascone—Road good, but hilly.
1 *Viterbo.*—A good inn, already mentioned. A third horse to the mountain.
1 La Montagna—Road good, but hilly.
1 Ronciglione—Two bad Inns. Road good.
1 Monterosi—Two Inns; *La Posta* the best. Road good.
1 Baccano—Inn, *La Posta*, and tolerably good.
1 Storta.
1¼ Roma—The road between Monterosi and the Ponte-Molle, from the spot where the Loretto and Siena routes join, is occasionally rough; but from the Ponte-Molle to Rome, excellent. Travellers who are provided with a *Lascia passare* for the Porta del Popolo, have no trouble with respect to Custom-house Officers; but persons not so provided, are obliged to drive, in the first instance, to the Custom-house; and give from five to ten Pauls, in order to save their Luggage from a tedious examination. An extra quarter of a post is charged on entering Rome; and an extra half post on quitting it.
—
23

ROUTE FROM FLORENCE, THROUGH PERUGIA, TO ROME.

1½ Ponte à Sieve—A post-royal.
1½ Incisa
2 Levane
2 Arezzo—Inn, *La Posta*.
1½ Castiglion Fiorentino
¾ Camuscia—Inn, La Posta.
1½ Case del Piano
1 Magione—A third horse to Perugia, and *vice versâ*.
1½ Perugia—Inn, *La Corona*, and good. The road from Florence to Perugia is excellent; unless it be during wet seasons; when the Lake of Thrasymenus sometimes overflows, and renders this route dangerous.
1 La Madonna degli Angeli—A third horse to Perugia, but not *vice versâ*.
1 Foligno—Inn, *La Posta*, and tolerably good.
1 Le Vene
1 Spoleto—Inn, *La Posta*, and good. A third horse to Strettura, and *vice versâ*. The mountain of La Somma, over which the road passes, is the highest point in this part of the Apennine. La Somma is supposed to derive its name from a temple dedicated to Jupiter-Summanus, which stood on its summit.
1 Strettura
1 Terni—Inn, *La Posta*, and very good.
1 Narni—A third horse from Narni to Otricoli, and *vice versâ*.
1 Otricoli—This town stands about two miles distant from what is supposed to have been the ancient *Otriculum*, which was seated on the Tiber.
½ Borghetto—Between this village and Otricoli the road crosses the Tiber on a fine Bridge, erected during the reign of Augustus, and repaired by Sixtus V. A third horse from Borghetto to Otricoli, but not *vice versâ*.
½ Civita-Castellana—*La Croce bianca* is a tolerable inn, though small.
1 Nepi—Inn not comfortable as a sleeping place.
½ Monterosi
1 Baccano
1 Storta
1¼ Roma—The road from Perugia to Rome is excellent.
—
27¾ posts.

ROUTE FROM GENOA, THROUGH BOLOGNA, RIMINI, SINIGAGLIA, ANCONA, LORETTO, AND TERNI, TO ROME.

3 Campo-Marone
4 Voltaggio
4 *Novi*

---

* The price of oxen per pair, for aiding post-horses to draw heavy carriages from Ponte-Centino up the mountain of Radicofani, is sixty baiocchi.

3½ *Tortona—La Croce bianca* is a good inn.
2¾ Voghera
1¼ Casteggio
1¾ Broni—Best Inn, *La Posta*.
2 Castel S. Giovanni—Between this spot and Piacenza the road traverses the bed of the Trebia.
2 Piacenza
2 Fiorenzuola—*The Albergo della Posta* is a good inn.
1 S. Donnino
1 Castel-Guelfo
1 *Parma*
1 S. Ilario
1 *Reggio*
1 Rubiera
1 *Modena*
1½ Samoggia
1½ *Bologna*—Between Samoggia and this city there is a bridge thrown across the Reno. Bologna is famous for quinces.
1¼ S. Niccolo—The road crosses the Savena on a bridge.
1¼ Imola—This town, the *Forum Cornelii* of the Romans, is seated on the ancient *Via Emilia*, which leads from Bologna to Rimini.
1 Faenza—Between Imola and this town the road crosses the Santerno on a bridge. Faenza, anciently *Faventia*, was heretofore celebrated for earthenware, to which it gave the name of *Faïence*. Part of the road between S. Niccoli and Faenza is, during wet weather, dangerous.
1 Forli—Anciently *Forum Livii*. The cupola of the Cathedral, painted by Cignani, and *the Chapel of the Madonna del Furco*, together with several pictures in other Churches, merit notice. The Square is one of the finest in Italy; and the Posthouse is a tolerable inn.
1½ Cesena—The road, previous to entering this town, crosses the Savio on a magnificent modern bridge. Cesena contains *a curious Library* belonging to the Minor Conventuals, and *a colossal statue of Pius VI*. Between two and three miles from this town, the road crosses the Pisatello, which flows into the Fiumecino, supposed to have been anciently called *the Rubicon*. Some authors, however, assert that the Pisatello itself was the stream which divided Cisalpine Gaul from Italy.
1 Savignano—Anciently *Compitum*.
1 Rimini—The road between this town and Fano is the ancient *Via Flaminia*. Rimini, the *Araminium* of the Ancients, and once a considerable city, still exhibits remains of former magnificence. The Bridge over the Marecchia, originally the *Arminum*, appears to have been either built or repaired by Augustus and Tiberius: it is situated at the junction of the Via Emilia with the Via Flaminia; and particularly merits observation. On quitting Rimini, the Pesaro road passes under a *Triumphal Arch*, erected in honour of Augustus.

Ravenna, the seat of Empire under Theodoric, is only four posts distant from Rimini, and merits notice, on account of its antiquities, and likewise because it contains the tomb of Dante. Best inn, *La Fontana*.

1½ Cattolica—Previous to arriving at this town, the road crosses the Conca on a bridge; but, when the Conca rises high in consequence of rain, this road is dangerous. Between Cattolica and Rimini are ruins of the ancient city of Conca, inundated by the sea; and at a distance, on the left, is the little Republic of San-Marino.

1 Pesaro—The great square, which is handsome, contains a statue of Urban VIII. Several antiquities and some fine paintings may be found in this town. The figs of Pesaro are deemed the best in Italy; and the Theatre is remarkably elegant.*

1 Fano—The modern name of this town seems to be derived from a *Fano*, or Temple of Fortune, which once stood here. The ancient name, according to Vitruvius, was *Colonia Fanestris*. The objects best worth notice at Fano are *the remains of the triumphal Arch of Constantine—the Library—the Theatre—and the Cathedral*, which contains paintings by Domenichino. The Inn here is tolerably good.

1 Marotta—Between Fano and Marotta the road crosses the Metro, anciently *Metaurus*, celebrated for the defeat and death of Asdrubal, during the second Punic war.

1 Sinigaglia—So called from its Founders the *Galli-Senones*. This town is enlivened by a celebrated Fair, during the last week of July.

1 Case-Bruciate

1½ Ancona—So called from being built in an angle resembling an elbow. This is a commercial town, with a fine Harbour, and a magnificent Quay. *The triumphal Arch* erected by the Roman senate, in honour of the Emperor Trajan, for having improved the Harbour of Ancona at his own expense, peculiarly merits notice; as it is finely proportioned, well preserved, and composed of larger blocks of marble than we find in any other ancient Roman edifice. Clement XII. made Ancona a Free-Port.

---

* The Villa, once inhabited by the late Queen of England, is about a mile from Pesaro: and in her pleasure grounds are two Monuments, the one erected to the memory of her Father, and the other to the memory of her Daughter, the amiable and ever to be lamented Princess Charlotte of Wales.

Oblong shell-fish called *Bellari*, or *Dattili del Mare*, are found alive in large stones on this coast: they were deemed a great delicacy by the ancient Romans, and are, according to Pliny, so luminous, that they shine in the mouth of the person who eats them.

1½ Osimo
1 *Loretto*—The road between Ancona and Loretto traverses a beautiful plain intersected by the rivers Musone and Aspido. Few of the original treasures of the celebrated *Santissima Casa* of Loretto now remain; but the liberal donations of the Bonaparte family, and other wealthy Roman Catholics, have, in some degree, compensated for the loss sustained, during the Pontificate of Pius VI., by the Church of the Madonna at Loretto. *This Church* is magnificent; and in its centre, immediately under the cupola, stands the *Santissima Casa*, cased with Carrara marble finely sculptured; and containing a picture of the Nativity, by Annibale Caracci, and a Holy Family, by Raphael; together with numerous treasures of various descriptions. The *Piazza*, fronting the Church of the Madonna, merits notice; as does *the subterranean Dispensary*, which is furnished with three hundred Gallipots, painted after the designs of Raphael, or Giulio Romano.

¾ Recanati
¾ Sambucheto
1 Macerata—*The Post-House* here is a good inn. The country between Loretto and Macerata is beautiful, and richly cultivated; and near the latter town are ruins of the city of *Heloia-Ricina*, built by Septimius Severus. Macerata is famous for artichokes.
1½ Tolentino—The Square in this town exhibits a well-preserved piece of ancient Sculpture. After quitting Tolentino, the road traverses a part of the Apennine.
1 Valcimara—The number of torrents which issue from the eastern side of the Apennine is so considerable, that Travellers should not venture to go by way of Ancona and Loretto to Rome, after recent inundations, caused either by hard rain, or the melting of snow.
1 Ponte-la-Trave
1 Seravalle
1 Case-Nuove.
1 Foligno
12½ *Roma*—See the Route from Florence through Perugia to Rome.
74½ posts.

ROUTE FROM MILAN, THROUGH BERGAMO, BRESCIA, VERONA, VICENZA, AND PADUA, TO VENICE, BOLOGNA, AND FLORENCE.

1½ Colombarolo—The country from Milan hither is beautiful.
1 Vaprio
¾ Osio
1 *Bergamo*—Near Canonica Travellers cross the Adda, anciently the *Adua*, in a ferry. The Bergamasco is highly cultivated, fertile, and populous; the town of Bergamo large, well fortified, and adorned with a handsome *Cathedral*, which contains paintings of the modern Venetian school: but the best pictures are in the *Church of S. Maria Maggiore*. Principal inn, *L'Albergo Reale*. Bergamo is called the birthplace of Harlequin. This town is enlivened by a celebrated Fair, during the latter part of August, and the commencement of September; and its resident inhabitants amount to above thirty thousand persons.
1 Cavernogo
1 Palazzolo
1½ Ospedaletto
1 *Brescia*—The road from Bergamo hither traverses a rich plain at the foot of the Alps. Brescia is a considerable town, seated at the base of a mountain, between the rivers Mella and Naviglio, and supposed to contain forty-five thousand inhabitants; its fortifications are strong, and defended by a citadel. *The Palazzo di Giustizia* is a remarkable edifice, built partly in the Gothic, and partly in the Grecian style, and contains fine frescos, together with other good paintings. *The Cathedral* is a handsome modern structure. *The Churches of S. Nazaro al Carmine*, and *S. Afra*, contain fine pictures of the Venetian school, as do several of the Palaces. *The Mazzucchelli collection of medals*, and *the public Library*, merit notice. *The Theatre* is handsome; and *Le due Torri* is deemed the best inn.
1½ Ponte S. Marco.
1 Desenzano—After passing Ponte S. Marco, the road lies on the luxuriant margin of the Lago di Garda; whose waters resemble a little sea, and contain a fish called *Carpione*, which was deemed particularly delicious by ancient Epicures. The Lago di Garda, formerly called *Lacus Benacus*, is about thirty-five miles in length; and, where widest, fourteen in breadth: the Alps in great measure surround it, and the picture it exhibits is beautiful.
1½ Castel-Nuovo
1½ *Verona*—On quitting the margin of the Lago di Garda, the road enters the Veronese, which is one of the most fertile parts of Italy; abounding in corn, wine, oil, fruits, mulberry-trees, rice, etc. Verona, pleasantly situated on the Adige (anciently *Atagis*), and

one of the oldest cities of Italy, is supposed to contain 50,000 inhabitants, including its suburbs. The fortifications were constructed by San-Micheli. Here is a *Triumphal Arch*, called *Porta dei Borsari*, and erected in the reign of Gallienus; and *an Amphitheatre*, supposed to have been built during the reign of Trajan, and almost perfect. It contains 23,484 spectators commodiously seated; and is composed of large blocks of marble without cement. Near this magnificent monument of antiquity, is *the modern Theatre*, a fine structure, the entrance to which is by a beautiful portico, built by Palladio. *The tombs of the Scaligeri Family* merit notice, as does *the Palazzo del Consiglio*, a noble edifice, built by San-Sovino. *The Chiesa di S. Giorgio* contains a picture of the martyrdom of that Saint, by Paolo Veronese; and *the Church of S. Bernardino* contains the celebrated Cappella-Varesca, by San-Micheli. Verona gave birth to the Poets Catullus and Æmilius Macrus; the Historian Cornelius Nepos; Pliny the Elder; Vitruvius the celebrated Architect of the Augustan age; Paolo Veronese; and many other persons of distinguished abilities.

The petrified fishes found in Monte Bolca, near Verona, are curious. Principal inns, *Le due Torri*, and *La Torre di Londra*.*

1 Caldiero
1½ Monte-Bello
1½ *Vicenza*—From Verona hither the road is bordered by mulberry-trees interlaced with vines; and exhibits a view of the Alps which divide Italy from Germany. Vicenza, anciently called *Vicetta*, is delightfully situated on the Bacchiglione, contains, including its suburbs, above 30,000 inhabitants; and is the birth-place of the celebrated Architect Palladio, who has adorned it with his finest works; namely, *the Olympic Theatre!! the Basilica*; and several *Palaces* in the town (where the House he once inhabited may still be seen); *the triumphal Arch* leading to the Campo Marzo; and *the Church of the Madonna del Monte*, not far distant. *The Rotonda of the Casa-Capra* was likewise built by Palladio. Best inn, *I due Rode*, and very comfortable. The wine of Vicenza has the reputation of being particularly wholesome; and the climate, during summer, is one of the best in northern Italy.

1½ Slesega—The country from Verona hither is beautiful.
1 *Padua—The Stella d'oro* has been already mentioned as a good inn: the *Aquila d'oro* likewise is a good one.
1½ Dolo
1½ Fusina—Road from Milan hither excellent.
Venice—by water, five miles.
Travellers who go by land to Fusina, usually return by water to Padua; whence the distance is—
1½ to Monselice
1½ *Rovigo*
1½ Polesella
1½ *Ferrara*—A Procaccio goes twice a week from Ferrara to Bologna, by water.
1½ Malabergo
1 Capodargine
1 *Bologna*
1½ Pianoro—Hence to Lojano a third horse, or oxen, to every calesse: and for all the sharp ascents of this passage of the Apennine carriages which usually travel with three horses must have four, and carriages which usually

---

* About half a mile distant from the walls of Verona, in a Garden, once the Cemetery of a Francescan Convent, is a Sarcophagus, called *the Tomb of Juliet;* and made of Verona marble; with a place for her head, a socket for a candle, and two holes for the admission of air. Juliet is supposed to have died in the year 1303, when Bartolomeo della Scala (or degli Scaligeri), was Lord of Verona: and Shakspeare probably intended to represent one of the Scaligeri, by his Escalus. The names of the rival families, whom our great Poet has immortalized, were Capello, and Montechio: the tomb of the former stood in the Cemetery of the Francescan Church; and they had a palace in the town of Verona: they were highly favoured by the Scaligeri; a circumstance which probably offended the Montechi, a more ancient and affluent family than the other, and possessors of the Castle of Montechio (situated about fifteen miles from Verona), and likewise proprietors of a palace in the Veronetta. After the marriage and fray, Juliet came to the Francescan Convent, under pretence of confession; and her confessor, Father Lorenzo (called, in the *Compendio*, from which this account is extracted, Leonardo of Reggio), gave her a powerful soporific; at the same time sending to inform her relations that she had been suddenly attacked by illness; and as the soporific took effect before their arrival, they thought her dead: consequently, she was not removed from the Convent; but immediately put into her coffin: and, according to a custom which still prevails, a lighted candle was placed in the coffin, near her head; and, after the funeral ceremony, the lid, according to usual practice, was put on in private. Father Lorenzo, when resolved to administer the soporific, sent a letter to Mantua, informing Romeo of this resolution; but before the letter arrived, he heard the report of Juliet's death, left Mantua, scaled the wall of the Cemetery belonging to the Francescan convent, and swallowed the poison. Next day Bartolomeo degli Scaligeri, and the two rival families, assisted at the obsequies of the unfortunate Romeo and Juliet.

travel with four horses must have six, beside oxen.

1½ Lojano
1 Filigare
1 Covigliajo
1 Monte-Carelli—On going from Monte-Carelli to Covigliajo a third horse, or oxen.
1 Cafaggiuolo
1 Fonte Buona
1 *Firenze.*

42½ posts.

ROUTE FROM MILAN TO BOLOGNA, THROUGH PIACENZA, PARMA, REGGIO, AND MODENA.

1½ Melegnano
1½ Lodi. Inns, *L'Albergo del Sole, 1 Tre Re*, etc.
1½ Casal-Pusterlengo
2 Piacenza
12 Bologna—See "Route from Genoa, through Bologna, Rimini, Sinagalia, Ancona, Loretto, and Terni, to Rome."

18½ posts.

ROUTE FROM MILAN TO TURIN.

1½ Sedriano
1 Buffalora
3 *Novara*—This is an episcopal city of high antiquity, and its *Cathedral* merits notice. Here are three inns, *Les Trois Rois, Le Poisson d'Or*, and *Le Faucon.*
1½ Orfengo
1½ *Vercelli*—Between Novara and Vercelli the country is marshy, and the air unwholesome. Rice grows luxuriantly here, and seems to be almost the only grain which is cultivated in this neighbourhood. Vercelli, seated at the confluence of the Cerva and the Sesia, is a considerable town; and *the Portico of its Cathedral* merits notice. The principal inns are, *Le Lion d'Or*, and *Les Trois Rois.*
1½ S. Germano
2½ Cigliano
1½ Rondissone
1 Chivasso
1½ Settimo
1½ Turin—Between Settimo and Turin the road is excellent, and the country

fertile, well cultivated, and watered by the rivers Doria, Stura, Molone, Orco, and Dora-Baltea, all of which descend from the Alps.

18 posts.

ROUTE FROM AOSTE TO TURIN.*

3½ Châtillon
3¾ Donas
3 *Ivrée*
2½ Caluse
1¾ Chivasso
3 Turin.

17½ posts.

ROUTE FROM TURIN, OVER THE MARITIME ALPS, TO NICE.

2½ Carignano
2½ Racconigi
1½ Savigliano
2¾ Centale
1½ *Coni*—Best inn, *La Posta.*†
1 Borgo S. Dalmazio
2½ Limone §
4 Tenda
2½ Breglio
2½ Saspello
2¾ Scareno
2½ *Nice***—Persons going this road should provide wine for their journey at Turin.

27½ posts.

ROUTE FROM TURIN, OVER THE BOCCHETTA, TO GENOA.

1½ Truffarollo
1¾ Poirino
1½ Dusino
1½ La Gambetta
1½ Asti—Inns, *La Rosa Rossa*, and *Il Leone d'Oro.*
1½ Annone
1½ Feliciano
2¾ *Alessandria*—This town contains, beside *The Albergo vecchio d'Italia*, already mentioned, two inns, namely, *I Tre Re* and *La Locanda d'Inghilterra.*††
3½ Novi §§
4 Voltaggio—A third horse for the passage of the Bocchetta.***

---

* There are no relays of post horses at the three first stations.

† There are no relays of post horses between Coni and Nice; therefore, on this road, it is necessary to travel *en voiturier.*

§ Between Limone and Scarena it is frequently difficult to travel in a carriage.

** *The Hôtel des Etrangers* (though not mentioned in the former part of this work), is one of the best inns at Nice.

†† An extra quarter of a post is paid on quitting Alessandria.

§§ A third and fourth horse all the year from Novi to Voltaggio, and *vice versâ*; together with an extra charge of twenty-five centimes per horse, on account of the badness of the road.

*** A third and fourth horse all the year from Voltaggio to Campo-Marone, and *vice versâ*; together with an extra charge of twenty-five centimes per horse, for the passage of the Bocchetta.

4 Campo-Marone—Inn, *La Posta*.
3 *Genoa*—The journey from Alessandria, over the Bocchetta to Genoa, with post-horses, seldom occupies more than ten hours.
—
27¾ posts.

ROUTE FROM ROME TO NAPLES.

Previous to undertaking this journey it is requisite for British Subjects to obtain passports from the British Consul-General, countersigned at the Police-Office, and likewise by the Neapolitan Minister at Rome.

Passports originally granted by a French Ambassador must be signed by the French Minister resident at Rome before they are presented to the Neapolitan Minister for his signature.

1½ Torre di mezza-via—Hence, to Rome, the charge is only one post and a quarter.
1 Albano
¾ Genzano—A third horse from Albano to Genzano (but not *vice versâ*); and for a carriage drawn with either four or six horses, two in addition.
1 Velletri

{ Pontine Marshes } A third horse from Velletri to Genzano (but not *vice versâ*); and for a carriage drawn by either four or six horses, two in addition. The journey from Velletri to Terracina, usually occupies from four to five hours, with post-horses.

1 Cisterna
1½ Torre de' tre Ponti
1 Bocca di Fiume
1 Mesa
1 Ponte Maggiore
1 Terracina

1½ Fondi—A third horse in addition to every pair, from Fondi to Itri.
1 Itri
1 *Mola*—From Mola to Itri a third horse, so far as the Cenotaph of Cicero. The price of this horse is ten grains.
1 Garigliano—The toll paid for every four-wheeled close carriage on springs, which crosses the Garigliano, is six carlini; and for every open carriage, four carlini. From Garigliano to S. Agata a third horse is added to every pair.
1 S. Agata
1 Sparanisi—A third horse in addition to every pair, from Sparanisi to S. Agata.

1 *Capua*—At the barrier here, four ducats are paid for every coach, or post-chaise; and two piastres for every open carriage on springs.
1 Aversa
1 *Naples*—An extra half post is paid on entering and on quitting this city.*
—
20¾ posts; real distance, 19¾ posts.

Persons in robust health, who travel post from Rome to Naples, may, by setting out very early the first morning, reach Terracina before the close of day; and again, by setting out very early the second morning, they may reach Naples that night. If, however, ill health, short days, or any other cause, compel Travellers to sleep two nights on the road, the best plan is to go to Velletri the first day, to set out soon after sunrise on the second day, drive to Mola di Gaeta, sleep there; and on the third day, by setting out early, it is practicable to reach Naples at the common hour for dinner. By pursuing this plan Travellers pass the Pontine Marshes at the wholesomest time, namely, between nine in the morning and three in the afternoon.

A light Carretella, containing two persons only, with but little luggage, usually goes from Rome to Terracina in ten hours and a half; and returns in nine hours—goes from Terracina to Naples in fourteen hours, and returns in eleven hours.

ROUTE FROM NAPLES TO PÆSTUM.

1½ Torre del Annunziata—A post-royal; on account of which an extra half post is charged.
1½ Nocera
1½ *Salerno*—From Nocera to Salerno an additional horse to every pair.
1 Vicenza
1 Eboli
2½ Pæstum, by way of Persano.
—
9½ posts, including the post-royal.

* Travellers, on entering Naples, are obliged to deposit their passports at the Police-Office; neither can they, till their departure, legally reclaim them.

ENVIRONS OF NAPLES.

Posts.
1 from *Naples* to Caivano.
1 from *Caivano* to Caserta.
½ from *Caserta* to S. Leucio.
1 from *Naples* to Pozzuoli.
1 from *Pozzuoli* to Fusaro, or Licola.
1 from *Naples* to Astroni.
½ from *Naples* to Capo-di-Monte.
1 from *Naples* to Portici, La Favorita, or Torre del Greco.

ROUTE, EN VOITURIER, FROM PISA TO MASSA AND CARRARA, WITH AN ENGLISH POST-CHAISE, DRAWN BY FOUR HORSES.

	Miles.	Hours.
Via-Reggio	19	6½
Pietra-Santa	6	1½
Massa	7	1½
Carrara	5	1½

ROUTE, EN VOITURIER, FROM ROME TO FLORENCE, THROUGH PERUGIA, WITH AN ENGLISH COACH DRAWN BY FOUR MULES.

	Hours.	
Monti-rosi	7	
Civita-Castellana	3½	
Terni	7½	
Spoleto	5½	Between Strettura and this town, to ascend the mountain of La Somma, we had two oxen in addition to our mules.
Foligno	4½	
Perugia	5½	To ascend the mountain on which Perugia stands, we had two oxen in addition to our mules.
Torricella	4½	
Camuscia	6	
Arezzo	5½	
San-Giovanni	6½	
Firenze	7	

It is deemed unwholesome to travel from Florence through Perugia to Rome from the time when the great heats commence, till after the autumnal rains have fallen: and it is almost equally unwholesome to travel from Rome through Siena to Florence, during the great heats.*

ROUTE, EN VOITURIER, FROM FLORENCE, THROUGH SIENA, TO ROME, WITH AN ENGLISH POST-CHAISE DRAWN BY THREE HORSES.

	Hours.	
Poggibonsi	7	First day.
Siena	4	
Buonconvento	4	
S. Quirico	3	Second day.
La Scala	3½	
Radicofani	3½	
Torricelli	2½	Third day.
S. Lorenzo-Nuovo	3½	
Bolsena	2	From S. Lorenzo-Nuovo hither the road lies on the margin of the Lake of Bolsena; the air of which has been already mentioned as unwholesome.
Montefiascone	3½	Fourth day.
Viterbo	2½	
Monterosi	7	Fifth day.
Roma	7	

ROUTE, EN VOITURIER, FROM ROME TO NAPLES, WITH AN ENGLISH POST-CHAISE, DRAWN BY THREE HORSES.

	Hours.	
Velletri	6	First day.
Terracina	9½	Second day.
Fondi	2	
S. Agata	6	Third day.
Capua	3½	
Naples	3½	

On returning from Naples to Rome, British Travellers must have passports from their own Ambassador in the first-named city, countersigned at the Police-Office, and also by the Roman Consul: and it is likewise advisable for persons who travel in their own carriage to endeavour to obtain from the British Consul-General at Rome a *Lascia passare* for Terracina, and an-

---

* Persons who wish to see the Cascade of Terni, and avoid sleeping at Torricella, where the inn is comfortless, should stop the first night at *Civita-Castellana*, the second at *Terni*, the third at *Spoleto*, the fourth at *Perugia*, the fifth at *Camuscia*, and the sixth at *S. Giovanni*; or *the Locanda del Pian della Fonte.*

other for the Porta di S. Giovanni at Rome. Persons who travel from Naples to Rome without having a *Lascia passare* for Terracina, are compelled, unless they go post, or hire horses of the Naples post-master for the whole journey, either to allow their trunks to be examined at Terracina, or to deposit four piastres for having them plumbed.

ROUTE, EN VOITURIER, FROM CALAIS TO ROME, DURING THE WINTER OF 1820, WITH AN ENGLISH POST-CHAISE, DRAWN BY FOUR STRONG HORSES.

The Voiturin was Emery; who charged, for the horses and two meals a day, with three good bed-rooms every night, for one master and two servants, a hundred and ten Louis-d'or; he defraying all expenses, except the customary fees to Servants at Inns. Had this journey been undertaken at a more favourable season, Emery would not have demanded so high a price.

Days.	Posts.		Inns.
1st	4½	Boulogne.................	Parker's Hôtel d'Angleterre.
2d		Montreuil................	Le Renard d'Or.
	7	Bernay..................	La Poste.
3d		Airaines.................	La Poste.
	9	Granvilliers.............	Hôtel d'Angleterre. (a)
4th		Beauvais.................	L'Écu de France.
	8	Beaumont................	Le Grand Cerf.
5th	4	*Paris*...................	Hôtel de Montauban.
6th		Montgeron...............	La Ville de Lyon.
	5½	Melun...................	La Gallère. (a)
7th		Montereau...............	Le Lion d'Or.
	8	Sens....................	Hôtel de l'Ecu.
8th		Joigny...................	Les Cinq Mineurs.
	7½	Auxerre.................	Hôtel de Beaune.
9th		Lucy-le-Bois............	Hôtel des Diligences. (a)
	8½	Rouvray.................	La Poste.
10th		Saulieu..................	Hôtel de S. Nicolas.
	About 6	Ernay...................	Hôtel de la Croix Blanche. (a)
11th		La Roche Pot............	Les Bons Enfans. (a)
	About 7	Chalons-sur-Saône.......	Les Trois Faisans. (a)
12th		Tournus.................	Hôtel du Sauvage.
	7½	Macon...................	Hôtel de l'Europe.
13th		Huit Franche............	Le Faucon. (a)
	8½	Lyon*...................	Hôtel de l'Europe.
14th	3¾	La Verpellier............	A country inn, not bad.
15th		Le Tour du Pin†........	Le Soleil.
	7¾	Les Echelles............	La Poste.
16th		*Chambery*..............	La Poste.
	5	Montmellian.............	Inn on the hill. (a)
17th		Aiguebelle...............	Hôtel de l'Union.
	7½	S. Jean de Maurienne §..	La Poste.
18th?		S. Michel................	Hôtel de Londres.
	4½	Modane..................	Hôtel du Lion d'Or.
19th	4	Lans-le-Bourg...........	Hôtel Royal.

Owing to an uncommonly rapid and heavy fall of snow upon Mont Cenis, it was found needful here to place the bodies of carriages in *traîneaux* so far as Molaret; though the wheels were drawn over the mountain without being taken off their axles. Voi-

---

(a) The Inns marked thus are unfit for sleeping places.

* Beyond Lyon the inns do not furnish tea.

† French and Savoyard Frontier Custom houses between Le Tour du Pin and Les Echelles.

§ A tolerable inn, called *L'Hôtel du petit S. Julien*, between S. Jean de Maurienne and S. Michel.

turins pay from twenty to thirty francs for conveying the body of of a carriage, in this manner, from Lans-le-Bourg to Molaret, or Susa: and Travellers, to avoid stopping at the former place, while their carriages are remounted, usually proceed to the latter. Carriages, generally speaking, are five hours in ascending in a *traîneau* from Lans-le-Bourg to La Grande Croix; and five hours in descending from La Grande Croix to Susa.

Days.	Posts.		Inns.
20th		La Grande Croix..........	*Delicious trout may be procured here.* (a)
	8	Susa	La Posta.
21st		S. Ambrogio.............	Albergo della Vigna.
	7½	*Turin*...................	Locanda d' Inghilterra.
22d		Villa Nuova.............	Albergo di S. Marco.
	7½	Asti	Il Lione d'Oro.
23d		Alessandria.............	Albergo Reale Vecchio d' Italia.
	8½	Tortona*................	La Croce Bianca.
24th		Broni....................	La Posta.
	7½	Castel S. Giovanni†.....	Albergo di S. Marco.
25th		Fiorenzuola.............	La Posta.
	5	Borgo S. Donino.........	La Croce Bianca.
26th		S. Ilario.................	La Posta. (a)
	5	Rubièra.................	Only one inn. (a)
27th		Castel Franco §.........	Albergo di S. Marco.
	4	*Bologna*................	Albergo Imperiale.
28th		Lojano...................	La Posta. (a)
	5	Covigliajo...............	La Posta.
29th		Le Maschere.............	A single house.
	4	*Florence*...............	Il Pellicano.

The road over the Apennine, between Bologna and Florence, is so well constructed as to be almost constantly passable, even during heavy falls of snow; but, on descending from Lojano to Florence, during frosty weather, it is sometimes needful to chain two wheels at the same moment, and always necessary to double chain one wheel.

Days.	Posts.		Inns.
30th		Tavernelle..............	Merely a resting place for horses.
	3	Poggibonsi..............	Il Lione Rosso.
31st		Siena	L'Aquila Nera.
	4	Buonconvento**.........	*Albergo del Cavalletto.* (a)
32d		Locanda della Scala.....	A single house. (a)
	5½	Torricelli	Only one inn. (a)

Torricelli is situated about six miles beyond the mountain of Radicofani; and Travellers who arrive late in the day, during winter, on the summit of this mountain, should not attempt descending till the next morning; as the descent, from being rapid, and near the brink of precipices, is dangerous without good driving light, though the road over Radicofani is at all seasons smooth and hard; but from the base of the mountain to Torricelli, and a short distance further, the road, from being intersected by a torrent, is very rough during winter.

* Just beyond Voghera a Bridge, which, unless drivers be careful, is dangerous.

† A frontier Custom-house, belonging to Maria-Louisa. Between Castel S. Giovanni and Fiorenzuola Travellers ford that celebrated torrent, the Trebia, which is sometimes dangerous after heavy rains.

§ A frontier Custom-house, belonging to the Pope.

** Oxen are requisite, during winter, to draw carriages up the hill near Buonconvento.

Days.	Posts.		Inns.
33d		Bolsena...............	La Posta.
	4½	Montefiascone	La Posta. (a)
34th		Ronciglione.............	Albergo del Angelo. (a)
	4	Monterosi	La Posta.
35th		Storta.................	
	3½	*Roma*	

Inns good, those marked thus (*a*) excepted. Road, in consequence of heavy rain, very indifferent between Lucy-le-Bois and Ernay, between La Roche Pot and Châlons, between Huit Franche and Lyon, and between Tortona and Broni; but, in every other part, perfectly good. After heavy winter rain, however, it is advisable to go from Turin to Milan, and thence to Bologna, instead of taking the shorter route through Alessandria.

ROUTE FROM FLORENCE, THROUGH BOLOGNA, VENICE, VIENNA, PRAGUE, AND DRESDEN, TO HAMBURGH.*

Posts		
23	Fusina—See "Route from Milan through Bergamo, etc., to Venice, Bologna, and Florence."	
	Venice, by water, 5 miles: and thence by water to *Mestre*, 5 miles.	
1½	Treviso—Principal inn, *La Posta*.	
1	Spresiano	
1	Conegliano	
1½	Sacile	
1	*Pordenon*†	
1½	Codroipo	
1½	Udine	
1½	Nogaredo	
2	Goertz	
1	Cernicza	
2	Wippach	
1	Prewald	
1	Adelsberg—See, under GERMANY, the route from Vienna to Trieste.	
1	Lasse	
1	Ober-Laybach	
1	*Laybach*—See, under GERMANY, the route from Vienna to Trieste.	

* See, under GERMANY, the price of post horses in that country.
† Travellers who take the Klagenfurt-road go from *Pordenon* to *S. Paternion*; crossing, previous to their arrival at the latter place, the *Tagliamento*, and then proceeding to

	Posts.
Villach	1½
Velden	1

1½	Potpetsch
1	S. Oswald
1	Franz
1½	Cilli
1½	Gannowitz
1	Freistritz
1	Mahrburgh—See, under GERMANY, the route from Vienna to Trieste.
1½	Ehronhaussen
1	Lebering
1	Kahlsdorf
1	*Gratz*—See, under GERMANY, the route from Vienna to Trieste.
1½	Pegau
1	Redelstein
1	*Bruck* on the Muhr
1	Moerzhofen
1	Krieglach
1½	Moerzuschlag
1	Schottwein
1	Neukirchen
1	Neustadt
2	Neudorf
1	*Vienna*
1	Enzersdorf
1	Stockerau
1	Malebern
1	Holabrunn
1	Jezelsdorf
1	*Znaim*
1	Freymersdorf
1	Budwitz
1	Schelletau
1	Stannern
1	*Iglau*
1	Stecken
1	Teutschbrodt
1	Steinsdorf
1	Benekau
1	*Czaslau*
1	Kolin
1	Planian
1	Boehm-brod
1	Bichowitz
1	*Prague*
1	Sarzedokluk
1	Schlan
1½	Budin
1	Lobositz
1½	Aussig
1	Peterswald
1	Zehist

Klagenfurt	1
S. Veit	1
Friesach	1
Neumarck . . .	1
Unsmarck . . .	1½
Judenberg . . .	1½
Knittelfield . . .	1
Graubath . . .	1
Leoben	1
Bruck . . .	1

1   *Dresden*
1½ Meissen
1½ Stauchitz
1½ Wermsdorff
1   Wurtzen
1½ *Leipzig*—See, under GERMANY, the route from Hamburgh to Leipzig.
1½ Landsberg
2   Coethen
1½ Kalbe
1½ *Magdeburgh*
2   Burgstall
2   Stendal
1½ Osterburgh
1   Arendsee
1½ Lenzen
2¼ Luhten
1½ Boitzenburg
2   Escheburg
1½ *Hamburg.*

126 posts.

ROUTE FROM FLORENCE, THROUGH MANTUA, AND BY THE TYROL, TO AUGSBURGH AND WURTZBURGH.

9   Bologna—See the last route.
1½ Samoggia
1¾ *Modena*
1½ Carpi
1   Novi
1½ S. Benedetto
1½ *Mantua*—This city, which contains above 24,000 inhabitants, is watered by the Mincio, anciently *Mincius*; and, being surrounded with inundations occasioned by that river, is very unwholesome during summer. *The Cathedral* here was built after the design of Giulio Romano, who painted its cieling and tribuna; and has likewise enriched Mantua with more of his works. Not far hence stands the Village of Pietole, also called *Andes*, the birth-place of Virgil. The principal inn at Mantua is *La Posta.*
1   Roverbella
1½ Villafranca
1½ *Verona*
1½ Volarni
1   Peri
1   Halla—Inn, *La Corona.*
1½ *Roveredo*—This town was anciently called *Roboretum*: its principal inns are *La Rosa* and *La Corona.*
1   Caliani
1½ *Trent*—From Verona hither the road follows the course of the Adige. Trent, anciently called *Tridentum*, is placed in a delightful valley, at the base of the Alps, between Italy and Germany. Its Cathedral, a Gothic edifice, contains an excellent Organ; and beyond the Gate of S. Lorenzo is a fine Bridge thrown over the Adige. The principal inn here is *L'Europa.*
1   Lavis

1½ Salorno
1   Egna
1   Branzolo
1   Botzen—The country from Botzen to Brixen is beautiful.
1   Deutschen
1   Kollman
1   *Brixen*
1   Ober-Mittewald
1   Sterzingen
1   Brenner
1   Steinach
1   Schoenberg
1   *Inspruck*—This city, the capital of the Tyrol, and supposed to contain 10,000 inhabitants, is placed in a romantic valley, watered by the river Inn, anciently called Ænus. The Mausoleum erected here, to record in *bassi rilievi* the principal incidents of the life of Maximilian, merits notice. *The Eagle*, *The golden Lion*, and *The Rose* are the best hotels at Inspruck.
1   Zirl—Few scenes can vie in sublimity with the passage of the Zirl.
1   Barwies
1   Nazareth
1   Lermos
1   Reiti
1   Füssen
1   Someister
1   Schwabich Brück
1   Hohenwart
1   Hurlach
1½ *Augsburg*—Principal inns, *The Three Moors* and *The White Lamb*. See, under GERMANY, the route from Frankfort to Augsburg.
1½ Metlingen
1   Donawert
1½ Nordlingen
1½ Dunckelsphul
1   Creilshiem
1½ Blaufelden
1½ Mergenthiem
1   Bischofheim
1½ *Wurtzburg*—Principal inn, *The Hôtel of Franconia*. See, under GERMANY, the route from Vienna to Ostend.

65¾ posts.

The road through the Tyrol, from Trent to Inspruck, was once excellent, and is still good; though it has been, of late years, injured by the heavy cannon and artillery waggons which have passed over it. The views in this country are picturesque, beautiful, and sublime: and where the road quits the plains of Italy to ascend the Rhætian Alps, are two gigantic and extraordinary rocks, which seem to have been severed by the hand of Nature for the purpose of affording a passage to the Adige; whose graceful sinuosities are a material embellishment to every scene in which they present themselves.

ROUTE, EN VOITURIER, DURING SUMMER, FROM ROME, THROUGH FLORENCE AND MILAN, BY THE SIMPLON, TO GENEVA; AND OVER THE JURA ALPS TO POLIGNY, DIJON, MELUN, PARIS, AND BOULOGNE.*

No British subject, who intends going by the above-named route to England, should leave Rome without being provided with a passport from the British Consul-General; which passport should be countersigned first at the Police-office, then by the Ambassador of Austria and Tuscany, and, lastly, by the French Ambassador.

From Rome to Boulogne the time employed in travelling is about thirty-two days, during summer, with a light English post-chaise, not heavily laden, and drawn by three strong horses.

First day,   .   Posts 4½ Baccano and Ronciglione.
Second day,   .   Posts 6½ Viterbo and San-Lorenzo Nuovo.
Third day,   .   Posts 6½ Radicofani and San-Quirico.

At Acquapendente, the next post to S. Lorenzo Nuovo, Travellers are obliged to show their passports, and to pay one paul per passport at the Police-Office there, as already mentioned. At the Custom-house on Radicofani Travellers usually pay from three to six pauls, according to the number of their trunks, for having them plumbed, and thus secured from examination in the Tuscan State.

Fourth day,   .   Posts 2½ Montaroni and Siena.

If luggage be not plumbed it is examined on going into Siena, by the Roman gate.

Fifth day,   .   Posts 5 Barbarino and Florence.

On entering the latter city Travellers usually give a few Pauls to the Custom-house Officers. *The Aquila Nera* is the inn usually resorted to by *Vetturini*.

Sixth day,   .   Posts 4½ Le Maschere and Pietramala.
Seventh day,   .   Posts 4½ Poggioli and Bologna.
Eighth day,   .   Posts 5 Modena and Marsaglia.
Ninth day,   .   Posts 4 Parma and San-Domino.
Tenth day,   .   Posts 4½ Piacenza and Casal-Pusterlengo.

Beyond Piacenza, on the opposite side of the Po, is a Custom-house where trunks, and even the inside of carriages undergo a strict examination; but where nothing appears to be considered as contraband, except silks, and other wearing apparel not made up. It is advisable to have luggage plumbed here.

Eleventh day,   .   Posts 4½ Melegnano and Milan.
Twelfth day,   .   Posts 4½ Cascina and Sesto-Calende.
Thirteenth day, .   Posts 7 Fariolo and Vogogna.

Travellers, (if the weather be favourable), usually send their carriages empty from Sesto to Fariolo; hiring for themselves, at Sesto, a boat, which costs a Napoleon, *buonamano* to the Boatmen inclusive; and which proceeds first to Arona, next to the Borromean Islands, and then to Fariolo.

Fourteenth day, .   Posts 6½ Domo d'Ossola and Simplon.
Fifteenth day,   .   Posts 6 Brigg
Sixteenth day, .   Posts 8¼ Tourtemagne and Sion.
Seventeenth day,   Posts 6¾ Martigny and S. Maurice.
Eighteenth day,   Posts 8½ S. Gingoux and Thonon.
Nineteenth day,   Posts 4½ Geneva
Twentieth day,   Posts 7½ Gex and Morez.

Travellers are obliged to have their passports signed at Gex: and at the French Custom-house between Gex and Morez, trunks are completely unpacked and rigorously examined; as likewise are the insides of carriages: nothing, however, seems to be considered as contraband by the searchers here, except wearing apparel, not made up, Roman pearls, and Geneva watches and trinkets for sale. At Morez, trunks, etc. are again examined.

Twenty-first day,   Posts 7 Champagnole and Poligny.

---

* So little care is now taken of the Simplon-road, that I would advise Travellers neither to attempt leaving nor entering Italy, by this route, sooner in spring than June, nor later in autumn than October.

ITALY—ROUTES.

On arriving at Poligny, Travellers are obliged to deliver up their Passports at the Sous-Préfecture; whence they are forwarded to Paris: while new Passports (the expense of which is fifty sous each) are substituted for those left at the Sous-Préfecture.

Twenty-second day,   Posts 6¼   Mont-sous-Vaudrey and Auxonne.
Twenty-third day,   Posts 6¼   Dijon and Pont-de-Pany.
Twenty-fourth day,   Posts 7¼   Vitteaux and Rouvray.
Twenty-fifth day,   Posts 8¼   Lucy-le-Bois and Auxerre.
Twenty-sixth day,   Posts 7¼   Joigny and Sens.
Twenty-seventh day, Posts 8   Montereau and Melun. Inn at the former town, The *Lion d'Or*, and bad; at the latter, The *Hôtel de France*, and very comfortable. Montereau is a large town, watered by the Yonne and Seine; but much injured in its appearance, by the bridges thrown over these rivers having been nearly destroyed by the merciless hand of war. The hill above Montereau commands a fine view of the Yonne and Seine.
Twenty-eighth day,   Posts 5½   Charenton and Paris.

The road from Fossard through Melun to Paris contains less pavement than does that through Fontainebleau; but is more hilly, and not so pleasant. The mode of proceeding with respect to Passports at Paris has been already mentioned.

Twenty-ninth day,   Posts 8½   Beaumont and Beauvais.
Thirtieth day,   . . . 7¾   Granvilliers and Airaines.
Thirty-first day,   . . . 7¼   Nouvion and Montreuil.
Thirty-second day,   . . 4½   Boulogne.

This is a handsome town; in the vicinity of which there are several villas, chiefly tenanted by English families: and here likewise is a Protestant School for young Ladies, kept by Mrs. and Miss Dowling.

It has been already mentioned that the passage from Boulogne to Dover is, generally speaking, accomplished in less time than from Calais to Dover: and Travellers who go to The *Hôtel de Londres* at Boulogne, and embark from that inn, are charged as follows:—

Breakfast, per head, francs two—dinner, francs four—beds, for one Master and one Servant, francs four—dismounting and embarking a four-wheeled carriage, francs sixteen—clearance of ditto and luggage, francs twelve—Permit, francs two—Passport, francs two—porters, from three to six francs, according to the quantity of luggage—Commissary (who exonerates Travellers both from trouble and expense at the Custom-house), francs ten.*

The Commissary belonging to the *London Hotel* at Dover charges ten and sixpence for getting an English carriage, with the luggage belonging to it, out of the packet, and then clearing them at the Customhouse; but British Travellers who design landing at Dover, should be careful not to bring with them a single article which pays duty, if they would wish to avoid detention, fatigue, and needless expense.

I travelled from Rome to Boulogne in my own landaulet, drawn by three horses, belonging to the Roman *Padrone di Vetture*, Balzani; and I paid for myself, another Lady, and two Servants, a hundred louis-d'or, *buona-mano* inclusive; together with one Louis and a half per day whenever I chose to rest. Balzani engaged to defray the expense of barriers and toll-bridges; to furnish extra horses whenever needful; to provide us with two meals a day, a sitting-room, and four good beds every night during the journey; and likewise during days of rest; and also to have taken us on to Calais, had we desired it; which engagement was so punctually fulfilled by his Postillion, who drove me, that I gave him three Napoleons as a present.†

From Rome I took with me as many Louis-d'or as served to pay Balzani; and as many Napoleons as I was likely to want for other expenses; and this proved an economical measure, because there is no *agio* upon gold at Rome.

---

* The charge at Boulogne, for embarking a carriage, depends upon whether it be dismounted or not; and as this hazardous operation is seldom, if ever, necessary when carriages are conveyed from France to England, or *vice versâ*, by Steam Packets, these vessels, which may now be found in almost every port, are the conveyance usually preferred for carriages.

† Balzani also paid the tax now levied in France upon foreign Voiturins.

410 APPENDIX. [CH. VI.

ROUTE, EN VOITURIER, FROM FLORENCE TO VENICE, MILAN, TURIN, AND OVER MONT CENIS TO PONT-DE-BEAUVOISIN, DURING THE SUMMER OF 1822, WITH AN ENGLISH LAUNDALET DRAWN BY THREE HORSES.

	Hours.	Days.	Inns.
Le Maschere	3½		A single house.
Pietramala	4½	1st	A single house.
Pogiole	5½		(Not far beyond Pietramala is the Barrier where luggage may be plumbed for Venice.)
Bologna	3¾	2d	S. Marco.
Il Te	2¾		A single house.
Ferrara	2½	3d	I tre Mori.
			For signing every passport at Ferrara the charge is five pauls.
Rovigo	7		La Posta.
Monselice	3½	4th	La Posta.
Dolo	5		La Campana.
Mestrè	4½	5th	La Campana.
Venice	2½	6th	Gran-Bretagna.
Padua	6½		Stella d'Ora.
Vicenza	4½	7th	I Due Rode.
Villa Nuova	4		A single house. (a)
Verona	3½	8th	I Due Torri.
Peschiera	3		Inn bad.
Ponte S. Marco	3½	9th	La Posta, and extravagantly dear.
Brescia	2		I Due Torri.
Antignate	4½	10th	Il Pozzo.
Gorgonzola	4¾		Albergo Grande al Ponte, (a) extravagantly dear.
			Gorgonzola is famous for cheese called Stracchini.
Milan	2	11th	Gran-Bretagna.
Magenta	3½		Albergo Grande.
Novara	3½	12th	I Tre Re.
Vercelli	3½		I Tre Re.
Cigliano	5	13th	La Corona Grossa.
Chivasso	2½		I Due Buovi Rossi.
Torino	3½	14th	La Buona Donna.
S. Ambrogio	4		La Vigna.
Susa	5½	15th	La Posta.*
Lans-le-Bourg	8		Hôtel d'Angleterre.
Modane	2½	16th	Hôtel des Voyageurs.
S. Jean de Maurienne	3½		La Poste.
Aiguebèlle	6	17th	Hôtel de l'Union.
Chavanne	4		A single house. (a)
Chambery	2	18th	La Poste.
Echelles	4½		La Poste.
Pont-de-Beauvoisin	2½	19th	Le Tre Corone.

* Post-horses were put to my landaulet from Susa to the Italian barrier.

CHAPTER VII.

AUSTRIAN DOMINIONS.

VENICE, MILAN, VIENNA, ETC.

Passports—Money of the Imperial Territories—Bankers' accounts—Vienna bank-bills—Price of Post-horses, etc., in the Austrian-German Dominions—Most profitable money Travellers can take from Tuscany to Germany—Persons going from Tuscany to Venice should have their baggage plumbed at Florence—Fees to Custom-house Officers at Bologna and Venice—Price of Apartments at Hotels in Venice—of Dinner—of a Gondola—Wages of a Valet-de-Place—Articles best worth purchasing—Arrival and Departure of Letter-Couriers—Milan—Lodging-houses—Hotels—Job Carriages—Hackney Coaches—Valets-de-Place—Boxes at La Scala—Arrival and Departure of Letter-Couriers—Vienna—Pound weight—Braccio—Charges at Hotels—Price of Dinner at a Table d'Hôte—of Dinner at a Restaurateur's—Wages of a Valet-de-Place—Price per night of one Bed-room at an Inn—Hackney Coaches—Sedan Chairs—Medical Men—Shops—Articles best worth purchasing, and their prices—Expense of going into the Parterre at the Opera-house—Usual Price of a Box—Travellers advised to go Post from Vienna to Dresden—Arrival and Departure of Letter-Couriers—Diligence—Prague—Articles best worth purchasing—Wages of a Valet-de-Place—Price of a Job Carriage—Hackney Coaches.

No Foreigner is allowed to enter the dominions of the Emperor of Austria, without exhibiting a passport, signed by an Austrian Ambassador.

MONEY OF THE IMPERIAL TERRITORIES.

Souverain, florins $6\frac{2}{3}$.
Ducat, florins $4\frac{1}{2}$.
Crown, or piece of two florins and sixteen krëutzers.
Piece of krëutzers 34.
Ditto of krëutzers 18.
Ditto of krëutzers 17.
Piece of one paul, or krëutzers 12.
Ditto of krëutzers 10.
Piece of krëutzers 5.
Ditto of groschen 1, or krëutzers 3.
Ditto of krëutzers 1.
An imperial sequin, and a ducat, generally are synonymous: sometimes, however, an imperial sequin is only four florins and thirty krëutzers: other sequins are four florins and twenty-eight krëutzers. The convention-dollar passes for two florins throughout Germany. Sixty krëutzers make one florin.

Bankers' accounts are kept in florins. It is generally difficult in Germany, to procure much gold or silver, without paying an agio for it; but the Vienna bank-bills, many of which are only five florins each, pass current every where throughout the imperial territories, and are always readily changed into silver.

PRICE OF POST-HORSES IN THE AUSTRIAN-GERMAN DOMINIONS.

The price of draught-horses throughout the Austrian dominions, and other parts of Germany, is fixed in the different monies of the respective countries.

A German post is, generally speaking, about two German miles; and one German mile is about four English miles and a half.

In Austria and Bohemia (according to the tariff), draught-horses are charged at thirty-five kreutzers each, per mile:* and the legal claim of Postillions is as follows:

No. of horses.	SINGLE POST.		POST AND A HALF.		DOUBLE POST.	
	Florins.	Kreutzers.	Florins.	Kreutzers.	Florins.	Kreutzers.
2	0	30	0	45	1	0
3	0	45	1	0	1	30
4	1	0	1	30	2	0
6	1	30	2	15	3	0

A German Postillion, like those of France and Italy, expects more than his legal claim; and seems to think he has a right to as much per post for himself, as Postmasters charge per horse: indeed, if he drive three horses, he expects to receive, per post, one third more than the price for each horse.

The expense of greasing wheels, if grease be found by the Traveller, is from ten to seventeen kreutzers; and Travellers are obliged to pay for greasing their wheels at every third post.

A carriage conveying but two persons, and but one trunk, is allowed to travel with two horses only; and carriages with four inside places, and two trunks, are seldom compelled to travel with more than four horses.

In the Empire, the price of every draught-horse is from one florin and fifteen kreutzers, to one florin and thirty kreutzers a post; and the price for greasing wheels is twelve kreutzers.

A *Calèche de Poste*, furnished by a Post-master, costs, in the Empire, twenty kreutzers per station.

Persons who intend travelling from Rome through Florence, to Venice, and thence to Vienna, or any other part of Germany under Austrian government, should provide themselves, at Rome, with as many Napoleons as they may be likely to want between that city and the confines of Germany: and they should also endeavour to purchase, of the money-changers at Florence, souverains and imperial sequins sufficient for the imperial dominions in Germany.

From the commencement of Saxony to the town of Hamburgh, Napoleons are the most profitable money for Travellers.

Persons going from Tuscany to Venice, should have their baggage plumbed at Florence; which operation usually costs about five pauls.

At the gate of Bologna the Custom-house Officers expect a present of five pauls per carriage; and at Ferrara, on quitting the town, Travellers are expected to make the same present.

VENICE.

Good apartments, containing from six to eight beds, cannot usually be procured, either at The Gran-Bretagna, or The Europa, for less than a Napoleon per night. Breakfast, for masters, costs two francs a head—dinner, five

---

* Travellers are sometimes compelled to pay more.

francs—and the charge, per head, for servants, by the day, is six francs.

A gondola, with only one gondoliere, costs four francs per day; and contains, in its cabin, four persons; who may secure themselves from rain; these boats being conveniently fitted up with glasses and Venetian-blinds: they are likewise furnished with handsome lanterns at night.

The wages of a *Valet-de-place* is from four to five francs a day.

The articles best worth purchasing at Venice are, gold chains, seals, etc., sold by weight, according to the price of gold—necklaces, and other personal ornaments, made with very small beads of various colours—wax candles—Mocha coffee—chocolate—books, and maps.

ARRIVAL AND DEPARTURE OF LETTER COURIERS.

Sunday, at eight in the morning, arrives the Courier from Padua—*at ten* arrive letters from Vienna, Trieste, etc.; Milan, Verona, Mantua, Brescia, Piedmont, Genoa, Switzerland, France, Spain, Great Britain, and the kingdom of the Netherlands.

Monday, at eight in the morning, arrive letters from Padua, Vicenza, etc.—*at ten* from Vienna—and *at four in the afternoon* from Milan, Brescia, Verona, France, Switzerland, Spain, Great Britain, the kingdom of the Netherlands, the Tyrol, Germany, Ferrara, the Ecclesiastical State, the kingdom of Naples, and the Duchy of Modena.

Tuesday, at eight in the morning, arrive letters from Padua, Vicenza, etc., and *at ten* from Vienna, Milan, Mantua, etc., and Tuscany.

Wednesday, at eight in the morning, arrive letters from Padua—and *at ten* from Vienna, Trieste, Milan, Verona, etc., Genoa, and Piedmont.

Thursday, at eight in the morning, arrive letters from Padua, and Rovigo—*at ten* from Vienna, Milan, Verona, etc.; France, Switzerland, Spain, Great Britain, and the kingdom of the Netherlands—and *at four in the afternoon* from Ferrara, the Ecclesiastical State, Naples, and Modena.

Friday, at eight in the morning, arrive letters from Padua—and *at ten* from Vienna, Trieste, etc.; Milan, Mantua, etc.; Tuscany, the Tyrol, and Germany.

Saturday, at eight in the morning, arrive letters from Padua—and *at ten* from Vienna, and Milan.

Sunday, at three in the afternoon, go letters for Vienna, Mestrè, Treviso, etc.; Trieste, Milan, Verona, Vicenza, etc.—and *at five in the afternoon* for Padua.

Monday, at three in the afternoon, go letters for Milan, Padua, Vicenza, Verona, etc.—and *at six in the afternoon* for Vienna, and the intermediate cities.

Tuesday, at noon, go letters for Ferrara, the Ecclesiastical State, Naples, and Modena—*at three in the afternoon* for Vienna, and Milan—and *at six in the afternoon* for Padua.

Wednesday, at six in the afternoon, go letters for Milan, Verona, Mantua, Parma, Piacenza, Tuscany, Brescia, Bergamo, Piedmont, Genoa, Switzerland, France, Spain, Portugal, Great Britain, the kingdom of the Netherlands, the Tyrol, Hamburgh and Germany, Vienna, Mestrè, Treviso, etc.; Trieste, and Padua.

Thursday, at three in the afternoon, go letters for Vienna, Milan, etc.—and *at six in the afternoon,* for Padua.

Friday, at noon, go letters for Padua, Ferrara, the Ecclesiastical State, Naples, and Modena—*at three in the afternoon* for Milan, Vicenza, Verona, etc.—and *at six in the evening* for Vienna, Mestrè, Treviso, etc., and Trieste.

Saturday, at half-past eight in the evening, go letters for the Ecclesiastical State, Naples, Milan, Verona, Mantua, Parma, Piacenza, Tuscany, Brescia, Bergamo, Piedmont, Genoa, Switzerland, France, Spain, Portugal, Great Britain, the kingdom of the Netherlands, the Tyrol, Hamburgh, and Germany; Padua, Treviso, Vienna, and Trieste.

The Post-office is always open from eight in the morning till five in the afternoon; and, on some days of the week, till a later hour.

MILAN.

Lodging-houses in this city are numerous, and not very high priced. Hotels are expensive. A job carriage usually costs from fifteen to sixteen francs per day; and the price of Hackney coaches is the same as at Paris. A *Valet-de-Place,* if hired for a very short time, and expected to act as a *Cicerone,* commonly demands five francs per day: and the expense of a good box, large enough to accommodate four persons, at *La Scala,* on Sundays, seldom amounts to less than from twenty-five to thirty francs, entrance-money inclusive; which is one franc and a half per head; but, on other days, a box may frequently be hired for ten francs. The price per head for admittance to the *Parterre* is one franc and a half.

ARRIVAL AND DEPARTURE OF LETTER-COURIERS.

Sunday, *arrive letters from* Switzerland.

Monday, *from* Genoa, Great Britain, France, Spain, Portugal, Turin, Venice, Germany, and other parts of northern Europe.

Tuesday, *from* Naples, Rome, Tuscany, Switzerland, etc.

Wednesday, *from* Genoa, Great Britain, etc., as on Monday.

Friday, *from* Genoa, Great Britain, etc., as on Monday—and *from* Tuscany, Rome, Naples, Venice, Germany, other parts of northern Europe, and Switzerland.

Saturday, *from* Switzerland, and the kingdom of the Netherlands.

Sunday, *at eleven in the morning, go letters* for Switzerland, and the kingdom of the Netherlands.

Monday, *at six in the afternoon,* for Venice, etc.—*at nine in the evening* for Genoa, Spain, etc.—and *at ten* for Turin, France, Great Britain, etc.

Tuesday, *at eleven in the morning,* for Switzerland.

Wednesday, *at one in the afternoon,* for Switzerland, and the kingdom of the Netherlands—*at six in the afternoon* for Venice, Germany, and other parts of northern Europe—*at nine in the evening* for Florence, Rome, Naples, Genoa, etc.—and *at ten* for Turin, France, Great Britain, etc., as on Monday.

Thursday, for Switzerland.

Saturday, *at nine in the even-*

ing, for Genoa, etc., as on Monday—and *at ten* for Venice, Germany, and other parts of northern Europe; Florence, Rome, Naples, Turin, France, Great Britain, etc., as on Wednesday.

The Post-Office is *opened*, at nine in the morning, every Monday, Tuesday, and Wednesday—at eleven every Thursday—and at nine, every Friday, Saturday, and Sunday: and it is *shut*, at six in the evening, every Monday—at nine, every Tuesday—at ten, every Wednesday and Saturday—at three, every Thursday and Sunday—and at nine, every Friday.

VIENNA.

The pound-weight at Vienna is eighteen ounces; and the common measure, called a *braccio*, is somewhat longer than that of Florence.

At one of the best Hotels in Vienna, I paid for six rooms, and dinner for three persons, linen, bread, beer, and table wine* inclusive, eighteen florins per day.

The price of dinner at a *Table d'Hôte*, varies from thirty-four krëutzers to a crown per head; and the price of dinner at a *Restaurateur's*, varies from five krëutzers to one florin per head.

A *Valet-de-Place* usually expects from thirty-four krëutzers to one florin per day.

It is seldom possible at Vienna, to procure a bed-room at any inn for less than one florin per night. There are in this city, excellent Hackney coaches to be hired by the hour; and good sedan chairs, into which the sick cannot be admitted. There likewise are several good physicians and surgeons.

The shops at Vienna are richly furnished; and the articles best worth purchasing seem to be, eyder-down, black lace, furs, household linen, Bohemian kerseymere, and broad cloth. Eyderdown is usually sold at nine florins the pound. Broad black lace costs from three to five pauls the *braccio*; kerseymere, if dyed in grain, three florins and three quarters the *braccio*; if not so dyed, three florins and one quarter only.

The usual price in the *parterre* at the opera-house is one florin; but, upon extraordinary occasions, two; the usual price of a box one ducat; but upon extraordinary occasions, two.

It is not pleasant to travel *en voiturier* from Vienna to Dresden; because the Post-masters between the above-named cities are so spiteful to *Voituriers* that the latter can neither procure extra horses, nor other necessary accommodations on the road.

ARRIVAL AND DEPARTURE OF LETTER-COURIERS.

Monday morning arrives the post from Italy, Spain, France, and Great Britain.

Tuesday morning from Saxony, and the northern countries.

Thursday morning from Italy.

Saturday morning from Saxony.

Monday afternoon at three o'clock, goes the post to Italy.

---

* Travellers should endeavour to procure old Austrian wine, which is more wholesome than are the common wines of Hungary. The Germans, if report speak true, frequently put a poisonous metallic substance into their white wines, particularly those of the Rhine.

Wednesday evening to Saxony, and the northern countries; Spain, France, and Great Britain.

Thursday evening to Italy.

Saturday evening to Spain, France, and Great Britain.

The posts of the Imperial German Dominions arrive and depart daily.

A Diligence sets out for Presburgh at eight o'clock every morning; another, for Italy, at half-past seven every Monday morning; and another for Prague and Dresden, at nine o'clock every Tuesday morning. One place in a German Diligence usually costs about thirty krëutzers per German mile.

PRAGUE.

The articles best worth purchasing here are, Silesia lawns, table-linen, Bohemian lustres, and other kinds of glass.

The wages usually demanded by a *Valet-de-place* is thirty-four krëutzers a day; and the price of a job-carriage two florins and thirty krëutzers a day.

There are good Hackney coaches in this city.

CHAPTER VIII.

DRESDEN, HAMBURGH, BERLIN, ETC.

Money of Saxony—Price of Post-horses—Dresden—Pound-weight—Common measure—Price of Apartments in the principal Hotels—Price of Dinner at Hotels, and at the houses of Restaurateurs—Wages of a Valet-de-Place—Price of Job Carriages, Sedan Chairs, Wine, and Bottled Beer—Articles best worth purchasing—Arrival and Departure of Letter-Couriers—Expense of franking letters for England—Diligence—Hamburgh—Money, Bankers' accounts, etc.—Pound-weight—Price per head for Dinner at a Table d'Hôte—Price of Claret—Cambrick the article best worth purchasing—Price of Post-horses, etc. in the Dominions of Prussia, Hesse, Brunswick, and Hanover—Roads in northern Germany—Wienerwagens—Marktschiffs—Private Vessels—Voyage from Frankfort on the Mein to Cologne—Ditto from Ratisbon to Vienna—Route from Hamburgh to Berlin—Population of that city, and objects best worth notice—Theatres, Clubs, etc.—Promenades—Hotels and Lodging-houses—Wages of a Valet-de-Place—Job Carriages—Hackney Coaches—Price of Dinner at a Restaurateur's—Environs—Route from Hamburgh to Leipsic—Population of Leipsic—Objects best worth notice—Promenades—Prices at the German Theatre—Best Inns—Fairs—Prices at Inns—Wages of a Valet-de-Place—Job Carriages, and Hacks—Route from Leipsic to Dresden—from Leipsic through Gotha to Frankfort on the Mein—from Leipsic to Brunswick—from Brunswick to Hanover—from Hanover to Gottingen—from Leipsic to Danzick—from Frankfort on the Mein to Augsburgh—from Augsburgh to Constance, Schaffausen, and Basle—from Augsburgh to Ratisbon—from Ratisbon to Munich—from Ratisbon to Prague—and from Vienna through Ratisbon and Brussels to Ostend—Packets from Colchester to Ostend; from Ostend to Harwich; and from Ostend to Margate—Route from Frankfort on the Meine through Cassel to Munster—Voyage on the Rhine from Mayence to Coblentz—Excursion from Gottingen to Harz—German Baths—Carlsbad—Expenses there—Pyrmont—Expenses there—Spa—Expenses there—Route from Vienna to Carlsbad, through Eger and Zwoda—from Hanover to Pyrmont—from Hamburgh to Pyrmont—from Brussels, through Aix-la-Chapelle and Liege, to Spa—from Vienna to Baaden—from Vienna to Presburgh—from Teusch Altenburg to Belgrade—from Presburgh to Kaschau and Tokay—and from Vienna to Trieste.

MONEY OF SAXONY.

Ducat.....................worth florins 4¾
Crown, or convention dollar......florins 2
Florin.........................groschen 16
Half-florin....................groschen 8
Quarter-florin.................groschen 4
Piece of groschen two, marked........"12" that number of these pieces making one dollar.*
Piece of groschen one, marked........"24" that number of these pieces making one dollar.
Piece of half a grosch, marked........"48" that number of these pieces making one dollar.
Piece of three pfennings.
Piece of one pfenning.

Bankers' accounts are kept in dollars and groschen; the former being an imaginary coin, worth one florin and a half.

Spanish dollars do not pass here.

PRICE OF POST-HORSES, ETC. IN SAXONY.

For every draught-horse the charge is ten groschen per mile; and every postillion, driving three or four horses, has a right to eight groschen. Couriers, whether travelling in a carriage or on horseback, pay twelve groschen a mile.

* These are not convention dollars, but those in which Bankers' accounts are kept.

Two persons, if travelling in their own carriage, are obliged to take three horses; but, if travelling in a Post-master's carriage, not more than two horses. The charge for a Post-master's carriage is four groschen per mile; and the charge for greasing wheels from three to four groschen.

DRESDEN.

The pound weight of Dresden is sixteen ounces; the aune, or common measure, two feet; and the foot twelve inches.

The best apartments in the principal Hotels usually let for one ducat per day; and dinner, in these hotels, is commonly charged at one florin per head; though Travellers may be tolerably well served at twelve groschen. *Restaurateurs* give good dinners at eight groschen per head.

The wages of a *Valet-de place* is one florin per day.

A job carriage, for the whole day, costs about three florins; for the half day, two florins and four groschen.

The price of a Sedan chair, in the old Town, is two groschen for going to any part of it; and two for returning: in the new Town exactly double; and the chairmen charge one grosch for every quarter of an hour when they are kept waiting.

Wine of the country is usually charged at ten groschen per bottle; and bottled beer at two groschen and six pfennings.

The articles best worth purchasing in this city are black and white lace, which may be bought of the Lace-makers.

ARRIVAL AND DEPARTURE OF LETTER-COURIERS.

Sunday afternoon arrive letters from Vienna, Prague, etc.; and likewise from Great Britain, France, Holland, Hamburgh, Amsterdam, Belgium, Hanover, Brunswick, etc.

Tuesday morning, from Italy, the Tyrol, Switzerland, etc.

Wednesday afternoon, from Vienna, Prague, etc.

Thursday afternoon, from Holland, Belgium, Hamburgh, etc.

Sunday morning, at eight o'clock, the post goes to Hamburgh, with letters for Great Britain, etc.

Monday afternoon, at three o'clock, to Holland and Belgium; and *at six,* to Prague, Vienna, etc.; Venice, Italy in general, and Switzerland.

Wednesday, at noon, to Holland, France, Denmark, etc.

Friday, at one in the afternoon, to Prague, Vienna, etc.

Letters must be sent to the post one hour, and parcels two hours, before the Courier sets out. Letters for Great Britain pay eight groschen each.

Wednesday morning, at eight o'clock, the Diligence sets out for Prague and Vienna; and Thursday morning, at the same hour, for Hamburgh.

HAMBURGH.

Accounts are kept in marks and skillings; a mark being from sixteen to eighteen pence, English, according to the exchange; and a skilling the sixteenth of a mark. Convention-dollars do not pass for quite two florins at

Hamburgh; no money being current but that of Hamburgh and Denmark.

The pound weight is sixteen ounces.

Several of the Inns contain a *Table d'Hôte*, at which the price, per head, for dinner, is from twelve skillings to two marks.

Claret is good and cheap; being usually sold at two marks a bottle.

Almost every article of commerce may be purchased at Hamburgh; but, though exempt from Port-duties, things in general are dear, cambrick excepted.

PRUSSIAN DOMINIONS.

Persons who travel post usually pay ten groschen per German mile for every draught-horse; and at Berlin one mile more than the actual distance is charged, it being a post royal. The Wagenmeister, or Superintendant of post-carriages, has a right to four groschen at every post; and Postillions are entitled to three groschen per mile. The price for greasing wheels is four groschen in Capital Cities, and other large towns; but, in Villages, only two groschen.

A light carriage, containing only two places, is allowed to travel with only two horses, provided it convey but one person and one trunk: if it convey two persons, they must take three horses; and carriages conveying three or four persons must have four horses. Every Berlin, or carriage with four inside places, must have four horses; and if it contain four persons, five horses; but if it contain from five to seven persons, six horses are indispensable: and if, moreover, it be heavily charged with baggage, Post-masters are authorized to put on eight horses.

The price of a *Calèche de Poste*, furnished by a Post-master, is six groschen per station.

Postillions are obliged to drive one German mile an hour on well-paved roads; one mile in an hour and a quarter on good roads not paved; and one mile within an hour and a half where the road is sandy.

On quitting Berlin every Traveller should have a passport from Government, which the *Wagenmeister* commonly procures. Travellers should likewise have their trunks plumbed.

HESSE.

Persons who travel post pay ten groschen per German mile for every draught-horse; and for Couriers' horses twelve groschen. If the post be from two miles and a half to three miles in distance, the postillion is entitled to eight groschen, provided he drive three or four horses; and he is entitled to ten groschen, provided there be six horses. If the length of the post be from one mile and a half to two miles only, and the Postillion drive three or four horses, he is entitled to six groschen; and provided there be six horses, he is entitled to eight groschen.

The legal claim of the *Wagenmeister* at each station, is two groschen; and the charge for greasing wheels from three to four groschen.

BRUNSWICK.

Persons who travel post pay twelve groschen per German mile for every draught-horse.

A Berlin conveying six persons,

servants inclusive, together with trunks not exceeding three quintals in weight, is allowed to travel with only four horses. A post-chaise conveying four persons, servants inclusive, is allowed to travel with only three horses; and if it convey but three persons, it is allowed to travel with only two horses.

HANOVER.

Persons who travel post pay twelve groschen per German mile for every draught-horse.

A postillion who drives two or three horses is entitled to six groschen; if he drive four horses, his claim is eight groschen; and he is entitled to sixteen groschen provided there be six horses: but, if a post be uncommonly long, namely, from four to five miles in distance, he is entitled to seven groschen, provided he drive two or three horses; nine, if he drive four horses; and eighteen, if there be six horses.

The *Wagenmeister's* claim is from three to six groschen per post; and the expense of greasing wheels, from three to four groschen.

In Hanover, the old Louis passes for only four crowns and sixteen groschen in paying either the post or the tolls; but is current for five crowns in paying for grease, *Tringeld* (drink-money), and expenses at inns.

The roads in the north of Germany are, generally speaking, bad; and the *mélange* of territories is an obstacle to their improvement: moreover, the distances from place to place are not determined with precision; and therefore Post-masters sometimes exact.

There is a kind of carriage, half open, and containing four persons, to which, if it be not encumbered with much baggage, Post-masters have no right to put more than two horses, except in the Hanoverian territories. This carriage is called a Wienerwagen.

The noble rivers which intersect Germany render travelling by water practicable and pleasant; there being, on many of these rivers, Marktschiffs (a sort of *Coche-d'eau*), which travel regularly from city to city.

Private vessels likewise may be procured.

The voyage from Frankfort on the Mein to Cologne is delightful; as is that from Ratisbon to Vienna.*

ROUTE FROM HAMBURG TO BERLIN.

1½ Eschenburgh
2 Boitzenburgh
1½ Lubthen
2¼ Lenzen——This town is charmingly situated. A ferry over the Elbe.
1½ Perleberg
1 Kleezke
1½ Kyritz
2 Fehrbellin
2 Bootzo
1½ *Berlin.*
———
16¾ posts.

Berlin, the metropolis of Prussia, and one of the most splendid cities in Germany, is watered by the Spree, and supposed to contain (including its garrison) one hundred and fifty-one thousand inhabitants. Some of the objects best worth notice here are—*The Château Royal — Monbijou — the Royal Stables — the Arsenal,* deemed the finest building of its kind in Europe; its Court con-

---

* A *Coche-d'eau* goes every Sunday from Ratisbon, and arrives at Vienna in three days, or three and a half. The passage-money, for a gentleman or lady, is a ducat; and for a servant, a convention dollar.

tains twenty-one masks, representing Death, by Schluter; and the Statue of Frederick I. is by Schluter and Jacobi—*the Italian Opera House*, which contains five thousand spectators—*the Royal Library*, built after the design of Frederick II.—*the buildings of the Royal Academy*—*the Theatre and Churches in the Place des Gens-d'armes*—*the Hôtel de Ville*—*the Bank*—*the Governor's Palace*—*L'Hôtel des Cadets*—*L'Hôtel des Invalides*—*the Palaces of Prince Henry, the Prince Royal, Prince Louis of Prussia, etc.*—*the Cathedral*—*the Church of S. Hedewige*—*the Church belonging to the Garrison*, and containing four pictures by Rhode, which represent the death of four celebrated Prussian Warriors—*the Church of S. Peter*—*the Church of S. Mary, and its Gothic Tower*—*the Church of S. Nicholas*, remarkable for its antiquity, paintings, and sculpture; and likewise for the monument of Puffendorff—*the Churches of S. Sophia and S. Dorothy*, the latter of which contains the monument of Count de Mark—*the Parochial Church*—*the Place de Guillaume*, ornamented with statues—*the colossal equestrian Statue of the Elector Frederick-William*, deemed the *chef-d'œuvre* of Schluter—*the Pont Royal*—*the magnificent Brandenburgh Gate*, built after the model of the Propylæum at Athens—*the Porcelain Manufactory*—and *the Iron Foundery*.

To the Italian Opera the audience are admitted gratis; Foreigners being placed in the second and third row of boxes.—At the Buffa Opera and the German Theatre, the price for each place in the first row of boxes is sixteen groschen; in the second row, twelve groschen; in the parquet, twelve groschen; in the amphitheatre, eight groschen; and in the gallery, four groschen.

Clubs, called *Resources*, and the Fishery at Stralau, on the 24th of August, serve to diversify the amusements of this city.

The principal Promenades are under the Lime-trees—the Place de Guillaume—the Place de Doehnhof—the Park—Le Cercle—Bellevue—the Garden of the Royal School—and the Coffee and Lemonade Gardens.

Here are three classes of Hotels, in the first of which may be placed *La Ville de Paris*—*L'Aigle d'Or*—*La Ville de Rome*—*Le Cerf d'Or*—and *L'Hôtel de Russie*.* A tariff, exhibiting the prices at these hotels (which prices are fixed by government), is open to the inspection of every Traveller. Ready-furnished lodgings are advertised in the newspaper; and the rent of two rooms in a good situation is from eight to twelve crowns per month.

The wages of a *Valet-de-Place* is twelve groschen a day, provided he be kept no longer than eight o'clock in the evening: and sixteen groschen if he remain beyond that hour.

The price of a job carriage is two crowns a day; and the fare in a hackney coach from six to eight groschen, according to the distance.

Restaurateurs charge for dinner from six to twelve groschen per head.

The environs of Berlin contain several objects worth notice; a-

---

* This is an excellent Inn, and contains a good *Table d'Hôte*.

mong which is *Sans Souci;* where the Gallery of Paintings exhibits a sketch of Moses, by Rembrandt — Roman Filial Piety, by Guercino — the four Evangelists, by Vandyck — and Venus attired by the Graces, together with the Judgment of Paris, by Rubens.

Persons who like water-parties, may go in boats to Treptow, Charlottenburg, etc.

ROUTE FROM HAMBURGH TO LEIPSIC.

- 7½ Lenzen
- 1½ Arendsee
- 1 Osterburgh
- 1½ Stendal — *The Cathedral of S. Nicholas* merits notice.
- 1½ Burgstall
- 1 Magdeburgh — This city is supposed to contain 36,000 inhabitants. Best hotels, *L'Auberge d'Allmer,* and *Le Roi de Prusse.*
- 1 Salze
- 1 Kalbe
- 1½ Cöethen
- 1 Zoerbig
- 1 Landsberg
- 1½ *Leipzig.*

20½ posts.

This town is supposed to contain above 32,000 inhabitants. The objects best worth notice are — *The Pleissenbourg* — *the Paulinum* — *the College of the Princes,* and *the Red College* — *the ancient Arsenal* — *the Hôtel de Ville* — *the Cour d'Auerbach* in Fair time — *the Exchange* — *the College of S. Thomas* — *the Manège* — *the Theatre* — *the Churches of S. Nicholas and S. Thomas* — *the House of Mr. Muller,* which contains thirteen ceilings by Oeser — *the Esplanade* — and *the Public Libraries.*

The Promenades are numerous and pleasant. The prices at the German Theatre are, for a box in the first row, four crowns; in the second row three crowns; in the third row, eight bons-groschen; and, for a place in the *parterre,* six bons groschen; unless it be Fair time, when something more is paid.

The three Fairs are held at Christmas, Easter, and Michaelmas; and at these Fairs as many books are said to be sold yearly as amount to 500,000 rix-dollars.

The principal inns are — *L'Hôtel de Saxe* — *L'Hôtel de Bavière* — and *L'Ange Bleu.*

The price of a front room, fuel inclusive, at an Inn, is one florin per day; and of a back room, eight bons-groschen. The wages of a *Valet-de-Place* is one florin per day; unless it be during Fair time, when he expects a crown. Job carriages and common hacks may always be found before the Gates of S. Pierre and Grimma.

Leipsic will henceforth be memorable for having given its name to one of the most important modern battles ever fought — a battle in which near half a million of men, commanded by three Emperors, a King, and an Heir-apparent to a throne, were engaged during little less than a hundred hours — they fought in a circle embracing above fifteen miles.

ROUTE FROM LEIPSIC TO DRESDEN.

- 1½ Wurzen — *The Cathedral* here merits notice.
- 1 Wernsdorf
- 1 Stauchitz
- 1½ Meissen — Best inn, *Le Soleil d'Or.*
- 1½ *Dresden.*

6½ posts.

ROUTE FROM LEIPSIC THROUGH GOTHA, TO FRANKFORT ON THE MEIN.

- 1 Lützen — Near this small town is the spot on which Gustavus Adolphus perished; and a stone marks the spot where this hero's body was found.
  Charles XII., being in the neighbourhood of Lützen, went to visit the field of battle; little thinking, perhaps, that treachery would soon de-

stroy his life, as it did that of his glorious model, Gustavus.

1 *Weissenfels*—The *Castle* here and its *Church* merit notice.

1 *Naumburgh*—The *Cathedral* here merits notice. Best inns, The Post-house, and *Le Cheval*. The wine of this neighbourhood resembles Burgundy.

1 *Auerstadt*—Between Naumburgh and Auerstadt the road traverses the mountain of Kœsen.

1½ *Weimar*

1½ *Erfurt*—This city is enriched with a University.

1½ *Gotha*—The inhabitants of Gotha are estimated at 11,000. The *Château*—the great *Terrace*—the *Arsenal*—the churches called *Kloster* and *Neumarkts Kirchen*—the *English Garden*—the *public Library* and that of the *Sovereign*—the *Royal Collection of Paintings*, etc.—and the *Gymnasium*, merit notice.

Best inns, *Le Nègre*, and *Le Grelot d'Argent*.

The road to Gotha is execrable in wet weather.

1½ Eisenach—*La Klemme* is a good inn. The Castle of Wartbourg, which stands on the summit of a hill in this vicinity, once served as an asylum to Luther.

1 Berka—A bad road from Eisenach to Berka.

1 Wach—Pavement from Berka hither.

1½ Hunefeld

1 Fulde—This city contains 12,000 inhabitants. The objects best worth notice are, the *Château*—the *Cathedral*—the *Churches of S. Boniface* and *S. Michael*—the *Convent of S. Sauveur*—the *Benedictine* and *Franciscan Convents*—the *Porcelain Manufacture*, and the *Library belonging to the University*.

The celebrated Baths of Bruckenau are near Fulde.

Best inns, The Post-house, and *Le Cigne*. The wine of S. John's mountain, in this neighbourhood, is excellent, and sold in sealed bottles out of the Prince Bishop's cellar.

1 Neuhof

½ Schlüchtern

1 Saalmünster

1 Gelnhausen—*Le Soleil* is a good inn.

1½ Hanau—A pretty town. The Castle merits notice.

1 Frankfort.

20½ posts.

The inhabitants of Frankfort are estimated at 43,000, beside near 7,000 Jews, who live detached from the rest of the people.

The objects best worth notice in this city are —*the Cathedral—the Church of S. Catherine—the Convent des Prédicateurs*, containing a celebrated Assumption, by Albert Durer—*the Hôtel de Ville—the Teutonic Palace—the Palace of the Prince of Thurn and Taxis—the Exchange—the Arsenals—the Foundery—the Hôtel Dieu—the Maison de Force—the Hospital of S. Esprit—the Theatre*—and *the Bridge*, thrown over the Mein.

Inns— *La Cour d'Angleterre—La Maison Rouge—Le Cygne Blanc*, etc.

Frankfort Fair is held twice a year; namely, at Easter, and during the latter end of Summer.

ROUTE FROM LEIPSIC TO BRUNSWICK.

1½ Groskugel

1¼ Halle—Inns, *L'Anneau d'Or—Prince Royal de Prusse—Lion d'Or*. Among the objects best worth notice here are *the Cathedral* and *the University*.

1½ Könnern

1½ Aschersleben—*The Church of S. Etienne—the Public School—and the Ruins of the Château d'Ascanie*, merit notice.

1 Quedlinburgh—*The Château—the Library*—and the Promenade called *Le Bruhl*, merit notice.

1 Halberstadt

1½ Roklum

1½ *Brunswick*.

11 posts.

Brunswick is supposed to contain 28,000 inhabitants. The objects best worth attention in this city are—*the Castle*, called *Grauen Hof—the New Hôtel de Ville — the Most-Haus*, in the Square, before which is an antique Statue of a Lion—*the Buildings of Carolinum—the Opera-house—the Cathedral—the Hospitals—the Fountain, in the Place de Hegenmarkt—the Church of S. Nicholas*, which contains two good pictures—*the Churches of S. Catherine* and *S. Andrew—the Old Hôtel de Ville—the Royal Collection of Natural History, Paintings*, etc.—and *the Carolinum Library*.

Brunswick is famous for a sort of beer called *Mumme.*

Best inn—*L'Hôtel d'Angleterre.*

At Wolfenbuttel, near this city, there is a valuable Library; and at the *Château de Salzdahlum* a good collection of Pictures.

ROUTE FROM BRUNSWICK TO HANOVER.

1½ Peine
1 Sehnde
1 Hanover.
———
3½ posts.

This city contains about 18,000 inhabitants; and the objects best worth notice are—*the Church belonging to the Château—the Opera-house—the Royal Stables—the Maison des États—the Arsenal—the Mint—the Cannon Foundery—the Monument of Werlhof,* in the public Cemetery—*the Monument of Leibnitz*—and *the Royal Library.* The principal Promenades are—the Countess of Yarmouth's Garden—Ellernreid Wood—Count Walmoden's Garden—and the drive to Herrnhausen, and Mont Brillant.

Best Inns—*La Taverne de Londres—Prince d'Eutin—*and *La Maison de Strelitz.*

ROUTE FROM HANOVER TO GOTTINGEN.

1 Tielenwiesen—This road is excellent.
1 Bruggen
1½ Eimbeck.
1 Nordheim—A famous Organ in the parochial Church.
1 *Gottingen.*
———
5½ posts.

The city contains near 8,000 inhabitants. The objects best worth notice are—*the six Churches—the Buildings of the University—the Observatory—the Lying-in Hospital—the Anatomical Theatre—the Botanic Garden—the Manège,* and *the Library belonging to the University.* This Library contains above 120,000 volumes, and is deemed the best in Germany.

Inns—*La Couronne—Le Roi de Prusse,* etc.

The environs of Gottingen are interesting; and especially so is the excursion to Hartz.

ROUTE FROM LEIPSIC TO DANTZICK.

Miles.
3 Torgau—The principal Church here contains the Tomb of Catherine a Boria, Luther's wife.
1½ Herzberg
1 Hohenbuckau
1 Luckau
1 Lubben
1½ Liberosa
1 Beeschow
1 Mühlrose
1½ *Frankfort on the Oder*—This city contains 12,000 inhabitants; and among the objects best worth notice are *the Churches of S. Mary* and *S. Nicholas—the Chartreuse—the Hôtel de Ville—the Casernes—the Hôtel Dieu—the Bridge—the Monument of Prince Leopold of Brunswick,* who was drowned in the Oder, by attempting to save the lives of others—and *the Monument of Kleist,* the Poet.

There is a University here: and among the best inns are, *Les Trois Couronnes, L'Aigle Noir,* and *Le Soleil d'Or.*

2 Custrin
2½ Neudamm
3½ Soldin
3½ Pyritz
3 *Stargard—The Church of S. Mary,* in this town, merits notice. The best inn is *Les Trois Couronnes,* near the Post-house.
2½ Massow
3 Neugard
2½ Plathow
2¼ Pinnow
2¾ Leppin
2¼ Coerlin
3¼ Cöeslin
3¼ Pankenin
3¼ Schlave
3¼ Stolpe—Famous for the amber found in its vicinity.
3½ Lupow
5 Godentau
3¾ Neustadt
3¾ Katz
3¼ Dantzig.
———
75 miles.

This city contains 48,000 inhabitants; and among the objects best worth notice are—*the Ex-*

change—the *Cathedral*, which is one of the finest churches in Europe—the *Lutheran College*—the *Hôtel de Ville*—the *Cour des Nobles*—the *Arsenal*—and the *Junker-Garten*.

Inns—*La Maison Anglaise*—*Les Trois Nègres*, etc.

ROUTE FROM FRANKFORT ON THE MEIN TO AUGSBURG.

Posts.
1 Hanau—Philipsruhe and Wilhelmsbad, in this neighbourhood, merit notice.
1½ Dettingen—Memorable for the battle of 1743.
½ Aschaffenburg
1 Obernburg
1 Milenburg
1 Hundheim
1 Bischofsheim
1 Mergentheim
1½ Blaufelden
1½ Crailsheim—Famous for its China Manufacture and mineral waters.
1 Dünkelsbühl—The Church of the Carmelites, in this town, is adorned with a fine picture.
1½ Nördlingen—A Crucifix, attributed to Buonaroti, and an excellent Painting by Albert Durer, embellish the principal Church here.
1½ Donauwörth
1½ Meidingen
1½ *Augsburgh*.
___
18½ posts.

Augsburgh, formerly denominated *Augusta Vindelicorum*, the largest city in Swabia, and supposed to be the most ancient, is seated between the rivers Lech and Wertach, and contains 36,000 inhabitants. The objects best worth notice are *the Cathedral*, which comprises twenty-four chapels; and is adorned with a celebrated picture of the Resurrection, by Zoll—the *Abbey of S. Ulric*—the *Church of S. Anne*—the *Hôtel de Ville*—the *Tower of Perlach*—the *Arsenal*—the *House of Correction*—the *Gate called Einlass*—the *public Fountains*—some *private houses*, which contain antique paintings in fresco—and *the Libraries* belonging to the Cathedral and S. Ulric; the latter of which possesses the drawings and sketches of Albert Durer.

Augsburgh exhibits vestiges of Roman Antiquities.

Les Trois Maures has been already mentioned as the best inn; *L'Agneau blanc*, in the Faubourg, likewise merits recommendation.

ROUTE FROM AUGSBURGH TO CONSTANCE, SCHAFFHAUSEN, AND BASLE.

1½ Schwabmünchen
1½ Mindelheim
1½ Memmingen
1½ Wurzach
½ Woltek
½ Ravensberg
1 Stadelle—The first view of the Lake of Constance is enchanting.
1 Moersburg
1 *Constance*—Travellers who pursue this route cross the Lake to Constance; and for a four-oared boat, large enough to convey a carriage, the common price is from three to four florins, together with about thirty kreutzers to the boatmen for drink-money.

The *Cathedral* at Constance is a fine edifice; and its doors merit observation.

The principal inn is *L'Aigle d'Or*.

Travellers should visit the Island of Meinau.

1 Zell
½ Singen—Near this place, on the summit of a rock, originally volcanic, is the Castle of Hohentwiel, which belongs to the Sovereign of Wurtemberg, and now serves as a State-prison.
1 *Schaffhausen*—The bridge here, constructed by a common carpenter, named Grubenmann, once merited observation; but the ruthless hand of war has destroyed it. *The public Libraries* deserve notice.

About one league from Schaffhausen, on the way to Zurich, is the celebrated *Fall of the Rhine*: and Travellers who wish to see the terrestrial rainbows which this stupendous Cataract exhibits, should visit it before nine o'clock in the morning.

2 Waldshut
1 Lauffenburgh—Here is another *Fall of the Rhine*; but not equal in beauty to that of Schaffhausen.
1½ Rheinfelden—Between Rheinfelden and Basle is Augst, anciently *Augusta Rauracorum*, where remains may be traced of Roman Antiquities.
1 *Basle*.
___
18½ posts.

This is a flourishing commercial

city, supposed to contain 15,000 inhabitants. The objects best worth notice here are, *the Arsenal—the Bridge* thrown over the Rhine—*the Cathedral*, a Gothic edifice which contains some Antiquities, together with the Tomb of Erasmus—*the Hôtel de Ville*, where there is an apartment painted by Holbein, who was a native of Basle—*The Dance of Death*, painted on the walls of the Cemetery, and supposed to have been done by a pupil of Holbein—and *the public Library*, which is embellished with paintings by Holbein, Antiquities, Natural History, etc. Basle contains a University: and among the best inns are, *Les trois Rois*, and *La Cigogne*.

There is a singular custom in this city, that of setting all the clocks one hour too fast.

ROUTE FROM AUGSBURGH TO RATISBON.

1½ Aicha—The ruins of the two Castles of Wittelsbach, from which family descend the Princes of Bavaria, render this small town remarkable.
1½ Waidhofen
1½ Geisenfeld
1½ Neustadt
1½ Saal
1½ *Ratisbon.*

8½ posts.

Ratisbon is seated on the Danube; and contains 22,000 inhabitants. The objects best worth notice in this city are, its *ancient Bridge,* three hundred and fifty yards in length—*the Cathedral—the Abbey of S. Emmeran—The Hôtel de Ville*—and *the Library of the Prince of Thurn and Taxis,* which is open to the public Mondays, Wednesdays, and Fridays, from ten till twelve in the morning, and from two till five in the afternoon. Persons who wish to see it on other days must apply to the Librarian. *The town Library*—and *the Library and Cabinet of the Abbey of S. Emmeran,* likewise merit attention.

The best inn is *Les trois Heaumes.*

ROUTE FROM RATISBON TO MUNICH.

1 Eglofsheim
1 Buckhausen
1 Ergolspach
1½ *Landshut*—The objects best worth notice in this town are, the Palace—the Gothic tower belonging to the Church of S. Martin—the Church of S. Job—the Church belonging to the Domenican Convent—the Abbey of Seeligenthal—and the Maison de Ville.
1 Mospurg
1 *Freysing*—The objects best worth attention in this town are, the Cathedral—the Benedictine Church—the Chapel and Cupola of S. Peter's—the Abbey of Weyhen-Stephan—the Collegiate Church of S. Veit—and the Benedictine Lyceum.
  Principal inns, *La Charrue,* and *Les sept Glands.*
1½ Garching
¾ *Munich.*

8½ posts.

Munich, the capital of Bavaria, is seated on the Iser; and contains above 40,000 inhabitants. *The Royal Residence* in this elegant city, though unpromising on the outside, is magnificent within; and exhibits a fine collection of pictures; among which are a hundred and thirty Miniatures, each of them being valued at two hundred louis-d'or. The Tapestry in this palace, representing the exploits of Otho de Wittelsback; the great Staircase; the Chapel, which contains a painting attributed to Buonaroti, together with the altar used by the unfortunate Mary, Queen of Scotland, during her imprisonment, and a particularly fine organ, all merit notice; as do the Treasury (which abounds with splendid jewels) and the Antiquary.* Other objects which deserve attention are, *the Cabinet of pictures belonging to the Duke of Litchenburg, ci-devant Beauharnois—the Museum of carved ivory—the new Theatre—the paintings in the Church of Notre-Dame—the Church of the Theatins*, which contains a good picture, by Sandrat, representing the Plague at Naples—*The Church of the English Nuns*, who educate young Ladies gratis—*the picture, by Tintoretto* (most provokingly cut in two, for the convenience of the candle-snuffer), in *the Augustine-Church—the Church dedicated to S. Peter*, which contains good Pictures—*the Libraries of the King, the Theatins*, and *the Academy of Science*—and *the royal Cabinets of Medals and Natural History.*

Principal inns, *L'Aigle—Le Cheval blanc*, etc.

There are several pleasant Promenades in the vicinity of Munich: the royal Villas of Nymphenburg, and Schlesheim, both situated at a short distance from the city, merit notice: Schlesheim contains a very large collection of pictures.

ROUTE FROM RATISBON TO PRAGUE.

1 Kurn
1 Nietenau
1 Neukirchen
1 Roez
1 Walmunchen
1 Klentsch
1 Temiz
1 Storkau
1 Staab
1 Pilsen—Best inn, *La Croix d'or.*
1 Rockizan
1 Manth
1 Czernowitz
1 Zditz
½ Beraun
1 Dusnik
1 *Prague.*
___
16½ posts.

ROUTE FROM VIENNA, THROUGH RATISBON AND BRUSSELS, TO OSTEND.

1 Burgersdorf
1 Sigbartzkirchen
1 Perschling
1 S. Poelten
1½ Moelk—*The abbey* here merits notice.
1½ Kemmelbach
1 Amstetten
1½ Strenberg
1 Ems
1½ *Lintz*—The last post in Lower Austria. This town contains 20,000 inhabitants. Best inn, *L'Aigle noir.* The women of Lintz are celebrated for their beauty.
1½ Efferding—The first post of Upper Austria.
1½ Baversbach
1 Sicharding
1 Sharding
1 *Passau*—A fine town. *The Cathedral* and its organ, *the Château*, *the Library de Lamberg*, and the prospect from the Garden of the Convent of Mariahilf, deserve attention.
2 Vilzhofen
2 Platling
2 *Straubing—The collegiate Church, the ci-devant Jesuits' College*—and *the Carmelite Convent*, which contains the Tomb of Duke Albert, merit notice; as does *the Abbey Ober-Altaich*, which is in the vicinity of Straubing.
1½ Psader
1½ *Ratisbon*
1½ Schambach
1 Teiswang
1 Theining
1 Postbaner
1 Feucht
1 *Nuremberg*—This city contains 30,000 inhabitants; and the objects best worth notice are, *the Cathedral*, dedicated to S. Laurence, and adorned with beautiful painted glass—*the Chapel of S. Anne*—*the Church of S. Claire*, which contains a painting upon glass executed in 1278—*the Chapel of Mendel*, adorned with several good pictures—*the Chapel Holzschouhe-*

---

* The Statues lately found at Ægina (a Greek Island in the *Mare Ægeum*) now enrich the collection of antiquities at Munich. They originally adorned the pediment of a temple consecrated to Minerva; and all represent warriors, one female figure excepted. These statues form an interesting link in the chain of ancient sculpture; as they are superior to the Egyptian style, though inferior to that of the most eminent Grecian sculptors.

rienne du S. Sepulcre—the imperial Château, embellished with valuable pictures; for showing which, the Custode expects a florin—*The Hôtel de Ville:* likewise embellished with good pictures; for showing which, the Custode expects two kopfstucks—*the Bridges*—*the Arsenal*, which contains two Cannon dated 1499—and *the Copper Mills.* Best inns, *Le Cheval Rouge,* and *Le Coq Rouge.*

1 Farnbach
1 Em kirchen
1 Langenfeld—The *Post-House* here is a good inn.
1 Bossenheim
1½ Kitzingen
1 *Wurtzburgh*—The road from Nuremberg hither is excellent. Wurtzburgh contains 16,000 inhabitants. The objects best worth notice are, *the Château*, remarkable for its staircase—*the Citadel*, in the centre of which is an ancient Temple—*the Arsenal*—*the Chapel of S. Mary*—*the Cathedral*—*the Church belonging to the Chapître de Neumunster*—*the Chapître de Haug*—*the Great Hospital*—*the Couvent de S. Benoit*—*the Picture-Gallery belonging to the Prince-Bishop*, containing a Magdalene by Fesel—and *the Library belonging to the University.* Best inns, *La Cour de Franconie*—*La Poste*—*Le Cygne.* The most celebrated wines of Franconia grow near Wurtzburgh, namely, the *Vin de Lieste,* the *Vin de Stein,* called *Vin du S. Esprit,* and the *Vin de Calmus.*

1 Remlingen
1 Esselbach
1½ Rohrbrunn
1 Besanbach
1½ Gottingen
1 Hannau
1 *Frankfort on the Mein*
1 Kœnigstein
1½ Wierges
1½ Limburg
1 Walnerod
1 Freylingen
1 Gulroth
1 Weyersbusch
1½ Ukerot
1 Siegburg
1½ *Cologne*—This city is supposed to contain above 30,000 inhabitants; and among the objects best worth notice are, the *Cathedral*—the *Church of the eleven thousand Virgins*—the *Church of the Maccabees*—the *Chapître de S. Géreon*—the *Archiepiscopal Seminary*—the *Hôtel de Ville*—the *Arsenal*—the *Hierosolomitanite Chapel,* which contains a celebrated painting—and the *Cathedral Library.*

Cologne is paved with basalt.—One of the principal inns is, *Le S. Esprit.*

1½ Bergheim
1½ Linnig
1 Gangelt
1½ Reckem
1½ Tongern
1½ S. Trond
2 Tirlemont
2 *Louvain*—The inhabitants of this town are supposed to amount to 40,000. One of the principal inns is, The *Hôtel de Cologne.*

1½ Cortenberg
1½ *Bruxelles*—This city, the capital of the Kingdom of the Netherlands, is watered by the little river Senne, and supposed to possess about 15,000 inhabitants. Its fortifications are destroyed; but its ramparts, being planted with trees, form pleasant walks round this city. *The Park*, or public Garden, is adorned with fountains and statues, and encircled by splendid buildings. *The Palace,* in which the Austrian Viceroy formerly resided, contains a Picture-Gallery, and a public Library, rich in finely illuminated Manuscripts. The *Hôtel de Ville* and its *Gothic Towers*—the *Theatre*—the *Church of S. Gudule,* and the *Chapel of Notre-Dame*—the *Church and Place de S. Michel*—the *Place de Sablon,* and *the canal,* merit notice. Brussels is celebrated for its Manufacture of Lace. Here are several good inns; namely, the *Hôtel d'Angleterre*—The *Hôtel de Belle-vue*—The *Hôtel de Flandre,* etc.

This may be called a cheap city for permanent residence, though house-rent is dear.

Not far hence, and in the neighbourhood of Genappe, a market-town on the river Dyle, is the celebrated Plain of Waterloo; where a small Band of British Heroes vanquished the gigantic power of France, and put to flight her ablest General.

1½ Asche
1½ Alost
1½ Quadrecht
1 Gand
2 Alteren
2 Bruges
2 Ostend—The *Hôtel de Ville,* and some Pictures, by Flemish Masters, which adorn the Churches in this town, merit notice. The best inn is, *Nicholson's Hotel.*

86½ posts.

Packets sail every Tuesday and Friday, weather permitting, from Colchester to Ostend; and the common passage is about twelve hours.

Packets usually sail twice a week from Ostend to Harwich; and the common passage, with a fair wind, is about twenty hours.

Packets likewise sail from Os-

GERMANY—CASSEL, COBLENTZ.

tend to Margate; and the common passage is about twelve hours.

ROUTE FROM FRANKFORT ON THE MEIN, THROUGH CASSEL, TO MUNSTER.

1½ Friedberg
1 Butzbach
1 *Giessen*—The University of Giess was founded in 1607. The *Library*—the *Pædagogium*—the *Château*—the *Arsenal*—and the *Church of S. Pancrace* merit notice.
1 *Marburgh*—The *Library* belonging to the *University*, here, is a fine one. The best inn is the *Post-House*.
1½ Holzdorf
1 Jessberg
1 Wabern
1½ *Cassel*—This city is supposed to contain about 20,000 inhabitants; and the objects best worth notice are, the *Château*—the *Palace*—the *Place de Fréderic* and the *Statue* by which it is adorned—the *Arsenal*—the *Roman Catholic Church*—the *reformed Church*—and the *Statue of the Landgrave, Charles*—the *Opera-House*—the *Museum Fredericien*—and the *Pictures in the Hall of the Academy of Painting*. The principal inns are, the *Hotel d'Angleterre* (already mentioned)—*Maupin's*—*The Stockholm*—and *L'Aigle*.
1 Wertuffeln
1 Ostendorf
1 Lichtenau
1 *Paderborn*—The *Cathedral* here—the *ci-devant Jesuits' Church*—and the *University*, merit notice. The source of the river Pader is in the middle of the town.
1½ Nienkirchen
2 Warensdorf
1½ *Munster*.

18½ posts.

This city contains 25,000 inhabitants; and *the Church of S. Lambert*—*the episcopal Palace*—*the Cathedral*—and *the Chapel of Bernard de Galen*, merit notice.

VOYAGE ON THE RHINE FROM MAYENCE TO COBLENTZ.

Persons who wish to make this excursion, should leave Mayence toward evening: and go either to *Mittelheim* or *Langenwinkel*. Next morning, about half an hour before sun-rise, they should walk to *Johannisberg;* and from the Balcony of the Castle there, contemplate the view.

From Langenwinkel to *Geisenheim*, the time occupied in going is about an hour; and at the latter place, Travellers should disembark, and visit *Neiderwald*, a Garden belonging to the Count d'Ostein, and embellished with delightful prospects. From Geisenheim to *S. Goaer*, the time occupied in going is about four hours; and here Travellers should sleep; rising, however, at five o'clock the next morning, in order to reach *Coblentz* by nine.

Two boats, one to convey a carriage, and the other to convey Passengers, usually cost about three Carolins (seventy-two francs); and for five Carolins, Travellers may be conveyed to Cologne, provided they do not choose to stop at Coblentz.

The principal inns at Coblentz are *Le Roi des Romains*, and The *Post-House;* and the objects most worthy of attention in this town are, *the collegiate Church of S. Castor* and *the Fort of Ehrenbreitstein*, originally a Roman work.

EXCURSION FROM GOTTINGEN TO THE MINES OF HARTZ.

Behind Kattlenburg rise the first hills which belong to the chain of the Hartz.

Osterode—This town contains 4,000 inhabitants—*Klausthal*—inn, *La Couronne*. This town contains 10,000 inhabitants. The richest Mines are *La Caroline*, which is 105 fathoms deep; and *La Dorothée*, which is 102 fathoms deep.

The *Georgestollen* is a remarkable work.

Ludwiger-Rechenhaus exhibits a collection of all the machines employed in the Mines.

Two miles from Klausthal is the ancient imperial city of *Goslar;* which has only 7000 inhabitants; though it contains from fourteen to fifteen thousand houses. This city is celebrated for its excellent beer called *Gose*, of which there are seven kinds; and that most esteemed is called *Beste Krug*. Half a league from this city is the *Rammelsberg*, the most ancient of the Mines of Hartz.

On the road leading from Isenburg to Brocken, not far from the Château de Stappelnburg, is a beautiful prospect; and from the summit of *Brocken* a plain is discoverable, which extends seventy leagues, and contains five millions of people.

From Brocken Travellers usually go to *Elbingerode*, in order to see *the Grotto* called *Bauhmanshôle*. The Stalactites which adorn this Grotto are beautiful and various; but the objects most interesting here are petrified human bones, supposed to be antediluvian. At *S. Andreasburgh*, in this neighbourhood, was found a piece of silver, weighing eighty pounds.

This excursion may be easily accomplished in a fortnight.

CELEBRATED GERMAN BATHS.

CARLSBAD.

Carlsbad contains about 3,000 inhabitants, and several lodging-houses. The price of apartments varies according to the number of persons who frequent the Baths; but a good suite of rooms, with several beds, seldom lets for more than ten florins a week.

The best *Traiteurs* usually charge eight groschen per head for dinner. At the *Salle de Bohéme*, and the *Salle de Saxe*, breakfast, either of coffee or chocolate, costs half a kopfstuck and twelve krëutzers. For loading, or unloading a travelling carriage, the price is a goulden. To the *Valet-de-Place*, who goes round with the visiting-tickets of Itinerants, when they arrive, and when they depart, the fee is two gouldens. For reading the gazettes during the whole season, the price is one goulden. The drawers of water at each spring expect from every customer a kopfstuck or two, as a farewell present; and the waiters at the *Salle de Bohéme*, and the *Salle de Saxe*, expect every person whom they have attended to give them at least one goulden as a parting compliment. The entrance-money at the balls is one goulden per head: and persons who require a physician, while they use the Baths, commonly give him four or five ducats when his attendance ceases.

The roads in this neighbourhood are abominable.

PYRMONT.

The Pyrmont season commences about the end of June. The new lodging-house at the Baths is a good one; and the price of each apartment is marked over the door. There are several other lodging-houses. Dinner costs from eight to sixteen groschen per head, according to its quality; and the public amusements here are numerous and various.

SPA.

The season at Spa commences about the end of May. Here are lodgings of all descriptions, and all prices. *Traiteurs* send out good dinners at four francs a head; and persons who like to dine at a *Table d'Hôte* are particularly well served for three francs a head. Saddle horses cost, by the day, from five to six francs each.

Spa, to lovers of gaiety, is pleasant; though, compared with many other places on the Continent, expensive.

ROUTE FROM VIENNA TO CARLSBAD, THROUGH EGER AND ZWODA.

1 Enzersdorf
1 Stockerau
1½ Weikersdof
1 Meisau
1 Horn
1½ Göffritz
1 Schwarzenau
1½ Shrems
1½ Schwarzbach
1½ Wittingau
1½ Budweis
2 Moldauthein
2 Pisek
1 Strakonitz
1 Horazdiowitz
1½ Grünberg
2 Pilsen
2 Miess
1 Tschernoschin
1 Plan
1 Sandau
1 Eger
1½ Zwoda
1½ *Carlsbad*—The best road to Carlsbad is this, through Eger and Zwoda.
32½ posts.

ROUTE FROM HANOVER TO PYRMONT.

1½ Springe
1 Hameln—A strong place.
1 *Pyrmont*—The *Chariot de Poste* goes from Hanover to Pyrmont during the months of June, July, and August.
3½ posts.

ROUTE FROM HAMBURGH TO PYRMONT.

½ Harburgh
1½ Tostedt
1½ Rotenburgh
1 Ottersberg
1½ Brême
1½ Bassum
1 Barenburgh
1 Ucht
1½ Minden—*La Ville de Berlin* is a good hotel.
1 *Rinteln*—This town contains a celebrated University.
1½ *Pyrmont*.
13½ posts.

ROUTE FROM BRUSSELS, THROUGH AIX-LA-CHAPELLE AND LIEGE, TO SPA.

1½ Cortenberg
1½ *Louvain*
2 Tirlemont
2 *S. Trond*
1½ Tongres
1½ Reckheim
1½ Sittart
1 Geilenkirchen
1 Juliers—The principal inn here is *La Cour Impériale*.
The distance from Juliers to Cologne is two posts and a half.
1½ *Aix-la-Chapelle*—This city contains above 27,000 inhabitants. *The Cathedral*, wherein is the Tomb of Charlemagne—*the Hôtel de Ville*—*the Baths*—and *the ci-devant Jesuits' College*, are the objects best worth notice. Here are several inns.
From Aix-la-Chapelle to Maestricht is three German miles.
1½ Balisse
1 *Liège*.
17½ posts.

This city is watered by the Maes, and supposed to contain above 80,000 inhabitants: its Citadel commands a magnificent prospect; and *the Hotel des Etats*—*the Hôtel de Ville*—*the Fountain in the Grande Place*—*the Cathedral*, dedicated to *S. Lambert*—*the Quay*, on the banks of the Maes, and *the Bridge* thrown over that river, all merit notice. Liege boasts a delightful Promenade, called *Coronmaes*.

Among the best inns are, *L'Aigle noir*, and *La Cour de Londres*.

German Miles.
3 *Spa*.

ROUTE FROM VIENNA TO BADEN.

1 Neudorf
1 *Baaden*—Celebrated for its mineral waters.
—
2 posts.

ROUTE FROM VIENNA TO PRESBURGH.

1 Schwachat
1 Fischament
1 Regelsbrunn
1 Teutsch-Altenburgh—The frontier town of Hungary.
1 *Presburgh.*
—
5 posts.

This city, in time past, the capital of Hungary, is not supposed at the present moment to contain above 22,000 inhabitants; though its population, previous to the removal of the seat of government to Buda, was estimated at 28,000. Presburgh is finely situated on an eminence overlooking an immense plain, watered by the Danube; and among the objects best worth notice here, are *an equestrian Statue,* by Donner, of S. Martin, which adorns the parochial Church—*another Statue*, by the same sculptor, in the Esterhazy-Chapel—*The Governor's Palace—the royal Chancery—The Theatre—the Public Granaries—the Caserne—the royal Château—the Cupola of the Church of S. Elisabeth—the royal Catholic Academy*—and, *the Lutheran Gymnasium.* The public amusements consist of operas, German plays, concerts, and balls. Here are some good private Libraries, and Cabinets of Natural History; together with a celebrated Collection of wry faces.

The Château de Lanschitz, near Presburgh, is worth seeing; as likewise is the Château d'Esterhazy.

ROUTE FROM TEUTSCH-ALTENBURGH TO BELGRADE.

1 Kittsee—A Royal Château.
1 Rackendorf
1 Wieselburgh
1 Hochstrass, *or* Hogstrass—A post and a half is sometimes charged here.
1 *Raab*—The population of this city is estimated at 13,000. Its Cathedral is magnificent.
1 Goenyo
1 Ais
1 Comorn—The Church which formerly belonged to the Jesuits merits notice.
1 Nessmely—Celebrated for excellent white wines.
1 Neudorf
1 Dorogh
1½ Wereschwar
1 *Ofen, or Buda*—The population of Buda (called by the Germans Ofen) is estimated at 55,000, including the town of Pesth, from which it is separated only by the Danube. At Buda the Hungarian *Regalia* are kept: and the Crown which was presented in the year 1000, by Pope Sylvester II, to Stephen King of Hungary, is an imitation of that worn by the Greek Emperors.
1 Teleny
1½ Ereschin
1 Adony
1 Pentele
1½ Foeldwar
2 Paksch
2 Tolnau
1 Sekare—Celebrated for its wines; which are deemed superior to Burgundy.
1½ Pobtaszek
1 Sekescoe
1 Mohacseh
2 Baranyawar
1 Laskafeld—The frontier town of Sclavonia.
1 *Esseck*—Vestiges of the ancient city of *Mursa* are discoverable here.
1 Verra
1 Wukowar
1 Oppatowaz
1½ Illok
1 Szuszek
2 Peterwaradin
1 Carlowitz-Unterleg
1 Poska
1 Cserevicz
1½ Banovzo
1½ *Semlin*—This town contains a Health-Office for purifying letters and merchandize which come from Turkey.
—
45½ posts.

From Semlin to Belgrade the time occupied in going is about one hour and a half.

ROUTE FROM PRESBURGH TO KASCHAU AND TOKAY.

1 Csekles
1 Sarfoë
1 *Tyrnau*—This town, adorned with nine large towers and several churches, makes a handsome figure at a distance. *The Cathedral—the Epis-*

copal Palace—and *the Académie des Nobles*, merit notice.

1½ Freystüdtel
1 Rippyn
1 Nagy-Tapolcsany
1 Nitra-Sambokreth
1 Westenics
1 Baymozs—There are *Hot Baths* in this town.
1 Rudno
1 Turocz-Sambokreth
1 Nolscova
1½ Rosenberg—*The Mineral Waters* and *the College* here are celebrated.
1 Pentendorf
1 Okolisna
1 Vihodna
1 Lusivna
1 Horka
1 Leutschau—*The Hôtel de Ville* is a handsome building: but the town is ill supplied with water.
1 Biaczovez
1½ Berthod
1 Eperies—Finely situated, and famous for its wines.
1 Lemesau
1 Kaschau—A strong town. *The Governor's House* is a handsome building. *The Baths* of Kaschau are celebrated; but the air is unhealthy.
1 Szinne
1 Wilmann
1½ Tallya—Famous for its wines.
2 Tokay—On the mountain of S. Thérèse, and in the vineyard of Szarwarsch, grow the best wines of Tokay, which, in stomach complaints, have been found particularly beneficial.*

Hungary abounds in excellent fruit, beef, wild-fowl, and venison; and the wines are so good, and at the same time so strong, that, to foreigners, they sometimes prove dangerous.

In Gallicia, and the Bukovine, Travellers ought to carry provisions with them; as little beside straw can be procured at the inns.

ROUTE FROM VIENNA TO TRIESTE.

1 Neudorf
1 Gunselsdorf
1 Neustadt
1 Neukirchen
1 Schottwien
1½ Moerzuschlag

1 Krieglach
1 Merzhofen
1 Bruck
1 Rettelstein
1 Peggau
1 *Gratz*—This town, the capital of Styria, is supposed to contain above 33,000 inhabitants; and among the objects best worth notice are, *the Imperial Château—the Maison des Etats—the Church de la Cour*, and *that* dedicated to *S. Catherine—the parochial Church*, adorned with a painting by Tintoretto—*the ci-devant Jesuits' College—the two Columns, and the Convent in the Fauxbourg of Muer—the Lyceum* and *its Library*—and *the Johannæum*. The Poor-house, which comprehends a general hospital, a lying-in hospital, a foundling hospital, an asylum for Lunatics, and another for the Aged, is a most benevolent and useful institution.

The promenades in and about this town are pleasant.

Best inn, *The Sun.*

1 Kalsdorf
1 Lebering
1 Ehrenhausen
1½ *Mahrburg*—This is the most populous town in Styria, Gratz excepted.
1 Feistritz
1 Gannowitz
1½ Cilli
1½ Franz
1 S. Oswald
1 Potpetsch
1½ *Laybach*—This city, the capital of the Duchy of Carniola, is supposed to contain about 11,000 inhabitants. *The Cathedral*, dedicated to S. Nicholas, merits notice; as does *the Church of S. Peter*, in the Fauxbourg.
1 Ober-Laybach
1 Lasse
1 *Adelsberg*—There is a celebrated *Grotto* in this town; and another, called *The Grotto of S. Madelaine*, at a short distance.

The Lake of Zirknitz is not very far from Adelsberg.

1 Präwald
1 Sessana
1 *Trieste*†—This is a free port, with § spacious and safe Harbour, and a population estimated at above 30,000. a
—— 32 posts.

The objects best worth notice here are, *the Mole—the Lazzaretti—the Cathedral—the Greek Church*—and *the Roman Antiquities.*

Principal inn, *Il Buon Pastore.*

* The Hungarians have eight sorts of wine somewhat similar in flavour to Tokay, and frequently sold under that name. The best Tokay is seldom if ever sold.

† From Trieste to Fiume, another Austrian free port, is a distance of five posts.

§ The population of Trieste did not amount to more than 18,000 a few years since.

CHAPTER IX.

PORTUGAL.

Expense of going in a Post-Office Packet from Falmouth to Lisbon—Days appointed for sailing—Money of Portugal—Lisbon—Hotels—Population—Objects best worth notice—Cork Convent—Cintra—Water, eatables, and asses' milk—Lodgings—Board—Fire-wood—Garden of the Convent of Necessitades—Public amusements—Price of draught-horses—Passports, etc.—Route from Lisbon to Oporto—Ditto from Lisbon to Madrid.

EXPENSE OF GOING IN A POST-OFFICE PACKET FROM FALMOUTH TO LISBON.

EVERY cabin passenger usually pays for passage and board (wine, tea, and sugar inclusive), twenty-three pounds, and every steerage passenger fourteen pounds. Female servants pay as cabin passengers. Children, under twelve months old, go free of charge; under four years old they pay as steerage passengers; and above that age as cabin passengers.

Lisbon-packets generally sail every Saturday; though every Friday is the time when they are ordered to sail, from April till October.

The accommodations on board these vessels are excellent. I would not, however, advise passengers to use the sheets, blankets, and pillows, belonging to the packet; but to provide plenty of their own: and this not merely to secure themselves from cold, and other unpleasant circumstances, during their voyage; but likewise because blankets and down-pillows are particularly needful at Lisbon. Invalids who visit this city during winter should wear very warm clothing, and live in an apartment which fronts the south.

MONEY OF PORTUGAL.

	l.	s.	d
A Ree.			
10 Rees, equal to a half Vintem.			
20 Rees, equal to a Vintem; in English money about........	0	0	1
5 Vintems, equal to a Testoon....	0	0	6
4 Testoons, equal to a Crusade of Exchange.............	0	2	3
24 Vintems, equal to a new Crusade.............	0	2	8
10 Testoons, equal to a Milree, (1000 Rees).......	0	5	7
48 Testoons, equal to a Moidore..	1	7	0
64 Testoons, equal to a Joannes....	1	15	9

Accounts in Portugal are kept in Rees.

LISBON.

Lisbon, anciently called *Olisippo*, and in Portuguese Lisboa, is a flourishing commercial city, seated near the mouth of the Tagus, or Tajo, embellished by one of the finest Harbours in Europe, and supposed to contain 200,000 inhabitants.

Among the objects best worth notice in this metropolis and its environs are, *the Royal Residence; the Exchange; the India-House; the Arsenal;* and *the equestrian bronze statue of Joseph I.;* all of which adorn the *Praça do Commercio*—the *patriarchal Church;* and *that belonging to the Convent of S. Roche*, which comprises an Asylum for Foundlings. In the last-named

Church is a Chapel dedicated to S. Roche, and considered as one of the most richly-decorated temples of the Christian world. The picture above the altar is a particularly well executed Roman Mosaic; as likewise is another picture on the right side of the Chapel: the pavement is wrought in Mosaic; the pilasters are formed of porphyry, verde antique, lapis-lazuli, and other precious marbles: the doors are bronze, beautifully worked and gilt: the candelabra and the lamps are of solid silver; and the altar is composed of lapis lazuli, amethysts, and gold; and ornamented with a scriptural Group in *alto-rilievo*, which is one entire block of silver.* Other objects that deserve attention in Lisbon and its environs are, *the new Church*, erected by the late Queen — *the Quays* — *the Aqueduct of Alcantara*, which consists of thirty-five arches: the largest being 249 feet in width, and 332 in height. This magnificent structure, built of white marble, was erected by John V.— *the Church and Convent of Belem*, where the Sovereigns of Portugal are buried —(Belem exhibits a kind of Gothic arabesque architecture, unknown in other parts of Europe) — *the Convent of Brancanas*, which contains a picture of the blessed Virgin finely executed—*the Cork Convent* on the summit of Cape S. Roche—and *Cintra*, which contains a good Inn, and exhibits ruins of a Moorish Palace.

Cintra is deemed the best summer-residence in the environs of Lisbon; but during winter and spring its excessive humidity renders it unwholesome.† The *Penha verde* at Cintra is usually visited by Travellers.

Lisbon possesses excellent water, good beef, fish, vegetables, fruit, and asses' milk; but eligible lodgings are scarce and dear; and a lady or gentleman can seldom board with a Portuguese family under seven shillings, English money, per day, lodging not inclusive.

Fire-wood likewise is dear at Lisbon.

The Garden belonging to the Convent of Necessitades, situated at the foot of Buenos-Aires, affords an agreeable promenade; and the public amusements of this city are, the Italian opera, the Portuguese theatre, bull fights, and assemblies at the houses of the English merchants.

Among the principal inns are, *Barnwell's English Hotel* — *Owens's Hotel*—*O'Keif's Hotel* —*L'Hôtel Piémontais* — and *La Calcada de Estrella*.

PRICE OF DRAUGHT-HORSES, ETC.

Draught-horses, or mules, in Portugal, are charged at eight testoons a pair, per league: the common mode of travelling is *en voiturier;* and a calash, containing two places, and drawn by two mules, may usually be hired for about fifteen francs a day, all expenses included.

Travellers going from Lisbon to any other part of Portugal, should

---

* When Junôt commanded at Lisbon, this *alto-rilievo*, together with most of the church-plate in the city, was packed up, for the purpose of being conveyed to France; but, owing to the suddenness and rapidity of his retreat, this valuable plunder was left behind.

The Chapel of S. Roche is reported to have cost the Portuguese nation a million of crusades.

† Many persons prefer Bellas to Cintra, because it is more quiet, and less liable to fogs, than the last-named place.

solicit, from the chief-magistrate of the quarter in which they lodge, a passport containing the names of the Travellers, the number of their horses, mules, and attendants; together with a permission to carry fire-arms.

Persons going to Spain must apply for a passport from the Spanish Minister at Lisbon; and this last-named passport, if presented to Spanish custom-house officers, and accompanied by a fee, prevents any examination of baggage.

ROUTE FROM LISBON TO OPORTO.

1st day   Alveria and Castenheda—About midway there is a ferry over the Tagus. The road lies between hedges of aloes and olives.

2d day   Olta and Tagarro—A sandy plain, abounding with Indian figs.

3d day   Venta—These Ventas are inns, established by order of government, at the distance of four or five Portuguese miles from each other. Government likewise regulates the charges at these inns, by a tariff, which is always exposed to public view.

4th day   Alcobaça.

5th day   Leyria—Travellers may stop, during this day's journey, at the *Convent of Batalha*, which has a fine Gothic church, with a beautiful tower.

The road is good, and the country adorned with plantations of olives and forests of cork-trees.

6th day   Pombal and Pondes—Travellers should visit the *Moorish Castle* on a hill near Pombal.

7th day   Coimbra and *Almahada*—Coimbra contains 13,000 inhabitants, and a University. Here are *a Roman Bridge* and *Aqueduct*, almost entire.

8th day   Albergaria, Antonio, Venta, *and* Villanova—Travellers, during this day's journey, pass two rivers, either on bridges or in a ferry.

9th day   Oporto—This city, the largest in Portugal, Lisbon excepted, is watered by the Douro, anciently the *Durius*, on which river gondolas, like those at Venice, are much used. Oporto is supposed to contain 30,000 inhabitants; and has long been famed for its wines, of which it is said to export yearly twenty thousand pipes. *The Quays* here are magnificent.

Time employed in travelling from Oporto to Almeida, 65 hours—from Oporto to Salamanca, 27 hours—from Salamanca to Valladolid, 36 hours—from Valladolid to Madrid, by Segovia and the Escurial, 50 hours.

Segovia is well worth seeing, on account of its Aqueduct, a noble monument of antiquity, and in perfect preservation. Some authors suppose it was erected during the reign of Trajan; but the Spaniards gravely assert, that it was the work of Hercules.

The Cathedral at Segovia is one of the handsomest edifices of its kind in Spain; and the Alcazar, or Castle, stands beautifully.

ROUTE FROM LISBON TO MADRID.

Leagues.
3 Aldea-Gallega—To this place Travellers are conveyed on the Tagus, in a large boat; but it is not prudent to set out if the river be much agitated.
5 Canna
3 Ventas-Nuevas—The road crosses a brook.
4 Montemornovo
3 Arayolos—The road crosses another brook.
3 Venta del Duque—From Aldea-Gallega to this place the road is tolerably good.
3 Estremos
3 Aleravazaz
4 Elvas—This is the last town of Portugal. Here travellers are waited upon by the Custom-house Officers, and desired to declare what articles of commerce, and what money they have with them, after having done which they receive an *Albara*.

One mile from Elvas the road traverses a rivulet, which divides Portugal from Spain.

3 Badajos—This town, the capital of Estremadura, is entered, on the Portuguese side, by a bridge thrown over the Guadiana, anciently called the Annas. It is a place of high antiquity.

Here Travellers are liable to have their baggage examined. The road from Estremos hither is, generally speaking, bad.

3 Talavera del Arrojo
2 Lobon
2 Arrorogo de San Servan.
2 Merida—This town was built by the Romans, and is entered on the Por-

	tuguese side by a bridge of sixty one arches, thrown over the Guadiana. Here are several Antiquities, among which is an equestrian Statue.
4	Venta del Desblado.
3	Meajadas
3	Puerta de Santa Cruz
3	Trujilo—The birth-place of Pizarro.
4	Jarajzejo—One hour distant from Jarajzejo Travellers are obliged to descend from their carriages, while the latter are conveyed, by the assistance of oxen, over a steep and rugged road; and after passing the river del Monte, on a bridge, carriages are drawn by oxen up a hill, which belongs to the chain called Sierra de Guadelupe.
	Jarajzejo contains considerable vestiges of Moorish architecture.
4	Casas del Puerto
2	Almaraz—Half an hour distant from Almaraz is a bridge thrown over the Tagus, beyond which river the road ascends a hill, thence becoming good, and continuing so the whole way to Madrid.
2	Navalmoral—The first town of New Castile.
4	Calcada de Oropesa
4	Venta
4	Talavera de la Reyna
2	Sotocochinos
3	Bravo
3	Maqueda
2	Venta del Gallo
3	Santa-Cruz del Retamar
2	Valmajado
3	Naval-carnero
2	Mostoles—Here stands *a Church*, the inside of which is completely covered with gilding.
3	Madrid—On approaching this city carriages are either driven through the Mançanares, or over it, by means of the fine Bridge of Segovia.
103	

The country between Badajoz and Madrid is, generally speaking, uncultivated, unless it be in the neighbourhood of towns and villages; and exhibits, to the left, a long chain of mountains.

It is practicable so to arrange this journey that Travellers may go by S. Ildefonso, the Escurial, or Aranjuez.

CHAPTER X.

SPAIN.

Money of Spain—Price of Post-horses, etc.—Articles particularly requisite for Travellers in Spain—Route from Bayonne to Madrid—Saragossa—Valencia—Valladolid—Burgos—Population of Madrid—Objects best worth notice there—Literary Establishments—Promenades—Public amusements—Manufactures—Inns—Environs—Job-carriages—Gates and Streets—Route from Perpignan to Barcelona—Climate of Barcelona—Population—Objects best worth notice—Inns—Promenades—Route from Barcelona to Saragossa—from Madrid to Grenada—Alhambra, and other objects best worth notice in the last-named city—Promenades—Climate—Route from Madrid to Malaga—Description of that city—Route from Madrid to Cordova, Seville, and Cadiz; together with a description of the three last-named cities.

VALUE OF THE MOST CURRENT SPANISH MONEY IN FRENCH FRANCS.

	Francs.	
Doblon	83	63
Pistole	20	91
Half-Pistole	10	45
Piastre	5	43
Real de à ocho	4	35
Escudo vellon	2	71
Real de à quatre	2	17
Peseta Mexicana	1	35

PRICE OF POST-HORSES, ETC.

The common charge, per post, is from ten to twelve reals for every draught-horse; a post being about two Spanish leagues, or three hours, in length. A Postillion cannot legally demand more than two reals per post; but expects a peseta, beside a dinner, or extra-money to provide one. For a carriage furnished by a Post-master, the price is four reals per post.

On entering and on quitting Madrid, and every other place where the King resides, Travellers pay a post-royal; which is double the price of a common post.

The post on great roads is well served; and the horses, when speed is compatible with safety, go remarkably quick: but the roads in Spain cannot, generally speaking, be called good; though, throughout the whole Signory of Biscay, and in some districts near Madrid, they are excellent.

The custom of taking journeys in a *Coche de Colleras* with six mules, or a *Calesa* with two, still predominates; but, for one person, a more economical way of travelling is to accompany the *Ordinario*, or to ride on a *Borrico*, attended by a muleteer on foot.

Voiturins usually charge for a calesa with two mules and their driver, the keep of mules and muleteer not inclusive, about fifteen francs a day: or for each mule, provender inclusive, two piastres a day.

The common day's journey of a Voiturier is about eight Spanish leagues; and each of these leagues contains 3,400 geometrical paces.

It is impossible to travel comfortably in Spain without a Servant who understands the language; because the Inns are so destitute of eatables, that Travellers are compelled to purchase their provisions in the large towns through which they pass; and likewise obliged, generally speaking, to have them cooked by their own servant: a pot for boiling meat, with a cover and padlock, to prevent theft, is therefore requisite; and travelling beds, in this country, are particularly needful.

Travellers should avoid taking snuff, new muslins, or new printed cottons, amongst their baggage, as these articles are contraband.

Servants should have fire-arms.*

ROUTE FROM BAYONNE TO MADRID.

Miniundo—A beautiful entrance to the Pyrenees; and the further the road advances the more picturesque is the scenery.

S. Jean Pié de Port—Near a spring of remarkably fine water, between this town and Roncesvalles, is the spot which divides France from Spain.

Roncesvalles—The road from Bayonne hither being dangerous for carriages, it is advisable either to go on mules, or to take the road by *Ostariz, Annoa, Maya, Berrueta, Lanz,* and *Ostiz,* to Pamplona.

The village of Roncesvalles is supposed to be the spot where Charlemagne's army was defeated, when the famous Roland lost his life.

14 Pamplona—The Inn at Pamplona is in the square. This town was anciently called *Pompelo*.
3½ Otriz
2½ Jaffala—A good road, which continues to Portacillo.
4 Marailla
3 Valtierra
4 Cintronigo
5 Agreda—Here the baggage of Travellers is visited and plumbed by the Custom-house Officers.
3½ Hinojosa
4 Zimayon
3½ Almazan—Here the road traverses the Douro on a stone bridge, near which there is a beautiful Promenade.
3½ Adradas
5 Lodares—The road lies over a mountain whose summit exhibits a large and well-cultivated plain.
2½ Bujarrabal
2½ Torremocha
3 Almodrones
2½ Grajanejos
3 Torija
3 Guadalaxara
3½ Venta de Meco
2½ Torrejon de Ardoz—Here the road crosses the Xarama on a bridge.
4 Madrid.

84½ leagues.

* Persons who wish to travel expeditiously in Spain should ride on post-horses. Several saddle-horses are kept at every post-house.

Many Travellers prefer going by Saragossa and Valencia; or by Valladolid, Burgos, and Vittoria.

Saragossa, the capital of Arragon, is seated on the Ebro, formerly called the *Iberus;* and contains *a Cathedral* and *a Moorish Tower,* which merit notice.

Valencia, supposed to contain above 70,000 inhabitants, is delightfully situated in the most fertile part of Spain. Its *Cathedral,* once a Mosque, is adorned with fine paintings. *The College of Corpus Christi* contains a celebrated picture; and several of the Convents and Monasteries are adorned with good paintings. *The Church of S. Nicholas*—*the University*—and *the public Libraries,* merit notice.

This city is lighted with handsome lamps, patrolled by watchmen, and encompassed with high walls, nearly circular. Its climate is so warm as to be oppressive during the day, even in winter.*

Valladolid, anciently called *Pintia,* contains a University; and, in *the Dominican Church of S. Paul,* two celebrated pictures, by Cardenas.

Burgos, the ancient capital of Old Castile, is built partly on the acclivity of a Mountain, and partly on the banks of the Arlançon. Its *Cathedral,* one of the finest Gothic structures in Europe, and some other Churches, merit notice.

Madrid, anciently denominated *Mantua,* is supposed to contain upward of 150,000 inhabitants. It has fifteen Gates, all composed of granite, and most of them handsome: its streets are clean, spacious, well paved, and well lighted; and the entrance to this city, through the gate of Alcala, is strikingly magnificent.

Among the objects which especially deserve attention are — *the Royal Residence,* called the New Palace, which is sumptuously furnished, and adorned with fine pictures — *the Royal Cabinet of Natural History* †—*the Churches of S. Isabella, S. Paschalis, S. Isidoro, S. Francesco de Sales,* and *S. Martino*—*the Convent of Las Descalzas Reales,* which contains a fine collection of pictures—*the Church of Las Salezas* —*the Royal Convent of S. Philip,* in point of architecture one of the finest buildings at Madrid— *the Domenican Church* — and *the Bridge,* thrown over the Mançanares.

This city is enriched with a University, a Royal College, called *Estudios Reales,* an Academy of Arts, and other literary establishments.

The principal Promenades are —the Prado—a fine Street, called Alcala—the Gardens of the Casa del Campo—and the banks of the Mançanares.

The Spanish Theatre, the Bull-fights, the *Tertullia,* and the *Refresco* (the two last being card-assemblies, balls, concerts, or *goûtés*), are the principal public amusements.

The Tapestry Manufacture; the China Manufacture at Buen-Retiro; and the Glass Manufacture at S. Ildefonso, merit notice.

Several of the Inns at Madrid are good; and one of the best is

---

* Murviedro, erected on the site of the ancient *Saguntum,* which was destroyed by Hannibal, is about four leagues distant from Valencia; and exhibits several vestiges of antiquity.

† This Cabinet contains ancient Peruvian pottery, very like that of Egypt.

the *Croix de Malte,* in the Alcala.

Provisions are cheap; and the common table-wines are those of La Mancha and Valdepenas.

There are no Hackney coaches in this city; but job-carriages may be hired by the day for eight or nine French livres.

The objects best worth notice in the environs of Madrid are— *the Buen-Retiro,* which is embellished with an equestrian Statue of Philip IV. by Pietro Tacca— *the Palace of Aranjuez,* and its Gardens—*the Palace of S. Ildefonso,* its Paintings, Sculpture, and Water-works—and *the Escurial,* which is situated about twenty English miles from Madrid, at the foot of the Guadarama mountains. This Palace, erected by Philip II., contains an immense collection of Pictures, some of which are classed among the finest existing; it is likewise rich in sculpture, gems, and precious marbles; and among its buildings comprises a Church, splendidly ornamented; and a Cemetery, called the Pantheon, where the Sovereigns of Spain, beginning with Charles V., are buried. The Escurial is likewise furnished with a Library particularly rich in Hebrew, Arabic, and Greek manuscripts.*

The road from Madrid hither is excellent, and the country beautiful.

ROUTE FROM PERPIGNAN TO BARCELONA.

2 Bollo—Near Fort Bellegarde is the Barrier between France and Spain; where every Traveller must produce a passport.
This road exhibits a fine view of the Pyrenees.

3 Jonquera
3 Figueras—A sandy soil, and cork-trees. Figueras is a fortified town.
3 Bascara—The road traverses the lofty mountain of Cuessa-Regia, the environs of which are beautiful.
3 *Gerona*—Anciently *Gerunda.* The *Cathedral,* and *the Arabian Baths,* merit notice.
4 Mallorquinas
2½ Hostalrich—Here Travellers ford a river which, after floods, is dangerous.
2 San Seloni
3 La Roca
2½ Moncade—The road skirts the banks of the sea.
2 *Barcelona*—The hedges near this city consist of aloes.
—
30 leagues.

Barcelona, anciently denominated *Barcino,* from Hamilcar Barcas, by whom it was built, is a fine city, charmingly situated, in a delicious climate, near the mouth of the Llobregat; and supposed to contain 111,000 inhabitants: its Port and Mole are handsome. *The ruins of the Roman Town,* and *the Temple of Hercules*—*the Arabian Baths*—*the Cathedral,* a light and elegant Gothic edifice—*the Church of Sa. Maria*—*the Palace of the Captain-General*—*the Exchange*—and *the Academy des Beaux Arts,* merit notice. The Hotels in this city are good; the streets well lighted at night; and the Promenades pleasant; especially those called *the Rembla,* and *the Esplanade. The Capuchin Garden,* at Sarria, is worth seeing; and the Villas near Barcelona are numerous, and well situated.

ROUTE FROM BARCELONA TO SARAGOSSA.

2 Martorell—*Hannibal's Bridge,* and *triumphal Arch,* render this village remarkable: the present Bridge, however, was not erected by Hannibal; but built with the materials of that which he erected.

---

* The books in this Library are placed with the edges of the leaves outward; a singular method introduced into the Escurial by a learned Spaniard of the sixteenth century. *The Casa Reale,* situated in the Park of the Escurial, contains fine pictures.

A fine and populous country.
2 San-Felix
3 Piera—Close to Piera, and isolated in the centre of a plain, rises Montserrat, so called from the word *Serras*, a saw; though its peaks are more like a multitude of sugarloaves, placed on rocks; which, including these peaks, are above three thousand feet in height. This extraordinarily-shaped mountain displays fine grottoes of stalactites: and, in its middle region, stands a Convent, where every stranger meets with a hospitable reception; and where Pilgrims, if poor, whether men or women, are fed for three successive days, whenever they visit the Convent; and if medical assistance be required, they receive it gratuitously. The Hermitages of Montserrat, twelve in number, merit notice; as do the almost endless variety of evergreens, and deciduous plants with which the mountain abounds.

Near the town of Cardona is a lofty hill, consisting of one block of Gemmæ Salt, with which candlesticks, boxes, etc., are made: and this substance is transparent, like rock-crystal.

3 Igualada—The road traverses the river Noya three times. The Inn at Igualada is a good one.
3 Santa-Maria
3 Cervera—This town is situated in a charming valley, and contains a University.
2 Tarraga—An excellent inn. The price of provisions, and of the *Ruido de Casa*, is fixed at every inn by the *Arancel*, or tariff.
4 Mollerusa
4 Lerida—Anciently called *Ilerda*.—Near this place Cæsar was defeated by one of Pompey's generals. There are several Antiquities at Lerida.
5 Fraga
4 Candasnos
3 Bujaralos
3 Venta de S. Luca
3 Aguilar—Here the road crosses the river Cinca. A fine country well cultivated. Road good.
3 La Puebla
3 *Saragossa*—This town was called by the Romans *Cæsar-Augustæ*.
51 leagues.

ROUTE FROM MADRID TO GRANADA.

8 Aranjuez—Viz. 2½ leagues to *Los Angeles*, 3 to *Espartinas*, 2½ to *Aranjuez*, whence to Madrid the road is excellent.
2 Ocanna—Windmills announce to the Traveller that he is entering the province of *La Mancha*, where the customs and manners described by Cervantes still prevail; and where every peasant talks of Don Quixote and Sancho. At the *Venta de Quesada* is a well, distinguished by the name of the Knight.*—Thus is genius immortalized, even by the lowest of the people!
3½ La Guardia—The Church here contains celebrated pictures by Angelo Nardi.
2 Tembleque
2 Canada de la Higuera
2 Madridejos
3 Puerta de Lapiche
2 Villalta—Here Travellers either drive through the Gijuela, or cross it on a bridge.
2½ Venta de Quesada
2½ Mançanares
2 N.S. de la Consolacion
2 Valdepenas—The wines of Mançanares and Valdepenas are much liked.
2 Santa Cruz—The plain of La Mancha begins near Tembleque, at La Concepcion de Almaradiel, the first of the new villages of the Sierra Morena.

The houses, surrounded with cypress-trees, which are seen on this road, belong to German families who came hither to people the country.

2 Almaradiel
3 Las Correderas
3 Las Carolinas
2 Guarraman
2 Baylen
2½ Casa del Rey
2½ Andujar
5 Jaen—Here Travellers are conveyed across the Guadalquivir (anciently the *Bœtis*), in a ferry.
3 Cambil
3 Alcala la Real—This place abounds with citrons, figs, and oranges; and its Abbey is the most amply endowed of any one in Spain.
4 Pinos Puente—Here the Road enters the celebrated Vega, or plain of Granada; and crosses the small river Cubillas.
4 *Granada*.

71½ leagues.

Granada, not long since, was supposed to contain 80,000 inhabitants; but now the population is estimated at only 50,000. *The Cathedral* here, a large and venerable pile, is embellished with fine paintings, by Don Pedro d'Athanasia, Spagnoletto, Risuenno, and John of Seville. *The Cartuxa—Los Angelos—S. Domingo*

* This well communicates with the subterraneous river Guadiana.

—and *the Capuchin Convent*, possess good pictures; and *the Collection of Moorish Antiquities* merits notice.

The Paseo is a pleasant Promenade; so likewise is that on the banks of the Xenil; and the climate is temperate and healthy.

Albambra, justly the pride of Granada, stands on a lofty eminence between the rivers Douro and Xenil, and derives its name from the red colour of the materials with which it is built; the word Alhambra signifying *the Red House*.

This ancient Palace of the Moorish Kings, in point of workmanship, perhaps the most beautiful structure extant, is so well described by Townsend, that I cannot do better than copy his account of it.

" The ascent to this edifice (unique in its style of architecture), is through a shady and well-watered grove of elms, abounding with nightingales. You enter first into an oblong court of 150 feet by 90, with a basin of water in the midst, of 100 feet in length, encompassed by a flower border. At each end is a colonnade. Hence you pass into the court of the lions, so called because the fountain in the middle is supported by lions. It is adorned with a colonnade of a hundred and forty marble pillars. The royal bed-chamber has two alcoves adorned with columns, and a fountain between them in the middle of the room; adjoining are two hot-baths. The great hall is about forty feet square, and sixty in height, with eight windows and two doors, all in deep recesses. Between this and the oblong court is a gallery of ninety feet by sixteen. All these lower apartments have fountains, and are paved either with tiles or marble, in checkers. The idea of the ceilings is evidently taken from stalactites, or drop-stones, found in the roofs of natural caverns. The ornaments of the friezes are arabesque, and perfectly accord with the Arabic inscriptions, which are here suited to the purpose for which each apartment was designed. Thus, for instance, over the entrance to the hall of judgment, is the following sentence: *Enter, fear not; seek Justice, and Justice thou shalt find*. A handsome staircase leads to a suite of apartments intended for the winter."

Adjoining to Alhambra is a Palace begun by Charles V., but never finished; and near it another Moorish Palace, called Xenalarlife, the entrance to which is adorned by two cypress-trees, reputed to have flourished during five ages; they are immensely large.

ROUTE FROM MADRID TO MALAGA.

52½ Andujar--See the preceding route.
 3 Porcuna
 5 Bajena
 4 Lucena
 3½ Alameda
 3½ Antequera
 3 Venta de Cantarrajan
 4 *Malaga*.

78½ leagues.

Malaga, anciently called *Malaca*, and supposed to contain above 45,000 inhabitants, is adorned with a handsome *Cathedral*, the interior of which is beautifully finished; the high altar and pulpit are of fine marble; and the choir is ornamented in a style of peculiar elegance.

The white wine of the mountains near Malaga, and the red wine, called *vino tinto*, are much esteemed, and the fruits are excellent.

Some vestiges of antiquities may be discovered here.

ROUTE FROM MADRID TO CORDOVA, SEVILLE, AND CADIZ.

52½ Andujar—See the route from Madrid to Granada.
3½ Aldea del Rio
3½ Carpio
1½ Cortijo de Casa Blanca
2½ Cordova.

64⅓ leagues.

Cordova, anciently denominated *Corduba*, and reputed to contain near 30,000 inhabitants, was built by the Romans, and subsequently became a Moorish capital. It stands in a charming situation, and is watered by the Guadalquivir. A considerable part of *the Roman Walls* still remain; and *the Cathedral*, once a mosque, is a splendid, though a fantastic edifice.

According to Strabo, Corduba was founded by Marcellus, and the first Roman Colony established in Spain; it boasts of having given birth to Seneca and Lucan.

3 Cortijo de Mango-Negro
3 Carlotta
4 Erija
3 Louisiana
3½ Venta de la Portuguesa
2½ Carmona
3 Jarazone la Vieja
3 *Seville.*

86⅓ leagues.

Seville, anciently denominated *Hispalis*, is supposed to contain above 80,000 inhabitants; and possesses an excellent inn, called *The Posada de la Bavière*. The city stands on the banks of the Guadalquivir, in a rich and beautiful plain: its walls, like those of several Spanish towns, are circular, and seem of Moorish construction. Some of its gates are handsome; and its *Cathedral*, a magnificent edifice, is embellished with a Tower deemed a *chef d'œuvre* of architecture. In the Cathedral are some very fine pictures; that called *The Gamba*, and painted by Luis de Vargas, especially merits notice, as do those of the admirable Murillo, who was born at Seville. The Organ is a very fine one; and the Episcopal Library consists of 20,000 volumes. The *Hospicio de la Caridad* contains the master-piece of Murillo; and *the Capuchin Church* is likewise enriched with several of his works. *The Church of Santa Cruz* contains a fine picture, by Don Pedro de Campanna, of the Descent from the Cross; *the Franciscan Convent* is embellished with paintings by Murillo; as are many other Convents, Churches, and private houses. *The Jesuits' College*, now the Inquisition, is a handsome structure; *the Alcazar, or ancient Moorish Palace*, and its Garden, deserve notice; as do *the Exchange, the University, the Cannon Foundery, the Aqueduct*, and *the Alameda*, or public walk.

One league distant from this city, at the ancient *Italica*, are ruins of an Amphitheatre.

2 Dos Hermanas
3 Venta vieja de Bran
4 Caberas
3½ Cortijos de Romaniana
3½ Xeres de la Frontera—This town is supposed to stand on the site of the ancient *Asti-Regia*, near which spot Roderic, last Monarch of the Visigoths, lost the battle that put a period to their dominion in Spain.
2½ Puerto de Santa Maria
3 La Isla de Leon
3 *Cadiz.*

113¾ leagues.

Cadiz, anciently called *Gades*,

was founded by the Phœnicians, and afterward became a Roman colony. It contains 80,000 inhabitants; is the most flourishing commercial city of Spain, and possesses a safe and very capacious harbour. Among the objects best worth notice at Cadiz are — *the New Custom-house — the Great Hospital — the Capuchin Church*, adorned with an *Ecce Homo*, by Murillo — *the Old* and *the New Cathedral — the Theatre — the Mall —* and *the Ramparts*.

The public amusements consist of bull-fights, French, Italian, and Spanish theatrical exhibitions; assemblies, balls, concerts, and parties of pleasure to Chiclona, a small town four leagues from Cadiz.

The best wines in this neighbourhood are Xeres and Pacaretti.

Travellers who visit Cadiz should take especial care to be supplied with water from the adjacent village, called Puerto de Santa Maria.

The churches and convents of Spain are peculiarly rich in plate and precious stones; but these treasures, however splendidly they may decorate an altar, do not deserve to be named among the objects most worthy of a Traveller's attention: persons who have sufficient leisure, however, would do well to examine them.

CHAPTER XI.

KINGDOM OF THE NETHERLANDS.

PROVINCE OF HOLLAND.

Money—Post-horses—Treckschuyts, etc.—Expense of travelling post from Naarden to Amsterdam—Expense of travelling in a Treckschuyt, etc.—Dutch Inns—Route from Amsterdam to Clêves and Cologne—and from Clêves to the Hague, Rotterdam, and Helvoetsluys—Prices, per Packet, from Helvoetsluys to Harwich—Days appointed for sailing—Route from Amsterdam to Munster—from Amsterdam to Emden—from Amsterdam to Utrecht, Bois-le-Duc, and Maestrich—from Amsterdam to Leyden, the Hague, and Rotterdam—from Nimeguen to Rotterdam and Helvoetsluys—from Nimeguen to Bois-le-Duc and Breda—from Bois-le-Duc to Anvers—from Bergen-op-Zoom to Anvers—from Amsterdam to Hamburgh—and from Hamburgh to Amsterdam, by Groningen and Leuwarden—Population of Amsterdam—Objects best worth notice—Public Amusements—Carriages—Inns—Villages of Broek and Saardam—Dock-yard belonging to the latter—Price of a boat to go and return from Amsterdam to Saardam—Voyage from Amsterdam to Utrecht.

MONEY.

	l.	s.	d.
A stiver, in English money about	0	0	1
A gilder, or florin, 20 stivers	0	1	9
A rix-dollar, 2½ florins	0	4	6
A dry-gilder, 60 stivers	0	5	4
A silver ducatoon, 3 florins 3 stivers	0	5	8
A gold ducat, 20 florins	1	16	0

In Belgium the greater part of the currency is French money.

POST-HORSES, TRECKSCHUYTS, ETC.

Persons who resolve to travel post through Holland, should nedeavour to procure from the first post-master who furnishes them with horses, a paper called *Un billet de Poste*, which enables them to proceed without unnecessary delays, and precludes disputes relative to the number of their horses.

A Traveller who procures this *Billet*, pays to the post-master who gives it the whole expense of his horses, from the place whence they set out to their journey's end; and presents a few stivers to his secretary. The usual price charged by post-masters for every draught-horse, is one florin an hour.*

EXPENSE OF TRAVELLING POST FROM NAARDEN TO AMSTERDAM (TWO DUTCH MILES IN DISTANCE), WITH THREE HORSES.

	Florins.	Stivers.
Horses	12	0
Master of the post-carriages	0	6
Greasing wheels	0	6
Driver	1	0
Tax for the roads	1	0
	14	12

Travelling post in Holland is always expensive, and often disagreeable; for many of the roads are bad: neither ought it indeed to be attempted during spring and autumn, on account of the rains and fogs, which render almost every road so wet and muddy, as to be dangerous; and this circumstance, united to the exorbitant sums usually charged for baggage, makes Dutch Diligences ineligible; therefore, the general mode of travelling is in Treckschuyts, or covered barges. These vessels contain two apartments, the after one, called *the roof*, being neatly fitted up, and appropriated to the best company; the other, to servants, etc. The roof holds from eight to twelve persons, according to the size of the vessel; the inferior apartment from forty to fifty. A Treckschuyt moves precisely at the rate of four English miles an hour; and is drawn by one horse, on whose back rides a lad, called the Conductor. This lad blows a horn as the signal of departure; and uses the same instrument whenever he wishes to have a drawbridge lifted up, and whenever he descries another vessel. Places in the roof should be secured a day before they are wanted. Places in the inferior apartment cost about six stivers each per mile; and places in the roof are something dearer. A roof-passenger is allowed to carry one hundred pounds weight of baggage, cost free.

The Conductor expects from every Passenger about one stiver.

Persons who wish to travel frugally and pleasantly in Holland, should not encumber themselves with much baggage: for Dutch porters are so exorbitant in their charges, and at the same time so notoriously addicted to theft, that it is necessary to make a bargain with them respecting price before trunks are removed; even from one Treckschuyt to another; and equally necessary never to lose sight of a trunk while it continues in their possession. The cheapest way of transporting heavy baggage from one town to another is by means of vessels called Packet-boats.

Dutch Inns are, generally speaking, clean and good: but it is re-

---

* Two leagues of Holland make one post, and two miles of Holland (about nine English miles) equally make one post.

quisite for persons who intend to reside long at any of them, to make an agreement with the innkeeper for the price of apartments, etc.

ROUTE FROM AMSTERDAM TO CLEVES AND COLOGNE.

2½ Naarden—Travellers who come from Germany find the first Treckschuyts here. Naarden stands on the Zuider-Zee.
2½ Amersfort—This town is famous for its manufactures of dimity and bombasins.
2 *Arnheim*—The ramparts here are pretty.
2 Nimeguen—*The Maison de Ville*, where the peace of Nimeguen was concluded in 1678, merits notice; as does *the old Château of Falkenhof*, built by Charlemagne.
2 *Cléves*—*The Castle here—the Hôtel de Ville—the lofty Tower*, from the summit of which above twenty-four towns are discoverable—and the Promenades, all merit notice.
1½ Calcar
1½ Xanten
1½ Rheinbergen
1 Hochstras
1 Undingen
2 Nous
2 Dormagen
1½ Cologne—See, under GERMANY, the route from Vienna, through Ratisbon and Brussels, to Ostend.
——
23 miles of Holland.

ROUTE FROM CLEVES TO THE HAGUE, ROTTERDAM, AND HELVOETSLUYS.

2 Nimeguen
2 Wageningen
5 *Utrecht*—This is a handsome town; and the ruins of its *Cathedral* merit notice; as does its *University* (though inferior to that of Leyden), and its *botanic Garden*. Utrecht is supposed to contain above 30,000 inhabitants.
4 Alphen
2 *Leyden*—The population of Leyden is estimated at 48,000. Its streets are spacious, clean, and well paved; its buildings elegant; and its public institutions useful. It stands on the ancient bed of the Rhine, and the street which contains the Stadt-house is of an extraordinary length. *The Stadthouse*, and *the Hospital*, in this street, are fine buildings; and the Halls of the former exhibit good pictures; the most celebrated of which (by Lucas Van Leyden), represents the last Judgment. Another picture, interesting on account of its subject, represents the famishing Inhabitants of Leyden, after they had compelled the Spaniards to raise the siege of the town, eagerly devouring the relief which was brought to them by their countrymen.
The University of Leyden, founded in 1575, is the most ancient in Holland; and has had among its professors and scholars some of the most learned men in Europe. It contains many objects of interest. The *botanic Garden* merits notice; and *the public Library* is famed for its collection of oriental manuscripts. In the centre of Leyden is *a Tumulus*, said to have been erected by Hengist, the Saxon Prince: it commands an extensive view.*

2 The Hague—This town, or to speak more correctly, this village, is supposed to contain near 40,000 inhabitants. The Voorhout is a fine street, adorned with several elegant buildings, and the Vyverburgh is a handsome oblong square. The Hague is paved with light-coloured bricks, which are kept remarkably clean.
Public entertainments here are reduced to the Dutch Theatre, opened only twice a week; and the price for admittance to the boxes is something more than half an English crown.
About one English mile from the Hague, in *The House in the Wood*, is the national Cabinet of Pictures; which contains a celebrated candle-light piece, by Schallen, the subject being a portrait of William III. of England.
Two English miles from the Hague is Scheveling, where the Stadt-holder embarked when he fled from his country. The road between the Hague and this village is perfectly straight, about twenty paces broad, and shaded by beeches, limes, and oaks, of so extraordinary a magnitude, that they form to appearance an impenetrable forest.
3 *Rotterdam*—This city, reputed to contain 56,000 inhabitants, stands near the confluence of the Rotte with the Maes.

---

* Haerlem is only fifteen English miles distant from Leyden; and well worth visiting, on account of *the Organ* placed in its principal Church, and said to be the finest instrument of the kind existing. Travellers may hear it at any time, by paying a ducat to the Organist, and a couple of guilders to the Bellows-blowers.
The length of the largest pipe is thirty-two feet, and its diameter sixteen inches; the Organ has sixty stops, four separations, two shakes, two couplings, and twelve pair of bellows.
Haerlem disputes with Mentz and Strasburgh the honour of having invented the Art of Printing; and its Bleacheries are famed for the whiteness they give to linen.
The city is neat and well built.

HOLLAND—HELVOETSLUYS, ETC.

The principal streets are intersected by canals, deep enough to receive vessels of three hundred tons burden; and the Boom-Quay is a fine street: but the buildings at Rotterdam are completely Dutch, and consequently inelegant.

The Market-place is adorned with a bronze statue of Erasmus, who was born here.

Concerts are the favourite amusements in this city. The Play-house is small, but neat.

4 Helvoetsluys—At this Port Travellers frequently embark for England.
—
24 miles.

PRICES, PER POST-OFFICE PACKET, FROM HARWICH TO HELVOETSLUYS; AND VICE VERSA.

	l. s. d.
Cabin, or whole Passenger	2 14 0
Half-passenger	1 7 6
Four-wheeled carriage, the charge for shipping it being paid by the owner	6 6 0

After-cabin, if a Family take it to themselves, from twenty-five to thirty guineas, according to the number of beds required.

These rates were established in 1815; but probably they may have been recently lowered, like those to and from Cuxhaven.

Provisions for the Passengers, wine and spirits excepted, are provided by the commander of the vessel, at his own expense.

Harwich packets sail to Helvoetsluys every Wednesday and Saturday, about two o'clock in the afternoon, weather permitting; and return twice a week, if possible.

ROUTE FROM AMSTERDAM TO MUNSTER.

7 *Arnheim*
2 Doesburgh
2 Lanaweert
2 Buckhold
2 Cotsfeld
4 Borken
2 *Munster*—See, under GERMANY, the route from Frankfort on the Mein through Cassel to Munster.
—
21 miles.

ROUTE FROM AMSTERDAM TO EMDEN.

5 Amersfort
1½ Worthluisen
2 Loo—*The Castle* here merits notice.
3 Zwolle—*The large Church*, in the Market-place, is worth seeing.
4 Hardenberg
2 Paylen
2 Sudlar
3 Schwetz
2 Nieuschanz
2 *Emden*—*The Maison de Ville*—*the Arsenal*—*the new Church*—*the great Church*—and *the Tomb of Count John II.* merit notice.
—
26½ miles.

ROUTE FROM AMSTERDAM TO UTRECHT, BOIS-LE-DUC, AND MAESTRICHT.

3 *Utrecht*
5 *Bois-le-Duc*—*The Maison de Ville* is a miniature-copy of the Stadt-house at Amsterdam.
3 Heydenhoren
2 Achelen
1½ Brée
½ Asch
2 *Maestricht*—This is a strong and flourishing town, seated on the Maes, and embellished with handsome public edifices, and pleasant Promenades: it also contains a Theatre.
—
18 miles.

A barge goes daily from Maestricht to Liege, and accomplishes the voyage in six hours. The price of each seat in this vessel is twelve stivers.

ROUTE FROM AMSTERDAM TO LEYDEN, THE HAGUE, AND ROTTERDAM.

3 *Leyden*
2 The Hague—Hence to Rotterdam the country is beautiful.
3 *Rotterdam*.
—
8 miles.

ROUTE FROM NIMEGUEN TO ROTTERDAM AND HELVOETSLUYS.

3½ Thuil
3 Gorinchem—The Maes (here called the Merwe,) abounds with salmon. *The Castle of Lovenstein*, not far hence, was the prison of Hugo Grotius.
3½ Kruympen
1½ *Rotterdam*
4 Helvoetsluys.
—
15½ miles.

ROUTE FROM NIMEGUEN TO BOIS-LE-DUC AND BREDA.

2 Grave
3 *Bois-le-Duc*
1½ Druynen
2 *Breda*—The *Palace* here is a fine building, well fortified.
———
8½ miles.

ROUTE FROM BOIS-LE-DUC TO ANVERS.

3 Eyndhoven
8 Tournhout
4 Oostmalle
4 *Anvers.*
———
19 miles.

ROUTE FROM BERGEN-OP-ZOOM TO ANVERS.

4 Puten
4 *Anvers.*
———
8 miles.

ROUTE FROM AMSTERDAM TO HAMBURGH.

11½ Zwolle
4 Hardenberg
4 Nienhaus
3 Lingen
2 Hoselunen—*The Castle of Clemens-werth*, in this neighbourhood, merits notice.
2 Loeningen
2 Kloppenburgh
3 Wildshausen
1 Delmenhorst
1 Brême
1 Obern-Neuland
1 Fischerhude
3 Kloster-Seven—The Convention of 1757 was concluded here.
4 Buxtehude
1½ Kranz
½ Blankensee—The situation of this village is picturesque.
2 Hamburgh—It is necessary to cross the Elbe in order to reach Hamburgh.
———
46½ miles.

ROUTE FROM HAMBURGH TO AMSTERDAM, THROUGH GRONINGEN AND LEUWARDEN.

4½ Hornburgh
4½ Bremervoerde
3 *Elsfleth*—Here the road crosses the Weser.
7 Barnhorst
1½ Ape
4 Detron
1 Nienschans
1½ Winschoten
1½ *Groningen*—The *Market-place* here, called the *Bree-Markt*, is magnificent; and *the Gothic Tower* of S. Martin's Church is the loftiest building in Holland. *The Library* belonging to the University merits notice; and *the Plantage* is a pleasant Promenade.
A variety of petrifactions are found in the vicinity of this town.
2 Strohbusch
2 Dockum
2 *Leuwarden*
1 Francker
1 Harlingen—This is a handsome town.
14 *Amsterdam*—In order to reach this city, it is necessary to cross the Zuider-Zee.
———
52½ miles.

Amsterdam, situated at the confluence of the Amstel with a rivulet called the Wye, is a fortified town, about nine miles in circumference, and supposed to contain 217,000 inhabitants. *The Stadt-House*, a justly celebrated edifice, is embellished on the outside with statues, among which is a fine colossal Atlas. The Hall where criminals receive sentence, and the Great Hall, together with its bronze Gates, merit notice. The Burgomaster's Apartment contains a fine picture, by Ferdinand Bol, representing Fabricius in the camp of Pyrrhus; and another of Curius at his frugal repast. The Council-chamber is adorned with paintings; one of which, by Vanderhelst, represents the entertainment given by the Burgomasters of Amsterdam to the Ambassadors of Spain, in consequence of the peace of Munster. Another picture, by Vandyck, represents an assembly of the States. The Stadt-house stands upon piles, in number said to be 13,659. *The New Church*, near the Stadt-house, contains Monuments to the memory of several distinguished Dutchmen; and *the Old Church*, called *Oudenkirk*, is enriched with an Organ little inferior, either in size or excellence, to that at Haerlem. This Church likewise contains fine painted glass, and some monuments. Among other public buildings, worth notice, are—*the India House* — *the West India House*—*the Exchange*—*the Bank*—*the Town Arsenals*—*the Admiralty, and its Arsenal*— and *the Orphan Asylum. The Synagogue* of the Portuguese Jews is a fine one: and the Jews have a Theatre in this city, and represent Hebrew plays: there is likewise a Dutch Theatre, and also a French one; but both are ill attended, Concerts being the favourite public amusement. The streets of Amsterdam are, generally speaking, intersected by canals, and adorned with trees. The carriages commonly used are fastened to a sledge, and drawn by one horse; and these vehicles may be hired for half the price of those which run upon wheels. Two of the principal inns are—*The Arms of Amsterdam*, and *The Doelen*.

Near this city stand the pleasant Villages of Broek and Saardam; and in the Dock-yard belonging to the latter, Peter the Great of Russia worked as a common carpenter. The cottage wherein he lived, while thus employed, is still shown to Travellers.

A boat, to go and return from Amsterdam to Saardam, usually costs from six to nine florins.

The voyage from Amsterdam to Utrecht occupies eight hours; and is the most pleasing, in point of scenery, that can be undertaken in Holland.

The Dykes of this country, constructed to preserve it from inundations, are stupendous works, which highly merit notice.

CHAPTER XII.

DENMARK.

Money of Denmark—Price of Post-horses, etc.—Day-book—Passports, etc.—Route from Hamburgh by sea to Helsingoer, and thence by land to Copenhagen—Route by land to Lubeck, or Kiel, and thence by sea to Copenhagen—Expense attendant upon crossing the Great Belt—ditto upon crossing the Little Belt—Copenhagen—Harbour—Population—Naval arsenal—other objects best worth notice—Inn—Environs—Route from Copenhagen to Hamburgh—Route from Copenhagen to Gothenborg.

MONEY OF DENMARK.

	l.	s.	d.
A skilling, in Eng. money about	0	0	0¾
16 skillings, called a mark	0	0	9
A crown, 4 marks	0	3	0
A rix-dollar, 6 marks	0	4	6
A ducat, 11 marks	0	8	3
A hatt-ducat, 14 marks	0	10	6

A mark is an imaginary coin. The Danes usually keep accounts in rix-dollars.

PRICE OF POST-HORSES, ETC.

The customary price of post-horses in Denmark is sixteen skillings a horse, per German mile.

Every postillion is entitled to four skillings per German mile; and for a carriage, furnished by a postmaster, the price is two skillings per German mile:

In the Isle of Funen the price is only ten skillings a horse, per German mile, during summer; but in winter, something more.

In Zeeland the price is fifteen skillings a horse, per German mile.

In addition to the price of post-horses, two skillings and a half per mile are paid at every barrier.

To every English carriage, containing four places, post-masters have a right to put six horses; and to every English carriage, containing two places, four horses: but three persons going in an open post-chariot of the country, and having only one trunk, are not compelled to take more than one pair of horses.

Persons who travel post in Denmark, and in the Duchy of Holstein, receive, at every post-house, a *billet*, containing the hour, and even the moment of their departure from that station. Postillions are bound to drive at the rate of one German mile an hour; and dare not stop, nor even smoke, without permission from the Traveller; who, on changing horses, gives his *billet* to the post-master; and at the same time mentions whether the postillions have behaved well or ill; and, in the latter case, they are severely punished.

At every post-house there is a day-book, in which the Traveller is required to write his name, the hour of his arrival, and that of his departure; making, on the margin, his observations, and complaints, if he think himself in any respect aggrieved.

No innkeeper can allow a Traveller to leave his house before this useful regulation has been complied with; and the day-books of every inn are examined once a month by Government.

Passports are always requisite in the Danish Islands: they are presented to the officer on guard, at the gate of every city; and, after having been inspected and signed, they are returned to their owners by a soldier, who solicits a trifling gratuity for his trouble.

Persons who like a sea voyage may embark at Hamburgh, in a vessel bound to the Baltic, and land at Helsingoër; where these vessels cast anchor; and where carriages returning to Copenhagen, which is only five German miles distant, may be met with constantly

Another way of accomplishing this journey is to travel by land either to Lubeck, or Kiel; and then proceed by sea to Copenhagen. From Hamburgh to Kiel is twelve German miles; from Hamburgh to Lubeck eight; and the voyage from the latter port to Copenhagen is shorter than from Kiel: but at Lubeck Travellers pay for every trunk a tax of one rix-dollar; and at Kiel considerably less.

EXPENSE ATTENDANT UPON PASSING THE GREAT BELT.

	Marks.	Skillings.
Embarkation of a carriage	1	8
Passage of ditto	21	0
Taxes, etc	3	2
Drink-money for the men who embark a carriage	1	2
Fees to soldiers who have the charge of passports	0	13
Landing a carriage, independent of drawing it from the water side to the post-house	0	12
Drink-money for the boatmen	1	0

The length of this passage is about four German miles.

EXPENSE ATTENDANT UPON PASSING THE LITTLE BELT.

	Marks.
Embarkation and passage of a carriage.	9
Disembarkation of ditto	3

The length of this passage, between Snoghoe and Middlefart, is only half a German mile: but between Aroe and Assens it is four times that distance.

No Foreigner is allowed to enter Copenhagen without exhibiting a passport; and, on quitting this city, it is necessary to procure, from the High-President, another passport, which costs three marks.

Copenhagen, the metropolis of Denmark, and called in the Danish language, *Kiobenhavn*, stands on the Island of Zeeland; and is defended by four royal castles, and embellished with a fine harbour, formed by a large Canal flowing through the city, and capable of receiving five hundred ships; though it admits only one at a time.

Copenhagen has suffered much from the ravages of war; but, some years since, it contained above 90,000 inhabitants, and a peculiarly fine *naval Arsenal*, which still merits notice. Among other objects best worth observation in this city are, *the University*, founded in 1745, and richly endowed—*the Library* belonging to the University—*the Cabinet of Natural History*—*the Royal Museum*—*the royal Library*, containing 120,000 volumes—*the Church dedicated to the Saviour*, and *that dedicated to the blessed Virgin*—*the Seminary for naval Cadets*—*the Academy of Painting and Sculpture*—*the Barracks*—*the equestrian Statue of Christian V.*—*the Exchange*—*the ruins of the Castle of Christianburgh*—*the Obelisk erected in 1793*, to commemorate the deliverance of the peasants from the chains of feudal slavery; which was effected by the interest of Frederick VI., when heir-apparent to the throne—*the Statue of Frederick V.*—and *the Theatre.**

The grand Hotel is a good inn.

About twenty English miles from Copenhagen is *Fredericsburgh*, the most splendid royal Residence in Denmark: and near Helsingoër, is *a royal Villa*, supposed to stand upon the ground formerly occupied by the palace of Hamlet's father: and in an adjoining Garden is shown the spot where, according to tradition, that Prince was poisoned.

Jaegerspreiss, about six German miles from Copenhagen, also belongs to the royal Family; and stands in a Park, which contains several ancient Tombs of northern Heroes; together with the Monuments of Tycho Brahe and Bernsstorf.

Marielust, a royal Villa about five German miles from Copenhagen, commands a remarkably fine view; and the road to Eenroom likewise exhibits beautiful scenery.

ROUTE FROM COPENHAGEN TO HAMBURGH.

German miles.

4 *Roeskilde*—The Cathedral here contains the tombs of the Danish Kings: and the water in this town is excellent.

4 *Ringstedt*—Between Ringstedt and Slangense is the celebrated *College of Sora*.
The principal Church at Ringstedt contains the tomb of Canute, and is likewise the burial place of other Danish Princes.

4 Slangense

2 Korsoër—Here Travellers embark upon the Great Belt.

4 Nyborg

4 *Odensee*—This is the capital of the isle of Funen.

---

* Several of the finest works of the Chevalier Thorwaldsen are destined to enrich the royal Collection of Sculpture at Copenhagen.

5 *Assens*—Here Travellers cross the Little Belt.
2 Aroësund
2 Hadersleben
4¼ Apenrade
4½ Flensborg—A safe port, capable of admitting very large vessels.
4½ *Sleswick*—This is the capital of the Duchy of Sleswick.
3¼ Rendsborg—Here the Eyder marks the boundary between Germany and Denmark.
3 Remmel
3 Itzcho
3¼ Elmshorn
2¼ Pinneberg
3¼ *Humburgh.*

62¼

ROUTE FROM COPENHAGEN TO GOTHENBORG.

German Miles.
6 Helsingborg — Between Copenhagen and Helsingborg Travellers cross the Sound, and enter Sweden.

Swedish Miles.*
1 Fleminge
1½ Engelholm
1¼ Margaretha-Torp—Hence to Karup, the road is very hilly.
1 Karup
1¼ Laholm—Here is a fine fall of the Loga-Strom.
2¼ Halmstat
1¼ Quibille
1¼ Sloeinge
1½ Falkenberg
1¼ Marup
1⅞ Warberg—This is a safe Port.
2 Bacha
1½ Alsa
1¼ Kingsbaka
1 Kjarra
¼ *Gothenborg.*

6 German miles.
21⅞ Swedish miles.

CHAPTER XIII.

SWEDEN AND NORWAY.

Money—Price of Post-horses, etc.—Route from Stralsund to Stockholm, through Carlscrona—Stockholm—Population—Harbour—Streets—Royal Residence—other objects best worth notice—Promenades—Public Amusements—Inns—Environs—New Upsala—Spot where the Kings of Sweden in ancient times were elected—Iron Mines—Route from Stockholm to Upsala—ditto from Stockholm to Gothenborg—Description of that town—Prices per Packet from Gothenborg to Harwich—Route from Gothenborg to Christiania and Bergen.

MONEY OF SWEDEN.

The common currency of this country is paper; of which there are two kinds, namely Bank-paper, and Government-paper, distinguished from each other by the word *Banco* being added to the first, and *Rixgeld* to the second. They are of very different value; Government-paper having suffered a depreciation of above thirty per cent; while Bank-paper continues at par. Calculations are generally made in Government-paper; so that payments either in Bank-paper, or copper, go for one-third more than their denomination.

Gold and silver coins can seldom, if ever, be met with; but the following copper coins are in common use.

Rundstychs . . 12 of which make 1 skilling.
Stivers . . . . 4 of which make 1 skilling.
Skillings . . . 8 of which make 1 dollar.

Forty-eight skillings, or six dollars, make one rix-dollar, in value from two to three English shillings, according to the exchange.

* One mile of Sweden is about one mile and a half of Germany.

The Bank notes are of the following kinds:

8 Skillings — 12 skillings — 24 skillings — 1 rix-dollar — 2 rix-dollars — 3 rix-dollars — and so on, up to 30 rix-dollars.

The Government notes are of the following kinds:

16 skillings — 32 skillings — 1 rix-dollar — 2 rix-dollars.

Accounts are usually kept in rix-dollars.

PRICE OF POST-HORSES, ETC.

The charge for every post-horse, per Swedish mile (rather more than six English miles and a half), is, at Stokholm, sixteen skillings Banco — in several other towns, twelve skillings Banco — but in some of the country villages only eight skillings Banco.

Every postillion is entitled to one skilling and a half per station; and with four skillings they are well satisfied.

The hostler at each station is entitled to one skilling.

To heavy carriages post-masters frequently put six or seven horses.

Foreigners who take their own carriage to Sweden, should likewise take harness; and also be especially careful to chain one of their wheels when going down hill.

Foreigners, on arriving in Sweden, should provide themselves with a passport from the Governor of the Province they happen first to enter. They should likewise solicit from the Governor of the first town through which they pass, an order for post-horses: it is also requisite, in many parts of this country, to send forward a person, called a *Forebud*, to bespeak the number of horses required by the Traveller at every post. The expense of employing a Forebud, is one silver dollar per station; though if horses thus ordered wait for the Traveller beyond the time appointed by him, the post-master has a right to one silver dollar an hour for this detention.

Every post-house contains a day-book, in which Travellers are required to enter their name and rank, the time of their arrival, the place they came from, and whither they are going; the number of horses they want, their complaints, if they have any to prefer against the post-master, and also the time of their departure. This day-book is inspected every month by Government.

The roads throughout Sweden are excellent; and no tolls are demanded, unless it be on crossing bridges; neither do robbers infest the highways: but postillions, during winter, are apt, in order to save ground, to drive over lakes not thoroughly frozen; and, during spring, for the same reason, to venture upon sheets of ice beginning to thaw; in consequence of which practice so many lives have been lost, that Travellers should never permit their drivers to quit the great road.

Foreigners who take their own carriage across the Sound pay high for its passage: but travelling carriages on sale, may frequently be met with at Helsingborg and Gothenborg; and open carriages of the country (a sort of cart, hung upon springs, and sufficiently large to contain two persons, and one trunk), may always be procured for eight or ten crowns.

The rate of posting in Sweden is from seven to ten English miles an hour.

Travellers should take provisions with them from city to city; because the eatables found in small towns and villages are not good.

ROUTE FROM STRALSUND, THROUGH CARLSCRONA, TO STOCKHOLM.

Persons who design crossing the Channel to Ystad should endeavour to announce their intention, either on a Saturday or a Monday morning, at the post-office at Stralsund. The public packet-boat sails from the last-mentioned town toward night, and arrives at Ystad next morning.

The prices per public Packet are—

	Crowns.	Skillings.
For every Cabin Passenger, one trunk and one portmanteau inclusive........	2	36
For every Servant..........	2	12
For every Horse	2	12
And for every four-wheeled Carriage............	4 or 5.	

A private yacht may be hired for seventy rix-dollars, drink-money and other trifling expenses not inclusive.

Stralsund contains near 11,000 inhabitants: its *Cathedral* merits notice; as do *the Church of S. Mary*, and its Organ; *the Town and College Libraries;* and *the Cabinet of Natural History*.

16 Ystad—This town is small, but well built; and the German inn is the best. In the vicinity of Ystad is the Castle of Marswinsholm.
⅞ Herrenstad
1⅞ Tranas
1½ Andrarum
1½ Degeberga
1¼ Nebbelof
1 *Christianstad*—This is a strong fortress, where Travellers should take care to have their Passports countersigned.

The gates of the town are shut every night at ten o'clock. The trade carried on here is considerable; and among the objects best worth notice are, *the Arsenal—the Governor's Residence—the principal Church*—and *the Bridge*.

1 Fielding
1½ Gadenry
1½ Norjo
1½ Assarum
1 Trensum
1¼ Stoby
1½ Ronneby
1½ Skillinge
1½ *Carlscrona*—This town, supposed to contain 16,000 inhabitants, possesses a Harbour capable of receiving a hundred ships of the line; and is celebrated for its covered Docks; and likewise for an artificial rise and fall of water, constructed to remedy the want of the ebb and flow of the tide.
⅞ Rubbetorp
1½ Killeryd
1½ Fur
1½ Emmeboda
1½ Ericksmala
1½ Kulla
1½ Lenhofta
1½ Nybbeled
1⅝ Stokdorp
2 Stwetland
1⅝ Bransmala
1½ Ecksioe—*The Church* here merits notice; and between this place and Berga are three Stones, inscribed with Runic characters.
1⅞ Bone, *or* Berga
2 Sathella
2⅜ Hester
1¼ Dala
¾ Moelby
1⅞ Bankeberg
1 *Linköping*—This town contains a celebrated *College* and a fine *Cathedral.*
1⅝ Kumla
1¼ Brink
1¼ *Norkœping*—This is one of the handsomest and one of the most commercial towns in Sweden: it contains 9,000 inhabitants.
¾ Oby—The lofty marble mountains of Kolmorden begin here.
1½ Krokek
1¼ Wreta—At Staffsia, near Wreta, there is a rich iron mine.
1⅛ Jaeder
1¾ *Nikœping*—This is a large and handsome commercial town.
2¼ Swardbro
2 Oby
1½ Pilkrog
1½ *Soedertellje*—From Soedertellje to Stockholm, Travellers have the option of going by water.
2 Fithie
1½ *Stockholm*—Two roads, the one eighty Swedish miles and one-eighth, the other eighty-one and seven-eighths, in distance, lead from Stralsund through Jonkoping to Stockholm.

———

84 Swedish miles.

The site of Stockholm, the metropolis of Sweden, is singular, romantic, and beautiful.

This city is built upon seven small rocky islands of the Baltic, beside two peninsulas: its edifices stand upon piles; and the number of its inhabitants is supposed to be 76,000.

The harbour, though difficult of access, is extensive and convenient; and of such a depth, that ships of the largest burthen can approach the Quay, which is lined with capacious warehouses. The streets rise above one another in an amphitheatrical shape, and are crowned by *the regal Palace,* a large, quadrangular, and magnificent structure. A long Bridge, composed of granite, forms the approach to this Palace; opposite to which (at the other extremity of the bridge), is a Square, adorned with an equestrian statue of Gustavus Adolphus, and containing two handsome edifices, namely, the Palace of the Princess Sophia, and the Italian Opera-house. The furniture of the regal Palace is superb; and among the pictures, several of which merit notice, is a celebrated Combat of Animals. The statues were collected by Gustavus III.; many of them are antique; and the Endymion belonging to this collection is particularly admired.

The Church of S. Nicholas contains a good picture of the last Judgment, and a statue of S. George—*the Church of Riddarholm* contains the Tombs of the Swedish Kings; and on that of Charles XII. are a Club, and a lion's skin—characteristic ornaments! Opposite to the Hôtel de Ville is *the statue of Gustavus Vasa;* and, on the Quay, *that of Gustavus III. The Maison des Nobles,* and *the Arsenal* are worth seeing; and the prospect from the Tower of S. Catharine is particularly beautiful.

Stockholm contains a royal Academy of Sciences; a royal Academy of Painting and Sculpture; a royal Cabinet of Natural History; and a royal Cabinet of Medals; all of which merit notice; as do the royal Library, the Library belonging to the Academy of Sciences, and the Studio of Sergel, a celebrated Sculptor.

The principal promenades are, the King's Garden; the royal Hop-Garden; the Park, and the Bridge of Boats. The public amusements consist of Italian operas, Swedish plays, concerts, and balls; the two last being given by Clubs, called the Amaranth, the Narcissus, etc.

Among the principal inns are, *The English Tavern; the Crown;* and *the Cave of Bacchus.* The English Tavern furnishes Travellers with breakfast and dinner; the other inns provide breakfast only:* there is, however, a Club, called the Selskapet, which furnishes a dinner daily to as many of the members as may choose to partake of it. The dinner costs about twenty-pence English a head; liquors, ice, and coffee, not included; and every member has power to introduce a Stranger for one month.†

In the neighbourhood of this city is the royal Palace of Ulricsdal, which contains the Library of Queen Ulrica Eleonora; a Cabinet of Natural History, arranged by Linnæus; some paintings, and a statue of King Frederick.

Drottningholm, a very large edifice, finely situated on the banks

---

* The price of breakfast at an hotel is about two English shillings per head, and the price of apartments from ten to fifteen English shillings a room per week.

† The price paid for washing linen in Sweden is exorbitant, and so likewise are the wages demanded by travelling servants.

of the Mœlar, is another royal Residence, in the vicinity of Stockholm; and contains a Cabinet of Natural History, arranged by Linnæus: here likewise is a Picture Gallery.

On the way to Drottningholm stands a rock, called The Royal Hat; and upon which an iron hat is now placed in memory of Eric II., who, being pursued by enemies, jumped off this rock, and thereby lost his hat, but saved his life.

Haga is a small and elegant royal Villa, situated very near Stockholm; and about forty-five English miles from this Metropolis is New Upsala, formerly the capital of Sweden, and built near, if not actually upon, the foundations of Old Upsala, a place of high antiquity; and, previous to the introduction of Christianity in Sweden, the abode of the high-priest of Odin.

Upsala, so called from the river Sala, which runs through it, is a well-built town, containing about 3,500 inhabitants, and the most celebrated University of northern Europe, instituted by Steno Sture, in 1476, and particularly patronised by Gustavus Adolphus. Its Library is open to the public on Wednesdays and Saturdays; and consists of above 60,000 printed volumes, and about 4,000 manuscripts; among which is the celebrated *Codex Argenteus*, or translation of the Gospels into the Gothic language: the leaves are stained with a violet colour, the letters are capitals, and were all originally done in silver, except the initial characters, and a few passages, which are done in gold.*

The Cabinet of Natural History and Botanic Garden were arranged by Linnæus.

The Cathedral, begun in the thirteenth century, under the direction of Bonneville, a Frenchman, is deemed one of the handsomest churches in Sweden, and particularly deserves attention on account of its monuments, ancient and modern (among which are those of Gustavus Vasa and Linnæus), the treasures of its Sacristy and the Shrine, wherein rests the mortal part of King Eric.

About seven English miles from Upsala is the spot where the Kings of this country, in very ancient times, were elected: it lies in the middle of the plain of Mora; and is distinguished by the remains of several Runic stones; on the largest of which, called The Morasten, the Sovereigns were enthroned; while their name and the year of their election were inscribed upon another of these stones.

Near Upsala is the iron Mine of Dannemora, reputed to produce the best iron in the world; and upward of ninety fathoms in depth.

This mine has been worked for near five centuries; and persons who wish to examine it descend in a bucket to the spot where the miners are employed.

ROUTE FROM STOCKHOLM TO UPSALA.

2 Rotebro
1¾ Mnerstadt
1¾ Alsike
1½ *Upsala*.

7 Swedish miles.

ROUTE FROM STOCKHOLM TO GOTHENBORG.

1½ Barkarby
1½ Tibble
2 Gran

---

* Ulphilas, a bishop of the Goths, flourished under the Emperor Valens, and was the first person who translated the Bible into the Gothic language: his translation of the Gospels is the only part of this work now extant.

SWEDEN AND NORWAY—GOTHENBORG.

1½ Lisslena
1 *Enköping*—Here are some Ruins of Convents and Churches.
1 Nigwarn
2 *Westeras*—The *Cathedral* here and its Tower merit attention.
2 Kolbek
1½ Kiœping
½ Oestuna
1 *Arboga*—The Canal of Arboga unites the Lakes of Hielmar and Mœlar. In the environs of Arboga are several Antiquities, supposed to have been the work of very ancient Northern nations; and a Forest, in which it is imagined that their religious ceremonies were performed.
1½ Faelingsbro
1½ Glantshammer
1½ *Orebro*
1 Mosos
1 Blakstad
2 Wiby
2 Bodame
2½ Hoswa
1¾ Walla
2 Binneberg
2 Skiaerf
1 Skara
1½ Wonga
2 Wedum
1¾ Siæfde
2½ Alingsos
1½ Ingarid
1⅔ Lerum
2 *Gothenborg.*

47¾ Swedish miles.

This town, supposed to contain 25,000 inhabitants, is placed in a picturesque situation on the banks of the Gotha: and among the objects best worth attention here, are, *the four Bridges—the Swedish Church*, and its *Cupola—the German Church—the College*, and its *Library—the India House—the little Gothic Castle of West-Gotha—the Vauxhall—the Promenades of Carlsport*, and *the view* from the summit of Otterhollen.

The Hotels at Gothenborg are expensive, but not good. An apartment, consisting of two rooms only, can seldom be obtained under a sum equivalent to twenty-five English shillings per week. Breakfast costs from eighteen-pence to two shillings, English money, per head; dinner these hotels do not furnish.

Harwich-Packets sail to Gothenborg every Wednesday and Saturday, about two o'clock in the afternoon, weather permitting; and return twice a week, if possible.

	l.	s.	d.
The price paid by a Cabin Passenger, unless recently lowered, is	14	5	6
The price paid by a Half Passenger	7	13	6
The price for conveying a four-wheeled Carriage	15	15	0

ROUTE FROM GOTHENBORG TO CHRISTIANIA.

2¼ Lahall
1¼ Cattleberg
1¾ Edet-Luck
1 Forss
1 Gerdeim
1 Trolhaëtta—The magnificent *Cataracts and Sluices of Trolhaëtta* are well worth notice.
1½ Wenersborg
1 Almas
1 Raknebo
1¾ Herrstadt
1½ Quistroëm
1¾ *Swarteborg*
1 Ratalshed
1½ Stede
1½ Skyalleryd
¾ Wick
1 Est
¾ Stroëmstadt
1½ Stogdal
1½ Helle
⅞ *Fredericshall*—Here are some handsome public buildings.
The spot where Charles XII. expired is usually visited by Travellers.
1½ Guslund
1½ Thune
1½ Kaelshuset
1¾ Willingen
1½ Soner
1 Sunbije
1 Korsegarten
1 Schutsjoryd
2½ *Christiania.*

38½ Swedish miles.

This town, the capital of Norway, is situated in a spacious valley, and supposed to contain between nine and ten thousand inhabitants.

ROUTE FROM CHRISTIANIA TO BERGEN.

2 Asker—The road leading to Asker is excellent, and the situation of that place beautiful.
Here are rocks of a stupendous height.

2 Bragernes
¾ Gusnestro
1¾ Simonstadt
1¾ Sunby
1¾ Nordby
¾ Hiemb
¾ Asken
1 Stecholt
¾ Hochstedt
1 Skeen
1¾ Brewig
1¾ Eeg
¾ Wallekirch
3 Krageron
2 Oster-Risoër
¾ Groenesund
¾ Moene
1¾ Ongestadt
½ Berge
1 Waagė
1½ Assen
1 Sansted
½ Nederneskongs
1 Grimsted
1 Hogested
1½ Magested
1½ Birkeland
1 Obel
1 Wee
2 *Christiansund*—This is a considerable town and port.
4 Mandal
1½ Spangelried
1½ Porshafen
1½ Farsund
1 Bistereid
2 Hitteroë
1½ Sognedall
2½ Eggersund
1½ Sirevog
1 Qualleen
1½ Hoberstadt
1½ Brune
½ Opevad
½ Ganu
2½ *Stavanger*—The Cathedral here is better worth notice than any other in Norway, that of Drontheim excepted.
5 Karsund
10 *Bergen.*

60 Swedish miles.

This is the largest and most commercial town in Norway, and contains near 20,000 inhabitants: its Port is remarkably safe; and its *Cathedral*—*German Church*—*Castle*—*Hospital*—and *Magazines*, merit notice. Here are public Seminaries; and a Society for the encouragement of useful enterprises.

CHAPTER XIV.

RUSSIA.

Money of Russia—Price of Post-horses, etc.—Podaroshna—other requisites for Travellers in Russia—Russian Voiturins—Passports—Route from Riga to Petersburgh—Population of Petersburgh—situation of that city—Streets—Admiralty—Admiralty-Quay—Isaac-Platz, and equestrian Statue of Peter the Great—Church of S. Isaac—Summer Palace—Marble Palace—Winter Palace and its Church—Hermitage—Imperial Collection of Paintings and Academy of Sciences—Fortress—Church of the Holy Virgin of Casan—other Edifices, etc. worth notice—Seminaries—Charitable Institutions—Manufactories—Cottage inhabited by Peter the Great—Promenade and other public Amusements—Inns—Cronstadt—Royal Villas—Formalities required before Foreigners can quit Petersburgh—Route from Petersburgh to Moscow—account of the latter city—Route from Petersburgh to the Frontier of Sweden—Route from Moscow to Grodno—Route from Moscow to Riga, and the Frontier of Prussia.

MONEY OF RUSSIA.

A copeck.... 2 denuscas—in English money something less than ½*d*.
An altin .... 3 copecks
A grievener . 10 copecks
A polpotin .. 25 copecks
A poltin..... 50 copecks
A rouble ....100 copecks
A Xervonitz. 2 roubles.

A copeck is an imaginary coin. Accounts are kept in roubles.

PRICE OF POST-HORSES, ETC.

The usual price of post-horses in Russia is two copecks a horse per verst (near two-thirds of an

English mile); unless it be a verst royal, when the price is doubled.

A Russian postillion cannot demand more than one copeck a horse per verst; but Travellers generally give five copecks per verst, which is deemed liberal payment.

Post-masters are directed, by the last Imperial Ukase, to put three horses to every carriage containing two or three persons.

Between Perm and the Government of Tobolsk, between that Government and Uffa, and likewise on the roads beyond these districts, only one copeck per verst is paid for each horse from October till April; and in the Governments of Tobolsk and Irkutsk only half a copeck. In the territory of Kolhivano and Vorsnesenki the price varies according to the season; one copeck being charged from April till October, and only half that sum from October till April.

No person is allowed to travel post without having first obtained an order for post-horses, signed by a Governor civil or military: and every Traveller, on receiving this order, which is called a *Podaroshna*, must pay a tax of one copeck per verst for every horse mentioned in the order.

The consequence of the low price of post-horses is, that Foreigners frequently find it difficult to obtain them; but, exclusive of this circumstance, the posts are well served. The horses go remarkably quick, whether harnessed to wheel-carriages or sledges; and at every verst stands a post, expressing the distance from the last town to the next. During winter it is usual to travel in sledges; which proceed with such velocity, that a journey of two hundred and fifty versts may be accomplished in twenty-four hours. The common Russian wheel-carriage, for travelling, is called a *Kibitka*, and resembles a cart.

Travelling beds and sheets are absolutely necessary in this country; a bed being a scarce commodity, even in cities, and always unattainable at a country-inn. It is likewise requisite to take provisions from town to town.

Russian Voiturins have fleet horses, and a great deal of custom. The real, if not the ostensible Voiturins are the Post-masters: for when their post-horses are not employed by order of Government, they have the privilege of letting them out for hire; charging five copecks per verst on the great roads; but on the cross roads only three: and when all the post horses are engaged, they furnish Travellers with what are called Peasants' horses; charging for these an advanced price, and demanding much more than they take.

No Foreigner can enter Russia without exhibiting a passport signed by a Russian Minister: and persons who travel in this country, should neither leave their carriages unlocked, nor unguarded; because the common people are inclined to thieve.

ROUTE FROM RIGA TO PETERSBURGH.

Riga, next to Petersburgh, the most commercial town of the Russian Empire, is seated on the Duna; and contains within its fortifications about 9,000 persons, and in its suburbs about 15,000. Among the most remarkable edifices here, are *The Hôtel de*

Ville—the Exchange—the imperial Palace—the Cathedral—the Arsenal—S. George's Hospital—S. Peter's Church—the Russian Hospital—the Theatre—and the Custom-house. The floating bridge thrown over the Duna, and the Garden of Vitinghof, are the principal Promenades.

Riga contains several good private lodgings; and two tolerable inns; the best of which is, *La Ville de Petersbourg.*

Versts.
11 Neuenmülhun—Government of Riga.
15 Kilkensfehr—A sandy road.
  Passage of the Aa
19 Engelhardshof
21 Roop—This town is adorned with handsome edifices.
22 Lenzenhof
18 Wolmar
18 Stakeln
21 Gulben
  Passage of the Embach
18 Toilitz
22 Kuikatz
24 Uddern
25 Dorpat
23 Iggafer
23 Torma
  Lake of Peypus, which divides the Governments of Riga and Petersburgh.
25 Nennal—Government of Petersburgh.
14 Rana-Pungern
24 Klein-Pungern—Here Travellers going to Petersburgh quit the Lake of Peypus.
20 Kiew—The Gulf of Finland is discoverable here.
11 Fokenhofs, *or* Kudley—The road lies near the banks of the Gulf.
17 Waiwara
22 Narva—Travellers whose Passports are not sealed by the Emperor, are visited by the Custom-house Officers here.
22 Jamburgh
  Passage of the Narowa
15 Opolie
25 Czerkowitz
22 Kaskowa
19 Kiepen
25 Strelna
17 *Petersburgh*—Superb villas, and other handsome buildings, form the avenues to this splendid capital.
——
558 versts, about 370 English miles.

The account given of Petersburgh by Mr. James, a modern Traveller, is so beautiful, and at the same time so accurate, that persons possessed of his " Journal of a Tour in Germany, Sweden, Russia, and Poland," can require no further information respecting the metropolis of the Russian Empire : but to persons who are not fortunate enough to possess his work, the following account may, perhaps, be acceptable.

Petersburgh is said to contain about 200,000 inhabitants, exclusive of Cronstadt, a Fortress which defends the entrance of the Neva, and is the principal station of the imperial navy. Petersburgh stands on both sides of the Neva, between the Lake Ladoga and the Gulf of Finland; and is built partly upon the continent, and partly upon islands in the mouth of the river; the right bank exhibiting the old town, and the left bank the new one; through which pass three Canals, adorned with Bridges, and magnificent Quays of Granite. The streets of the new town are, generally speaking, spacious; three of them, which meet at the admiralty, being of an extraordinary length; and these streets are intersected by others embellished with handsome esplanades. *The Admiralty* exhibits a façade of more than a quarter of an English mile in length, adorned by six porticos, and surmounted with a gilt dome and spire; and at the back of this immense structure is the Dock-yard. The *Admiralty-Quay*, erected by Catherine II., does honour to her memory. Among several other objects which merit the attention of a traveller are *the Isaac Platz*, ornamented with an equestrian statue, in bronze, of Peter the Great, done by Falconet; and representing Peter in the act of mounting an eminence, the summit of which he has nearly attained: his right hand is stretched out, as if he were blessing his people; while with the left, he holds the reins. An enormous rock of granite which, when transported to Petersburgh from the morass wherein it was found, weighed above fifteen hundred tons, forms the pedestal. The statue is said to be a striking likeness of Peter, and cost the Empress Catherine II., by whom it was erected, 424,610 roubles.— *The Church of S. Isaac*, a magnificent, though a heavy edifice, of hewn granite—*the imperial summer Palace* (a beautiful specimen of architecture) and *its public Garden*—*the marble Palace*, built by Catherine II. for Prince Orloff— *the imperial winter Palace*, which contains the Jewels of the Crown, and the famous diamond purchased by the Empress Catherine of a Greek, to whom she paid for it 450,000 roubles, and a pension of 100,000 livres-tournois for life —*the Church belonging to this palace*—*the Hermitage*, which, notwithstanding its name, contains magnificent apartments, and a summer and winter garden; the first, in the Asiatic style, occupying the whole level roof of the edifice, the other being a spacious hothouse, adorned with gravel-walks, orange-trees, and parterres of flowers, and peopled with birds of various climates—*the imperial collection of Paintings* — *the imperial Academy of Sciences*, which contains a Library rich in Chinese and Sclavonian manuscripts: (here also are instructions relative to a code of laws, written by the hand of the Empress Catherine.) The Academy likewise contains a Museum of Natural History particularly rich in ores (among which is a mass of native iron 1656lbs. in weight); a collection of Rarities, comprising a variety of ornaments found in the tombs of Siberia, many being of massive gold and very elegant workmanship; idols brought from Siberia; arms and dresses of the various inhabitants of the Russian Empire; among which are Japanese habits and armour, a collection of coins; and a waxen figure of Peter the Great, the features of which were taken from a mould applied to his face after death. — The Fortress, or Citadel, which is surrounded by walls of brick faced with hewn granite, and contains *the cathedral of S. Peter and S. Paul*, is a noble edifice adorned with a spire of copper gilt. Here are deposited the remains of Peter the Great, and most of his successors: and in the Fortress is preserved a four-oared boat, said to have been the origin of the Russian navy, and called by Peter, the Little Grandsire. *The Church of the Holy Virgin of Casan;* a splendid edifice, recently built, and supposed to have cost 15,000,000 roubles, The architect was a Russian slave. by name Woronitchki, and educated at the imperial Academy— *the Lutheran Church of S. Anne* —*the convent and Church of S. Alexander Newski* — *the new Exchange*—*the statues of Suwarrow and Romanzow*—*the great Theatre*—*the Quays of Newa, Fontaka, and Koika*— *the great Market*—*the new Bank*—and *the Arsenal*, which contains trophies and armour belonging to various nations.

The Corps des Cadets, the Couvent des Demoiselles nobles, and the Institute of Catherine, are excellent seminaries for the education of the nobility, and some children of inferior rank. The annual income of the first is 30,000l. sterling; and the two last are richly endowed; and likewise enjoy the advantage of being patronised and constantly inspected by the Dowager Empress.

The general Hospital, the Foundling Hospital, the Asylum for the Deaf and Dumb, and the Asylum for Widows and Orphans are munificently endowed, and remarkably well conducted charities.

The imperial cotton Manufactory, the imperial plate-glass Manufactory, the imperial tapestry, porcelain, and bronze Manufactories, and the iron Foundry, merit notice.

The cottage inhabited by Peter the Great, while he constructed the Fortress, stands in the old town; and is still shown to Travellers. It contains but three rooms, only eight feet in height, and the largest not more than fifteen feet square. A boat, made by the Czar himself, is kept near this cottage.

The most frequented promenade at Petersburgh is the Boulevards, which consist of three avenues of trees carried round three sides of the Admiralty: the public amusements are concerts, given in the Hall of Music, and exhibitions in the Theatres.

The best inns are, *La Ville de Londres—La Ville de Grodno—La Ville de Paris*—and *L'Hôtel de Madrid.*

The Fortress of Cronstadt, its Arsenal and Docks, merit notice; but cannot be seen without permission from the Governor.

There are twelve royal Villas in the neighbourhood of Petersburgh. *Tschesme* contains portraits of the reigning Princes of Europe—*Tzarskoe-Zelo*, about fifteen English miles from the metropolis, contains a room incrusted with amber, and a garden which merits notice; but the house is too gaudy—*Peterhof*, about five miles further distant, is called the Versailles of the North.

It is necessary that Foreigners, previous to quitting Petersburgh, should have their names advertised three times in the gazette; which added to the formalities required for obtaining the *podaroshna* and passports, occupies some time.*

ROUTE FROM PETERSBURGH TO MOSCOW.

Versts.
- 22 S. Sophia—District town. Government of Petersburgh.—A few versts from Petersburgh begins the wooden road constructed by Peter the Great; and consisting of a platform of small trees, which, when not neatly joined together (and this frequently occurs), is so rough, that the Russians, in order to mitigate the inconvenience, fill their travelling carriages with soft pillows.

  The country between Petersburgh and Moscow is covered, generally speaking, with thick forests of birch and fir.
- 11 Igiora
- 25 Tosna
- 32 Pomerania—Government of Novgorod.
- 25 Tischoudovo
- 24 Spaskaja-Poliste
- 24 Podberezie
- 22 *Novgorod*—Government town. Novgorod, supposed to have been founded in the fifth century, and once so potent as to have been called *The Resistless*, possessed, during the plenitude of its power, upward of

---

* The distance from Petersburgh to Cronstadt is, by land, 47 versts.
From Petersburgh to Vyborg, 139 versts.
From Petersburgh to Smolensko, 838 versts.
From Petersburgh to Archangel, 1,145 versts.
From Petersburgh to Astracan, 1,479 versts.
The Almanack published yearly by the Academy of Sciences at Petersburgh contains a table of the Russian towns, with their distances from Petersburgh and Moscow.

400,000 inhabitants: and though now depopulated, and hastening fast to decay, it still exhibits vestiges of former magnificence; among which are *the Walls of the Kremlin*, and *the Church of S. Sophia*, containing the Tombs of Valdomir and Feodor; together with curious specimens of architecture, and paintings supposed to have been executed previous to the revival of the Arts in Italy. Its brazen Gates are reported to have been brought from the Crimea at the time of Valdomir's expedition against the Greek Empire.

35 Bronnitzi
27 Zaiffova
31 Krestzi—District town.
16 Rachino
22 Jagelbitzi
22 Zimogorie
20 Jedrovo
36 Kotilovo
36 Wischnei-Wolotzek—District town. Government of Tver.
33 Widropouskoe
38 Torjock—District town.
33 Mednoe
30 *Tver*—Government town; handsome, very commercial, and seated on the Volga.
26 Wosskresenkoe
31 Zadivovo—Government of Moscow.
26 Klin—District town.
31 Pecheki
22 Tschernaia-Griasse
28 *Moscow*.

728 versts, about 520 English miles.

Moscow, the ancient capital of the Russian empire, and thirty-five versts in circumference, is watered by the Moskwa; and before the French invaded Russia possessed upward of 300,000 inhabitants. The Kremlin, or citadel, which stands on an eminence in the centre of the town, is a large walled circle, containing a gaudy mass of Asiatic, Grecian, and Gothic edifices; and comprehending the Holy Gate, through which every passenger walks bareheaded; the Trinity Church; together with those of S. Nicholas and the Assumption; the Chapel and Palace of the Czars; and the lofty Tower of Ivan Veliki, crowned by a steeple and gilt dome. The Palace of the Czars is a gorgeous structure in the Hindoo style, and was erected about two hundred years ago. The domes of the various buildings are many of them gilt, the roofs stained either green or red, and the walls and towers covered with glazed tiles of various colours, or adorned with paintings which represent scriptural histories.

The imperial palace was gutted by the French; as was an ancient edifice containing an apartment which is used as the public hall of audience at the coronation of the Russian sovereigns. Part of the walls of the Kremlin, and one of the towers near the river, the church of S. Nicholas, the four great bells of Moscow, the walls of the arsenal, and a piece of the gate of S. Nicholas, were blown up, and the tower of Ivan Veliki rent from the top to the bottom, by mines prepared and exploded at the command of Napoleon, when he was compelled to relinquish his long-looked-for asylum in Moscow, by a master-stroke of Russian policy, which reduced the greater portion of the town to ashes, and thereby, in all probability, saved the empire from being conquered by France.

Moscow is now rising rapidly from its ashes, though vestiges of the conflagration still remain. The most frequented Promenade here is the Boulevards; and *The German Hotel* is one of the best inns.

ROUTE FROM PETERSBURGH TO THE FRONTIER OF SWEDEN.

Versts.
24 Dranichenikovo
15 Beloostrofskoe
25 Lindoula—Government of Vyborg.
20 Pampala
19 Souvenoia
20 Kemera
22 Vyborg—Government town.
20 Tervaioki
17 Vilaioki
23 Ourpala

16 Puterlakce
18 Grenvic
16 Frideriksham—District town.
23 Kiumene-Gorodock
22 Puttice—Last station in Russia.
5 Aborforce—Upon the river Kiumene.

305 versts, about 200 English miles.

ROUTE FROM MOSCOW TO GRODNO.

Versts.
27 Perkouchekovo—Government of Moscow.
26 Koubinskoe
22 Chelkova
24 Mojaisk—District town.
27 Gridnevo—Government of Smolensko.
29 Ishatsk—District town.
30 Teplouka
29 Viasma—District town.
26 Semlovo
23 Giachekova
28 Dorogobusch—District town.
23 Mikailovka
24 Pneva
17 Bredikino
23 *Smolensko*—Government town. There is a fine Cathedral at Smolensko.
23 Koritnia
23 Krasnoi—District town.
18 Liadi—Government of Mogilew.
16 Koziani
14 Doubrovna
17 Orcha—District town.
28 Kokanova
18 Tolotzine
15 Maliavka
15 Kroupki
23½ Lochenitzi—Government of Minsk.
17 Borysow—District town.
17½ Jodino
17½ Smolevitzi
15½ Jouchnovka
21 Minsk—Government town.
21½ Gritchina
18½ Koidanovo
14½ Komel
21½ Novoc-Svergino
25 Nesvig—District town.
28 Mire—Government of Lithuania.
24 Korclitzi
21 Novogrodok—District town.
36½ Belitza
28 Joloudoke
14 Tstouchino
14 Kamenka
21 Skidel
35 *Grodno*—Frontier town.

996½ versts, above 700 English miles.

Grodno is the capital of Lithuania, and contains *a Palace*, erected by Augustus III.; *a medicinal College*, and *a botanic Garden*; together with several decayed buildings which evince its ancient splendour.

ROUTE FROM MOSCOW TO RIGA, AND THE FRONTIER OF PRUSSIA.

Versts.
489 Orcha—See the route from Moscow to Grodno.
20 Orcki
18 Babinovitzi—District town.
25 Poloviki
22 Vitepske—Government town.
21 Staroe—Government of Vitepske.
21 Kourslofschina
17 Doubovike
22 Ostrovliani
15 Peroutina
12 Polotske—District town.
9 Gamzeleva
26 Logofka
25 Proudniki
25 Driza—District town.
19 Tschourilova
18 Drouia
20 Koesslavle
22 Plokcha
22 Dinaburg—District town.
17 Kirousska
17 Avcenova
20 Livenhof
16 Tripenhof
22 Glazmaneke
24½ Kopenhausen
21 Remershof
16 Jounternhof
23 Ogershof, *or* Iskile
21 Kirkholm, *or* Choupel
14 *Riga*—Government town.
19 Alaie
20¾ *Mittau*—Government town.
   Mittau, the capital of Courland, is extensive, but not populous. The *Ducal Château* merits notice, as do the *Reformed Church* and the *Academy*.
28 Doblene—Government of Courland.
24½ Berggof
29½ Frauenburg
28½ Strounden
24 Gross-Drogen
19 Taideken
25½ Ober-Bartau
27 Routzau
21 Palangen—Government of Lithuania. A Custom-house on the Frontier of Prussia.

1346½ versts, above 960 English miles.

AN ALPHABETICAL LIST

OF

TOWNS, RIVERS, GULFS, ISLANDS, ETC.

WITH

THEIR ANCIENT NAMES.

Towns.	Ancient Names.	
Abano	Aponum	Italia.
Acerenza	Acherontia	Magna Græcia.
Adra	Abdera	Hispania.
Agen	Aginum	Gallia.
Aix	Aquæ-Sextiæ	Gallia.
Albenza	Albium Ingaunum	Italia.
Alba	Alba-Pompeia	Italia.
Alcara de Henares	Complutum	Hispania.
Almasa	Numantia	Hispania.
Almaden	Sisapo	Hispania.
Alicant	Lucenium	Hispania.
Almeria	Murgis	Hispania.
Algesiras	Tingentera	Hispania.
Amiens	Ambianum	Gallia.
Angers	Andevacum	Gallia.
Antibes	Antipolis	Gallia.
Aousta	Augusta-Prætoria	Italia.
Arezzo	Aretium	Italia.
Arras	Atrebates	Gallia.
Ascolo	Asculum	Magna Græcia.
Assisi	Asisium	Italia.
Augsburgh	Augusta-Vindelicorum	Germania.
Auch	Ausci	Gallia.
Autun	Augustodunum	Gallia.
Auxerre	Antissiodurum	Gallia.
Avignon	Avenio	Gallia.
Baca	Basti	Hispania.
Baia	Baiæ	Magna Græcia.
Balaguer	Bergusa	Hispania.
Balbastro	Balbastrum	Hispania.
Barcelona	Barcino	Hispania.
Bari	Barium	Magna Græcia.

ALPHABETICAL LIST OF TOWNS.

Towns.	Ancient Names.	
Benevento	Beneventum	Magna Græcia.
Besançon	Vesontio	Gallia.
Bergamo	Bergomum	Italia.
Bevagnia	Mevania	Italia.
Bilboa	Flaviobriga	Germania.
Bisignano	Besidiæ	Magna Græcia.
Bologna	Bononia Felsinia	Italia.
Bolsena	Volsenum	Italia.
Bourdeaux	Burdigala	Gallia.
Boulogne	Gessoriacum	Gallia.
Boianno	Bovianum	Magna Græcia.
Bregentz	Brigantium	Germania.
Brest	Brivates	Gallia.
Briançon	Brigantia	Gallia.
Brindisi	Brundisium	Magna Græcia.
Calais	Portus-Iccius	Gallia.
Canapina	Capena	Italia.
Canosa	Canusium	Magna Græcia.
Casal-novo	Manduria	Magna Græcia.
Castel di Brucca	Velia	Magna Græcia.
Castel-à-mare	Stabiæ	Magna Græcia.
Catania	Catana	Sicania-Sicilia.*
Carthagena	Carthago-nova	Hispania.
Capua	Casilinum	Magna Græcia.
Cadiz	Gades	Hispania.
Calahorra	Calaguris	Hispania.
Cambray	Camaracum	Gallia.
Cahors	Cadurci	Gallia.
Cajazzo	Calatia	Magna Græcia.
Castigliano	Carsula	Italia.
Castro-Vetere	Causon	Magna Græcia.
Cassano	Cosæ	Magna Græcia.
Castro-Giovanni	Henna	Sicilia.
Caserta	Staticula	Magna Græcia.
Cerveteri	Cære	Italia.
Ceuta	Abyla	Hispania.
Chieti	Teate	Magna Græcia.
Chiusi	Clusium	Italia.
Chartres	Carnutes	Gallia.
Châlons	Catalauni	Gallia.
Châlons-sur-Saône	Cabillonum	Gallia.
Citti di Castello	Tifernum-Tiberinum	Magna Græcia.
Civita-Castellana	Fescennium	Italia.
Civita-Vecchia	Centumcellæ	Italia.
Civita della Vigna	Lanuvium	Italia.
Como	Comum	Italia.

* These names it derived from the Sicani and Siculi, who peopled a considerable part of the country: it was also called Trinacria and Triquetra, from its triangular figure.

ALPHABETICAL LIST OF TOWNS.

Towns.	Ancient Names.	
Cochile	Sybaris *	Magna Græcia.
Cortona	Coritus	Italia.
Cologne	Colonia Agrippinæ	Germania.
Collioure	Caucoliberis	Hispania.
Cordova	Corduba †	Hispania.
Conza	Compsa	Magna Græcia.
Cronstadt	Prætoria	Germania.
Crotona	Croton	Magna Græcia.
Cuma	Cumæ	Magna Græcia.
Denia	Dianeum §	Hispania.
Dijon	Dibio	Gallia.
Elche	Illici	Hispania.
Embrun	Embrodunus	Gallia.
Essek	Mursa	Germania.
Eugubio	Iguvium	Italia.
Evoli, or Eboli	Eburi	Magna Græcia.
Evora	Ebora	Hispania.
Faenza	Faventia	Italia.
Faro	Ossonoba	Hispania.
Fano	Fanum Fortunæ	Italia.
Faro di Messina	Mamertini	Sicilia.
Fermo	Fermum	Italia.
Fiesole	Fæsulæ	Italia.
Florence	Florentia	Italia.
Foligno	Fulginium, or Fulginas	Italia.
Fondi	Fundi	Italia.
Forli	Forum-Livii	Italia.
Forlim-Popoli	Forum-Popilii	Italia.
Frascati	Tusculum	Italia.
Genoa	Genua	Italia.
Genzano	Cynthianum	Italia.
Gibraltar	Calpe	Hispania.
Girgenti	Agrigentum	Sicilia.
Granada	Eliberis, or Garnata	Hispania.
Grenoble	Gratianopolis	Gallia.
Guadix	Acci, or Colonia Accitana	Hispania.
Guardamar	Alone	Hispania.
Huesca	Osca	Hispania.
Imola	Forum-Cornelii	Italia.
Joigny	Joviniacum	Gallia.
Ispello	Hispellum	Italia.
Itri	Urbs Mamurrarum	Italia.
Ivrea	Eporedia	Italia.
Lamentana	Nomentum	Italia.

* Afterward called Thurii; and here Herodotus lived and died.
† Called, by the Romans, Patricia.   § Called, by the Greeks, Artemisium.

ALPHABETICAL LIST OF TOWNS.

Towns.	Ancient Names.	
Langres	Lingones	Gallia.
La Riccia	Aricia	Italia.
Larina	Larinum	Magna Græcia.
Lavinia	Lavinium	Italia.
Leghorn	Portus Labronis Herculis	Italia.
Lerida	Ileuda	Hispania.
Leyden	Lugdunum Batavorum	Gallia.
Lintz	Lentia	Germania.
Liria	Edeta	Hispania.
Lisbon	Olisippo, Olyssipo, Ulyssipo *	Hispania.
Limoges	Lemovices	Gallia.
Lodi	Laus Pompeia	Italia.
Lorca	Eliocroca	Hispania.
Lucero	Luceria†	Magna Græcia.
Ludove	Luteva	Gallia.
Lyons	Lugdunum	Gallia.
Marubio	Marrubium	Italia.
Madrid	Mantua	Hispania.
Malaga §	Malaca	Hispania.
Marseilles **	Massilia	Gallia.
Marburgh	Mattacum	Germania.
Matteo	Indibilis	Hispania.
Macon	Matisco	Gallia.
Messina	Messana	Sicilia.
Mentz	Maguntiacum	Germania.
Merida	Augusta-Emerita	Hispania.
Mequinenza	Octogosa	Hispania.
Metz	Divodurum	Gallia.
Milan	Mediolanum	Italia.
Miranda	Deobriga	Hispania.
Miseno	Misenum	Sicilia.
Milasso	Myle	Sicilia.
Modena	Mutina	Italia.
Modica	Mutyca	Sicilia.
Mola di Gaëta	Formiæ	Italia.
Monaco	Portus Herculis Monœci	Italia.
Monte Leone	Mutusca	Italia.
Montpellier	Agathopolis	Gallia.
Monselice	Mons-Silicus	Italia.
Murcia ††	Vegilia	Hispania.

* Said to have been founded by Ulysses. † Famed for its wool.
§ Built by the Phœnicians, who called it מלח (salt), from the quantity of salt-fish sold there.
** Once inhabited by a colony of Phœnicians.
†† Murcia was likewise called Tadmir; that is, *productive of palm-trees*; with which the southern part of Spain abounds; there being, near Alicant, a forest, reported to contain above two hundred thousand.

ALPHABETICAL LIST OF TOWNS.

Towns.	Ancient Names.	
Murviedro	Saguntum	Hispania.
Narni	Narnia, or Nequinum	Italia.
Narbonne	Narbonensis	Gallia.
Nantes	Condivicum	Gallia.
Nato	Netum	Sicilia.
Nevers	Nivernum	Gallia.
Nissa	Naissus	Germania.
Nismes	Nemausus	Gallia.
Nipi	Nepete	Italia.
Norsia	Nursia	Italia.
Norma	Norba	Italia.
Noyon	Noviodunum	Gallia.
Novara	Novaria	Italia.
Nocera	Nuceria	Magna Græcia.
Nuremburgh	Norica	Germania.
Orihuela	Orcelis	Hispania.
Orléans	Aureliani	Gallia.
Otranto	Hydrantum	Magna Græcia.
Otricoli	Ocriculi, or Ocriculum	Italia.
Paderno	Hybla	Sicilia.
Padua	Patavium	Italia.
Pavia	Ticinum	Italia.
Palestrina	Præneste	Italia.
Pæstum	Posidonia	Magna Græcia.
Palermo	Panormus	Sicilia.
Pampeluna	Pompelo	Hispania.
Paris	Parisii vel Lutetia	Gallia.
Perugia	Augusta-Perusia	Italia.
Pesaro	Pesaurum	Italia.
Perigueux	Petrocorii	Gallia.
Piacenza	Placentia	Italia.
Pistoja	Pistoria	Italia.
Piperno	Privernum	Italia.
Pignerol	Pinarolum	Gallia.
Pisa	Pisæ	Italia.
Piombino	Populonia	Italia.
Pozzuoli	Puteoli *	Magna Græcia.
Poictiers	Pictavi	Gallia.
Porto-Venere	Portus-Veneris	Italia.
Ponte-Corvo	Fregellæ	Italia.
Prattica	Lavinium	Italia.
Ratisbon	Reginum	Germania.
Ragusa	Epidaurus	Germania.
Resina	Retina	Magna Græcia.
Reggio†	Rhegium Lepidi	Magna Græcia.
Rennes	Redones	Gallia.

* Called, by the Greeks, Dicæarchia.   † The birth-place of Ariosto.

ALPHABETICAL LIST OF TOWNS.

Towns.	Ancient Names.	
Rheims	Durocorturum	Gallia.
Ricti	Reate	Italia.
Rimini	Ariminum	Italia.
Rome	Roma	Italia.
Roma-Vecchia	Pagus Lemonius	Italia.
Roveredo	Roboretum	Germania.
Rouen	Rotomagus	Gallia.
Rosas, or Roses	Rhoda	Hispania.
Ruvo	Rubi	Magna Græcia.
Salobrina	Selimbena	Hispania.
Sassina	Sarsini	Italia.
S. Maria dei Faleri	Falerii	Italia.
S. Donato	Appii-Forum	Italia.
S. Vitorino	Amiternum	Italia.
Salerno	Salernum	Magna Græcia.
Saragossa	Cæsar-Augusta	Hispania.
Salamanca *	Salamantica	Hispania.
S. Lucar	Fanum Luciferi	Hispania.
Saintes	Santones	Gallia.
St. Paul-trois-Châteaux	Augusta-Tricastrinorum	Gallia.
St. Quentin	Aug.-Veromanduorum	Gallia.
S. Mareo	Calacta	Sicilia.
S. Lorenzo	Laurentum	Italia.
Saleme	Halicyæ	Sicilia.
Salpi	Salpia	Magna Græcia.
Saragusa	Syracusæ	Sicilia.
Seville	Hispalis †	Hispania.
Setuval	Cætobrix	Hispania.
Segorbio	Segobriga	Hispania.
Sens	Senones	Gallia.
Sezze	Setinum	Italia.
Sermoneta	Sulmona	Italia.
Siena	Sena-Julia	Italia.
Sisseg	Siscia	Germania.
Sorrento	Syrentum	Magna Græcia.
Soissons	Augusta-Suessonum	Gallia.
Spoleto	Spoletum	Italia.
Spire	Noviomagus	Germania.
Starmonetta	Sulmo	Italia.
Susa	Segusium	Italia.
Tarracon	Turiago	Hispania.
Tarento	Tarentum	Magna Græcia.
Tangiers	Tingis	Hispania.

* A Roman road may be traced from Salamanca through Merida to Seville.
† Founded by Scipio Africanus, according to some authors; and by others supposed to have been built by the Phœnicians, and afterward called, by the Romans, Julia.

ALPHABETICAL LIST OF TOWNS.

Towns.	Ancient Names.	
Tariffa	Mellaria	Hispania.
Tarragona	Tarraco *	Hispania.
Termini	Thermæ	Sicilia.
Temeswar	Tibiscus	Germania.
Terni	Interamna	Italia.
Tertosa	Dertosa	Hispania.
Tivoli	Tibur	Italia.
Tiano	Teanum	Italia.
Tortona	Dertona	Italia.
Torre di Mare	Metapontum	Magna Græcia.
Tours	Turones	Gallia.
Toledo	Toletum	Hispania.
Toulouse	Tolosa	Gallia.
Trepani	Eryx	Sicilia.
Triers, or Treves	Augusta-Trevirorum †	Germania.
Troyes	Augusta-Tricassium	Gallia.
Trent	Tridentum	Germania.
Trieste	Tergeste	Germania.
Turin	Augusta-Taurinorum	Italia.
Valladolid	Pintia	Hispania.
Valencia	Valentia	Hispania.
Valence	Valentia	Gallia.
Venosa	Venusia §	Magna Græcia.
Vera	Urci	Hispania.
Verdun	Varodunum	Gallia.
Venafro	Venafrum	Magna Græcia.
Venice	Venetiæ	Italia.
Vegel	Besippo	Hispania.
Viterbo	Volturnum	Italia.
Vienna	Vindebonna	Germania.
Vicenza	Vicentia	Italia.
Vicenza	Picentia **	Magna Græcia.
Villa-Franca	Carthago-Vetus	Hispania.
Voltera	Volaterræ	Italia.
Worms	Borbetomagus	Germania.
Xeres de la Frontera	Asta Regia	Hispania.
Xativa	Setabis	Hispania.
Zamora	Sentice	Hispania.

Rivers.	Ancient Names.	
Adaja	Areva	Hispania.
Adige	Athesis, or Atagis	Italia.
Aisne	Axona	Gallia.
Almone	Lubricus Almo	Italia.

* Founded by the Scipios. † Supposed to be the most ancient city of Europe.
§ Where Horace was born. ** Near Pæstum.

ALPHABETICAL LIST OF RIVERS.

Rivers.	Ancient Names.	
Arno	Arnus	Italia.
Cicabo	Cyane	Sicilia.
Danube	Danubius *	Germania.
Dauro	Dat-aurum	Hispania.
Douro	Durios, or Durius	Hispania.
Durance	Druentia	Gallia.
Ebro	Iberus	Hispania.
Elbe	Albis	Germania.
Farsa	Fabaris	Italia.
Fiumecino	Rubicon	Italia.
Foglia	Isaurus	Italia.
Freddo	Crinisus	Sicilia.
Galeso	Galesus	Italia.
Garigliano	Liris	Italia.
Garonne	Garumna	Gallia.
Giaretta	Simœthus	Sicilia.
Girona	Gerunda	Hispania.
Guadalete	Lethe	Hispania.
Guadiana	Anas	Hispania.
Guadalquiver	Bœtis	Hispania.
Inne	Oenus	Germania.
Isère	Isara	Gallia.
Lamo	Lamus	Italia.
Liquienza	Liquentia	Italia.
Loire	Ligeris	Gallia.
Llobregat	Rubrigatus	Hispania.
Marne	Matrona	Gallia.
Magra	Macra	Italia.
Mein	Mœnus	Germania.
Metaro	Metaurus	Italia.
Mincio	Mincius	Italia.
Moselle	Mosella	Germania.
Mugnone	Minio	Italia.
Negro	Tanager	Italia.
Nera	Nar	Italia.
Ofanto	Aufidus	Magna Græcia.
Ombrone	Umbro	Italia.
Pisatella	Rubicon †	Italia.
Po	Padus	Italia.
Pretatore	Ufens	Italia.
Rhine	Rhenus	Germania.
Rhone	Rhodanus	Gallia.
Saône	Arar	Gallia.
Savio	Sapis	Italia.
Sarno	Sarnus	Magna Græcia.
Segura	Terebus, or Tader	Hispania.

* Called at its mouth the Ister.
† So denominated because it flows into the Rubicon.

ALPHABETICAL LIST OF RIVERS, LAKES, ETC.

Rivers.	Ancient names.	
Serchio	Ausar	Italia.
Seine	Sequana	Gallia.
Silaro	Silarus	Magna Græcia.
Tajo	Tagus	Hispania.
Teverone	Anio	Italia.
Tesino	Ticinus	Italia.
Tevere	Tiberis, or Albula	Italia.
Tiferno	Tifernus	Magna Græcia.
Topino	Tinia	Italia.
Var	Varus	Italia.
Velino	Velinus	Italia.
Volturno	Vulturnus	Magna Græcia.
Xenil, or Genil	Singulis	Hispania.
Xucar	Sucro	Hispania.

Lakes and Bays of Italy.	Ancient Names.
Bolsena, Lake of	Vulsinus.
Bonifaccio, Straits of	Fossa Fretum.
Bracciano, Lake of	Sabatinus.
Celano, Lake of	Fucinus.
Chiama, Lake of	Clanius, or Clany.
Como, Lake of	Larius.
Constance, Lake of	Brigantinus.
Fondi, Lake of	Fundanus.
Garda, Lake of	Benacus.
Genoa, Gulf of	Mare-Ligustium.
Maggiore, Lake of	Verbanus.
Manfredonia, Gulf of	Urias Sinus.
Messina, Straits of	Fretum Siculum.
Naples, Bay of	Crater Sinus.
Perugia, Lake of	Trasymenus.
Policastro, Gulf of	Laus Sinus.
Quarnaro, Gulf of	Flanaticus Sinus.
Salerno, Gulf of	Pæstinus Sinus.
S. Euphemia, Gulf of	Hippinates Sinus.
Spezia, Gulf of	Portus Lunæ.
Squillace, Gulf of	Scylacius Sinus.
Venice, Gulf of	Adriaticum Mare.

Spain.	Ancient Name.
Alicant, Bay of	Illici Sinus.

Islands in the Mediterranean Sea, anciently called Mare Internum.

Capri . . . . *anciently*	Caprea.
Corsica	Cyrnus.
Elba, or Elva	Ilva.*
Hieres	Stæchades.
Ischia . . . , ...	Inarime, or Ænaria.
Malta	Melita.†
Nisida	Nesis.
Procida	Prochyta.
Stromboli	Strongyle.
Sicily	Sicania-Siciliæ.

* Noticed by Virgil for its mines of iron.
† Supposed, by some authors, to be the island where St. Paul was shipwrecked.

ADDENDA.

SICILY.

Concise History of the Island—most eligible months for visiting it—Palermo—Ægesta—Trapani—Marsala—Selinuntium—Sciacca—Agrigentum—Licata—Terranova—Biviere di Lentini—Syracusæ—Catania—Ætna—Giarra—Castagno di cento Cavalli—Francavilla—Taurominium—Messina—Melazzo—Rheggio—Lipari Islands—Cefalu—Mermini—Character of the Sicilians—Productions of Sicily—Climate—Manner of Travelling—Prices paid by Travellers—Requisites for Travellers—Routes, and Distances from place to place.

SICILIA, or, as it is usually called, Sicily, the largest island in the Mediterranean Sea, was anciently denominated *Sicania, Trinacria,*[1] *Triquetra,* and *Sicania-Siciliæ.* Its form is triangular; each of the extremities being terminated by a promontory; one of which, anciently called *Lilybæum,* faces Africa; another, called *Pachynum,* faces the Peloponnesus; and the third, called *Pelorum,* faces Italy. Tradition says, Pelorum was thus named by Hannibal, in honour of his Pilot, Pelorus. The last mentioned Promontory now bears the appellation of Capo del Faro (from the Pharos erected there); Pachynum is called Capo Passaro, and Lilybæum Capo di Boco. Two Rocks, not far from the Sicilian shore, have long been the dread of mariners and the theme of poets; that, named Scylla, situated a few miles from Messina, on the Calabrian side; and, on the opposite side, in the Straits of Messina, was the other, called Charybdis. During tempestuous gales, the noise of the waves, dashing violently against Scylla, and then precipitating themselves into caverns at its base, still resembles the howl of dogs and beasts of prey.

" Dire Scylla there, a scene of horror forms;
And here, Charybdis fills the deep with storms:
When the tide rushes from her rumbling caves
The rough rocks roar, tumultuous boil the waves."

But though Scylla still is, occasionally, the terrific monster thus described by Homer, Charybdis has ceased to resemble the appalling Whirlpool he mentions: indeed, it is almost a matter of difficulty, now, to ascertain the identical situation of this Whirlpool; notwithstanding we are told by writers, long subsequent to Homer, that the rapidity of the currents, and the irregular and violent flux and reflux of the sea, in the Straits of Messina, once made Charybdis most dangerous.[2]

Sicily is computed to be about sixty-six leagues in length, and in breadth forty-five; but its size does not seem precisely known. It contains several lofty mountains; and elevated above them all towers Ætna, a double-headed giant, continually vomiting sulphur and flames. Several rivers fertilize the Island, which was once denominated the Granary of Rome: and were this soil properly tilled, it would produce more corn than any country of its size existing.

---

[1] From its three Promontories of Lilybæum, Pelorus, and Pachynus.
[2] See HOMER, *Odyssey,* Book xii.—STRABO, 6.—MELA, ii. c. 7.—PAUSANIAS, iv. c. 23.—DIODORUS SICULUS, 4.—THUCYDIDES, i. etc.— and HERODOTUS, vi. c. 23, 1. 7. c. 28.

The pasturages, flocks, and herds sacred to Apollo, were celebrated by ancient Bards; the plain of Enna[1] was famed for delicious honey; and, according to Diodorus Siculus, hounds lost their scent in hunting, on account of the odoriferous flowers which profusely perfumed the air: an anecdote worthy of credit, as the flowers in Sicily, during Spring, are, at the present day, abundant and fragrant beyond description. The surrounding sea teems with excellent fish; in short, nature appears to have lavished all her treasures on this Island.

As to its political history, Sicily, like the Kingdom of Naples, properly so called, may be compared to a Brilliant of the first water, which has, from time immemorial, excited the cupidity of Princes; and alternately fallen into the hands of those, for the moment, most powerful. Its original inhabitants were, according to received opinion, a very gigantic race; and skeletons of a most uncommon length have certainly been found in Sicilian tombs. These Aborigines, called Cyclops, and Læstrygones, are reported to have been Anthropophagi; what became of them is unknown; but, when the Sicani colonized in Sicily, the greater part of the Island was uninhabited. They are supposed to have been Spaniards, who dwelt near the Sicanus, a small river in Spain; and from these Settlers Sicily acquired the name of Sicania. They erected towns on the heights; and each little State was governed by its own Chief. During the reign of these petty Princes Hercules is said to have landed on the Island, and embellished it with a Temple, not far distant from Argyra, the birth-place of Diodorus Siculus. The Cretans likewise, led by Minos, invaded the Sicani, in pursuit of Dædalus, who took refuge among them, after having justly offended the Monarch of Crete: but the Ruler of the Sicani, while promising to give up the culprit, and at the same time receiving Minos with dissembled friendship, treacherously put him to death. This event occurred thirty years previous to the Trojan war, and, at a subsequent period, the Tomb of Minos was discovered by labourers, who were making the Walls of Agrigentum.[2] At length the Siculi (a nation of Campania, driven from their possessions by the Opici) passed, on rafts, the Strait[3] which separates Magna Græcia from Sicily, invaded the Island, and obtained a permanent footing on its shores. This occurred above a thousand years previous to the Christian era, and gave birth to perpetual warfare between the Sicani and the Invaders; till at length both parties agreed to divide the Island between them: and attracted by the great renown for wisdom and virtue enjoyed by the sons of Æolus, King of the Æolides, they likewise agreed to invest these Princes with sovereign power over Siculi, as the Island seems, at that period, to have been called; and they had no cause to repent their determination. But when this Royal Race was extinct, the Si-

---

[1] Now Castro-Giovanni.

[2] These Walls were solid indigenous rocks, cut into the form of walls; and ancient Sicilian Tombs are frequently found in rocks.

[3] This Strait, called from the Siculi, *Siculum Fretum*, is fifteen miles long; but, in some places, so narrow that the barking of dogs may be heard from shore to shore: the Strait is supposed to have been formed by an earthquake, which separated Sicily from the Continent.—Plin. iii. c. 8.

cani and Siculi (become one people) chose their Sovereigns from among their own compatriots; which measure unfortunately occasioned feuds and civil war, the cankerworms of national strength. These feuds, however, did not prevent the people of Siculi, or Sicania-Siciliæ, as it was then denominated, from receiving with humanity the ill fated Trojans, who sought an asylum among them, after the destruction of Troy: but the Phœnicians and Greeks, aware of the diminished force of a country distracted by internal commotions, took advantage of this circumstance, by planting Colonies there; and at length the Carthaginians became masters of the whole Island, till dispossessed, by the Romans, during the Punic wars. Its most celebrated Cities, when it fell under the Roman yoke, were Syracusæ, Messana (anciently *Zancle*), Leontium, Lilybæum, Agrigentum, Gela, Drepanum, and Eryx: and the inhabitants of these Cities were so prone to luxury, that *Siculæ mensæ* became proverbial. When the Greeks colonized here, they inspired the Sicilians with a passion for the Muses. Stesichorus, a native of Himera in Sicily, who flourished above six hundred years before the Christian era, was a celebrated Poet; insomuch that Phalaris, Sovereign of Agrigentum, exhorted the citizens of Himera (a town subsequently destroyed) to erect a temple to his memory; and offered to provide them with money and workmen for this purpose; at the same time advising that all their temples should become the depositories of the poems of Stesichorus. Sicily may be called the birth-place of Pastoral Poetry, as Theocritus, in both senses of the word, the first of pastoral Poets, was born at Syracuse. Epicharmus, a native of the same town, introduced Comedy there, about four hundred years previous to the Christian era, and, according to some opinions, was the Inventor of this species of composition. Sicily likewise gave birth to Tragic Poets; among whom were Empedocles, grandson to the philosopher, and Dionysius II, Sovereign of Syracuse. She was also famed for the eloquent oratory of her sons: and produced, among several renowned philosophers, the illustrious Empedocles; whose works were so enlightened, that Lucretius seems to question whether their author was a mortal; and whose virtues were so eminent, that his compatriots repeatedly offered him the sceptre of their country, which he as repeatedly refused. Tradition says, this unambitious man precipitated himself into the crater of Ætna; thinking that his sudden disappearance might induce a belief of his having been received among the gods: more probably, however, he accidentally fell into the crater, while prosecuting his philosophical researches: his sandals, being made of bronze, were disgorged by the Mountain, and thus proclaimed the manner of his death. Diodorus, as already mentioned, was a Sicilian: he composed a Universal History, in forty parts; travelled through most of the countries which he describes, and was thirty years in writing his Work. Ancient authors, fearful of being erroneous, never wrote in haste—they respected the public. Archimedes, too, was a Sicilian, born at Syracuse; and when the Roman Consul, Marcellus, besieged that city, Archimedes, in consequence of his wonderful knowledge of geometry, defended it for three years, by constructing machines which suddenly lifted into the air the Roman vessels stationed in the Bay, and then precipitated them with such violence into the water, that they immediately sank. He likewise set one of the Roman fleets on fire with burning glasses. Marcellus, however, at length succeeded in taking the City; at the same time issuing strict orders to his soldiers to respect the Life of Archimedes; and even offering a reward to any one who would bring the Philosopher unhurt into his presence. But these precautions proved useless. The Philosopher, absorbed in solving a problem, and ignorant that the Besiegers were possessed of the City, was slaughtered by a Roman, for having refused to follow him. Marcellus raised a monument over the remains of Archimedes; placing upon it a cylinder and a sphere: and Cicero, during his Questorship in Sicily, discovered this Monument overgrown with brambles, near one of the gates of Syracuse. But although the Romans encountered great difficulties in subjugating the Sicilians, they fell, comparatively speaking, an easy prey to the Saracens. That brave, but cruel, and fanatic People, made a descent upon the Island in 669; surprised and plundered Syracuse, and then re-embarked for their own territories. In 827, they were recalled by a vindictive and powerful Sicilian Nobleman, to revenge his private quarrel; and aided by this villain, they enslaved his country. Messina defended itself with great valour against the Invaders; but was compelled to capitulate. All the cities which endeavoured to maintain at the moment, or afterwards recover their freedom, suffered dreadfully; and Syracuse, which was among the latter, having been long besieged, and reduced to extremities the most repugnant to human nature, was taken by assault, sacked, and burnt—even its walls were razed. Sicily languished under the Saracenic yoke above four centuries: but, at length, Roger, surnamed Guiscard, a Norman by birth, delivered the Island from the dominion of the Infidels; re-established its Churches; and became the first of its Norman Rulers, under the title of Conte Ruggiero. His family reigned in succession; subsequent to which period the Sicilian sceptre has been swayed by divers potentates of Europe; and several of the present customs of the Island are derived from its Spanish Sovereigns.[1]

The Arts of Painting and Sculpture were highly cultivated in early ages, by the inhabitants of Sicily: and *Greco-Siculi* Vases furnish some of the most splendid specimens of pottery existing.

The principal Ports in this Island are those of Messina, Syracuse (called, in Italian, Siragusa), and Trapani; each being situated near one of the great Promontories; and those of Palermo and Catania, situated between the others. There are likewise several small landing-places; and, to avoid being surprised by Corsairs, the Sicilians have encircled themselves with Martello Towers.

The most eligible months for visiting Sicily are those of March,

---

[1] In 1282, the memorable Sicilian Vespers placed Peter of Arragon on the throne of Sicily: from him its crown devolved on Ferdinand of Castile, and remained annexed to that of Spain, till, by the treaty of Utrecht, it was given to Sardinia.

April, May, and June, as the flowers which enamel the Island are then in high beauty; the sun is not sufficiently fervent to be dangerous, (if Travellers guard their heads properly against it); neither is there at this season, much *Mal' Aria*. During Spring, Summer, and Autumn, a Steam Packet usually goes from Naples to Palermo (a hundred and eighty-four miles), in about twenty-four hours.[1] The approach to the latter Town presents fine scenery. The Æolides form a beautiful group on the left, near Sicily, while Ustica appears far off on the right, and Ætna is likewise seen at a distance. The mountains which back Palermo, the deep blue sea, from whose bosom rise the most picturesque rocks imaginable, the Cape of Zafarano, and the Monte-Pellegrino, all contribute to render the entrance to the capacious Harbour of this Metropolis delightful. The best Hotel here is *The Prince of Wales*, kept by Mr. and Mrs. Page: the latter is an Englishwoman.

The gaiety and Asiatic appearance of Palermo are peculiarly striking; an effect produced, in part, by numerous palm-trees, and a species of weeping cedar, which flourishes here. Palermo, however, displays other features of an Asiatic Town; some of its buildings are Saracenic; and the Chaldee Inscription, already mentioned, as having been found within its walls, gives strength to the opinion of several learned Sicilians, who suppose it was originally built by Emigrants from Chaldæa and Damascus, transported hither by the Phœnicians; and aided in their work by that wealthy mercantile People, and some Israelite Adventurers.

This Town, anciently called *Panormus*,[2] and once the strongest hold of the Carthaginians in Sicily,[3] is supposed to possess, at present, about a hundred and sixty thousand inhabitants; and stands at the base of a natural amphitheatre, formed by lofty and barren hills, between which and the Town lies an uncommonly luxuriant and beautiful valley. Palermo (one of the most regularly built Cities in Europe), has a splendid Quay,[4] called *the Marina*, and furnished with Marble Seats, and a small Theatre; where, during summer, a select Band of Musicians execute music, generally of their own composing, to amuse the Palermitan Nobility, who drive daily, and even twice a day, to the Marina, for the benefit of sea-breezes: and here may usually be seen idle Palermitans, of the lower rank, assembled round a Story-teller, whose histories, though not equal, perhaps, in merit, to "The Arabian Tales," excite the interest of his auditors.[5] This exhibition

---

[1] One of these Vessels, (*The Real Ferdinando*) managed by Englishmen, went from Naples to Palermo and Messina, and *vice versâ*, about once a fortnight during the Summer and Autumn of 1826; the price for each Chief Cabin Passenger, being twenty ducats, from Naples to Palermo, bed and board inclusive; the price for each second class Passenger, bed, but not board, inclusive, nine ducats; and the price for each third class Passenger three ducats, without either bed or board.

[2] Two large and profound inlets of the sea anciently formed the Harbour of Palermo; and, according to Diodorus Siculus, this City was called Παν-ορμος (Panormus), because the word signifies, in Greek, *a deep Harbour*. Palermo and its environs were denominated by the Latins, *Aurea Valle* and *Hortus Siciliæ*.

[3] Amilcar defended himself on Ereta, now Monte-Pellegrino, near this City, for three years.

[4] Foreigners, on arriving in the Harbour of Palermo, are welcomed by a boat filled with a Band of Music.

[5] These Story-tellers exhibit all the year round, at a given hour, in Palermo, delivering

eems to be derived from the Asiatics: for "The Arabian Tales," translated into English, owe their existence to a description of Storytellers who have, from earliest times, belonged to the suite of Asiatic Princes, for the purpose of entertaining them with fabulous histories. *The Upper Marina Terrace*, and *Public Gardens* adjoining the Marina, are likewise favourite promenades. In these Gardens are walks shaded by orange and lemon-trees; fountains which nourish aquatic plants; and Canary-birds living and singing in capacious aviaries, with one side open to the air. *The Botanic Garden* merits notice, as it has in some degree recovered from the injuries it sustained during the last civil commotions. The two principal Streets of Palermo, one of which, called *the Toledo*, is a favourite Drive, intersect each other at right angles; and lead into a handsome octangular Piazza, called Quattro Cantoni, from the centre of which both parts of each Street, and the four principal Gates of the City, are seen. These Gates, about half a mile distant from each other, display good architecture. The Streets are noisy and crowded, like those of Naples. The Shops (open in front, and almost innumerable)[1] usually constitute the ground-floor of private houses and likewise of Religious Establishments for Females, who are placed in the attic stories; and the long grated projecting Galleries belonging to each of these Monasteries, form a striking feature of the Toledo. Every window in this Street has its Balcony, supported with wooden props; by no means consistent with splendid architecture; but, nevertheless, the Toledo is handsome; owing chiefly to its being quite straight, and a mile in length. The *Piazza* in which *the Duomo* stands is likewise handsome; and this Church, a spacious Italian Gothic Structure, exhibiting Saracenic ornaments, and dedicated to Saint Rosalia, the Patroness of Palermo, contains the Tomb of the Saint; whose relics are preserved in silver, studded with diamonds.[2] The Duomo was built in 1185; its exterior has been restored at one end, and displays inlaid figures, and black and white ornaments. The Capitals of the Columns of the Portal are thickly fretted leafwork, in the Saracenic style. The interior of the Church is ornamented by eighty Columns of oriental granite, with Capitals shaped like a turban. The Bishop's Throne, and Canons' Stalls, are embellished with Gothic work well carved in wood; the High-altar is rich in marbles; and the Ciborio is fifteen feet in height, and composed entirely of lapis lazuli. A side-chapel contains four porphyry Sarcophagi, which enclose the remains of the Norman Conte Ruggiero, his Consort, and other Royal Persons. The porphyry is red, and very fine; and the Tombs stand under two gilt Mosaic Canopies, each supported by six columns.[3] *The Chiesa del Angelo Custode* merits notice; and *the Chiesa di*

---

expositions of Ariosto, Tasso, etc., alternately exciting the laughter and the tears of their hearers; and receiving, as a recompense from each of them, a grain or two.

[1] The signs over these Shops are carved and painted in imitation of life; and the Barber's Shop proclaims the Doctor.

[2] This Tomb is near the Choir; and not exhibited to public view, except when the Fête of the Saint is celebrated.

[3] Modern whitewash, the bane of architectural beauty, has destroyed the grandeur of the interior of the Duomo.

S. Simone, likewise called *La Martorana*, is an interesting specimen of the combination of Greek, Arabic, and Norman architecture. This Church (rich in marbles) contains, on one side of its splendid High-altar, a solid verde antique Table. The Nuns' Gratings, near the Altar, are silver. The spacious *Chiesa di S. Giuseppe* is remarkable for its immense marble Columns, supposed to be antique. *The Chiesa dell' Olivella* abounds with costly decorations, and contains a Picture of S. Ignatius, attributed to Caravaggio; though more probably the work of Filippo Paladino.[1] *Sa. Tita* exhibits a fine Picture of the Deposition from the Cross, attributed to Vincenzo Anemole; it is an imitation of Raphael's celebrated Painting on this subject. The Picture of the Magdalene was done by Monrealese.[2] *The Palazzo Reale*, in the twelfth century a Fortress, and the Residence of Ruggiero when Monarch of Sicily, has, since that period, been considerably enlarged and improved. The Court of this Edifice is furnished with three tiers of Corridors, some of them double; and by their connexion with staircases, they present a singular view of arches and columns; appropriate, however, to a warm climate. The Chapel Royal (on the second floor) was begun by Ruggiero, in 1129, and finished thirteen years after. It is a chaste Building of the *Greco-Araba-Normanna* School. The Royal Apartments are embellished with excellent Tapestry, representing the Exploits of Don Quixote: and the view from the Terraces is enchanting. *The Bronze Rams*, transported by Charles III, from Syracuse to Palermo, merit notice: they are about five feet long, three feet high, in a recumbent posture, and very beautiful.[3] *The Palazzo Butera* consists of magnificent, splendidly furnished, and comfortable Apartments, with a delightful Promenade three hundred feet in length, and an awning for Summer, situated above the second Marina. *The Torre della Cuba*, in a Garden, near Palermo, is a curious Saracenic rectangular Edifice, with two doorways having pointed Arches: its Roof is a semicircular Dome; and its upper edgings exhibit Arabic Characters: if the blind Windows were ever open (which, according to appearance, they were not), this edifice must have been peculiarly light and elegant; at all events, however, the architect who erected it was well aware of the beautiful effect produced by light and lofty arches. On the outside of the Porta-nuova, but near the City, is *the Torre della Ziza*, another Saracenic Structure, which, though injured by earthquakes, still retains a Fountain, a Portico, Columns, and Mosaics, belonging to the original Edifice. *The Villa Butera*, called *Villa-Wilding*, abounds with luxuries. Here are Public Gardens laid out in the English manner; and, amidst a great variety of exotics, flowering in the open air, are most of those plants which require hothouses in England. Here, like-

---

[1] In a Side-chapel is a Holy Family, attributed to Raphael.

[2] Pietro Novelli, surnamed Monrealese, and born at Monreale, in 1608, studied at Rome, and was a painter of distinguished merit.

[3] The entrance to the Senate House displays several Latin Inscriptions of the time when Sicily was governed by the Romans: and in the Cortile di Spedale, once magnificent, but now a neglected building, is the Fragment of a very animated Fresco, by Monrealese; and an old Picture of Death on the Pale Horse.

wise, collected from various countries, is a Menagerie of Birds, and among them the Egyptian Ibis.

The Royal Chinese Villa called *La Favorita* is embellished with pretty Drives, about four miles in extent.[1] The Road from Palermo to Monreale, a distance of near four miles, is excellent. *This archiepiscopal Town*, originally a Saracenic Hamlet, was enlarged by William II, surnamed "The Good," who, in 1177, erected its Cathedral; which Edifice, not long ago, suffered considerably from fire; and is now repairing at a very large expense, that it may correspond with the rest of the Structure: which displays costly Gates of bronze; ancient Columns of granite with elegant Capitals; Columns of porphyry; a beautiful Pedestal, belonging to a bronze Statue of S. John the Baptist, and the Tomb of William I. (the Pedestal and the Tomb are porphyry); the Tomb of William II; and, in the Choir, superb Mosaics.

On the Staircase of the annexed Monastero dei Canonici Benedettini is a celebrated Painting, by Monrealese; which represents William the Good blessed by S. Benedict. Monreale stands on an elevated spot, commanding a lovely view: and higher still, on the right, is another Benedictine Convent, *the Monastero di S. Martino*, supereminent in beauty of situation, riches, and splendour, appropriated to Noblemen only, and more like a royal residence than a religious retirement.[2] In the superb Hall of entrance is a picture of S. Martino on Horseback, giving his mantle to an indigent man. The Rails of the Staircase are alabaster and Sicilian marble; the Corridors are spacious; and the Refectory contains a fine Fresco by Monrealese, for which he received two hundred and ten ducats. This Convent likewise possesses other good Paintings, namely, the Annunciation by Monrealese; the Daughter of Herodias, attributed to Guercino; a Holy Family, by Titian; and S. John preaching in the Desert, by Paladino. The Church is handsome, its Organ celebrated; and nothing can exceed the splendour of the Sacerdotal Vestments in the Sacristy. The Library contains a Chinese Manuscript Dictionary; some beautiful Manuscript Bibles; and a Copy of Luther's Works, with Notes, and Revisions, said to be his own. The Museum, though not large, is valuable; and comprises a Collection of ancient Sicilian Vases and Medals; a beautiful ancient Glass Cup; a Head of Friendship, supposed to be Grecian sculpture, and bearing a Greek Inscription; together with a great variety of Sicilian Marbles, Jasper and Agates.[3] There is a Carriage-road, in extent about eight miles, hilly and not good, the whole way from Palermo to this Convent. Returning hence, Travellers may usually obtain permission to go through *the Docca di Faleo*, a Royal Drive.

The Convent of the Coppuccini,

---

[1] This Villa cannot be seen without an order. One room below stairs, near the Bath, contains English Prints—on the first floor is a circular Dinner-Table, so arranged that the dishes are raised from below—on the same floor, in the large room, is a Table of Petrified Wood, said to have been brought from Pompeii; the outside edges resemble agate; and in the adjoining bed-room are two more Tables of Petrified Wood. The floor over the dining-room contains bed-rooms—still higher are the State Apartments; and above them is a Prospect-room, which exhibits magnificent views.

[2] On the way to the Monastero di S. Martino is a Castle, built by the Normans.

[3] Ladies are not allowed to enter this Convent.

about one mile distant from Palermo, attracts the notice of Travellers, because the defunct Brethren are dried, dressed, and placed upright in niches, belonging to the Catacombs under the conventual Church, that their Friends may visit and pray by them, annually, on the second of November. On the floor are wooden coffins enclosing the remains of persons who were not in Holy Orders.[1] These Catacombs contain Vaults, secured by iron doors, where the bodies of deceased Monks are deposited for half a year: at the end of which period they join the assembly of Mummies. *Monte-Pellegrino* is famed for having been the Retreat of the amiable Niece of William the Good, Saint Rosalia, who, in the prime of youth and beauty, withdrew from the world, and devoted herself to religious observances. It rises perpendicularly at the distance of one mile and a half from Palermo, to the height of nineteen hundred and sixty-three feet above the level of the sea; and Travellers usually ascend this Mountain on donkeys by a path called *La Scala*,[2] to *the Church of Saint Rosalia*; in which Priests celebrate Mass daily, and receive the offerings made by Pilgrims. This Church leads to a *Chapel*, constructed in *a Grotto* covered with Stalactites; and where, according to tradition, the Saint secluded herself, and ended her days. Her Statue, well executed in white marble, lies under the Altar of the Chapel; and represents a young and lovely person praying fervently: a Book, a Skull, and a Crucifix are placed at her side: but the Statue loses its effect, by being covered with a robe of solid gold enriched by precious stones. The Grotto is capacious and sombre. Beyond this spot stands a pretty Building, the roof of which is ornamented with a Statue of Saint Rosalia: and here parties frequently come from Palermo to dine, and enjoy the view; which comprehends Ustica (twenty leagues distant), Alicudi, and Felicudi (the most Western of the Æolides), together with the Valley of La Favorita, profusely rich, and highly cultivated. A Festival in honour of Saint Rosalia is held annually, by the Palermitans, in the month of July, and continues several days; during which period Palermo is splendidly illuminated every night, and a splendid display of Fireworks exhibited. This Festival commences with a pompous general procession of the Dignitaries of the Church, and other Clergy, the State Officers, the Military, and other Inhabitants, who conduct through the streets a Triumphal Car, preceded by trumpets and kettle-drums. A Platform, about three-quarters the height of the Machine, contains a numerous band of Musicians, who, at intervals, execute, in honour of the Saint, vocal and instrumental music. The length of the Machine is seventy feet, the breadth thirty, and the height above eighty: it terminates in a Dome, resting on six Corinthian Columns, ornamented with Figures of Saints and Angels: and, elevated on the summit of this Dome, stands a Semi-colossal silver Statue of Saint Rosalia. Orange-plants, Vases filled with Flowers, and artificial Trees of Coral, garnish the Machine. But

---

[1] These bodies are dried and preserved, like those of the Monks.

[2] There is, however, a Carriage-road to the foot of Monte-Pellegrino.

the most splendid part of the Festival is the Illumination with which it concludes; and which takes place in the Duomo: where twenty-thousand wax lights, multiplied by mirrors innumerable, are tastefully disposed in upward of five hundred lustres. Placed on an eminence, near the other end of the *Concha d'oro*, as Palermo is poetically called, stands *the Monastero di Santa Maria di Gesù*, which should be visited by Travellers, because it commands a particularly fine view of Palermo.[1] The Rocks close to the Convent are very beautiful; and in this vicinity are Ruins of an Aqueduct. A Carriage-road leads to the Convent.[2] A Carriage-road likewise leads to a Village about ten miles distant from Palermo, and called *La Bagaria;* where a Sicilian Nobleman, Prince Palagonia, built a whimsical *Palazzo;* and squandered a large property in having all the most hideous combinations of beings, real or imaginary, represented by the best sculptors he could engage to work for him: and a few scattered Monsters, on the approach to the Palazzo, together with one semicircular Court still remaining, show how successfully he gratified his eccentric taste. The interior of the Mansion contains one Room (now going fast to decay), with a Looking-glass, Ceiling, and Walls inlaid with Porcelain and Coloured Glass; the effect of which, when lighted up, must have been splendid: and another Room with a Looking-glass Ceiling, a beautiful Floor, and Walls completely covered by Marble, and Paintings to imitate marble, so well executed, and skilfully overspread with Glass, that it is difficult to detect the deception. This Room contains China, an elegant Table, and other costly furniture, in good condition, Prince Butera has a *Villa* at La Bagaria, remarkable only for *a small Casino in its Garden*, representing a Convent, and containing the Story of Adelaide and Comegio, superbly executed in Waxwork.[3] *The fine Bassi-rilievi, brought from Selinuntium to Palermo*, should be enquired for by Travellers, as Antiquities which particularly merit notice.[4]

The Opera at Palermo is, generally speaking, good; but the Theatre cannot vie with that of S. Carlo at Naples.[5]

The Palermitans are lively, acute, intelligent, and particularly civil and obliging to British Travellers. Music and poetry appear to be the favourite studies of the upper rank of persons; and several Palermitans are versed in the Arabic and ancient Greek languages.

Travellers who wish to make the Tour of the Island, usually set out on the Carriage-road, which extends some way; ordering their Mules, or Lettigo (a litter), to be in waiting at its termination.

---

1 Ladies are not admitted into this Convent.

2 Near the path which leads to the Convent is an ancient square Sepulchral Chamber, delved in a rock, and containing a Well at one end.

3 In this vicinity, on an eminence, now called Monte—Catalfano, stood the ancient *Solus*.

4 Among these *Bassi-rilievi* is the head of Medusa, represented as being covered with hair, instead of serpents: it seems, therefore, that the latter was, comparatively speaking, a modern invention.

5 Gloves and stockings fabricated with the beard of the Pinna Marina, which is found in large quantities at Tarento, may frequently be purchased at Palermo; and are well calculated for Travellers who mean to ascend to the summit of Ætna; being so peculiarly warm that medical men recommend them, as a cure for rheumatic pains in the limbs.

The Carriage-road passes through Monreale to *Alcamo*, thirty-one miles distant from Palermo, and furnished, at the present moment (1827), with an Hotel kept by an Abate; which, though small, possesses the comfort of cleanliness. The olive-trees, seen from this road, are remarkably large; the country between Monreale and Alcamo is beautiful; and the Butterflies here, and in all parts of Sicily, are superb. The Town of Alcamo abounds with Churches and Religious Establishments; and the neighbouring Mountain produces superb yellow Marble.[1] After sleeping at Alcamo, Travellers usually proceed, through a dreary country, to the ancient Ægesta, and thence to *Trapani*, a distance of thirty miles. The Temple of Ægesta, and the Site of the Town, are nine miles from Alcamo.

Ægesta, or, as it was likewise called, *Segesta*, founded by Ægestus, a Siculian, soon after the Trojan war, owed its destruction to the Potter's son, Agathocles, who subjugated the whole island:[2] and about a hundred paces from the Site of this Town, marked by a few scattered masses of ruins covered with herbs, is an object of peculiar interest, an ancient quadrilateral Grecian Doric Edifice, simple, grand, and almost entire, standing solitary, on an isolated circular hill, in a bold but desolate country. Gigantic Steps, three in number, lead up to the Platform on which rests this Temple (as antiquaries suppose it to have been), and each of the three first Steps is one foot and a half in width. The Edifice has two Fronts, both terminated by a Pediment. Six Columns, without bases, and placed a few inches within the verge of the Platform, adorn each Front; each side presents twelve Columns, making thirty-six in all. The exterior of the Temple seems to have bidden defiance to time, one Column excepted; which, being damaged, was restored (though unskilfully) in 1781. The length of the Temple is a hundred and eighty-two Paris feet, taken from the centre of the angular Columns; and the breadth sixty-eight feet. The Columns, composed of stone, smooth, but neither stuccoed nor fluted, are about six feet in diameter, and thirty feet high; the intercolumniations being unequal; the Capitals measure three feet four inches in height. The construction of the Fabric is such, that, supposing it to have been a Temple, the high-altar must have fronted the east; but no vestiges remain of a Cella.[3] When

---

[1] Several Travellers have taken the Abate, who keeps the Hotel at Alcamo, as their Guide to the Sulphureous Hot Springs, and Ruins of Ægesta.

[2] Scipio Africanus the younger, at the close of the third Punic War, is said to have restored to the inhabitants of the district of Segesta a famous bronze Statue of Diana, which the Carthaginians had purloined; and which Cicero saw, during his Sicilian Quæstorship.

[3] Judging from the description given by Vitruvius of Greek Temples, and also from there being no remains of a Cella, this Edifice was more probably a Basilica, than a Temple, though its elevated position bespeaks it the latter kind of building; because the ancient Greeks, (as already mentioned), impressed with an idea that when the deities of Olympus visited their earthly temples they might find it more convenient to alight on an eminence than in a plain, always placed these sacred structures in as lofty a situation as possible. The dimensions of the Edifice in question, in Paris feet, are taken from Ferrara's account of the Antiquities of Sicily: its dimensions, in English feet, are computed to be as follows. Exterior length, two hundred feet—breadth, eighty-eight feet four inches—diameter of the columns, six feet eight inches—intercolumniations, about the same. This Edifice, supposed to be more modern than the other Grecian Doric Temples of Sicily, is less excellent with respect to architecture.

this Edifice was built is unknown; and to which of the heathen divinities it was consecrated, seems uncertain. It in some measure resembles the Temple of Neptune at Pæstum; and has much the advantage of that Temple, in point of situation; but in nothing else. On the side of a neighbouring Eminence are *Ruins of a Theatre*, the external Wall of which is composed of large masses of stone; and rests against the approximate Rock. The form of the Theatre may be completely traced; but no vestiges remain of its Scena; and its Seats are nearly destroyed. It stands under the ruins of *an ancient Castle*, which commands a fine view of *Mons-Eryx*, where the presumptuous Challenger of Hercules was buried.[1] Two miles distant from the ancient Ægesta are *Sulphureous Hot Springs*, called *Acque Segestane*; which, according to Diodorus, gushed from the earth by order of the Wood Nymphs, to refresh Hercules after the fatigues of his voyage to Sicani. On the road to Trapani, about one mile distant from that Town, is a Church with a Norman door, and containing the famous Madonna of Trapani, covered with splendid jewels. This Town, in shape like a Scythe (whence its original name, *Drepanum*),[2] stands on an isthmus, near the side of Mount Eryx; possesses a safe Harbour (mentioned by Virgil), and is famed for having been the place where Anchises died, and where Æneas celebrated funeral games in his father's honour. From the Port may be seen the Rock described by Virgil, Æn. III. V. Trapani is strongly fortified, and enriched by Coral and Thunny Fisheries. Ivory, Coral, Conchs, and Alabaster, are manufactured in the town; but the *Incisori* here cannot vie with those at Rome. The Hotel at Trapani is a bad one. In this Town the Carriage-road terminates. After sleeping at Trapani, Travellers frequently make *an excursion to the summit of Eryx*, the highest Mountain of Sicily, Ætna excepted. The ascent is easy, though tedious, and exhibits beautiful scenery. *Fragments of granite Columns and a Fountain*, are called the remains of the celebrated Temple of Venus, which once embellished this spot: but of the Tomb of Anchises there are no vestiges. Travellers who ascend Eryx, usually finish their day's journey at *Marsala*, eighteen miles from Trapani;[3] the mule-track, between which Towns, lies within view of the sea.[4] Marsala was erected by the Saracens, on the Promontory of Lilybæum, and on the site of an ancient City, likewise called *Lilybæum*, and a peculiarly strong place; which, during the wars between the Romans and Carthaginians, stood a ten years' siege. Diodorus gives it the appellation of "impreguable:" its Harbour, which the Romans vainly endeavoured to destroy, is

---

[1] Eryx, relying on his great personal strength, challenged all Strangers to contend with him in the combat of the cestus. Hercules accepted the challenge, and Eryx fell. Eryx erected a Temple to Venus on this Mountain, which bears his name; and where, we are told, was the tomb of Anchises.

[2] Δρεπανον, *faulx*.

[3] Travellers, who do not ascend Mount Eryx, usually proceed from Trapani, through Marsala and Mazzara, to Castel-Vetrano; a distance of thirty-eight miles.

[4] This mule-track, though not good, is interesting; because it displays a view of three Islands, called *Aræ*, by Virgil; on one of which Ulysses is supposed to have been shipwrecked; and upon these Rocks Æneas lost the greater part of his fleet.

mentioned as having been capacious and excellent;[1] and its vicinity to the African coast rendered it a place of great consequence. Near this Port the Romans were defeated, B.C. 249, by the Carthaginians, under Adherbal; and the Carthaginians, under Hanno, lost, near this Port, a battle which terminated the first Punic war, B.C. 242.[2] *The principal Church* at Marsala, *the Convento de' P. P. Carmelitani*, and *the Campanile*, merit notice. The town is clean, and contains twenty-five thousand inhabitants. After sleeping here, Travellers usually proceed through Mazzara to the Stone Quarry south of Campo-Bello; and thence to *Castel-Vetrano*, a distance of twenty-eight miles. The mule-track to Mazzara crosses a dreary heath; but the Town is environed by a fruitful country, and contains, in its Cathedral, three Sarcophagi, one of which displays good sculpture. The Walls of Mazzara are fortified with brick Towers, twelve feet square, and placed about sixty feet from each other. The ride to *the Stone Quarry*, near Campo-Bello, is dreary; but the Quarry excites a peculiar interest; because the stone of which it is composed, whether destined for shafts of pillars, or other purposes, was hewn out of this Quarry in shape and size precisely such as the builder required; instead of being cut into large shapeless blocks, and fashioned afterwards, according to modern wasteful practice. The Quarry lies east and west: its unworked part appears to be about forty feet high; and in some places the two sides remain, from between which the stone has been taken; leaving a kind of street. One shaft of a pillar stands by itself, with the lower end still joined to the natural bed of stone; its diameter is ten feet: several blocks for columns, of the same diameter, lie scattered here and there; and among a large number is one piece of twelve feet in diameter, resting on its side. That part of the Quarry where the finished columns, etc. were worked out below the level of the ground, contains two Shafts, quite perfect, of ten feet in diameter; and their component parts appear to have been shaped by a circular groove, three feet wide, ten feet deep, and just large enough for a man to work in it. The economy, both with respect to room and stone, in this Quarry, is curious; and as no other ancient quarry has been found in the neighbourhood, as the stone this Quarry produces is similar to that of which Selinuntium and its Temples were built, and as the dimensions of the columns, found here, correspond with those which ornament the Temples, it seems probable that the materials of which the Town and Temples were composed came from this Quarry, although between it and Selinuntium runs an unfordable river. Near Castel-Vetrano the scenery improves; and the Hotel there is clean and tolerably good. After sleeping at Castel-Vetrano, Travellers usually proceed to Selinuntium, and *Sciacci;* a distance of thirty miles.

---

[1] Charles V. destroyed it.
[2] It is reported that the violent rains of October, 1826, by washing away the soil on the Beach of Capo Boco, where the Harbour of Lilybæum was situated, have laid open remains of ancient Walls composed of soft stone stuccoed, Bases and Capitals of Columns, a Mosaic Pavement sixteen Palmi in length, Floors of white marble, etc., etc.

The ride to Salentium, through lanes bordered with white roses, and a path shaded with ilexes as it approaches the sea, is lovely; and the first view of the three largest Temples is most striking; in consequence of the colossal mass of ruins they exhibit. *Selinuns*, or *Selinuntium*, so called from the Greek word, σελινον, parsley, which herb grew there in profusion, was founded, A. U. C. 127, by a colony from Hybla-Megara, on Two Hills, sloping down gradually toward the sea, between the rivers Hypsa and Selinus.[1] The Hill furthest from the sea displays stupendous Ruins of the aforesaid *Grecian Doric Temples*, denominated by the Sicilians, *Pileri dei Giganti*. That toward the east has only one of its Columns standing; and this is without a capital; the whole edifice being thrown down, scattered, and disjointed; though but few things are broken. All the Columns of these three Temples have fallen outward; and apparently an earthquake, which came from east to west, laid them, and every sacred edifice at Selinuntium, prostrate. The Temple in question seems to have stood upon a Platform, encompassed by Steps about two English feet in depth, and to have been about three hundred and thirty-three English feet in length, and near one hundred and forty-seven in breadth. The exterior angular Columns were channeled, and those which supported the Portico plain: the Cella was enclosed by small Columns: the Capitals which lie uppermost in this stupendous pile of gigantic Ruins are elegantly curved; and the quadrilateral pieces of stone have two, four, or six, semi-elliptical grooves, to receive the ropes for their elevation. One solid mass of stone which seems to have formed part of an Architrave, is near forty feet long, seven broad and three deep; and one or two of the Columns (so situated that they can be measured) are twelve feet in diameter; others ten feet ten inches. About thirty paces from these Ruins are remains of *a Temple*, every part of which lies prostrate, except one tottering Pilaster. This Edifice is computed to have been about two hundred English feet in length, and about eighty feet in breadth; and its Portico was supported by thirty-six fluted Columns, each being one solid piece of stone. Toward the west are ruins of *a third Temple*, about two hundred and forty-two English feet in length, and about seventy-seven and a half in breadth: its Columns were fluted; and the only part now standing of this Edifice is one square Pilaster, probably a portion of the Cella. The Steps of the east Front are visible. Not far removed from one of the angles of these prostrate Temples, lies the Capital of a Column, simple like the Capitals at Pæstum, and fourteen feet in diameter: and several Capitals which present themselves among the remains of the largest Temple, appear to be of a similar size. These stupendous Edifices stood equidistant from each other, commanding an extensive and beautiful view of the sea: and the superb *Bassirilievi* from Selinuntium, already mentioned as being now at Palermo, were discovered by two Eng-

---

[1] Called, by Virgil, "*Palmosa Selinus;*" on account of the plant, *Palmetta*, with which the spot abounds.

lish Artists, among the ruins of the central Temple. Three quarters of a mile distant, at the foot of the Hill nearest to the Beach, are Ruins supposed to have been *Magazines* belonging to the Port: and on this *Hill* are *vestiges of the Town*, remains of *two Towers*, and also of *three Temples*, apparently not completed at the period when they were thrown down. These Temples stood within the Walls of Selinuntium. *The middle Edifice* had, on each side, seventeen Columns; and, at each end, seven, those at the angles included: the Columns were channelled; and (according to a Fragment which remains of one of them), about twenty feet long. The eastern entrance to the Cella, the outer Wall, and part of the interior Wall, may be traced. *The Temple furthest from the sea* had, on each side, sixteen Columns; and, at each end, six, those at the angles included. Here, likewise, the Cella may be traced; as may the Steps which led to the eastern Front of the Edifice. Contiguous to this Temple is *a Well*, formed of pottery, with pipes jointed together, and notches in the sides. This Well, probably an ancient Reservoir for purifying water, is twenty-three palmi deep, and sufficiently large for a man to descend into it. The Steps leading to the Portico of *the third Temple* have been excavated, and are much worn away.[1] Shelter may be obtained at a Farm-house near Selinuntium; but there is no village in this vicinity.[2] The commencement of the road to Sciacci is dull; it crosses the Ponte Belici,[3] a Bridge built with stones which belonged to the fallen Temples; and traverses (near the sea) another river, on a bar thrown up at its mouth; thence passing over a tedious heath to a fertile spot embellished with beautiful broom, and afterwards descending to the sea shore, in order to cross another river, near Sciacca, the ascent to which Town is steep, and the only Hotel it contains intolerable.[4] Sciacca, called *Termæ Selinuntiæ* from its Baths, said to have been constructed by Dædalus, is beautifully situated in a rich country embellished with magnificent palm-trees: its inhabitants are numerous; though not in appearance healthy: their Manufacture of Pottery merits notice; as every utensil is made in an elegant antique form. This Place gave birth to Agathocles, whose father was a manufacturer of the *Greco-Siculi* Vases. On the south side of the Town are celebrated *Hot Springs*, from which the water issues boiling: its smell is offensive; and it deposits, in the channel through which it passes, a white sulphureous sediment. At the side of

---

[1] Perhaps it might be in one of these Temples that the Matrons of Selinuntium took refuge, when their Town was stormed, 244 years after its foundation.—See DIODORUS SICULUS, *Lib.* xiii.

The Segestines, B.C. 410, having been oppressed and attacked by the Selinuntians, implored aid from Carthage; who sent to their assistance Hannibal, the Son of Giscon: and this general, B.C. 409, captured Selinuntium, and nearly destroyed it.

[2] At Memfrici, about seven miles from Selinuntium, Travellers, furnished with a letter of recommendation, are hospitably received, and provided with good beds, by Don Bastiano Ravita; who has, about three miles from Selinuntium, a Cassino, which he sometimes lends to Travellers who wish to examine the Temples at leisure. It should, however, be remembered, that the Marsh at Selinuntium produces *Mal' aria*.

[3] The river Belici, over which this Bridge is thrown, was anciently denominated the *Hypsa*.

[4] Travellers, if compelled to sleep at Sciacca, usually endeavour to obtain a private Lodging.

the Baths, formed by these Springs, is a small open *Well*, containing water reputed to perform miracles if taken daily: and contiguous are remains of part of the Baths supposed to have been constructed by Dædalus. The hill containing these Hot Springs is now called S. Calogero.[1] Travellers, who sleep at Sciacca, usually proceed, next day, to San Patro, a solitary House on the banks of the Platanus,[2] and thence to *Siculiana*, in all thirty miles. Between Sciacca and San Patro the road traverses several rivers, on embankments constructed to dam up their mouths for the purpose of irrigating immense rice-fields: and the air in this neighbourhood must, consequently, be unwholesome during warm weather. The country is dreary, and Siculiana is a wretched town with a bad Inn.

Travellers, who sleep here, usually proceed next morning to *Girgenti*, a distance of about twelve miles. Not far beyond Siculiana are magnificent Tamarisk-trees, with stems one foot in diameter: on approaching Girgenti the road is bordered by superb aloes; and the first view of the Town crowning a hill eleven hundred feet above the level of the sea, is most beautiful. *The Porto Nuovo*, or Mole, four miles to the south of Girgenti, presents a busy scene: here are immense quantities of sulphur-cake,[3] with other articles for exportation, lining the shore; ships taking in their respective cargoes; and boats loading with corn, by porters who wade more than knee deep through the water, carrying their burden in sacks on their heads and shoulders. The modern Mole of Girgenti may indeed be called an emporium for corn, the staple commodity of Sicily: and in this neighbourhood are a considerable number of deep Pits, made in the dryest of the indigenous rocks, and shaped somewhat like an egg with the small end upward: an opening is left for the admission of the corn; which, when perfectly free from damp, is thrown into the Pit, and excluded from air, by the immediate and secure stoppage of the aperture. The corn, thus preserved, keeps good for several years: it is thrashed in Sicily, as in Calabria, by means of the hoofs of oxen.

The Hotel at Girgenti (served by the Bishop's Cook) is tolerably comfortable; and Sig. Politi, an Artist who keeps for sale a collection of *Greco-Siculi* Vases, found in the Tombs at Agrigentum, has fitted up Apartments for the accommodation of Travellers. Modern Girgenti stands near the Site of the Citadel of the ancient Agrigentum; and though apparently magnificent, when seen from a distance, is found, on closer examination, to consist of small houses, and narrow streets. The present number of its inhabitants is computed to be about twenty thousand; and *its Cathedral* contains *a Baptismal Font*, originally a Sarcophagus discovered in the Ditch of ancient Agrigentum, and ornamented with superb Grecian Sculpture, representing the History of Hippolytus. The *Rilievi* on the north side of this Font are, however, less good than those on the other three sides. The north

---

[1] The Rocks, about Sciacca, are thickly covered with the Ice Plant.
[2] Anciently *the Halycus*.
[3] There are Sulphur Mines in this neighbourhood; and several Travellers think them worth visiting.

Aisle contains a valuable picture of the blessed Virgin and Infant Saviour, by Guido; and the Echo in the Cathedral merits notice.¹ About three quarters of a mile distant, on the declivity of the Hill crowned by the modern Town, is *the site of ancient Agrigentum*, or, as some authors call it, *Agragas*, from a contiguous river so denominated. This City is said to have owed its existence to Cocalus; who after receiving and protecting Dædalus, employed him in erecting a Fortress here, on a perpendicular Rock, to which there was but one avenue; and that one so narrow, and winding, as to be defensible by three or four men only.² Other writers, without noticing this circumstance, suppose the City to have been founded either by a Rhodian or an Ionian Colony: during its most flourishing state, it contained two hundred thousand inhabitants. Its government was at first monarchical; then democratic; and afterwards again monarchical under Phalaris: and in the fourth year of the ninety-third Olympiad it was taken and sacked by Amilcar. The ancient inhabitants of Agrigentum were particularly celebrated for their hospitality, their love of the Arts, and their luxurious style of living. Plato was so much struck by the solidity of their dwellings, and the sumptuousness of their dinners, that he said, "they built, as if they thought themselves immortal, and ate, as if they expected never to eat again." Diodorus likewise speaks of their luxury; and mentions that their large vases for water were commonly made of silver, and their carriages of ivory richly adorned: he also says, that one of the citizens of Agrigentum, when returning, victorious, from the Olympic Games, entered his native Town followed by three hundred cars, each drawn by four white horses sumptuously caparisoned: and Diodorus adds, the horses of Agrigentum were highly prized for their beauty and swiftness.³ Pliny, indeed, asserts, that funeral honours were paid to those who had frequently proved victorious at Olympia; and that superb monuments were raised to their memory; a cirumstance confirmed by another classic Writer, who says he observed, at Agrigentum, sepulchral pyramids, erected to the memory of horses.⁴ In order to see the Antiquities here, without losing time by going needlessly out of the way, Travellers should proceed either on foot or on mules, from the modern Town to *the Garden of the Convento di S. Nicolò*, which contains a fine ancient Cornice of marble; and, close by, is a well-preserved *Ædicula*, in shape quadrilateral, and of the Doric Order; its Walls being composed of stones beautifully united without cement. Not far distant are remains of a spacious *Doric Temple*, which was *consecrated to Ceres and Pro-*

---

1 Riedesel mentions that the modern Town of Girgenti contains a Spring of Water, which, on flowing into a basin, has its surface covered with oil, capable of burning equally well with that extracted from the olive.

2 Beyond the Porta di Mazzara of the modern Town, is *the site of the Citadel* supposed to have been constructed by Dædalus; and at the Porta del Cannone is *the Narrow Path* by which the Rock was scaled.

3 Silius Italicus praises the Agrigentine horses; and this district is still famous for a peculiarly fine breed, with short necks, very thick near the chest, like those represented in the Frieze of the Parthenon.

4 When these noble animals grew old, and unable to work, they were fed and attended with the kindest solicitude by the people of Agrigentum:—and it is to be wished that the moderns would imitate this humane example!

serpine; and, according to some opinions, the oldest sacred Edifice at Agrigentum; it is now partly transformed into the Church of S. Biagio.[1] Further on, at the eastern extremity of the ancient City, stands the *Temple of Juno Lucina*, beautifully situated, and commanding a magnificent prospect of the sea, mountains, plains, and modern Town of Girgenti. This Temple is placed on a highly elevated Platform, encompassed by four very deep Steps, which rest on a Base of four immense layers of stone. The size of the Structure seems to have been about one hundred and fifty-four English feet in length, and about fifty-five in breadth. The exterior Columns were thirty-four in number, of the Grecian Doric Order, fluted, without bases, and composed of soft bad stone: but the whole presents, externally, a picturesque clay colour, those parts excepted which have been disfigured by modern reparations. The eastern Front, where (according to general custom) was the principal entrance to this Temple, displays remains of an exterior Court. The Cella is perfect, and at its upper end are four Steps, leading to a Platform; beyond which, another Step leads to what probably was the Sanctuary: but this division of a Cella is uncommon. The Stones on the inside of the Cella are reddened by fire; and some of the internal work of other parts of the Edifice is coloured with Tyrian purple: thirteen Columns, with their Architrave, still remain standing on its northern side.[2]

The southern Ridge, leading from the Temple of Juno Lucina to that of Concord, displays *a Line of Tombs and Sepulchral Chambers* apparently delved in the solid rocks, of which the Walls of the ancient City were composed: and several Vases, all lying on their sides, have been found among these Sepulchres, which are quite in ruins.

The Temple of Concord, by far the most perfect of any sacred Edifice of the ancient City, seems to have been erected at a period when Grecian Doric architecture had reached its zenith of perfection. This sublime and beautiful Structure, which corresponds in dimensions with the Temple of Juno Lucina, rests upon a lofty Platform encompassed by six Steps. Its exterior Columns, thirty-four in number, stand uninjured in their original position, and are of the Grecian Doric Order, without bases, each composed of four blocks of stone. The principal Entrance fronts the east, as does the Entrance to the Cella, which is quite perfect; except that Arches are cut in its Walls, and part of one Wall is removed: dilapidations supposed to have taken place during the middle ages, when this Temple was dedicated to S. Gregorio, and used for Christian worship. The Wall of the Cella contains Winding Steps, which lead to the upper part of the Edifice.[3] In this vicinity are *remains of a Temple*, supposed to be that consecrated to Hercules; and which Cicero describes as being near the Forum, now totally de-

---

[1] Riedesel mentions that he saw, near S. Biagio, *Wheel-tracks made by ancient Cars*, and not further distant from each other than three Roman palmi.

[2] This Temple once contained the celebrated Picture of an earthly Venus, by Zeuxis.

[3] By ascending these Steps a sight may be obtained of large holes, apparently cut to receive beams for supporting a roof.

stroyed.¹ This Temple rested on a Platform encompassed by four Steps, and corresponded in dimensions with the two last named Edifices: it is now a confused pile of ruins, with only one Column standing. Its columns were channelled. To the west of the Temple of Hercules are sufficient remains of one of *the ancient City-Gates*, to prove that it was Doric architecture: and not far hence is supposed to have been *the ancient Port*. On the outside of this Gate is a well-preserved *Sepulchral Monument*; simple and unpretending; ornamented with Ionic Columns and Triglyphs above them; but, in shape, Egyptian. It is called *the Tomb of Theron*, an excellent Prince who reigned sixteen years over the Agrigentines, and died B.C. 472, universally beloved and lamented.² The architecture of the Tomb in question appears, however, of a more recent date; and some antiquaries are of opinion that it was the Grave and Monument of a Horse. Its Cornice is destroyed. Beyond this Tomb, and near the sea, is *a modern Edifice*, one Wall of which, fabricated with large square stones, seems to have originally made part of *the Temple of Æsculapius*, which had Grecian Doric Columns, fluted, without base, and their diameter was half buried in the Walls of the Temple. These Walls, or, more properly speaking, that which remains, exhibits an internal Winding Flight of Steps, similar to the one already described in the Cella-Wall of the Temple of Concord.³ Travellers on returning from the Temple of Æsculapius, before they re-enter the ancient Gate, should notice *the Sarcophagi formed in the City Walls*; huge masses of which lie prostrate, and seem to have slid down from their original position. On re-entering the Gate, it is usual to proceed northward, to *the colossal Temple of Jupiter Olympicus*, called, by Diodorus, the largest sacred Edifice in Sicily; and described as a striking proof of the magnificence of its founders; but, at the present moment, little more than an immense pile of ruins. It was, in length, about three hundred and sixty-eight English feet; in breadth about one hundred and eighty-eight; and the diameter of its Columns was thirteen feet four inches: they were channelled; and, according to Diodorus, each channel was sufficiently wide and deep for a man to stand in it.⁴ The Edifice rested on a lofty Platform, encompassed by several steps.⁵ On the north and south sides were fourteen Columns; to the east seven; and to the west only six. These Columns were semi-circular on the outer part, and squared within: the intercolumniations presented a Wall; thus forming

---

1 The Temple of Hercules once contained a celebrated picture of Alcmena, by Zeuxis.

2 Diodorus Siculus reports, that when the Carthaginians, under the command of Hannibal, the Son of Giscon, were destroying the Tombs on the outside of the Walls of Agrigentum, a flash of lightning struck Theron's Sepulchre, indicating that it was protected by Jove: and Diodorus adds, that a pestilence ensued in the Carthaginian camp; that Hannibal and several other persons died of this pestilence, and that the destruction of the Tombs was consequently abandoned.

3 Cicero mentions a beautiful little Statue of Apollo (marked on the thigh, in small silver letters, with the name of Myron), as having graced the Temple of Æsculapius at Agrigentum; and adds, that the Carthaginians possessed themselves of this Statue; which was restored to its original owners by Scipio.

4 The channels were twenty-two inches and a half in width.

5 On the north side are remains of five.

an exterior Temple to contain the Cella. This Temple, immense in height, and splendid beyond description, had two Fronts, each adorned with a Pediment, containing in its Tympanum superb sculpture: that of the eastern Pediment represented the War of the Giants; that toward the west, the Capture of Troy; and here, contrary to usage, is supposed to have been the principal Entrance; because this Front had only six Columns: but it does not seem likely that a religious custom should have been departed from, in the construction of a sacred Edifice. The Gates of the Temple were prodigious in magnitude, and transcendent in beauty. Each Triglyph belonging to the exterior architectural decorations, was ten feet high; and the Cella had twenty-four Pilasters. A great number of seashells are observable in the stone which formed this Edifice; and probably, to fill up the natural cavities of the stone, the whole building was encrusted with a strong stucco. Amidst this stupendous mass of ruins lies the Statue of an enormous Giant, measuring twenty-seven feet in length: the curls of his hair form a kind of garland; the legs are each in six pieces; the joints of each leg correspond; the head is in one piece;[1] and between the head and legs are four pieces, being alternately bisected; so that, in the body, are six rows of pieces. This Statue is composed of the same soft stone as the Temple; and was evidently stuccoed; for on and about the eyes, stucco may still be seen. Fragments of two other gigantic Statues of the same description lie near their Fellow-Monster: and it is said that fragments of ten or twelve more of these Giants have been found not far distant from the three already mentioned; and, like them, with elbows bent, and hands raised, in the attitude of supporting a weight above their heads: they are, therefore, supposed to have been Perses,[2] which formed a second row of Pillars, and rested upon the Capitals of immense Pilasters let into each Side-Wall of the interior part of the Temple.[3] Channels to receive ropes are visible in the largest stones belonging to this Edifice; which, owing to perpetual wars with Carthage, ultimately the destruction of Agrigentum, appears to have been never finished.[4] *The next Temple*, proceeding in rotation, *is that of Castor and Pollux*, where part of one Wall may be traced; two channelled Columns likewise remain; and appear to have been covered with superb white stucco. Westward, and beyond the ancient Walls, are two fluted Columns and some other remains of an Edifice denominated *the Temple of Vulcan*, but without good authority; as every ves-

---

[1] Some persons think it consists of two pieces.

[2] It is mentioned, in the first Chapter of this Work, speaking of Caryatides, that the conquerors of Caria (once called Phœnicia, because it was the abode of a Phœnician Colony), in order to commemorate their triumph over its inhabitants, erected public edifices, in which the figures of the female part of the subjugated people were used instead of columns; and when male figures were used in the same manner, the appellation given to them was "Perses."

[3] These Gigantic Figures were seen supporting parts of the Cornice, till the eleventh century.

[4] See DIODORUS SICULUS, *Lib.* xiii. *cap.* 24. According to this Author, the Temple of Jupiter Olympicus, at Agrigentum, seems to have been about three hundred and forty feet long, by one hundred and sixty feet wide. Other Writers say, it was three hundred and forty-five feet long, by one hundred and sixty-five wide: but neither of these measurements appears quite correct.

tige of that Temple, which once stood near Agrigentum, is supposed to be annihilated. *The ancient Bridge thrown over the Agragas*, merits observation, though almost destroyed; its materials being used daily, in modern buildings. *The Cloacæ*, cut through the rocks, and terminating in a *Cloaca Maxima*, likewise deserve notice.[1]

The stupendous Temples of Agrigentum, better worth seeing than any other antiquities Sicily contains, are eminently picturesque in point of situation; and the Temple of Concord is peculiarly striking, because nearly perfect: but neither the transcendent beauty of this Edifice, nor the simple grandeur of that at Ægesta, are so imposing and venerable as the Temple of Neptune at Pæstum; which, like the interior of S. Peter's at Rome, impresses the human mind with awe, and fits it for the worship of its Creator.

From Girgenti Travellers usually proceed through Palma to *Licata*, a distance of twenty-eight miles. Palma is pleasantly situated in a luxuriant valley: but between this rich district and Licata, the ancient *Phintia*, lies a dreary plain. Phintia, situated near the mouth of the Himera, now the Salso, was built by Phintias, an Agrigentine Prince, who transported thither the inhabitants of Gela, when he destroyed that town, about four centuries after its foundation; and the Promontory stretching into the sea, on the right of the river, is the *Ecnomos*, mentioned by Polybius, Diodorus, and Plutarch; where stood the Castle of Phalaris, which contained the bronze Bull, his famous instrument for torturing his subjects.[2] Licata has risen on the ruins of Phintia; and displays wider streets than are common in Sicily. Persons fortunate enough to procure a letter of recommendation to Sig. Giuseppe Paraninfo, are most hospitably received, and comfortably lodged, by that Gentleman, who resides at Licata: but those who are under the necessity of going to the Hotel, are wretchedly accommodated. Travellers frequently rest half a day at Licata; and then proceed to *Terranova*, a distance of eighteen miles, in the afternoon. The road lies on the sea shore; and the Hotel at Terranova is tolerably good: but persons acquainted with Mr. Wilding, Prince Butera's brother, and a resident here, are entertained at his house most sumptuously. This Town, built by the Emperor Frederick II, stands near the Site of the ancient *Gela*; which received its name from the *Gelas*, a small neighbouring river, and was founded by a Rhodian and Cretan Colony, above seven hundred years before the Christian era; and, according to Thucydides, forty-five years after Syracusæ. About three hundred paces to the east of Terranova are Remains of large Edifices, which mark the Site of the ancient City. On Medals found here, is the word "Gelas;" the ancient name of the river which now flows near Terranova: and moreover, the Greek Inscription relative to Gela, and found at Licata, was previously taken from among the Ruins near Terranova. After sleeping in the last named Town,

---

[1] A Banker, named Granot, who resides at Girgenti, and speaks English, is very kind and useful to Travellers.

[2] Amilcar carried this Bull to Carthage: but when that City was taken by Scipio, he restored the Bull to the Agrigentines.

Travellers usually proceed to Caltagirone, a distance of twenty-four miles.[1] The road passes through a corn country: the ascent to the Town is long and rapid; the Hotel very tolerable. Caltagirone, famous for a Manufactory of small Figures of *terracotta*, beautifully executed, and representing the lower class of people in coloured costumes, is a busy Town, and more extensive than Girgenti. After sleeping at Caltagirone, Travellers usually proceed to Palagonia and *Lentini;* a journey of thirty miles.[2] The commencement of the road is rough and steep; but presents a distant view of Ætna, with Mineo[2] finely placed on a commanding eminence. Multitudes of volcanic stones cover the soil: and near Palagonia is a pass through which a torrent of Lava appears to have rolled. Palagonia stands in a picturesque situation, on the side of a hill, near rocks of Lava finely broken: and beyond this spot beds of Lava and heaps of Volcanic stones present themselves great part of the way to the *Biviere di Lentini;* which Lake lies near the Town, and causes exhalations so peculiarly noxious, that they poison the surrounding country with *Mal' aria*.[3] The Town of Lentini is the ancient *Leontium;* once inhabited by the Læstrygones; whence its fields were denominated *Læstrygonii Campi:* its present appearance is that of a sickly poverty-stricken place; and its wretched Hotel affords no mattresses clean enough to sleep upon. After spending the night here, Travellers usually proceed to *Syracuse*, a distance of thirty miles. The first part of the road exhibits Ætna towering majestically above every other object, and Carlentini, built and fortified by Charles V.[4] The country is volcanic and beautiful; and the road, on approaching Agosta, presents a view of the sea, passes along a pretty water-lane, and goes within sight of what appears like a series of Craters united by a contiguous torrent. One of these Craters is very perfect; and its lava seems particularly ancient. The road crosses the torrent, which is ornamented with superb oleanders; and beyond it are groves of orange-trees and pomegranates: but, further on, the face of the country changes, and presents a dreary, barren, and rocky waste.

On the approach to Syracuse is *the Trophy which was erected to Marcellus*, opposite the Peninsula of Magnesi, formerly Tapso: and

---

1 Persons who wish to see the Museum and Excavations of the Barone Gabriele Judica, usually go from Terranova to Syracuse either by *Biscari*, or *Chiaramonte, Palazzola*, (the Baron's place of residence), and part of *Hybla Minor:* but this road is extremely bad: and may, indeed, be called dangerous. Baron Judica receives Travellers with great kindness and hospitality: his Museum consists of Vases and other antiquities, found in approximate Tombs, and Excavations, made on the spot where a Town, belonging to the Phœnicians, who colonized in Sicily, appear to have been buried. Remains of Public Baths, and a Theatre, may be seen in this Town; and the Tombs near it are square, or oblong cavities, delved in natural rocks. The Museum contains two curious Stone Foot-paths—an elegant bronze Lamp, shaped like a crab— Egyptian Idols—Votive Offerings—Moulds for casting Masks, and small Statues—a large Phœnician Vase, on which five rows of African Animals are painted—several of the *Greco-Siculi* Vases—a splendid Collection of Medals, etc. etc., all of which Antiquities the Baron wishes to sell. Near Palazzola are Statues, about ten feet high, hewn in the natural rocks.

2 Anciently *Minoa*, or *Heraclea* (for it had both names), and built by Minos, when he came to Sicily in quest of Dædalus.

3 The Lake of Lentini contains myriads of Leeches, which might endanger the life of any person tempted to bathe in its pestiferous waters.

4 This Prince invited the Inhabitants of Lentini to remove to his new Town; which is placed in a wholesome air: but they would not abandon the tombs of their ancestors.

after passing this Trophy the mule-path ascends the *Scala Græca*, goes through *Acradina*, and then unites itself with an excellent newly made road, in a rich and well cultivated country; where, fortified by drawbridges, stands the modern Siragusa, famous for its *Hotel*,[1] which contains large airy apartments, and is, in every respect, comfortable.

Syracusæ, likewise called, by the Ancients, *Pentapolis*, from comprising within its Walls five Cities, was founded above seven hundred years before the Christian era, by Archias of Corinth, one of the Heraclidæ; and in its most flourishing state comprised twelve hundred thousand inhabitants, extended above twenty-two English miles in circumference, and maintained an army of a hundred thousand foot, and ten thousand horse, together with a navy consisting of five hundred armed vessels. It was divided into five Parts, namely, *Ortygia*, *Acradina*, *Tycha*, *Neapolis*, and *Epipolæ*; and had three Citadels, treble Walls, and two capacious Harbours; the largest of which is computed to have been in breadth one mile and a quarter, in length two and a half, and in circumference six and a half. Its Edifices, public and private, were massive and stately; and its citizens remarkable for being eminently virtuous, or as eminently wicked: and this was exemplified in two of its most celebrated Characters, Archimedes, and the elder Dionysius. Syracusæ was attacked by the Athenians, both by sea and land, B.C. 414, but the following year the Athenians were discomfited; and their Leaders, Nicias and Demosthenes, both killed. Dionysius the elder distinguished himself greatly in the wars waged by his countrymen against Carthage; but abusing the power with which they entrusted him, he became their Sovereign and their Tyrant. This great bad man died B.C. 368, after having possessed the sceptre of Syracusæ thirty-eight years; and was succeeded by Dionysius the younger, whose cruel conduct toward Plato and Dion (the son of Hipparinus) provoked the latter to raise an army and expel him. This event occurred B.C. 357: ten years afterwards, however, he regained his sceptre; but was finally expelled by the Corinthians under Timoleon; and became a schoolmaster at Corinth (as Cicero observes), "that he might still continue to play the tyrant, and, because unable any longer to command men, exercise his power over boys." B.C. 212, the Syracusans who had been for three years closely besieged by Marcellus, at length relaxed in their military duties, during the nocturnal festival of Diana: and the Romans, taking advantage of this circumstance, made a forcible entry at one of the Gates, captured the City, and placed it under the yoke of Rome; which was much enriched and embellished by the paintings and sculpture of Syracusæ.[2] Little now remains of a Place once so populous and powerful, but a few almost unintelligible ruins, scattered here and there, among vineyards, orchards, and fields of corn. *The Island of Ortygia* lies southward. The

---

[1] The *Albergo del Sole*, near the Duomo. There is another, but very inferior Inn at Syracuse, *The Leone d'oro*.

[2] Marcellus, however, was too good to commit sacrilege; and therefore respected the statues of the gods, and left them in their temples.

ground rises toward the north; and becomes, toward the west, a Ridge about three miles and a half in length; at the extremity of which is *Epipolæ*. *Arcadina* occupied the shore from Ortygia to Trogilus; *Tycha* occupied the remainder of the plain to Epipolæ; and *Neapolis* was between the Great Harbour and a Ridge to the west of Ortygia. *Traces of eighteen Gates*, belonging to the ancient Walls, are discoverable. In the Island of Ortygia, now modern Syracuse, is *the Fountain of the Nymph, Arethusa;*[1] who, when changed, according to poetic license, into this stream, received divine honours, as the Patroness of the ancient City: but (though celebrated by Poets, and said, by Strabo and Diodorus, to have been of such magnitude that it contained shoals of sacred fishes, incredibly large), this Fountain is now reduced to a Tank for washerwomen; and presents nothing more than a rill of water flowing from an Aqueduct.[2]

A Temple of the ancient Doric Order and originally consecrated to Minerva, likewise stands in the modern Town. This Edifice, which appears to have possessed the beautiful simplicity and grandeur common to ancient Doric temples, was cruelly injured about the seventh century, by being transformed into a Church; and is now become the Cathedral of Syracuse: it suffered again in the twelfth century, when an earthquake shook down its roof. It was erected on a raised quadrilateral Platform, and displayed forty Columns fluted and without base; the shafts being about twenty-five English feet in height, and the capitals about three feet four inches. The Cella was enclosed by Walls composed of large stones, nicely joined together without cement; which walls have been cut through, to form communicating Arches with the side-aisles, when it became a Church. The Columns, on the north side of the Edifice, are damaged and built into the north wall; where eleven of them may be traced; those on the south side are better preserved: and at the west end two are still visible. *In order to visit the Rivers Anapus and Papyrus*, (two branches of the same stream), *and the district of Epipolæ*, it is requisite to provide a Boat for crossing the *Portus Magnus*, and ascending the Rivers. The mouth of the Anapus is little more than three boat-lengths in width, but very deep; the false Papyri (for there are two kinds) grow on its banks; which, about midsummer, are covered with myriads of flies peculiar to this spot, and having four dark coloured wings, and a black body tipped with red under the tail: and at the junction of the Anapus with the Papyrus, but no where else, is found a peculiar sort of shell, called by the Syracusan boatmen *Cozzola*, the inside of which resembles mother of pearl. The Papyrus is so narrow that a boat in ascending this River touches the reeds and canes on its banks, and is towed along. Near the river stand *two gigantic Doric Columns*, channelled to within a few feet of the ground; and these Columns, with some *fallen Fragments*, are the only remains now visible of a once magnificent Edi-

---

[1] Arethusa, one of the Sicelides, is fabled to have been transformed into a fountain by Diana.

[2] Charles V. when he fortified Syracuse, totally altered the appearance of this Fountain.

fice consecrated to Olympic Jove; whose Statue here was adorned by Hiero II. (a Syracusan Monarch famed for his virtues), with a mantle of gold wrought from the spoils of the Carthaginians: but Dionysius I. (prone to sacrilege) possessed himself of it, saying, "The Son of Saturn had a garment too heavy for summer, and too cold for winter; and should, therefore, be provided with one made of woollen cloth, fit for both seasons." The Prætor, Verres, the most rapacious of the Roman Governors of Sicily,[1] removed this statue to Rome; from which period the Temple went to decay. Near the ruins of this Edifice is *an oblong Well*, from twenty to twenty-five feet deep; and probably an ancient Receptacle for purifying water. Hence Travellers usually ascend the river to *the Fonte Ciane*, passing through fields of hemp.[2] Large quantities of the true and very fine Papyri grow near the Fonte Ciane, which has a capacious and deep *Basin*, furnished with remarkably pellucid water, and abounding with fish. The adjacent country presents a pestiferous marsh. At this place Travellers usually dismiss their boat; and mounting mules (sent hither expressly to wait for them) cross the Anapus on a bridge, and proceed to that portion of ancient Syracusæ denominated *Neapolis*. This ride presents a view of *the ruined Walls of Tycha*; and after ascending a narrow track, the road leads to *the site of the ancient Gate* where Demosthenes made a forcible entry; it then crosses *the Aqueduct*, whose source is thirty miles distant, and passes *a small Naumachia*; hence crossing several *ancient Wheel-tracks* to the *Quarries of the Philosophers*,[3] the ancient *Walls* on the left of which merit notice; they are nine feet thick. Passing to the north side of Fort Labdalus, the road goes through *a Gateway*, between the northeast angle of the Fort and a line of Walls to the north; and this is supposed to have been *one entrance to Epipolæ*.[4] Ruins of *Fort Labdalus still remain*; and, to the west, is a deep Moat. The Walls of Neapolis and Tycha united at the south side of the Fort; and Hybla Minor is a conspicuous object from this spot. Near Fort Labdalus is an interesting and very extensive *Subterranean Passage*, nine feet wide, cut through solid rocks, lofty enough to admit cavalry, and supposed to have been made for the conveyance of troops and provisions from one quarter of the ancient city to another.[5] Returning hence, and following the course of the Aqueduct, Travellers are shown several openings into the Subterranean

---

[1] See Cicero's *Orations*.

[2] It is asserted, by the Sicilians, that the farina of hemp in blossom causes *Mal' aria*; and that no person who values health, should sleep near hemp fields in blossom.

[3] So called, because supposed to have been the prison in which Dionysius confined the Poet Philoxenus, and certain Philosophers, for not having praised his poetical compositions.

[4] Here, according to Diodorus Siculus, began a Wall, erected by Dionysius the Elder, in twenty days; and extending, according to some opinions, seven miles. Six thousand masons were employed in this work, besides two hundred peasants, six thousand oxen, and a great number of persons who cut the stone in the quarries. One architect was assigned to every acre. Some of the stones which composed this Wall were eighteen feet long; and part of it was very perfect till thrown down by Charles V, at the period when he dismantled Fort Labdalus, and fortified Ortygia. *The Gate* by which Marcellus entered the *Epipolis* may still be traced.

[5] This Passage has been explored for some miles; and probably might have served, among other purposes, as a Sallyport from the strong Fortress of Labdalus.

Passage, and then conducted to *the descent into the Theatre;* leaving, on the right, *the ancient Entrance to Tycha*, which is cut through a solid rock, and bordered on both sides with small tombs, and marks of Marble Slabs, reported to have borne Greek Inscriptions. Above the level of the Theatre the Aqueduct terminates in *a Nymphæum*[1] delved in a solid rock: but the water which produced this Fountain is all drawn away to supply Mills, one of which now stands amidst the Seats of the Theatre, at present used as foot-paths for the animals who carry corn to the Mill. *The Theatre*, hewn out of a rock, was called by Cicero "*Maximum;*" and Diodorus thought it the most beautiful edifice of the kind in Sicily: the view from its summit is even now delicious, and must have been astonishingly magnificent when Syracusæ shone in all its glory. Few vestiges remain of the Scena; as the materials with which it was composed were used by Charles V. in his fortifications. The shape of this immense Theatre exceeds a semi-circle by twenty-seven feet four inches, and resembles a horse-shoe: its diameter is one hundred and sixteen feet; and it held forty thousand spectators.[2] Two Corridors remain; as do several of the Seats: and those in the lowermost rows appear to have been cased with marble. The first Seat of the lowest division is singularly cut at the back; and, perhaps, a piece of marble was inserted here, to form a magisterial chair. Under the Site of the sixth Seat, which no longer exists, is a Channel for Water.[3] The spectators enjoyed the accommodation of an Awning; marks, where the poles which supported it were fixed, being still visible. Against the back of the upper Corridor are Greek Inscriptions (one to each Cuneus); what remain appear to have been as follows.

Second Cuneus, ΒΑΣΙΛΙΣΣΑΣ ΝΗΡΗΙΔΟΣ
Third, ΒΑΣΙΛΙΣΣΑΣ ΦΙΛΙΣΤΙΔΟΣ
Fourth, ΒΑΣΙΛΕΟΣ ΙΕΡΩΝΟΣ
Fifth, ΔΙΟΣ ΟΛΥΜΠΙΟΥ
ΑΙ   ΣΣ   ΣΡΑΣ   ΦΡΟΝ

Riedesel supposes that the inhabitants of Tycha (from their situation) occupied the upper part of the Theatre; those of Acradina the middle; and those of Neapolis the lowest part; as they inhabited the plain. The district called *Neapolis*, in which this Theatre stands, was the last built, largest, and most magnificent part of ancient Syracuse;[4] and adjoining to the Theatre are the celebrated *Stone*

---

[1] Supposed to have resembled that at Athens; and to have been the Edifice, on which were inscribed the names of those persons who gained the prize for musical compositions in the Theatre; and likewise the place where the Tripod of Apollo was deposited, and consecrated.

[2] This Edifice is wider than the Theatre at Athens, by eighty-two Roman palmi; and supposed to be the most ancient Grecian Theatre extant. It seems almost impossible that the actors could have been heard in so immense a Fabric, notwithstanding the aid afforded them by masks which contained speaking trumpets, by sounding-plates of bronze, and by the still more powerful aid of the approximate rock.

[3] There is, in this Theatre, a contrivance for preventing the feet of the person behind from interfering with the comfort of his neighbour in front, by the stone, at the back of each row of seats, being *a little raised*. The same thing may be seen in the Tragic Theatre, at Pompeii.

[4] *Neapolis* did not exist till after the Peloponnesian war.

Quarry, and *Ear of Dionysius*. The latter is fifty-eight English feet in height at the entrance, about seventeen feet wide, and two hundred and ten feet long: the sides slope gradually to the summit, and terminate in a small Channel, which conveyed every sound in the Cave to an aperture near the entrance. Thus the sounds in this Prison were all directed to one common Tympanum; which communicated with a small private Apartment, where Dionysius spent his leisure hours in listening to the discourse of his prisoners. The echo produced by tearing a piece of dry paper is distinctly heard throughout the Cave; and that produced by firing a pistol is like the report of a cannon, and lasts ten seconds. In the Cave are remains of *one Bath*, just large enough to contain *one person*: an extraordinary circumstance, for which antiquaries cannot account. The Entrance to the Ear of Dionysius is *from the Quarry*, supposed to have been likewise used as a State Prison, and so large that it has now become a Rope Walk. Near the entrance to this picturesque Quarry are Marks where monumental tablets were inserted. *The Amphitheatre* is contiguous: it had four Entrances, and was partly masonry, and partly hewn out of solid rocks. Under the south Entrance is *an Aqueduct*. The semi-diameters of this Edifice are one hundred and thirty-four by eighty-three English feet; and the Wall of the Podium is about eight feet six inches in height.[1] Near the Amphitheatre are *Catacombs*, now called *Le Grotte di S. Giovanni*, peculiarly well constructed, and so immensely large as to resemble a subterranean city. They are entered by a Passage six feet high, eight feet wide, and excavated in a right line, so as to form the principal street, above which is an opening for the admission of light and air. Other streets branch off in various directions; and are all bordered with Columbaria, Sepulchral Chambers for families, and an infinite number of oblong Cavities, made to receive the remains of adults, and likewise of Children. *A Stone Quarry* situated in the ancient *Acradina*, and now *the Garden of the P. P. Cappuccini*, merits notice; as this Garden, part of which is near an hundred feet below the level of the soil, exhibits a scene peculiarly picturesque and beautiful: it has been hewn out of a rock hard as marble; and consisting of gravel, petrified shells, and other marine substances; and the bottom of this vast Quarry, whence, in all probability, most of the materials for building Syracusæ were taken, is at present covered with a bed of vegetable earth, so fertile as to produce superb oranges, citrons, pomegranates, etc. Part of the Quarry is cut like the Ear of Dionysius; and on one of the perpendicular masses of stone (left to support the roof), steps are visible, near its summit. Some Greek letters, graven in the rock, have led antiquaries to conjecture that the Athenians, made prisoners in consequence of the defeat of Nicias and Demosthenes, and

---

[1] The Amphitheatre, a Roman work, being too small for the ancient population of the City, is supposed to have been constructed during its decline.

Contiguous to this Edifice are *three Columns of marble*, called the remains of a Temple erected by the Romans, and dedicated to Ceres and Proserpine.

afterwards liberated for repeating verses from Euripides, were confined here. Under a fig-tree, contiguous to this spot, was found a headless statue of Venus, now in the Syracusan Museum, and a small Statue of Æsculapius; the former being excellent Greek sculpture. Travellers, not pressed for time, should visit the *Piscina, under the little Church of S. Nicola*, and a most magnificent ancient reservoir for Water. *The remains of the ancient Walls* of Syracusæ likewise deserve minute examination, as they are beautiful specimens of masonry. The exterior part was perpendicular, the interior shaped into steps; and triangular stones are said to have formed the upper part of the parapet. Modern Syracuse, computed to be about two miles in circumference, exhibits narrow streets, and a dejected, sickly population, not amounting to more than fourteen thousand persons: for the contiguous Marshes, and the extreme heat of the sun, which is said never to have been obscured one whole day at Syracuse, make the climate very unwholesome. The modern Town contains *a Public Museum*, in which *the Venus*, already mentioned as having been found without her head, is by far the finest piece of sculpture. Here, likewise, are the Inscriptions, taken from the Street of the Tombs, etc.; several Sarcophagi; the lower part of a fine *Basso-rilievo*, and two small Vases of ancient coloured glass. The Syracusan wine is particularly good, and of twelve kinds: and the olive-trees in this neighbourhood are of an astonishing size and age; some of them being more than two centuries old.

They produce delicious oil. The number of Papyri growing near the Fontana Papiria (or Ciane), is somewhat reduced at present; because the farmers cut and dried them to bind sheaves of grain: but this practice is now prohibited; and paper, resembling the ancient papyrus, has been recently made with this plant. The castor-oil shrub grows in large quantities at the sides of the roads near Syracuse. Travellers, on leaving this Town, to proceed to *Catania*, a distance of forty-two miles, retrace their steps through ancient Syracusæ, and pass *a Tomb called that of Archimedes*, but not corresponding with Cicero's description of the Tomb he saw. Two fluted Doric Columns support an Architrave and Frieze with Triglyphs, above which is a pediment; all these are hewn out of a solid rock; and the interior contains niches for urns, and a Sarcophagus. Adjoining is *a similar Tomb*. The road, after passing these Sepulchres, descends the *Scala Græca*, cut sloping on the sides of precipitous rocks, which extend on the west toward Fort Labdalus, and are equally precipitous along the sea coast toward Ortygia. Near the sea are Stones laid regularly, in various places, as for a road: and further on, to the left, is *a Wall*, apparently of Cyclopian work, and standing where Marcellus pitched his Camp. The contiguous *Trophy*, erected in honour of that great and amiable Roman, displays a base twenty-four palmi square, and sixteen high, on which is a Fragment, probably of a fluted Column. This Trophy was, according to report, much injured by the earthquake of

1542.[1] Further on, the road presents a prospect of Mililli,[2] together with Augusta (built by Frederick II.), and its Harbour; and then becomes dreary, till it advances toward the sea, and exhibits a fine view of Ætna. Beyond this spot Travellers cross the River Giarretta, anciently the *Symethus*, in a ferry-boat; thence traversing a large bed of Lava, which extends to Catania, and was produced by an Eruption of Ætna, in 1669.

The first view of Catania and its Saracenic domes is striking. Ætna, with its thickly inhabited base, towers behind it: and running out in a line before the Town, and beyond the present Port, is a stream of black Lava, of 1669, which again appears at the end of the Corso, and is a fearful sight; although the blocks are now mouldering into dust. The Strada-Messina may be called handsome: but houses with all their windows shattered, cracked walls, and columns declining from their perpendicular, proclaim the nature of the contiguous Mountain.

Catania, anciently *Cataetna* (Town of Ætna), was, according to some writers, founded by the Cyclops, and one of their first built Cities. Other records say it was founded by a Colony from Chalcis, seven hundred and fifty-three years before the Christian era. It now contains above thirty thousand inhabitants, and the only University in the Island; and is, moreover, the See of a Bishop; whose revenues are very considerable; owing, in great measure, to the produce of the snow on Ætna: for this Mountain not only furnishes Sicily with that healthful commodity, but likewise supplies Malta and several other places. Frozen snow is, strictly speaking, the staff of life in Sicily, both of the nobleman and the peasant; each of whom dreads a want of it, more than a famine. Catania was severely injured by the eruption of 1669, and almost entirely destroyed by the earthquake of 1693, when great part of its inhabitants were buried under the ruins of their houses and churches: but it rose again, Phœnix like, from its ashes, so much increased in beauty as to rival, if not eclipse, every other City of the Island—may it never again fall a prey to volcanic eruptions!—It contains good Hotels; *The Elephant Inn*, Piazza del Duomo, which is very comfortable; and the *Corona d'oro*; the master of which Hotel, Sig. Abbate, is an excellent Guide to the summit of Ætna. The Cathedral at Catania was originally built, and the See founded, by Ruggiero, in 1193. *The existing Cathedral* is the most chaste and elegant Church Sicily possesses: in its Façade are several Columns of granite, taken from the Scena of the ancient Theatre: its Cupola is superb; the Frescos, on the ceiling, are by Corradino; and on the left side of the Edifice is a good Picture of

---

[1] Not far remote from Syracuse is Nota, a beautiful little Town, containing a collection of Medals, etc. on sale.

[2] This district was once famous for Sugar Canes, which were sedulously cultivated during the period when Sicily was obliged to furnish a thousand cwt. of sugar, annually, for the Knights of Malta. In the Village of Avola, eighteen miles distant from Syracuse, small Sugar Plantations may still be seen: but they are kept up merely as objects of curiosity and pleasure; the superior quality of West Indian sugar having put an end to the cultivation of the Sugar Cane in Sicily, as an article of commerce. This plant is said to be indigenous to the Island: but whether its use was known to the ancients, or is a modern discovery, seems uncertain.

S. Agata, by Paladino. The Arabesques of the doors of the Cross Aisle, and the *Bassi-rilievi*, are by Gagini; and a Chapel to the north of the Choir contains fine specimens of Lava and Alabaster; one piece of the red Lava being equally beautiful with rosso antico, though somewhat paler.[1] The Piazza del Duomo is ornamented with *an Obelisk of red Egyptian granite*, placed on the back of an Elephant sculptured in lava. The Obelisk displays Hieroglyphics, and is supposed to have been made by the ancient inhabitants of Catania, in imitation of the obelisks of Egypt. The Elephant is one of the works of the lower ages. *The Monastero dei Benedittini* especially deserves notice, on account of having been so nearly destroyed by the Lava of 1699, that its preservation seems miraculous. The existing Garden belonging to this Convent is situated upon the Lava; which, after approaching within five yards of the Edifice, turned off to the left; on the north side it came within ten yards, and turned the corner near the Church, which was also untouched. But the earthquake of 1693 made it necessary to rebuild this Convent; and the present Structure is vast and magnificent: its Church would be handsome, but for the abominable whitewash with which the modern inhabitants of the two Sicilies have spoilt their public edifices. The Choir is ornamented with fine Carving in wood: some of the Paintings are by Cavallucci; the Organ is excellent, the singing fine, and the whole service performed with dignity and devotion. The Monks belonging to this Confraternity are the sons of noblemen; and appear to be persons of education. They possess a valuable Museum, which, except it be at their dinner hour, is shown to Travellers of the male sex. This Museum contains above three hundred ancient Sicilian Vases, exquisitely shaped and beautifully painted — one vase, with a black ground and red figures, displaying Etruscan Characters—a collection of Penates in *terracotta*, and bronze—a superb Venus-Anadyomene in bronze—an ancient circular Lamp for twelve lights—another Lamp for five lights—a collection of ancient Sacrificial and Family Utensils—a Roman Legionary Eagle—upward of a thousand ancient Medals of Sicily, Magna Græcia, and Greece, properly so called—Shells—Petrifactions, and Lavas from Ætna—two Tables of Petrified Shells polished—two Tables of Ebony and Ivory, representing the principal events in the Roman History—a Table comprising two hundred varieties of Marbles—and likewise several ancient Tiles; one displaying the figure of a Woman, and another that of a Rabbit.[2] *The Church* belonging to the large and wealthy *Convent of S. Nicola d'Asena* is three hundred and fifty English feet in length, by two hundred and forty in width; and contains an Organ with seventy-four stops,

---

[1] The Sacristy, belonging to the Duomo, contains a Fresco, which represents the terrible Eruption of 1669.

[2] The Arches of the ancient subterranean Structures, at Catania, are formed with tiles, placed, alternately, between pieces of lava: and the tile marked with a Rabbit, or a Hare, for it is difficult, in pottery, to distinguish the one from the other, was probably manufactured at Messina; as Anaxilaus, Sovereign of Rhegium, is said to have brought hares, or rabbits, most likely the latter, to Messina, where that quadruped was previously unknown; and in consequence, ancient Messinian medals bore the stamp of a hare, or a rabbit, whichever it might be.

one being imitative of drums and cymbals. This Instrument, which is considered as a *capo d'opera*, was made by a citizen of Catania. *The University* founded in 1444, by Alphonso, at that period Monarch of Sicily, contains a very large and valuable Library. *The Museum formed during the last century by the Principe Ignazio Biscari*, a most amiable, enlightened, and patriotic nobleman, highly deserves notice; and Travellers, anxious to see it to advantage, should signify their wish, over night, to the principal Custode; a gentlemanly, well informed person; who, thus called upon, shows the Museum himself. The Court-yard contains a small ancient Obelisk of granite, charged with Hieroglyphics, like that in the Piazza del Duomo—ancient Mill-stones, and Sarcophagi, of Lava—and a Pedestal supporting a Vase of Lava, also ancient and ornamented with *Bassi-rilievi*.[1] Among the collection of Bronzes, are—a Wrestler—Adonis—a Drunken Fawn—Antinous—Julius Cæsar—several Statues of Venus—Mercury—and a small Hercules. The collection of Egyptian, Etruscan, and Latin Antiquities, is large; and one of the Balances has a Weight representing the figure of Rome. Here, likewise, are ancient Tools, used by Mechanics—Sacrificial Utensils, and others, used in Public Baths—Kitchen Utensils—an ancient Ploughshare— magnificent bronze Vases, and elegant Lamps, one of which, shaped like a Scenic Mask, may be divided so as to make two. Among the collection of Statues in marble is a Torso, semi-colossal, and found in the ancient Forum of Catania. According to Riedesel it represented Bacchus, and is in the very finest style of Grecian sculpture!! This gallery likewise contains a Cornice, and a Capital of one of the Columns of the ancient Theatre, excavated by Prince Biscari—a Statue of Hercules, found in ancient Catania, with one leg wanting, which has been ill restored— a fine Pedestal—busts of Jove, and Caracalla—Venus, with a modern nose—a Hero—Scipio, with a Scar on the Head—Julius Cæsar—Adrian in the character of Mars—the Statue of a Muse, found in the ancient Theatre, and beautifully draped—and Ceres crowned with ears of corn, and supposed to represent Livia. Among the *Bassi-rilievi* is a beautiful Female Figure seated on one side of an altar, and a graceful manly figure on the opposite side, with his hand extended, as if he were in the act of adjuration; and behind the Altar is a third Figure, witnessing the scene. Another *Basso-rilievo* represents the head of Medusa, and is a fine Fragment. The Museum contains a large collection of Penates—a Cabinet of old Sicilian Costumes; eight thousand Medals, Roman, Sicilian, and Greek, four hundred of which are gold: and this collection comprises the whole series of Consular, and likewise of Imperial Roman Medals.[2] Here also is a Philosophical Cabinet, which contains two exquisite Lachrymatories of ancient coloured glass — a collection of Armour,

---

[1] Ancient *bassi-rilievi* of Lava were not uncommon at Catania; several of them having been found there in the ancient Baths.
[2] Many of the Sicilian medals record the filial piety of Anapius and Amphinomus, natives of Catania, who, as already mentioned, saved their parents from death, during an Eruption of Ætna.

and curious Musquetry—a good collection of Shells, and Sicilian Marbles—Specimens of the Ætna and Lipari Lavas—together with upward of four hundred ancient Sicilian Vases of pottery, found in and near Catania; some of them magnificent in point of size, all beautifully shaped, and several superbly painted. One of these Vases is highly prized for having a white ground, not often met with; and another exhibits four horses harnessed to a war-chariot. Catania contains a Silk Manufactory; and fine Specimens of Amber may be purchased in this City.[1] The remains of the ancient Town are, generally speaking, subterranean; and were chiefly discovered by Prince Biscari. Previous to the year 1669, the Castle stood on the sea shore, near the magnificent Mole formed in the sixteenth century by an Eruption of Ætna,[2] and contiguous to the ancient Wall of the Town, with a delicious Spring and Stream of water at its base. But the Lava of 1669, which ran from the Monti-Rossi (near Nicolosi), in a direct line to this point, accumulating till it rose above the Wall (near sixty feet high), filling up the sea to a vast extent, and destroying the Mole, had left, near the half-buried Castle, a small aperture, which enabled Prince Biscari to ascertain where the Wall of the Town was situated: and, in consequence, he made an excavation, and recovered for his compatriots their regretted Spring of water; to which Travellers are now conducted down, by a Staircase of sixty-three Steps in the midst of solid Lava. This Spring is perfectly translucent. *The Greek Theatre*, over which modern houses are now built, appears to have stood on the side of a hill, and was larger than the Theatre of Marcellus at Rome. Its columns were used by Ruggiero to ornament the Cathedral erected at his command; and the hand of Ignorance seems to have destroyed, during the dark ages, most of its decorations. Three Corridors and seven Rows of Seats have been excavated; and enough of the Scena remains to show the Three Doors of Entrance for the actors.[3] *An Aqueduct* is likewise discoverable here. The present Entrance is by the ancient Stairs of the Theatre; and to the right of these, are several other ancient Steps, leading to *the Odeum*, which was only one hundred and forty-five feet in diameter. Both Theatres were constructed with Ætna Lava; and perhaps, in the dramatic exhibitions here, Tisias, surnamed Stesichorus, who resided and died at Catania, might have first taught the Chorus to become stationary and chant, accompanied by music. Near the Porta di Aci, likewise called Porta Stesicorea, from the Tomb of Stesichorus having been placed here, are subterranean remains of *the immense Amphitheatre* erected by the Roman Colony Augustus established at Catania. But, when gladiatorial shows were abolished,

---

[1] The fruit, wine, and indeed all the productions of Catania, and its environs, are excellent.

[2] Nature had not given Catania a good Harbour; but Ætna fully supplied this deficiency, by the above-named Mole, beyond the power of man to have constructed.

[3] We are told that this Theatre existed during the second attack of the Athenians upon the Syracusans; and that Alcibiades, the Athenian general, pronounced an oration here. The Upper Corridor seems to have been furnished with Boxes, for female Spectators.

this colossean Edifice was neglected; and at length became a mass of ruins: in consequence of which, the people of Catania asked permission of Theodosius, to use some of the materials for repairing their walls; which permission was given, and profited by, in other instances. The circumference of this Edifice is reported to have been a thousand feet: several of its Corridors are excavated; and the lowest exhibits Dens for wild-beasts. On the western side are large Channels for Water; which might probably have been let into the Arena when naval combats were represented. The Amphitheatre was built on the side of a hill. In *the Vapour Baths*, excavated by Prince Biscari, the Waiting-room, and Furnaces, still exist:[1] and *under the Convento de' Carmelitani is another ancient Structure*, supposed to have belonged to Public Baths. Its form is octagonal: its diameter thirty-three feet; and it has a hemispherical Cupola. The style of the Edifice, and the Inscriptions, are Roman. *Behind the Monastero dei Benedittini*, in the midst of Lava, are *several Arches of a magnificent Aqueduct*, which brought water to Catania from Licodia, sixteen miles distant: this, too, is Roman work. *The Garden of the P. P. Cappuccini* contains a well-preserved *circular ancient Tomb;* together with ruins of *an ancient Pyramid*, small, but similar in construction to those of Egypt. Toward the northern part of the modern City, *near the Bastione degl' Infetti*, are remains of a large Structure of excellent Greek masonry, supposed to be part of *the celebrated Temple of Ceres*, to which females only were allowed access; and whence a peculiarly fine Statue of the goddess was stolen, by Verres. Westward, beyond the Walls of the City, are a considerable number of *ancient Tombs. At the Chiesa della Mecca* is a well-preserved *Columbarium;* and another may be found in *the Garden belonging to the Minoriti*. Beyond the Palermo-Gate of Catania, and extending for some miles, is a good Carriage-road; and the whole way between Catania and Termini a Carriage-road is forming.

Persons who mean to ascend Ætna, in order to view the rising sun from its summit, should provide themselves with strong thick-soled half-boots; those lined with fur are the most comfortable; gloves lined with fur; woollen stockings; and travelling caps lined with fur. Thick veils are likewise extremely useful to guard the eyes, and prevent the sulphureous clouds which frequently roll down Ætna from affecting the breath. Light, but very warm pelisses, or great-coats, are also needful; and Sicilian travelling cloaks, with hoods, the whole made of leather, are particularly convenient, as they exclude rain. A strong walking-stick, with an iron spike at the end, is likewise a great convenience between the Casa degli Inglesi and the summit of the Mountain. Mattresses, Coverlids, a Tinder-box and Matches; Lamp-oil, a Lantern containing a Lamp, Water, and a Kettle for heating it; *Carbo-*

---

[1] Balls of Lava, found near the Furnaces, have led antiquaries to conjecture that these balls were made red-hot, and used for keeping up the heat of fires.

nella;[1] an earthen Pipkin filled with strong Soup in jelly; Coffee, Sugar, Wine, powerful enough to be mixed with hot water, and Rum, or Brandy, for the Guides, are necessary appendages to this expedition. Travellers, however, should, on no consideration, follow the example of their Guides, by drinking spirits, to fortify themselves against the intense cold in the uppermost region of Ætna; as the purpose would not be answered; and illness might probably ensue. It has been already mentioned that the Master of the Corona d'oro at Catania is an excellent Guide for Ætna: but, in case of danger, the Mules and Guides of Catania cannot be so much depended upon as those of Nicolosi; and therefore Travellers often prefer the latter.[2]

An ascent to the summit of Ætna is unprofitable, and seldom practicable, unless the weather be serene and settled.

This mountain rises more than ten thousand feet above the level of the sea.[3] Pindar mentions it as an active volcano: Homer is silent on the subject.[4] Probably, therefore, no Eruption had taken place in his days. Plato's first visit to Sicily originated merely from a wish to examine the Crater of Ætna; and Adrian ascended this mountain to contemplate the rising sun from its summit. Its Base, computed to be above forty leagues in circumference, is full of Conical Hills; and this *first Region* likewise displays Villages, Gardens, Vineyards, Fields of Flax and Hemp, Hedges of Aloes; Olive and Orange-trees, and the Date-bearing Palm. *The second Region*, called Bosco di Paterno, is covered with Ilexes; and, toward the north, with Pines. The soil here being Lava converted by the hand of Time into rich vegetable earth, yields aromatic Herbs, and Flowers of various descriptions, mingled with Fern: but beyond the Grotta delle Capre, formerly used as a shelter for Travellers, the trees become fewer in number, deformed, and dwarfish, till, at length, they degenerate into shrubs, and are lost amidst volcanic sand. Here commences *The third Region*, consisting of Scoriæ, Ashes, and Snow; and leading to a Platform, in the centre of which is the Crater. The ascent to this platform presents no difficulty with respect to its steepness; but the excessive coldness of the air on so elevated a spot, and the gusts of wind, and clouds of sulphur, which sometimes assail Travellers, are distressing; and if not properly guarded against, dangerous. There are now two *Refuges*, or Resting Places, for Travellers on Ætna, *the Casa della Neve*, consisting of one room only, about thirty feet long, and originally built to shelter peasants employed in collecting snow; and *the Casa degli Inglesi*, consisting of three rooms, a small kitchen, and a stable for mules; and erected at the expense of British Officers quartered in Messina, A.D. 1810.[5] The warm clothing re-

---

1 Persons who intend sleeping at the Casa degli Inglesi, on Ætna, where there is a kitchen, would find Charcoal more useful than *Carbonella*.

2 The peasants of Ætna are celebrated for being robust, intrepid, civil, and honest.

3 According to Ferrara, it is ten thousand one hundred and ninety-eight Paris feet above the level of the sea; and, according to English measurement, ten thousand and thirty-two feet above the same level.

4 Homer's descriptions of countries are *even now* geographically true; and therefore his silence is strong presumptive proof.

5 The Key of the Casa degli Inglesi is kept at Nicolosi, by Sig. Mario Gemellara, who re-

quisite for Travellers who ascend to the Crater, should be put on in the first Refuge: and it is likewise advisable to have extra-wrappers, carried by the Guides, to be worn by Travellers on their arrival at the Crater.

The great object in visiting Ætna is *to see, from its summit, the rising of the sun, the Pyramid formed by the Shadow of the Cone, and the panoramic View over the whole Island.*

To the east of the path which descends from the Crater are Ruins, called *La Torre del Filosofo*, and supposed to have been an Altar or Ædicula, raised by the Romans, when they possessed Sicily, to Ætnean Jove.[1]

An English Gentleman and his Wife, who ascended to the Crater of Ætna at Midsummer, 1826, under the direction of *Vincenzo Carbonaro*, a judicious Nicolosi Guide, give the following report of their journey.

" The weather being favourable and the mountain clear, we set out, at half-past eight in the morning, from Catania; where Fahrenheit's thermometer was 71: and soon leaving the new road which leads to Messina, reached an immense sheet of Lava, commonly called *the Port of Ulysses*, and supposed to have been that, described by Homer, as 'commodious;'[2] but Ætna has so completely filled it with Lava, that this Port cannot easily be traced. From Catania to Nicolosi the country is covered with small villages, well cultivated farms, and a profusion of fruit: and in sight of Nicolosi is a small Crater of an inconsiderable depth, near the road. We reached Nicolosi, which is twelve miles from Catania, at a quarter past eleven: and at ten minutes after twelve, mounted fresh mules, and took two Muleteers, together with *Vincenzo Carbonaro*, and another Guide. We then travelled over a plain of fine sand; having, on our left, *Monte-Rosso*, whence issued the destructive torrent of Lava, which, in 1669, overwhelmed Catania. Clouds now began to form on Ætna; and thunder resounded like cannon: but, nevertheless, our Guides said, the weather would prove favourable. After crossing a field of Lava, we reached *the Bosco*, or *woody Region*, which resembles a park: and here we heard the *Cucco* and saw May in full blossom: but, owing to various streams of Lava, we were obliged to take a zigzag path, in some places unpleasant. The Bosco consists chiefly of stunted ilexes; and as we ascended through it, the thunder continued; though the clouds did not conceal the summit of Monte-Agnola. We now perceived a sensible difference in temperature; and, before our arrival at the *Refuge*, the thermometer fell to 66. This *Refuge*, seven miles from Nicolosi, and called *the Casa della Neve*, we reached at a

---

sides there; and Travellers should call for it as they pass.

[1] Diodorus says, there were several Altars, in Sicily, thus dedicated.

[2] See HOMER's *Odyssey*, Book IX. Homer's description, however, cannot be expected to agree in this instance with present appearances; as all the Eruptions of Ætna, (immense in number) are supposed to have taken place subsequent to his time. He flourished, according to the Arundelian Marbles, above nine hundred years before the Christian era; and Pindar, who, as already mentioned, gives the first account of an eruption of Ætna, was not born till more than five hundred years after the death of Homer. Thucydides is, next to Pindar, the earliest authority who speaks of an Eruption: and he describes it as having occurred between the eleventh Olympiad, B. C. 736, and the seventy-fifth Olympiad, B. C. 479.—*Bell. Pelop.* L. 3.

quarter before two. The Hut has no door; and several of the tiles have been blown off its roof; but placing our Mattresses in the dryest part of the wet pavement, and nailing a coverlid over the doorway, we dined, and went to bed. The Guides and Muleteers slept round an immense fire, on the outside of the Hut; and at ten o'clock at night we got up, took coffee and bread, and put on warm clothing. The clouds had dispersed; the stars shone brightly; and the Guides said, we should have a fine ascent; especially as the wind (the thing of all others they fear most) had subsided. At half-past eleven, when the moon rose, we set out; leaving our mattresses, etc. in the care of a lad: and, before quitting the Bosco, we passed the *Grotta delle Capre*, a small Cave formed by Lava. On quitting the Bosco, we found the degree of cold increase; the ascent likewise became steeper; and a slight wind arose. Here the moon, reflected in the Biviere di Lentini, was a beautiful object. Previous to reaching the snow the ascent became much steeper; the cold increased, and one of our party lost, for a short time, the use of a finger. On reaching the snow, we found it hard, and very slippery; insomuch that the mules could scarce keep upon their legs: however, we arrived without any accident at the *Casa degli Inglesi* (during Summer the usual sleeping-place on Ætna.)[1] about a quarter past two in the morning. The distance from the Casa della Neve to the Casa degli Inglesi is eight miles. The floors of the latter Refuge were covered with ice; and the chairs and table wet with drippings from the roof. Having made a fire and boiled some snow, we took soup, and warm wine and water: after which, leaving the mules in the Refuge, we proceeded, at three o'clock, on foot, accompanied by our Guides; who told us the Walk to the Crater would occupy about an hour.[2] Between the Refuge and the Base of the Cone we crossed a considerable tract of frozen Snow and Lava; finding the walk over the former not unpleasant; but, owing to the want of daylight, it was very troublesome to cross the Lava. On approaching the summit of the Cone we found ourselves in a cloud of sulphur; and were ordered, by the guides to move quickly to the westward; by doing which we soon got out of this smoke, so dense, that it nearly blinded us for the moment. The edge of the Cone of Ætna is much wider than that of Vesuvius, less sandy, and the path round it perfectly safe to walk upon. The ascent likewise, though longer, is preferable to that of Vesuvius; being firmer, and abounding with large stones, which afford good footing. We sat down on the Lava, which was heated by its numerous vapour apertures; but, nevertheless, could not keep ourselves tolerably warm. In a quarter of an hour, however, a gleam of light over Calabria, announced a brilliant sunrise: and, though the sun was partially concealed by clouds, their tints increased the beauty of the scene. Other clouds, floating

---

[1] The snow which during winter had accumulated in the Casa degli Inglesi, owing to the roof being out of repair, was only just cleared away when the party in question went to the summit of Ætna; and the Refuge was consequently so wet, that to sleep in it would have been dangerous.

[2] It is however advisable to allow an hour and a half; in order not to be disappointed of seeing the sunrise.

on the sea, looked like wool, and almost hid the tops of Lipari and Vulcano: but these clouds soon dispersed; and we then saw Stromboli, and the neighbouring Islands, distinctly. Our view over the circuit of Sicily was magnificent. Every mountain we looked upon seemed shrunk to a hillock; but Melazzo, Castro-Giovanni, the Biviere di Lentini, Augusta, and ancient Syracusæ, were very conspicuous objects. When the wind cleared away the vapours, we occasionally saw down the Crater of Ætna; which, in some places, is not precipitous: to walk round it occupies about an hour: but it has none of the grandeur displayed by the Crater of Vesuvius, which is nearly twice its size, with respect to circumference. A most curious and singular sight was *the shadow of the Cone of Ætna, in the shape of a Pyramid*, formed, apparently at a distance, over the south side of Sicily. As the sun rose, this Pyramid decreased in height. The thermometer, on the summit of Ætna, fell to thirty. We quitted this stupendous scene with the greatest regret: and passing, once more, through sulphur vapours, commenced our descent, at a steady walking pace. The loftiness of the Cone was now apparent; and we felt surprised to see how high we had ascended. After taking refreshments at *the Casa degli Inglesi*, we remounted our mules. Hence the descent was rapid; snow nearly covered the Piano del Lago; and, passing Montaguista, we went close to piles of Lava, and had the steepest part of Ætna to descend: but about eight in the morning we reached the Bosco; took off our extra-clothing at *the Casa della Neve*, and arrived, by ten o'clock, at Nicolosi; where, not being expected till a much later hour, we were detained some time in changing the mules. During the descent it was interesting to observe the numerous Craters; but, proceeding rapidly without diverging from our course to examine any of them, we reached Catania a quarter before one: and Abbate declared ours was the quickest return he knew of. The thermometer in the shade at Catania, about an hour after our arrival, was 77."

A party of English Gentlemen, who ascended to the Crater of Ætna the end of November, 1824, under the direction of Abbate, give the following account of their journey.

"Being advised, by Abbate, to sleep at the first Refuge, the Casa della Neve, we did not set out from Catania till eleven in the morning. The conical hills in the first Region of Ætna appear to be formed by ashes, stones, etc., which the earth emits at the point where it opened to discharge lava: and, after a certain length of time, curious crystals are found in these hills. Dining at *Nicolosi*, we recommenced our journey soon enough to arrive just before night at *the Casa delli Neve;* which stands at the top of the Bosco. This *Refuge* is a hut with half its tiles off; and the table, chairs, and door, it once possessed, have all been burnt by half frozen Travellers. Here were ourselves, and six mules, the Muleteers, the Guides, etc., a fire made with green wood, and a thick smoke, which threatened to stifle us all, for it would not draw through the holes among the tiles; and the Hut has no chimney. We had provided mattresses: and after supper lay down to sleep, if we could, wrapped in our leathern Sicilian cloaks; which proved most useful. The Guides, Muleteers, etc. sat round the fire: and soon after two o'clock in the morning we all started for the Casa degli Inglesi; which our Guides told us was a three hours' ride. On quitting the Bosco, we found the cold excessive; insomuch that it was scarce possible to speak, till we reached the shelter of *the Casa degli Inglesi*. Here, one of the servants became sick and giddy;[1] and one of the Gentlemen found his feet so completely benumbed that it was some time before he recovered the use of them. However, this Refuge was in better repair than the other; and a good fire cheered us all.[2] The situation of the Casa degli Inglesi is so elevated that even during Summer, when Travellers usually sleep here, they are obliged to have fires. On quitting this Refuge, we found the weather good; and experienced no inconvenience in our ascent to the Crater, except a difficulty of breathing; and this partly resulted from the hoods of the Sicilian cloaks, which the extreme cold compelled us to put on. The sun had risen a quarter of an hour before we reached the summit of Ætna, and was a little (though a very little) clouded; but overhead, and all around us, we had a beautiful clear sky, except toward the north, where clouds lay close upon the land. It was a few minutes past eight when we arrived at the Crater; whence huge volumes of sulphureous smoke were issuing: and the wind, being high, involved us in a small portion of this smoke, toward the latter part of our ascent. The Crater is angular, and of a prodigious depth; it was partially obscured by vapours; which, on rising into the air, were tinted with a variety of brilliant colours by the sun: but the cold was so intense that we could scarce continue for a quarter of an hour in this exalted situation (where Fahrenheit's thermometer fell to 18); although our feet, from having sunk some way into the sooty ground, were warm: and on removing part of the soot to look for sulphur spars, we found the heat as strong as the hand could bear. These specimens of sulphur are the most beautiful, and the most deceptive things imaginable: for their delicate and lovely bloom rubs off with the slightest friction. On our descent we visited *the Torre delle Filosofo*, thence proceeding eastward, till the Guides bandaged our eyes, and led us to a point, *the Brink of the Val del Bue*, where, on sight being restored, we beheld a lofty precipice, and a tremendous Crater. Hence we descended to *the Casa della Neve*: and, the day being much advanced, were under the necessity of sleeping at *Nicolosi*, in an Hotel more distinguished for the civility and attention of its Landlord, than for his means of rendering the house comfortable."

On leaving Catania, Travellers usually proceed to *Giarra*, a distance of twenty-four miles. Be-

---

[1] The common effect of intense cold upon Foreigners, on the heights of Ætna, after drinking spirits.

[2] Travellers should be careful not to approach very near these fires: for a Peasant, who attended this party of Gentlemen, suffered agonies, and became indeed extremely ill, by putting his bare feet close to a large fire.

tween Catania and L'Ognina, which stands on part of the site of what is called (perhaps erroneously) the Port of Ulysses, the road traverses the Lava of 1669; and soon after passes Castello di Aci, a strongly situated Fortress built upon ancient Lava which ran into the sea, and surrounded on three sides by that element. The next objects of interest, during this ride, are *the Scopuli Cyclopum*, at Trizza. The largest of these Islands is volcanic and basaltic; and the substruction is a species of yellowish chalk, which contains small crystals. On the summit is a Spring of fresh water. The next Island contains very fine basaltic Columns. In all there are seven Islands adjoining each other; though only three bear the name of *Scopuli*. Some writers conjecture that these are the Rocks described by Homer, as being near the Cave of the Cannibal, Polyphemus, who feasted on the ill-fated followers of Ulysses: but as these Rocks are decidedly Volcanic, and apparently the offspring of Ætna, they could not have existed till long after Homer's death. Between Trizza and Aci Reale the road crosses huge blocks of ancient Lava mixed with thick turf; which renders the footing for mules in several places very unpleasant. Near Aci Reale, on the sea shore, is another object of interest, *the Scali di Aci, or Steps of Acis*: according to fabulous history the spot where that Shepherd was murdered by his Rival. These Steps consist of ancient strata of Lava, one above another, with a layer of vegetable earth between each. There are, at least, nine strata; all formed by different eruptions: and a considerable time must have elapsed between each Eruption, to have allowed the formation of soil. The mule-track in the environs of Aci, though it traverses beds of Lava, is not bad: and the country, the whole way hence to Giarra, is beautiful. This Town contains a tolerable Hotel, furnished with clean beds; and the neatness of the houses, and the number of vessels building in the Port, announce the prosperity of the inhabitants. After sleeping here, Travellers usually *make an Excursion*, which occupies about five hours, to visit *some gigantic Chesnut-trees*, one of which is called *Castagno di cento Cavalli*. It now looks like six trees close together: and the fact seems to be, that it is a fine old Stock, whence the common kind of chesnut underwood was cut; and that six sprays were allowed to form the six trees in question; which are computed to be a hundred and ninety feet in circumference at three feet from the earth. Near this Tree are others, of an extraordinary size: but the soil being the richest in Sicily, all its productions luxuriate. The distance from Giarra to the Chesnut-trees is about six miles: and although the path is steep, and the footing for mules slippery and disagreeable, the peculiar beauty of the country renders the ride delightful. Travellers tempted by the hospitality of the British Vice-Consul, or any other cause, to rest half a day at Giarra, usually take, next morning, *a circuitous route, by going to Francavilla*; another delightful ride; and thence to *Giardini*; which is only eleven miles from Giarra; though, taking the circuitous route, this ride occupies eleven hours: but Travellers are amply repaid by the beauty of the scene. The mule-track from Giarra to Francavilla passes through Calatabiano, a picturesque village, overhung by a Castle: thence it follows the course of the river Alcantara, up a lovely valley, adorned with a view of Motta, crowning a lofty rock; and likewise with a view of Castiglione, finely placed on a conical mount. After crossing a wild brook, with a cascade, this sweetly variegated path reaches Francavilla; where Travellers should ascend the hill, to see a magnificent prospect; in which the Capuchin Convent forms the grand object. Travellers may vary this scene, by going to Francavilla on one side of the Alcantara, and returning on the other. Thrown over the river is an ancient Bridge, now a pile of ruins, whence the retrospective view may, with truth, be called enchanting. The distance from Giarra to Francavilla is eighteen miles; and thence to Giardini, ten. After sleeping at the latter place, which contains a tolerable Hotel, Travellers usually proceed through Taormina to *Messina*, a distance of thirty-four miles.

Taormina, about two miles from Giardini, and approached by a steep ascent, is beautifully and strongly situated on the declivity of wild and lofty rocks, in a salubrious air, and crowned with an ancient Castle. This, now inconsiderable, Town was once the magnificent City of *Taurominium*, supposed to have been so called from the small river *Tauromini̇us*, which flows near it. The Zancleans, and Hybleans, in the age of the elder Dionysius, built this City, amidst hills, at that period celebrated for the grapes they produced, and the prospects they exhibited:[1] and, at the present moment, the red wine of Taormina is excellent. Here are interesting monuments of antiquity. *The Naumachia*, four hundred and twenty-five palmi long, and one hundred and ninety-six broad, is a parallelogram, containing, on one side, thirty-seven Niches, alternately large and small. Channels of masonry to conduct water into the Edifice are likewise discoverable; and the whole structure appears to be Roman, some of the Bricks having Roman characters stamped upon them. Above the Naumachia are remains of *five Piscinæ*; similar in form, but not in size: they were lined with the *Opus Signinum*; and the smallest of the five is in the best preservation. A row of eight Pillars divides it into two Aisles, one hundred and twenty-eight palmi long, forty-eight wide, and thirty high; and the apertures for the entrance of the water are visible. *The Church of S. Pancrazio* is evidently the Cella of an ancient Grecian Temple, of which the Walls are still preserved: they consist of large blocks of white marble, joined together without cement; and are supposed to have been taken from the famous marble Quarry in this neighbourhood. Contiguous to the Church are ruins of *an Aqueduct*, and likewise *remains of a Wall* cased with white marble, and probably the ruins of a Temple erected to Apollo, by the inhabitants of Naxos, when they found an Asylum in Taurominium. The size of this Structure seems to have been immense. In

---

[1] See DIODORUS SICULUS, 16.

the Valley, which leads to Messina, are two *ancient quadrilateral Tombs*. But the most precious monument of antiquity now left in Taurominium is *its Theatre*. A peculiar hollow, in the upper part of a rock, was chosen for the site of this Edifice; which stands above the modern Town, in a lovely situation, commanding a view of the Straits of Messina, Giarra, Aci, Ætna, and the whole country near Taormina, which is highly cultivated, and richly clothed with olive and mulberry-trees. The shape of the Theatre is semi-circular, the order of architecture Corinthian. The Scena (of masonry, and nearly perfect) had three entrances from the Postscenium; the centre door being large, the others small. Between the large door, and each of the small ones, were three niches; and beyond each of the small doors was a Niche. The Proscenium is only five palmi in breadth; but might, nevertheless, have been large enough to contain the Chorus: the Orchestra, likewise, is narrow in proportion to the rest of the Edifice. Under the Proscenium and Scena is a subterranean Passage, or Gallery, in part open to the Theatre. The use of this Gallery is not known; but some antiquaries suppose it was for the Prompter; and that he read the parts, while the Actors merely supplied gesticulation. The Scenic Masks, however, comprising a kind of speaking trumpet, and universally worn by all the ancient Actors, Mutes excepted, prove this last conjecture groundless; although the Prompter's station, notwithstanding, might have been here. Under the Theatre are *an Aqueduct*, and *a Reservoir for water:*[1] and on each flank of the Scena are *square Structures*, probably Dressing-rooms for the Actors, and Withdrawing-rooms for the audience in case of bad weather. None of the Seats remain. The Walls appear to have been covered with white marble, fragments of which are visible: and in consequence of an excavation made during the years 1748 and 1749, a considerable number of Columns of Granite, Cipollino, Porta-Santa, and Saravenza Marble, were found here:[2] a variety of other architectural ornaments have been discovered, sufficient to evince the magnificence of this Theatre; and such is its perfection, with regard to the conveyance of sound, that words uttered in the lowest tone of voice, on or near the Scena, are heard distinctly, even in the Corridor which terminates the Edifice. Hence to the sea-coast the descent is very rapid: and after passing a hedge of oleanders in front of some cottages, and a Fortification called Fort Alessio, and constructed by the English, Travellers usually rest themselves and their mules for two or three hours at a place fourteen miles from Giardini, and then proceed, through a beautiful country, to Messina; where *The Britannia* is a very clean and comfortable Hotel.

Messina, called by the Siculi *Zancle* (a Sickle), from its Beach,

---

[1] The aqueduct was probably constructed to convey away the water which fell in the Theatre; a needful precaution, there being no roof.

[2] The marbles indigenous to Taurominium were celebrated for their beauty; but, nevertheless, foreign marbles seem to have been preferred as decorations for the public edifices of this Town.

formed like a crescent, was founded, according to tradition, sixteen hundred years before the Christian era: and some of the classic writers report that Anaxilaus, Sovereign of Rhegium, made war against the Zancleans, with the assistance of the Messenians of Peloponnesus; and, after proving decisively victorious, called the conquered city *Messana*, in compliment to his allies. This event is supposed to have taken place about four hundred years previous to the Christian era. In aftertimes the Mamertini (mercenary soldiers) took possession of Messana, subsequent to which, it fell into the hands of the Romans; and was, for a considerable period, their chief hold in Sicily. The modern Messenians aided Count Roger in delivering their country from the Saracenic yoke; and were recompensed with great privileges, some of which they still retain. But the misfortunes of Messina, in modern times, have been great. The Plague, in 1743, swept away full fifty thousand of its citizens: and the earthquake of 1783 nearly destroyed its magnificent Quay, and most of its superb edifices. The splendid crescent of houses, fronting the Marina, was reduced to piles of ruins; and the narrow streets were universally blocked up by fallen buildings; though some of the public structures, owing to their solidity, remained standing; and among these was the Cathedral: but the almost total destruction of private dwellings compelled the inhabitants to encamp in huts of wood. The dreadful effects of this earthquake were not occasioned by one shock only, but by several, which succeeded each other from the fifth to the seventh of February. The first was the most violent: providentially, however, an interval of a few minutes, between the first and second, enabled the inhabitants to escape from their tottering houses, and take refuge in the country. At the entrance of the Straits of Messina, on the Calabrian side, a violent shock of this earthquake being felt about noon, the people of the neighbourhood fled to the sea shore; where they remained in safety till eight o'clock at night; when, owing to another shock, the sea swelled immensely, and suddenly precipitated its waves upon the beach, ingulphing upward of a thousand persons: and the same tremendous swell sunk the vessels in the port of Messina, and destroyed the Mole. The dogs in Calabria appeared to anticipate this awful convulsion of nature, by howling piteously: the sea-fowl fled to the mountains: and a noise, like that of carriage-wheels running round with great velocity over a stone pavement, preceded the first shock of the earthquake; while, at the same moment, a dense cloud of vapour rose from Calabria, gradually extending to the Faro, and the Town of Messina. The loss of property here, public and private, was incalculable: splendid churches, works of Art, libraries, and records, being all involved in the common ruin: but such was the probity of the Messenian Merchants, that no one of them declared himself a bankrupt, in consequence of this severe visitation.

Messina is most beautifully situated in a climate at all seasons salubrious; and cooler than any other part of Sicily during summer. The houses are large and commodious; the environs abound with lovely and shady promenades; the necessaries of life are, generally speaking, cheap and abundant; the fish is particularly good; and the people are lively, intelligent, penetrating, and courteous; especially to the British Nation. Travellers, on arriving at Messina, usually visit *the Faro;* to which there is a Carriage-road made by the British Troops, when stationed here: and this drive occupies something more than an hour. *On walking to the Lighthouse*, it is not difficult to discern *the Current* now reported to run in and out of the Straits, alternately every six hours: and *this Current* at less than a mile from the shore, occasions *Breakers*, called *Charybdis;* but no longer dangerous.[1] *Scylla*, on the opposite coast, and about three miles distant, has the appearance of a gigantic Rock, separated, by some accidental circumstance, from the main land.[2] *The Promenade on the Marina* displays exquisite scenery, and a magnificent Port crowded with shipping: but, from want of means, the line of new houses in this vicinity have only their lower stories finished. *The Billiard-room*, and *Reading-room*, merit notice; as the situation in which they are placed is beautiful; and the scale on which they are built superb. *The Cathedral*, a spacious Edifice, contains a Marble Pulpit, by Gagini; and a High-altar richly embellished with Florentine Mosaics, and six Columns of Lapis Lazuli, supporting a representation of the Madonna, under a gold canopy. The Plate in the Sacristy is the *Capo d'Opera* of Guevara. *The Church belonging to the Convent of S. Gregorio* contains a fine Copy of the celebrated Picture of that Saint, at Bologna. *The Noviziato de' Gesuiti* is deliciously situated; and possesses a few good Pictures of the Roman School. The Town, backed by highly cultivated and thickly wooded mountains, looks to peculiar advantage from the Ramparts near the Citadel; which, on this side, is strongly fortified. Silks; knitted silk stockings; light cloth; and carpets similar to those of Turkey, are fabricated at Messina. *The Walk to the Telegraph* and *that to Tinamara*, are famed for commanding fine views.[3] The Roads, or, more accurately speaking, the mule-tracks round Messina, generally lie in the beds of torrents; after hard rain extremely dangerous; though several houses are scattered on their banks: the bridle-road to Melazzo is, however, good; and the Town worth visiting, as the descent thither displays bold scenery; and the Place is supposed to have been the ancient *Myle*, where Ulysses's Companions slew the Oxen of the Sun:[4] and between Melazzo and Lipari was the battle fought by Octavius Cæsar and Marcus Agrippa, against Sextus Pompey, which put an end to the power of that piratical Commander; who fled, by night, to Melazzo, and thence

---

1 It is, nevertheless, affirmed, that a Transport, not many years since, was whirled round, three times, by the eddy at Charybdis; and that the Currents in the Straits are still remarkably strong and irregular.

2 This Rock is not completely, though nearly, separated from the Calabrian shore.

3 It is said that *a ruinous Tower*, below the Castellacio, which commands Messina, was erected by Richard I., of England.

4 Homer tells us the Herds consecrated to Apollo were kept "on Sol's bright Isle," Trinacria. See *Odyssey*, Book XII.

These Herds were labouring oxen, employed in Tillage: and it was esteemed, by the Ancients, a particular profanation to destroy a labouring ox, and criminal to eat of it.

took refuge with Mark Antony. Melazzo is enriched by a Thunny Fishery, from the middle of April to the end of June; and from the beginning of August till September.

An excursion, by water, is frequently made from Messina, to visit Scylla, and land at Rheggio, about four leagues distant, and whither it is sometimes necessary to be towed up by oxen, on account of the strength of the Current. Rheggio, anciently *Rhegium*, displays melancholy traces of the earthquake of 1783. One handsome street, in which stands the Cathedral, is, however, capable of being restored without great expense. *The Cathedral* deserves notice: *the University* contains curious imitations of Plants: *the Manufactory of Bergamotte Oil* is worth seeing; and in this Town Travellers are shown a house, called the birth-place of Ariosto; although Reggio in Italy *(Rhegium Lepidi)* is generally supposed to be the spot where that great Poet was born. The Country about Rheggio merits observation.

Travellers, in order to complete their Tour round the seacoast of Sicily, usually prefer embarking in a *Speronaro*[1] at Messina, visiting the Lipari Islands, and going thence to Cefalù; instead of going by land to the latter Place: for although the muletrack, as already mentioned, is good as far as Melazzo, it is bad and mountainous thence to Cefalù. This little voyage, generally speaking, occupies about three days: and the following account is an extract from the journal of an English Gentleman and his Wife, who went from Messina to Cefalù, by sea, during Midsummer, 1826.[2]

"We set out at seven in the morning, in our Speronaro, with ten boatmen and two boys. The rowers stand upon the deck. There was a fixed awning, under which we sat and slept; having hired mattresses at Messina. After passing the Faro, we found the wind unfavourable; and, taking in our sails, rowed to *Acqua-Nero*, landing there at one o'clock. At a quarter past five the wind dropped, the sea was calm, and we resumed our voyage. A fair breeze during the night brought us near *Stromboli*, where, with occasional rowing, we arrived at nine in the morning. By the aid of a letter of recommendation to a Priest, called Don Giuseppe, we procured a room to dine in; and feasted on exquisite figs. At halfpast two we set out for *the summit of the Mountain;* finding the ascent rapid, and the heat excessive. The depth of the sand, and the steepness of the path, render this ascent more toilsome than those of Ætna and Vesuvius; it occupied near three hours. From the summit we saw *the Crater* about half way down; and the sight was grand and imposing. The Eruptions were only occasional; and resounded like cannon, shaking the ground. At eight in the evening we re-embarked, and rowed under the Island, till we came in sight of its beautiful little *Volcano*. Two small Mouths threw up fire incessantly; that on the south being the most active; and, at intervals,

---

[1] A *Speronaro* is a very safe kind of boat, with from six to ten oars, according to its size, and a helmsman.

[2] The hire of a *Speronaro*, large enough to convey from four to six passengers, is about fifteen ounces, forty-five Neapolitan ducats.

its force increased; while a northern Mouth, between every sixth and tenth minute, threw up large quantities of stones; but they were ejected with less violence than those thrown from the opposite side. The finest Eruption we saw startled us; for it began with a sound like the discharge of artillery; which was followed by a shower of stones so vivid that the whole side of the Mountain glowed with these bounding red-hot balls. Some of the largest broke to pieces as they rebounded against others; but, before they reached the sea, their heat was nearly gone. These Eruptions, reflected in the water, were magnificent. Leaving this extraordinary scene, we steered with a fair wind for Lipari; and about half-past seven in the morning were close to its remarkable Hill of white Pumice; which is exported in large quantities, and a source of wealth to the Island. We cast anchor close to the Lazzaretto at ten o'clock; and remained on board till one, waiting for our passports; because the Authorities were not quickly found, it being a Festa. At one, however, the British Consul, hearing of our arrival, invited us to his house, and received us most hospitably. Lipari contains *Hot Baths*, about four miles from the Port, in a rocky, narrow valley. We slept on this Island; and embarking next morning at a quarter before four, reached *the Bay of Vulcano*, at a quarter before five. The Bay exhibits wild rocks: the Island rose out of the sea two hundred and two years previous to the Christian era; and was consecrated, by the Greeks, to Vulcan.[1] We landed at five; and in a quarter of an hour reached *the base of the Crater; to the summit of which* the ascent is gradual, the path good, and the time occupied in ascending about forty minutes. We went down by an easy descent into the Crater; which is deep, grand, and exceedingly splendid with respect to the colours of its crystal sulphurs; large numbers of which are continually collected. On retracing our steps, we reached the summit at ten minutes past seven; and embarked in our Speronaro at eight. Having cleared Vulcano, we steered for Cefalù: but the appearance of a strange sail made us cautious, as we had been told of pirates: and soon after passing Capo d'Orlando, we coasted along to *Cefalù;* arriving there about midnight. Next morning we got pratique, settled with our Captain, gave his Men a *buonamano*, and did not regret having made this little voyage, by which we were much interested, though considerably fatigued. The situation of Cefalù is beautiful: and, while our mules were preparing, we visited *its Cathedral*, which contains ancient Mosaics at the end of the Edifice, and ancient Columns, and Capitals, in the Nave and Choir. The two Pillars between the Nave and Transept display Figures of Men supporting the Abacus. Cefalù is the ancient *Cefaloedis*. After a short detention at the Custom-house here, we mounted our mules about a quarter before nine, in order to proceed to *Termini;* a distance of twenty-four miles, through a lovely road, especially the first part, which lay between

---

[1] All the Lipari Islands were denominated *Vulcani Insula*.

coppices of aloes and myrtles, the latter in full blossom. At two o'clock we reached Termini; and found its Hotel tolerable. This Town was anciently called *Thermæ Himerensis*, on account of its hot Baths: it still contains Warm Salt Baths; and remains of an ancient Edifice, supposed to have been a Theatre, may be traced in the Senate House, and Prison. After sleeping at Termini, whence there is a good Carriage-road, in distance twenty-four miles, to Palermo, we set out for that City at half-past eight, and reached Page's Hotel at a quarter past twelve, driving the whole way between gardens with fences of magnificent aloes bursting into flower."

The Sicilians, taken collectively, are good humoured (though prone to momentary wrath, and addicted to jealousy), acute, animated, eloquent, and endued with considerable talents; especially for poetry; but owing to that fickleness of disposition common to the descendants of the ancient Greeks, seldom pre-eminent in arts and sciences, from want of perseverance. They are proud of what their country once was; and by no means deficient in that chivalrous spirit which might, if encouraged, render them again a powerful People. For hospitality to Strangers they were always famed; and, respecting this virtue, the present race have not degenerated from their ancestors; as the poorest Sicilian peasant will offer the best of every thing his cottage affords, to the traveller who pauses at his door. The populace are civilized, sober, and honest; easily governed by gentle means, though indignant when treated with harshness. All ranks seem partial to the British Nation. On the northern and eastern coast of Sicily, the natives, of both sexes, are handsome; their countenances being perfectly Grecian: and the female peasants on Mont Eryx, at Syracuse, about Catania, on Ætna, at Giarra, and on the road to the Castagno di cento Cavalli, are likewise very handsome: their costume throughout the Island is Grecian: but, in all the Towns, females wear black silk cloaks, which cover the head and face, according to the Spanish mode. A black leather cloak and hood, covering the whole person, is universally worn, in winter, by the male sex, when out of doors. The manners, customs, and domestic economy, of the Sicilian peasants, are said to be, at this day, what Theocritus represents them. The oxen throughout the Island are handsome animals of a dun colour, and remarkable for particularly fine horns, both with respect to length and thickness: and the nightingales seem to be as plentiful as the flowers, making the air resound with their harmony. The vegetable productions of Sicily are more various, and more abundant, than of almost any other country: and besides those mentioned in the foregoing pages, and several which, owing to the narrow limits of this Work, must be passed over in silence, is a Tree resembling the ash, which yields Medicinal Manna. An incision is made in the bark of this tree, near the root, at the commencement of August; and from this incision issues the juice which, when dried by the sun, becomes manna. The bread throughout the Island, except at Giardini and Taormina, is excellent, and especially so at

Girgenti: the Hybla honey has long been celebrated. Near Mazzara, and in some other places, the females spin cotton; and large quantities of hemp are grown in several districts. There is likewise a variety of fine fish on every part of the Sicilian coast; and the Thunny, and Pesce Spada, are particularly esteemed.

The climate of Sicily is excellent during Winter, and the six first weeks of Spring: but in Summer, Autumn, and even till the middle of November, *Mal' aria* prevails in several spots of the Island; especially at Selinuntium, at, and near, Lentini; and likewise at, and near, Syracuse. Even during winter, Sicilian scenery, so far as relates to colours, is gay and brilliant; the sky, in general, being cloudless, and the sunrise and sunset magnificent beyond description: during summer the brilliancy and beauty of the scenery is, of course, augmented; and the months of June and July are those most proper for an ascent to the Crater of Ætna. Sicily, however, is not, at any season, like several parts of Magna Græcia, uniformly beautiful: for although some tracts are luxuriant to excess, and cultivated to perfection, others are dreary, wild, and neglected: but if the plan of making a good post-road, to form an inland communication between Palermo and Messina, should be carried into effect, it may probably prove the means of inducing Sicilian noblemen to work the waste lands, and thereby complete the beauty, and increase the wealth, of their country.

Sicily does not, at present, contain above one million and a half of inhabitants.

No regular post-roads having yet been established, Travellers (Pedestrians excepted) are under the necessity of going from place to place throughout the Island, either in a Lettiga, or on mules. A Lettiga, the national carriage, holds two persons; and is, in shape, something like the body of a Vis-à-vis. This Vehicle, provided with strong poles, resembling those of a Sedan-chair, is carried by very powerful porter-mules, as the body of a travelling carriage was, in past times, conveyed over the Mont-Cenis. Two mules go before, and one behind, accompanied by a muleteer on foot, armed with a stick, ten or twelve feet long, to guide the mules; and another muleteer mounted, and riding at the head of the Cavalcade. A Lettiga is not usually furnished with cushions to sit upon; but has a dirty lining, and a gaudy outside: it goes up and down every hill, however steep, and makes the neighbourhood resound with mule-bells; which are hung, in a triangular shape, on the back of the leading mule. The motion of a Lettiga is fatiguing, and apt to produce drowsiness: and, moreover, the country cannot be seen to advantage in these Vehicles: neither can Travellers, thus conveyed, stop when they wish it; as the mule-bells prevent the muleteers from hearing, when called to; and besides this, a chair is indispensable for getting out of, or into, a Lettiga. The noise of the mule-bells may likewise prove an inconvenience, from impeding conversation. Travellers, who ride, usually furnish themselves with one mule for each gentleman, or Lady; ditto, for each Servant; ditto, for the Guide, who also acts as Cook and Purveyor; and ditto, for luggage.

The difference between Sicilian and Neapolitan money is as follows:—

10 grana of Naples make	1 Tari of Sicily.
5 ditto . . .	1 Carlino.
1 ditto . . .	1 Baioccho.
½ ditto . . .	1 Grano.

The price of a Lettiga carried by three mules is about thirty carlini per day, while Travelling; and about fifteen carlini for every day of rest. Mules for persons who ride may be engaged at Palermo, and throughout the Island, for ten tari each mule, on travelling days, and five on resting days; unless it be during harvest, when the price on resting days is six tari. The muleteers expect a trifling *buonamano* at the end of the journey.

At Catania the hire of mules is somewhat cheaper than at Palermo. An English Gentleman, not long ago, paid per day for the same mule, from Catania to Palermo, eight carlini on travelling days, and four on resting days; and other Travellers have lately engaged mules from Catania to Palermo at the rate of nine carlini for every travelling day, and five on resting days. For every mule from Nicolosi to Ætna, the price is fifteen tari; and for every Guide from Nicolosi to the summit of Ætna, including his mule, and charcoal for the Casa degli Inglesi, the price is two piastres and a half. At Catania, Messina, Syracuse, and Page's Hotel in Palermo, beds are six tari each person; and dinners eight: but it is necessary for Travellers, especially at Syracuse, to make their bargain beforehand. In smaller towns beds for masters are four tari each, beds for servants two tari each; and the Guide belonging to the Travellers, provides the table. This Guide, who, as already mentioned, acts as Cook, and Purveyor, and who is an indispensable appendage to every party of Travellers in Sicily, expects, for wages, one piastre a day, and a mule provided at the expense of his employers.[1] On this mule, however, he does not object to take a block-tin tea-kettle and the stew-pans, etc., requisite for cooking. Besides these articles Travellers should furnish themselves with Leather Sheets, Linen Sheets, Table-Linen, Towels, Knives, Forks, Spoons, a Lantern, and Tinder-box, common strong Cups and Saucers, the former without handles; a block-tin Tea-pot; a Coffee-pot; Rummers of double flint glass, or Bohemian crystal; Sugar, Tea, Coffee, Maccaroni, Parmesan Cheese, Hams, Poultry, and potted Butter; as butter cannot be procured in Sicily, except at Palermo and Messina. Large double Silk Parasols, and Straw Hats and Bonnets, double-lined with thick post-paper, are needful securities, at all seasons, against a *coup de soleil:* and some Travellers, who do not regard the expense of an extra-mule, take Mattresses; though they are seldom required, except on ascending Ætna; the mattresses at Hotels being, in general, good.

At Palermo the best Guides for Travellers who purpose making the Tour of the Island, are *Camello Catalani* and *Francesco Marsalona.*

---

[1] Two Masters and one Servant travelling on mules, with one luggage-mule, a Purveyor, and his mule, usually spend, in Sicily, about two pounds sterling a day in road expenses, the wages of the Purveyor inclusive.

Letters of recommendation to all the Civil Authorities from the *Luogotenente* at Palermo, are desirable; and letters of recommendation, from the British Consul General to all the Vice-Consuls, are, for British Travellers in Sicily, most useful.[1] Passports, on leaving Naples to visit this Island, on leaving Palermo to make a Tour round the sea-coast to Catania and Messina, and on leaving Messina to visit Rheggio, or the Lipari Isles, are, at present, indispensable.

ROUTE ROUND THE SEA-COAST OF SICILY, ON MULES; BETWEEN THE LATTER PART OF MAY AND THE EARLY PART OF JULY, 1826.[2]

1st day. From PALERMO to *Sala di Partinico*,+ miles 19. Hours employed in riding, 5¼.
From *Partinico* to *Alcamo*,* miles 12. Hours employed in riding, 3½.
Objects best worth notice; Morreale—its Cathedral—Picture, by Morrealese, in the Benedictine Convent— View of the Valley.

2d day. *Temple of Segesta*,+ miles 9. Hours employed in riding, 3.—*Trepani*,* miles 21. Hours employed in riding, 6¾. Objects best worth notice; Temple of Segesta—Theatre.

3d day. *A Vineyard.*+ Hours employed in riding, 4.—*Marsala*,* miles 18, from Trepani. Hours employed in riding, 2½.
Object best worth notice; Monte S. Giuliano, the ancient Eryx.

4th day. *Mazzara*,* miles 12.— Hours employed in riding, 2¾. *Stone Quarry*+ near Campo-Bello, miles 8.—Hours employed in riding, 2.—*Castel-Vetrano*,* miles 8.—Hours employed in riding, 2.
Object best worth notice; the Stone Quarry.

5th day. *Selinuntium*,+ miles 9. Hours employed in riding, 2½. —*Sciacca*,* miles 21.—Hours employed in riding, 4½.
Objects best worth notice; two Sets of Temples; three in each, at Selinuntium. Hot Springs at Sciacca.

6th day. *San Patro*, on the banks of the Platanus,+ miles 19.— Hours employed in riding, about 4¾.—*Siculiani*,* miles 11.—Hours employed in riding, about 2¾.

7th day. GIRGENTI,+ miles 12. Hours employed in riding, 3½. Objects best worth notice; the Mole—the Temples, and other Antiquities—the Cathedral, its Baptismal Font, and Echo.

8th day. Occupied in seeing the remains of Agrigentum.

9th day. *Palma*,+ miles 16.— Hours employed in riding, 5¼. *Licata** (commonly called Alicata), miles 12.—Hours employed in riding, 3½.

10th day. Half a day of rest. *Terranova*,* miles 18. Hours employed in riding, 5.

11th day. *A Barn*,+ miles 17.— Hours employed in riding, 4¼. *Cultagirone*,* miles 7. Hours employed in riding, 2¾.
Object best worth notice; a celebrated Manufacture of small Clay Figures, at Cultagirone.

---

[1] Travellers experience great civility from Messrs. Donandy and Campo, who frequently furnish them with introductory letters.

[2] Dining places, in the following Route, are marked with a cross; sleeping places with an asterisk. Persons who make the Tour of Sicily during fine weather find it pleasanter, and more economical, to dine out of doors, in a shady situation, near a spring, or stream of good water, than in a country Hotel.

12th day. *A Brook,*+ beyond Palagonia, miles 17.—Hours employed in riding, rather more than 5½.
*Lentini,** miles 13. Hours employed in riding, 3¾.
Object best worth notice, the Biviere di Lentini: an extensive, but very unwholesome Lake, well stored with fish.

13th day. *Walnut-trees,*+ miles 17. Hours employed in riding, 5¼.—SIRAGUSA,* miles 13.—Hours employed in riding, 3¾.
Objects best worth notice at Syracusa;— Amphitheatre—Theatre—Ear of Dionysius—Tomb called that of Archimedes—Strada Sepulcrale—Catacombs—Remains of Fort Labdalus—Subterranean Passage for Cavalry, etc.—Garden of the P. P. Cappucini — River Anapus—Temple of Jupiter Olympicus — Papyri — Fonte-Ciane—Duomo—Statue of Venus, in the Museum.

14th, 15th, and 16th day, at Syracuse.

17th day. *Scaro d'Agnuni,*+ miles 24.—Hours employed in riding, 6½. CATANIA,* miles 18. Hours employed in riding, 4¼.
Objects best worth notice; on leaving Syracuse, Scala Græca—Trophy erected in honour of Marcellus. At Catania; Theatre—Amphitheatre—Baths—and other Subterranean Antiquities—Duomo—Church of the Benedictines, their Garden and Museum—Prince Biscari's Museum.

18th, 19th, and 20th day, at Catania.

21st and 22d day. Expedition to Ætna, now called Mongibello.

23d day, at Catania.

24th day. *Trizza,*+ miles 7.—Hours employed in riding, about 2. *Giarra,** miles 17.—Hours employed in riding, 3½.
Object best worth notice; *Scopuli Cyclopum*, at Trizza. As the ride from Catania to Giarra occupies only half a day, Travellers frequently employ the other half in visiting the Castagno di cento Cavalli, situated about six miles from Giarra.

25th day. *Francavilla,*+ miles 18.—Hours employed in riding, about 5. *Giardini,** miles 10. Hours employed in riding, about 3.

26th day. *Dining Place*, miles 14.—Hours employed in riding, and visiting the Ruins of Taurominium, 2 miles beyond Giardini, 5¼. MESSINA,* miles 20. Hours employed in riding, about 5.
Objects best worth notice; Church of S. Pancrazio—ancient Piscinæ—Naumachia—Theatre, and View from it, at Taormina. At Catania; Convent of S. Gregorio—Cathedral—Citadel—Faro—surrounding Country.

27th, and three following days, Messina.

28th day, by Sea—From MESSINA to *Acqua Nero*, hours 6.

29th day, at nine in the morning *Stromboli*. To examine the Crater here occupies the better part of a day.

30th day, at ten in the morning. *Lipari*. To examine this Island occupies the better part of a day, and Travellers usually sleep here.

31st day, at five in the morning. *Vulcano*. The walk to and from the Crater here, occupies hours 2¾. And if the wind be tolerably fair, *Cefalù* is reached before midnight.

32d day, on mules, from *Cefalù*

to *Termini*,+ miles 24. Hours employed in riding, 5¾. PALERMO, miles 24—in a four-wheel carriage, hours 3¾.

ROUTE FROM CATANIA TO THE SUMMIT OF ÆTNA.[1]

Nicolosi, miles 12.—Hours employed in riding, 2¾.
Casa della Neve (winter sleeping place), miles 7.—Hours employed in riding, 1¾.
Casa degli Inglesi (summer sleeping place), miles 8.—Hours employed in riding, 2¾.
Walk to the summit of the Cone—hours 1½.
Descent to the Torre del Filosofo, Val del Bue, Nicolosi, and CATANIA, from 10 to 12 hours.

The intense cold on the summit of Ætna is so apt to affect the health, that Travellers are often compelled to stop an hour, or more, either at the Casa degli Inglesi, or the Casa della Neve, to recover themselves. A party, who ascended on the 29th of May, found Fahrenheit's thermometer, at half-past seven in the evening, 50½—at eleven, 45—at half-past twelve, 41½—at two in the morning, 30—at thirty-five minutes past two, near the Casa degli Inglesi, 27½—at a quarter before four, at the Casa degli Inglesi, 20, and on the summit of the Mountain, at five o'clock, 19½.

To shorten the time spent in the cold Regions of Ætna, and likewise to avoid the trouble and expense of carrying mattresses and coverlids thither, Travellers, capable of bearing long-continued exercise, should set out from Catania about noon—proceed to Nicolosi—repose there—then sup—leave Nicolosi seven hours before sunrise—proceed to the Casa della Neve—remain there one quarter of an hour only, to put on warm clothing—thence ride to the Casa degli Inglesi—remain there half an hour only, to procure hot soup and warm wine and water—and thence walk to the summit of the Mountain. The ascent, thus managed, occupies six hours and three quarters.

The Author feels that it would be assuming a merit to which she has little claim, did she not most thankfully acknowledge how much the foregoing account of Sicily has been improved by the minute, accurate, and valuable observations, in manuscript, of E. I. RUDGE, Esq.; and the Notes of other intelligent British Travellers, who have recently visited the Island.

[1] Travellers who engage the same mules to take them from Palermo to Messina, usually employ these animals to convey them as far as Nicolosi, on their ascent to the Crater of Ætna.

ROUTE FROM GENOA THROUGH LUCCA TO PISA, BY THE NEW ROAD.

3 *Recco*—A gradual ascent. A third horse from Recco to the next post, both going and returning. An extra half-post is paid on quitting Genoa.

1½ *Rapallo*—A third horse to the next post, both going and returning.

1¾ *Chiavari*—A third horse to the next post, going but not returning. Two good Hotels at Chiavari.

2¾ *Bracco*—A third horse to the summit of the Mountain. Price one livre and five sous, buona-mano inclusive.

1½ *Mattarana*—A small Inn; not a good one.

1½ *Borghetto*—A third and fourth horse from Borghetto to Mattarana, but not *vice versá*. Inns at Borghetto, *L'Hôtel de Londres*, and *L'Hôtel d'Europe*; latter very bad; former very tolerable. A third and fourth horse from Borghetto to La Spezia, and *vice versá*.

3 *La Spezia*—Inns, *L'Hôtel d'Europe*, *L'Hôtel de Londres*, and *L'Hôtel de l'Univers*: the first very comfortable; the second by no means a bad Inn; the third uncommonly dirty and ill provided. Road from Recco to La Spezia very mountainous.

2¾ Sarzana—Inn, *La Lunigiana*, and good. This is the last Town in the Genoese Territories.

1½ *Lavenza*—Road to Massa not good.

1 *Massa*—Inn, *Hôtel des quatre Nations*, and good.

1 *Pietra Santa*—Inn, *La Posta*, and good.

1 *Montramido*.

1½ *Lucca*—Inns, *The Albergo Reale della Croce di Malta*, and *The Pellicano*.

2 *Pescia*.

1½ *Pistoja*—Inn, *Il Sole*, and tolerable.

1½ *Prato*.

4½ *Florence*.

29¾ posts.

This Road, the seven miles between Lavenza and Massa excepted, is smooth, hard, and excellently made. The ascents and descents, though numerous, are not rapid; but they require additional parapet walls, to ensure the comfort and safety of Travellers. For further particulars see, at the end of this Chapter, " Route en Voiturier from Naples through Genoa, and by the Mount-Cenis, to Calais, in the Spring of 1827."

ROUTE FROM GENOA TO TURIN, BY THE VAL DI SCRIVIA.

2½ *Pontedecimo*—A third and fourth horse from Pontedecimo to Ronco, and *vice versá*.

2½ *Ronco*.

2 *Arquata*—A third horse from Arquata to Ronco; but not *vice versá*.

ROUTE FROM CALAIS TO BOLOGNA.

1½ Novi—Inn, *Hôtel d'Europe*.
3½ Alessandria—Inns, *Grande Albergo d'Italia—Locanda Reale*. An extra quarter of a post is paid on quitting Alessandria.
2½ Felizzano.
1½ Annone.
1½ Asti—Inn, *The Leone d'oro*.
1½ Gambetta.
1½ Dusino.
1½ Poirino—Inn, *L'Angelo*.
1½ Truffarello.
1½ Torino—An extra half-post is paid on entering and on quitting Turin. This Road, by the Val di Scrivia to Novi and thence to Turin, is excellent; and equally —— good at all seasons.

24¾ posts.

ROUTE, EN VOITURIER, FROM CALAIS, BY PONTARLIER, TO NEUCHATEL; AND THENCE THROUGH LAUSANNE AND BEX, BY THE SIMPLON, TO BOLOGNA.

From Calais to Auxonne, this Route is the same as that from Rome to Calais. Vide page 409.

1st day's journey from	Auxonne, *Mont-sous Vaudrey*. . hours	5½
"	Salins, Inn *Le Sauvage*.	4
2d "	Levier, Inn *Le Sauvage*.	4½
"	Pontarlier, Inn *Le Lion d'or*.	3¾
3d "	Couvez, Inn *Le Lion d'or*.	3½
"	Neuchatel, Inns, *Le Faucon—Les Balances*.	4½
4th "	Concise, Inn *L'Ecu de France*.	4½
"	Orbe, Inn *La Maison de Ville*.	3¾
5th "	Lausanne, Inns, *Le Faucon—La Couronne*.	5
6th "	Vevay, Inns, *Les trois Couronnes—La Croix de Malthe*.	3
"	Bex, Inn *L'Hôtel de l'Union*.	4
7th "	Martigny, Inn *Le Cigne*.	2
"	Sion, Inn *Le Lion d'or*.	4
8th "	Tourtemagne, Inn *Le Lion d'or*. . . .	5
"	Brigg, *Hôtel d'Angleterre*.	4
9th "	Village of Simplon, Inn *La Poste*. . .	6½
10th "	D'Omo d'Ossola, Inn *La Posta*.	4½
"	Fariola, Inn *Il Leone d'oro*.	4
11th "	Sesto-Calende, Inn *La Posta*.	5½
"	Cascina, Inn *La Posta*.	3½
12th "	Milan, Inn *Hôtel Suisse*.	4½
"	Lodi, Inn *La Posta*.	4½
13th "	Piacenza, Inn *Albergo delle tre Ganasce*.	5
"	Fiorenzola, Inn *La Croce Bianca*. . .	4
14th "	Parma, Inn *Il Paone*.	5

14th	"	Reggio, Inn *Albergo Reale*.	4
15th	"	Modena, Inn *Hôtel de S. Marco*.	4½
	"	*Samoggia*, Inn *La Corona*.	3
16th	"	Bologna.	4

The road from Auxonne to Salins is good, till it approaches the latter Town, situated in a dell of the department of the Jura, and consisting of old houses and dirty streets execrably paved, but surrounded with picturesque scenery. Beyond Salins the road ascends a steep and lofty mountain; passes through a fine wood of firs; and then descends to Levier and Pontarlier. The verdure in this country is beautiful; and the turf, which resembles velvet, is enamelled, during spring and autumn, with multitudes of Alpine flowers. Pontarlier stands in a pretty situation; and its streets are broad and clean: almost immediately beyond it, in the Village of Verrieres, is the French Frontier Custom-house; and near this spot the road divides into two branches; one going to Neuchatel, the other to Lausanne. The Neuchatel road passes through a narrow gorge of the Jura to a plain, whence it is carried midway up a mountain, and formed into a magnificent gallery, the soil above which is prevented from falling, by means of very strong hurdles placed one row above the other: and beyond this gallery the extensive Lake of Neuchatel, and the Glaciers of Berne (called The Young Fry), suddenly present themselves to view. The road then descends to the margin of the Lake, where the scenery is bold, rich, and beautiful. Neuchatel, a large Town, contains two Inns, *Le Faucon* and *Les Balances*. There are several handsome villas in the neighbourhood: and the new and excellent road from Pontarlier hither, is a superb work. From Neuchatel to Lausanne the road passes through a lovely country to Concise: where the Inn is clean and comfortable; and thence it proceeds to Orbe; which, though a small village, has a tolerable Inn.

This Passage of the Jura, by Salins, through Pontarlier, to Lausanne, is far preferable to that by way of Poligny; there being only one steep hill in the Pontarlier-road, and nothing to alarm the most fearful Traveller. The road from Lausanne by Vevay and Bex, to the Swiss Frontier, is likewise good and flat, one steep hill between Lausanne and Vevay excepted.

The Custom-house at Verrieres is no great annoyance to persons who travel in their own carriage; and small fees at the Swiss and Italian Custom-houses prevent baggage from being searched.

ROUTE, EN VOITURIER, FROM NAPLES TO ROME, SIENA, FLORENCE, LUCCA, GENOA, TURIN, AND BY THE MONT-CENIS TO PONT-DE-BEAUVOISIN, PARIS, AND CALAIS, DURING THE SPRING OF 1827, WITH AN ENGLISH LANDAULET DRAWN BY FOUR HORSES.[1]

If Travellers, instead of going by way of Florence, turn off at Poggibonzi, passing through Cammiano, La Scala and Piza, to Lucca, they save about twenty miles; and make this by far the shortest road from Naples to Calais, that by the Simplon excepted.

Days.		Roman miles.	
1st.	Capua.	16	Road tolerably smooth. Inn, *the Post-house*, and cleaner than it used to be.+
	S. Agata.	16	Road excellent. Inn, *the Post-house*.
2nd.	Mola.	17	Road excellent. Inn, *the Cicerone*.
	Terracina.	24	Road excellent. Inn improved.
3rd.	Pontine Marshes.	26	Road excellent. Inn opposite the *Braschi Villa*.+
	Velletri.	14	Road excellent. Inn, *Albergo Nuovo, Piazza del Duomo*.
4th.	Albano.	11	Road from Genzano to Albano in bad condition. Inn, *L'Europa*.
	Rome.	16	Road excellent.
5th.	Monterosi.	24	Road excellent. Inn *close to the Lake*.
	Ronciglione.	10	Road excellent. Inn, *Il Leone d'Oro*.
6th.	Montefiascone.	27	Road excellent. Inn *outside of the Town*.
	Acquapendente.	21	Road excellent. Inn, *the Post-house*.
7th.	La Scala.	12	Road excellent, the bed of the torrent excepted. Inn, *a single house*.
	Buonconvento.	16	Road excellent. Inn, *Le Cheval Anglais*.
8th.	Siena.	16	Road excellent. Inn, *L'Aigle noir*.
	Poggibonzi.	16	Road excellent. Inn, *Albergo della Corona*.
9th.	Florence.	24	Road excellent.
10th.	Pistoja.	20	Road good. Inn, *Il Sole*.
	Lucca.	25	Road good. Inn, *La Croce di Malta*.
11th.	Massa.	25	Road good. Inn, *Hôtel des quatre Nations*.
12th.	Sarzana.	14	First seven miles a narrow, rough, and, in wet weather, a swampy road; which may be avoided by going round Carrara. Inn, *Albergo della Lunigiana*.

[1] The bad Inns are marked with a Cross.

Days.		Roman miles.	
	Spezia.	13½	At a short distance beyond Sarzana, Travellers ford the Magra during summer, and pass it in a ferry during winter. Road good, but it crosses the beds of two small torrents. Inn at Spezia, *L'Hôtel d'Europe.*
13th.	*Borghetto.*	14	A high hill beyond Spezia; after passing which the road descends to the side of the Magra: a gallery is constructing to avoid that river; but the present road is rough for a mile and a half near Borghetto. Inn there, *L'Hôtel de Londres.* The Passage of a part of the Apennine, called the Bracco, commences at Borghetto, and terminates at Sestri.
14th.	*Sestri.*	20	Inns, *Hôtel de la belle Europe* and *Il Ponte*—former best. From Borghetto to Mattarana is an ascent of eight miles; the inclination of the road being about the same as that of the Simplon; but the width is not so great, a circumstance much to be regretted; as this road lies at the brink of precipices, and is not sufficiently guarded by parapet walls. Mattarana contains a small Inn, where Travellers, in case of necessity, might sleep. Hence the ascent continues for four miles; the road being cut in the side of a very lofty mountain, composed of white, yellow, and green marble, and crowned with beautiful grey granite. This part of the passage, being unsheltered, would, in stormy weather, be dangerous. The descent to Sestri is in length about eight miles; and with regard to smoothness and hardness, the whole road from Borghetto to Sestri is perfection.
15th.	*Routa.*	15	Inn, *Gran-Bretagna*, a small breakfasting-place. From Sestri the road lies on the sea-shore as far as Chiavari, where it begins to ascend another branch of the Apennine, and is again cut through marble rocks at the brink of a precipice which overhangs the sea. About midway be-

Days.		Roman miles.	
			tween Sestri and Routa it passes through two Grottoes delved in a rock of hard yellow marble, and lined with masonry; which destroys the beauty of the work. Near these Grottoes there is a sad want of parapet walls. On coming to Routa, the road passes through another Grotto, the length of which is very considerable; but a lining of masonry hides the superb marble in which it is formed.
	Genoa.	15	The goodness of the road between Sestri and Chiavari, and thence to Genoa cannot be exceeded even in Italy; where fine roads are now almost universal.
16th.	*Ronca.*	18	Inn, *L'Europa.* Road excellent, it passes for five miles through a flat country, and then ascends a lofty mountain of the Apennine, not exposed to every blast of wind, like the old road over the Bocchetta; but securely sheltered throughout the whole Passage, which terminates at Ronca.
	Novi.	20	Inn, *L'Hôtel d'Europe.* The road, which is flat and good, passes through a lovely little valley almost circular, and embellished by a waterfall.
17th.	*Alessandria.*	12	Inns, *Grande Albergo d'Italia, Locanda Reale.* Between Novi and Alessandria the Bridge over the Bormeda is broken; and a Bridge of Boats substituted in its stead; but this Bridge, after floods, is not always passable. Road good.
	Assi.	18	Inn, *Il Leone d'oro.* Road good.
18th.	*Poerino.*	15	Inn, *L'Angelo.* From Asti hither there is a gentle descent almost the whole way. Road good.
	Turin.	12	Road excellent.
19th.	*S. Ambrogio.*	12½	Inn, *La Vigna.* Road excellent.
	Susa.	10	Inn, *La Posta.* Road in want of trifling repairs.
20th.	*Lanneslebourg.*	20	Inn, *Hôtel Royal.* Road excellent to the first Post-house. Hours, in ascending, two and a half. Near the Valley embellished with a pretty

Days.		Roman miles.	
			miniature Lake, an Avalanche seems to have fallen recently; the trees and fences being broken by immense masses of snow; but the road remains uninjured. Hours, in ascending from the first Post-house to La Grande Croix, about two and a half. Road excellent, and thus far free from snow. From La Grande Croix to Lanneslebourg, some snow in the road, and an immense quantity on each side. Time employed in going, two hours and fifty minutes. Beyond the Post-house for a considerable distance, the road on the 16th of May was a sheet of ice bordered with walls of snow twenty feet high; and the Lake of Mont-Cenis was completely frozen.
	Modane	14	Inn, *Le Lion d'or.* The road from Lanneslebourg to Modane suffered by the last inclement winter: one of the Galleries gave way; and considerable quantities of earth fell from the heights above it. These mischiefs, however, are repaired.
21st.	*S Jean de Maurienne.*	20	Inn, *La Poste.* Road excellent.
	Aiguebelle.	16	Inn, *L'Hôtel de l'Union.* Road excellent.
22d.	*Montmellian.*	14	Inn, *La Poste.*+ Road excellent.
	Chambery.	10	Inn, *Hôtel du Petit Paris.* Road excellent.
23d.	*Pont de Beauvoisin.*	24	Inns, *La Poste — L'Hôtel de Savoie.* Road excellent.
	La Tour du Pin.	16	Inn, *Hôtel Cholat.*+ Road requires some trifling repairs.
24th.	*La Verpillière.*	18	Inn, *Le Chapeau rouge.* Road tolerable.
	Lyon[1]	18	Inn, *Hôtel du Parc.* Road tolerable.
25th.	*S. Georges.*	24	Inn, *Hotel du Chéne verd.* Road tolerable.
	Macon.	20	Inn, *Hôtel d'Europe.* Road in bad condition.
26th.	*Tournus.*	18	Inn, *Le Sauvage.* Road bad.
	Chalons-sur-Saône	16	Inn, *Les trois Faisans.* Road better than near Macon.
27th.	*Rochepot.*	18	Inn, *Le Chevreuil.* Road paved for two miles beyond Chalons, and afterwards tolerable.

[1] A Steam-packet runs daily between Lyon and Chalons.

CH. XV.]   ROUTE FROM NAPLES TO CALAIS.   533

Days.		Roman miles.	
	Ernay.	20	Inn, *La Croix blanche.* Road from Rochepot to Ernay extremely bad.
28th.	Saulieu.	18	Inn, *Le Dauphin.* Road bad.
	Rouvray.	14	Inn, *La Poste.* Road very bad, especially in the town of Saulieu.
29th.	Vermanton.	27	Inn, *Hôtel de Notre Dame.* Road very bad.
	Auxerre.	16	Inn, *Hôtel de Beaune.* Road tolerable.
30th.	Joigny.	19	Inn, *Hôtel des cinq Mineurs.* Road tolerable; some part of it paved.
	Sens.	18	Inn, *L'Ecu.* Road heavy, and ill kept.
31st.	Montereau.	23	Inn, *Le grand Monarque.* Some part of the road is paved, the rest extremely heavy and ill kept.
	Melun.	23	Inn, *L'Hôtel de France.* Near Melun the road is paved and in bad condition.
32d.	Montgeron.	18	Inn, *La Ville de Lyon.* Road indifferent.
	Paris.	15	Road tolerably good.
33d.	Beaumont.	20	Inn, *Le Paon.* Road paved, and well kept.
	Noailles.	16	Inn, *Hôtel de Calais.* Road tolerably good.
34th.	Marseille-sur-l' Oise.	24	Inn, *L'Epée Royale.* Road tolerably good.
	Poix.	16	Inn, *Le Berceau d'or.* Road good.
35th.	Abbeville.	26	Inn, *La Tête de Bœuf.* Road good.
	Bernay.	13	Inn, *La Poste.* Road good.
36th.	Samer.	27	Inn, *La Tête de Bœuf.* Road good, except the pavement and hill in the Town of Montreuil.
	Boulogne.	11	Inn, *Ancien Hôtel d'Angleterre.* Road good.
37th.	Calais.	22	Inn, *Roberts's Hôtel.* Road good.

Numb. of Roman miles 1235
Numb. of English miles from Calais to London by the Steam-packet. 126

It is difficult to ascertain, with any degree of precision, the distance from Naples to Calais; because French posts are not all of the same length; and the length of Italian posts varies materially: added to which, there are no mile-stones placed regularly in any part of the Route: and consequently the foregoing calculations with respect to the number of Roman miles from one stage to another may sometimes be erroneous: but the state of the roads in May 1827 (after a long series of heavy rain), is given with accuracy; and the best Inns are recapitulated, for the convenience of Persons who travel *en voiturier*

PASSAGE OF SPLUGEN. NEW ROAD.

(See page 360.)

Persons travelling from Suabia, or the Canton of the Grisons, to Venice, or Milan, find this the shortest route; though nobody should attempt to cross the Mountain of Splugen at the season of Avalanches.[1] But after the winter snow has fallen, and become sufficiently hard for a sledge to glide smoothly over its surface, or during the months of July, August, and September, when the winter snow is, generally speaking, melted, Travellers may, without danger, indulge themselves by exploring this Passage of the Alps; which very much surpasses in magnificent, sublime, and awful scenery, every other Carriage-road of Europe. It must, however, be acknowledged that the Galleries of this fine road, from the base to the summit of Splugen, on the side of the Grisons, are too narrow, and the turnings too sharp for English travelling carriages with four horses: and one of the Grottoes, on the Italian side, wants height; but this inconvenience will, it is supposed, be remedied in the course of a twelvemonth.

The Routes which lead through the Grisons to Splugen unite at *Bourg de Ragaz*, two leagues from which Town are the celebrated Baths of Pfeffers. From Ragaz to *Coire* (the Capital of the Canton of the Grisons) is five leagues. The road crosses the Rhine by the wooden Bridge of Tardis, and traverses by another Bridge the formidable torrent of Lanquart, which has often menaced the surrounding country with destruction. Here commences the superb road which joins, at three quarters of a league from Bellinzone, that of the Canton of the Tessin; and forms a communication between Italy, eastern and northern Switzerland, and Germany. From Coire[2] to the village of *Splugen* (eleven leagues), the road resembles a majestic avenue to an immense park. Two leagues from Coire the two arms of the Rhine, namely, the Vorder-Rhein, and the Hinter-Rhein, unite in face of the picturesque Castle of Richnau; and the Road passes over these brawling and impetuous streams by two splendid single-arched wooden Bridges; one of which was the work of a common village carpenter. From Richnau to the small Town of *Thousis* (three leagues and a quarter), the road lies at the base of the luxuriant Mont-Heinzenberg, in the Valley of Dornleschg, rendered sterile by the inundations of the Hinter-Rhein and the Torrent of Nolla. Here, in a peculiarly picturesque situation, are Ruins of the Castle of Réalta (called likewise Hohen Rhétièn), supposed to have been built by Tuscan Emigrants during some part of the middle ages. From Thousis to *Andeer* (near three leagues), the road passes through

---

[1] When there is such an accumulation of snow that the pointed rocks on the summits of the Alps are covered, Avalanches may be expected hourly.

[2] A Tariff containing the number of Posts, and the expense of Post-horses, Guides, and dismounting and remounting Carriages, on this new Road, has been published by the Government of the Grisons, and may be found at Coire.

the Valley of Schams; crossing by a fine Bridge, near Thousis, the destructive torrent of Nolla, and approaching, by a Grotto pierced through a solid rock, the wild, magnificent, and stupendous Ravine, called the Rheinwald, or Valley of the Forest of the Rhine,[1] through which that River and the Road wind amidst perpendicular Rocks not less than three thousand feet high, and clothed to their summits with stately firs, the branches of which seem to canopy the narrow Glen beneath them. The Rhine boils and foams along with appalling rapidity close to the Road; which has no defence against its impetuous neighbour but a slight parapet wall. From Andeer to *Splugen* is near three leagues; and on approaching that Village the Ravine widens, and displays magnificent cascades. This Defile between Coire and Splugen bears undeservedly the name of "Via-Mala." *Splugen*, situated in the Valley of the Rheinwald, contains a good Inn;[2] as do two other Villages in this Valley, those of Naffenen and Hinter-Rhein: the last stands at the base of the Bernardino; and about a league and a half from this Village the Valley is terminated by the immense Glacier of Vogelberg, the Source of the Rhine. From Splugen to *Chiavenna* the drive usually occupies about seven hours and three quarters; full five of which are spent in passing the Mountain.[3] The Austro-Lombardo Custom-house is two leagues beyond Splugen.

The distance from the Village of Hinter-Rhein to *the first Refuge* (Berghans) is near two leagues; and three hours are usually occupied in going. Berghans is a large edifice, situated in a wild country on the margin of a Lake, whose sable waters give birth to the impetuous torrent of the Moësa, which falls into the Ticino, about three quarters of a league from Bellinzone. The road to Chiavenna is formed into Terraces; and the descent so gradual as to preclude the necessity of using a drag-chain. From Berghans to the Hamlet of S. Bernardino is one league and a half; and midway the road passes the Moësa on a lofty Bridge. S. Bernardino is frequented during summer, on account of its Mineral Waters; and consequently, during summer, Travellers find the Inn at this Village provided with a well-stocked larder; and frequently take eatables thence to the next baiting place, *Misocco*, where the Inn is ill-provided and its master very imposing. From S. Bernardino to *Misocco* is three leagues. Here the road enters a cheerful Valley, which displays, as the Traveller advances, the rich culture of Italy; till at length the hills of Chiavenna, covered with fruit-trees, present themselves to view; and the mildness of the Italian climate compensates for the coldness of the Alps. From Misocco to *Bellinzone* is six

---

[1] The Forest of the Rhine contains Firs of so uncommon a magnitude, that one of them is said to measure twenty-five ells round the trunk; and the Fall of the Rhine in this Forest exhibits one of the sublimest objects in nature; which, while it fills spectators with awe, affords them the pleasure of contemplating scenes in the creation beyond the power of any pencil to imitate.

[2] Travellers going post over Splugen usually sleep here.

[3] The ascent, on the Rheinwald side of the mountain, commonly occupies about two hours.

leagues and a quarter: and three quarters of a league from Bellinzone, at the bridge of the Moësa, the new Route of the Bernardino joins the superb High-road of the Canton of the Tessin, which terminates at the base of S. Gothard.

Travellers, during summer, may reach the High-road to Milan, by going from Bellinzone to *Magadino* on the Lago Maggiore; whence (the season permitting), a Steam-boat starts every Thursday, Friday, Saturday, Sunday, and Monday morning, at six o'clock, for *Sesto-Calende*; where it arrives about noon. The price paid by a Chief-cabin Passenger, in this vessel, from Magadino to Sesto, is six Italian livres; the charge for the transport of a Berlin or English Post-chaise, is fifty livres; and the charge for the transport of a Calèche, forty livres.

Travellers may likewise reach the High-road to Milan by means of the Steam-boats (managed by Englishmen), which ply daily on the Lake of Como,[1] the season permitting: and persons who avail themselves of these vessels, embark at *La Riva*. Another way of reaching the High-road is to go by *Lugano, Ponte di Tresa*, and *Varese, to Sesto*.[2]

ROUTE FROM COMO, BY THE MONT-SPLUGEN TO ZURICH.

(Given on the authority of an English Traveller, who passed this new road in August, 1827.)

The Steam-packet, managed by Englishmen, conveys Passengers and Carriages about thirty-five miles, from *Como* to *Domaso;* and usually reaches the latter place at one o'clock, P. M. Small Boats take Passengers thence through the shoals to *La Riva;* and Boats of a larger size convey travelling Carriages. The distance from La Riva to Chiavenna is about twelve miles; and if the wind be adverse, the Boats employed to bring travelling Carriages from the Steam-packet to La Riva, seldom arrive till night; a serious inconvenience; as La Riva, during summer, is liable to *Mal'aria*, and therefore a dangerous sleeping-place. Small four-wheeled chaises may, however, be hired at the Post-house, for nine Austrian zwanzigers (*buonhomo* not inclusive), to convey Travellers to Chiavenna, about an hour's drive; and the Post-master undertakes to forward travelling carriages from La Riva to Chiavenna.

---

[1] The Lake of Como, anciently called *Lacus Larius*, is computed to be fifty miles in length; from three to six miles in breadth; and from forty to six hundred feet in depth. This Lake, combined with the Town of Como, anciently *Comum*, forms a beautiful landscape. Pliny the younger was born at Como; and in the front of the Cathedral is his Statue. The distance from Como, through Barlassina to Milan is three posts and a half.

[2] An economical and a safe mode of crossing the Mountain of Splugen, is to go under the guidance of the *Messager;* who travels every week from Lindau to Milan; and undertakes, for a certain price, to defray all the expenses of the Passage, board and lodging inclusive. But in whatever way Travellers cross this Mountain, they ought not to attempt the Passage during the months of May and June when the winter snow is melting. Several English Families have nearly lost their lives by crossing in June.

1½	from *Chiavenna* to *Isola*—A horse.
2	*Splugen* — A third horse. The drive from Chiavenna to Splugen occupies eight hours.
1¾	*Tusis*.
1½	Coire—The drive from Splugen to Coire occupies seven hours and a half.
1¼	*Bourg-de-Ragaz*—Two hours and a half.
1½	Wallenstatt—Four hours.
9¾	

At Wallenstatt the Post is discontinued: but good Boats and careful Boatmen may usually be found to convey Travellers down the picturesque *Lake of Wallenstatt*, (which is twelve miles in length), to *Wesen*, where Voiturins are always ready to furnish horses for *Rapperschwyl*, beautifully situated on the Lake of Zurich. This drive occupies about four hours and a half; and that from Rapperschwyl to Zurich about five hours.

The new road, during the month of August, 1827, was free from snow, safe, and in good order; and *La Couronne*, at Chiavenna—*La Poste*, at Splugen—*La Croix blanche*, at Coire—*Le Sauvage*, at Bourg-de-Ragaz—*La Poste*, at Wallenstatt—*L'Epée*, at Wesen, and *Le Paon*, at Rapperschwyl, were considered by the Traveller from whose journal this Route is an extract, as comfortable Inns.

INDEX.

	Page.
ABANO, Baths of	301
Abbey of S. Denis	2
Camaldoli, near Florence	85, 289
Del Bosco, near Novi	110
Abbeville	*Appendix*, 335
Adelsberg	ap. 433
Adrian's Villa	219
Agata, S.	229
Agnano, Lake of	255
Agnello, S.	289
Aicha	ap. 426
Aiguebelle	ap. 391
Aix-les-Bains	ap. ib.
Aix-la-Chapelle	ap. 431
Aix-en-Provence	ap. 345
Albano	224
Alessandria	109
Alicant	ap. 323
Alphabetical List of Towns, Rivers, etc., with their ancient Names	ap. 465-474
Alps, Jura chain, passage of	28
Alps, Maritime, ditto	106
Alps, Rhætian, ditto	ap. 407
Amalfi	290
Amiens	ap. 335
Amsterdam	ap. 448
Amphion, source of	37
Ancient marine festival at Sorrento	292
Ancona	ap. 398
Angers	ap. 356
Antibes	ap. 346
Antiquities between Baccano and Rome	121-123
Anvers	ap. 448
Aquapendente	121
Arboga	ap. 457
Arcy, Grottos of	27
Arezzo	297
Arona	45
Arqua	301
Aschersleben	ap. 423

	Page.
Assens	ap. 452
Assisi	296
Asti	109
Astroni	256
Avallyon	27
Avernus, Lake of	252
Aversa, Lunatic Asylum at	230
Austrian Dominions—Passports—Money—Post-horses—Best Money to take from Tuscany into Germany	ap. 411, 412
Avignon	ap. 345
Augsburgh	ap. 425
Augst	ap. 425
Auray	355
Aussig	342
Autun	ap. 342
Auxèrre	27
Auxonne	28
Baden	ap. 432
Baccano	123
Badajos	ap. 436
Bagni di Lucca	114
Bagni di Pisa	99
Baiæ, excursion to	250
Bank-notes, where to exchange them for Napoleons	ap. 326
Bargains with Innkeepers	ap. ib.
Bar-le-Duc	ap. 354
Barcelona	ap. 323, 440
Basle	ap. 425
Bataglia	301
Baths, German, namely, Carlsbad, Pyrmont, Spa	ap. 430
Baveno	44
Bayonne	ap. 349
Beauvais	2
Bellinzone	ap. 358
Belgirata	46
Benoît, S., Cascade of	ap. 392
Bergamo	ap. 399
Bergen	ap. 458
Berlin	ap. 419, 420

INDEX.

	Page.
Bernard, S., passage of	ap. 358
Besançon	ap. 353
Best road from Calais to Paris through Beauvais	ap. 335
Bocchetta, passage of	ap. 363, 400
Bois-le-Duc	ap. 448
Bologna, description of that city and its Environs — Masters for the Instruction of young Persons	54, 55
Bolsena, Lake of	122
Town of	121
Bonneville	32
Bordeaux	ap. 349
Borgo, S. Donino	51
Borromean Islands	45
Boulogne	ap. 334, 409
Breda	ap. 448
Brescia	ap. 399
Brest	ap. 349
Brieux, S.	ap. ib.
Brigg	40
Brîs, S.	27
Bronze Statues first brought to perfection in Etruria	61
Brunswick, price of Post-horses, etc.	ap. 419
Brunswick, description of that city	ap. 423
Brussels, description of	ap. 428
Budin	312
Buonconvento	121
Burgos	ap. 439
Cadiz	ap. 443
Caen	ap. 355
Cahors	ap. 354
Calais	1
Calais, distance from, to Paris	ap. 332
Cambray	ap. 335
Campo-Marone	111
Camuscia	ap. 397
Canal of Languedoc	ap. 333
Capri, description of	291
Capua, modern	229
Capua, ancient	256
Careggi de' Medici	83
Carignano	108
Carlscrona	ap. 454
Carrara	102
Cascade of Terni	295
Caserta, excursion to	256
Castel-à-mare	291
Cassel	ap. 429

	Page.
Cattolica	ap. 399
Cava, La	278
Cenis, Mont, passage of	ap. 363, 391
Chaldee Inscription at Palermo	283
Châlons-sur-Marne	ap. 351
Châlons-sur-Saône	ap. 343
Chambery	ap. 344
Chamois, its agility and sagacity	36
Chamouni, Valley of	33
Champagnole	29
Chapeau, excursion to	34
Charity, a peculiar trait of it	248
Chartres	ap. 354
Château of Fontainebleau	25
Chateauroux	ap. 348
Chaumont	ap. 352
Cenotaph of Cicero	228
Chède, Cascade, and Lake of	33
Cherbourg	ap. 355
Chiandola, La	106
Christiania	ap. 457
Christianstad	ap. 454
Christiansund	ap. 458
Civita Castellana	294
Cleves	ap. 446
Climates of the Continent	ap. 321
Cluse	32
Coffee, when first known as a beverage	268
Coimbra	ap. 436
Col de Ténèbres	ap. 360
Cologne	ap. 428
Como, Lake of	ap. 359
Coni	107
Conegliano	304
Constance, Lake and Town of	ap. 425
Copenhagen, and its environs, decription of	ap. 451, 452
Cora	227
Cordova	ap. 443
Corneto	122
Cortona	297
Cretins and Goîtres, by what means diminished in the Maurienne	ap. 391
Cumæ, excursion to	254
Custom-house between Gex and Morez	ap. 408
Custom-house near Piacenza	ap. ib.
Custom-houses at Pont-de-Beauvoisin	ap. 343
Custom-house at Ponteba	305
Cuxhaven	319

INDEX. 477

	Page.
Czaslau	311
Dantzig	ap. 424
Dejean and Emery, Voiturins	ap. 329
Denmark, Money — Price of Post-horses—Passports, etc.	ap. 449, 450
Dieppe	ap. 336
Dijon	28
Diligence from London to Paris	ap. 329
Doccia, Monastery of	84
Dole	28
Domo-d'Ossola	44
Dovaine, Frontier Custom-house	36
Douay	ap. 335
Dover, best Inn	ap. 329
Dover, Custom-house	ap. 409
Dresden, Population, Architecture, Religion, Character of Inhabitants, Inns, objects best worth notice	313
Royal Gallery of Pictures	314
Treasury	316
Cabinet of antique Sculpture and China	316, 317
Distance from Vienna to Dresden, and from Dresden to Hamburgh	317
Dresden, [Appendix.] Money of Saxony—Price of Post-horses —Weights and Measures— Prices at Hotels — Restaurateurs—Wages of a Valet-de-place — Carriages — Sedan-chairs, etc.——Articles best worth purchasing— Post-Office — Diligences — Expense of franking Letters for Great Britain	ap. 417, 418
Dunkelsbubl	ap. 425
Dunkerque	ap. 350
Eboli	284
Eohelles, passage of	ap. 343, 363
Ecksioe	ap. 454
Eger	ap. 431
Elvas	ap. 436
Emden	ap. 447
Emissario, near Albano	224
Enkoping	ap. 457
Environs of Florence	83
Erfurt	ap. 423
Esseck	ap. 432
Etrurians, the first comedians who exhibited in Italy	85

	Page.
Evian	36
Excursion from Geneva to Chamouni, etc.	32
Excursion from Plymouth to Orleans	ap. 331
Expense attendant upon continental travelling	ap. ib.
Faenza	ap. 398
Family expenses in various parts of the Continent, comparative view of	ap. 390
Famine in the Apennine	116
Fano	ap. 398
Ferrara	300
Fiesole	84
Fiorenzuola	51
Florence, origin of that city	57
Palazzo-Vecchio	ib.
Loggia	58
Piazza del Granduca	ib.
Royal Gallery of Sculpture and Paintings	58-65
Palazzo-Pitti	65-67
Giardino di Boboli	67
Museo d'Istoria Naturale	ib.
Duomo, Campanile, and Baptistery	68, 69
Church of S. Marco	69
S. S. Annunziata	70
S. Maria Maddalena dei Pazzi	71
Santa Croce	72
S. Lorenzo, new Sacristy, old Sacristy	74
Capella de' Medici	ib.
Libreria Mediceo-Laurenziana	75
Church of S. Maria Novella	ib.
Orsanmichele	76
San Spirito	ib.
Carmine	77
S. Trinità	78
S. Ambrogio	ib.
S. Gaetano	ib.
Reale Accademia	ib.
Oratorio dello Scalzo	ib.
Palazzi Gerini, Riccardi, Corsini, Mozzi, Buonaroti, Strozzi, Uguccioni	79
Casa dei Poveri	80
Spedali di Bonifazio, S. Maria nuova, degl' Innocenti — Columns, Bronze Wild Boar, and other Sculpture	ib.
Ponte Santa Trinita — Theatres — Mosaic Work — Ac-	

	Page.
cademia della Crusca — Hotels — Markets — Wine, Water — Climate — English Physician — Boarding-houses.	81
List of objects best worth notice, as they lie contiguous to each other	82
Festivals	ib.
Character of the Florentines.	85
Tuscan Peasantry	86, 87
Anecdote relative to a poor Foundling	88, 89
Florence, [Appendix.] Price of apartments at Hotels — Private Lodging-houses — where to apply for information respecting the latter — Boarding-house — prices of various articles — shops — Fire-wood — Fees to medical men — Masters — Artists — Bankers — Best *Padrone di Vetture* — Post-office — Country houses near Florence	373–376
Foligno	296
Fondi	228
Fontainebleau, Forest of	25
Forli	ap. 398
France, tax on English carriages	ap. 329
Money of France	ap. 330
Price of Post-horses	ap. 340
Public Diligences, etc.	ap. 333
Canal of Languedoc — Messagerie à Cheval — distance from Calais to Paris	ap. 334
Distance from Ostend to Paris — Dieppe to Paris — Havre to Paris	ap. ib.
Frangy	ap. 391
Frankfort on the Mein	ap. 423
Frankfort on the Oder	ap. 424
Frascati, excursion to	222
Fredericshall	ap. 457
Frejus	ap. 346
Freysing	ap. 426
Fulde	ap. 423
Gaëta	229
Garda, Lake of	ap. 399
Garigliano	229
Geneva, description of that town	30, 31
Geneva, Lake of	31

	Page.
Geneva, [Appendix.] Draught-horses — Money — Post-office — Expense of living at Geneva — Diligences — Price of Post-horses	357, 358
Genlis	28
Genoa, description of	103, 104
Hotels — Provisions — Climate — Character of the Genoese	105
Genzano, and the Festival of Flora	226
Genèvre, Mont, passage of	ap. 394
Gerona	ap. 440
Gex, passports	ap. 408
Giessen	ap. 429
Gingoux, S.	37
Gotha	ap. 423
Gothard, S., Passage of	ap. 358
Gottingen, description of	ap. 424
Gottingen, excursion thence to Hartz	ap. 429, 430
Gothenborg	ap. 457
Granada, description of that city and the Fortress of Alhambra	ap. 441
Gray	ap. 353
Gratz	ap. 433
Grenoble	ap. 353
Grodno	ap. 464
Groningen	ap. 448
Grotto-Ferrata	222
Hague, the	ap. 446
Halle	ap. 423
Hamburgh, description of	318
Hamburgh, [Appendix.] Money — Bankers' accounts, etc. — Pound weight — price of dinner at a table d'hôte — price of Claret — Cambric, the article best worth purchasing.	418
Hanau	ap. 423
Hanover, price of post-horses, etc.	ap. 420
Hanover, description of	ap. 424
Hannibal's Route into Italy	297
Helvoetsluys	ap. 447
Herculaneum	258-260
Hesse, price of post-horses, etc.	ap. 419
Hollabrun	310
Horace's Farm	221
Hours when Churches and Palaces in Italy are shown	47
Hyères	348

INDEX.

	Page.
Iglau	311
Imola	ap. 398
Inspruck	ap. 407
Ischia, description of that island	293
Itri	ap. 228
Jezelsdorf	310
Judenburgh	307
Juliers	ap. 431
Kaschau	ap. 433

Kingdom of the Netherlands, Holland — Money — Post-horses—Treckschuyts, etc.— Expense of travelling post— expense of travelling in a Treckschuyt—Dutch inns ap. 444, 445

Klagenfurt	306
Krieglach	307
Lago-Maggiore	45
Landshut	ap. 426
Lands-le-bourg	ap. 392
Lariccia, or Aricia	226
Lascia Passare	ap. 396, 397, 408
Laval	ap. 349

Lauffenburgh, fall of the Rhine ap. 425

Laundresses, their prices at Florence ... 375
at Rome ... 383
at Naples ... 388

Lavinium	226
Laybach	ap. 433

Leghorn, description of that Town and Port—Inns—Protestant Chapel ... 111, 112

Leghorn, [Appendix.] Prices of various articles—Things best worth purchasing — Provisions — Public conveyances from Leghorn to Pisa—Post-office ... 367-369

Leipsic, description of that city — prices at the Theatre — Fairs — Hotels—Wages of a Valet-de-place—Carriages ap. 422

Length of an Italian post	ap. 362
Lenzen	ap. 422
Leoben	ap. 307
Lerida	ap. 441
Leutschau	ap. 433
Leuwarden	ap. 448
Leyden	ap. 446
Liege	ap. 431
Lille	ap. 335
Limoni	107
Limoges	ap. 348
Linkoping	ap. 454
Lintz	ap. 427

Lisbon, description of the city, and its environs — water — eatables—lodgings—board— fire-wood — amusements— Hotels ... ap. 123, 124

Lodi	50
L'Orient	ap. 355
Louvain	ap. 428

Lucca, description of that city —Inn ... 112-114

Marlia — Road to the Bagni di Lucca ... 114

Peasantry—Mode of cultivatting this part of the Apennine —Villas between the Baths and the city ... 116, 117

Price of Post-horses in the Lombardo-Venetian Realm, Tuscany, the Principality of Lucca, the Ecclesiastical territories, and the Kingdom of Naples ... ap. 362, 366

Lützen ... ap. 422

Lyon, description of that city, ap. 343

Macon	ap. ib.

Madrid, description of that city and its environs ... ap. 439

Maestricht	ap. 447
Magdeburgh	318, and ap. 422
Maglan, Valley of	32
Malaga	ap. 442
Mans, Le	ap. 356
Mahrburgh	ap. 433
Mantua	ap. 407
Marburgh	ap. 429
Marengo, Plain of	110
Marino, San, Republic of	ap. 398
Martorell	ap. 440
Marseille	ap. 343
Martigny	38
Massa di Carrara	102
Massa di Sorrento	290
Maurice, S.	37

Means of preserving health during a long journey ... ap. 326

Meillerie, Rocks of	37
Meissen	347, and ap. 422
Melun	ap. 409
Mer de Glace	34, 35
Merida	ap. 436

INDEX.

	Page.
Merzhofen	307
Mestre	301
Midi, Dent du	38
Milan, description of that city and its Environs	47-50
Milan, [Appendix.] Lodging-houses—Hotels—Carriages—Valets-de-place—Boxes at La Scala—Post-Office	414
Mile, German, length of	ap. 412
Minturnum	229
Misenum	253
Mittau	ap. 464
Modena	53
Moelk	ap. 427
Mola di Gaëta	229
Molaret	ap. 394
Montanvert	35
Montauban	ap. 354
Mont Blanc	34
Monte di Fo	56
Montefiascone	122
Montmeillant	ap. 391
Monte Nuovo	252
Montereau	ap. 409
Montpellier	ap. 347
Monterosi, Lake of	123
Mont Rose	45
Montserrat	ap. 441
Monza	50
Morcles, Dent de	38
Moscow, description of	ap. 463
Moulins	ap. 344
Munich, description of	ap. 426, 427
Munster	ap. 429
Nancy	ap. 352
Nant d'Arpenas, Cascade of	32
Nantes	ap. 356
Naples, situation, Bay, etc.	230
Studii Publici	234-239
Naples — Museo Borbonico, when open to the public	239
Naples — Travellers advised to obtain an introduction to the Canonico Don Andrea di Jorio	ib.
Palazzo Reale	ib.
Chiesa di S. Ferdinando	ib.
Castel Nuovo	240
Castello dell' Uovo	ib.
Chiesa di S. Maria del Parto	ib.
di S. Brigida	ib.
di S. Giovanni di Fiorentini	ib.

	Page.
Chiesa di l'Incoronata	240
della Pietà de' Torchini	ib.
di S. Maria della Nuova	ib.
di Monte Oliveto	ib.
di Gesù Nuovo	ib.
di S. Chiara	ib.
di S. Giovanni Maggiore	241
del Salvatore	ib.
di S. Domenico Maggiore	ib.
dello Spirito Santo	ib.
di S. Maria della Sanità	ib.
di S. Giovanni a Carbonara	ib.
de' S.S. Apostoli	ib.
Arcivescovado	242
di S. Filippo Neri	243
di S. Paolo Maggiore	ib.
di S. Maria Maggiore	244
di S. Pietro à Majella	ib.
Cappella di S. Severo	ib.
Chiesa della Nunziata	ib.
di S. Maria del Carmine	245
di S. Martino de' Certosini	ib.
Castello di S. Elmo	246
Palazzo-Berio	ib.
Albergo de' Poveri	ib.
Theatres	ib.
Promenades	247
Forum Nundinarium	ib.
Monument to the memory of Eustace	ib.
Water	ib.
Climate of Naples	ib.
Society and Festivals	248
Hotels	ib.
Character of the Neapolitans	ib.
List of objects best worth notice, as they lie contiguous to each other	249
Naples, [Appendix.] Passports—Fees to Custom-house Officers—Money of Naples—Exchange	ap. 384
Bankers — Common measure — Weights — Hotels, and other Lodging-houses, prices at, and situation—Carriages--Servants' wages — Price of various articles — English warehouses — English medical men--Masters—Boxes at Theatres—Post-Office	ap. 385-389
Narbonne	ap. 354
Narni, Augustus's Bridge at	294

INDEX.

	Page.
Naumburgh	ap. 423
Nepi	ap. 397
Neptune, Grotto of, at Tivoli	220
Nero, Baths of	253
Nevers	ap. 344
Neukirken	307
New road from Genoa through Lucca to Pisa	102
New road from Genoa through the Val di Scrivia to Turin, avoiding the Bocchetta	109
Nice, description of that city and its climate	106
Nikœping	ap. 454
Nimeguen	ap. 447
Niort	ap. 355
Nisida	251
Nismes	ap. 347
Nocera	278
Nordheim	ap. 424
Nordlingen	ap. 425
Norkœping	ap. 454
Novara	ap. 401
Novgorod	ap. 462
Nuremberg	ap. 427
Odensee	ap. 451
Ofen, or Buda	ap. 432
Oneglia	106
Oporto	ap. 436
Orange	ap. 345
Orléans	ap. 348
Orvietto	122
Ossaia	296
Osoppo	304
Ostend	ap. 428
Otricoli	ap. 397
Packets from Cuxhaven to Harwich	319
Falmouth to the Mediterranean	ap. 322
London to Calais	ap. 327
Dover to Calais	ap. 328
Dover to Ostend	ap. ib.
Brighton to Dieppe	ap. ib.
Southampton to Havre	ap. ib.
Plymouth to Bordeaux	ap. 329
Plymouth to Guernsey	ap. 334
Colchester to Ostend	ap. 428
Ostend to Harwich	ap. ib.
Ostend to Margate	ap. ib.
Helvoetsluys to Harwich	ap. 447
Falmouth to Lisbon	ap. 434
Stralsund to Ystad	ap. 454
Paderborn	ap. 429

	Page.
Padua	300
Pæstum, excursion to	278-285
Paintings found in Herculaneum and Pompeii — Painting, Art of, its rise and progress	260
Palestrina, excursion to	223
Pollone, game of	83
Pamplona	ap. 438
Paris, improvements in that city	3
Musée Royal	4-16
Musée du Luxembourg	16
École Royale des Beaux Arts	ib.
Bibliothèque du Roi	ib.
Mazarine	ib.
de S. Génevière	17
de l'Arsenal	ib.
de la Ville	ib.
du Musée d'Histoire Naturelle	ib.
de la Faculté de Médecine	ib.
Musée d'Histoire Naturelle and Jardin du Roi	17-18
Theatres	18
Manufacture Royale des Glaces	ib.
Manufacture Royale des Tapisseries	ib.
Colonne de la Place Vendôme	ib.
Arc de Triomphe de l'Étoile	ib.
Porte S. Denis	ib.
Porte S. Martin	ib.
Tribunal du Corps Législatif	19
Basilique de Nôtre-Dame	ib.
Pantheon	ib.
Garde Meuble	ib.
Hôtel Royal des Invalides	ib.
Institution Royale des Sourds-Muets	20
Hospice de la Saltpêtrière	ib.
Hôpital des Enfans-Trouvés	ib.
Observatoire	ib.
Palais du Temple	ib.
Palais de la Bourse	21
Greniers de Réserve	ib.
Abattoirs	ib.
Halle au Blé	ib.
Halle aux Vins	ib.
Marché à la Volaille	ib.
Bridges	ib.
Fontaine du Boulevard de Bondi	22
des Innocens	ib.
de Grenelle	ib.
de la Bastille	ib.
Cimetières and Catacombes	22, 23

2 T

	Page.
S. Cloud	23
Sèvres	ib.
Versailles	ib.
Present State of Society at Paris	23, 24
Paris, [Appendix.] Hotels, etc. — Eatables and wine — Restaurateurs	336
Cafés — Wages of a Valet-de-place — Carriages — Public Boats — Provisions — Shops — Masters — English Library and Newspapers — Notary public — English Surgeon — Apothecaries, Chemists, etc. — Prices at the Theatres — Messageries Royales — Offices of the Coche d'eau — Voiturins — General Post-Office — Petite Poste	337-341
Parma	51, 52
Particulars relative to travelling in Italy	ap. 364-367
Passau	ap. 427
Passignano	296
Passports, how to proceed respecting them on leaving London for Paris	ap. 323
Passports, how to proceed respecting them previous to quitting Paris; and how, on quitting England, to prevent detention at Paris respecting them	24
Passports for returning from Rome to England	ap. 402
Pavia	50
Peasants' ball at Careggi de' Medici	87
Posilipo, Grotto of	254
Perigueux	ap. 348
Perpignan	ap. 354
Perugia	296
Pesaro	ap. 398
Pescia	117
Petersburgh and its environs	ap. 460-462
Peterswald	343
Peypus, Lake of	ap. 460
Piacenza	50
Pietole, birth-place of Virgil	ap. 407
Piperno	227
Pisa, description of that city and its environs	90-100
Character of the Pisans — Hotels — Fountain-water — Theatre — and Battle of the Bridge	100
Illumination in honour of S. Ranieri	101
Carnival	ib.
Climate	ib.
Pisa, [Appendix.] Fees to Custom-house Officers, etc. — Lodging-houses — Prices of various articles — Masters — Fees to medical men, etc. — Post-Office — Diligence from Pisa to Florence	369-372
Pisevache, Cascade of the	38
Pistoja, description of that city	117
Poggibonsi	ap. 396
Poggi-à-Cajano, near Florence	117
Poggi Imperiale, near Florence	84
Poitiers	ap. 355
Poligny, passports	ap. 408
Pompeii, excursion to, and description of, that city	264, 277
Ponte Centino	121
Ponte de Beauvoisin	ap. 343
Ponteba, Custom-house there	305
Ponte Molle	123
Ponte Mammolo	249
Ponte Sanguinetto	296
Pontine Marshes	227
Pordenon	304
Portici	260
Porto Venere	103
Portugal, money of	ap. 423
Price of draught-horses, etc.	ap. 434
Prato Fiorito, near Lucca	115
Pratolino, near Florence	84
Prague, description of that city — Inns	341, 342
Prague, [Appendix.] Articles best worth purchasing — Wages of a Valet-de-place — Carriages	416
Presburgh	ap. 432
Prices at Inns in France	ap. 330
Prices at Inns in Italy	ap. 365
Prices usually demanded by Voiturins	ap. ib.
Procida	293
Prussian dominions — Price of post-horses, etc.	ap. 419
Passports	ap. ib.

INDEX.

	Page.
Prussian dominions.—Quedlinburgh	ap. 423
Raab	ap. 432
Radicofani	121
Ratafia, a deadly poison, as now made in France and Italy.	ap. 339
Ratisbon	ap. 426
Ravenna	ap. 398
Reggio	52
Rheims	ap. 354
Rennes	ap. 355
Requisites for Invalids, and other Travellers, on leaving England	ap. 324
Rhine, Fall of, in the Rheinwald	ap. 361
Rhine, Fall of, at Schaffhausen	ap. 425
Riga	ap. 459
Rimini	ap. 398
Ringsted	ap. 454
Rinteln	ap. 431
Ro, Church there	46
Road, from Genoa to Nice	105
Rochelle, La	ap. 355
Roeskilde	ap. 454
Rome, Mal'aria	
Best situations	
Society	
Excavations made by the French	123-125
Travellers advised to visit the Ruins for the first time by moonlight	126
Roman filial piety	158

Antiquities within the Walls of Rome, namely:—

Foro Romano	126
Tempio di Giove Tonante	ib.
Tempio della Concordia	ib.
Arco di Settimio Severo	ib.
Tempio di Saturno	127
Colonna di Phocas	ib.
Tempio di Antonino e Faustina	ib.
Tempio di Giove Statore	ib.
Chiesa di S. Maria Liberatrice	ib.
Tempio di Remo	128
della Pace	ib.
di Venere e Roma	ib.
Arco di Tito	129
Colosseo	129, 130
Arco di Costantino	130
Chiesa di S. Teodoro	ib.

Antiquities of Rome, etc.   Page.

Arco di Settimio Severo in Velabro	131
Arco di Giano Quadrifronte	ib.
Cloaca Maxima	ib.
Chiesa di S. Maria in Cosmedin	ib.
Tempio di Vesta	132
della Fortuna Virile	ib.
Palazzo de' Cesari	132-134
Circus Maximus	134
Chiesa di S. Gregorio sul Monte-Celio	135
Termi di Tito	ib.
Sette Salle	ib.
Chiesa di S. Martino in Monte	ib.
di S. Pietro in Vincoli	136
di S. Maria della Navicella	ib.
di S. Stefano Rotondo	ib.
Obelisk of the Piazzo del Popolo	137
of the Trinità de' Monti	ib.
Villa Medici	ib.
Statues and Obelisk in Piazza di Monte-Cavallo	ib.
Chiesa di S. Bernardo	ib.
di S. Maria degli Angeli	138
The Pope's Oil Cellar	139
Obelisk of S. Maria Maggiore	ib.
Column in Piazza di S. Maria Maggiore	ib.
Basilica di S. Maria Maggiore	ib.
Obelisk di S. Giovanni in Laterano	140
Battisterio di Costantino	ib.
Basilica di S. Giovanni in Laterano	ib.
Scala Santa—Triclinium	141
Anfiteatro Castrense	ib.
Basilica di Santa Croce in Gerusalemme	ib.
Chiesa di S. Bibiana	142
Tempio di Minerva Medici	ib.
Arco di Gallieno	ib.
Remains of Aqueducts	ib.
Chiesa di S. Prassede	ib.
Campidoglio	ib.
Chiesa di S. Maria d'Aracœli	144
di S. Pietro in Carcere	ib.
Palazzo del Senatore	ib.
Palazzo de' Conservatori	145-147
Museo Capitolino	147-151
Travellers advised to visit the Museums by torch-light; and how to obtain permission for so doing	147

INDEX.

Antiquities of Rome, etc.   Page.

Tempio di Pallade	151
Tempio e Foro di Nerva	152
Foro e Colonna Trajana	ib.
Dogana Pontificia	354
Obelisk of Monte Citorio	ib.
Colonna Antonina	ib.
Mausoleo d'Augusto	ib.
Campo Marzo	ib.
Mausoleo-Adriano	ib.
Tempio del Sole	154
Obelisk in Piazza S. Maria sopra Minerva	ib.
Chiesa di S. Maria sopra Minerva	155
Pantheon	155-157
Bagni d'Agrippa	157
Piazza Navona	ib.
Chiesa di S. Agnese, Piazza Navona	ib.
Teatro di Marcello	158
Portico d'Octavia	ib.
Tempio d'Esculapio	ib.
Chiesa di S. Cecilia in Trastevere	159
Basilica di S. Maria in Trastevere	ib.
Chiesa di S. Prisca	ib.
di S. Sabina	160
di S. Alessio	ib.
Sepolcro di Cajo Cestio	ib.
Terme di Caracalla	ib.
Sepolcro de' Scipioni	161
Porta S. Sebastiano	ib.
Antiquities near Rome, namely, Basilica di S. Sebastiano alle Catacombe	ib.
Circo di Caracalla	162
Sepolcro di Cecilia Metella	163
Public Ustrina	ib.
Basilica di S. Paolo	ib.
Chiesa di S. Paolo alle tre Fontane	164
Excavations	ib.
Chiesa di S. Urbano	ib.
Fontana della Dea Egeria	165
Tempio di Redicolo	ib.
Porta Pia	ib.
Chiesa di S. Agnese fuori di Porta Pia	ib.
Chiesa di S. Costanza	ib.
Mons Sacer	166
Porta S. Lorenzo	ib.
Basilica di S. Lorenzo	ib.
Porta Maggiore	ib.
Tor de' Schiavi	167

Antiquities of Rome, etc.   Page.

Porta S. Giovanni	167
Temple of Fortuna Muliebris	ib.
Roma Vecchia	ib.
Porta Angelica	ib.
Porta Latina	ib.
Porta Pinciana	ib.
Porta Portense	ib.
Porta di S. Pancrazio	ib.
Pons Ælius, now Ponte S. Angelo	168
Pons Triumphalis	ib.
Ponte Sisto	ib.
Pons Fabricius, now Ponte dei Quattro Capi	ib.
Pons Cestius	ib.
Pons Palatinus	ib.
Pons Sublicius	ib.
Basilica di S. Pietro	169-174
Vaticano	174
Cappella Sistina	175
Cappella Paolina	ib.
Stanze di Raffaello	175-179
Easel-Paintings	179
Method of seeing the Statues of the Vatican Museum by torch-light	180
Museo Chiaramonti	180-182
Pio-Clementino	182-188
Libraria Vaticano	188-190
Chiesa dei P. P. Cappuccini	190
Palazzo Barberini	ib.
Chiesa di S. Maria della Vittoria	191
Fontana di Termine	ib.
Chiesa di S. Andrea à Monte Cavallo	ib.
Palazzo Pontificio	192
Palazzo Rospigliosi	192, 193
Fontana di Trevi	193
Chiesa di S. Maria del Popolo	ib.
di S. Carlo al Corso	ib.
di S. Lorenzo in Lucina	194
di S. Ignazio	ib.
de S. S. Apostoli	ib.
di S. Maria di Loretto	ib.
di Gesù	ib.
di S. Andrea della Valle	195
della Trinità de' Pelegrini	ib.
di S. Carlo à Catenari	ib.
di S. Giovanni de' Fiorentini	196
di S. Maria in Vallicella	ib.
di S. Maria della Pace	ib.
di S. Agostino	197

INDEX.

Antiquities of Rome, etc.	Page.
Palazzo Borghese	197
Sciarra	198
Doria	199
Bracciano	200
Colonna	201
Giustiniani	ib.
Massimi	ib.
Braschi	202
Farnese	ib.
Spada	203
Mattei	ib.
Costaguti	204
Falconieri	ib.
Farnesina	205
Corsini	ib.
Accademia di S. Luca	ib.
Villas near Rome, namely—	
Villa Olgiata	ib.
Borghese	ib.
Ludovisia	207
Albani	ib.
Mattei	209
Doria-Pamfili	ib.
Madama	210
Hospitals	ib.
Mosaic Manufacture	ib.
Basilicæ, when open—Palaces, Villas, and Museums, how to obtain admittance when they are not open to the public, and what fees are expected by the persons who show them	ib.
Artists	211
Bankers	ib.
Theatres	ib.
Carnival	ib.
Remnant of the ancient Saturnalia	ib.
Amusements during Lent	212
Ceremonies of the Holy Week, Easter-day, etc.	212-216
Promenades—Hotels	217
List of objects best worth notice as they lie contiguous to each other	ib.
Rome, [Appendix.] Current coins—Bankers' accounts—Weights—Measures—Hotels and other Lodging-houses—Water—Air—Prices of various articles—Confectioner—Medicines—Roman pearls—Masters—Best shops for antiquities, modern works of art, etc.—Theatres—Unfurnished apartments—Procaccio—Best Voiturin—Post-Office	378-384
Ronciglione	122
Rosenberg	ap. 433
Rotterdam	ap. 446
Roveredo	ap. 407
Rovigo	300
Rubicon	ap. 398
Russia, Money of — Price of Post-horses—Other requisites for Travellers— Russian Voiturins—Passports	ap. 458, 459
Salenche	33
Salerno	279
S. Jean de Maurienne	ap. 391
S. Lorenzo Nuovo	121
S. Malo	ap. 356
S. Quirico	121
S. Quentin, Tunnel at	ap. 351
Samogia	ap. 398
Saorgio	107
Saragossa	ap. 439, 440
Savigliano	108
Scarena	106
Schaffhausen	ap. 425
Schlan	342
Schottwien	307
Sculpture, Art of, its rise and progress	4
Secheron	32
Sedan	ap. 351
Segovia	ap. 436
Semlin	ap. 432
Sesto-Calende	46
Sestrières, Col de	ap. 395
Seville	ap. 443
Siena, Wine — Water — Eatbles—Character of the Sanesi—Objects best worth notice—Maremma	118-121
Sierre	39
Simplon, The, passage of	40-44
Price of post-horses to ascend the mountain	ap. 363
Sion	39
Sleswick	ap. 452
Smolensko	ap. 464
Soedertellje	ap. 454
Soissons	ap. 350
Sorrento—Description of that city and its Piano	285-290
Sorrento, [Appendix.] Lodging-houses — Provisions —	

2 T 2

INDEX.

Boats—Best mode of conveying a Family from Naples to Sorrento—Post-Office ... 389, 390
   Physician 390
Sospello 106
Spain, Money of—Price of Post-horses, etc.—Requisites for Travellers in that country, *ap.* 437, 438
Spilimbergo 304
Spilonga 296
Splugen, passage of .... *ap.* 360
Spoleto 295
Stargard .... *ap.* 424
Stavanger .... *ap.* 458
Stendal .... *ap.* 422
Stockerau 310
Stockholm, description of that city and its environs, *ap.* 454, 455
Stones, shower of, at Pienza ... 264
Stralsund .... *ap.* 454
Strasburgh .... *ap.* 352
Straubing .... *ap.* 427
Susa .... *ap.* 394
Sweden, Money of—Price of Post-horses, etc. .... *ap.* 452, 453
Switzerland, Post-horses, etc.—Best mode of travelling—Money, etc. .... *ap.* 357
Tagliamento, Torrent so called 304
Tavernettes .... *ap.* 393
Temple of Clitumnus 296
Tenda, Col di 107
Terracina 227
Terni 295
Thrasymenus, Lake of, 296, and *ap.* 397
Tivoli, excursion to 218
Tokay, wine of .... *ap.* 433
Torgau .... *ap.* 424
Torre del Greco, destruction of 263
   della Nunciata 264
   di tre Ponte 227
Torrecelli 121
Tortona .... *ap.* 405
Toulouse .... *ap.* 354
Tours .... *ap.* ib.
Tourtemagne, Cascade of 39
Traskirken 307
Trebia, Torrent so called, 51, and *ap.* 398
Trent .... *ap.* 407
Treviso 304
Trieste .... *ap.* 433
Trolhaëtta, Cascades of .. *ap.* 457

Troyes .... *ap.* 352
Tver .... *ap.* 463
Turin, description of that city—Hotels—Climate—Water—Environs 108, 109
Tuscany, current coins of—Weights—Measures—Prices at Hotels—Wages of Valet-de-place .... *ap.* 366
Tusculum 222
Tyrnau .... *ap.* 432
Valencia .... *ap.* 323, 439
Valence .... *ap.* 345
Valladolid .... *ap.* 439
Vall-Ombrosa 85
Vannes .... *ap.* 355
Velleia, Ruins of 52
Velletri 226
Venice, objects best worth notice there—Promenades—Theatres—Hotels—Water 301-304
Venice, [Appendix.] Price of Apartments and Dinner at Hotels—Price, per day, of a Gondola—Wages of a Valet-de-place—Articles best worth purchasing—Post-Office. 412, 413
Vercelli .... *ap.* 401
Verona, description of that city, and of Juliet's Death and Tomb .... *ap.* 399, 400
Vesuvius, excursion to 257
Vezoul .... *ap.* 352
Vicenza, description of .. *ap.* 400
Vico, Lake of 122
Vienna—Custom-house—Hotels—Objects best worth notice—Coffee-houses—Water—National dish—Theatres—Fireworks—Distance from Florence 308-310
Vienna, [Appendix.] Pound weight, and braccio—Prices at one of the Hotels—Restaurateurs—Wages of a Valet-de-place—Carriages and Sedan-chairs—Medical men—Shops—Articles best worth purchasing—Prices at the Opera-house—Post-Office—Diligences 415, 416
Vienne .... *ap.* 345
Via-Reggio .... *ap.* 395
Vietri 278

INDEX.

	Page.
Villach	305
Vionnaz	ap. 358
Viterbo	122
Voltaggio	111
Voltaire's Villa at Ferney	31
Voyage from Amsterdam to Utrecht	ap. 447
from Bordeaux, up the Garonne, to Toulouse	ap. 333
from Dresden, down the Elbe, to Hamburgh	317, 348
from Ferrara to Venice	300
from Frankfort on the Mein to Cologne	ap. 420
from Francolino to Venice	301
from Genoa to Leghorn	111
from Genoa to Nice	105, 106
from Guernsey to S. Malo	ap. 331
from Hamburgh, down the Elbe, to Cuxhaven	318, 319
from Leghorn to Pisa, by the Canal	ap. 368
from Lyon, down the Rhone, to Avignon	ap. 346
from Mayence, down the Rhine, to Coblentz	ap. 429
from Naples to Procida and Ischia	293
from Naples to Sorrento	285
from Sorrento to Amalfi	290
from Sorrento to Castel-à-Mare	291
from Sorrento to Capri	ib.
from Orleans, down the Loire, to Nantes	ap. 331
from Ratisbon, on the Danube, to Vienna	ap. 420
from Toulouse, on the Canal of Languedoc, to Beziers	ap. 334
Upsala	ap. 456
Utrecht	ap. 446
Water Diligence	ap. 334
Weissenfels	ap. 423
Wurtzburgh	ap. 428
Wurzen	ap. 422
Xeres de la Frontera	ap. 443
Yeselles, or Isella	44
Ystad	ap. 454
Znaim	310
Zwolle	ap. 448

APPENDIX—ROUTES.

FRANCE.

	Page.
From Calais, through Amiens, to Paris	334
Calais, through Beauvais, to Paris	335
Ostend, through Lille, to Paris	ib.
Dieppe, through Rouen, to Paris	336
Havre, through Rouen, to Paris	ib.
Paris, through Dijon, to Geneva	342
Lyon to Geneva, by Cerdon and S. Germain-de-Joux	ib.
Paris, through Lyon, to Chambery	ib.
Paris, through Nevers and Moulins, to Lyon	344
Lyon, through Avignon and Aix, to Nice	345
Avignon to Nismes and Montpellier	347
Aix to Marseilles and Toulon	ib.
Paris to Bordeaux and Bayonne	348
Paris to Brest	349
Paris to Dunkirk	350
Lille, through Ypres, to Ostend	ib.
Lille to Bruxelles	ib.
Paris, through Bruxelles, to Ostend	ib.
Paris, through Rheims and Sedan, to Liege	351
Paris, through Châlons-sur-Marne, to Strasburgh	ib.
Paris to Strasburgh, through Troyes, Langres, Vezoul, Befort, and Basle	352
Paris, through Langres, to Besançon	353
Paris to Grenoble	ib.
Paris, through Toulouse, to Perpignan	354
Paris, through Chartres, to La Rochelle	ib.
Paris, through Caen, to Cherbourg	355
Paris, through Rennes, to L'Orient	ib.

	Page.
From Paris to Nantes	355
Nantes, through Rennes, to S. Malo	356

SWITZERLAND.

	Page.
From Geneva, by the Simplon, to Milan	357

ITALY.

	Page.
From Geneva to Chambery	394
Chambery, over the Mont-Cenis, to Turin	ib.
Nice, through Genoa, to Pisa, with an account of the Bridle-road	395
Leghorn, through Pisa, to Florence	ib.
Pisa, through Lucca and Pistoja, to Florence	396
Pisa to Modena	ib.
Florence, through Siena, to Rome	ib.
Florence, through Perugia, to Rome	397
Genoa, through Bologna, Rimini, Sinagalia, Ancona, Loretto, and Terni, to Rome	ib.
Milan, through Bergamo, Verona, Vicenza, and Padua, to Venice, Bologna, and Florence	399
Milan to Bologna, through Piacenza, Parma, Reggio, and Modena	401
Milan to Turin	ib.
Aoste to Turin	ib.
Turin, over the Maritime Alps, to Nice	ib.
Turin, over the Bocchetta, to Genoa	ib.
Rome to Naples	402
Naples to Pæstum	ib.
Environs of Naples	403

En voiturier.

	Page.
From Pisa to Massa and Carrara	ib.
Rome to Florence, through Perugia	ib.
Florence, through Siena, to Rome	ib.

	Page.
From Rome to Naples	403
Calais to Rome, during the winter of 1820	404
Florence, through Bologna, Venice, Vienna, Prague, and Dresden, to Hamburgh	406
Florence, through Mantua, and by the Tyrol, to Augsburgh and Wurtzburgh	407
Rome, through Florence and Milan, and by the Simplon, to Geneva; and over the Jura Alps to Poligny, Dijon, Melun, Paris, and Boulogne, during summer	408
Florence, during the summer of 1822, to Venice, Milan, Turin, and over Mont Cenis, to Pont de Beauvoisin	410

GERMANY.

	Page.
From Hamburgh to Berlin	420
Hamburgh to Leipsic	422
Leipsic to Dresden	ib.
Leipsic, through Gotha, to Frankfort on the Mein	ib.
Leipsic to Brunswick	423
Brunswick to Hanover	424
Hanover to Gottingen	ib.
Leipsic to Dantzic	ib.
Frankfort on the Mein to Augsburgh	425
Augsburgh to Constance, Schaffhausen, and Basle	ib.
Augsburgh to Ratisbon	426
Ratisbon to Munich	ib.
Ratisbon to Prague	427
Vienna, through Ratisbon and Bruxelles, to Ostend	427, 428
Frankfort on the Mein, through Cassel, to Munster	429
Vienna to Carlsbad, through Eger and Zwoda	431
Hanover to Pyrmont	ib.
Hamburgh to Pyrmont	ib.
Bruxelles, through Aix-la-Chapelle and Liege, to Spa	ib.

INDEX.

	Page.
From Vienna to Baaden	432
Vienna to Presburgh	ib.
Teutsch-Altenburgh to Belgrade	ib.
Presburgh to Kaschau and Tokay	ib.
Vienna to Trieste	433

PORTUGAL.

From Lisbon to Oporto	436
Lisbon to Madrid	ib.

SPAIN.

From Bayonne to Madrid	438
Perpignan to Barcelona	440
Barcelona to Saragossa	ib.
Madrid to Granada	441
Madrid to Malaga	442
Madrid to Cordova, Seville, and Cadiz	443

NETHERLANDS.

From Amsterdam to Cleves and Cologne	446
Cleves to the Hague, Rotterdam, and Helvoetsluys	ib.
Amsterdam to Munster	447
Amsterdam to Emden	ib.
Amsterdam to Utrecht, Bois-le-Duc, and Maestricht	ib.
Amsterdam to Leyden, the Hague, and Rotterdam	ib.
From Nimeguen to Rotterdam and Helvoetsluys	447
Nimeguen to Bois-le-Duc and Breda	448
Bois-le-Duc to Anvers	ib.
Bergen-op-Zoom to Anvers	ib.
Amsterdam to Hamburgh	ib.
Hamburgh to Amsterdam, by Groningen and Leuwarden	ib.

DENMARK.

From Copenhagen to Hamburgh	451
Copenhagen to Gothenborg	452

SWEDEN AND NORWAY.

From Stralsund, through Carlscrona, to Stockholm	454
Stockholm to Upsala	456
Stockholm to Gothenborg	ib.
Gothenborg to Christiania	457
Christiania to Bergen	ib.

RUSSIA.

From Riga to Petersburgh	469
Petersburgh to Moscow	462, 463
Petersburgh to the Frontier of Sweden	463
Moscow to Grodno	464
Moscow to Riga, and the Frontier of Prussia	ib.

ADDENDA.

SICILY, concise history of that Island	475-478
Most eligible months for visiting it	478
Palermo and its environs	479-484
Alcamo	485
Ægesta, and its temple	485, 486
Acque Segestane	486
Madonna di Trapani	ib.
Town of Trapani	ib.
Mount Eryx	ib.
Marsala	ib.
Mazzara	487
Stone Quarry near Campo Bello	487
Castel-Vetrano	ib.
Selinuntium, and its Temples	487, 488
Sciacca, and its Hot Springs	489
Siculiana	490
Girgenti, and its Mole	490, 491
Agrigentum, and its Temples	491-495
Licata, the ancient *Phintia*	495
Terranova, near the ancient *Gela*	ib.
Caltagirone	496

INDEX.

	Page.
Palagonia	496
Biviere di Lentini	ib.
Town of Lentini	ib.
Approach to Syracuse	ib.
Modern Town	497
Ancient Syracusæ	497-502
Antiquities on the road to Catania	502
Catania	503-507
Requisites for Travellers who ascend Ætna	507
Description of Ætna	508
Journey to the Crater during midsummer, 1826	509-511
Ditto during winter, 1824	511, 512
Castello di Aci	513
Scopuli Cyclopum	ib.
Scala di Aci	ib.
Giarra	ib.
Castagnoi di cento Cavalli	ib.
Francavilla	ib.
Giardini	ib.
Taormina, and remains of the ancient *Taurominium*	514, 515
Messina, by whom founded—earthquake of 1773—description of the city	515, 516
Charybdis	517
Scylla	ib.
Melazzo	518
Excursion by water to Scylla and Rheggio	ib.
Excursion to the Lipari Islands and Cefalù	548, 520
Termini	519
Character of the Sicilians	520
Cattle, vegetable productions, and fish of Sicily	ib.
Climate	521
Population	ib.
Manner of Travelling	ib.
Sicilian money	522
Price of a Lettiga	ib.
Price of Mules	522
Hire of Ætna Guides, and Charges at Hotels	ib.
Wages of other Guides, and Requisites for Travellers who make the Tour of the Island	ib.
Route round the sea-coast	523-525
Routes from Catania to the summit of Ætna	525
Siena, description of that city	127-129
Maremma	129
Splugen, passage of	534-536

ROUTES.

From Genoa, through Lucca, to Pisa, by the new Road	526
Genoa to Turin, by the Val di Scrivia	ib.
Calais, by Pontarlier, to Neuchatel, and thence by Lausanne and Bex over the Simplon to Bologna	527, 528
Naples to Calais	529-533
Como, by Mount Splugen, to Zurich	536, 537

www.ingramcontent.com/pod-product-compliance
Lightning Source LLC
Chambersburg PA
CBHW062123160426
43191CB00013B/2178